THE SECOND COMING

THE SECOND COMING

A Mysterious Interpretation to the Gospel of Matthew

CYRENE

PARTRIDGE
A Penguin Random House Company

ISBN:	Hardcover	978-1-4828-2116-1
	Softcover	978-1-4828-2115-4
	eBook	978-1-4828-2114-7

To order additional copies of this book, contact
Partridge India
000 800 10062 62
www.partridgepublishing.com/india
orders.india@partridgepublishing.com

CONTENTS

How wondrous this, how mysterious!
I carry fuel, I draw water.

A Zen Saying

PREFACE

The inspiration to study the Gospel came to me out of the blue. Looking back I wonder why the idea occurred to me at all. After all, I was never a religious Christian by any stretch of imagination. My church visits were few and far between. Even when I visited, I was merely a passive spectator of the proceedings from one of those rear pews. I merely accepted religion as part of my environment. To me, it was a *tamasha* adults played, and I was generally suspicious of those who took their roles too seriously. Considering such a backdrop, I am unable to understand why this urge suddenly occurred to me. Perhaps it was the 2012 frenzy that literally set the Web ablaze with all kinds of wild rumours or, perhaps, it was the frightening realization that I am nearing sixty. Whatever it was, I thought it would a shame if I passed away without knowing the Gospel.

I admit that I am not a hard-core Christian. But it does not mean that I am an atheist or that I am not spiritual. In fact, I am deeply spiritual. Right from childhood, I was attracted to mysticism. It was a kind of fatal attraction, like the moth's attraction to fire. I have mysticism in my genes, as it were. Even as a young lad, I was seeking. What it was that I was seeking, I had no clue then. Nevertheless, I was seeking; and there was an air of urgency and expectation to it. It seems to me now that I was driven by a question—the abstract question *what*. Whenever I entered a bookstore or library, it was with the expectation that the book I picked up would reveal to me a great secret. And I have spent a small fortune, buying books. Over the past 40-plus years I have read quite a few books and articles, belonging to a wide variety of genres. With the arrival of the Internet, especially, the Google search engine and Wikipedia, the extent and depth of my search increased considerably.

There is a scene in the Gospel of Matthew where Jesus calls Matthew to follow him. Jesus sees him sitting at the receipt of custom and says to him, "Follow me." Matthew simply rises and follows Jesus; no questions asked, no questions answered. Looking back, my situation too was somewhat like that of Matthew's. Just like him I too was engaged in a colorless job when the call came. At the time, I was teaching Strategic Management in a local business school as an Associate Professor. Many may consider it a colorful job; but to me, the whole thing smacked of hypocrisy. Somehow, the academic scene seemed to me suffocating—more noxious and unbearable than the industrial scene. I had joined the Institute only a year ago, after throwing away a senior management position in a leading media company. Anyway, when the call came, like Matthew I too got up and got out. It did not occur to me to consult anyone before taking the decision. I simply walked out without a plan in mind.

Ironically, what helped me most in this work is my lack of Christian conditioning. Because of that, I could approach the Gospel without any preconceived notions. I could approach it with an open mind and see it in a fresh light. Ironically, what many may consider as weakness turned out to be my strong point. I simply followed my heart. But, each time I sat down to write, I prayed to God for guidance. It was a short prayer: "God, lead me in the truth." That's all. The prayers were always directed inwards. And each time, the thought that followed surprised me. It seemed as if the thoughts sprang from my body; so convincing they seemed to me. This Gospel exposition is the compilation of those thoughts. I have not tried to moderate them to make them compatible with the accepted doctrine. I leave it to you to judge it yourselves.

The true hero of this book is the Self, although he is behind the book all the time. He is the final authority on truth. If a particular revelation feels right to him, then it is right indeed, no matter what others have said about it in the past or what they might say about it in future. That's what I believe. Therefore, you may not find extensive citations in this book, although I have used references extensively. Unlike scientific works, which depend on others' approval for validation, a spiritual work does not require others' approval; it only needs Self-validation. As far as I am concerned, a piece of information authoritative if I am convinced about it; it doesn't matter who postulated it. The Self is the source of authority, not others. And the Gospel reveals him to us through an allegory. And that hero is you, and I.

Because the Self is the subject of this book, I have consistently used masculine gender in the book's narration. There is no particular reason for choosing the masculine gender other than the simple reason that I am a male. Gender really does not matter since the Self is genderless; it is neither male nor female; it is both male and female. Perhaps, some of the views expressed in this book may not seem politically-correct to some of you. But, the Self has nothing to do with group or political-correctness.

Because the Gospel describes the Self, and because the Self is non-dualistic in its essence, a true Gospel interpretation cannot be authoritative; it can only be speculative. Speculation does not necessarily imply lack of knowledge; rather, it is the nature of truth. In that respect, it is very much similar to the idea of *uncertainty* in Heisenberg's Uncertainty Principle.

This book is not exactly written for you. It is the by-product of my own efforts to understand the Gospel meaningfully. It is the compilation of the thoughts that went through me as I tried to grapple with the Gospel, as I tried to explain it to myself in an internally consistent manner. And I consider this book truly spiritual because its content was revealed to me by the Self (the spirit). The interpretation is mine, and mine alone. Perhaps, you may not agree with me. The book may not seem spiritual to you, but that's only natural. Only you can make your spiritual interpretation. Others' interpretations can, at best, be literal interpretations; but, they may perhaps serve you as a guide. But, it cannot be the truth itself; because the truth is you; it is your Self. Perhaps, it explains why a number of Gospels and Gospel interpretations came up during the early days of Christianity.

In developing this exegesis, I have consciously avoided other Gospel interpretations; I have also not followed their rules of hermeneutics. The reason is this: if you follow someone else's map, you will only reach where they have reached; you will never discover the Self. Nevertheless, in order to guide me through the work and to make the exegesis internally consistent, I have framed seven rules of my own. They have been my guiding beacon throughout the preparation of this work.

This exposition is my understanding of the Gospel; this is how I make sense of it. And this is the only way I can make a meaningful and internally-consistent explanation to the Gospel. I call it spiritual interpretation for two reasons: firstly, it is my (Self) interpretation; secondly, it is purely speculative. But, my gut feeling tells me that it has the flavor of truth. So I venture to present it before you. Perhaps, some of my thoughts may inspire you to write your own spiritual interpretation of the Gospel.

The Author

SPIRITUAL MEANING OR LITERAL MEANING?

It is virtually impossible to make an honest interpretation of the Gospel without defining the terms *spiritual* and *literal.* More importantly, the Gospel interpreter should at least have a clear conception as to what it is *not* spiritual. Yet, there is a great deal of confusion surrounding these terms. To many, *spiritual* simply means "concerning religion." Such a definition is problematic and could lead us in the wrong direction. Therefore, let us first define the terms accurately.

At the simplest level, the term *spiritual* means "concerning meaning"; it has nothing to do with history. According to the English dictionary, *spiritual* means "of or concerning the spirit." But, what is spirit? The word *spirit* is defined as follows:

1. The principle of conscious life; the vital principle in humans, animating the body.
2. A principle that inspires, animates, or pervades thought, feeling, or action.
3. The seat of feelings or sentiments, or as prompting to action.

The term *spirit* means "knowing" or "awareness." But, the adjective, *spiritual* implies "inner knowing," or "body-awareness." It refers to knowing revealed by the body. Knowledge received from outside, according to this definition, cannot be called spiritual. Moreover, spiritual knowledge is experiential knowledge. It is empirical, direct, firsthand, and personal knowledge.

Spiritual meaning is the inner (esoteric) meaning, whereas literal meaning is the outer (exoteric) meaning. The latter is determined by tradition, and it is the meaning generally accepted by society. Literal meaning is the consensual meaning; it is the traditional, limited, and frozen meaning. It is derived by the mind.

The table below highlights the important differences between literal meaning and spiritual meaning:

Literal Meaning	Spiritual Meaning
Outer meaning	Inner (esoteric) meaning
Generally-accepted	Individualistic
Revealed by others (not-Self)	Revealed by the Self
Revealed by the mind	Revealed by the body
Authoritative	Speculative
Solid, Frozen	Fluid, Probabilistic
Limited	Unlimited

Spiritual interpretation of scripture is always a personal interpretation, and it is up to each man to discover it for himself. Others' interpretations can only be literal interpretations, at best.

The literal scripture is only the map. The spiritual scripture, on the other hand, is the territory. And that territory is the human body.

The literal understanding is the broad way; the spiritual understanding is the narrow way.

> *Enter ye in at the straight gate: for wide is the gate, and broad is the way, that leadeth to destruction, and many there be which go in thereat: Because straight is the gate, and narrow is the way, which leadeth to life, and few there be that find it.*
> Matthew 7:13-14

Gödel, Escher, Bach: An Eternal Golden Braid is a book by Douglas Hofstadter that explores the mystery behind meaning. Given below is an extract from the Preface of the book:

> *. . . the most crucial aspect of Gödel's work is its demonstration that a statement's meaning can have deep consequences, even in a supposedly meaningless universe. Thus it is the meaning of Gödel's statement G (the one that asserts "G is not provable inside PM") that guarantees that G is not provable inside PM (which is precisely what G itself claims). It is as if the sentence's hidden Gödelian meaning had some kind of power over the vacuous symbol-shunting, meaning-impervious rules*

> *of the system, preventing them from ever putting together a demonstration of G, no matter what they do.*
>
> Gödel, Escher, Bach: an Eternal Golden Braid, Douglas R. Hofstadter (PM: *Principia Mathematica* by Alfred North Whitefield and Bertrand Russell)

Spiritual meaning is also known as *mystery*. The Greek word for *mystery* is *mystērion* (G3466). It is derived from the root word *myō*, which means "to shut up." In that sense, spiritual meaning is the 'shut up' meaning. The only way to access it is through speculation. And only body-aware human beings possess that faculty (computers cannot speculate). Mystery is the state of non-duality. In physics, it is called the *Quantum-mechanical state*. The human DNA is the physical expression of that very same Mystery.

THE FATHER OR GOD?

It is impossible to discern the spiritual meaning of the Gospel without a clear conception of the terms *Father* and *God*. According to the Gospel, Jesus comes from the Father.

The Gospel defines the term *Father* as follows: "*I and my Father are one*" (John 30:1). Every human being addresses himself as "I." In other words, the term "I" refers to the 'Self', or the collective 'self'. And the word "one" suggests unity, or wholeness. The term "one" also means "not two" and, therefore, suggests non-duality. According to the Gospel, the Self and Father are identical. And they denote wholeness (unity) and non-duality.

In addition to the term *Father*, the Gospel also uses the term *God*. For example, in Matthew 5:8 Jesus says, "*Blessed are the pure in heart: for they shall see God.*" Spiritually, the term *heart* refers to the DNA. Therefore, according to the Gospel, purity of DNA and God are interrelated. Perhaps, they are one and the same. Therefore, it follows that the corrupt DNA is the devil.

The Biblical definition of God is given in the opening verse of the Old Testament: "*In the beginning God created heaven and the earth*" (Genesis 1:1). According to this definition, God is the creator of heaven and earth. The word "create" has the following connotations:

1. To cause to come into being, as something unique that would not naturally evolve.
2. To evolve from one's own thought or imagination, as a work of art or an invention.
3. To cause to happen; bring about; arrange, as by intention or design.

The word *create* implies arranging, or assembling; it involves *time*. Creation can happen only in time. In other words, creation implies duality. The Hebrew word for *create* is *bārā* (H1254), which means "to cut down," "to select," or "to choose." According to this definition, creation is a conceptualization (cutting, choosing, and labeling) process. It is a mental process. The creator God is like a super 'program' and the created world is its 'application', or projection. The scriptural God is the scripture itself.

The term Father, however, refers to the Self. It is the ultimate, indivisible reality which manifests itself in everything, and of which all things are parts. It is the All, the unity and mutual interrelation of all things and events. It is both immanent in and transcendent to everything. And it is the Self in man, and it is non-dualistic in nature. It is called *Brahman* in Hinduism, *Dharmakāya* (Body of Being) in Buddhism, and *Tao* in Taoism. Because it transcends all concepts and categories, Buddhists also call it *Tathata* or *Suchness*. It is paradoxical in nature. It is beyond language. It is beyond scripture. It is beyond God.

God (DNA) is the creator of the world (mind) and ego, and the master of both. It is the bio-chemical expression of man's deeply-help beliefs, or scripture. The outer or literal scripture is merely reflection of the inner scripture, or DNA. But, the outer scripture, if accepted, can influence the inner scripture and even modify it.

As one's belief system changes, one's God changes too. The truth is that God is a programmable entity that can be shaped in any form. However, to do that, one has to first establish link with the Father. But, due to ignorance, we leave the job of shaping God to others. Religion, education and media continually shape God as a slave driver for the Establishment. That is why the Establishment maintains such tight control over religion, education, and media. But, the Establishment has no direct control over the Father. Body-awareness is the manifestation of the Father in you. And the voice of the Father is called intuition.

I shall try to give a different spin to the concepts of Father and God with the help of a diagram.

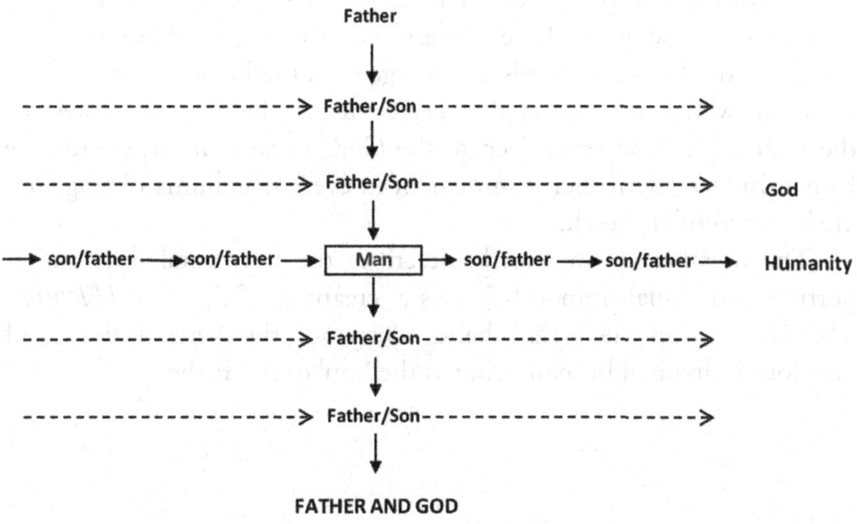

In the above diagram, the horizontal line at the centre represents our world and humanity. It is a chain of father-son relationships, and it represents the history of humanity—from the indefinite past to the indefinite future. The horizontal line flows from left to right and it represents the arrow of time. Here, each father gives rise to a son and then dies after some time.

The vertical line represents several (perhaps infinite) tiers of worlds and their humanity. And the vertical line is a chain of Father-Son relationships. The vertical line represents timelessness or eternity—the NOW. It is ever present. Each level of humanity gives rise (creates?) to a new generation humans (humanity) and then fades away (perhaps like the Atlanteans). To the lower level humanity, the higher level humanity is God, or *Elohim* and they venerate it. The vertical line, or the totality of worlds and their humanity is called the Father.

It is also possible that each world may have few individuals (gods) from the higher world(s) that provide the necessary continuity between the worlds. They are the carriers of wisdom, and they possess the more evolved DNA of the gods. These wise men are called the Evites, or Prophets.

The higher level, or the world of the gods, is considered the 'heaven' for those in the lower level. And the lower level, or the world of the creatures, is considered the 'hell' for those in the higher level. Those who corrupt their DNA, takes rebirth in a lower level. Those who improve the purity of their DNA, take rebirth in a higher level. But, those who those understand the truth—those who are enlightened—bypass all levels and merge with the Father.

Man, who is situated at the very center of the diagram represents the Father. He is superior even to the Gods because he represents the Father. In fact, the Father is immanent in every true human being. Yet, He is transcendent to all.

The literal scripture merely describes the horizontal line, and it portrays individual human being as a 'creature' of the gods (*Elohim*). The Gospel, on the other hand, describes the vertical line, and positions individual human being as the 'son' of the Father.

THE BOOK OF GENESIS—A PRIMER TO THE GOSPEL

"*The path up and down are one and the same*" said Heraclitus, the pre-Socratic Greek philosopher who lived in the Greek city of Ephesus during the fifth century BC. The path to heaven is also the path to hell; where you end up depends on the direction of your journey. That two-way path is called scripture.

The Hebrew word for *scripture* is *ketāb* (H3791), which means "something written," that is, a writing, a record, or a book. The word *ketāb* is derived from the root word *kātab* (H3789), which means "to scribe." The Greek word for *scripture* is *graphē* (G1124), which means "a document." The word is derived from the root word *graphō* (G1125), which means "to scribe." The book (*ketāb*) that we are referring to here is the Scripture.

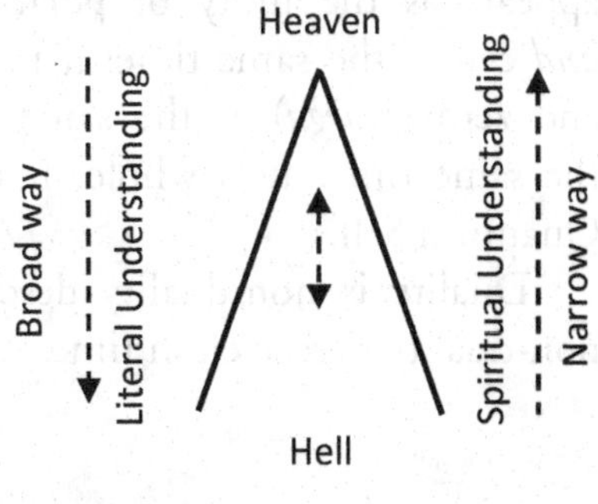

Scripture – The Two-way Path

The Bible opens with the verse, "*In the beginning God created the heaven and the earth.*" The Hebrew word for *create* is *bārā* (H1254), which means "to cut down", "select" or "choose." According to this definition, creation is a *cutting and choosing* process. In other words, creation implies *fragmentation*. The concept of creation embeds in itself the concepts of objectivity, locality, and causality. In other words, creation implies *duality*; it involves fantasy or delusion. However, the verse also suggests that the state prior to creation is *wholeness* or *non-duality*. That is, in the beginning there was only the Self. The Hindu epic, *Srimad Bhāgavadam* articulates this truth clearly:

Ahamēvāsamēvāgrē nānyad yat sadasatparam
Srimad Bhāgavadam 2.9.32
("In the beginning, only I (Self) was there; good and evil did not exist then.")

To perceive non-duality (Self) as a world (of polar opposites) created by a God is duality. Duality is the essence of religion.

The Bible may be understood dualistically (literally) or non-dualistically (spiritually). The former is the path down; it leads the *follower* to hell (the world of duality and delusion). The latter is the path up; it leads the *seeker* to heaven (non-duality or enlightenment). Dualistic understanding is *literal* or *classical* understanding; religion is its interpreter. Non-dualistic understanding is *spiritual* or *quantum* understanding; the Self is its interpreter.

Non-duality appears paradoxical from duality perspective; it appears as the unity of polar opposites. Non-duality is *both* good *and* evil at the same time; it is *neither* good *nor* evil. It is one (*alpha*) and zero (*omega*) at the same time. It is beginning and the end at the same time. It is whole. It is called *pūrṇam* in Sanskrit. It is the Quantum Self.

Duality is non-duality described and understood classically; it is non-duality perceived in time. And it is cyclical (serpentine) in nature.

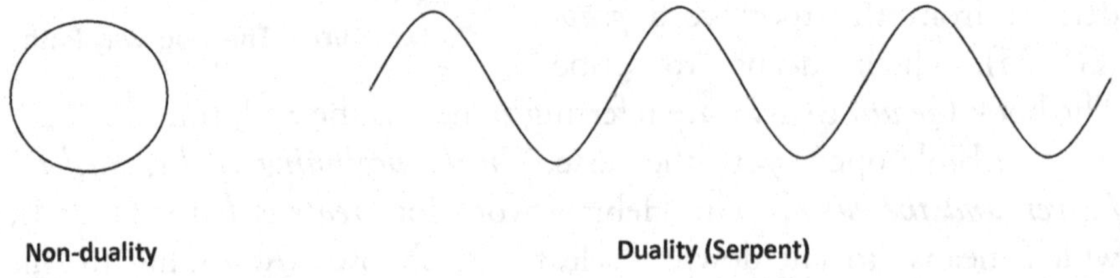

The Hebrew word for *serpent* is *nāhās* (H5175). It is derived from the root word *nāhas* (H5172), which means "to hiss." Therefore, the term *serpent* is generally interpreted as "snake." But, the word *nāhas* has another meaning, which is "to whisper a magic spell." Perhaps, the Bible uses the term in this latter sense. Bible describes the *serpent* as follows:

Now the serpent was more subtil than any beast of the field which the LORD God had made.
Genesis 3:1

The word *subtil* (Hebrew: *ārum* H6175) is generally interpreted as "cunning." The word *cunning* actually means "parasitic," because the parasite uses cunning to entrap, enslave, and exploit its host. The word *subtil* also means "thin, or tenuous" or "difficult to perceive or understand." The Sanskrit word for *subtle* is *sūkṣma*, which means "extremely small," "not perceivable" or "clever." From the above, two salient features of serpent stand out: one, it is subtle (microscopic, difficult to understand, and parasitic); two, it is created (artificial).

The minutest organism in the world is the virus. The average virus is about one one-hundredth the size of the average bacterium. Most viruses are too small to be seen directly with an optical microscope. They are difficult to understand; they can neither be classified as living nor can they be classified as dead; they are both living and dead. They have been variously described as "organisms at the edge of life." A virus is essentially a book; it simply contains the genetic information for creating another virus. In a sense, it is a spirit—an evil spirit. The word *spirit* means "knowing"; therefore, the term *evil spirit* implies "evil knowing," "false knowing," or "ignorance." In other words, the virus embodies ignorance. The virus needs a cell (a host) to come to life, and it employs cunning to entrap, enslave, and exploit its host. Once captured, the virus transforms the host into a virus-generating factory. Metaphorically speaking, the virus *proselytizes* the host to become an *evangelist* for it! The virus is the perfect example of a parasite.

The Biblical serpent is the "evil spirit" known as duality. And it is a serpent that can cast a magic spell known as delusion. Its victims lose individuality (body-awareness) and turn into 'members'. Serpent-bitten humans exhibit two symptoms:

1. They tend to lump together into groups. Such groups include religion, political parties, secret societies, mobs, etc. Infected persons are possessed by *group spirit* (Sanskrit: *krōdha*). War is the chief manifestation of this spirit.

2. They tend to perceive *value* in worldly (worthless) objects. Infected persons tend to measure everything in terms of an imaginary quantity called *value* (Sanskrit: *kāma*)

The Serpent lives in the *tree of the knowledge of good and evil.* In the Book of Genesis of the Bible, there is mention of two special trees in the Garden of Eden: one of them is called the *tree of the knowledge of good and evil*; the other, the *tree of life*. The Hebrew word for *tree* is *ēs* (H6086); it is derived from the primitive root *āsa* (H6095), which means "to fasten" or "make firm", i.e. "to close the eyes." Spiritually, the term *tree* refers both to scripture and DNA.

The Hebrew word *ēs* (tree) also means "gallows." A *gallows* is a wooden frame, consisting of a crossbeam on an upright, on which condemned persons are executed by hanging. In other words, the term *tree* refers to the *cross*. The *tree of the knowledge of good and evil* is the literal or duality-based scripture, also known as the Serpent. The *tree of life* is the spiritual scripture—the human body (DNA). The *cross* represents both.

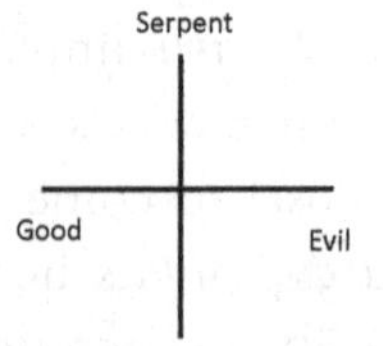

The Tree of the Knowledge of Good and Evil (Lucifer)

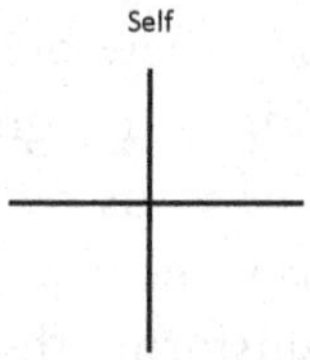

The Tree of Life (Christ)

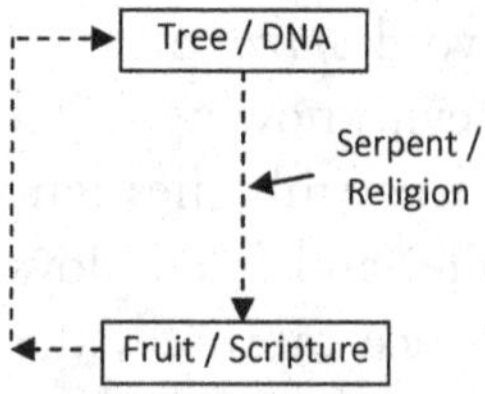

The Fall

The *fruit* (seed) of the tree of the knowledge of good and evil is the literal understanding. Just as any other seed, this seed too can become a tree (DNA) if planted in a fertile ground (imaginative mind) and regularly irrigated (worshipped with belief). Eventually, the new tree too will bear fruit (seed), which in turn, produces another tree, and the cycle goes on and on. This downward spiraling of human consciousness is called delusion or *death*.

God warns Adam, the first human, about the dire consequences of consuming the 'forbidden' fruit:

> *But of the tree of the knowledge of good and evil, thou shalt not eat of it: for in the day that thou eatest thereof thou shalt surely die.*
> Genesis 2:17

Surely die, says God. The Hebrew word for *death* is *māwet* (H4194), which, figuratively, means "ruin." The word *death*, in this context, implies spiritual death or delusion. The consequence of eating the *forbidden fruit* is spiritual death; it's a certainty for Adam. However, God does not issue the same warning to Eve, Adam's mate. Perhaps, she is genetically more evolved than Adam and, therefore, resistant to the 'forbidden fruit.' Both Adam and Eve consume the fruit. But, only Adam dies spiritually; Eve escapes death. Adam becomes a slave to the Serpent; Eve is unaffected. Their progeny, however, is affected in that they belonged to two distinct groups:

1. Offspring having Adam's 'fallen' genetic structure, also known as the "Sons of Serpent." For the purpose of this exposition, we shall designate them as *Adamites*. Adamites carry the Serpent seed, and they constitute a small fraction of human population.
2. Offspring having Eve's uncorrupted genetic structure, also known as "Sons of God." For the purpose of this exposition, we shall designate them as *Evites*. Evites carry the pure human seed, and they constitute almost the entirety of the human population.

Although the Evites constitute the large majority among humans, it does not imply that all of them are leading true Evite existences. Many Evites lead Adamite-like existence, totally deluded like the Adamites. These unfortunate people have been tricked by the Serpent into eating the forbidden fruit. Fortunately, they are not totally dead, thanks to their true nature, but only under a deep spell. For the purpose of this exposition, we shall call them the *Mortals*. However, Mortals can be woken up from their slumber if they are able to eat the fruit of the Tree of Life.

According to the Book of Genesis, the Adamites are spiritually dead and are incapable of understanding the scripture spiritually.

And the LORD God said, Behold, the man is become one of us, to know good and evil: and now, lest he put forth his hand, and take also of the tree of life, and eat, and live for ever: Therefore the LORD God sent him forth from the garden of Eden, to till the ground from whence he was taken. So he drove out man; and he placed at the east of the garden of Eden Cherubims, and a flaming sword which turned every way, to keep the way of the tree of life.
Genesis 3:24

The expression, "to know good and evil" implies the power of discrimination; it implies intelligence. It also implies *discretion*, which manifests as the *tendency to disobey*. In other words, the Adamites are intelligent, disobedient, and they lack body-awareness. The expression, "flaming sword which turned every way" refers to non-duality. The Adamites cannot tolerate non-duality.

In Biblical parlance, genetic structure is called *seed*. There is mention about two kinds of seeds in the Book of Genesis. The situation: God upbraiding the Serpent for deceiving the humans.

And I will put enmity between thee and the woman, and between thy seed and her seed; it shall bruise thy head, and thou shalt bruise his heel.
Genesis 3:15

The term, *thy seed* refers to the Adamites who carry the Serpent seed. They lack conscience and empathy. The majority of the Adamites are deluded religious zealots. Adamites worship the Serpent. They have only group-awareness; they lack self-awareness. They are practically insane. An Adamite is a potential *priest*.

The term, *her seed* refers to the Evites, who carry the pure human seed. They are totally sane people who are in touch with reality. Evites are body-aware and are impervious to religion. They worship the Father (Self). They are also known as the *righteous* or the *just*. An Evite is a potential *prophet*.

Adamites and Evites represent the two states of human existence, rather than two separate races. The division, however, is not on gender lines; there are many women who have Adamite qualities and there are many men who have Evite qualities. The salient characteristics of the two groups are given below:

Adamite	**Evite**
Group-aware	Self-aware
Insane	Sane
Controlled by thoughts	Controlled by feelings
Materialistic	Spiritual
Rational	Intuitive
Religious	Prophetic
Believer	Faithful
Clever, manipulative	Innocent, naïve
Dualistic	Non-dualistic
Extroverts	Introverts
Domineering	Meek and gentle
Competitive	Cooperative
Loves order	Loves freedom
Worships system	Worships truth

The Adamites are materialistic people who are totally focused on achieving, and are engrossed in worldly pursuits. They are fanatical about the group to which they are affiliated. Adamites are the backbone of society, and they are its elite class. Evites co-exist with the Adamites, but are not religious like the Adamites. Awakened Evites pursue truth rather than wealth, power and fame.

The Serpent's main pray is the Evites and its attack is two-fold: first, it attacks physically by corrupting the DNA genetically; second, it attacks spiritually by corrupting the belief system (scripture). For the latter attack, the Serpent uses the weapon known as *meme*. The word *meme* is a shortening of *mīmēma* (from Ancient Greek), which means "to imitate" or "imitated thing." The term meme was coined by the British evolutionary biologist Richard Dawkins in his book *The Selfish Gene* (1976). A meme is an idea, behavior, or style that spreads from person to person within a culture. A meme acts as a unit for carrying cultural ideas, symbols, or practices that can be transmitted from one mind to another through writing, speech, gestures, rituals, or other imitable phenomena. Memes are regarded as cultural analogues to genes in that they self-replicate, mutate, and respond to selective pressure. Whereas, the physical virus corrupts the body, the meme corrupts the mind. The Serpent is assisted by Adamites in capturing the Evite.

The term *Serpent* refers to dualistic religion and its duality-based scripture. Non-duality based religions do not corrupt humans. In fact, a non-duality-based religion is not a religion at all, but a state of being. It is the state of being truly human. The Hindus call it the *Sanātana Dharma*, which means "Quantum Self." It is the science of 'humanity'. To be a follower of *Sanātana Dharma* means to be a true human being. It means to be in touch with reality, to be totally sane. *Sanātana Dharma* is the true 'religion' of India. A true follower of *Sanātana Dharma* is also a true Christian, and vice versa.

THE MYSTERY OF ADAM AND EVE

Try to recollect a dream you had recently. Now, while you were in that dream, you really believed you belonged to that world. And it seemed so real to you. You actually experienced the pleasures and pains of that world. But now, looking back at the dream from the real world, you realize that it was merely a fantasy of your mind, and that it had no reality to it. But, what do you say about your present world? How can you be certain that it is real? It reminds us of the Zhuangzi parable about the butterfly.

In many ways dream is like a movie. Just as the movie, the dream too has a time-like continuity and a space-like extension to it. And it has a rather flexible storyline, like the TV soaps. Within the dream you have a body, but it is a virtual body; it has no truth to it. It is your *self* in the dream, and it is the mental projection of the real you. The self may be compared to a character in a movie that has no control over the movie. It is this dream self that is allegorically represented in the Genesis story as *Adam*. He is a *spiritual being* in that he is merely a *form of knowing*. But, he is also real in that he has a real body in the real world. In other words, he has a *soul*.

Adam's real body that exists in the real world is called the *Self*. The Gospel calls it the *Father*. It is always present with Adam, although he is not aware of it. But, he can feel it if he really focuses attention on himself in a special way. The Self is present in Adam as body-awareness. It is his real mate, the *Eve*. It is not the other Eve who is Adam's worldly mate—the literal Eve—but it is his spiritual mate; his inner body.

Just as a movie has its source in a script, the dream world too has its source in a script. And that script is called DNA, and it exists inside Adam. It is also known as *spiritual scripture*. Just as the movie is the visual presentation of the script, and the world is the projection of the spiritual scripture—the DNA. But, Adam mistakes it for *God* because, to him, it seems to control his destiny. What Adam really does not know is that this God is actually a program and that it is programmable. However, to program it, he has to enter into his real body. In other words, Adam has to become body-aware to control his God and his destiny. And that process is called meditation, or prayer.

It is the movie script that manifests as the film-roll, and it is the film-roll that translates as the movie in the light of the projector. Similarly, it is Adam's DNA (scripture) that translates as the world in the light of his Self. The light of the Self has the power to project infinite possibilities of every 'word' in the DNA (scripture). But, what Adam does not realize is that his beliefs can alter his scripture (DNA) and, therefore, his world.

The dream (God/Scripture/DNA) contains two inherent forces: one, a force that pushes it outwardly, which tends to extend the dream; two, a force that pulls it inwardly, which tends to terminate the dream. The term *Adamite* refers to humans who are children of the outwardly-acting God (Serpent). Their role is to help extend the dream. They are followers of the literal scripture. The term *Evite*, on the other hand, refers to humans who are children of the inwardly-acting God. Their role is to terminate the dream. They are followers of the spiritual scripture. Evites are body-aware, inherently. However, many Evites lead Adamite existences, engrossed in the world and out of touch with their bodies. Adam is really an Evite who acts and behaves like an Adamite. You are Adam. And Eve is your real body (soul), which is one with the Father.

	Outward-acting	**Inward-acting**
God	Serpent (Anti-Christ)	Christ
Scripture	Literal Scripture	Spiritual Scripture
DNA	"Thy seed" / Adamite	"Her seed" / Evite
Awareness	Delusion	Body-awareness

THE FORBIDDEN FRUIT AND THE SPELL

In a sense, the Genesis creation story itself is the "forbidden fruit." If you really believe in the literal story, then you are led to believe that the universe and man are the creations of an external entity called God. Thus, the Genesis story can transform your pure (non-duality) consciousness into duality-consciousness, leading to fragmentation of consciousness. However, at the spiritual level, the Genesis story reveals that very same secret to you. Thus the Genesis story is fiction and truth at the same time. This leads to a situation somewhat like the *Epimenides paradox*. Thomas Fowler (1869) states the paradox as follows: "Epimenides the Cretan says, 'that all the Cretans are liars,' but Epimenides is himself a Cretan; therefore he is himself a liar. But if he be a liar, what he says is untrue, and consequently the Cretans are veracious; but Epimenides is a Cretan, and therefore what he says is true; saying the Cretans are liars, Epimenides is himself a liar, and what he says is untrue. Thus we may go on alternatively proving that Epimenides and the Cretans are truthful and untruthful."

The Genesis story can cause a spell-like state in human consciousness, which is akin to a confused or paradoxical state of mind, which is called *Babylon*. The name *Babylon* is derived from the Hebrew word *bābel* (H894), which means "confusion." The word originated from the Greek version of Akkadian word *Bab-ilani* which means "the gate (portal) of the gods." In other words, the Genesis story is a *dimensional portal*.

The structure of the Genesis story may lead to a cognitive complication (knot) known as *Tangled Hierarchy*. The state of confusion created by it is called the *Strange Loop*, also known as "the spell." A strange loop, technically called *tangled hierarchy consciousness*, arises when, by moving only upwards or downwards through a hierarchical system, one finds oneself back where one started. Strange loops may involve self-reference and paradox. The concept of a strange loop was proposed and extensively discussed by Douglas Hofstadter in *Gödel, Escher, Bach*, and is further elaborated in his book *I am a Strange Loop*, published in 2007.

A tangled hierarchy is a hierarchical consciousness system in which a strange loop appears.

A strange loop is a hierarchy of levels, each of which is linked to one other by some type of relationship. A strange loop hierarchy, however, is 'tangled', in that there is no well defined highest or lowest level; moving through the levels, one eventually returns to the starting point, i.e., the original level. Examples of strange loops that Hofstadter offers include: many of the works of the artist M.C. Escher, the information flow network between DNA and enzymes through protein synthesis and DNA replication, and self-referential Gödelian statements in formal systems. (For example, scripture may be considered a formal system.)

> *And yet when I say "strange loop", I have something else in mind—a less concrete, more elusive notion. What I mean by "strange loop" is—here goes a first stab, anyway—not a physical circuit but an abstract loop in which, in the series of stages that constitute the cycling-around, there is a shift from one level of abstraction (or structure) to another, which feels like an upwards movement in a hierarchy, and yet somehow the successive "upward" shifts turn out to give rise to a closed cycle. That is, despite one's sense of departing ever further from one's origin, one winds up, to one's shock, exactly where one had started out. In short, a strange loop is a paradoxical level-crossing feedback loop.*
>
> *I Am a Strange Loop*, Hofstadter (PP. 101-102)

Strange loops take form in human consciousness as the complexity of active symbols in the brain inevitably lead to the same kind of self-reference which Kurt Gödel, the Austrian-American logician, mathematician, and philosopher, proved was inherent in any complex logical or arithmetical system in his *Incompleteness Theorem*. Gödel showed that mathematics and logic contain strange loops: propositions that not only refer to mathematical and logical truths (literal truths), but also to the symbol systems expressing those truths (spiritual truths). This leads to the sort of paradoxes seen in statements such as "This statement is false," wherein the sentence's basis of truth is found in referring to itself and its assertion, causing a logical paradox.

Hofstadter argues that the psychological self (ego) arises out of a similar kind of paradox (spell). We are not born with an ego—it emerges only gradually as experience shapes our dense web of active symbols into a tapestry rich and complex enough to begin twisting back upon itself. According to this view the psychological self (ego) is a narrative fiction, something created only from the intake of symbolic data and its own ability to create stories about itself from that data.

These are the premises on which this exposition is based. The reader may check if it has been validated at the end of this exposition. Validation, however, does not mean validation by consensus. If the reader is convinced that the hypothesis has been validated, then it is indeed valid as far as he is concerned, irrespective of what others might say.

KEY TERMS DEFINED

The definitions of key terms as applied in this exposition are given below:

The Father:	The Self; The All; Non-duality
God	The DNA; The scripture
The Holy Ghost	Body-awareness; Self-awareness
The Son	Carrier of Holy Ghost; True human being
The Serpent:	Dualistic religion and its dualistic scripture; The Virus
Jesus:	The uncorrupted human body; The literal Gospel
Christ:	The true human DNA; The spiritual Gospel
Satan:	Dualistic (literal) scripture; The Serpent DNA
Adamites:	Carriers of virus DNA
Evites:	Carriers of true human DNA
Mortals:	Deluded Evites

There is only one Father, and he is the All—the Father of everything, everywhere. He is non-duality—the unity of polar opposites. He is immanent in everything, yet transcendent to everything. He is present in everything as the *form.*

However, there are many Gods; there are as many Gods as there are DNAs (scriptures). The God of the Adamites is not the God of the Evites. When Adamites talk about God, they are talking about their God, the Serpent; they worship him. When Evites talk about God, they are talking about their God, the Christ; they worship him. Mortals, however, worship the Serpent thinking that they are worshipping Christ. The term *worship*, here, means "to obey orders."

Christ represents the true human DNA, and the resurrected Jesus symbolizes it. An awakened Mortal—one who has known Christ—realizes his true Evite nature and is enlightened. The Gospel facilitates the knowing of Christ.

THE RULES OF EXEGESIS

And I saw in the right hand of him that sat on the throne a book written within and on the backside, sealed with seven seals. And I saw a strong angel proclaiming with a loud voice, Who is worthy to open the book, and to loose the seals thereof?
Revelation 5:1-2

The seven rules of exegesis used in this exposition are given below:

1. The Jot and Tittle Rule
   The first and foremost is the rule of the *Jot and Tittle.* It stipulates that we take every detail of the Gospel text on faith, as infallible truths. This may seem incredulous to the scientifically-minded person who may say, "Show me the proof, then I will accept." But, the Gospel says, "First accept on faith, then you will see the proof."
   Scriptural authority: The King James Bible, Authorized Version
2. Never ignore a paradox
   Whenever the essential nature of things is analyzed by the intellect, it must seem absurd or paradoxical; because truth is paradoxical. Therefore, never underestimate the paradox. Encounters with it are literally encounters with the Self.
3. Gospel: The Book written within and on the backside
   The Gospel is a book written both *within* and *on the backside.* The writing within is the spiritual Gospel and the writing on the backside is the literal Gospel. While the literal content is visible to all, the spiritual content is visible only to those who are able to 'open' it.
4. Gospel words are divine
   Gospel words are divine; they have a light-like quality about them. Just as white light enfolds multiple colors, the Gospel

words enfold multiple meanings. It is up to the interpreter to choose the meaning(s) that *feels* right to him. Choosing, however, is not an "either-or" kind of operation; rather, it is a "both-and" kind of operation.

5. Gospel terms define classes not instances
   Gospel terms define spiritual principles rather than names of particular objects, persons, or places. In other words, the Gospel terms define classes (generalities) rather than instances (particularities). The Gospel story is a vehicle for carrying spiritual truths. It is an allegory rather than a historical account.
6. Truth is seen, not heard
   The emphasis on seeing in mystical traditions should not be taken too literally, but has to be understood in a metaphorical sense, since the mystical experience of reality is an essentially non-sensory experience. When mystics talk about seeing, they refer to a mode of perception which may include visual perception, but which always and essentially transcends it to become a non-sensory experience of reality. What they do emphasize, however, when they talk about seeing, looking or observing is the empirical character of their knowledge. *Seeing* implies personal or direct experience of the truth, whereas *hearing* implies second-hand or indirect knowledge.
7. Truth cannot be seen from within a religion
   At least two lines are required to define a point. If we consider the point as analogous to truth and line as analogous to path (religion), then it is easily seen that the truth cannot be determined from within a religion. The seeker of truth has to approach it from at least two different angles; only then the truth can be discerned. However, the only requirement is that the selected paths (religions) be straight (non-dualistic).

GOSPEL OF MATTHEW

THE EXEGESIS

CHAPTER 1

In the beginning

MATTHEW 1:1

"The Book of the generation of Jesus Christ, the son of David, the son of Abraham."

The Gospel of Matthew is a crypt with two gates of entry: one of them, conspicuous and wide; the other, hidden and narrow. The wide gate is open and the path it leads to is easy to follow. Casual visitors to the Gospel—the Gospel tourists—choose the wide gate to enter it. But, they see only the *dead Jesus*—the literal Gospel. The narrow gate, on the other hand, is difficult to find and is locked, and the path it leads to is arduous. Only the Gospel adventurers find it, open it and dare to enter through it. But, these brave men see the *living Jesus*—the spiritual Gospel.

The very first statement of the Gospel of Matthew is mysterious, and unraveling it correctly is critical to the Gospel's exposition. But, for unraveling, we need special tools. Therefore, we shall first familiarize ourselves with a powerful exegetical tool—the *Strong's Concordance.*

The Strong's Concordance is a concordance of the *King James Bible* (KJV) that was constructed under the direction of Dr. James Strong (1822-1894) and first published in 1890. Dr. Strong was Professor of exegetical theology at Drew Theological Seminary at the time. The Strong's Concordance is an exclusive cross-reference of every word in the King James Bible back to the word in the original text.

According to the Strong's Concordance, the Greek word for *book* is *biblos* (G976), which means "a scroll of writing." And *scroll* is a roll of papyrus, parchment or paper which has been written, drawn or painted on for the purpose of transmitting information. The Greek word for *generation*, according to the Strong's Concordance, is *genesis* (G1078), which means "nativity." If we trace the origin of the word *genesis*, we arrive at the word *ginomai* (G1096), which means "to cause to be" or "to come into being." The word also means "to have a self." In short, the word *generation* implies *genetics*.

genesis ⟵ *genea* ⟵ *genos* ⟵ *ginomai*
G1078 ⟵ G1074 ⟵ G1085 ⟵ G1096

Applying the implications of the words *book* and *generation*, we translate the expression, "the book of the generation of Jesus Christ" as "the scroll of genetics of Jesus Christ." The *scroll of genetics*, in scientific parlance, is known as DNA. Therefore, the expression "the book of the generation of Jesus Christ" may be translated as "the DNA of Jesus Christ." In other words, the opening verse of the Gospel of Matthew introduces the Gospel as the DNA of Jesus Christ!

DNA (*Deoxyribonucleic Acid*) is also known as the "Book of Life." It encodes the genetic instructions used in the development and functioning of all living organisms and many viruses. Nearly every cell in human body has the same DNA, and most of it is located in the cell nucleus. The information in DNA is stored as a code made up of four chemical bases: *adenine* (**A**), *guanine* (**G**), *cytosine* (**C**), and *thymine* (**T**). The human DNA consists of about 3 billion bases, and more than 99 percent of those bases are the same in all people. The order, or sequence, of these bases determines the information available for building and maintaining an organism, similar to the way in which letters of the alphabet appear in a certain order to form words and sentences of a book.

DNA bases pair up with each other, A with T and C with G, to form units called *base pairs*. Each base is also attached to a sugar molecule and a phosphate molecule. Together, a base, sugar, and phosphate are called a *nucleotide*. Nucleotides are arranged in two long strands that form a spiral called a *double helix*. The structure of the double helix is somewhat like a ladder, with the base pairs forming the ladder's rungs and the sugar and phosphate molecules forming the vertical sidepieces of the ladder. An important property of DNA is that it can replicate, or make copies of itself. Each strand of DNA in the double helix can serve as a pattern for duplicating the sequence of bases. This is critical when cells divide because each new cell needs to have an exact copy of the DNA present in the old cell.

The expression "*the book of the generation*" appears only in two places in the entire Bible. The first appearance is in the Book of Genesis (5:1), where it says, *"This is the book of the generations of Adam."* The other is the opening verse of the Gospel of Matthew (1:1). In other words, the Bible talks about two kinds of DNAs: the first is the DNA of the "corrupted" Adam (mind); the other is the DNA of the "uncorrupted" Adam (body), also known as Eve.

MATTHEW 1:2-17

"Abraham begat Isaac; and Isaac begat Jacob; and Jacob begat Judas and his brethren; And Judas begat Phares and Zara of Thamar; and Phares begat Esrom; and Esrom begat Aram; And Aram begat Aminadab; and Aminadab begat Naasson; and Naasson begat Salmon; And Salmon begat Booz of Rachab; and Booz begat Obed of Ruth; and Obed begat Jesse; And Jesse begat David the king; and David the king begat Solomon of her that had been the wife of Urias; And Solomon begat Roboam; and Roboam begat Abia; and Abia begat Asa; And Asa begat Josaphat; and Josaphat begat Joram; and Joram begat Ozias; And Ozias begat Joatham; and Joatham begat Achaz; and Achaz begat Ezekias; And Ezekias begat Manasses; and Manasses begat Amon; and Amon begat Josias; And Josias begat Jechonias and his brethren, about the time they were carried away to Babylon: And after they were brought to Babylon, Jechonias begat Salathiel; and Salathiel begat Zorobabel; And Zorobabel begat Abiud; and Abiud begat Eliakim; and Eliakim begat Azor; And Azor begat Sadoc; and Sadoc begat Achim; and Achim begat Eliud; And Eliud begat Eleazar; and Eliazar begat Matthan; and Matthan begat Jacob; And Jacob begat Joseph the husband of Mary, of whom was born Jesus, who is called Christ. So all the generations from Abraham to David are fourteen generations; and from David until the carrying away into Babylon are fourteen generations; and from carrying away into Babylon unto Christ are fourteen generations."

The genealogy of Jesus Christ is as given below:

1. Abraham
2. Isaac
3. Jacob
4. Judas (and his brethren)
5. Phares (and Zara *through* Thamar)
6. Esrom
7. Aram
8. Aminadab
9. Naasson
10. Salmon
11. Booz (*through* Rachab)
12. Obed (*through* Ruth)
13. Jesse
14. David (the king)
15. Salomon (*through* her that had been wife of Urias)
16. Roboam
17. Abia
18. Asa
19. Josaphat
20. Joram
21. Ozias
22. Joatham
23. Achaz
24. Ezekias
25. Manesses
26. Amon
27. Josias
28. Jechonias (and his brethren, about the time they were carried away to Babylon)
29. Salathiel (after they were brought to Babylon)
30. Zorobabel
31. Abiud
32. Eliakim
33. Azor
34. Sadoc
35. Achim
36. Eliud

37. Eleazar
38. Matthan
39. Jacob
40. Joseph (the husband of Mary)
41. ?
42. Jesus (who is called Christ)

The genealogy of Jesus presents us a problem. According to Matthew 1:17, there are 42 generations from Abraham to Jesus—14 generations from Abraham to David, 14 from David to Jachonias (up to the time of carrying away into Babylon), and 14 from Jachonias to Jesus. That adds up to 42 generations from Abraham to Jesus. But, the genealogy lists only 41 generations! We cannot simply gloss over this anomaly because, according to the principle of the *Jot and Tittle,* every word of the Gospel, even the minutest detail, is beyond reproach. Therefore, we must resolve this anomaly before we can continue with the exegesis.

To resolve this anomaly, we first locate Jesus at the 42nd position in the genealogy, as mentioned in Matthew 1:17, and then start listing the generations from Abraham. When we do so, we find the 41st position empty. We find only empty space between Joseph's generation (40th) and Jesus' generation (42nd). There is a clear *discontinuity* in the genealogy of Jesus suggesting that Jesus is not a descendant of Abraham and David in the literal sense. Discontinuity, according to Thomas Samuel Kuhn, the American physicist, historian and philosopher of science, is indicative of a paradigm shift. Based on Kuhn's definition of scientific paradigm, Fritjof Capra defines a *social paradigm* as follows:

> *. . . a constellation of concepts, values, perception, and practices shared by a community, which forms a particular vision of reality that is the basis of the way the community organizes itself.*
>
> Fritjof Capra, The Web of Life, p.5

Here, the paradigm shift is from the Adamite worldview to the Evite worldview; from insanity to sanity; from darkness to light; from Serpent to Jesus Christ; from *thy seed* to *her seed.*

The empty space in the 41st position naturally raises the question "What"—the abstract concept that potentially contains all *possible* answers, or knowledge. The Hindu vēdas call it *Kā*, which means "pure awareness" (Sanskrit: *śuddha bhōdham*). The universe is the manifestation of *Kā*. It represents the Brahman—the Self.

In Matthew 1:16 we read: *"And Jacob begat Joseph the husband of Mary, of whom was born Jesus, who is called Christ."* According to the Gospel, Joseph and Jesus are related via Mary, who is the connecting link between the two. The Father and the Son are related through the Holy Ghost. And the Holy Ghost is body-awareness.

THE GENEALOGY OF JESUS CHRIST—DEMYSTIFIED

If we take the names in the genealogy of Jesus Christ simply for their word meaning, I repeat, simply for their word meaning, ignoring the histories of the persons behind those names, then we realise that the genealogy of Jesus Christ is telling a miraculous story—the story of the transformation of the Adamite DNA (scripture) into the Evite DNA (scripture).

To demystify the genealogy, we have to strip off the literal (historical) content of the names and take only their spiritual essence.

At the very top of the list is Abraham. The name *Abraham* is derived from the Hebrew word *abrāhām* (H85), which means "father of a multitude." Abraham represents the *Father* or the Self. He is not merely the father any particular nation, but the father of all. Abraham represents the dreamer. Or, he may be thought of as the author-reader of a fantastic story. Abraham begets Isaac.

The Greek word used in the Gospel for *beget* is *gennaō* (G1080), which means "to procreate" or "to regenerate." The word is derived from the root word *ginomai* (G1096), which has many connotations and is used with great latitude. The word *ginomai* means "to cause to be," "to pass down," or "to publish," among others. Spiritually, the word *beget* means both "to create" and "to author." It implies both physical evolution (DNA evolution) as well as spiritual evolution (scriptural evolution).

The name *Isaac* is derived from the Hebrew word *yiṣḥāq* (H3327), which means "laughter" or "mockery." Isaac is the only Biblical patriarch whose name is not changed, and the only one who does not leave Canaan. Ugaritic texts dating from the 13th century BCE refer to the Canaanite deity *El* who has a benevolent smile. Isaac represents the creator God, who is an *epiphenomenon* ('mockery') of the Father. Isaac represents both the dream and the dream-script. Alternatively, he may be thought of as a book, which Abraham (the author-reader) scribes. And its story is flexible. It is made up of dreamer's beliefs. As the dreamer's beliefs change, the dream changes too. Isaac represents the belief system, the God, and the true human DNA, also known as the living book. Isaac begets Jacob.

Jacob represents Adam who is the progenitor of man. The name *Jacob* is derived from the Hebrew word *ya'aqōb* (H3290), which means "heel-catcher" or "supplanter." He is a *supplanter* because he is Father himself disguised as a character in the dream (book). However, as character, he is not aware of his true nature. He is a *heel-catcher* because he is connected to the Father (Self) by an unseen umbilical-cord-like link called body-awareness (Holy Ghost). In other words, Jacob is actually Father himself mistaken as man because of the spell cast by the 'book'. Jacob is also known as *Israel*, which signifies humanity.

Jacob begets Judas. The name *Judas* is derived from the Hebrew word *yehūda* (H3063), which means "celebrated." The word *yehūda* is derived from the root word *yāda* (H3034), which literally means "to use the hand", but it also means "to revere" or "to worship" (with extended hands). Judas represents devotion, or body-awareness. Judas begets Phares and Zara through Thamar.

Thamar is the daughter-in-law of Judas who tricks him into having intercourse with her. She eventually bears him the twins, Phares and Zara, in that illegitimate union. The name *Thamar* is derived from the Hebrew word *tāmār* (H8558), which means "fruit" or "tree." Thamar represents the Serpent, and the "forbidden fruit" that the Serpent gave to the humans. The Serpent is an alien virus—the *enemy*. The forbidden fruit is the Serpent seed (DNA). And that fruit contains a deadly poison that can cast a death-like spell (delusion) in humans. In other words, the virus fruit can cause fatal infection in humans. The seed of the fruit can take root in human body. A major symptom of the infection is the feeling of sin, which is the root of religion. Religion, in turn, can break or separate human consciousness into mind and body. In other words, religion separates humanity into two genetically separate groups: the Adamites and the Evites.

The name *Phares* is derived from the Hebrew word *peres* (H6556), which means "a break" or "a breach." The name Phares signifies fragmented consciousness (mind). He represents the "fallen Adam," or deluded humans known as the Adamites. The name *Zara* comes from the Hebrew word *zerah* (H2225), which means "a rising of light." Zara represents the body; Zara represents body-aware humans known as the Evites. The expression, "*Judas begets Phares and Zara of Thamar*" may be interpreted as follows: "dualistic religion caused the separation of pure consciousness into mind and body by the spell known as sin." Phares begets Esrom.

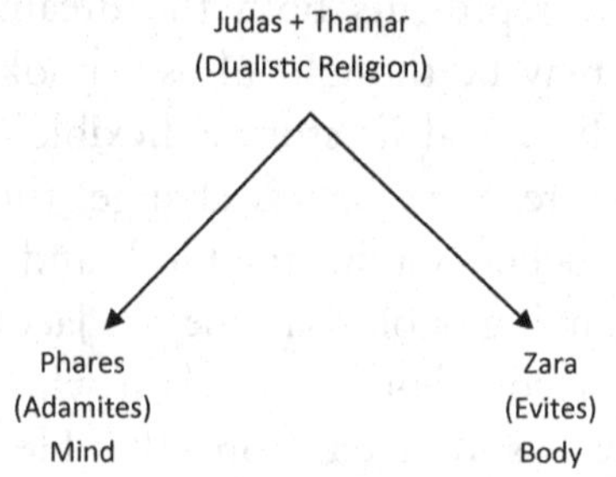

THE FALL

The name *Esrom* is derived from the Hebrew word *heṣrōn* (H2696), which means "court-yard." It is derived from the root word *hāṣēr* (H2691), which means "a hamlet surrounded by walls." Esrom represents a house of worship, or a temple. It represents a religious gathering. Esrom begets Aram.

The name *Aram* is derived from the Hebrew word *rām* (H7410), which means "lifting." The word *rām* is derived from the root word *rum* (H7311), which means "to raise", "to exalt", "to lift up" or "to promote." Aram represents religious fervor, or religiosity. It is also called "the fear of God." Aram begets Aminadab.

The name *Aminadab* is derived from the root words *am* (H5971), which means "congregation" and *nādab* (H5068), which means "volunteer" or "soldier." Spiritually, the name Aminadab represents the religious fanatics. Aminadab begets Naasson.

The name *Naasson* is derived from the Hebrew word *nahṣōn* (H5177), which means "enchanter." It is derived from the root word *nāhas* (H5172), which means "to hiss" or "to whisper a magic spell." Naasson represents the *Serpent-children*. Naasson represents the priestly class. Naasson begets Salmon.

The name *Salmon* is derived from the Hebrew word *salmōn* (H8012), which means "investiture." The word investiture means "the act or process of investing"; it implies formal bestowal. The word *salmōn* is derived from the root word *salma* (H8008), which means "a dress" or "garment." Therefore, the name Salmon represents ordained priesthood. Salmon begets Booz of Rachab.

The name *Rachab* is derived from the Hebrew word *rāhāb* (H7343), which means "a proud Canaanitress." The Canaanites are also known as Phoenicians. Phoenicia was an ancient Semitic civilization situated on the western coastal part of the Fertile Crescent (Babylon) and centered on the coastline of modern Lebanon. It was an enterprising maritime trading culture that spread across the Mediterranean from 1550 BC to 300 BC. The Phoenicians were famed in Classical Greece and Rome as 'traders of purple', referring to their monopoly on the precious purple dye of the Murex snail, used, among other things, for royal clothing, and for their spread of the alphabet, from which almost all modern phonetic alphabets are derived. Purple and scarlet are signature colors of the Phoenicians. The Phoenician alphabet is the basis for most languages written and spoken today; the Phoenician city of Byblos gave the Bible its name (Greek: *Ta Biblia*, meaning "the books"). Byblos was a great exporter of papyrus in ancient times. Spiritually, *Rachab* represents the Babylonian scripture in written form. Rachab also represents the *Scribe*.

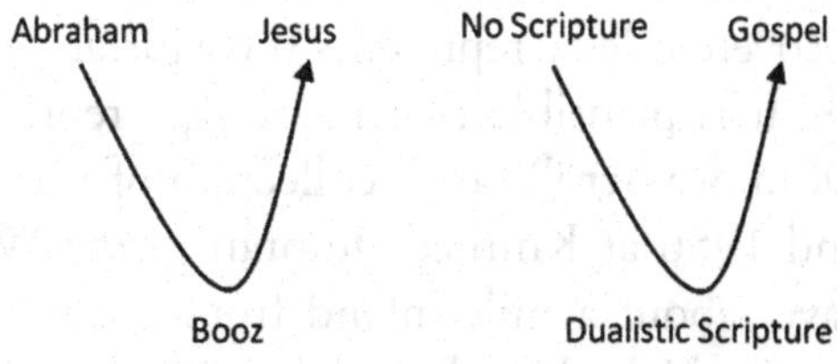

THE EVOLUTION

Booz is the offspring in the marriage between Salmon and Rachab. In other words, Booz represents the Serpent priesthood's adoption and adaptation of the Babylonian scripture, which is essentially a dualistic doctrine. The name *Booz* is derived from the Hebrew word *bō'az* (H1162), which refers to the name of a pillar in front of the temple. It is a phallic symbol, and is symbolized by the *obelisk*. Boaz represents the alien virus DNA in verbal form. It also represents the dualistic (literal) scripture. Boaz marks the nadir of the Adamites' genetic and scriptural evolution. Booz begets Obed through Ruth.

Ruth is a Moabite woman. The name *Moab* is derived from the Hebrew word *mo'ab* (H4125), which means "seed of the Father." Ruth represents the Evites. The marriage of Booz and Ruth represents the mixing of non-dualistic and dualistic scriptures. It also represents the mixing of Evite and Adamite DNAs. The product of that marriage is Obed.

The name *Obed* is derived from the Hebrew word *obēd* (H5744), which means "tilling" or "working." The word is derived from the active participle of the word *abad* (H5647), which means "to work," "to serve," or "to till." To till means to labor, as by plowing or harrowing, upon land for producing crops. Spiritually, the word "tilling" implies *cloning*. Therefore, the name Obed suggests genetic modification of the Adamite DNA. It represents *recombinant* DNA. Recombinant DNA molecules are formed by laboratory methods of genetic recombination (such as molecular cloning) to bring together genetic material from multiple sources, creating sequences that would not otherwise be found in biological organisms. Obed also signifies the reformation of dualistic scripture. Obed begets Jesse.

The name *Jesse* is derived from the Hebrew word *yīsay* (H3448), which means "to extant." It has the same meaning as the word *yēs* (H3426), "to stand out" or "to exist." Spiritually, the verb "to exist" implies "to be real." Jesse represents the real scripture, or scripture freed from corruption. Alternatively, he represents the real human DNA, or DNA freed of corruption. In other words, Jesse (*yīsay*) is Isaac (*yiṣḥāq*) recovered. Jesse represents the Mortal.

It is plausible that name *Jesse* represents the *Dead Sea Scrolls*. The Dead Sea Scrolls are a collection of 972 texts discovered between 1946 and 1956 at Khirbet Qumran in the West Bank. They were found in caves about a mile inland from the northwest shore of the Dead Sea, from which they derive their name. The texts are of great historical, religious, and linguistic significance because they include the earliest known surviving manuscripts of works later included in the Hebrew Bible Canon, along with extra-biblical manuscripts which preserve evidence of the diversity of religious thought in late Second Temple Judaism. The scrolls have traditionally been identified with the ancient Jewish sect called the *Essenes*. The Dead Sea Scrolls are regarded as "*The Torah according to the Essenes*," which suggests the evolved state of their scripture. Jesse represents the Essene and their scripture. Jesse begets David the king.

The name *David* is derived from the Hebrew word *dawīd* (H1732), which means "loving." The word is derived from the root word *dōd* (H1730), which means "to boil" or "to love." David represents a true body-aware human being (Evite). Unlike his predecessors, he is not afraid of expressing physical love for fear of committing sin. He has the presence of the Father with him constantly and, therefore, he is confident that he cannot falter. David begets Solomon through a woman, who was formerly the wife of Urias. Physically, David represents a sect of Essenes and their scripture.

The name *Urias* is derived from the Hebrew word *uriya* (H223), which means "the light of East." The word is derived from the root word *ur* (H217), which means "the East," or "the region of light." Urias is a Hittite man, which suggests that he is from India. Spiritually, Urias represents the non-dualistic teaching of India. In other words, the expression "*. . . and David the king begat Solomon of her that had been the wife of Urias*" actually means "the fusion of Essene scriptures and the non-duality teachings of India gave rise to *Gnosticism*." Solomon represents Gnosticism.

The name *Solomon* is derived from the Hebrew word *salmon* (H8012), which means "investiture." The word investiture implies formal bestowal. The word *salmōn* is derived from the root word *salma* (H8008), which means "a dress" or "garment." Here, the name Salmon suggests a new line of priesthood, who are not priests in the regular sense of the word, but mystics or truth-seekers. The garment that drapes them is body-awareness. The new line of priesthood is also known as the *Prophets*. In India, they are known as *yōgis*. Salomon begets Roboam.

The name *Roboam* is derived from the Hebrew word *rehab'*ām (H7346), which means "a people has enlarged." Spiritually, the word *enlarged* implies "evolved." The name Roboam signals the birth of a new bloodline known as the "*line of David*." It is the line of body-aware Evites known as the *Royal Sages*. In Hindu mythology, these royal sages are known as the *rājarṣi*. The term is derived from the Sanskrit roots *rāja*, meaning "king" and *ṛṣi*, meaning "sage." Given below are the prophetic words of Prophet Isaiah:

> *For unto us a child is born, unto us a son is given: and the government shall be upon his shoulder: and his name shall be called Wonderful, Counsellor, The mighty God, The everlasting Father, The Prince of Peace. Of the increase of his government and peace there shall be no end, upon the throne of David, and upon his kingdom, to order it, and to establish it with judgment and with justice from henceforth even for ever . . .*
>
> Isaiah 9:6-7

Roboam begets Abia. The name *Abia* is derived from the Hebrew word *abiyāhu* (H29), which means "worshipper of Father." The Davidic line is the line of prophets who are worshippers of the Father rather than worshippers of God. Spiritually, the name Abia signifies the prophetic words, "*The Everlasting Father.*" Abia begets Asa.

The name *Asa* is derived from the Hebrew word *āsā* (H609). Its derivation is unknown, but the name suggests the name of a king and a Levite. Spiritually, the name Asa implies "royal priesthood," which is translated as *Rājariṣi*, or *Rājayōgi* in Sanskrit. Spiritually, the name Asa signifies the prophetic words, "*The Prince of Peace.*" Asa begets Josaphat.

The name *Josaphat* is derived from the Hebrew word *yehōśāpāt* (H3092), which means "YHWH-judged." It is derived from the root words *YHWH* (H3068), which means "the Father," and *śāpat* (H8199), which means "to judge" or "to govern." Spiritually, the name Josaphat refers to Prophet Micah's prophesying (Micah 5:2) regarding the coming of the "Governor." The name implies self-governance, or independence from religion. Spiritually, the name signifies the prophetic words, "*The Counsellor.*" Josaphat begets Joram.

The *Joram* is derived from the Hebrew word *yehōrām* (H3088), which means "YHWH-raised." The name Joram means "saved by the Father." Spiritually, the word *saved* implies eternity; it refers to the prophetic words "no end," and "for ever." Joram begets Ozias.

The name *Ozias* is derived from the Hebrew word *uzziya* (H5818), which means "strength of God." Spiritually, the name Ozias signifies the prophetic words, "*The Mighty God.*" Ozias begets Joatham.

The name *Joatham* is derived from the Hebrew word *yōtām* (H3147), which means "YHWH is perfect." It is derived from the root word *tām* (H8535), which means "complete." The words *perfect* and *complete* refer to the *Circle of Self*, which signifies the *Quantum Self* (Sanskrit: *pūrṇam*). Spiritually, Joatham signifies "*The Wonderful.*" Joatham begets Achaz.

The name *Achaz* is derived from the Hebrew word *āhāz* (H271), which means "possessor." It is derived from the root word *āhaz* (H270), which means "to seize," often with the accessory idea of holding in possession. The name Achaz implies possession of body-awareness (soul). Achaz alludes to the prophetic expressions, "the throne of David" and "his kingdom." Achaz begets Ezekias.

The name *Ezekias* is derived from the Hebrew word *yehizqiyāhu* (H2396), which means "strengthened of YHWH." It is derived from the root word *hāzaq* (H2388), which means "cured" or "repaired." The name means "cured by the Father." Ezekias begets Manasses.

The name *Manasses* is derived from the Hebrew word *menaśśeh* (H4519), which means "causing to forget." The word is derived from the root word *nāśa* (H5382), which means "to remit" or "to forget." The word, *remit* means "to pardon or forgive an offence." The name Manasses signifies salvation. Manasses begets Amon.

The name *Amon* is derived from the Hebrew word *āmōn* (H525), which means "trained" or "skilled." The word is derived from the root word *āmān* (H542), which means an "expert." Amon signifies equanimity, or faith. Amon begets Josias.

The name *Josias* is derived from the Hebrew word *yōśiah* (H2977), which means "founded of YHWH." Spiritually, it means "planted by the Father." The name Josias suggests *Immaculate Conception.* Josias begets Jechonias and his brethren before they were taken away to Babylon.

The name *Babylon* is derived from the Hebrew word *bābel* (H894), which means "confusion." The word is derived from the root word *bālal* (H1101), which means to "overflow" or "mix." Babylon signifies corruption—corruption of DNA and corruption of scripture. The expression "*before they were taken away to Babylon*" actually implies "before the attempt to corrupt them was made." Here, the genealogy of Jesus Christ talks about a second attempt to corrupt the Evite scripture and DNA.

The name *Jechonias* is derived from the Hebrew word *yekonyāhu* (H3204), which means "YHWH will establish." It is derived from the root word *kun* (H3559), which means "to be erect" or "set aright." Jechonias represents the Evite DNA, which could not be corrupted by genetic mixing; Jechonias also represents the Evite scripture which could not be tampered with. However, concurrently, it also suggests that Jechonias' brethren were destroyed by Babylon.

A word of caution: If you take the genealogy of Jesus Christ as history, then you are led into the literal Bible. According to the Bible story, Jechonias is known as *Jehoiachin*. He is the grandson of Josias, not his son, as mentioned in the Gospel. The name *Jehoiachin* is derived from the Hebrew word *yehoyākin* (H3078), which means "YHWH will establish." However, in the literal Bible we come across another character by the name *Jehoiakim* as the son of Josias, and as the father of Jehoiachin. Jehoiakim is a cursed figure. He is cursed by the Prophet Jeremiah (Jeremiah 22:24-30) never to be able to occupy the throne of David. The name *Jehoiakim* is derived from the Hebrew word *yehūyāqim* (H3079), which means "Jehovah will raise." Surprisingly, the name *Jeremiah* (H3414) too has a similar meaning ("Jah will rise"). In other words, one who takes the genealogy as history is led into *confusion*. It is this descending into confusion that is allegorically depicted as "taking away into Babylon." In other words, Babylon is nothing but a metaphor for literal Old Testament. It is the *Mystery Babylon*!

Jechonias begets Salathiel while he was in Babylon. The name *Salathiel* is derived from the Hebrew word *se'altiēl* H7597, which means "I have asked God." Spiritually, it means "I have asked the body"; it signifies meditation. The name Salathiel suggests that the Evite directly asks his body—the spiritual scripture—for revelation of truth. Salathiel begets Zorobabel.

The name Zorobabel is derived from the Hebrew word *zerubbābel* (H2216), which means "descended of Babylon." The word is derived from the root words *zārab* (H2215), which means "to flow away." Spiritually the word *zārab* means "to come out of." As we have seen before, the term *bābel* (H894) refers to Babylon. Therefore, the name Zorobabel means "to come out of Babylon." Zorobabel represents DNA that has safely "come out of" genetic corruption. Zorobabel represents the scripture that has "come out of" (escaped) corruption. Zorobabel begets Abiud.

> *And I heard another voice from heaven, saying, Come out of her, my people, that ye be not partake of her sins, and that ye receive not of her plagues.*
> Revelation 18:4

The name *Abiud* is derived from the Hebrew word *abihūd* (H31), which means "father of renown." Spiritually, it means "the Self that is known." The name Abiud refers to the *form* of the human body; it represents body-awareness. In other words, Abiud signifies meditation. Abiud begets Eliakim.

The name *Eliakim* is derived from the Hebrew word *elyāqim* (H471), which means "God of raising." It is derived from the root words *ēl* (H410), which means "God" and *qum* (H6975), which means "to lift up again," "to establish," or "to enjoin." Eliakim suggests the saving of human DNA from corruption. It also signifies the saving of Evite scripture. Here, it may be noted that although an Evite cannot really become an Adamite, he could lead an Adamite existence if he forgets the Father, that is, if he loses body-awareness. Eliakim signifies "the return," or *repentance*. Eliakim begets Azor.

The name *Azor* is derived from the Hebrew word *azzūr* (H5809), which means "helpful." The word is derived from the root word *āzar* (H5826), which means "to surround" or "to protect." The name Azor suggests that body-awareness will protect the Evites from evil like a shield. Azor begets Sadoc.

The name *Sadoc* is derived from the Hebrew word *sādoq* (H6659), which means "just." It is derived from the root word *sādaq* (H6663), which means "to be right" or "righteous." The Evites are also known as "the Just" or "the Righteous." Sadoc begets Achim.

The name *Achim* is derived from the Hebrew word *yōqim* (H3137), which is derived from the root word *yehūyāqim* (H3079), which means "YHWH will raise." Achim begets Eliud.

The name *Eliud* is derived from the Hebrew words *ēl* (H410) and *hōd* (H19350. Together they mean "God of majesty." Eliud begets Eleazar.

The name *Eliazar* is derived from the Hebrew word el'*āzar* (H499), which means "God is helper." The word is derived from the root word *āzar* (H5826), which means "to surround" or "to protect." Eleazar begets Matthan.

The name *Matthan* is derived from the Hebrew word *mattān* (H4977), which means "a gift." The word is derived from the root word *nātan* (H5414), which is used with great latitude with many meanings. The word means "to put forth" or "to print" among others. The name Matthan signifies Matthew and represents the spiritual Gospel. Matthan begets Jacob.

The name *Jacob* is derived from the Hebrew word *ya'aqōb* (H3290), which means "heel-catcher" or "supplanter." If the first Jacob signifies the imperfect Adam, then the second Jacob signifies the perfect Adam. He represents the new scripture that supplants the old one. Spiritually, the latter Jacob implies enlightenment. Jacob begets Joseph, the husband of Mary.

The name *Joseph* is derived from the Hebrew word *yōsēp* (H3130), which means "let him add." The word is derived from the root word *yāsap* (H3254), which means "to add," "to augment," or "to continue." Joseph represents "the one who adds"—the one who writes the Gospel.

Spiritually, Joseph represents the Father. But, he is known to the world only as the husband of Mary. The name *Mary* is derived from the Hebrew word *miryām* (H4813), which means "rebelliously." It is derived from the root word *mēri* (H4805), which means "to rebel." Mary represents turbulent consciousness, or mind. Mary is Joseph's (the Father's) creative mind. She represents the story—the world. In other words, the Father manifests as the Son in the world. And he is called the "Son of man," or "human being."

The statement, "*And Jacob begat Joseph, the husband of Mary, of whom was born Jesus, who is called Christ*" suggests that Joseph wrote the Gospel in the form of a historical allegory. It is the birth of the Gospel that is portrayed in the Gospel as the birth of Jesus. Joseph puts down his enlightened DNA in verbal form to give birth to the Gospel. The name Christ refers to the Father. Son of Man is the Christ. The Gospel is the DNA (*generation*) of Jesus Christ.

The genealogy of Jesus describes the evolution of man in a new light. Each name in the genealogy describes a certain stage in human evolution rather than a generation in human history. In other words, the interval between two generations in the genealogy represents an indefinite period rather than one human lifetime. The Gnostics call it an *aeon*. The word *aeon* is a Latin literal translation from the *koine* Greek word *ho-aion*, which means "age," "forever," or "for eternity." Its meaning is more or less similar to the Sanskrit word *kalpa* and the Hebrew word *olam* (H5769). Although the term *aeon* may be used in reference to a period of a billion years (especially in geology, cosmology or astrology), its more common usage is for any indefinite period.

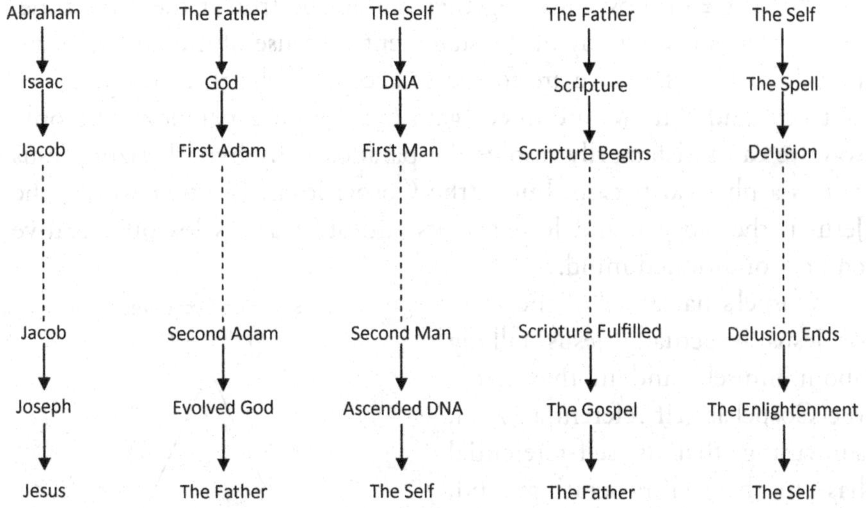

THE EVOLUTION

MATTHEW 1:18-21

"Now the birth of Jesus Christ was on this wise: When as his mother Mary was espoused to Joseph, before they came together, she was found with the child of the Holy Ghost. Then Joseph her husband, being a just man, and not willing to a make her a publick example, was minded to put her away privily. But while he thought on these things, behold, the angel of the Lord appeared unto him in a dream, saying, Joseph, thou son of David, fear not to take unto thee Mary thy wife: for that which is conceived in her is of the Holy Ghost. And she shall bring forth a son, and thou shalt call his name JESUS: for he shall save his people from their sins."

The Gospel presents before us three propositions:

1. Jesus is the son of Joseph, a progeny in the line of Abraham and David.
2. Jesus was immaculately conceived in Mary by the Holy Spirit.
3. Mary was still a virgin when Jesus was born

The three propositions, together, cannot be true at the same time. Yet, we cannot reject any of the statements because of the *Jot and Tittle* principle. Therefore, we are forced to accept all the three propositions as truth, and thus we are once again faced with a paradox. The only way we can satisfactorily resolve the paradox is by hypothesizing Jesus not as a physical person, but as the Gospel itself. In other words, the Jesus is the Gospel, and Joseph is its author; Mary is Joseph's creative and unconditioned mind.

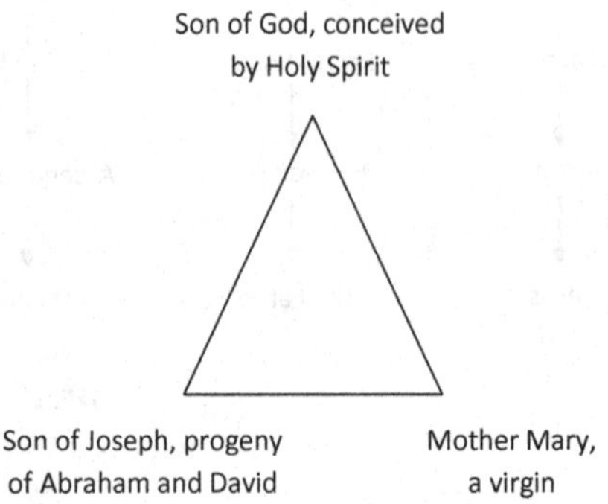

THE PARADOX

Gospel's narration of the story of Jesus is actually Jesus talking about himself, and in that sense, the Gospel is self-referential. And, something that is self-referential has to be self-generating and, therefore, a living being. The Gospel, it seems, is autopoietic.

What is *autopoiesis*? The word autopoiesis is derived from the Greek roots *auto* and *poiesis*. The word *auto* means "self" and refers to the autonomy of self-organizing systems; and *poiesis*—which shares the same Greek root as the word *poetry*—means "creation." Autopoiesis literally means "self-creation" or "self-generation." The term was introduced in 1972 by Chilean biologists Humberto Maturana and Fransis Varela. An autopoietic entity is one that is organized as a network of processes of creation, transformation, and destruction of components, which through their interaction and transformation continuously regenerate and realise the network of processes (relations) that produced them, and constitute the entity as a concrete unity in the space in which it exists. The space defined by an autopoietic system is self-contained and cannot be described by using dimensions that define another space. Autopoiesis was originally presented as a system-description that was said to define and explain the nature of living systems. An autopoietic system is to be contrasted from an *allopoietic* system, such as a factory, which uses raw materials and components to *create* a product (an organized structure) which is something *other* than the factory itself. Metaphorically speaking, the output of an autopoietic system is called a *son*, whereas the output of an allopoietic system is called a *creation*.

The Gospel is a living system in that it is the set of relationships between its motifs. It is an *organization* rather than a *structure*. According to Maturana and Varela, the organization of a living system is independent of the properties of the components, so that a given organization can be embodied in many different manners by many different kinds of components. According to this principle, as you change the meaning given to the Gospel motifs, another Gospel could arise that embodies the same set of relationships but tells a different story. The spiritual Gospel reveals the organization of the Gospel. The literal Gospel, on the other hand, describes the structure of the story.

This self-referencing, self-generating, self-organizing nature of the Gospel accounts for its holiness. Therefore, Jesus is the Gospel. He is *"Word made flesh."* In the words of Apostle John:

> *In the beginning was the Word, and the Word was with God, and the Word was God. The same was in the beginning with God. All things were made by him; and without him was not anything made that was made. In him was life; and the life was the light of men. And the light shineth in darkness; and the darkness comprehended it not.*
> John 1:1-5

The Greek word for *Gospel*, as used in the Gospel, is *euangelion* (G2098), which means "good message." But, the English word *Gospel* originates from the Anglo-Saxon word *Godspell*, which means "a narrative of God." The equivalent Sanskrit word for Gospel is *Bhāgavadam*. It is defined as follows: *Bhāgavata idam Bhāgavadam*, which means "the body of *Bhagavān* (God) is *Bhāgavatam* (Gospel)." The term *God*, here, refers to the true human (Evite) DNA. In other words, the Gospel describes the true human DNA. It implies that the Evite body is the manifestation of Gospel. Another Sanskrit definition of Bhāgavadam states: *Bhāgavadam ayam Bhāgavata*. According to this definition, one who understands Gospel becomes a God (Evite). In other words, the Gospel can purify corrupted DNA. Yet another definition of Bhāgavadam states: *Kāla dēsāvathibhyām nirmuktam iti Bhāgavadam*. It means that the Gospel is free from space and time. It is a narrative free from space and time. And such a narrative cannot be history; it has to be myth.

According to the Hindu epic *Padma Purāṇa*, Bhāgavadam was first narrated at a place called *Naimiṣāraṇya*. The term *Naimiṣāraṇya* is defined as follows: *Nemi śīryate yatra tat naimiṣa*. According to this definition, Naimiṣāraṇya is where the wheel stops spinning. Naimiṣāraṇya is mind free of thoughts. It suggests that the Gospel arises in still mind. Virgin Mary—the still mind of Joseph—represents the Naimiṣāranya—the womb of the Gospel.

If the Gospel is Jesus, then the Gospel meaning is the *flesh* and *blood* of Jesus. The literal meaning of the Gospel is the flesh of Jesus; and the spiritual meaning is his blood. The 'flesh' of Jesus has the

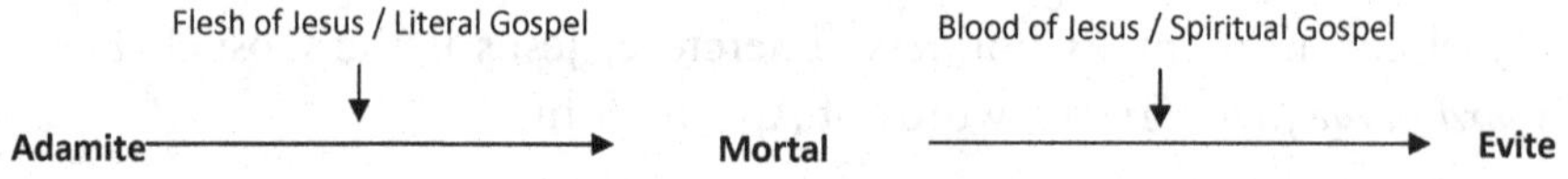

THE TRANSFORMATION

power to transform an Adamite into a Mortal; the 'blood' of Jesus has the power to transform a Mortal into an Evite, or *Son of God* (Jesus). The 'blood' of Jesus has the power to transform an Evite into an enlightened Evite (Christ).

> *But as many as received him, to them gave he power to become the sons of God, even to them that believe on his name.*
> John 1:12

The spiritual meaning of the Gospel is the blood Jesus shed for us on the cross. The term *cross* refers to the literal Gospel. Those who can truly understand the spiritual meaning of the Gospel are freed from ignorance and delusion, and are freed from religion.

Virgin Mary represents Joseph's unconditioned mind; the Holy Spirit, the spiritual meaning of the Gospel; Jesus is enlightenment. The implication: if the Gospel reader's mind is still, open, and free from external influences, then the Gospel seed impregnates it to give birth to Jesus (enlightenment). The reader is thus transformed into a *son of God*, an Evite.

The Gospel uses the Greek term *pneuma* (G4151) for Holy Spirit; it means "a breath of air"; it implies divine *inspiration*. The Hebrew term used in the Old Testament for Holy Ghost is *ruach ha-kodesh*, which means the "Spirit of God." Holy Ghost or Holy

Spirit in Hebrew generally refers to the divine aspect of revelation. In Jewish *Midrashic* literature, Holy Spirit is used as a hypostatization or metonym for God. The term *hypostatization* means "regarding something abstract as a material thing"; *metonym* means "a word that denotes one thing but refers to a related thing."

Joseph, the father of Jesus, is described in the Gospel as a *tekton*. The word *tekton* (G5045) has been traditionally translated into English as *carpenter*. But *tekton* is a rather general word implying "makers of objects" in various materials, even words. The Hebrew word for carpenter is *hārāŝ* (H2796) and it means "a fabricator of any material." It is derived from the word *hāras* (H2790), which means "to engrave" or "to devise." Very little other information about Joseph is given in the Gospel. He is never quoted. Perhaps, Joseph is actually the *tekton* of the Gospel. The characters in the Gospel are hypostatization of spiritual principles. For example, Joseph hypostatizes the Father; it is a metonym for the author of the Gospel. Jesus hypostatizes the Son; it is a metonym for the Gospel itself. Virgin Mary, the mother of Jesus, hypostatizes the Holy Ghost; it is a metonym for Joseph's creative mind. It is considered a *virgin* because it is free from religious conditioning.

Perhaps Joseph belonged to the *Essene* sect. The Essenes were a sect of Second Temple Judaism that flourished from the 2nd century BCE to the 1st century CE, which some scholars claim seceded from the Zadokite priests. Being much fewer in number than the Pharisees and Sadducees, the Essenes lived in various cities but congregated in communal life dedicated to asceticism, voluntary poverty, and daily immersion (meditation). Many separate but related religious groups of that era shared similar mystic, eschatological, messianic, and ascetic beliefs. These groups are collectively referred to by various scholars as the *Essenes*. Josephus, the first century Romano-Jewish scholar, historian and hagiographer, records that Essenes existed in large numbers and thousands lived throughout Roman Judaea.

The Gospel is a homiletic method for transforming Adamites into Evites; it is the path of enlightenment and sanity. The Father takes birth in Joseph's innocent mind as the Gospel (Jesus) through *Immaculate Conception*.

The Nativity account tells the story of a man—an Evite—who by divine inspiration writes a book (the Gospel) that challenges the established doctrine of his religion that he is afraid to publish it for fear of public ridicule and punishment. He, at first, considers discarding the document, but an inner *voice* tells him to go ahead and publish the book because the spiritual message contained in it has the power to transform the world. Intuition tells Joseph to give the book the name *Jesus*.

Joseph, the earthly father of Jesus, is an ignored character in the New Testament. He is one of the least understood personalities in the Bible. Yet, in our exposition, Joseph occupies a pivotal position. He is the corner stone—*"the stone that the builders rejected."* The Joseph of the New Testament is an echo of the Joseph of the Old Testament who is a pre-figuration of Jesus. The story of Joseph prepares us for the coming of Jesus in the Gospel. But, he is also the victim of the persecutions of his own brethren who mistake his innocence for conceit. Joseph's story provides us the hermeneutical framework for understanding the Jesus story in the Gospel. The major theme in the Joseph story is one of jealousy and betrayal—the betrayal of an Evite by Adamites, and yet saved by Providence. This very same theme is evoked in the parable of the murderous tenants in the vineyard, in the Gospel. The parable is an important key to understanding how Jesus' rejection and death is to be understood. The evil-doing tenants plot and kill the son of the vineyard owner, saying, *"This is the heir; come let us kill him and the inheritance will be ours"* (Matthew 21:38).

MATTHEW 1:22-25

"Now all this was done, that it might be fulfilled which was spoken of the Lord by the prophet, saying, Behold, a virgin shall be with child, and shall bring forth a son, and they shall call his name Emmanuel, which being interpreted is, God with us. Then Joseph being raised from sleep did as the angel of the Lord had bidden him, and took unto him his wife: And knew her not till she had brought forth her firstborn son: and he called his name JESUS."

The *Tanakh* is the canon of the Hebrew Bible. It is also known as the *Masoretic Text* or *Miqra*. The name Tanakh is an acronym of the first Hebrew letter of each of the Masoretic Text's three traditional subdivisions: *Torah* ("Teaching", also known as the Five Books of Moses), *Nevi'im* ("Prophets") and *Ketuvim* (*"Writings"*)—hence **T**a**N**a**Kh**. The term Tanakh means "that which is *read*." It refers to the literal Scripture. However, the Gospel expression, "that which was *spoken* of the Lord by the prophet" refers to the spiritual Scripture. The expression, "that it might be fulfilled which was spoken" is mentioned 9 times in the Gospel of Matthew, and nowhere else. Similarly, the expressions, "that which was spoken," or "it was spoken" are mentioned 14 times in the Gospel of Matthew, and nowhere else.

The Gospel echoes the words of Prophet Isaiah in announcing the birth of Jesus:

> *Behold, a virgin shall be with child, and shall bring forth a son, and they shall call his name Emmanuel, which being interpreted is, God with us.*
> Isaiah 7:14

The Greek word *Emmanouēl* (G1694) is derived from the Hebrew word *Immānuēl* (H6005) which means "with us is God." The Hindu equivalent for *Emmanuel* is *Vāsudēva*. The name *Vāsudēva* originates from two Sanskrit roots—*vāsa*, meaning "living," and *dēva* meaning "God." Combined together, it reads "living God." Vāsudēva is the earthly *avatar* of Lord Vishṇu. The Sanskrit root *vish* means "to enter"; therefore, the term *Vishṇu* means "he who has entered everything"; the Gospel calls it the Father.

The Gospel reveals two secrets:

1. The Gospel is the DNA of Jesus Christ
2. Jesus lives in uncorrupted human bodies

From these two facts we may infer that the Gospel or Jesus refers to the uncorrupted human (Evite) DNA. In other words, the DNA is the God that lives in us. Thus, the Gospel reveals to us the identity of God and the Serpent:

1. The term *God* refers to the uncorrupted human DNA
2. The term *Serpent* refers to the virus that corrupts human DNA

"Then Joseph being raised from sleep did as the angel of the Lord had bidden him, and took unto him his wife: And knew her not till she had brought forth her firstborn son and he called his name JESUS." Joseph decides to go ahead with his work, having found inner conviction, and does not yield to distractions of mind until the book was published. He names his book "Jesus."

CHAPTER 2

The Going Out

MATTHEW 2:1-2

"Now when Jesus was born in Bethlehem of Judaea in the days of Herod the king, behold, there came wise men from the east to Jerusalem, Saying, Where is he that is born King of the Jews? for we have seen his star in the east, and are come to worship him."

Jerusalem is the holy city of the Jews. It is called *Yeruśalayim* (H3389) in Hebrew, which means "a dual" (in allusion to its two main hills). Jerusalem symbolizes duality. It represents religion. Jerusalem signifies the 'group spirit,' or the Adamite spirit. Bethlehem is the name of a Palestinian city located in the central West Bank, neighboring south Jerusalem. The name *Bethlehem* (H1035) means "house of meat," or "house of bread." It refers to the Evite body, which is, literally, a house of meat. The expression, "house of bread" refers to the Gospel. The Gospel articulates the idea as follows:

> *And as they were eating, Jesus took the bread, and blessed it, and brake it, and gave it to the disciples, and said, Take, eat, this is my body.*
> Matthew 26:26

The Greek term for Judaea is *Ioudaia* (G2449) and it derives from the Greek word *Ioudaios* (H2453), meaning "belonging to the Jews." So, the phrase "Bethlehem of Judea" may be interpreted as "the body of Jew," or "scripture of Jews." Therefore, the expression, "Jesus was born in Bethlehem of Judaea" implies that the Gospel is the evolution of the

Tanakh. In other words, the expression implies that the Gospel fulfills the Tanakh. The word *fulfill* originates from the Greek word *plērēs* (G4134), which means "to make complete, or whole." The word *fulfill* does not suggest similarity between Tanakh and the Gospel; rather, it suggests just the opposite.

Herod was the Roman *client king* of Judaea. A client king is the ruler of a *client state*—a state that is economically, politically, or militarily subordinate to another more powerful state in international affairs. Herod is described by historians as a 'madman' who murdered his own family and a great many others. Herod was a *Judanized Edomite* He was an alien pretending to be a native. Judaea was a client state of Rome and Herod was her client king, ruling on and in behalf of the powers in Rome. Symbolically, Rome represents the alien masters—the Serpent. Herod represents the political establishment that is merely a puppet in the hands of the alien masters.

The word *east* literally means "a location in the eastern part of a country." But spiritually, the term suggests wisdom. *East* refers to India and non-duality. The Sanskrit word for *east* is *pūrva*, which means "before" or "ancient." Therefore, the expression "east of Jerusalem" means "before duality"; it implies non-duality. The wise men that came from east to Jerusalem represent the wisdom teachings of India—the *Advaita* (non-duality) teachings of India. It suggests the influence of pagan philosophies on Judaism (represented by Urias in the genealogy of Jesus).

The wise men ask King Herod, *"Where is he that is born King of the Jews? for we have seen his star in the east, and are come to worship him."* The phrase "King of the Jews" is used four times in the Gospel of Matthew: the first time in the above verse, and three times in Chapter 27, in connection with the crucifixion of Jesus.

The term *king* used in the above verse is significant. The word *king* is used in the Old Testament of the King James Bible 1677 times. In 1487 of those cases, the Bible uses the Hebrew word *melek* (H4428), which means "king" or "royal." The word *melek* is very similar to the Arabic word *mālik,* which means "master." The word *mālak* (H4427) is used 43 times; it means "to reign"; inceptively, "to ascend the throne"; causatively, "to induct into royalty." The word *mālak* is used mostly in connection with David who commences the royal dynasty of the Israelites. David was an ordinary man (Mortal) who got inducted into royalty by the grace of YHWH. David's line is a line of Evites, and Joseph belongs to it. The Aramaic word *melek* (H4430) is used for *king* 147 times, but, mostly in connection with foreign (alien) kings. The Gospel, however, uses the Greek word *basileus* (G935). The etymology of the word *basileus* is unclear. Most linguists assume that it is a non-Greek word that was adopted by Bronze Age Greeks from a preexisting linguistic substrate of the Eastern Mediterranean. The term, in all probability, refers to the Evite. The phrase, "King of the Jews" actually implies "master of the Jews" rather than "leader of the Jews."

The term *master* has the following connotations:

1. A person with the ability or power to use, control, or dispose of something
2. An owner of a slave, animal etc.
3. An employer of workers or servants
4. A person eminently skilled in something
5. A person whose teaching others accept or follow
6. A victor or conqueror
7. An original document, manuscript, etc., from which copies are made
8. Jesus Christ

The term *star* refers to any celestial body, a point of light that is visible from earth in darkness. From a non-dualistic perspective, the "star of the east" refers to the Gospel; it implies non-duality. The "star of the east" is the "inner sun" that dispels the darkness of ignorance and delusion caused by duality (religion). However, from the dualistic perspective, the "star of the east" refers to the rising sun. It is the physical (literal) source of light that dispels darkness. It is the *illuminator* of the world. It is the "outer sun," and it is called *Lucifer*. Lucifer represents duality. Religion and science are its left and right arms.

The term *star* also implies brilliance or fame. Therefore, the statement, *"Where is he that is born King of the Jews? for we have seen his star in the east, and are come to worship him"* may be translated as follows: "Where is that non-dualistic teaching (Gospel) whose fame we heard even in India. We have come to study it."

MATTHEW 2:3-6

"When Herod the king had heard these things, he was troubled, and all Jerusalem with him. And when he had gathered all the chief priests and scribes of the people together, he demanded of them where Christ should be born. And they said unto him, In Bethlehem of Judaea: for thus it is written by the prophet, And thou Bethlehem, in the land of Juda, art not the least among the princes of Juda: for out of thee shall come a Governor, that shall rule my people Israel."

Herod represents governments that betray their people and serve alien masters. Jerusalem is the head-quarters of Herod's government. Jerusalem represents the politico-religious establishment. The alien rulers and their minions are worried about the emergence of the Gospel (Jesus) that is awakening people from the spell cast by religion. The entire ruling hierarchy is concerned about the Gospel and its teachings.

Herod convenes a conclave of government officials, religious heads and intellectuals to discuss ways and means of locating the document's source and arrest the spread of the non-dualistic (*gnostic*) ideology. The term *gnostic* means "pertaining to knowledge," especially spiritual or self knowledge; it implies non-duality.

The term *Christ* comes from the Greek word *Christos* (G5547), which means "anointed." To anoint means to pour perfumed oil on people and things to symbolize the introduction of a sacramental divine influence, a holy emanation, or spirit. Here, the "perfumed oil" is the Holy Spirit, or body-awareness. The term *Christ* refers to someone who is anointed with the Holy Spirit—someone who is totally awake and body-aware. The term also refers to a book containing non-dualistic (*gnostic*) teachings.

The Adamite intelligentsia identifies the Gospel as the source of the trouble. They quote from the Bible prophesy concerning the coming of a *Messiah*—the anticipated savior of Mortals:

> But thou, Beth-lehem Ephrata, though thou be little among the thousands of Judah, yet out of thee shall he come forth

> unto me that is to be ruler in Israel; whose goings forth have been from of old, from everlasting.
>
> Micah 5:2

Beth-lehem represents the Evites; *Judah*, the Adamites; and *Israel*, the Mortals. The Biblical prophesy foretells the arrival of a *Messiah* who will liberate humanity from the hypnotic spell cast by religion. The expression, "whose goings forth have been from of old, from everlasting" may be read as follows: "whose story is old, yet new." According to the Hindus, a story that is old and new at the same time is called *purāṇa*. The word *purāṇa* is derived from the Sanskrit roots *purā*, meaning "old" and *nava*, meaning "new." The term *purāṇa* also means "myth." Therefore, the prophesied *Messiah* is a mythical story—the Gospel.

MATTHEW 2:7-10

"Then Herod, when he had privily called the wise men, enquired of them diligently what time the star appeared. And he sent them to Bethlehem, and said, Go and search diligently for the young child; and when ye have found him, bring me word again, that I may come and worship him also. When they had heard the king, they departed; and, lo, the star, which they saw in the east, went before them, till it came and stood over where the young child was. When they saw the star, they rejoiced with exceeding great joy."

Herod is Rome's proxy. And Rome is the Serpent, the cohesive *network* that operates as a single entity, the unseen master of the world. Herod represents the Politico-Religious Establishment that serves Rome. He is concerned about the influence of the new book, popularly known as Jesus, or the Gospel, on the Mortals. He is worried because he knows that the non-dualistic (gnostic) teachings of the Gospel can destroy duality (religion) and liberate the Mortals from his stranglehold. Therefore, he requests the intelligentsia to carefully examine all newly published gnostic documents ("search in Bethlehem") and locate the Gospel (Jesus)—the book that can destroy religion. The Gospel is the star that leads to the "young child," which is enlightenment.

Herod eagerly asks the wise men the time the star appeared. He wants to know when the wise men first came to know about the Gospel. Then he says to the wise men, *"Go and search diligently for the young child; and when ye have found him, bring me word again, that I may come and worship him also."* Here, Herod represents the Establishment and the young child, truth. The Establishment wants its intelligentsia to search diligently and find the truth. But its intentions are evil; it wants the truth only to distort and kill it.

". . . and, lo, the star, which they saw in the east, went before them, till it came and stood over where the young child was. When they saw the star, they rejoiced with exceeding great joy." The wise men follow the Gospel's trail of fame and, finally, locate it, and are overjoyed. But, we can interpret the verse in a different way using the key given.

THE KEY	
Term / Phrase	**Interpretation**
"them"	Truth-seekers
"the star, which they saw in the east"	The non-dualistic (spiritual) interpretation of the Gospel
"went before them"	Guided them
"till it came and stood over where the young child was"	Till they received enlightenment

The spiritual implication of the verse: "The non-dualistic interpretation of the Gospel guided the truth-seekers to enlightenment and bliss."

The word "lo" is an interesting term. It is used 8 times in the Gospel of Matthew. It generally signals the presence of non-duality ("I am") wherever it is mentioned. Numerically, the word "lo" represents the number 10, where 1 represents *Alpha* and 0 represents *Omega*.

> *I am alpha and Omega, the beginning and the end, the fist and the last.*
> Revelation 22:13

MATTHEW 2:11-12

"And when they were come into the house, they saw the young child with Mary his mother, and fell down, and worshipped him: and when they had opened their treasures, they presented unto him gifts; gold, and frankincense, and myrrh. And being warned of God in a dream that they should not return to Herod, they departed into their own country another way."

"And when they were come into the house, they saw the young child with Mary his mother." The Hebrew term for *house* is *bayit* (H1004), which means "inside." Here, the house represents the Gospel, the book. The content of the Gospel represents the inside of the house. The *young child* is the new insight; it is the spiritual Gospel. "Mary, his mother" represents the *outside*; it refers to the literal Gospel. Mary symbolizes the story in which the Gospel truth is embedded. The wise men are the Evites. Therefore, the verse may be interpreted as follows: "When the Evites read the Gospel, they see the truth couched in allegory." The Sanskrit word for *insight* is *darśanam*. However, the word *darśanam* also suggests falling and worshipping a God.

The *inside* represents the quantum field; it is the field of possibilities. The state inside is paradoxical or mythical; it defies logic. We can never really know the *inside*. Even if we cut it open and peep inside, all we see is the *outside*. Inside is inside; it can never become outside. In Quantum Mechanics, the *Schrödinger's Cat* paradox proves this beyond a shred of doubt. Schrodinger's Cat is a thought experiment, devised by Austrian physicist Erwin Schrodinger in 1935. It illustrates the problem of the Copenhagen interpretation of quantum mechanics applied to everyday objects. The Gospel calls the *inside*, the *kingdom of heaven*. All we can do is speculate about it in multifarious ways, which is the right thing to do. The Gospel expresses it as "falling down and worshipping."

The expression, "Mary, his mother" also refers to duality or the mind. Mary symbolizes the Tanakh, which gave rise to the Gospel. According to Eastern mystics, there is only non-duality. To them, opposites are merely abstract concepts belonging to the realm of thought, and as such they are relative. By the very act of focusing our attention on any one concept, we create the opposite. Duality gives birth to Non-duality.

> *When all in the world understand beauty as beautiful, then ugliness exists; when all understand goodness as good, then evil exists.*
>
> Lao Tzu

The wise men kneel and worship the young child. It signifies the Evites' acceptance of the Gospel as a deity. They pay their respect to the young child by presenting gifts of gold, frankincense and myrrh. Gold signifies great value. Frankincense is a substance that can purify atmosphere, and therefore, denotes purity, or truth. Myrrh was used by ancient Egyptians for the embalming of mummies. Myrrh signifies eternal life. Therefore, the presentations of gold, frankincense and myrrh signify the great value, the cleansing power and the life-giving potential of the Gospel.

"And being warned of God in a dream that they should not return to Herod, they departed into their own country another way." Here, the Gospel uses the Greek word *chrēmatizō* (G5537) for God; it means "inner revelation." It implies revelation by the body (DNA). The first thing that occurs to the wise men after they visit the young child is that they should not return to Herod. To "return to Herod" means "to go back to religion, or duality." The implication: when the truth-seeker finds the hidden message of the Gospel, he is transformed, and he abandons his dualistic religion and pursues a new path—the path of truth, the path of non-duality, the path of self-awareness.

MATTHEW 2:13-15

"And when they were departed, behold, the angel of the Lord appeareth to Joseph in a dream, saying, Arise, and take the young child and his mother, and flee into Egypt, and be thou there until I bring thee word: for Herod will seek the young child to destroy him. When he arose, he took the young child and his mother by night, and departed into Egypt: And was there until the death of Herod: that it might be fulfilled which was spoken of the Lord by the prophet, saying, Out of Egypt have I called my son."

The Greek word for *Lord* is *kurios* (G2962); it refers to the Self. The Greek word for *angel* is *angelos* (G32), which means "a messenger." Therefore, the expression, *angel of the Lord* means "messenger of the Self," or intuition.

The term *Egypt* is derived from the ancient Greek name *Aiguptos* (G125), which is a corruption of an earlier Egyptian name, *Hwt-ka-Ptah*, meaning "home of the ka (soul) of Ptah." In Egyptian mythology, *Ptah* is vocalized as *Pitah*, and it means "father." In other words, *Egypt* means "home of the Father" or "the home of the Self"; it refers to the human body. And Egypt signifies "the inside," or "the inner body." Egypt signifies mystery. The word *mystery* means "something that defies understanding" or "something that cannot be explained." Egypt represents the true human body—the Self. Interestingly, the Sanskrit words for *father* and *mystery* are *pitāh* and *gupt* respectively.

Joseph, the author of the Gospel, is afraid that the Politico-Religious Establishment might kill the Gospel if it ever finds out the real implication of its non-dualistic message. His intuition tells him to encode the Gospel message in an allegory so that the Adamites, who are spiritually blind, would not perceive it.

The angel of Lord instructs Joseph: *"Arise, and take the young child and his mother, and flee into Egypt, and be thou there until I bring thee word."* Intuition warns Joseph not to reveal the true meaning of the Gospel openly. The Gospel, even today, remains in that encrypted form. The true meaning of the Gospel will be revealed only when it is time for the Establishment to leave. In other words, the revelation of the true meaning of the Gospel will ring the death knell of the Politico-Religious Establishment. It is the end of the 'world'. The revelation of the true meaning of the Gospel is the *Second Coming of Jesus Christ.* The prophets of Israel have foretold that it would happen.

The emergence of the true meaning of the Gospel from the allegory is implied in the prophetic words: *"Out of Egypt have I called my son."* It means: "from inner body comes the Gospel." It also means "from the spiritual Gospel comes the literal Gospel."

> *And there appeared a great wonder in heaven; a woman clothed with the sun, and the moon under her feet, and upon her head a crown of twelve stars: And she being with child cried, travailing in birth, and pained to be delivered. And there appeared another wonder in heaven, and behold a great red dragon, having seven heads and ten horns, and seven crowns upon his heads. And his tail drew a third part of the stars in heaven, and did cast them into the earth: and the dragon stood before the woman which was ready to be delivered, for to devour her child as soon as it was born. And she brought forth a man child, who was to rule all nations with a rod of iron:*

> *and her child was caught up to God, and to his throne. And the woman fled into the wilderness, where she hath a place prepared of God, that they should feed her there a thousand two hundred and threescore days.*
> Revelation 12:1-6

In the above verse, the *woman* represents the creative mind of the Evite; the *man child*, the Gospel; the *great red dragon*, religion. The expression, "rod of iron" refers to sword, which implies non-duality. The term *God* refers to the true human DNA. And that God lives in Egypt, or the inner body (cell).

MATTHEW 2:16-18

"Then Herod, when he saw that he was mocked of the wise men, was exceeding wroth, and sent forth, and slew all the children that were in Bethlehem, and in all the coasts thereof, from two years old and under, according to the time which he had diligently enquired of the wise men. Then was fulfilled that which was spoken by Jeremy the prophet, saying, In Rama was there a voice heard, lamentation, and weeping, and great mourning, Rachel weeping for her children, and would not be comforted, because they are not."

The name *Bethlehem* means "house of bread" and, therefore, refers to the collection of spiritual documents. The expression *"children that were in Bethlehem and in coasts thereof"* refers to gnostic documents written by Evite authors in the Roman-Judaea region. Slaying by Herod of all the children, two years and under, in Bethlehem and nearby places refers to the confiscation and censoring of all gnostic books, published in Palestine during the past two years, by the Establishment.

The Gospel talks of a great lamentation in the land: *"In Rama was there a voice heard, lamentations and weeping, and great mourning, Rachel weeping for her children and would not be comforted, because they are not."* What is the meaning of these mysterious words? Literally interpreted, the words of prophet Jeremiah refers to the cry of a mother (Rachel) over her children, and with them the weeping over the fallen destiny of Israel, and over the calamities about to come upon her. But, spiritually, the words suggest something else. The name *Rama* is derived from the Hebrew word *rāma* (H7413), and it refers to the feminine active principle. The name *Rachel* is derived from the Hebrew word *rāhēl* (H7353), which means "a ewe" (the females being the predominant element of a flock). The terms *Rama* and *Rachel,* together, point to the Evites. The cry of Rachel signifies the cry of *Mother Wisdom,* or *Sophia* over the destruction of thousands upon thousands of priceless gnostic works by the Politico-Religious Establishment.

Sophia is a central idea in Hellenistic philosophy and religion, Platonism, Gnosticism, Orthodox Christianity, Esoteric Christianity, as well as Christian mysticism. *Sophiology* is a philosophical concept regarding wisdom, as well as theological concept regarding the wisdom of the Biblical God.

Rama probably refers to Ramallah, the Palestinian city in the central West Bank, located 10 kilometers north of Jerusalem. Ramallah was historically a Christian town, but today Christians are only a minority there. The lamentation of Rachel still echoes in the streets of Ramallah.

MATTHEW 2:19-23

"But when Herod was dead, behold, an angel of the Lord appeareth in a dream to Joseph in Egypt, Saying, Arise, and take the young child and his mother, and go into the land of Israel: for they are dead which sought the young child's life. And he arose, and took the young child and his mother, and came into the land of Israel. But when he heard that Archelaus did reign in Judaea in the room of his father Herod, he was afraid to go thither: notwithstanding, being warned of God in a dream, he turned aside into the parts of Galilee: And he came and dwelt in a city called Nazareth: that it might be fulfilled which was spoken by the prophets, He shall be called a Nazarene."

The expression, "land of Israel" implies "land of the Mortals," which is the world. Intuition tells Joseph, the author of the Gospel, that the time has come for presenting the Gospel before the world—to reveal truths unknown to Mortals since the beginning of time—in the form of an allegory. The reason he is encouraged to go ahead with the publication of his book is the news about the death of Herod; the end of an oppressive regime and the onset of a more people-friendly one. Herod's son *Archelaus* represents democracy. The name *Archelaus* (G745) actually means "the people's ruler." Joseph decides to publish the book after sensing a general easing of the political climate. Yet, he is cautious because he knows that Archelaus is after all is of the same stock as Herod and, therefore, potentially as brutal as his father, despite his humane exterior. As a precaution, Joseph avoids going into Judaea; instead, he settles in Nazareth, a city in Galilee.

The name *Judaea* (G2449, G2453) means "land of Jews." The name Judaea signifies the Jews. *Galilee* (H1551, G1056) means "a circle"; it signifies the Mortals. Nazareth is the largest city in the North District of Israel and is known as the Gentile capital of Israel. The name Nazareth is not mentioned in pre-Christian texts, but appears in many Greek forms of the New Testament. The name is derived from one of the Hebrew words for *branch*, namely *neser* (H5342), and reminds us of the prophetic words of Isaiah: *"And there shall come forth a rod out of the stem of Jesse, and a Branch shall grow out of his roots"* (Isaiah 11:1). The Hebrew word for *rod* is *cho er* (H2415), meaning "a twig." The twig signifies life. There is an alternative interpretation for the name Nazareth. According to this interpretation, the name is derived from the verb *nazar* (H5341), meaning "to watch" or "to guard," and is understood in the sense of "watchtower" or "guard place." Nazareth implies self-awareness, and its inhabitants are known as *Nazarenes*. They are Evites.

The Gospel says Joseph *"being warned of God in a dream, he turned aside into the parts of Galilee; And he came and dwelt in a city called Nazareth."* The expression, "Nazareth, part of Galilee" means "Gentile Evites"; it means "self-aware humans." Joseph's intuition tells him to avoid the Adamites and to settle among the Evites, who are gentiles. He decides to present his Gospel only to the Gentiles.

CHAPTER 3

And He Called

MATTHEW 3:1-2

"In those days came John the Baptist, preaching in the wilderness of Judaea, And saying, Repent ye: for the kingdom of heaven is at hand."

The Greek name *John* is derived from the Hebrew name *Yohanan* (H3110), which means "Graced by YHWH." The word, Baptist is derived from the Greek word *baptizō* (G907), which means "to make whelmed," or "to make fully wet." The term refers to ceremonial ablution, especially of the ordinance of Christian baptism. Spiritually, the term *baptism* suggests conversion, or proselytization into another religion. Spiritually, the expression, "wilderness of Judea" refers to the Old Testament.

There are two aspects to John the Baptist: a higher aspect and a lower aspect. In the higher aspect, John represents repentance; in the lower aspect, John represents the literal Gospel, or the Christian Church.

But, here, we shall discuss the higher aspect. Spiritually, John denotes repentance. The Greek word for *repentance* is *metanoeō* (G3340), which means "to think differently or afterwards," that is, "to rethink." The word is commonly interpreted as "to morally feel compunction." But, spiritually, the term implies redirecting focus of awareness from the world to the body. The advent of John the Baptist signifies the inner urge to know the truth. The phenomenon of *metanoeō* does not happen to everyone. It happens by pure chance.

One has to be *graced* by the *Father* to experience it. The word *graced* actually means "to come into favor."

The advent of John the Baptist heralds the arrival of Jesus Christ. In a sense, John represents the state of readiness of mind and body before discovering the Gospel truth. The Hindus call it *Brahma-jijnāsā*, which is the pre-requisite for enlightenment. The very first *sūtra* (aphorism) of the *Brahma Sūtra*, one of the three canonical texts of Hindu religion, states:

> *Athātō Brahma-jijnāsā*
> Brahma Sutra 1:1
> ("Then the urge to know the truth.")

Baptism is a ceremonial immersion in water. It is the initiatory rite of passage of a sect, and represents the act of cleansing, both physically and mentally, a novice before admitting him into the sect. Water signifies awareness; therefore, the baptism rite signifies the dawning of body-awareness. It symbolizes coming out of delusion (mind) and coming in contact with reality (body). The baptism ritual also symbolizes the "washing away" of sins (conditioning). A child does not require baptism because it has only body-awareness, and no social-awareness. Therefore, the baptism of the Church is actually reverse baptism in that it is the rite of passage into religion, society and mind. It is the rite of passage into the world—the beginning of conditioning.

The message of John the Baptist is direct and terse: *"Repent ye: for the kingdom of heaven is at hand."* The term *heaven* is a much misunderstood one. We think of it as a pleasurable place located somewhere out there. The Sanskrit word for heaven is *vaikunda*, and it is defined as follows: "*Vikunditha buddhir-yathra bhavēth,*" meaning "where delusion does not exist." According to this definition, heaven is not a place, but the state of mind that is free from delusion. It suggests freedom from religion.

The expression, "at hand" has two implications: one, it suggests temporal proximity (now); two, it suggests spatial proximity (here). John probably meant both when he said, "The Kingdom of heaven is at hand." The expression, "at hand" implies "here and now." That which is always here and now is the body.

A kingdom is the domain of a king. The kingdom of heaven that John refers to is the human body. And the king of the human body is the Self. Therefore, what John says is this: "Turn towards your body and feel God." John's message echoes the Hindu *mahāvākya* (great saying) "*Tat Twam Asi,*" which means, "You are that."

MATTHEW 3:3

"For this is he that was spoken of by the prophet Esaias, saying, The voice of one crying in the wilderness, Prepare ye the way of the Lord, make his paths straight."

The name *Esaias* is derived from the Hebrew word *yĕśaya* (H3470), which means "YHWH has saved." The name refers to an Evite. It also hints at the saving power of the Gospel.

Spiritually, the term *wilderness* suggests deluded mind, especially, the Adamite mind. According to the Gospel story, John the Baptist is the mystic who preached in Judaea. His message is concise and pithy: *"Prepare ye the way of the Lord, make his paths straight."* The *Lord* John refers to is not an external God, but the Father—the Self—whose "way" is inwards, not outwards. The word *straight* literally means "without bend, angle, or curve." Morally, it means "righteous"; but, spiritually, it means "direct." In other words, John is saying, "Make his paths direct." And the direct path to the Self is the body; every other path is indirect in that they all employ mind. And John says, *paths,* implying that there are as many paths to the Self as there are humans. Alternatively, the expression, "straight path" suggests "straight religion," or non-duality.

A righteous person is one who is body-aware; he is aware of his thoughts, actions, sensations, and feelings. He is in touch with reality, and, therefore, escapes the trap set by the Serpent. To be truly righteous means to be fully human. An automaton or an artificial intelligence entity cannot be righteous. And righteousness suggests the presence of the Father.

In a sense, the statement, "Prepare ye the way of the Lord, make his paths straight" is an elaboration of the statement, "Repent ye: for the kingdom of heaven is at hand."

If Jesus is the Gospel, the book, then John the Baptist is the preface to it.

MATTHEW 3:4-6

"And the same John had his raiment of camel's hair, and a leathern girdle about his loins; and his meat was locusts and wild honey. Then went out to him Jerusalem, and all Judaea, and all the region about Jordan, And were baptized of him in Jordan, confessing their sins."

Camel's hair is called *sūf* in Arabic, and one who wears raiment of camel's hair is called a *Sūfi*. A Sūfi is a prophet—an Evite. Prophet Elijah, the *Tishbite*, is described in the Bible as a hairy man, suggesting his Evite nature.

> *And they answered him, He was an hairy man, and girt with a girdle of leather about his loins. And he said, It is Elijah the Tishbite.*
> 2 Kings 1:8

Was John the Baptist a Sūfi mystic? Does his entrance in the Gospel suggest the influence of Gnosticism on the Gospel?

Sūfism is most prevalent in the middle-east and the Mediterranean region, particularly in Egypt, Syria, Iraq, Turkey and Arabia. Many people are drawn into Sūfism because of its emotional and personal ways of knowing God. Sūfism has come to mean as the path (straight path) of those who are interested in finding a way or practice toward inner awakening and enlightenment. The movement developed as a protest against the corrupt Politico-Religious Establishment and against the legalism and formalism of worship that paid more attention to the form than the content of the faith.

John wearing the "leathern girdle about the loin" implies a state of *vigilance*; it signifies body-awareness. John's food was "locusts and wild honey," suggesting that a truth-seeker will not worry about sustenance. Jesus says,

> *Therefore I say unto you, Take no thought for your life, what ye shall eat, or what ye shall drink; nor yet for your body, what ye shall put on. Is not the life more than meat, and the body than raiment?*
> Matthew 6:25

"Then went out to him Jerusalem, and all Judaea, and all the region about Jordan, And were baptized of him in Jordan, confessing their sins." The term *Jerusalem* is derived from the Hebrew word *yerūšalaim* (H3389), which means "a dual" in allusion to its two main hills. Jerusalem refers to duality or dualistic religion. The term *Judaea* is derived from the Greek word *Ioudaios* (G2453), which means "belonging to *Jehudah*." Judaea refers to Judaism. The term *Jordan* is derived from the Hebrew word *yardēn* (H3383), which means "a descender." The word is derived from the root word *yārad* (H3381), which means "to go downwards" or "to fall." The terms *Jerusalem*, *Judaea*, and *Jordan*, together, point to the Adamites. In other words, John's message (the preface) inspired many deluded Adamites to read the Gospel.

MATTHEW 3:7-10

"But when he saw many of the Pharisees and Sadducees come to his baptism, he said unto them, O generation of vipers, who hath warned you to flee from the wrath to come? Bring forth therefore fruits meet for repentance: And think not to say within yourselves, We have Abraham to our father: for I say unto you, that God is able of these stones to raise up children unto Abraham. And now also the axe is laid unto the root of the trees: therefore every tree which bringeth not forth good fruit is hewn down, and cast into the fire."

There is no mention of Pharisees or Sadducees in the Old Testament. These Jewish sects are said to have originated only about 150 years before Christ. We find mentions about them in the writings of the Romano-Jewish historian Josephus around that time. The Pharisees were the most numerous and wealthy sect of the Jews. They derived their name from the Hebrew word *pārāṣ* (H6567), which means "to set apart," or "to separate." The Pharisees separated themselves from the rest of the people, and professedly devoted themselves to special strictness in religion. They considered themselves to be special and maintained a holier-than-thou attitude. The Pharisees were at various times a political party, a social movement, and a school of thought among the Jews during the Second Temple Period.

The Sadducees were contemporaneous with the Pharisees, and they were the upper social and economic echelon of Judean society. As a whole, the Sadducees sect fulfilled the various political, social, and religious roles, including maintaining the Temple. The Sadducees were widely assumed to have been named after *Zadok*, a priest in the time of King David and King Solomon.

The Pharisees and Sadducees are prototypes of religious fundamentalists. They are over-zealous and hypocritical in their behavior. They are also cunning, calculative and upwardly mobile. A quality that typifies both Pharisees and Sadducees is vanity. The Pharisees and the Sadducees represent the religious fundamentalists in the Jewish society who have surrendered their individuality for religious/tribal identity. Traditions, as stipulated by the *Talmud*, dictate their behavior. Metaphorically speaking, the Pharisees and Sadducees are those who sold their souls to the Serpent. They are religious fanatics. However, John is quite surprised to see some of the Pharisees and Sadducees seeking the truth, and he questions them: *"O generation of vipers, who has warned you to flee from the wrath to come?"* implying, "O religious fanatics, do you think you can escape perdition?"

Spiritually, the expression, "generation of vipers" implies "DNA of the Serpent." According to John, the Pharisees and the Sadducees are the carriers of virus-infected DNA—the Serpent-children. It is probable that they have been infected by the virus during their sojourn in Babylon.

Surrendering individuality to society/religion is an essential requirement for becoming a public figure. In other words, to become a public figure, one has to serve or worship the Serpent, one has to have the Serpent DNA, or one has to be an Adamite. Serving or worshipping the Serpent means accepting societal norms (social and religious traditions) as the sole guide to behavior. In that sense, public figures are those who have sold their souls to the Establishment (Serpent) in exchange for worldly gains, such as wealth, power and fame.

The Sadducees' belief system reflects their hopelessness:

1. They believe that there is no resurrection, neither angel nor spirit; and that the soul of a man perishes with the body
2. They reject the doctrine of fate or decrees

While the Pharisees consider the Talmud as their most important scripture, the Sadducees reject the Talmud, but accept only the Torah. However, it is the non-dualistic scripture that John describes as the "fruit meet for repentance." It is the scripture that will help one turn inwards. Alternatively, the expression, "fruit meet for repentance" refers to individuality. In order to repent, one should first of all have the sense of "I am." Here, John stipulates the criterion for repentance: "In order to repent, one has to be an individual, first of all." In order to realise "I have erred," one should have the sense of "I am." A socialite (Adamite) does not have individuality, and therefore, cannot repent. And to repent means to repent to the Self, not to the public.

John adds, *"And think not to say within yourselves, We have Abraham to our father: for I say unto you, that God is able of these stones to raise up children unto Abraham."* What John says is this: "Do not think that you are human simply because you call yourselves human. Without individuality, you are but a lifeless thing like the stone."

John continues, *"And now also the axe is laid unto the root of the trees: therefore every tree which bringeth not forth good fruit is hewn down, and cast into the fire."* The term *tree*, here, refers to the DNA. The fruit of that tree is the scripture. Good fruit refers to non-dualistic scripture, and evil fruit refers to dualistic scripture. Alternatively, the term tree refers to the body, and the fruit refers to awareness (mind). Here, the good fruit refers to body-awareness or individuality, and the evil fruit refers to world-awareness, religious-awareness, or delusion.

According to John, the tree that does not bear good fruit is hewn down or cut to the root. In other words, the DNA (race) that has not produced non-dualistic scripture will be destroyed. A tree that is cut to the root will never sprout again. Alternatively, John's statement also implies that the Adamites who have not 'received' the Gospel will not receive eternal life, and they perish with this life. To receive the Gospel means to spiritually understand the Gospel.

Contrary to popular belief, the Gospel advises man to develop individuality. Individuality is essential for experiencing life fully, and to learn the lessons from life experiences. A person who does not have individuality has little chance of awakening. But, the Establishment, especially organized religions, lays great emphasis on suppressing individuality. It only wants slavish-minded people, not free-thinking individuals.

The *Mṛthyunjaya mantra* of the Hindu Rig Vēda reveals the secret of individuality. The name *Mṛthyunjaya mantra* actually means "the death-conquering mantra."

> *OM tṛyambakam yajāmahe sugandhim puṣti-vardhanam*
> *Urvārukam—iva bandhanān mṛtyōr-mukṣīyamāmṛtāt*
>
> ("Om, we worship the fragrant Self who nourishes and nurtures all beings. As a ripened pumpkin is freed from its bondage to the creeper, may He liberate us from death to immortality.")

It is very difficult to detach the raw pumpkin fruit from its vine by force; but, when the fruit is fully ripened, it drops off from the vine on its own. It is the fully ripened individuality that John calls "*the fruit meet for repentance.*" Individuality too, like the fully ripe pumpkin, falls off the world on its own and merges with Father, the Universal Self.

MATTHEW 3:11-12

"I indeed baptize you with water unto repentance: but he that cometh after me is mightier than I, whose shoes I am not worthy to bear: he shall baptize you with the Holy Ghost, and with fire: Whose fan is in his hand, and he will thoroughly purge his floor, and gather his wheat into garner; but he will burn up the chaff with unquenchable fire."

John the Baptist preached in the wilderness of Judea. He represents proto-Christianity (esoteric Judaism) which is an admixture of Jewish scripture and pagan mythology. The fact that John preached in the "wilderness of Judaea" implies that his esoteric teaching was accepted only by a fringe group in the Jewish community.

John the Baptist represents ego. Baptism signifies the rising of ego. Ego is a Latin and Greek word meaning "I", often used in English to mean the "self", "identity" or other related concepts. Ego is individuality, but false individuality; nevertheless individuality.

John says, "*. . . but he that cometh after me is mightier than I, whose shoes I am not worthy to bear: he shall baptize you with the Holy Ghost, and with fire.*" John the Baptist represents ego, and that which follows it is body-awareness. John represents an Adamite who has transformed into an Evite by the grace of the Father. Alternatively, he represents the literal meaning of the Gospel.

Baptism by John makes the infected Adamite realise that he is infected, and that he needs cure. The cure is Jesus Christ, the true meaning of the Gospel. John's declaration, "*. . . he that cometh after me is mightier than I whose shoes I am not worthy to bear*" may be translated as follows:

1. "The body-awareness that follows ego is so potent that a Mortal cannot fathom it."
2. "The spiritual understanding that follows literal understanding is so powerful that a Mortal cannot fathom it."

John describes "he that cometh after" as follows: "*Whose fan is in his hand, and he will thoroughly purge his floor, and gather his wheat into garner; but he will burn up the chaff with unquenchable fire.*" The term *fan*, here, refers to the winnowing fan. The winnowing fan is used to segregate wheat from chaff. It refers to the spiritual Gospel. But, the expression "fan in his hand" has a deeper esoteric meaning. It refers to the *Sudarśana Chakra.* According to Hindu mythology, the *Sudarśana Chakra* is the spinning fan-like super weapon which Lord Vishnu holds in his rear right hand. (Lord Vishnu holds the *śhanka* (a conch shell) in his left forehand, a *gada* (mace) in his left rear hand, and a *padma* (lotus) in his right forehand.) Lord Vishnu is the Hindu equivalent of Christ. The word *Sudarśana* is derived from two Sanskrit roots—*su* meaning "real," "good," or "divine," and *darsana* meaning "vision." The term *Sudarśana* implies enlightenment. It represents non-duality, or the *Tetralemma*, also known as *Dharma*.

"Purging of floor" signifies the separation of the wheat and chaff. Wheat kernel is the good fruit of the wheat plant. The wheat plant represents human being, and the wheat kernel represents body-awareness. The chaff looks like the wheat kernel, but does not have seed inside. Chaff represents the piety of the religious fanatics. According to the Gospel, only the wheat is stored in the granary; the chaff is burnt. One who remains an Evite at death reincarnates again as an Evite. However, one who remains an Adamite at death goes to perdition. The enlightened Evite, however, merges with the Father on death, and escapes delusion permanently.

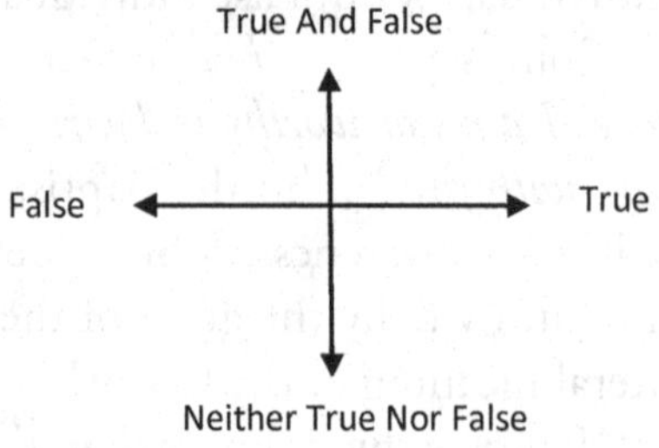

TETRALEMMA / DHARMA

MATTHEW 3:13-17

"Then cometh Jesus from Galilee to Jordan unto John, to be baptized of him. But John forbad him, saying, I have need to be baptized of thee, and comest thou to me? And Jesus answering said unto him, Suffer it to be so now: for thus it becometh us to fulfill all righteousness. Then he suffered him. And Jesus, when he was baptized, went up straightway out of the water: and, lo, the heavens were opened unto him, and he saw the Spirit of God descending like a dove, and lighting upon him: And lo a voice from heaven, saying, This is my beloved Son, in whom I am well pleased."

Baptism by John is the beginning of a necessary path that an Adamite must tread before he is *converted* as an Evite. The path entails first a descending (baptism by water), and then an ascending (baptism by fire). At the end of the path, the Adamite is cured of his infection. He recovers body-awareness and comes to know the Father, or his true Self. To be baptized by John refers to the literal understanding of the Gospel.

The name *Jordan* comes from the Aramaic word *Yārden* (H3383) meaning, "one who descends." Jordan represents the literal Gospel. The descent signifies literal understanding of the Gospel; the ascent signifies spiritual understanding.

Alternatively, Jordan represents society. Baptism by John signifies the descending into or immersing in the delusionary world. It is essential for the development of a healthy ego, for the eventual sacrifice at the altar of the Self. But, in the Baptism of the organized Church, a soul descends into Jordan and is drowned!

Baptism by John signifies the *Grihasta āśrama* of the Hindu tradition. *Āśrama* is one of four stages in an age-based social system, as laid out in Hindu religion. The four *āśrama* are: 1) *Brahmacharya*, 2) *Grihastha*, 3) *Vānaprastha*, and 4) *Sanyāsa*. During the *Brahmacharya āśrama* (student life, age: 8-18), a male child would leave his family to live in a *Gurukula* (house of the *guru*), acquiring knowledge of science, philosophy, scriptures, and logic, practicing self-discipline and celibacy, learning to love a life of *dharma* (righteousness). The initiation to this stage is called *Upanayana*. During the *Grihastha* āśrama (household life, age: 18-40), man spends his life enjoying family life, carrying out one's duties to family and society, and involved in gainful labor. The initiation to this stage is called *Samāvartana*. During the *Vānaprastha āśrama* (retired life, age: 40-65), man completes his household duties, and gradually withdraws from the world, freely shares his wisdom with others, and prepares for the complete renunciation of the final stage. During the *Sanyāsa āśrama* (renounced life, age: 65-demise), man completely withdraws from the world and starts dedicating to spiritual pursuits, the seeking of *mōksha* (freedom from delusion), and practicing meditation to that end.

In the above Gospel verses, we see the meeting of two men: Jesus of Galilee and John of Jordan. The term *Galilee* is derived from the Hebrew word *galil* (H1551), which means "a circle." However, the Greek word for Galilee is *Galilaia* (G1056), which means "the heathen circle." The name *Galilee* signifies Evites or body-aware humans. The phrase "Jesus from Galilee" means "Jesus, the Evite," and "John from Jordan" means "John, the transformed Adamite." Their meeting signifies the confluence of spiritual and literal meanings in the Gospel.

John also represents a teacher, but an unenlightened one. He can teach the great truths, but he himself has not experienced them directly. It is reflected in John's words, *"I have need to be baptized of thee, and comest thou to me?"* In reply, Jesus says to John, *"Suffer it to be so now: for thus it becometh us to fulfill all righteousness"* It means: "Let us not violate the *āśrama dharma*." The *Sanātana Dharma* does not advise young men to choose the ascetic path, but wants them to be active members of the society and to develop healthy ego. At the same time, it advices older people to gradually withdraw from the public arena, and pursue the spiritual path.

The Gospel gives us a dramatic depiction the enlightenment process: *"And Jesus, when he was baptized, went straightway out of the water: and, lo, the heavens were opened unto him, and he saw the Spirit of God descending like a dove, and lighting upon him: And, lo, a voice from heaven, saying, This is my beloved Son, in whom I am well pleased."* Jesus coming "straightway out of the water" signifies the spontaneous rising of body-awareness. The opening of *heavens* signifies the opening of mind, the erasing of conditioning. Spirit of God descending like a dove and alighting on Jesus represents enlightenment, the dawning of TRUTH. The process describes the inner revelation of the spiritual (non-dualistic) meaning of the Gospel. The voice that says, *"This is my beloved Son, in whom I am well pleased"* is the Evite's realization, *"I and my Father are one."*

If we consider Jesus as representing the Gospel, then the baptism by John refers to the *dipping* of the Gospel in reader's body-awareness. John represents the true Christian Church that facilitates the meeting between the reader and the Gospel.

CHAPTER 4

In the Desert of

MATTHEW 4:1-4

"Then was Jesus led up of the Spirit into the wilderness to be tempted of the devil. And when he had fasted forty days and forty nights, he was afterwards an hungred. And when the tempter came to him, he said, If thou be the Son of God, command that these stones be made bread. But he answered and said, It is written, Man shall not live by bread alone, but by every word that proceedeth out of the mouth of God."

The word *then* in the above verse actually implies "after baptism" in this context. After baptism, Jesus was *"led up by the Spirit into the wilderness to be tempted of the devil."* If we take Jesus as the Gospel, the book, then his baptism is analogous to the book's exposition. The term *Spirit* is derived from the Greek word *Pneuma* (G4151), which literally means "a current of air." However, spiritually, it means "the vital principle," which is the Self. In this context, the term *Spirit* refers to the author's (Joseph's) intention. The term *wilderness* is derived from the Greek word *erēmos* (G2048), which means "desert," or "wasteland." It is derived from the Greek root *chōra* (G5561), which means "a space or territory including its inhabitants." Spiritually, the term *wilderness* refers to Judaea. The word *tempt* is derived from the Greek word *peirazō* (G3985), which means "to assay." It means "to examine or analyze." For example, we assay gold ornaments to determine their gold content. Similarly, we also assay books to determine their truth content. The term *devil* is derived from the Greek word *diabolos* (G1228), which means "a traducer," specifically Satan.

The word *traducer* means "to speak maliciously and falsely of," or "to defame." The term *Satan* is derived from the Hebrew word *śāṭān* (H7854), which means "an opponent." The word is derived from the Hebrew root *śāṭan* (H7853), which means "to attack." In this context, it refers to the harsh and wily critics of the book. In a sense, the Gospel is describing the trials it undergoes immediately after its release in Judaea.

Alternatively, baptism refers to the initiation of a man into the public arena. Devil, the tempter, is the Establishment (the society). The *wilderness* is the delusionary world of dualities. The Spirit leading Jesus into the wilderness is the man's freewill opting for the dualistic, materialistic, worldly path during the *Grihastha* phase of life.

When the Grihastha phase of life is over, around the age of forty, man has a critical decision to make: either remain as an independent and free-thinking individual or surrender to society and become a public figure. The choice is between independence and slavery. If he chooses the former, he gradually detaches himself from the public arena and enters the *Vānaprastha* and *Sanyāsa* phases of life. The man then chooses the path of non-duality, the path of truth-seeking and renouncement. The prize to win is enlightenment, and the price to pay is wealth, power and fame. On the other hand, if he chooses the latter, then he chooses the path of duality, which is the path of achieving and losing—the path of opposites. The prize to win is wealth, power and fame, and the price to pay is his soul. Those who choose this path choose a dualistic religion, its dualistic scripture and its dualistic conception of God—the all-powerful entity who bestows wealth, power and fame on those who serves him.

The choice between independence and slavery is the test. And it happens when man reaches the age of forty. The Serpent is the tester. If one is successful in this test from the Serpent's viewpoint, then one is in the path of materialism, with the potential rewards of wealth, power and fame. If one fails, then one is in the path of spiritualism, and the potential rewards are enlightenment, peace and satisfaction. Winning one means losing the other. No one can opt for both choices at the same time. If anyone says it is possible, he is most likely an agent of the Serpent.

Only the Evites (Sons of God) are given the test because only they possess freewill. The test is not carried out on Adamites.

Jesus had fasted forty days and forty nights, and was "an hungred," before he was put to test by the devil. Here, "forty days and forty nights" refers to the first half of a man's life, which is generally devoid of any significant material achievements. By the age of forty, man is really hungry for wealth, power and fame. It is at this point that the devil conducts the test.

The test includes three challenges. The first: *"If thou be the son of God, command that these stones be made bread."* Stone is a lifeless object, whereas bread contains life. Here, the devil is asking Jesus to transform lifeless matter into a living thing. Literally interpreted, the devil is asking Jesus to perform magic. But, the real implication of the challenge is much deeper. It represents the societal pressure on man to accept the notion of *Objectivity*. Objectivity is the belief that the perceived world is real, and independent of the human observer and the process of knowing. It is diametrically opposed to the *Advaita* truth, *Barahma satyam jagath mithya,* meaning, "The Self is real; the world is only an illusion." Therefore, the first challenge of devil is: "Accept Objectivity."

Jesus evades the devil's challenge, and quotes from scripture: *"It is written, Man shall not live by bread alone, but by every word that proceedeth out of the mouth of God"* (Deuteronomy 8:3). The expression, "it is written" may be interpreted both as "it is written in the scripture," and as "it is written in the DNA." The *word* that comes from the Self is self-reference (body-awareness), or truth. The spiritual implication of the words is this: "It is truth that sustains man." Man is both a physical organism and a spiritual principle. Whereas the physical organism is nourished by food, the spiritual principle is nourished by truth. Physical food is required only in the physical (dualistic) world; it is not required in the spiritual (non-dualistic) world. In the spiritual world, man can sustain on body-awareness.

The first test of the devil is essentially the first *conditioning* by society: "Believe that the world is real." Countering the challenge, the Gospel states the first *de-conditioning* principle of the Self: "Accept that the Self is the truth, and that it is nourished by truth."

At the core, man is the *principle of existence*, but it expresses itself dualistically as DNA. The DNA is a particular (bio-chemical) way of describing the principle of existence. But, the principle itself can be described in many different forms, or formalisms. And each of them represents an organism and its environment. The true human DNA is called Gospel, or *Bhāgavatam*. And the corrupt (infected) human DNA is known as Satan. The *principle of existence* is known as the Self, Father, "I am," or *OM*.

MATTHEW 4:5-7

"Then the devil taketh him up into the holy city, and setteth him on a pinnacle of the temple, And saith unto him, If thou be the Son of God, cast thyself down: for it is written, He shall give his angels charge concerning thee: and in their hands they shall bear thee up, lest at any time thou dash thy foot against a stone. Jesus said unto him, It is written again, Thou shalt not tempt the Lord thy God."

The term *holy city*, literally, refers to Jerusalem; but, here, it refers to the mind, or the world. Similarly, the term *temple* refers to the Jerusalem Temple; but, here, it refers to the human body. Therefore, "pinnacle of the temple" refers to the summit, or centre of human body, which is the Self. The devil is the Establishment (society). Here, Jesus represents the man, the Evite. Alternatively, if Jesus is taken as the Gospel, then the pinnacle represents the Gospel truth.

The devil asks Jesus to *cast* himself down from the pinnacle of the temple. The expression, "cast down" means both "to hurl down" and "to lower someone's spirit." In other words, the society is asking the man to deny the Self. Jumping down from the temple suggests the separation of awareness from body. It represents the jump from truth to falsehood. Thus, the devil offers his second challenge: "Separate awareness from body and focus it on the world." Alternatively, it implies: "Denounce individuality and join the mob."

If we take Jesus as the metonym for the Gospel, then the jumping down from the pinnacle of the temple refers to the "collapse" of truth—the myth—into history.

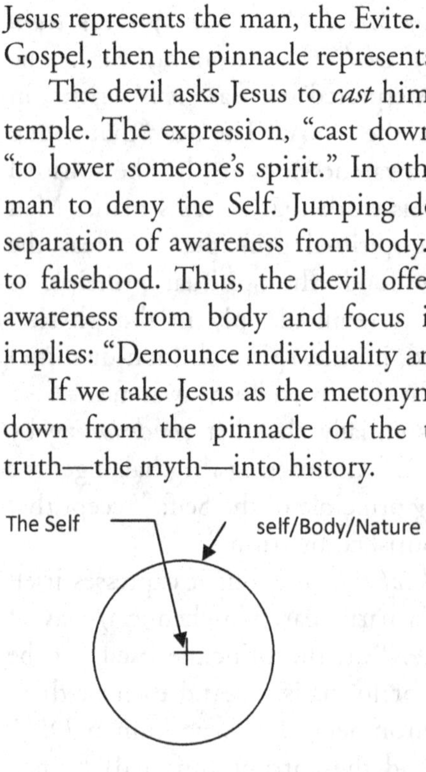

THE CIRCLE OF SELF

The circle represents the principle of existence. At the center of the circle is the Self; the circumference represents his *self*, or the body. For a circle, the circumference and the centre are equivalent. Similarly, man's *self* (body) and the *Self* too are equivalent. According to the Hindu Vedanta, the circle represents the unity of *Ātma* and *Brahman.* Just as the circle, the Evite too is in harmony with his body and his nature; there is no separation at all between the Self, body and nature. The Adamite, on the other hand, denies the Self, his body and nature, and identifies totally with the mind. He is under great delusion.

The notion that "I am separate from the environment" is known in Physics as *Locality*. When you accept the notion of Locality, you lose the sense of oneness with body and nature; you lose body-awareness. Thus you gets alienated from nature first, and then from your own body.

Devil's second test, in fact, has two clauses:

1. Deny the Self and surrender to the soceity (religion, government etc.)
2. Accept notion of Locality

Devil's argument goes like this: "If you think reality is non-local, why don't you jump from this building? If there is no separation between you and nature, how can you possibly hit the ground or dash your feet against a stone? If not, accept the notion of Locality." Devil's argument reflects the cleverness of the common-sens*e* (classical) logic. The Gospel episode reminds us of an excerpt from the book *Life of Samuel Johnson*, which relates to an incident that happened between idealist philosopher Bishop George Berkeley and the famous lexicographer Samuel Johnson, as narrated by biographer James Boswell.

> *"After we came out of the church, we stood talking for some time together of Bishop Berkeley's ingenious sophistry to prove non-existence of matter, and that everything in the universe is merely ideal. I observed that though we are satisfied his doctrine is not true, it is impossible to refute. I never shall forget the alacrity with which Johnson answered, striking his foot with mighty force against a large stone, till he rebounded from it—'I refute it thus!'"*
>
> Life of Samuel Johnson, James Boswell

The devil quotes scripture: *"For he shall give his angels charge over thee, to keep thee in all thy ways."* (Psalm 91:11). Jesus counters the devil quoting the same scripture: *"Ye shall not tempt the LORD your God, as ye tempted him in Massah"* (Deuteronomy 6:16). *Massah* (H4531) is one of the locations which the Torah identifies as having been travelled through by the Israelites, during their Exodus from Egypt. The Biblical text states that the Israelites argued with Moses about the lack of water, with Moses rebuking the Israelites for testing YHWH, hence the name Massah, which means "querulous testing." Spiritually, Egypt represents the inside of the Circle of Self; Canaan represents the outside. The exodus is from inside to outside; *Massah* represents the circumference of the Circle of Self, or non-duality. It is neither inside nor outside; it is both inside and outside. Similarly, the expression, "lack of water" means "lack of meaning"; it denotes paradox. In other words, Jesus says: "Do not deny the Self."

The second test of the devil is essentially the second *conditioning* by society: "Accept Locality." Countering the devil's argument, Jesus states second *de-conditioning* principle of the Self: "Accept the non-local nature of the Self."

MATTHEW 4:8-11

"Again, the devil taketh him up into an exceeding high mountain, and sheweth him all the kingdoms of the world, and the glory of them; And saith unto him, All these things will I give thee, if thou wilt fall down and worship me. Then saith Jesus unto him, Get thee hence, Satan: for it is written, Thou shalt worship the Lord thy God, and him only shalt thou serve. Then the devil leaveth him, and, behold, angels came and ministered unto him."

Spiritually, the term *mountain* refers a hierarchical structure, or system. The "exceeding high" mountain to which the devil takes Jesus is classical logic. The expression, "kingdoms of the world" refers to various formalisms—science and religion.

It is these formalisms that the Gospel refers to as the *devil*, *Satan* or the *Serpent*. Rules are the fundamental ingredient of formalisms. But, the truth cannot be perceived within formalisms. To see the truth, one has to go outside formalisms. Mechanical systems, such as the computer, can operate only within formal systems. Only human beings have the capacity to go outside formalisms and perceive the truth. But, if a human being constrain himself to a formalism, then he is only a *formalist*, not a truth-seeker. He is, in fact, a worshipper of the devil.

Given below is a quote from the Gospel of John, where Jesus rebukes the Jewish scholars, the Scribes and the Pharisees, for their hypocrisy:

> *Ye are of your father the devil, and the lusts of your father ye will do. He was a murderer from the beginning, and abode not in the truth, because there is no truth in him. When he speaketh a lie, he speaketh of his own: for he is a liar, and the father of it.*
> John 8:44

Alternatively, the mountain represents the various sub-systems of the world—political, religious, military, financial, media and entertainment, commerce and so on. Showing off the extent of his domain, the devil throws his third and final challenge at Jesus: *"All these things will I give thee, if thou wilt fall down and worship me."*

The third test of the devil is essentially the third *conditioning* by society: "Accept the notion of *Causality*!" Causality is the notion that an *external causal agency* (God) is the creator and controller of the world. Causality is closely connected with the concept of *monotheism*. In a sense, the devil is saying, "Accept monotheism!" Only an external ruler would ask you to fall down and worship him; the Self would never say that. How can you fall down and worship your own Self?

Most of the ancient religions are pantheistic and idol-worshipping. In the Hindu religion, there are 330,000,000 gods! The contingent of gods is so large that each man can have his own private God! But, that 'personal' God is known as the Self, or "I am." The name "I" is common to all, and yet it is private to each one of us. In that sense, it is both transcendent and immanent.

Jesus responds to the devil with a rebuke: *"Get thee hence Satan: for it is written, Thou shalt worship the Lord thy God, and only him shalt thou serve."* The phrase, "get thee hence" means "get behind," or "be subservient." Here, Gospel uses the term Satan instead of devil. Satan is a manifestation of the devil. It is the evil spirit that possesses Adamites, who are the leaders of governments, religions, and other forms of social systems. Devil's test is always executed through Satan. Countering the devil Jesus states the third principle of the Self: "The true human being (Evite) is the master of the world."

In the temptation episode, we see devil trying to gain lordship over Jesus. The devil represents the society and Jesus represents the individual. Therefore, the temptation of Jesus by the devil is an allegory that exposes society's strategies for controlling the individual. Two major arms of the society (Establishment) are government and religion, both of which complement and supplement each other. Religion bestows the needed authority and legitimacy to the rulers. Rulers, in turn, are dependent on religion for psychologically controlling the masses into submission. Both serve the same master—the Serpent. Jesus' rebuke, "*Get thee hence, Satan*" is actually directed at the leaders.

Jesus quotes from the scripture (Deuteronomy 6:13) in rebuking the devil: *"Thou shalt worship the Lord thy God, and him only shalt thou serve."* The expression, "Lord thy God" refers to the Self. The implication of the words is this: "Man's Self is his master; therefore, he should be self-aware."

Although it may appear strange and counter-intuitive to commonsense, Jesus argues against monotheism. A monotheistic God is an external power centre. And that power center wants individuals to convert into *members*. That power is duality—the magic spell cast by the Serpent. Monotheism is an inherently dangerous mental construct. It establishes a *throne* for a *one-world ruler*, but leaves the throne vacant by not clearly defining its occupant. Thus, it facilitates Satan to occupy the vacant throne through subterfuge. The organized religions and media have conditioned mankind to believe that there is something inherently good about monotheism, and that pantheism is inherently bad. Whose interests are they actually serving?

> *It is clearly extremely important that no part of what originates in the response of memory be missed or left out of awareness. This is to say, the primary 'mistake' that can be made in this field is not the* <u>*positive*</u> *one of wrongly assigning what originates in thought to a reality independent of thought. Rather, it is the* <u>*negative*</u> *one of overlooking or failing to be aware that certain movement originates in thought, and thus implicitly treating that movement as originating in non-thought.*
>
> David Bohm, *Wholeness and the Implicate Order*

Perhaps, worshipping a physical idol is a lesser evil than worshipping a mental idol.

A concept similar to monotheism, in the political arena, is the concept of democracy. Theoretically, democracy is the rule by the people, of the people and for the people. But who is this *people*? There is no such entity called the people. It is only a word, a mental construct. In democracy a throne called *people* is created and left vacant for to Satan to occupy. The imposter in the throne has all the powers, but with no accountability. The proponent of both the monotheistic form of religion and the democratic form of government is one and the same—the Serpent.

Devils temptation of Jesus reveals the basic criteria of materialism:

1. Accept the notion of Objectivity (Accept the world)
2. Accept the notion of Locality (Accept religion)
3. Accept the notion of Causality (Accept monotheism)

Objectivity, Locality and Causality are the *cardinal sins*. The Hindu Vēdanta calls it the *thāpathraya*, meaning "the sin trio"—the root of ignorance.

Jesus' replies to the devil reveal the criteria of spirituality:

1. Self is the truth, and it is sustained by truth
2. Do not deny the Self
3. The Self is the true master; therefore, be self-aware

MATTHEW 4:12-16

"Now when Jesus had heard that John was cast into prison, he departed into Galilee; And leaving Nazareth, he came and dwelt in Capernaum, which is upon the sea coast, in the borders of Zabulon and Naphthalim: That it might be fulfilled which was spoken by Esaias the prophet, saying, The land of Zabulon, and the land of Naphthalim, by the way of the sea, beyond Jordan, Galilee of the Gentiles; The people which sat in darkness saw great light; and to them which sat in the region and shadow of death light is sprung up."

The name *Capernaum* (H3723, H5151) literally means "Nahum's village." Nahum was a minor Hebrew prophet, and the name means "comforter." Spiritually, *Capernaum* represents the literal Gospel, and John the Baptist represents Gnostic Gospels. Therefore, John's imprisonment suggests the confiscation of Gnostic Gospels, and the imposition of restriction on individual freedom of speech.

The name Nazareth refers to the spiritual Gospel. Therefore, these Gospel verses tell us that Joseph, when he hears about the prohibition on esoteric writings and the restriction on freedom of speech by the Establishment, decides to be cautious; he stops *preaching* the spiritual Gospel, instead, starts preaching the literal Gospel—the Jesus story. It may be noted that the word *preach* implies both speaking and writing.

Term	Spiritual Meaning
John the Baptist	Gnosticism
Imprisoning of John the Baptist	Banning of gnostic books
Capernaum	The literal Gospel
Nazareth	The spiritual Gospel
Naphthalim	Struggle
Zabulon	Gift of God
Esaias	Salvation
Jordan	The "Establishment"
Galilee of the Gentiles	Humanity

The name *Naphthalim* (H5321) means "my wrestling," or "struggle." Spiritually, the name denotes the "outside." The name *Zabulon* (H2074) means "gift," or "gift of God." Spiritually, it represents the "inside." Therefore, Jesus settling in Capernaum of Galilee in the borders of Zabulon and Naphthalim means that the truth lives in the literal Gospel as non-duality. It also implies that the Self lives in the human body as "the form."

The prophesy of Isaiah says,

> *Nevertheless the dimness shall not be such as was in her vexation, when at the first he lightly afflicted the land of Zebulon and the land of Naphtali, and afterward did more grievously afflict her by the way of the sea, beyond Jordan, in Galilee of the nations. The people that walked in darkness have seen a great light: they that dwell in the land of shadow of death, upon them hath the light shined.*
>
> Isaiah 9:1-2

The Prophesy says that truth of the Gospel is "beyond Jordan" in the "Galilee of the nations." The name *Jordan* refers to the Politico-Religious Establishment. The phrase, "Galilee of the nations" represents humanity. The Esaias prophesy says that truth lies in the body of Evites. It is enlightenment that is referred here as "the great light."

MATTHEW 4:17

"From that time Jesus began to preach, and to say, Repent: for the Kingdom of heaven is at hand."

Kingdom of heaven is a much misunderstood concept. We think of it as a place somewhere out there—a utopian paradise that is free from pain and misery and oppression. We think of it as the domain of God, where we go after death. But is that the real implication of the term?

Kingdom of heaven refers to the *quantum field*. The term *field* means:

1. An expanse of ground, especially a piece of land suitable for agriculture.
2. A sphere of activity, interest etc., within a particular business of profession.
3. Physics: The influence of some agent, as electricity or gravitation, considered as existing at all points in space and defined by the force it would exert on an object placed at any point in space.
4. Mathematics: A number system that has the same properties relative to the operations of addition, subtraction, multiplication, and division as the number system of all real numbers; a commutative division ring.
5. Psychology: The total complex of interdependent factors within which a psychological event occurs and is perceived as occurring.

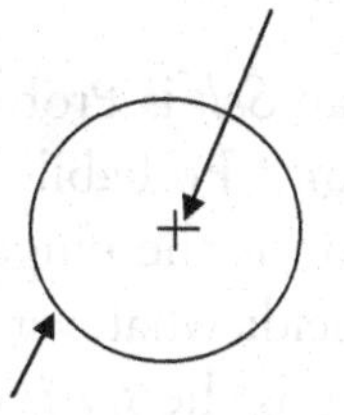

KINGDOM OF HEAVEN

I will give a different spin to the phrase, *"kingdom of heaven."* I think kingdom of heaven is analogous to the mathematical concept of *probability distribution*. But, before we talk about probability distribution, let us first understand what probability is. *Probability* is a measure or estimation of how likely it is that something will happen or that a statement is true. The first attempt at mathematical rigor in the field of probability, championed by Pierre-Simon Laplace, is known as the *classical definition*. Developed from studies of games of chance (such as rolling dice) it states that probability is shared equally between all the possible outcomes, provided these outcomes can be deemed equally likely.

The Self is Probability. It is not simply an abstract mathematical concept, but existence itself.

> *I am Alpha and Omega, the beginning and the ending, saith the Lord, which is, and which was, and which is to come, the Almighty.*
> Revelation 1:8

Probability, just as light, exists in two states: one, as probability (point/particle/Omega); two, as probability distribution (circle/wave/Alpha). Probability has the following properties:

1. It is ineffable. It cannot be described as anything specific.
2. It is a point. But, probability distribution is a field.
3. It is non-duality; it represents balance or homeostasis.
4. It is a paradox; it is represented by the equation, A = (not-A).
5. Probability is the *form* of everything in probability distribution.
6. The sum of all the values in probability distribution is unity or whole.
7. Every point in probability distribution is *potentially* probability itself.
8. Every point in probability distribution is connected to every other point; a change in one point affects every other point.
9. Probability distribution is an ever-expanding circle with uncertain circumference.

Human *Self* is Probability, and the human body (*self*) is probability distribution. Probability is the Father, the King, and probability distribution is the kingdom of heaven. The kingdom of heaven is like a fertile field; whatever sown there, grows and multiplies abundantly. Probability is the *spirit* operating in the field. For example, if you sow the concept *tree* in this field, it will manifest all possible forms of trees. If you sow good seeds in this field, it will generate good trees; if you sow bad seed in this field, it will generate bad trees.

Consider this: Can we see the *inside* of our bodies? Well, it's impossible! Even if we cut open the body and look inside, what we are seeing is only the *outside*. The inside is for ever inside; we can see only the outside. The *inside* exists as probability space, as probability distribution. It is a space where everything—all that has happened, all that is, and all that is to happen—is present as possibilities at every instant. It is a field of potentiality, a quantum field. It is this inner body, the probability space, the field of potentiality, the quantum field that the Gospel calls as the kingdom of heaven.

Now, let us come back to the Gospel verses.

The expression, "from that time" may be interpreted as: "after Jesus settles down in Capernaum on the border between Naphthalim and Zebulon." It suggests that the truth is embedded in the literal Gospel non-dualistically. And that truth is this: *"Repent: for the Kingdom of heaven is at hand."* The message is similar to that of John the Baptist's, but the Gospel message is two-pronged. It points to both the *goal* of the Gospel, and the *means* to achieve it. The goal is the realization of truth (the kingdom of heaven), and the means to achieve it is the human body (the kingdom of heaven). However, to *see* the body, one has to *turn* towards the body. The act of turning towards the body is called *repentance*.

The crux of Jesus' message is this: "Freedom is within your reach; but, first, know your body." Freedom is not obtained by conquering external enemies, but by conquering the internal enemy (the Serpent). When you the fight and destroy the evil inside, the evil outside dies too. It is this secret that Lord Krishna tells Arjuna in *Bhagavad Gīta*, urging him to fight the great fight.

By the way, the name Arjuna is derived from the Sanskrit root *ṛij*, meaning "straight," "not-crooked," "upright," or "righteous." Arjuna represents a righteous man—an Evite. Arjuna is also known as *Bhāratha*, which means "one who is self-aware." Another name for Arjuna is *Anakha,* which means "the sinless one." There is stark resemblance between Arjuna (and his five brothers) and Jesus. Arjuna's birth too is by Immaculate Conception. His mother Kunti was miraculously conceived by god Indra to give birth to Arjuna. Arjuna's earthly father, Pāndu, is not his real father. In the Hindu epic *Mahābhārātha*, the Pāndava race represents the Evites. Their elder cousins who are also their arch-enemy, the Kauravā race, represent the Adamites.

The *Kingdom of heaven* refers to the (inner) human body. Thus, the Gospel reveals to you a potent weapon to kill the Serpent—the body. But, only a body-aware man can wield it. A deluded man cannot fight the Serpent because he has already surrendered his weapon to it. According to the Gospel, body (body-awareness) is the truth; mind is a liar.

Kalidasa, the great poet-dramatist-philosopher of ancient India states this truth in his famous drama-poem *Kumārasambhava*:

> *Śarīram-ādyam khalu dharma sādhanam"*
> Kumārasambhava (Canto 5:33)
> ("Body is the primary instrument for seeking truth.")

The story of *Kumārasambhava* is mysterious in that it is rife with esoteric symbols. The name Kumārasambhava means "birth of a child." *Thārakāsura* (*thāra*: star; asura: demon), an alien demon, was given a boon by Lord Shiva that no one could kill him except Shiva's own son. The demon repeatedly defeats the gods until heaven was on the verge of collapse. The gods then pray to Lord Shiva for salvation from the evil demon. But, Shiva is helpless because he is unable to beget a son; he had already killed *Kāmadēva,* the god of love. *Pārvathi*, a virtuous woman, performs great spiritual penances and wins the love of Lord Shiva. Consequently, Shiva resurrects *Kāmadēva* and then marries *Pārvathi* to have a son named *Kārtikēya*, who then kills *Thārakāsura* and restores the glory of gods. In this mythical story, the gods represent the Evites; Lord Shiva represents the Self; Pārvathi represents awareness, or pure mind; *Kāmadēva* represents love; and their son *Kārtikēya* represents enlightenment. The killing of the alien demon *Thārakāsura* by *Kārtikēya* represents the conquering of ignorance (darkness) by wisdom (light).

MATTHEW 4:18-20

"And Jesus, walking by the sea of Galilee, saw two brethren, Simon called Peter, and Andrew his brother, casting a net into the sea: for they were fishers. And he saith unto them, Follow me, and I will make you fishers of men. And they straightway left their nets, and followed him."

Spiritually, the word *sea* means a large number of people. The term *Galilee* denotes Evites. Therefore, the phrase, "Jesus walking by the Sea of Galilee" suggests that the Gospel circulated among the Evite population. Alternatively, the term "sea of Galilee" denotes pagan literature, and Jesus represents the enlightened Joseph. Therefore, the phrase suggests that Joseph, the author of the Gospel, searched pagan literature for suitable stories to use as the Gospel vehicle.

The Gospel story, fundamentally, is about a dying and resurrecting godman. The term *godman* refers to the Evite. An Evite is called a *godman* because he is both god and man; he is god manifested as man. (The term *god* refers to the true human DNA.) The dying godman represents deluded man; the resurrecting godman, the enlightened man.

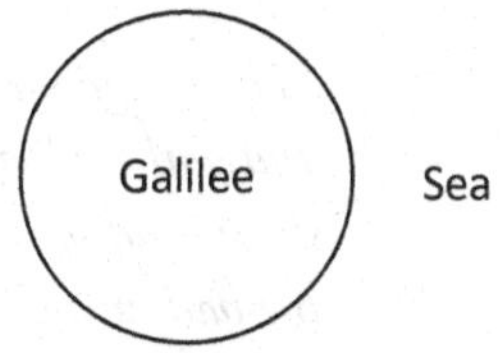

THE SEA OF GALILEE

There are a number of pagan mythologies of the ancient world that echoes this "dying and resurrecting godman" theme. In Egypt the godman is called *Osiris;* in Greece, *Dionysus*; in Syria, *Adonis;* in Asia Minor, *Attis,* in Mesopotamia, *Marduk;* in Persia, *Mithras*; and so on. These pagan mythologies form the basis of the Gospel story. However, in the Gospel, they are presented as disciples of Jesus. In that sense, the Gospel is a *syncretistic* combination of pagan mythologies. The notion that disciple Thomas came to India to preach Gospel, actually suggests the Hindu influence on the Gospel. Similarly, the story of Judas' betrayal of Jesus suggests the corrupting influence of duality-based scripture on the Gospel. While the general belief is that the disciples of Jesus went out to preach to the world, the truth may be that the world came to Jesus, the Gospel, to shape it.

The Hebrew equivalent of Simon is *Śīmōn* (H8095, H8085), which means "he who has heard." Simon represents a true human being—an Evite. Spiritually, the name Simon means "hearing" and, therefore, implies meaning. The name *Peter* is derived from the Greek word *petros* (G4074), which means "rock," which is a lifeless object. Perhaps, the name Simon Peter denotes some pagan mythology, which is fiction (Peter) on the outside, but embeds great spiritual truths (Simon) in the inside. Alternatively, Simon Peter represents an Evite who leads the life of an Adamite.

The name *Andrew* is derived from the Greek name *Andreas* (G406), which means "man" or "manly." The name Andrew also means "strong," "courageous," or "warrior." The Sanskrit word for truth-seeker is *dhīrāh*, meaning "courageous." Andrew also represents an Evite.

The Gospel says, *"Simon called Peter, and Andrew his brother, casting a net into the sea . . ."* What is meant by "casting a net into the sea"? The Gospel gives us a hint:

> *"The Kingdom of heaven is like a net, that was cast into the sea, and gathered every kind: which, when it was full, they drew to shore, and sat down, and gathered the good into vessels, cast out the bad away."*
> Matthew 13:47

The Greek word for *net* is *sagēnē* (G4522), which means "a bag of netted rope used for catching fish." Spiritually, the term *sea* refers to a *field*, or body-awareness. Net is a matrix, which, in this context, denotes formalism. In literary theory, formalism refers to the critical approaches that analyze, interpret or evaluate the inherent features of a text. These features include not only grammar, and syntax but also literary devices such as meter and tropes. The formalist approach reduces the importance of a text's historical, biographical, and cultural context. Formalism is an elaborate conceptual structure that is built on the foundation of a set of axioms, and a set of rules. The content of the formalism, acquires meaning within the structure of the formalism, but has no meaning intrinsically. A mythical story is a good example of formalism.

Jesus says to Simon and Andrews, *"Follow me, and I will make you fishers of men."* The expression, "casting a net into the sea" has two implications: one, it refers to the act of creating a story; two, it refers to the act of making someone body-aware. The Gospel uses the expression in both senses. On the one hand, Simon Peter and Andrew, represent two pagan mythologies (Roman perhaps) that went into the making of the Jesus Story. Gospel offers to make these myths "fishers of men." In other words, the Gospel offers to elevate these pagan mythologies as vehicles of spiritual truths, as instruments of salvation. On the other hand, Simon and Andrew represent the two fishes caught in the net—two body-aware humans, two Evites.

MATTHEW 4:21-22

"And going on from thence, he saw other two brethren, James the son of Zebedee and John his brother, in a ship with Zebedee their father, mending their nets; and he called them. And they immediately left the ship and their father, and followed him."

It is extremely unlikely that a person, a fisherman, a Jewish fisherman at that, would leave his trade and his father at the mere call of a total stranger. If so, what is it that the Gospel trying to tell us?

The name *Zebedee* is derived from the Greek name *Zebedaios* (G2199). It has its root in the Hebrew word *zebed* (H2065), which means "*a gift,*" or "dowry." The name *James* is derived from the Hebrew name *yāqōb* (H3290), meaning "heel-catcher." The name *John* is derived from the Hebrew name *yehōhānān*, (H3076) which means "*Graced by* YHWH." Perhaps Zebedee represents the Greek literature, which has *gifted* (as dowry) the two great epics to Adamites (and humanity)—the *Iliad* and *Odyssey*. Alternatively, James and John also denote two Evites.

The Sanskrit word for epic is *purāṇa*. The term *purāṇa* is defined as follows: "*Pura api nava iti purāṇa.*" *Purāṇa* is both old and new; it is neither old nor new. It is timeless, and therefore, superior to history. Characters in *purāṇa* are archetypes rather than historical characters.

MATTHEW 4:23-25

"And Jesus went about all Galilee, teaching in their synagogues, and preaching the gospel of the kingdom, and healing all manner of sickness and all manner of disease among the people. And his fame went throughout all Syria: and they brought unto him all sick people that were taken with divers diseases and torments, and those which were possessed with devils, and those which were lunatick, and those that had the palsy; and he healed them. And there followed him great multitudes of people from Galilee, and from Decapolis, and from Jerusalem, and from Judea, and from beyond Jordan."

Jesus commences his ministry with the message: *"Repent: for the Kingdom of heaven is at hand."* At the outset, the message sounds apocalyptic and foreboding, but really, it is good news. It says, "Freedom is now within reach: turn to your body." The essence of the message is that God resides within man, and not in temples outside. There is also the cue that man is fundamentally sinless (Sanskrit: *anakhan*). It is indeed good news for a people obsessed with morality, law, sin and religion.

"And Jesus went about all Galilee, teaching in their synagogues, and preaching the gospel of the kingdom, and healing all manner of sickness and all manner of disease among the people." The word *synagogue* is derived from the Greek word *synagōgē* (G4864), which means "an assemblage of persons." The word is derived from the Greek root *syn*, which means "together," and *agein*, which means "to bring, or lead." Surprisingly, the word synagogue is not mentioned anywhere in the Old Testament; instead, it uses the term temple. The Hebrew word for temple is *hekāl* (H1964), which means "a large public building such as a palace or temple." Therefore, it is plausible that Jesus (Gospel) taught small gatherings of people, and did not preach in Jewish temples as is commonly believed.

Spiritually, the expression, "Gospel of the kingdom" means "Gospel of the body." The principle of the "Gospel of the kingdom" is similar to that of the *Rāja Yōga* of India. The term *Rāja Yōga* means "royal union" and is one of the six schools of *Sanatana Dharma* philosophy. Its principal text is the *Yōga Sūtras* of Pātānjali. *Rāja Yōga* is concerned primarily with the cultivation of the truth-seeker's mind using a succession of steps, such as meditation (*dhyāna*) and contemplation (*samādhi*). Its objective is to further one's acquaintance with the Self, achieving awakening (*mōkṣa*) and eventually enlightenment (*kaivalya*). The yogic physical culture has another branch in addition to Raja yoga. It is the *Hatha yōga*. Its focus is mainly physical and attempts to balance mind and body via physical postures (*āsanās*), purification practices (*ṣatkrīya*), controlled breathing (*prāṇāyāma*), and the calming of mind through relaxation and mediation.

The phrase, "And Jesus went about all Galilee" suggests that the Gospel circulated among the Evites. Perhaps, Joseph went around preaching to the Evites the *Gospel of the Human Body*, revealing the secret of using the human body to fight delusion. The phrase, "all manner of sickness and all manner of diseases" refers to both mental and physical illnesses caused by the Serpent's 'poison'. The Gospel, by exorcising the Serpent's spell, heals all manner of sicknesses and diseases.

The Gospel says, *"And his fame went throughout all Syria."* The Hebrew name for Syria is *arām* (H758), which means both "the high-land" and "Syrians." It is derived from the root word *armōn* (H759), which means "to be elevated". Therefore, the verse suggests that the Gospel became famous in the *Levant*, and those who practiced the Yōga of the Gospel were relieved of their afflictions, both mental and physical.

All manner of sick people were brought to Jesus to heal. The Gospel classifies the afflicted people into three broad categories:

1. Those possessed with devils
2. Those who are lunatick
3. Those who have palsy

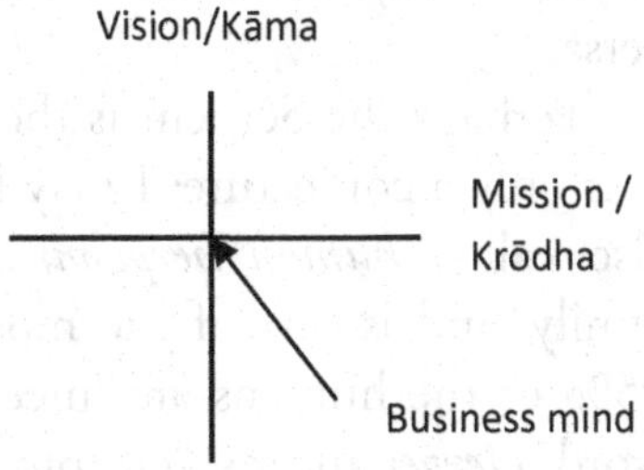

THE BUSINESS MIND

A businessman is business-aware, but not body-aware. The Gospel portrays business-awareness as an evil spirit. The exchange of body-awareness for business-awareness is like selling soul to the devil. The insatiable desire to grow (*kāma*) and the fierce competitive spirit (*krōdha*) are the two wings of the devil. In management parlance, they are known as business *vision* and business *mission* respectively. A real businessman is, in a sense, a psychotic.

Lunaticks are the *moon-struck* people. The word *lunatic* is an informal term referring to people who are considered mentally ill, dangerous, foolish or unpredictable. A lunatic has lost touch with reality or truth. He thinks of himself as someone else. He suffers from a mental disorder known as Dissociative Identity Disorder (DID), also known as Multiple Personality Disorder (MPD). It is a mental disorder characterized by at least two distinct and relatively enduring identities or dissociated personality states that alternatively control a person's behavior, and is accompanied by memory impairment for important information not explained by ordinary forgetfulness. In other words, a lunatic is alienated from himself. All Adamites are lunatics of varying degrees of severity.

The term *palsy* refers to paralysis, wherein a local body area is incapable of voluntary movement. In the spiritual sense, the person afflicted by palsy is not body-aware; it implies spiritual paralysis.

Jesus heals all sorts of sicknesses, suggesting that the Gospel is capable of dispelling all ignorance and delusion.

The Gospel exposes religion, especially religious fanaticism, as the disease afflicting humanity, not just figuratively speaking, but literally. It is the infection (magic spell) caused (cast) by an alien virus (the Serpent). The infection spreads using two *vectors*: one, an ideology (*meme*) that infects the mind; two, a physical virus that infects the physical body. Infection of the mind could spread to the body and vice versa.

Perhaps the Serpent is the *Epstein-Barr* virus, which is a retrovirus. It is only a conjecture; I may be wrong. The Epstein-Barr virus (EBV), also called *human herpesvirus 4* (HHV-4), is a virus of the herpes family, and is one of the most common viruses in humans. Close to 95% of the humans are infected by this virus. By the way, the Greek word *Herpes* means "creeping"; and in Latin it means "Serpent" or "Snake." The most effective weapon (anti-virus treatment) against the Serpent is Jesus Christ, the Gospel.

Most children become infected with EBV and gain adaptive immunity. Infants become susceptible to EBV as soon as maternal antibody protection disappears. Many children become infected with EBV, and these infections usually cause no symptoms or are indistinguishable from the other mild, brief illnesses of childhood.

"And there followed him great multitudes of people from Galilee, and from Decapolis, and from Jerusalem, and from Judaea, and from beyond Jordan." Decapolis is a district in Syria. But, the Greek term *Decapolis* (G1179) refers to a ten-city region. Spiritually, the term refers to the human body, with its five organs of perception (*jnānēndriya*) and the five organs of action (*karmēndriya*). The expression "beyond Jordan" implies "beyond delusion." Judea signifies a fringe group among the Jews who followed Jesus. In other words, those who followed Jesus were body-aware human beings; they were Evites.

CHAPTER 5

Spoken Words—The First Sermon

MATTHEW 5:1-3

"And seeing the multitudes, he went up into a mountain: and when he was set, his disciples came unto him: And he opened his mouth, and taught them, saying, Blessed are the poor in spirit: for theirs is the kingdom of heaven."

The Greek word for *multitudes* is *ochlos* (G3793), which means "a mob," or "a rabble." Spiritually, it denotes duality. The Greek word for mountain is *oros* (G3735), which means "a rising above the plain." The word is derived from the root word *ornis* (G3133), which means "a bird, as rising in the air." Spiritually, the term refers to the higher state of consciousness, or body-awareness. Therefore, Jesus withdrawing to a mountain on seeing the multitude has the following connotations:

1. The literal Gospel transforming into the spiritual Gospel.
2. An Evite entering the meditative state of consciousness.

The expression "when he was set" refers to the meditative posture (Sanskrit: *āsana*). In Zen Buddhism it is called *zazen*, which means "seated meditation." It is a meditative discipline that practitioners perform to calm the body and the mind, and to be able to concentrate enough to experience insight into the nature of existence and thereby gain enlightenment.

The disciples represent body functions (*prāṇa*). Therefore, the gathering of disciples around Jesus suggests the withdrawing of senses towards the Self. Here, the Gospel gives us the picture of an Evite entering the meditative state.

Deep in meditation, the first insight that occurs to the Evite is: *"Blessed are the poor in Spirit: for theirs is the Kingdom of heaven."* Spiritually, the expression, "poor in spirit" means "poor in mind," or "poor in religion." A man "poor in mind" is a body-aware man. He is an innocent man. He is a righteous man. He is an Evite.

The Greek word for *blessed* is *makarios* (G3107), which means "supremely blest." The word is derived from the root word *makar*, which means "blessed," "fortunate," or "happy." However, the Hebrew word (used in the Old Testament) for *blessed* is *barāk* (H1288), which has an entirely different connotation. It means "to kneel"; by implication to *bless* God (as an act of adoration), and vice versa man (as a benefit); also (by euphemism) to *curse* (God or the king, as treason). Here, the Gospel uses the term *blessed* to refer to the Evite. According to the Gospel, the poor, the meek, and the gentle are the "chosen ones." However, to the Adamites, the rich, the famous, and the powerful are the chosen ones. The Gospel, thus, repeals a basic societal norm.

The first tenet of the Gospel: *The Evites are the chosen ones, not the Adamites.*

The fundamental truth that the Gospel reveals is that the *blessed* is one who is guided by the body, not by religion. But, according to the society, the blessed one is one who is rich, famous, or powerful—the one who is guided by the mind. In the Hindu tradition, the Evite is called *sātvika.*

MATTHEW 5:4-10

"Blessed are they that mourn: for they shall be comforted. Blessed are the meek: for they shall inherit the earth. Blessed are they which do hunger and thirst after righteousness: for they shall be filled. Blessed are the merciful: for they shall obtain mercy. Blessed are the pure in heart: for they shall see God. Blessed are the peacemakers: for they shall be called the children of God. Blessed are they which are persecuted for righteousness' sake: for theirs is the kingdom of heaven."

"Blessed are they that mourn: for they shall be comforted." The Greek word for *mourning* is *pentheō* (G3996), which means "to grieve" (the feeling or the act). It suggests a loss—loss of something dear to heart. It implies break in the relationship with an object or a person. It is the net of relationships that ensnares man as a captive to the world. Therefore, losing relationships means gaining freedom. The Sanskrit word for relationship is *sanga*; therefore, the Blessed is one who is *asanga*. The true God takes away the possessions of his beloved. The Hindus call him *Hari*, which means "he who steals." Alternatively, the term *mourning* suggests *empathy*. The Blessed is one who is able to empathize with his fellow-creatures.

"Blessed are the meek: for they shall inherit the earth." The Greek word for *meek* is *praus* (G4239), which means "mild." It is generally interpreted, by implication, as "gentle." But, the term *mild* really means "not extreme." Spiritually, it denotes the "middle path," or non-duality. The Hebrew word for earth is *eres* (H776), which means "to be firm." Spiritually, the term denotes reality, or sanity. Therefore, according to the Gospel, the Evite is sane and follows the middle path.

"Blessed are they which do hunger and thirst after righteousness: for they shall be filled." The Greek word for righteousness is *dikaiosynē* (G1343), which means "equity of character or act." The word *equity* implies equanimity, which is mental or emotional stability. According to the Hindu Vēdānta, equanimity is the blessed state known as *yoga*—the union of body and mind. The Bhagavad Gita defines it as follows: "*Samatvam yoga uchyate.*" It equates yoga with equanimity. The Hebrew word for righteous is *sadiq* (H6662), which means "one who is self-justified." Spiritually, the term self-justified means "self-aware." Righteousness, therefore, denotes self-awareness, or body-awareness. In other words, the Evite is body-aware and righteous. Spiritually, the expression "to hunger and thirst after righteousness" means "to be body-aware." Therefore, according to the Gospel, the Evite finds the truth.

"Blessed are the merciful: for they shall obtain mercy." The Greek word for *mercy* is *eleos* (G1653), which means "compassion." The Hebrew word for mercy is *raham* (H7356), which means "compassion"; by extension "the womb cherishing a foetus"; by implication "a maiden." It suggests tender love. The Sanskrit word for compassion is *karuna*. He who is compassionate is kind and forgiving; he does not judge others. Compassion arises from the feeling of

oneness with nature. A compassionate person is kind to nature because he knows that it is his own body. Arising from compassion is the attitude of non-violence (*ahimsa*). Therefore, the Evite is non-violent.

"Blessed are the pure in heart: for they shall see God." The Greek term for *heart* is *kardia* (G2588). Figuratively, it refers to (the center of) thoughts or feelings. The Hebrew word for heart is *lēb* (H3820), which means "the centre." The term *heart* refers to the human DNA. Therefore, to be "pure in heart" means to be pure in DNA—to be an Evite. According to the Gospel, the Evites have pure DNA and are, therefore, body-aware.

"Blessed are the peacemakers: for they shall be called the children of God." Peace is the state or condition conducive to, proceeding from, or characterized by tranquility. The Greek word for *peace* is *eirēne* (G1515), which means "to set at one again." The word originates from the primary verb *eirō*, which means "to join," or "to yoke." The Sanskrit equivalent of the word is *yōga*. In other words, the Gospel declares that Evites are *yogis, or* "sons of God."

"Blessed are they which are persecuted for righteousness sake: for theirs is the kingdom of heaven." Righteousness is a property of the Evites. Individuality and body-awareness are the chief characteristics of the Evite. The term "Blessed" simply means "Evites." The Adamites hate the Evites for being different from them, for being individualistic, and for being sane. The attitude of the Adamites towards Evites is clearly described in parable of the evil-doing tenants: *"This is the heir; come let us kill him and the inheritance will be ours."* (Matthew 21:38). According to the Gospel, the Evites are the inheritors.

The eight *beatitudes* by Jesus at the *Sermon on the Mount*, define the Evite, who is the primary target audience of the Gospel.

The beatitudes are not platitudes; they are important pronouncements. It is good news for Evites, but bad news for Adamites. In fact, it is the *winnowing fan* that segregates the wheat from the chaff.

MATTHEW 5:11-12

"Blessed are ye, when men shall revile you, and persecute you, and shall say all manner of evil against you falsely, for my sake. Rejoice, and be exceeding glad: for great is your reward in heaven: for so persecuted they the prophets which were before you."

The beatitudes of Jesus actually define the Evite; it specifies the qualities of a true human being. Here, Jesus describes the attitude of *men* (Adamites) towards *man* (Evite). The Hebrew word for *men* is *ĕnōs* (H582), which means "mortal." It differs from the more dignified term *ādam* (H120), which means "true human being," or "individual." The term "men" denotes duality and, therefore, the Adamites. The Hebrew word for *man* is *īś* (H376), which means "man as an individual." It denotes the Evites.

Adamites hate the Evite for the very qualities Jesus calls him *the Blessed*—individualistic, child-like, curious, detached, pacifist, meditative, and loser. It may be compared to the murderous hatred of an impostor towards the true inheritor. The Gospel explains why Adamites revile and persecutes the Evite: "for my sake"—for being a true human being.

The life of an Evite in this world is not easy. The world hates him for being special, and it labels him as evil. They called even Jesus a Samaritan and said that he had a devil (John 8:48). Who are the *Samaritans*? The Samaritans are a mixed group, believed to have been descendents of intermarriages between Jews and Gentiles, notably the Syrians. The Samaritans had a relatively simple faith, similar to that of the Jews, but using only the Torah, and rejecting the other sections of the Tanakh. Their worship focused towards a mountain in Samaria rather than the mountain in Jerusalem, and their version of the Torah differed from the Jewish Torah in naming this mountain as the center of the worship. The Samaritans were considered second-class citizens in Israel. The Jews did not want to risk their social position by associating with Samaritans, and the Samaritans too wanted minimal interaction with the hypocritical Jews.

Just as the Jews reviled Jesus calling him a Samaritan, the Adamites revile Evites calling them the *Nephilim* or the *Fallen Ones*. Jesus tells Evites to be happy when Adamites makes such an accusation because it is a reconfirmamation of their special status as prophets, or Evites.

MATTHEW 5:13

"Ye are the salt of the earth: but if the salt have lost his savour, wherewith shall it be salted? it is thenceforth good for nothing, but to be cast out, and to be trodden under foot of men."

The term *ye* in the above verse, refers to the Blessed—the true human being (Evite). Jesus compares him to the salt of the earth.

The Greek word for *salt* is *halas* (G217), which, figuratively, means "prudence." The word *prudence* suggests wisdom, or body-awareness. The Greek word for "losing savour" is *mōrainō* (G3471), which means "to become insipid," or "to become a fool." Spiritually, it implies ignorance, or delusion.

Salt is a chemical compound (Sodium Chloride) belonging to the broader class of *ionic salts*. It is absolutely essential for animal life, but can be harmful in excess quantities. It is one of the oldest, most ubiquitous food-seasoning, and salting is an important method of food preservation. The taste of salt ('savour') is one of the basic human tastes. And salt is composed of equal number of *cat-ions* (positively charged ions) and *an-ions* (negatively charges ions) so that the substance is *electrically neutral* (without a net charge). Salt performs its essential function by dissolving itself, and lending its savour—saltiness—to other objects (food). In other words, salt "sheds its lifeblood for the good of others." And salt can exist in two states: as salt (as particle), or as saltiness (as field) in other substance. In that respect, it exhibits particle-wave duality like the photons. A *photon* is an elementary particle, the quantum of light and all other forms of electromagnetic radiation, and the force carrier for the electromagnetic force.

By comparing true human beings (Evites) to salt, Jesus is telling something important about them. The first and foremost is that they are needed for the existence and good of the world. Their presence makes the world 'savory'. They preserve and sustain life. Just as ionic salts, their essential nature is neutrality, or non-duality. That is, they follow the *middle path*. Their essential function is to shed their life force, or blood (savour) for the good of others. In a sense, the Evites are like the *sacrificial lambs*. This self-sacrificing nature of Evites is called *altruism*. It is the principle or practice of unselfish concern for or devotion to the welfare of others.

The Gospel then asks, *". . . but if the salt have lost his savor, wherewith shall it be salted?"* If saltiness is analogous to blood, then losing saltiness is analogous to corruption of blood. And blood is the physical manifestation of body-awareness, and vice versa. Therefore, if a person's blood is corrupt, then serious consequences follow: firstly, he loses body-awareness; secondly, he becomes selfish; and, finally, he loses individuality. But, what corrupts the blood? The chief corruptors of blood are the *antigens*—the proteins that *adhere* to the blood cells. Spiritually, antigen is analogous to sin.

The Gospel explains the consequences of losing body-awareness: *"It is thenceforth good for nothing, but to be cast out, and to be trodden under foot of men."* It implies that a man whose blood is corrupt is "good for nothing." Spiritually, the expression, "good for nothing" means "selfish." The expression, "to be trodden under the foot of men" means "to be a *member.*" A *member* is slavish to the society, party, community, taxon, or other bodies to which he is affiliated; he lacks individuality. According to the Hindu tradition, such a person is incapable of performing *svadharma.* The Sanskrit word *svadharma* is derived from the roots *svam*, which means "Self," and *dharma*, which means "truth." *Svadharma* means "true Self." One who has lost body-awareness descends to the level of a herd animal ("sheeple"), and, therefore, loses his *elect* status.

MATTHEW 5:14-16

"Ye are the light of the world. A city that is set on an hill cannot be hid. Neither do men light a candle, and put it under a bushel, but on a candlestick; and it giveth light unto all that are in the house. Let your light so shine before men, that they see your good works, and glorify your Father which is in heaven."

"Ye are the light of the world." Here, Jesus is addressing the Evites; and the theme of the address is *svadharma.* Earlier Jesus compared the *svadharma* of Evites to the *svadharma* of salt (savour). Here, he compares it with that of light.

Light has two states of existence: one, as particle; the other, as wave. Light, as particle, is called a *Photon*; light as wave is called a *probability wave.* The point Jesus makes is this: just as salt discharges its *svadharma* by dissolving, just as light discharges its *svadharma* (creativity) by dissolving into a probability wave, the Evite discharges his *svadharma* through altruism.

"A city that is set on an hill cannot be hid." Jesus compares the Evite to a "city that is set on a hill." What is special about the city that is set on a hill? It stands out! It does not get merged and lost into the background. The implication is that an Evite is an individual.

"Neither do men light a candle, and put it under a bushel, but on a candlestick; and it giveth light unto all that are in the house." Again, Jesus compares the Evite to a candle. A candle discharges it *svadharma* by melting down, while providing light for others. In a sense, the light emitted by the candle is its lifeblood shed for others. The Greek word for *bushel* is *modios* (G3426), and it means "a measure." It is the unit of dry measure containing four *pecks*. A bushel is *a container of limited capacity*. It represents the world. The world is light *measured out*. In other words, the world is wave-function collapsed. Man's true nature is light; the world is just an expression of that light. In Quantum Mechanics, the limited state of the wave-function is called the *collapsed state*. The one who hides his candle under the bushel is called an Adamite.

Only an individual can discharge *svadharma*; a member, cannot. When man becomes an individual, something magical happens: he becomes one with everything. But, for that he has to overcome selfishness. Becoming an individual is not a matter of *works*. One cannot become an individual by one's own effort. The simple truth is that no one can become an individual by volition. It is a matter of being, not of becoming. It is a birthright. Only a *son* has it; a *creature* cannot have it. An Adamite cannot have it. Only by the grace of the Father can one become a *son*. According to the Hindu tradition, a soul takes human birth after millions of reincarnations. According to the great Hindu Advaita philosopher Ādi Śankarāchārya:

> *Janthūnām nara-janmam durlabhamatha pumstham tatō—vipratha*
>
> ("To be born as a human being is rare for a creature; to be born an individual is even rarer; to be an enlightened individual is extremely rare.")

"Let your light so shine before men, that they see your good works, and glorify your Father which is in heaven." The phrase, "*good works*" means more than merely good actions; it implies discharging *svadharma*. For example, the *svadharma* of sun is to shine. In the sunlight rain falls, plants grow, and life on earth is sustained. But the sun is not shining with the intention of sustaining life on earth. Sun simply shines; it simply discharges its *svadharma*. Similarly, the Evites, by their very existence, discharge their *svadharma*.

In the above Gospel verse, the term *Father* refers to the Self. Therefore, the phrase "glorifying your Father" means "glorifying your Self." So the implication of Jesus' words is this: "When you discharge your *svadharma*, everything receives satisfaction." It sounds very similar to the advice of Lord Krishna gives to Arjuna in Bhagavad Gīta:

> *Śreyān svadharma vigunah paradharmāt svanuṣtitāt*
> *Svadharme nidhanam śrēya paradharmō bhayāvahah*
> B.G. 3:35
> ("Better is your svadharma, however lowly it may be, than imitating the dharma of another, however lofty it may be. There is satisfaction in being yourself; but, to be a hypocrite is indeed frightful.")

The term *paradharma* means "another's nature." It means "hypocrisy."

MATTHEW 5:17

"Think not I am come to destroy the law, or the prophets: I am not come to destroy, but to fulfill."

The term *law* refers to the principles and regulations established in a community by some authority and applicable to its people, whether in the form of legislation or of custom and policies recognized and enforced by judicial decision. In the Gospel context, the term *law* is generally attributed to the Torah. The *prophet* is like a referee. He cries fowl whenever there is departure from the law. Spiritually, however, the term *law* refers to the human DNA.

The Greek word for *fulfill* is *plēroō* ((G4137), which means "to make whole," "to finish," or "to make perfect." But, the organized Christian Church uses this Gospel verse as the endorsement for the Old Testament. But what is the real implication of the verse? According to the dictionary, the word *fulfill* has the following connotations:

1. To carry out, or bring to realization prophesy or promise
2. To satisfy or do, as duty; obey or follow, as commands
3. To develop the full potential of something
4. To bring to an end; finish or complete, as a period of time

The Gospel is generally believed to be the fructification of the Old Testament prophesies. But, we can also argue that the Gospel fulfills in the sense that it heals the scripture from the corruption caused by literalism (duality). In a sense, the arrival of the Gospel finishes the Old Testament. It makes it obsolete.

Alternatively, the Gospel heals man's DNA from the corruption caused by the Serpent.

The other implication of the verse is that we cannot discard morality and traditions altogether, and embrace individuality, just as we cannot discard the evil completely and embrace the good. The Gospel advocates the middle-path—the path of non-duality. Only through duality can man know that his essence as non-duality. The Gospel urges us to know non-duality through duality.

MATTHEW 5:18-19

"For verily I say unto you, Till heaven and earth pass, one jot or one tittle shall in no wise pass from the law, till all be fulfilled. Whosoever therefore shall break one of these least commandments, and shall teach men so, he shall be called least in the kingdom of heaven: but whosoever shall do and teach them, the same shall be called great in the kingdom of heaven."

The organized Christian Church uses these verses as an endorsement for the infallibility of the Bible. But, it seems the Gospel is telling something different.

The *tittle* is a small distinguishing mark, such as a diacritic, or the dot on a lowercase "j" or a lowercase "i." The tittle is an integral part of the glyph "i" and "j," but diacritic dots can appear over letters in various languages. The Greek word for *jot* is *iōta* (G2503), and the word for *tittle* is *keraia* (G2762). *Iōta* is the smallest letter of the Greek alphabet. Alternatively, it may represent the *Yod*, the smallest letter of the Hebrew and Aramaic alphabets. *Keria* is the hook or *serif*, possibly referring to the other Greek diacritics.

i j

DOT AND TITTLE

The "jot and tittle" represents the "least commandments." It denotes something physically insignificant, or immaterial, but spiritually having great impact on the environment. Salt is a good example of such a thing. Similarly, the insignificant diacritical marks can make a big difference to the meaning of written text in that it can make it readable or unreadable. Physically, the "jot and tittle" refers to the *genes* in DNA. The Hindus call it *karma*.

Therefore, Jesus says, *"Verily I say unto you, Till heaven and earth pass, one jot or one tittle shall in no wise pass from the law, till all be fulfilled."* The Greek word for the preposition "till" is *heōs* (G2193), which means "until," or "even." Although the term is generally interpreted as "even though," its spiritual implication is "until." Similarly, the expression, "heaven and earth" denotes duality, and it refers to the dualistic scripture (Adamite DNA). The Greek word for *pass* is *parerchomai* (G3928), which means "to perish." The term *law* refers to the non-dualistic scripture (Evite DNA). The expression, "till all be fulfilled" implies "till it is made perfect."

The Gospel verse may be split into three parts:

1. The condition: *Till heaven and earth pass* (Until the dualistic scripture perishes)
2. The consequence: *One jot or one tittle shall in no wise pass from the law* (The *karma* cannot be escaped)
3. The limiting condition: *Till all be fulfilled* (Till it becomes non-dualistic scripture)

Therefore, the spiritual implication of the verse is this: "Until the dualistic scripture (corrupt DNA) is made whole (non-dualistic), man will reincarnate again and again. This is the truth." The scripture becomes whole only when it substituted by the Gospel. However, literally, the verse is an endorsement for the infallibility of the Gospel words.

Reincarnation is the religious or philosophical concept that the soul or spirit, after biological death, begins a new life in a new body that may be human, animal or spiritual depending on the moral quality of the previous life's actions. The process goes on indefinitely until the soul is freed of all *karma.*

Jesus adds, *"Whosoever therefore shall break one of these least commandments, and shall teach men so, he shall be called the least in the kingdom of heaven; but whosoever shall do and teach them, the same shall be called great in the Kingdom of heaven."* In a sentence, the *least commandment* is a diacritical mark. If we break or disregard the diacritical marks, then the sentence becomes corrupted. Spiritually, breaking the least commandments suggests genetic modification. The term *Kingdom of heaven* refers to the human body. Therefore, the expression, "least in the Kingdom of heaven" means "least in body," which suggests loss of body-awareness, or soul. Therefore, the implication of the verse is this: "If an Evite's DNA gets corrupted, he becomes an Adamite."

The secret the Gospel reveals here is that genetic modification can happen not only though physical means but also through spiritual means. That is what it implies by the term "teaching." Teaching men to break the least commandments means altering scripture, the book, through addition, deletion, or modification of words. The scripture affects man's belief system, which in turn affects his mind. Eventually, the corruption passes from the mind to the body (DNA) through genetic ("*mematic*") modification.

MATTHEW 5:20

"For I say unto you, That except your righteousness shall exceed the righteousness of the scribes and Pharisees, ye shall in no case enter into the kingdom of heaven."

The term *righteousness*, in this context, refers to self-nature or *svadharma*. The expression, "kingdom of heaven," refers to body-awareness. The Scribes and Pharisees represent the Adamites. The "righteousness of the Scribes and Pharisees" is overzealous religiosity and hypocrisy. In other words, the Adamites lack body-awareness. Alternatively, the term *righteousness* denotes DNA. Therefore, the expression, "righteousness of the scribes and Pharisees" refers to the Adamite DNA. Therefore, the Gospel says: "Unless you have the Evite DNA, you cannot have body-awareness."

The "kingdom of heaven" which the Scribes and Pharisees are awaiting is a one-world Government, wherein they are the privileged class.

The Gospel completely opposes the scripture (DNA) of the Adamites. According to it, the truth can be known only through the human body. Mind is a liar and cannot be trusted. However, duality-based religions are mind-based religions, and its followers are "mental." They lack contact with truth. In other words, the Adamites are under the magic spell of the Serpent.

MATTHEW 5:21-26

"Ye have heard that it was said by them of old time, Thou shalt not kill; and whosoever shall kill shall be in danger of the judgment: But I say unto you, That whosoever is angry with his brother without a cause shall be in danger of the judgment: and whosoever shall say to his brother, Raca, shall be in danger of the council: but whosoever shall say, Thou fool, shall be in danger of hell fire. Therefore, if thou bring thy gift to the altar, and there rememberest that thy brother hath ought against thee; Leave there thy gift before the altar, and go thy way; first be reconciled to thy brother, and then come and offer thy gift. Agree with thine adversary quickly, whiles thou art in the way with him; lest at any time the adversary deliver thee to the judge, and the judge deliver thee to the officer, and thou be cast into prison. Verily I say unto thee, Thou shalt by no means come out thence, till thou hast paid the uttermost farthing."

Here, the Gospel demonstrates how to "exceed" the righteousness of Scribes and Pharisees by repealing the Mosaic laws one by one, and replacing them with new laws, which are cosmic in nature.

The phrase "ye have heard that it was said by them of old time" actually refers to the Mosaic Law. The Gospel distances itself from dualistic religions by calling it "them of old time." The expression, "said by them of old time" refers to Mosaic laws.

The Mosaic Law stipulates, *"Thou shalt not kill"* (Exodus 20:13). Here, Jesus, instead of making the law lighter, makes it harder to comply: so hard that no one can ever comply with it. According to Jesus' revised rule, even if you are merely angry at your brother, even then you are in danger of punishment. If you call your brother "useless" (Aramaic: *Rhaka* G4469), then you should be condemned by the council. If you call your brother "fool," then you are in danger of hell fire. Or, if you come to the temple for a sacrifice and then remember that you have a grouse against your brother, then you should leave your gift at the altar and go and settle the issue with him. In other words, Jesus expands the scope of the Mosaic Law from the external world of actions to include the internal world of intentions also. According Jesus, even thinking harm in mind is unlawful. The Mosaic Law only deals with actions.

In a sense, the Jesus is mocking at the hypocritical Adamite Laws. He is using the technique of *hyperbole* and *parody* to highlight the inherent hypocrisy in the Adamite moral laws. The very notion of killing another, arise from duality—from the belief that you are separate from others. That is why Jesus says, ". . . except your righteousness shall exceed the righteousness of the Scribes and Pharisees, ye shall in no case enter into the kingdom of heaven." The righteousness of the Adamites is duality. The point Jesus makes is this: it is duality that creates the murderer. The Bhagavad Gīta puts it in a different way:

> *Ya ēnam vētti hanthāram yaschynam manyate hatam*
> *Ubhau tau na vijānītah nāyam hanthi na hanyate*
> (B.G: 2:19)
> ("He who regards self as slayer and he who thinks he is slain, both are ignorant. He slays not, nor is he slain.")

The Mosaic Law is founded on the premise of duality—the separation between "I" and the "other." It is moralistic in its essence. Unfortunately, moralistic laws will only transform man into a hypocrite. We see this phenomenon in action all around us. For example, we see leaders who talk incessantly about peace acting as aggressors. We see champions of prohibition drinking in private. There are many examples.

The strange and diabolic aspect of moral laws is that they promote the very same evil that they purport to avert! The reason for this strange behavior may be found in human nature. Man's essential nature is freedom, and therefore, he has an innate tendency to resist limitations. The Establishment knows this and uses it to its advantage. Therefore, its laws may superficially appear beneficial to people, but the intention behind them is usually malicious. We can observe this principle in action in liquor prohibition.

Moral laws also take the form of tradition. In another context, Jesus asks these hypocrites: *"Why do ye also transgress the commandment of God by your tradition?"* (Matthew 15:3)

The Mosaic Law says, "Do not kill," but Jesus says, "Remove the cause of murder."

MATTHEW 5:27-32

"Ye have heard that it was said by them of old time, Thou shalt not commit adultery: But I say unto you, That whosoever looketh on a woman to lust after her committed adultery with her already in his heart. And if thy right eye offend thee, pluck it out, and cast it from thee: for it is profitable for thee that one of thy members should perish, and not that thy whole body should be cast into hell. And if thy right hand offend thee, cut it off, and cast it from thee: for it is profitable for thee that one of thy members should perish, and not that thy whole body should be cast into hell. It hath been said, whosoever shall put away his wife, let him give her a writing of divorcement: But I say unto you, That whosoever shall put away his wife, saving for the cause of fornication, causeth her to commit adultery: and whosoever shall marry her that is divorced committeth adultery."

The Gospel repeals yet another Mosaic law: *"Thou shalt not commit adultery"* (Exodus 20:14).

The Gospel again uses the technique of hyperbole and parody to highlight the absurdity of Mosaic laws. It expands the scope of the term *adultery* to include even looking at another with lust in mind, thus, expanding the scope of the term to include both actions and intentions. As per the revised definition, all are guilty of the crime of adultery. But, the religious establishments are only concerned with the actions.

When everyone is guilty of a crime, then it is crime no more; it is called a *tradition.*

What is adultery? Adultery is the voluntary sexual intercourse between a married person and someone other than the lawful spouse. What is meant by "lawful spouse"? Whose law—God's or man's? What claim does a human being have over another? Can society grant such a claim through the *social contract* known as marriage? Jesus says, no. Marriage is not a natural law of nature. It is an artificial system created by man, purportedly for the benefit of society.

According to the Gospel, it is impossible for man to commit adultery because no one owns another. (However, rape is a different matter, because it is not consensual.) It again uses the technique of hyperbole and parody to raise some rhetorical questions:

1. Will you pluck out your right eye simply because it saw something morally objectionable?
2. Will you cut off your right hand and throw it away simply because it did something morally objectionable?

How you answer these questions is important. If your answer to these questions is yes, then, the chances are that you are an Adamite.

The Gospel also addresses the issue of divorce. Jewish tradition allows a man to divorce his wife by giving her a divorce notice. But, the Gospel asks, "If you say that marriage is a sacrament blessed by God, how can you annul it simply by issuing a divorce notice?" We read In Genesis 1:27: *"So God created man in his own image, in the image of God created he him; male and female created he them."* God created the first humans as male and female, not as husband and wife. The institution of marriage is not a creation of God; it is the creation of society (religion). The Gospel is opposed to attributing too much sanctity to the social contract called marriage. The binding agent in a social contract is fear—fear of reprisal from the society. It is not love. It is because of fear of society that many couples suffer the ordeal of marriage even when love has gone from their marriage. According to Jesus, love should be the *glue* binding man and woman.

The term *fornication* implies consensual sex between two unmarried persons or two persons not married to each other. But, spiritually, fornication means consensual, lustful, but love-less sex between man and woman. Married couples can have consensual but lustful sex even when they do not love each other anymore. According to the Gospel, lustful and loveless, sex is wrong. According to this revised definition, many married couples are guilty of fornication. However, in the eyes of society, there is nothing morally objectionable in those marriages.

The Mosaic Law says, "Do not commit adultery," but the Gospel says, "Do not commit fornication."

MATTHEW 5:33-37

"Again, ye have heard that it hath been said by them of old time, Thou shalt not forswear thyself, but shalt perform unto the Lord thine oaths: But I say unto you, Swear not at all; neither by heaven; for it is God's throne: Nor by earth; for it is his footstool: neither by Jerusalem; for it is the city of the great King. Neither shalt thou swear by the head, because thou canst not make one hair white or black. But let your communication be, Yea, yea; Nay, nay: for whatsoever is more than these cometh of evil."

The Mosaic Law says, *"Thou shalt not forswear thyself, but shall perform unto the Lord thine oaths."* The Greek word for *forswear* is *epiorkeō* (G1964). It is derived from the roots *epi* (G1909), which means "superimposition," and *horkos* (G3727), meaning "a restraint," or "an oath," which implies commitment. The word *epiorkeō* actually means "to renege on the commitment." What the Mosaic Law really saying is: "Honor the commitment to the Lord; don't renege on it."

The Greek word for *Lord* is *kurios* (G2962), and it refers to the Father. But the Father is ALL, and does not need any promise from man. He who needs man's obeisance is another Lord—the Serpent, who is also known as *Baal.* It is a Semitic word signifying "Lord, master, owner (male), keeper, or husband," which became the usual designation of the great weather-god of the Western Semites. The term Baal simply means "boss."

The Gospel calls attention to the act of *swearing* (Greek. *omnuō* G3660). To swear means to bind oneself by oath. The essential form of an oath is: "I will do" or "I will not do." An oath is a solemn promise made before an *external* power centre—a power center other than the Self. Oaths are made before powerful people such as the judge, the king, or the priest, who represent external power centers. They represent the Baal. Spiritually, the term "forswear" means "to accept as boss."

But the Gospel says, "Swear not at all," implying that Evites should not accept any external authority as his master. It implores them not to make oaths to any Lord, be it an inside Lord or an outside Lord; because the inside-Lord does not need it and the outside-Lord does not deserve it. The Gospel says, *"Swear not at all; neither by heaven; for it is his throne: Nor by the earth; for it is his footstool; neither by Jerusalem; for it is the city of the great King."* The term *heaven* refers to the inner body; *earth,* the outer body, which is nature. Jerusalem, the city of the great King, refers to mind; it also refers to the scripture. In short, according to the Gospel, you are the "great King."

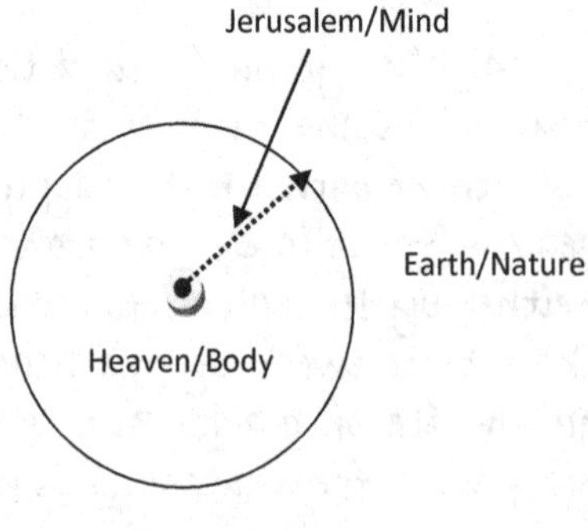

CITY OF THE GREAT KING

Jesus adds: *"Neither shalt thou swear by the head, because thou canst not make one hair white or black."* The term *head* refers to any formal system, such as scripture, which is the God of dualistic religions. But, according to the Gospel, no formal system can alter reality.

Swearing always involves a Lord, an external power center, and it is always a representative of Baal.

The Mosaic Law says, "Obey the boss," but the Gospel says, "You are the boss." In these verses, Jesus rips apart the Mosaic Law and exposes it as a ruse by the Establishment to exploit human beings.

MATTHEW 5:38-42

"Ye have heard that it hath been said, An eye for an eye, and a tooth for a tooth: But I say unto you, That ye resist not evil: but whosoever shall smite thee on thy right cheek, turn to him the other also. And if any man will sue thee at the law, and take away thy coat, let him have thy cloke also. And whosoever shall compel thee to go a mile, go with him twain. Give to him that asketh thee, and from him that would borrow of thee turn not thou away."

The Mosaic Law states, *"And if any mischief follow, then thou shalt give life for life, Eye for eye, tooth for tooth, hand for hand, foot for foot, Burning for burning, wound for wound, stripe for stripe"* (Exodus 21:23-25). Here, the Gospel repeals the Mosaic Law of retribution and replaces it with a law that is cosmic in nature. The Gospel seems to say, "How can you negate evil with more evil? How can you put out fire with fire? It does not make sense." Fire can be put out only by water, which is opposite in nature to fire. The logic is straight forward. Yet, we find it hard to follow.

If the law of retribution does not make sense from the logical perspective, why then do we follow it? The answer is: because of the public. We think that our public image would be affected if we do not avenge the harm in equal measure. But, we try to rationalize our illogical action by arguing that retribution deters potential offenses. Public image is the reflection of the Self in mind's mirror.

The Mosaic Law of Retribution is based on the notions of *me* and *mine*; it is based on duality. In other words, the Mosaic Law is based on the premise of separation between self and (not-self). Fear arises from this assumed separation. It is the fear that the *other* would destroy *me* and take way what is *mine*. It is this paranoia that gives rise to violence.

The Gospel, however, is based on non-duality. It is based on the premise that there is really no separation between self and (not-self). According to the Gospel, the aggression of the *other* towards me is the manifestation of my own inner fears. Therefore, the remedy for violence is the elimination of fear. Only a truly fearless man can show the other cheek when struck on one. Violence cannot come near such a man. And, fear is eliminated only through freedom from duality. Fear is eliminated only by curing the spell cast by the Serpent. The most effective vaccine against the Serpent poison is the spiritual Gospel. The Gospel logic is counter-intuitive, but true.

Action comes into being when the reaction potentially exists. Action and reaction occur simultaneously. They are like two sides of a coin. The time gap that we perceive between action and reaction is only illusory. Action cannot manifest if reaction is not forthcoming. It is the principle behind the Gospel admonition, *"Resist not evil."* Evil comes into being when you prepare for it. The "good news" of the Gospel is that you can control the outside by controlling the inside.

The Mosaic Law says, "Avenge evil by evil," but the Gospel says, "Conquer your fears."

MATTHEW 5:43-48

"Ye have heard that it hath been said, Thou shalt love thy neighbor, and hate thine enemy. But I say unto you, Love your enemies, bless them that curse you, do good to them that hate you, and pray for them which despitefully use you, and persecute you; That ye may be the children of your Father which is in heaven: for he maketh his sun to rise on the evil and on the good, and sendeth rain on the just and on the unjust. For if ye love them which love you, what reward have ye? do not even publicans the same? And if ye salute your brethren only, what do ye more than others? do not even the publicans so? Be ye therefore perfect, even as your Father which is in heaven is perfect."

The Mosaic Law says, *"Thou shalt not avenge, nor bear any grudge against the children of thy people, but thou shalt love thy neighbor as thyself: I am the LORD"* (Leviticus 19:18). The expression, "children of thy people" means "our people." The Mosaic Law is parochial; its definition of *neighbor* is too narrow. The law is silent about the Gentiles. The Mosaic love is not universal; the love it propounds is tribal, clannish love. On the other hand, the Gospel advocates universal love, which arises from the realization that there is no separation between "I" and the "other". Whereas the Mosaic Law advocates dualistic love, the Gospel advocates non-dualistic love.

The Gospel says, *"Love your enemies, bless them that curses you, do good to them that hate you, and pray for them which despitefully use you, and persecute you."* The essence of the Gospel message is this: "Counter the negative with the positive." When the negative is opposed by the positive, the result is balance. Hindu Vēdānta calls it *Samatvam*, which means equanimity. Samatvam is *Yōga*—the *union* of *Jīvātma* (self) and *Paramātma* (Self).

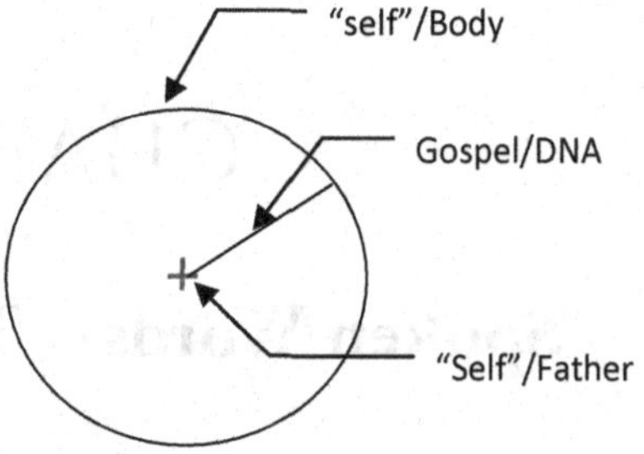

CONCEPT OF MAN

Truth is non-dual. It is the state of *samatvam*. It is the "kingdom of heaven." Therefore, when you realise truth, you realise the "kingdom of heaven." You become an Evite. Perhaps, that is what the Gospel implies when it says, "*That ye may be the children of your Father which is in heaven.*" Because truth (body-awareness) is non-dual; it does not make differentiations such as good-evil, just-unjust and so on. The Gospel describes the non-dual nature of the Self: "*. . . for he maketh his sun to rise on the evil and on the good, and sendeth rain on the just and on the unjust.*"

Therefore the Gospel says, *"Be ye therefore perfect, even as your Father which is in heaven is perfect."* The word, *perfect* means "balanced", in this context. The "Father which is in heaven" is the Self. According to the Gospel, when man attains the state of balance, or non-duality, he becomes one with the Self; he attains *Yōga.*

Given below are the Mosaic Laws that have been modified by the Gospel:

	Mosaic Law	**Gospel Law**
1	Do not kill	Remove the cause of murder.
2	Do not commit adultery	Do not commit fornication
3	Obey the boss	You are the boss
4	Avenge evil by evil	Conquer your fears
5	Love your people	Love your enemies

CHAPTER 6

Spoken Words—The Second Sermon

MATTHEW 6:1-4

"Take heed that ye do not your alms before men, to be seen of them: otherwise ye have no reward of your Father which is in heaven. Therefore when thou doest thine alms, do not sound a trumpet before thee, as the hypocrites do in the synagogues and in the streets, that they may have glory of men. Verily I say unto you, They have their reward. But when thou doest alms, let not thy left hand know what thy right and doeth: That thine alms may be in secret: and thy Father which seeth in secret himself shall reward thee openly."

Having modified the Law of the Adamites, the Gospel focuses on their traditions (the Prophets).

The term, *men* is used frequently in the Gospel. It refers to the public, which is the visible and active aspect of society. The term *society* refers to a group of people related to each other through persistent relations. Human societies are characterized by patterns of relationships between people who share distinctive culture and institutions. *Relationship* is the *thread* with which the fabric called society is woven. While individuals are real, society is only a mental construct. Yet, its power and influence are very real and palpable. The term "men" also refers to duality and mind.

To the Adamites, the public (manifested as the Establishment) is their God, although they don't admit it. What they call "fear of God" is actually fear of the public. Society is the creator and maintainer of Adamite laws and morality. And it is like a stern father—strict, domineering, judgmental, punitive, derisive, comparing, and harsh. It is also a beast in that it continually devours human lives through murders, suicides, genocides and wars. Many live in misery because of it. It is called the *Legion*—the army of the Serpent. In a sense, mind itself is the internalization of society, and society is the externalization of mind. Just as society is a network of relationships, mind too is a network of relationships. It is the God of duality-based religions; religion and government are its left and right arms.

Hypocrite is an oft-repeated word in the Gospel of Matthew. The word, in its many forms, is used 26 times in the New Testament—18 times in the Gospel of Matthew alone. In contrast, it is used only 14 times in the entire Old Testament—8 times in the Book of Job, 4 times in the Book of Isaiah, once each in Psalms and Proverbs. The Greek term for hypocrite is *hypocritēs* (G5273), which means "an actor under an assumed character." The Hebrew word for *hypocrite* is *hānēp* (H2611), which means "soiled with sin." The word is derived from the root word *hōnep* (H2612), which means "moral filth." A hypocrite is one who pretends to have virtues (moral or religious), and principles that he does not actually possess, especially one whose actions belie stated beliefs. He is one who feigns some desirable or publicly approved attitude, especially one whose private life, opinions, or statements belie his public statements. A hypocrite is "an actor under an assumed character." The assumed character may differ from person to person, but the actor is always the same: the Serpent.

According to the Bhagavad Gīta, a hypocrite is one who does *paradharma*—one who does another's *dharma*. The Bhagavad Gīta says,

> *Swadharme nidhanam śrēya paradharmo bhayāvahah*
>
> B.G. 3:35
>
> ("It is better to die as oneself; to die as someone else is indeed frightening.")

Whatever the hypocrite does is hypocrisy. And hypocrisy is the state of promoting or trying to enforce standards, attitudes, lifestyles, virtues, beliefs, and principles that one does not actually hold and may regularly violate. Hypocrisy involves deceiving others as a way of life. The word *hypocrisy* is derived from the Greek word *hypokrisis* (G5272), which means "jealous," "play-acting," "acting out," "coward," or "dissembling."

The public figure often turns out to be a hypocrite because the standards, attitudes, lifestyles, virtues, beliefs, and principles set by society are often hard to comply with. Therefore, the so-called public figure is often compelled to play act. That is the reason we find more hypocrites in religion and politics.

The Gospel says, *"Take heed that ye do not your alms before men, to be seen of them: otherwise ye have no reward of your Father which is in heaven."* The Greek word for the expression, *"Take heed"* is *prosechō* (G4337). It denotes caution. The word, "alms" commonly refers to the money, food or other donations that is given to the poor or needy. But the Greek word for alms is *eleēmōsyne* (G1654), which means "compassion, as exercised towards the poor." It is much broader in scope. The *Father which is in heaven* is the Self, and the *reward* from him is self-satisfaction. Therefore, the crux of the Gospel warning is this: "Do not pretend compassion for popularity sake because it never begets self-satisfaction."

Why do hypocrites show off? The Gospel says, *". . . that they may have glory of men."* A public figure derives a kind of 'high' when he receives public recognition. It is not self-satisfaction, but a cheap imitation of it. Public recognition is the public figure's reward from his master, the Establishment. And the 'high' that he derives is a sense of *competitive advantage*. But, self-deception destroys the man's self-respect.

Almsgiving of the hypocrite is like trading: he trades a portion of his wealth in exchange for public recognition. He is a trader at heart. His God is pleased only by public display, because the public is his god.

After describing the nature and fate of the hypocrites, the Gospel lays down the conduct for Evites. The God of the Evite is the Father—the Self. And he resides in his body. Therefore, the Gospel advises: *"But when thou doest alms, let not thy left hand know what thy right hand doeth: That thine alms may be in secret: and thy Father which seeth in secret himself shall reward thee openly."* Contrary to popular belief, the concept of almsgiving is repugnant to true spirituality. How can anyone *offer* anything, when one does not really own anything in this world? Nevertheless, it is obligatory for a householder (*Grahastha*) to share his wealth with others. But, he has to do it discretely. Man's attitude when *sharing* wealth with fellow-men shall be as prescribed by the Vēdic mantra, which says, "*idam na mama,*" meaning "this is not mine." Almsgiving is done for self-satisfaction, and not for public recognition. The Greek word for right hand is *dexter,* which means "good," and it denotes the individual; the word left hand is *sinister*, which means "evil" and it denotes the public. Almsgiving becomes real when the public does not come to know what the individual has done. That is the implication of the statement, "*Let not thy left hand know what thy right hand doeth.*"

MATTHEW 6:5-6

"And when thou prayest, thou shall not be as the hypocrites are: for they love to pray standing in the synagogues and in the corners of the streets, that they may be seen of men. Verily I say unto you, They have their reward. But thou, when thou prayest, enter into thy closet, and when thou hast shut thy door, pray to thy Father which is in secret; and thy Father which seeth in secret shall reward thee openly."

After warning the Evites not to emulate the Adamites in giving alms, the Gospel warns them not to emulate the Adamites in praying.

The term *Father* is mentioned 43 times in the Gospel of Matthew, and the term *God* is mentioned 54 times. However, the term *Jehovah* is not mentioned anywhere in the Gospel, or the New Testament.

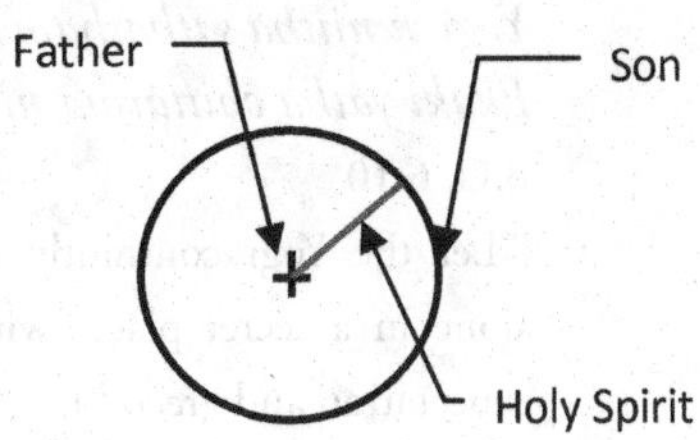

THE TRINITY

The Greek word for Father is *patēr* (G3962), which simply means "father." The term *Father* suggests blood relationship, which is direct and intimate. The term is equivalent to the Hindu concept of *Brahman*, which is the origin and support of the phenomenal universe. It is sometimes referred to as the *Absolute* or *Godhead*, which is the divine ground of all being. The Father is ALL. The term *God*, on the other hand, refers to the dreaming state of the Father when he exercises his creative will and sets in motion the creative process. The term *God* actually refers to the human DNA, and it is the basis of scripture. In fact, the Adamite God and the Evite God are entirely different, even antithetical to each other. So are the Adamite scripture and the Evite scripture. The God of the Adamite is the Serpent. Another name for God is Spirit. The Evite God is known as Holy Spirit, and the Adamite God is known as Evil Spirit, or Devil.

The Greek word for prayer is *proserchomai* (G4334), which means "to come near," or "to draw near." Spiritually, it means "to draw near to Self." It suggests focusing awareness inwards. On the other hand, the Hebrew word for prayer is *tepilla* (H8605), which means "intercession," or "supplication," both of which suggest focusing awareness outwards. In both cases, the term *prayer* implies communication. The direction of the hypocrites' prayer is outward, and it is directed at the public. And for the public to take notice, they have to pray publicly. Therefore, they *"love to pray standing in the synagogues and in the corner of streets, that they may be seen by men."* But, the Gospel asserts, *"Verily I say unto you, They have their reward."* Getting noticed by the public, and the 'high' they derive from it, is their only reward.

The Gospel teaches the Evites how to pray: *"But thou, when thou prayest, enter into thy closet and when thou hast shut thy door, pray to thy Father which is in secret; and thy Father which seeth in secret shall reward thee openly."* The expression implies more than just praying in private. Spiritually, the term *closet* refers to the human body, and the term *door* (Sanskrit: *dwāra*) refers to the sensory openings, especially, the eyes. In other words, closing eyes and focusing awareness on body are the two most important steps in prayer. And they are the basic steps in Yoga meditation. The Bhagavad Gīta describes the process:

> *Yogī yunjītha sathatham atmānam rahasi sthitha*
> *Ekākī yatha chittātma nirāśīraparigraha*
> B.G. 6:10
> ("Let the Yogi constantly engage with his self in yoga, remaining alone in a secret place, with thoughts and ego subdued, free from expectation and greed.")

The Bhagavad Gīta also describes the reward the *Father* bestows on the Yogi:

> *Yunjanēvam sadātmānam yogi vigatha kalmashah*
> *Sukhēna brahma-samsparsham athyantham sukham-ashnuthe*
> B.G. 6:28
> ("The Yogi, who thus, yoking 'self' with the 'Self' is freed from all sins, and enjoys the infinite bliss of contact with the Eternal.")

MATTHEW 6:7-8

"But when ye pray, use not vain repetitions, as the heathen do: for they think that they shall be heard for their much speaking. Be not ye therefore like unto them: for your Father knoweth what things ye have need of, before ye ask him."

The word *heathen* literally means an 'unconverted' individual of a people that do not acknowledge the *true God*. The Greek word for heathen is *ethnikos* (G1482), and it is derived from the root word *ethnos* (G1484), which means "foreign people," or "aliens." According to this definition, heathen are a group of people who live among others who are not of their kind. They are parasites in some sense. However, spiritually, a heathen is an unrepentant person: one who has not known the true God (body). In other words, a heathen is one who is not body-aware. As per this definition, most of the so-called believers would qualify as heathens. All Adamites are heathens. And their God is the public who hears prayers only if it is done publicly. The prayers he hears are protests, demonstrations, revolutions and wars.

The Greek word for "vain repetition" is *bottologeō* (G945), which means "to prate." It means to utter in empty or foolish talk: to prate absurdities with the greatest seriousness. The operative word here is *vain*. The word, *vain* means excessively proud of or concerned about one's own appearance, qualities, and achievements; it means "conceited." "Vain repetitions" actually refers to the pompous religious rituals. Therefore, the Gospel advises: *"Be not ye therefore like unto them: for your Father knoweth what things ye have need of, before ye ask him."* Here, the word *ye* refer to the Evites and, *them*, the Adamites.

Who knows your needs most intimately? You! Your inner Self (Father) knows your needs more than anybody else. You are the one who is most concerned about your welfare. Do you have to ask yourselves for a favor? No! Therefore, the Gospel says, "For the Evite, even the notion of prayer is redundant." By the way, the word *redundant* actually means "vain repetition"!

MATTHEW 6:9

"After this manner therefore pray ye: Our Father which art in heaven, Hallowed be thy name."

After explaining the preparations for the prayer, the Gospel explains the form of a true prayer. The first and foremost thing about true prayer is that it is addressed to *Our Father* and none else. The term "Our Father" implies that:

1. He is *my* Father
2. He is the Father of all

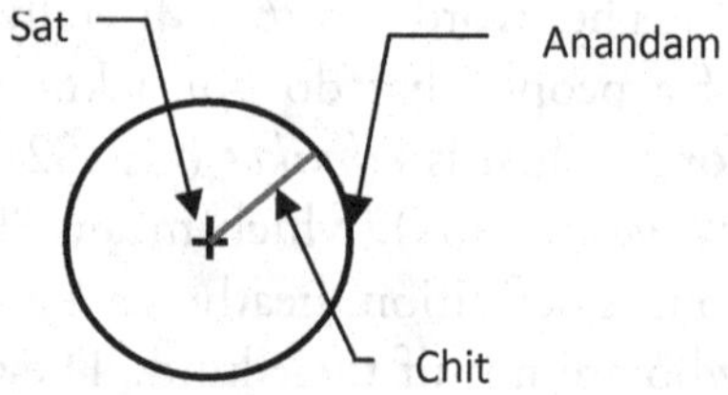

SACHIDANANDAM

The term refers to man's inner Self. It is him that we address as "I." Our individual selves are manifestations of that One Universal Self. And he knows himself through each of us. We are his *eyes* ("I"s). The Hindus call him *Brahman*. He is also known as *Sachidānandam,* meaning *truth* (*sat*), *mind* (*chit*), and *bliss* (*ānandam*).

The Greek word for *hallowed* is *hagiazō* (G37), which means "to make holy" or "to purify." The Hebrew word used in the Old Testament, is *qādas* (H6942), which means "to pronounce ritually clean," which has a dualistic connotation. Spiritually, the word *hallowed* means "halo-ed." A *halo* is a circle, or ring, traditionally representing the radiance around the head of saints. It represents self-awareness. The expression, "hallowed be thy name" actually means, "Thy name is, *The Haloed*"! According to the Gospel, The Self is a point surrounded by a circle.

> *The greatest of all lessons is to know your Self, for when a man knows himself he knows God.*
>
> Clement of Alexandra, the Christian Gnostic

For the Gnostics, the search for self-knowledge is identical with the search for God, because when we discover our deeper identity, we discover God. For the Gnostics, God is "pure knowing," or "pure awareness" (Sanskrit: *śuddha-bōdham*) in which everything exists as ideas. And God manifests through us as "the Self" or "I". Therefore, at the innermost depths of each of us we are one, although outwardly, we may appear to be separate individuals, and our shared identity is one: the Self, or "I." It is the invisible root of the tree of which we are branches.

According to the Gnostics, human beings have three essential aspects: body, soul and spirit. And they employed the notion of "Circle of Self" to elucidate their teachings. The circumference of the circle represents the body, which the Gnostics called the *physis.* It is the *distinction* that separates the *inside* from the *outside.* It represents our *outer self.* The radius of the circle represents the *psyche,* or soul. It represents the DNA, the *Word,* or the spiritual scripture. In relationship to the body, we experience it as the *inner self,* or soul (Sanskrit: *jīvan*). It is psyche that we call God. At the centre of the circle is our essential identity, which the Gnostics called *Pneuma*, or *Nous.* It is the witness (Sanskrit: *sākshi*) of all our experiences. Plotinus, the famous Greek philosopher (205-270 CE), describes it as "the knowing principle." It is the Nous that "knows," and the subject of every experience. It is that we call "I". It is our "sense of being." It is what we are. It is also known as Consciousness.

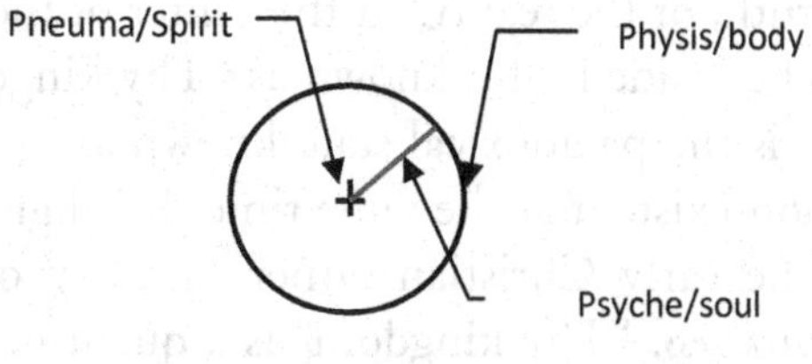

CIRCLE OF SELF

The circle is an extremely mysterious geometrical form. The true circle exists only in the mathematical realm (heaven), because the transcendental number ϖ exists only in the mathematical realm. Yet, we have an intuitive conception about circle; because that is what we are.

MATTHEW 6:10

"Thy kingdom come. Thy will be done in earth, as it is in heaven."

Deluded man is an outward-looking entity. He does not realize that the world that he sees outside is just an illusion created by him. It is a distorted and dark view of the reality. The light in which he sees objects in the outer world is the light of intellect—that of the brain and the sense organs. And the outside world is a synthetic world, or a created world. If man is the "Circle of Self," then the illusory world represents the outside of the Circle. The Gospel calls it the e*arth*.

The inside of the circle is called the *kingdom of heaven*. It is the truth, or the reality. At the center of the Circle is the Self, or the Father. The inside is also known as "Thy kingdom," or "kingdom of the Self." It is the paradoxical state known as non-duality. It is *both* existent *and* non-existent at the same time. It is light and darkness at the same time. The early Christian father Gregory of Nyassa called it the *dazzling darkness*. "Thy kingdom" is a quantum mechanical state. It is the field of pure potentiality, where anything is possible. It is a probabilistic (mythical) state, yet it has being. The Gospel expression, "Thy kingdom come" suggests enlightenment.

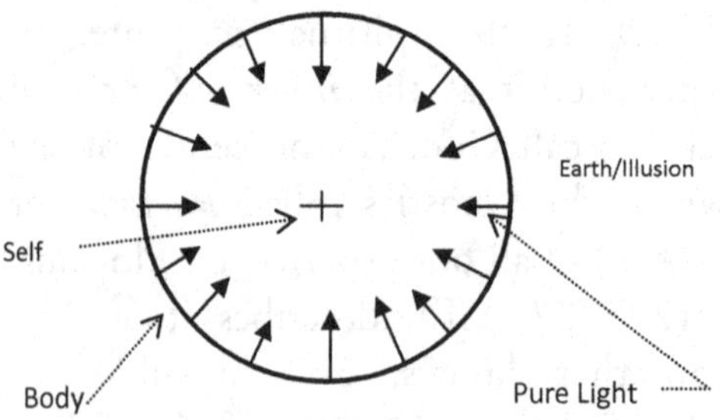

Thy Kingdom Come

Dividing heaven (truth) and earth (falsehood) is man's body, which is in contact with both at the same time. Therefore, it is the portal to heaven.

The expression, "Thy will" refers to "Self-will." It is also called "freewill." It is freewill that makes man unique. The Hindu Vēdānta defines it as follows: "*Kartum vā akartum vā anyadhā kartum vā*," describing freewill as the power to do, not do, or do differently. It is the ability to "do differently" that makes man unique. According to science, freewill is the ability of agents to make choices unconstrained by factors such as metaphysical constraints (logical, or theological), physical constraints (such as chains or imprisonment), social constraints (such as threat of punishment, or censure), and mental constraints (such as compulsions or phobias, neurological disorders, or genetic predispositions). In other words, what makes man truly human is his inherent tendency *to disobey*. This may come as a great shock to Christians who are fed on the steady diet of obedience.

The notion of freewill and the notion of causality cannot go together. You have to make a choice (assuming you have freewill). But western (dualistic) religions embrace both and futilely struggle to reconcile them.

MATTHEW 6:11

"Give us this day our daily bread."

The expression "this day" calls for special attention. An Evite prays for today's sustenance, but not for tomorrow's. For tomorrow's sustenance he prays tomorrow. In other words, an Evite prays daily. And that prayer is not "vain repetitions," but mediatation.

The expression, "daily bread" suggests that the Evite is not concerned about saving for future. Planning is not for him. The term *planning* has the inbuilt assumption of scarcity; it also assumes an external power centre that controls availability.

The Greek word for *give* is *didōmi* (G1325), which is a prolonged form of a primary verb, and is used with great latitude. It means "bestow," "grant," or "show" among others. Spiritually, the word *give* implies "show." Therefore, the Evites pray: "Show us this day, our daily bread." The Self shows the opportunity; the Evite work for it. In other words, the Evite believes in abundance, not scarcity.

But the Adamite's position is hypocritical. On the one hand he says that his God is all-powerful, merciful, and all, but, on the other, he struggles hard to eke out a living. What does that indicate? It means only one thing: he doesn't really believe in that God. But, such a logical conundrum does not arise for the Evite who says the Self is his provider. It makes perfect sense: he (the Self) works and feeds himself (the Self); if he doesn't work, he cannot feed himself. But, the Self shows the possibilities.

MATTHEW 6:12

"And forgive us our debts, as we forgive our debtors."

The term *debt* implies a liability or obligation to pay to or perform for another. In theology, however, debt means an offense requiring reparation; a sin; a trespass.

The notion of sin arises in duality. It has its basis on the assumptions of Objectivity, Locality, and Causality *(thāpathraya)*, which are the fundamental assumptions of duality. The concept of sin acquires meaning only if you believe the world is real. Sinning is possible only if you believe that you are separate from others. Sinning is possible only if you believe you are the doer. But, all these assumptions are fundamentally erroneous.

Sin, in the western context, is defined as any act of transgression, especially willful or deliberate violation of some religious or moral principle. For the Adamites, sin is the act of violating God's will, which is nothing but violating religious canons. However, spiritually, the word debt *has* a different connotation. The Greek word for *debt* is *opheilēma* (G3783), which literally means "something owed." Morally, it implies a fault. The word *opheilēma* is related to the word *ophelos* (G3786), which means "to accumulate," "to take advantage," or "to profit." Therefore, the spiritual implication of the prayer is this: "Forgive us for taking advantage of others, as we forgive others of taking advantage of us." The crux of Gospel message: "Do not exploit others."

According to the *Advaita Vēdānta*, the term *sin* (Sanskrit: *pāpam*) refers to actions done under delusion. Exploiting fellowmen is definitely a sinful activity. The exploiter is a firm believer in duality: he believes the world is real; he believes he is separate from others; and, he believes he is the doer. In that sense, business, in its essence, is a sinful activity. However, it is also true that society cannot function without business. Hence, the prayer.

MATTHEW 6:13

"And lead us not into temptation, but deliver us from evil: For thine is the kingdom, and the power, and the glory, for ever. Amen."

One of the key secrets of the Gospel lies hidden in the prayer, *"And lead us not to temptation, but deliver us from evil."* The word "temptation" has the following implications:

1. The *act* of tempting
2. The *object* that tempts
3. The *state* of being tempted

The word *temptation* points to an act, an object and a state. The Gospel equates it with evil. The word has another connotation. It suggests wavering of mind, or doubt. In other words, temptation implies alternation of consciousness. Temptation arises when you think you have a choice, when you look at situations as *either-or* choices. Temptation implies duality. The Greek word for *temptation* is *peirasmos* (G3986), which means "putting to proof" (by experience of duality).

The word *lead* has the following connotations:

1. To go before or with to show the way
2. To conduct by holding or and guiding
3. To influence or induce; cause
4. To guide in direction, course, course action, opinion, etc.

The tempter (the evil) is the one who lead us away from "Thy kingdom" (body-awareness) into delusion. It is who we trusted to guide and lead us. And who is that guide? Religion and its dualistic scripture!

The word, *deliver* means "to set free or liberate." Therefore, according to the Gospel, "salvation" is the deliverance from religion.

The final words of the prayer, *"For thine is the kingdom, and the power, and the glory, for ever and ever"* is called the *doxology* of the prayer. It is not there in Luke's Gospel, nor is it present in the earliest manuscripts of Matthew.

The Hebrew word for Amen is *āmēn* (H543), which means "true," or "faithfulness." The Sanskrit equivalent of the word is OM. Also known as *Omkāra* or *Praṇava*, OM is a mantra and a mystical Sanskrit sound of Hindu origin, sacred and important in various *Dharmic* religions such as Hinduism, Buddhism, and Jainism. The syllable OM is described as all-encompassing mystical entity in the *Upaniṣads*. OM is another name for Brahman. In Bhagavad Gita, Lord Krishna defines it:

> *Om tatsat-iti nirdēśo Brahmans-trividhah samratah*
>
> B.G. 17:23
>
> ("OM, tat and sat has been declared as the triple appellation of Brahman, who is Truth, Consciousness and Bliss.)

MATTHEW 6:14-15

"For if ye forgive men their trespasses, your heavenly Father will also forgive you: But if ye forgive not men their trespasses, neither will your Father forgive your trespasses."

A key milestone in the spiritual quest is the identification of the enemy, the evil. When it is identified, the battle is half won. The Church calls this enemy "the devil," or "Satan," but it does not clearly identify who the enemy is, but only describes it as a dark, ugly, fearsome monster from another realm. But, Apostle Peter describes the enemy as a clear and present danger:

> *Be sober, be vigilant; because your adversary the devil, as a roaring lion, walketh about, seeking who he may devour.*
> 1 Peter 5:8

The Gospel reveals that invisible, powerful and present enemy: it is duality-based religion and its scripture. And the protection against this enemy is sobriety and vigilance, or, in other words, body-awareness. There is an interesting episode in the Gospel of Mark about Jesus encountering a devil-possessed man:

> *And they came over unto the other side of the sea, into the country of the Gaderenes. And when he was come out of the ship, immediately there met him out of the tombs a man with an unclean spirit, Who had his dwelling among the tombs; and no man could bind him, no, not with chains: Because that he had been often bound with fetters and chains, and the chains had been plucked asunder by him, and the fetters broken in pieces: neither could any man tame him. And always, night and day, he was in the mountains, and in the tombs, crying, and cutting himself with stones. But when he saw Jesus far off, he ran and worshipped him, And cried with a loud voice, and said, What have I to do with thee, Jesus, thou Son of the most high God? I adjure thee by God, that thou torment me not. For he said unto him, Come out of the man, thou unclean spirit.*

And he asked him, What is thy name? And he answered, saying, My name is Legion: for we are many."
Mark 5:1-9

The unclean spirit identifies himself as *Legion*, and then defines it: "we are many." Thus, the devil reveals his identity as duality.

The Greek word for trespass is *paraptōma* (G3900), which means "a slide-slip" (lapse or deviation), i.e. (unintentional) error or (willful) transgression. The word *trespass* also implies crossing the boundary into another's domain. The Gospel rubbishes the notion of trespass or sin, along with the notion of duality. How can characters in a story have freewill? How can a character in a story be held responsible to his actions? If you accept the notion that ordinary men don't have freewill, then you cannot attribute any motives for their actions. You then tolerate their trespasses as random events, and do not react to them emotionally. Thus, you find it easier to forgive others' trespasses. By the same token, you also do not blame yourselves for your own ignorant actions. Thus, you are freed from sin and guilt. Thus, you escape the clutches of religion and priests. However, you can forgive others' and your own trespasses only if you truly believe in non-duality. On the contrary, if you find it hard to forgive other's trespasses, it means that you believe in duality. And if you believe in duality, then you believe in doership and, therefore, sin follows.

There are two kinds of trespasses: one, *men* trespassing into you; two, you trespassing into *men*. The former trespass implies sensual stimuli entering you. *Forgiving* this trespass means not reacting or responding to external stimuli. The latter trespass implies your own actions under delusion. Such actions are called *karma* or sins. Only the Heavenly Father (inner Self) can forgive such sins, and it entails realizing the truth. When you realise the truth, you find it easy to condone others' trespasses and your own trespasses.

MATTHEW 6:16-18

"Moreover when ye fast, be not, as the hypocrites, of a sad countenance: for they disfigure their faces, that they may appear unto men to fast. Verily I say unto you, They have their reward. But thou, when thou fastest, anoint thine head, and wash thy *face; That thou appear not unto men to fast, but unto thy Father which is in secret: and thy Father, which seeth in secret, shall reward thee openly."*

There are two types of people in this world: the Evites who are known as *the righteous*, and the Adamites who are known as the *hypocrites*. The God of the Evites is the Self, and the God of the Adamites is the public. The Adamites worship their god by conspicuous actions, and considers their prayers answered if they receive favorable opinion from the public.

Fasting is fundamental to Adamite religions. It is the act of willingly abstaining from all food, drink, or both, for a period of time. And, the idea of fasting has the inbuilt assumption of *doership*. The fasting man says, "I decided to fast." Fasting is an action against the body; it is an action against the Self (the Father).

The Gospel does not ask us to fast, yet it says, "*When ye fast . . .*" implying that even the Evites have to fast from time to time. At the outset, it may seem like a contradiction, but it is not. The Gospel is referring to a different kind of fasting. When you truly accept the principle *"Give us this day our daily bread,"* fasting comes with it naturally in that you are forced to fast when there is no food. Now, it is Providence that decides the timing and duration of this fasting, not religion. The Bhagavad Gīta explains that attitude:

> *Yadruschaya lābha santhuṣta dwandathīto vimatsara*
> *Sama siddhāvasiddhou ca kṛutwāpi na nibadhyate*
> B.G. 4:22
> ("Content with whatsoever God provides, free from duality and striving, unaffected by success and failure, the righteous, even though acting, is not bound.")

The Gospel seems to say, "When you have food, eat it heartily, and having eaten, wait for the next meal." The righteous prays: *"Lead us not to temptation."* It is the fervent prayer of the Evite to save him from the temptation to believe "I earned my food." It is the belief in doership that eventually leads us into the snare of the enemy.

Because the Adamite's god is the public, he has to put on appearances to impress it. Gospel says, "They have their reward" implying that the *high* the Adamite receives from the farce is his only reward.

Can you call "not eating" as *fasting* if the public does not acknowledge it as such? Not at all! It is then called *starving.* Fasting necessarily needs public acknowledgement. Therefore, the Gospel advises the Evites: "Do not fast."

MATTHEW 6:19-21

"Lay not up for yourselves treasures upon earth, where moth and rust doth corrupt, and where thieves break through and steal: But lay up for yourselves treasures in heaven, where neither moth nor rust doth corrupt, and where thieves do not break through nor steal: For where your treasure is, there will your heart be also."

The term *treasure* refers to something greatly valued or highly prized. Man's treasure is his awareness. It is his most prized possession. Awareness is also called "pure mind." The term *heart* refers to the center of the Circle of Self. It refers to man's being. Heart is the source of awareness.

The term *earth* refers to the phenomenal world. It denotes the "outer body," or mind. Spiritually, the term *earth* refers to the literal scripture. The term *heaven,* on the other hand, refers to the "inner body." It refers to the spiritual scripture. The Gospel calls it the "kingdom of heaven." Modern physics calls it the *quantum field.* It is the underlying fundamental entity, which is the essence of all phenomena in this world. It is the only reality.

> *We may therefore regard matter as being constituted by the regions of space in which the field is extremely intense . . . There is no place in this new kind of physics both for the field and matter, for the field is the only reality.*
>
> Albert Einstein

According to Plato, heaven is the ideal plane—the plane of *archetypes.* In heaven there exist only abstract principles, not physical objects. Heaven represents the inside of the Circle of Self.

The Gospel warns: *"Lay not up for yourselves treasures upon earth."* It means:

1. "Do not focus awareness on the outside."
2. "Do not focus awareness on the world (mind)."
3. "Do not focus awareness on the literal scripture."

The Gospel explains why you should not keep your 'treasure' upon 'earth': *". . . where moth and rust doth corrupt, and where thieves break through and steal."* Everything in the phenomenal world is subject to change and flow. They are transitory in nature. Like modern physicists, the mystics see all objects and processes in a universal flux and deny existence of any material substance. In the dynamic world views of Eastern mysticism and of modern physics, there is no place for static shapes, or for any material substance. The basic elements of the universe are dynamic patterns; transitory stages in the "constant flow of transformation and change." It is this constant flow of transformation and change that the Gospel describes as *"where moth and rust doth corrupt, and where thieves break through and steal."*

Therefore the Gospel advises: *"But lay up for yourselves treasures in heaven, where neither moth nor rust doth corrupt, and where thieves do not break through nor steal."* It means:

1. "Focus your awareness on the inside, which is unchanging."
2. "Focus your awareness on the body, which is the reality."
3. "Focus your awareness on the spiritual scripture, which is the truth."

The Gospel gives the rationale behind the counsel: *"For where your treasure is, there will your heart be also."* It means this: "You become that which you focus awareness on." In other words, the Gospel says, "The scripture you invest awareness in becomes your DNA." In other words, the scripture devours the soul.

> *Be sober, be vigilant; because your adversary the devil, as a roaring lion, walketh about, seeking who he may devour.*
> 1 Peter 5:8

MATTHEW 6:22-23

"The light of the body is the eye: if therefore thine eye be single, thy whole body shall be full of light. But if thine eye be evil, thy whole body shall be full of darkness. If therefore the light that is in thee be darkness, how great is that darkness!"

In order to truly understand this Gospel verse, we have to first understand the spiritual implication of the term eye. The eye represents man's worldview. It is through the eye man sees the world. In other words, the eye represents man's belief system—the scripture. The tem eye refers to the Self-DNA combination. The Self is also known as light. In the movie analogy, the Self represents the projector (light); DNA, the film roll; and, the world, the movie. The DNA becomes the body/world in the quantum-mechanical light of the projector. In this analogy, the eye represents the working projector.

The term *body* refers to man's physical body, which is also known as the "self." It is a projection of DNA. The world is also a projection of DNA, but a much larger one.

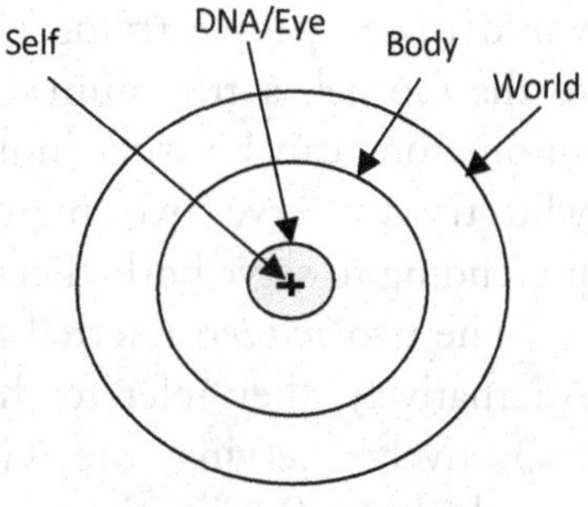

LIGHT OF THE BODY

The term *single* means "not-two." It denotes non-duality. Therefore, the expression "if thine eye be single" means "if your outlook is non-dualistic," or "if your scripture is non-dualistic." The expression, "thy body shall be full of light" means "you are body-aware," or "you are an Evite." Therefore, the statement, *"If therefore thine eye be single, thy whole body shall be full of light"* means, "If your outlook is non-dualistic, then you are an Evite" or, "If your scripture is non-dualistic, then you are body-aware."

Spiritually, the term evil refers to duality (Sanskrit: *dwanda*). It is the spell cast by the Serpent. The term *darkness* refers to delusion. It also implies corruption. Therefore, the phrase, *"But if thine eye be evil thy whole body shall be full of darkness" means,* "But, if your outlook is dualistic, then you are an Adamite." Or, "If your scripture is dualistic, then you live in delusion."

"If therefore the light that is in thee be darkness, how great is that darkness!" Spiritually, the expression, "if therefore the light that is in thee be darkness" suggests "if therefore you lack body-awareness." Therefore, the implication of the verse is this: "If you are an Adamite, you live in total delusion."

Term / Phrase	**Spiritual Implication**
Light	The Self / Truth
Eye	Belief System / Scripture
Single	Non-duality
Body	"self"
Evil	Duality
Darkness	Corruption / Delusion

MATTHEW 6:24

"No man can serve two masters: for either he will hate the one, and love the other, or else he will hold on to the one, and despise the other. Ye cannot serve God and mammon."

The term *man* refers to an individual human being. Gospel says that no *man* can serve two masters. But, it is commonplace in the world to see people trying to serve two or more masters. According to the Gospel, a true human being can serve only one master. Only automatons can be truly indifferent to the masters they serve. Those who try to serve two masters, end up actually serving one, but pretending to serve both. They end up hypocrites.

The two *masters* referred to in this verse are God and the Serpent. Alternatively, they refer to the spiritual scripture and literal scripture respectively. Serving the God means to be body-aware, to be non-dualistic. Serving the Serpent means to be deluded, to be dualistic.

Can a medical doctor really be spiritual? Can he serve medicine and God with equal fervor? Will a doctor dispense prayers to his patients instead of medicines? Yet many doctors say that they are firm believers in God. Isn't that hypocritical? The Gospel says it is impossible to serve two masters. The doctor who claims he is a true Christian is a hypocrite. It is the same for every other worldly profession. Therefore, should a professional discard spirituality? Yes, at least when he is a practicing professional.

The Gospel uses two interesting expressions here: they are "the one," and "the other." The expression, "the one" refers to the Self, or non-duality; "the other" refers to the Serpent, or duality. He who serves the Self is called an Evite; he who serves the Serpent is called an Adamite. The Gospel does not use the word *serve* in the literal sense. It uses the Greek word *douleuō* (G1398), which means "to be a slave to," or "to be in bondage."

The Gospel describes what happens if one tries to two masters: "*. . . for either he will hate the one, and love the other, or else he will hold on to the one, and despise the other. Ye cannot serve God and mammon.*" The Gospel does not clarify who *mammon* is, but describes him to be antithetical to God. As we have seen before, the term *God* refers to the true human (Evite) DNA, or the spiritual scripture. Therefore, the term mammon must be referring to the corrupt (Adamite) DNA, or the literal scripture.

The term *mammon* is one of bible's best kept secret. Scholars do not agree about the etymology of the word, but it is theorized that the term *mammon* derives from Late Latin *mammon*, from Greek *mammōnas* (G3126), from Syriac mamona ("riches"), from Aramaic *mamon* ("riches, money"), from a loanword from Mishnaic Hebrew *mamon* ("money, wealth, or possessions"), although it may also have meant "that in which one trusts." Perhaps, the latter is a more accurate definition of mammon.

The Philosophy of Money (1900) is a book on economic sociology by the German sociologist and social philosopher, George Simmel. Simmel believed people created value by making objects, then separating themselves from those objects and then trying to overcome that distance. In other words, distance (unavailability) makes objects desirable, and therefore, valuable. The very act of distancing generates desire. Moral laws operate on the same principle. They create the very evil they purport to avert. That is why the Gospel advises us to "resist not evil." Perhaps, the Gospel is referring to the literal scripture as mammon. What it says is this: "You cannot follow the literal scripture and the spiritual scripture at the same time. The former promises success in this world, but actually delivers delusion; the latter promises nothing in this world, but delivers truth.

MATTHEW 6:25-26

"Therefore I say unto you, Take no thought for your life, what ye shall eat, or what ye shall drink; nor yet for your body, what ye shall put on. Is not the life more than meat, and the body than raiment? Behold the fowls of the air: for they sow not, neither do they reap, nor gather into barns; yet your heavenly Father feedeth them. Are ye not much better than they?"

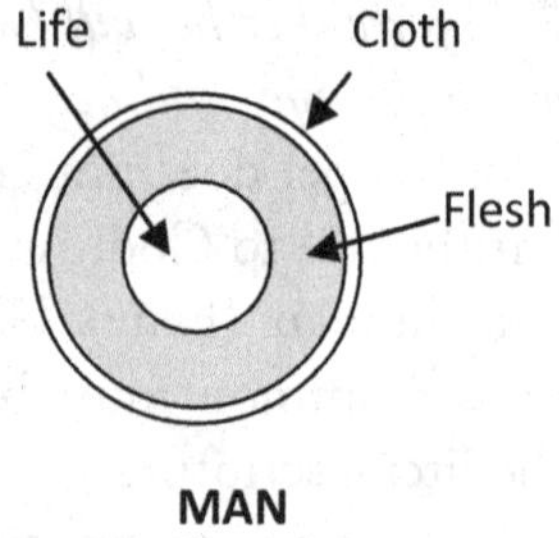

In the above verse, the word "therefore" implies "because you (Evites) serve the Self." The expression, "take no thought for your life" means "do not worry about livelihood." The point the Gospel makes is that the body-aware Evites do not have to worry about livelihood; the Self will take care of it. Its rationale: *"Is not life more than meat, and the body than raiment?"* The Gospel asks, "Which is more important, life or food; body or clothes?"

The Gospel uses the Greek word *trophē* (G5160) for "meat," which means "flesh" or "food." The equivalent term in Sanskrit is *annam*, which means "food" or "matter." Human body is essentially life (spirit) enclosed by flesh, or matter. Cloths cover the human body to create man's outward appearance. The order of priority is life, flesh, and lastly cloths. It is a causal chain. Life is the cause of physical body, and the physical body is the cause of worldly objects. The worldly priority, however, is in the reverse order: matter come first; then the body; lastly, life. We think life is an epiphenomenon of matter.

The Gospel advises the Evites to get their priorities straight, and reveals that cause has the inherent power to create the required effects, whatever it may be. The Self is the *Original Cause*, and it has the potential to generate everything that man needs. Therefore, those who serve the Self don't have to worry about livelihood. The Gospel takes the example of the birds of the air as proof that Existence provides for its creation. It then asks, *"Are ye not much better than they?"* implying that the primary concern of Evites should be serving the Self. The Bhagavad Gīta echoes this truth:

> *Ananyās-chintayanto mam yeh janāh paryupāsate*
> *Tēṣham nityābhiyuktānām yōgakṣēmam vahāmyaham*
> B.G. 9:22
> ("To those who serve the Self, not thinking about others, to those righteous men, I provide sustenance.")

The underlying theme of the Gospel is that man's Self is the original cause of the Universe, and it is concerned about its/his well-being. It is the lack of faith that prevents him from manifesting his real potential. The Gospel takes birds as an example to prove the point. The birds do not plan their lives, yet they live. They lead a care-free life instinctively trusting in the ability of nature to feed them. Do birds believe in God? Or, do they believe in nature? Absolutely not! They simply exist. If at all they 'believe' in anything, it is existence.

The Gospel message: It is the Father (Self/Existence) who sustains everything.

MATTHEW 6:27-30

"Which of you by taking thought can add one cubit unto his stature? And why take ye thought for raiment? Consider the lilies of the field, how they grow; they toil not, neither do they spin: And yet I say unto you, That even Solomon in all his glory was not arrayed like one of these. Wherefore, if God so clothes the grass of the field, which to day is, and to morrow is cast into the oven, shall he not much more clothe you, O ye of little faith."

The question, *"Which of you by taking thought can add one cubit into his stature"* is usually interpreted as, "No one can change his height by thinking about it." But, the Gospel is not talking about improving stature at all. On the contrary, it is asking, "Who can transform thoughts into physical effects?" hinting that it is possible for some. So, the issue here is the ability to transform thoughts into physical effects. It is relevant because the Gospel is discussing about livelihood.

To prove the point, the Gospel presents the lotus motif—the symbol of creation. The expression, "lily of the field" actually refers to the lotus. But, the term lily is commonly interpreted as something insignificant. Spiritually, the lily, or the lotus motif is highly significant. It is a sacred symbol in Hinduism and Buddhism. With its roots in mud, the lotus rises above the murky water to blossom clean and bright, symbolizing purity and elevation. The lotus symbolizes the Evites who rise above the chaos and delusion of the world. Moreover, the lotus flower has an affinity towards the sun, which symbolizes the Evites' affinity towards truth. Just as water cannot wet the lotus flower, sin cannot blemish the Evites. The eight-petal lotus that is used in Buddhist *mandalas* symbolizes cosmic harmony, and the thousand-petal lotus represents spiritual illumination. Among its many meanings and significance, the lotus is a symbol of self-generation, and so it also represents divine birth, spiritual development and creation itself. The bud of the lotus symbolizes potential, particularly of spiritual nature. The lotus symbolizes non-duality.

MATTHEW 6:31-32

"Therefore take no thought, saying, What shall we eat? or, What shall we drink? or, Wherewithal shall we be clothed? (For after all these things do the Gentiles seek:) for your heavenly Father knoweth that ye have need of all these things."

The crucial term that has to be understood in this verse is *Gentiles*. The Hebrew word for Gentiles is *goy* (H1471), which means "a foreign nation," "a troop of beasts," or "a flight of locusts." The term Gentiles suggests aliens. They are unrighteous people who don't serve the Father (Self). Their God is *Beelzebub*, who is also known as "lord of the flies." Spiritually, the expression, "lord of the flies" means "lord of the viruses," which is the Serpent. The term *Gentiles* actually refers to the Adamites. And the term *righteous* refers to the Evites.

The God of the Gentiles is Baal—the Establishment. Since the Gentiles do not serve the Father, they have to worry about their food, shelter and clothing. The term *Gentile* is derived from the Latin word *gentilis*, which means "of or belonging to a clan or tribe." The typical characteristic of a Gentile is that he is tribalistic, or clannish.

If you are body-aware, then you can be certain that you not a Gentile; if not, you are a Gentile. But no one can say if the other person is a Gentile or not. But, the Evite status is a birthright; it is a gift from the Father. However, an Evite could lose his birthright and live *like* an Adamite, or an Adamite could usurp an Evite's birthright and live *like* an Evite.

The Gospel reverses the definition of Gentile and the non-Gentile. According to it, a Gentile is one who does not know the Father; he is a faithless one. The Gentile only believes in the public, and his actions are dictated by it. The non-Gentile, on the other hand, is faithful to his Self, which knows his needs more than anyone else. Therefore, the Gospel says, "*. . . your heavenly Father knoweth that ye have need of all these things.*"

MATTHEW 6:33-34

"But seek ye first the kingdom of God, and his righteousness; and all these things shall be added unto you. Take therefore no thought for the morrow: for the morrow shall take thought for the things of itself. Sufficient unto the day is the evil thereof."

The expression, "all these things" refers to the three basic concerns of man, as mentioned in the previous verse:

1. "What shall we eat?"
2. "What shall we drink?"
3. "Wherewithal shall we be clothed?"

The Gospel assures the Evite that the Father will take care of his needs. But, there is a condition: *"But seek ye first the kingdom of God, and his righteousness . . . "* The condition: "First, know the body closely." According to the Gospel, the body is capable of satisfying man's needs.

Therefore the Gospel counsels: *"Take therefore no thought for the morrow: for the morrow shall take thought for the things of itself. Sufficient unto the day is the evil thereof."* The Greek word for *morrow* is *aurion* (G839), which means "rough wind." The word is derived from the root word *aēr* (G109), which means "circumambient wind." Spiritually, the term *morrow* refers to the mind. Therefore, the spiritual implication of the verse: "Don't fall into mind's trap. Leave him alone. This miserable world itself is his creation."

The word *morrow* (*aurion*) also means "the next day". Therefore, the Gospel says that the Evite is not concerned about future. He knows that each day comes with its uncertainties, and, therefore, there is no point in worrying about it. This is the literal implication of the verse. But, it has another implication. Just as the notion "two" (duality), the notion "next" is also a mental construct. *Next* never arrives! Therefore, it is fundamentally insatiable. That is the *evil* the Gospel is alluding to.

Human misery falls into two categories: one, frustrations; two, worries. While frustrations relate to the past, worries relate to the future. Frustration and anxiety are the two pillars of this delusionary world.

The Evite is not perturbed by uncertainty. His mantra: *Atithi dēvō bhava*. It means, "The guest is God." The mantra exhorts us to treat guests with respect. But, spiritually, it has another meaning. The word *atithi* is derived from two roots: the prefix "a," meaning "not"; and, "*tithi,*" meaning "date." Therefore, the term *atithi* means "not date." The term *atithi* refers to events that occur unexpectedly in life. And that *atithi* is *Uncertainty*! Therefore the `mantra says, "Uncertainty is God." Modern physics confirms it. According to Heisenberg's *Uncertainty Principle*, uncertainty is the very stuff of reality. And it is rife with potentiality. It is the Self of man.

According to the Hindu tradition, a man receives four great truths at four key stages of his life. The first is: *Māthru dēvō bhava*; it means "Mother is God." Man receives this mantra at birth, and it is uttered to him silently by nature. That *atithi* is instinct. Guided by it, he gravitates towards mother for sustenance. Man receives the second mantra, when he is able to fix his gaze. The mother utters this mantra, pointing towards the father: *Pithru dēvō bhava*; it means "Father is God." Later, when he reaches about eight years of age, the father takes him to a teacher, and pointing at the teacher he utters the third mantra: *Āchārya dēvō bhava*; it means "The teacher is God." Man receives the fourth and final mantra several years later, perhaps after several lives (*janmās*) and after several teachers later, by sheer grace of God, when a *Guru*, utters to him the final mantra: *Athithi dēvō bhava.* The man now understands the truth with his whole being and gets enlightened.

CHAPTER 7

Spoken Words—The Third Sermon

MATTHEW 7:1-2

"Judge not, that ye be not judged. For with what judgment ye judge, ye shall be judged: and with what measure ye mete, it shall be measured to you again."

Judging is based on the assumption of separation. I judge others, or others judge me. Without the separation, judging is not possible. In other words, in real love, there is no judgment.

The separation between "I" and the "other," or (not-I) is just an illusion. It is the root of human cognition, which is the basis of our waking consciousness. In reality, there is no separation between I and (not-I). Reality is a continuous, unbroken field with no boundaries at all. Such a medium will not appear as such to those living in it. It would appear more like space. And that medium is called pure consciousness, or simply Consciousness.

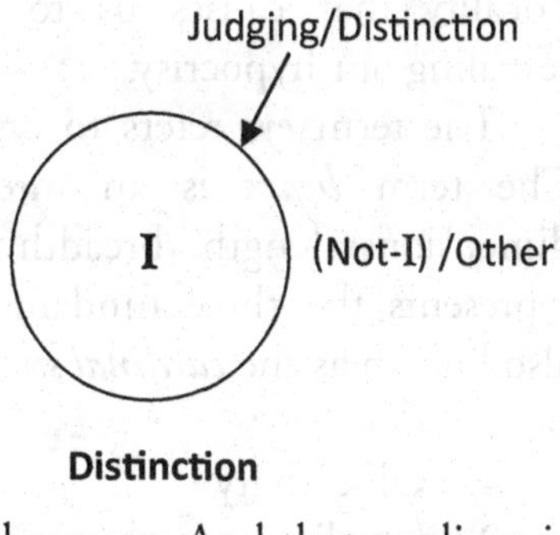

Just as every action in the physical space is opposed by an equal and opposite reaction every thought in spiritual space (consciousness) is opposed by an equal and opposite thought. It is an absolute certainty. However, there may be time delay action and reaction, since consciousness is timeless. When we judge someone, we are also judged, simultaneously.

The separation between "I" and (not-I) arise due to ignorance. The illusion of separation is one of the cardinal sins of man. It is called the *Ādhibhauthika thāpa* in the Hindu Vēdānta. The Sanskrit word "thapa" means "heat," or "misery." *Ādhibhauthika thāpa*" is the misery caused by objects and entities (the *other*) in space. In physics it is known as the assumption of Locality.

The word *measure* presumes separation between the "measured," the "measurer," and the "meter." However, in a continuous medium, where there is no separation between the "measured" and the "measurer," the "measurer" becomes the "measured".

MATTHEW 7:3-5

"And why beholdest thou the mote that is in thy brother's eye, but considerest not the beam that is in thine own eye? Or how wilt thou say to thy brother, Let me pull out the mote out of thine eye; and, behold, a beam is in thine own eye? Thou hypocrite, first cast out the beam out of thine own eye; and then shalt thou see clearly to cast out the mote out of thy brother's eye."

In the previous verse we saw how delusion arises from the assumption of Locality. We also saw that it is the assumption of Locality that causes us to judge others, despite our own faults, revealing our hypocrisy.

The term *eye* refers to one's worldview. It is our "point of view." The term *beam* is an interesting metaphor. A beam has three dimensions: length, breadth and width. The term *beam*, therefore, represents the three fundamentally faulty assumptions about reality, also known as the *cardinal sins* (Sanskrit: *thāpathraya*). They are:

1. Objectivity
2. Locality
3. Causality

It is these faulty assumptions that the Gospel calls as "the beam that is in thine own eye." The cardinal sins cloud our perception of reality. The term *mote* refers to a splinter of the beam. The mote originates from the beam. It implies that the fault that we see in others fundamentally originates from our faulty assumptions about reality.

The Gospel is not talking about morality here, as is generally perceived. It discusses the much more serious issue of *ignorance*. It is these faulty assumptions about reality that deludes man to consider the other as a separate entity, and therefore, to judge him. When the *beam* of ignorance is removed from our worldview, both the "other" and the "mote" disappear from our worldview simultaneously.

MATTHEW 7:6

"Give not that which is holy unto the dogs, neither cast ye your pearls before swine, lest they trample them under their feet, and turn again and rend you."

A thing is considered *holy* if it possesses the *seed* quality—the quality of self-generation. The seed encapsulates in itself its past and future. It is a "bundle of potentiality." Just like the seed, the Gospel is also timeless, and, therefore, holy. The Word (Evite DNA) too is a bundle of potentiality, and it manifests in multifarious forms (stories). And each of these manifestations is a spiritual interpretation of the Gospel. The *seed* quality of the Gospels is not apparent to the Adamites.

Earlier, we compared the Gospel to the Srimad Bhāgavatam of the Hindus. The Bhāgavatam opens with the *Adhikāri Skandha*. The Sanskrit word *adhikāri means* "the rightful owner," or the "keeper." The *Adhikāri Skandha* is the section of Bhāgavatam that defines who is eligible to *hear* the Gospel. It also defines the qualities of one who possess it. The word, *hear* means much more than simply hearing; it implies understanding the spiritual meaning of the content. The rightful owner of Bhāgavadam is *King Parīkshit*—the righteous king, who is born in the line of *Pāndavas*. He represents the Evite. Similarly, the rightful owner of the Gospel—the one who is eligible to understand the spiritual meaning of the Gospel—is the Evite.

The Gospel says, *"Give not that which is holy unto the dogs."* The phrase, "that which is holy" refers to the spiritual meaning of the Gospel words. The use of the term, "dogs" is significant. The Hebrew word for *dog* is *keleb* (H3612), which means "to yelp" or "to attack." What are the characteristics of dogs? They bark; they fight among themselves; they bite; they can be conditioned (trained). All these are characteristics of the Adamite.

The Hebrew word for *swine* is *hāzir* (H2386), which is derived from an unused root probably meaning "to enclose," or "to pen." The term *swine* refers to those who are possessed by the group spirit, or duality—those who are clannish. Swine are ugly and gluttonous creatures that live in filth. Therefore, the term *swine* refers to materialistic people.

Pearls signify rare and valuable objects. Pearls are rare and are found only in deep oceans, and great effort is required to acquire them. Pearls are spherical and luminescent. In the past, pearls came from India and Sri Lanka. The term *pearl* refers to the *Advaita* teachings of India.

The Gospel implores the Evites not to indiscriminately reveal the Gospel secrets to the Adamites. The reason: Adamites, who lack body-awareness, are incapable of understanding the true meaning of the Gospel's non-dualistic message; they may reject it and then accuse you of blasphemy.

MATTHEW 7:7-8

"Ask, and it shall be given you; seek, and ye shall find; knock, and it shall be opened unto you: For every one that asketh receiveth; and he that seeketh findeth; and to him that knocketh it shall be opened."

Can computers ask questions? I mean, really ask questions? No! Only a conscious, self-aware entity can ask questions. Only humans can ask questions. Computers can only mimic it. A cleverly designed program may trick you into believing that it is really asking questions. "Asking," "seeking," and "knocking" are different forms of the question "what."

The Gospel declares in no uncertain terms: *"For every one that asketh receiveth; and he that seeketh findeth; and to him that knocketh it shall be opened."* The reason? The question is the answer! Question is like the seed; it is a bundle of potentiality. All possible answers are contained in the question "what"; the seeker has only to manifest the appropriate answer into actuality. But, to manifest it he requires unwavering faith.

What is the secret of manifesting the right answer from the question? The Gospel explains in John 14:14: *"If ye shall ask any thing in my name, I will do it."* The Gospel words are very clear; there is no ambiguity there. If we analyze John 14:14, we find the two important points:

1. The real prayer has the form of a question (asking).
2. The question has to be asked in "my name."

To be effective, the prayer should be in the form of a question. But, our prayers are like begging. We pray like slaves begging to their master. The effective prayer is addressed to no one. It is simply a question, nothing more, nothing less. Now, what is meant by asking in "my name"? We assume that the term "my name" refers to Jesus, and we ardently pray in Jesus' name, but to no avail. The truth is that the term "my name" refers to the pronoun "I" ("Self"), which is my real name, as well as everyone's. "My name" is "The Self"; therefore, asking in "my name" implies asking with body-awareness, or asking with faith.

The Gospel promises that when you ask the Self a real question with self-awareness, it will be answered.

MATTHEW 7:9-11

"Or what man is there of you, whom if his son ask bread, will he give him a stone? Or if he ask a fish, will he give him a serpent? If ye then, being evil, know how to give good gifts unto your children, how much more shall your Father which is in heaven give good things to them that ask him?"

In the earlier verse, we saw the Gospel promising the Evite that whatever he asks the Self (Father) with self-awareness will be given to him. Here, it contrasts the gifts given by the Father with the gifts given by the Creator, and emphasizes that whatever the Father gives is, ultimately, for the good of the progeny. In the case of the creator, it need not necessarioy be so.

The Evites are called "sons" because they are 'born' of the Father. In contrast, the Adamites are called "creatures" because they are 'created' by a Creator in his image. The Father gives his sons bread when they ask for bread and fish when they ask for fish. The Creator gives his creatures stone when they ask for bread and serpent when they ask for fish. While the Father is concerned about the good of his children, the Creator is only concerned about controlling his creatures.

The Gospel introduces the motifs *bread* and *stone* to contrast the good (spiritual) gifts provided by the Father and the evil (material) gifts provided by the Creator. Bread is a substance that sustains and nourishes life. Spiritually, it refers to the spiritual scripture, the Gospel. The circle represents bread. Stone, on the other hand, refers to a lifeless thing, something that does not nourish life. The stone only create obstructions and pain. Spiritually, the term *stone* refers to the literal scripture. The polygon represents stone.

Spiritually, the expression, "son asking bread" refers to man's physical needs. The Father gives his children things that are ultimately good for them, whereas the Creator gives his creatures worldly pleasures, which can harm them ultimately.

The Gospel introduces two more motifs - the *fish* and the *serpent* - to contrast the gifts given by the Father and the Creator. What is the difference between a fish and a serpent? Fish is a living thing, which is a wholesome food. And fish lives in water (consciousness). The *Vesica Pisces* symbol represents fish. The symbol also represents Jesus Christ, the Gospel.

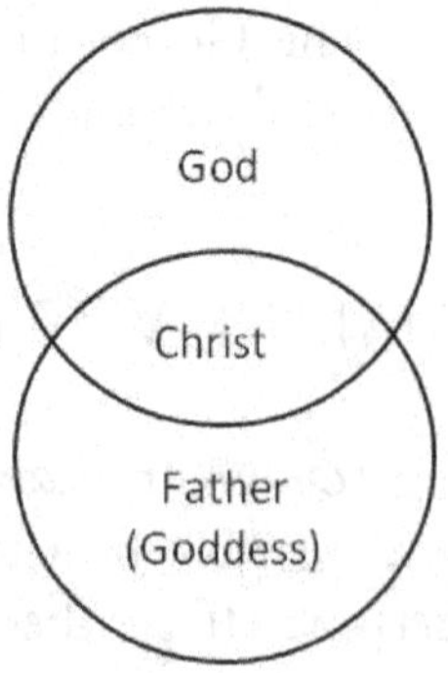

THE VESICA PICSES

In the earliest traditions, the Supreme Being was represented by a sphere, the symbol of a being with no beginning and no end, continually existing, perfectly formed and profoundly symmetrical. The addition of a second sphere represented the expansion of unity into the duality of male and female, god and goddess. By overlapping the two spheres, the god and goddess created a divine offspring. The *Vesica Pisces* motif (and its derivatives, the Flower of Life, Tree of Life, and fundamentals of geometry) has a history of thousands of years and easily predates virtually all major religions of the current era. Fish represents true human DNA.

Serpent, on the other hand, is a venomous creature. Its poison is deadly. Serpents crawl in dust (matter). And it is represented by the *sine curve,* which 'simulates' the circle in time. The sine curve is open ended, but seems to continue forever. The sine curve is but a simulation of the circle in space-time. Serpent represents virus DNA.

Spiritually, the expression, "son asking fish" refers to man's spiritual needs. The Father gives his children the spiritual scripture (the Gospel) for nourishment, whereas the Creator gives his creatures the literal scripture (the Law), which can kill him spiritually.

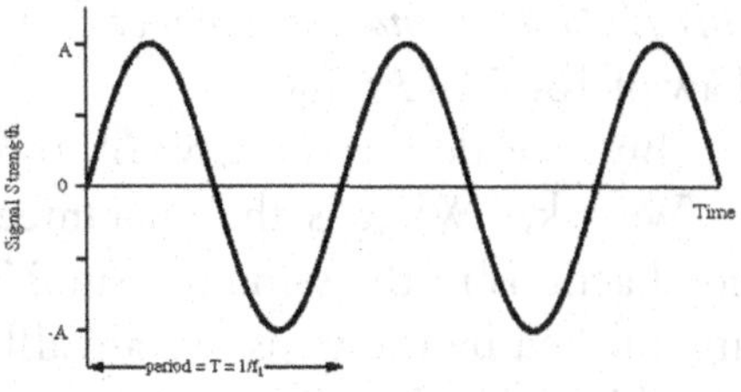

(a) Sine Wave

THE SERPENT

Therefore, the Gospel asks the Evite, "If you are so much concerned about your children's welfare, won't the heavenly Father (the Self) be more concerned about you, his child?"

MATTHEW 7:12

"Therefore all things whatsoever ye would that men should do to you, do ye even so to them: for this is the law and the prophets."

Imagine a universe of gel. Also imagine that everything in that universe is made of gel. Imagine yourself to be in that universe, and that your body itself is made of gel. Now, in this strange world, if you want something to be done to you, the best way would be to do the same thing to the "other"—the medium. Since the medium is continuous and integral, your action will go around and then come around to you. Let us call it *the Law of Toroidal Action.*

Now, take our universe. Everything in our universe is made of energy, and therefore, in terms of energy, our cosmos is a continuous and integral medium just like the gel universe we imagined. Energy is a form of consciousness. Therefore, our cosmos too is a continuous and integral field of consciousness. Naturally, the Law of Toroidal Action should apply to all our actions and thoughts in this universe; the effect may be delayed or not, but it is a certainty.

The Gospel says, *"Therefore all things whatsoever ye would that men should do to you, do ye even so to them."* If you want others to be nice to you, you be nice to them. If you want others to respect you, you respect them first. You cannot deceive others and then expect others to be honest with you. Whatever you want others to do to you, you do it to them. According to this law, the violence, poverty, and misery that we experience in this world are self-inflicted. The Gospel says, "*. . . for this is the law and the prophets*"; it replaces the Mosaic Law with the Law of Toroidal Action.

But, we doubt the Law of Toroidal Action; we are suspicious of it. We ask, "What is the guarantee that the world would return our good actions in the same measure? The reason we doubt is because we are infected by the virus; we are afflicted by cardinal sins (*thāpathraya*) of Objectivity, Locality and Causality. We are unable to imagine the universe to be one single, integral whole called Consciousness. The idea of separation is deeply ingrained in our consciousness. Thus, the Gospel echoes the Upaniṣad mantra, *Īśāvāsyam idam sarvam* which means, "There is only It, nothing else." And it is the continuous, integral field in which we have our being.

> *For in him we live, and move, and have our being; as certain also of your poets have said, For we are also his offspring.*
> Acts 17:28

MATTHEW 7:13-14

"Enter ye in at the straight gate: for wide is the gate, and broad is the way, that leadeth to destruction, and many there be which go in thereat: Because straight is the gate, and narrow is the way, which leadeth unto life, and few there be that find it."

The word *gate* literally means an opening permitting passage through an enclosure. The Sanskrit word for gate is *dwāra*, which means an opening, not only of physical things, but of spiritual things also. In the latter sense, our eyes, ears, nose, tongue, and skin are gates through which information enters into our awareness.

The Gospel speaks of two types of gates and two types of paths:

		First Type	Second Type
1.	Gate	Straight gate	Wide gate
2.	Way	Narrow path	Broad path

The first type of gate is known as the *straight gate.* It refers to the human body. Alternatively, it refers to the spiritual scripture. The second type of gate is called the *wide gate* and it refers to sense-openings (*dwāra*), such as eyes, ears, nose, tongue, and skin, through which awareness flows out into the world of delusion. Alternatively, it refers to the literal scripture.

The first type of path is known as the *narrow path.* It is the arduous path of self-searching, or truth-searching. That path leads inwards. It is called the path of repentance (*vairāgya*). But, the narrow path leads to life and enlightenment. The other path is called the *broad path;* it is the path of delusion. The wide path is called religion. It is a broad and easy path and *many* take this path. The word *many* refers to the Adamites. But, this path leads only deeper and deeper into delusion, and eventually to destruction.

The Greek word for gate is *pylōn* (G4440), which means the doorway of a building or city. However, the word Gospel uses is *pylē* (G4439), which means "a gate," that is, the leaf or wing of a folding entrance. Spiritually, it refers to the outer cover of a book - the scripture.

MATTHEW 7:15

"Beware of the false prophets, which come to you in sheep's clothing, but inwardly they are ravening wolves."

The most important word in this verse is the term *prophets.* Literally, the word *prophet* refers to a man chosen to speak for God or a man who speaks by divine inspiration. The term also refers to one of a class of persons in the early church, next in order after the apostles, recognized as inspired to utter special revelations and predictions (1 Cor. 12:28). It refers to the priests who are ordained by the Church, and who do not possess the divine inspiration. They are merely employees of the Church. Perhaps, it is this group that the Gospel refers to as *false prophets.* And they have a dress code: they wear long garments called *melotes.* There is an allusion about it in the Gospel of Mark (12:38) in connection with the Scribes: "*. . . which love to go in long clothing, and love salutations in the marketplaces.*" *Melote* is also known as the "goodly Babylonian garment" that Achan coveted and stole from the Canaanite spoils (Joshua 7:20-21.). It refers to a monastic cloak. The greed and rapacity of the false prophets comes through in this Old Testament story.

The goodly Babylonian garment symbolizes Mystery: Babylon the Great, the Mother of harlots and abominations of the earth. It represents every departure from the true path. Babylon symbolizes the rebellious attitude of them that say, *"We will not walk therein"* (Jeremiah 6:16).

> *And upon her forehead was a name written, MYSTERY, BABYLON THE GREAT, THE MOTHER OF HARLOTS AND ABOMINATIONS OF THE EARTH.*
> Revelation 17:5

Spiritually, the term "prophets" refers to the Evites and their spiritual scripture. Therefore, the term "false prophets" refers to Adamites and their literal scripture, also known as the Serpent. The Greek word for "false prophet" is *pseudoprophētēs* (G5578), which means "a religious imposter." The word is derived from the word *psuedēs* (G5571), which means "wicked" and *prophētēs* (G4396), which means "a foreteller." The Greek word for *sheepskin* is *mēlōtē* (G3374). It is commonly used in book-binding. Spiritually, "the false prophet that comes to you in sheep's clothing" actually refers to a book which gives false prognostications. It is an indirect reference to the literal scripture. Therefore, the Gospel warning, "Beware of the false prophets, which come to you in sheep's clothing" is a warning against false scriptures. The Gospel depicts the *false prophets* as ravening wolves. The word *ravening* implies predatory, rapacious, raptorial, or voracious nature. They want more than flesh; they want souls. They corrupt the human DNA.

The Greek word for *apostle* is *apostolos* (G652), which means "a delegate," specifically, an ambassador of the Gospel. The word is derived from the root word *apostellō* (G649), which means "set apart," i.e. by implication "to send out on a mission." The term apostle is found only in the New Testament; it is not found anywhere in the Old Testament.

Why does the Gospel compare the false prophets to wolves? The first and foremost reason is that they are ravening and rapacious like the wolves. The other is reason is that they hunt in packs like wolves. Wolves don't hunt alone; they hunt as a *pack*. Each pack is a congregation, and each has a leader. In nature, wolf packs are less about ferocity and more about order. Wolves follow an incredibly sophisticated group hierarchy. Each pack has an *alpha male* and an *alpha female*. The pack leader need not be the alpha male; it can be an alpha female too. The *Beta wolf* comes next. Beta wolf acts as the Second-in-Command, taking over if the Alpha male dies. At the bottom rung of the ladder are the *Omega wolves*. The Omega wolf is the weakest and the least cared for in the pack. Wolf is an extremely social animal.

MATTHEW 7:16

"Ye shall know them by their fruits. Do men gather grapes of thorns, or figs of thistles?"

Here, the Gospel talks about identifying the false prophets. It says, *"Ye shall know them by their fruits."* Literally, the word *fruit* means "any product of plant growth useful to humans or animals." Fruit is the developed ovary of a seed plant with its contents and accessory parts. If we compare seed to the DNA, then the ovary refers to the body-cell. Therefore, in this context, the term "fruits" refers to man's body-cells. In other words, the Gospel tells us that we can identify the false prophets by their body-cells! Amazing!

Alternatively, the Gospel is also saying that the false prophets can be identified by their actions. On the action side, these false prophets preach lofty principles, but never practice them. Their words and actions do not match. They are hypocrites. On the being side, they can be identified by their microbiology. Perhaps, the Gospel is telling us that there is something in the human body-cell that exposes the false prophet.

To elucidate the point, the Gospel takes two fruits and two plants as examples. The fruits considered are the grape and the fig; and the plants, thorns and thistle. *Grape* is a fruit that is sweet and edible. It comes in *red* or *blue* colors. The juice of grape can be converted into *spirit*. Spiritually, the grapes denote the human blood. *Fig*, on the other hand, is an edible fruit consisting of a mature *syconium* (fleshy part) containing numerous one-seeded fruits. Spiritually, the fig denotes human flesh containing numerous mononucleate cells. The fig and grape, together, represents the Evite (true human being).

The *thorn*, also known as the *common hawthorn* (genus: *Crataegus*; family: *Rose*) is a species native to Europe, northwest Africa and western Asia. It has been introduced in many other parts of the world where it entered as an invasive weed. Spiritually, thorn represents the *invasive virus* that has infected humanity. *Thistle* is the common name of a group of flowering plants characterized by leaves with sharp prickles on the margins, mostly in the family of *Asterceae*. The thistle is an ancient Celtic symbol of nobility of character as well as of birth. It is an invasive alien species that has invaded whole earth. These plants are good for nothing and they choke the native plants. The thorn and the thistle, together, represent the *invasive alien virus* (the Serpent). By the way, the thorn represents England; and, thistle represents Scotland. Rose (a thorn) is the national flower of England; and, thistle that of Scotland. Spiritually, the expression, "thorn and thistle" refers to Babylon.

MATTHEW 7:17-18

"Even so every good tree bringeth forth good fruit; but a corrupt tree bringeth forth evil fruit. A good tree cannot bring forth evil fruit, neither can a corrupt tree bring forth good fruit."

As we have seen before, spiritually, the term *tree* refers to the DNA. And the fruit of that tree is scripture. According to the Gospel, there are two types of trees: the good trees and the corrupt trees. Spiritually, they represent "her seed" (true human DNA) and "thy seed" (virus DNA) respectively. The *good fruit* refers to the spiritual scripture; the *evil fruit* refers to the literal scripture.

Those who have corrupt DNA are fundamentally bad; whatever they do, even if it appears noble and kind outwardly will ultimately turn out to be bad for humanity because they are fundamentally bad in their being. In other words, the corrupt trees simply cannot bear good fruits. Those who have true human DNA are fundamentally good; whatever they do, even if it appears evil outwardly will ultimately turn out to be good for humanity because they are fundamentally good in their being. In other words, the good trees simply cannot bear evil fruits.

MATTHEW 7:19-20

"Every tree that bringeth not forth good fruit is hewn down, and cast into the fire. Wherefore, by their fruits ye shall know them."

According to the Gospel, true human beings (Evites) and corrupt human beings (Adamites) can be distinguished by the nature of their DNA, or scripture. As we have seen before, the good fruits of the good tree denote flesh and blood. Spiritually, they represent faith (body-awareness) and freewill.

The Gospel says that the corrupt trees will be hewn down. The word, *hew* means "to strike forcibly with an ax, sword, or other cutting instrument." Spiritually, *hewing* suggests the disintegration of the corrupt DNA, and the corrupt scripture. And the instrument that breaks them down is the sword. Spiritually, the term *sword* denotes non-duality. Moreover, according to the Gospel, the hewn-down tree is cast into the fire. And *fire* represents truth. In other words, the Gospel says that the ignorance of the literal scripture will be destroyed by truth.

MATTHEW 7:21

"Not everyone that saith unto me, Lord, Lord shall enter into the kingdom of heaven; but he that doeth the will of my Father which is in heaven."

He who calls constantly utters "Lord, Lord" is called a religious fanatic. He has subsumed his individuality to his religion, and is overeager to fulfill his religious obligations. He is a religious fundamentalist.

Spiritually, the term "kingdom of heaven" refers to the human body, or truth. Therefore, expression, "to enter into the kingdom of heaven" means "to be body-aware," or "to be sane." According to the Gospel, the religious fanatic is not a sane man. He is under severe delusion.

According to the Gospel, a sane man is one who does *"the will of my Father which is in heaven."* What does that imply? The expression, "my Father which is in heaven" refers to the Self. Therefore, "the will of my Father which is in heaven" suggests Self-will, or freewill. One who acts according to his freewill is called an individual. He is an Evite.

The real essence of freewill is the power to alter a decision after it is made. In other words, discretion is the essence of freewill. It is the essential quality of a true human being (Evite). Compassion arises from discretion. One who lacks discretion cannot show compassion; he simply quotes the rules and regulations.

According to the Gospel, only the individual find the truth.

MATTHEW 7:22-23

"Many will say to me in that day, Lord, Lord, have we not prophesied in thy name? and in thy name have cast out devils? and in thy name done many wonderful works? And then will I profess unto them, I never knew you: depart from me, ye that work inequity."

The Greek word for *iniquity* is *anomia* (G458), which means "violation of a law." Its Hebrew equivalent word is *ōla* (H5766), which means "evil." Spiritually, the term *iniquity* implies duality. The Bhagavad Gita equates equity (*samatvam*) with Yoga. Therefore, iniquity (*asamatvam*) means "lack of Yoga," or "delusion." In short, the term iniquity suggests duality, or delusion. The expression, "ye that work iniquity" actually refers to the Adamites.

The expression, "many will say to me" actually means "many will wonder." The term "me," refers not to Jesus, but to the Self of every human being. The term, "that day" refers to the *Day of Judgment*, which is nothing but death. The soul of the Evite will reincarnate after death to continue its journey until it realizes the ultimate truth. But the soul of the Adamite perishes with death. His journey ends because his vehicle (body/DNA) is corrupted beyond repair. No more reincarnations for him. And the Adamite realizes it just before death. And that is his judgment. It is not a verdict given an external entity. However, the Adamite can indirectly continue his earthly sojourn by leaving a male offspring.

The Adamite will wonder at the time of death:

1. "Did I not give inspired sermons in church?"
2. "Did I not proselytize unbelievers?"
3. "Did I not join the Communion every Sunday?"

Then his Self will say to him, "*I never know you.*" Its implication: "You do not know your own Self." And then pronounces its harsh indictment: *"I never know you: depart from me, ye that work inequity."*

The Ancient Greek aphorism "know thyself" (Greek: *gnōthi seauton*) is one of the Delphic maxims and was inscribed in the forecourt of the Temple of Apollo at Delphi. The maxim is interpreted differently by different philosophers. The *Suda*, a 10th century encyclopedia of Greek Knowledge says: "the proverb is applied to those whose boasts exceed what they are." Plato employs the maxim "Know Thyself" extensively by having the character of Socrates use it to motivate his dialogues.

MATTHEW 7:24-27

"Therefore whosoever heareth these sayings of mine, and doeth them, I will liken him unto a wise man, which built his house upon a rock: And the rain descended, and the floods came, and the winds blew, and beat upon that house; and it fell not: for it was founded upon a rock. And every one that heareth these sayings of mine, and doeth them not, shall be likened unto a foolish man, which built his house upon sand: And the rain descended, and the floods came, and the winds blew, and beat upon that house; and it fell: and great was the fall of it."

Gospel gives us another test for distinguishing between Evites and Adamites. The test: "Can you hear *these sayings of mine*?" Here, the expression, "these sayings of mine" refers to the spiritual meaning of the Gospel message. The word, *hear* implies understanding. Therefore, the phrase, "whosoever heareth these sayings of mine" means "whosoever truly understands the Gospel message." He who understands the spiritual meaning of the Gospel is an Evite. The Gospel calls him a wise man. And it explains why it calls him a wise man; because, he has built his house upon a rock. Here, the term *house* refers to the soul or belief system. The term *rock* denotes unchanging nature; it refers to non-duality, or truth. In other words, the Evite's soul is based in truth; it is, therefore, eternal.

The Greek word for rain is *brochē* (G1028). It is derived from the root *brechō* (G1026), which "to moisten," especially by rain. The Greek word for *floods* is *potamos* (G4215), which means "a current." The Greek word for winds is *anemos* (G417), which means "four quarters of earth," or "wind." The Gospel words echoes the Bhagavad Gita:

> *Nainam chhindanthi śaśtrāṇi nainam dahati pavakāh*
> *Na caimam klēdayanthyāpah na śōśayati māruthah*
> Bhagavad Gita 2:23
> ("The Atman cannot be cut by weapons nor it is burnt by fire; it cannot be moistened by water nor dried by the wind.")

The Greek word for *sand* is *ammos* (G285), which means "sand, as heaped on the beach." Spiritually, the term *sands* refer to the words of a book. According to the Gospel, the soul of the Adamite is based on his scripture. It is not eternal, but perishes with death.

MATTHEW 7:28-29

"And it came to pass, when Jesus had ended these sayings, the people were astonished at his doctrine: For he taught them as one having authority, and not as the scribes."

The Greek word for *doctrine* is *didachē* (G1322), which means "teaching." The word is derived from the Greek root *daō*, meaning "to teach." But, the Hebrew word for *doctrine* is *leqah* (H3948). It means "something received" (mentally), or "instructions." It refers to the canons. The term *leqah* also means, in a sinister sense, "inveiglement." To *inveigle* means "to entice, lure, or ensnare by artful talk."

The people were astonished at Jesus' doctrine because it was something totally new and exciting, but opposite to what they have been taught by religion. The word *astonished* means "to be filled with sudden overpowering surprise or wonder." The word also means "to be bewildered, to be confused, to be dumbfounded, or to be shocked." In other words, the Evites who heard the Gospel message were overpowered with wonder, but the Adamites were bewildered, confused, and shocked by it.

"For he taught them as one having authority, and not as the scribes." Authority is the power to determine, adjudicate, or otherwise settle issues or disputes. Discretion is the essence of authority. One who has real authority has discretion too. Without discretion, one is merely a proxy of a higher authority. And discretion is the power or right to decide or act according to one's own judgment. It is the power to overrule or bypass law; it implies freewill. Therefore, the Gospel implies that Jesus taught like an individual, not like the theologians. In other words, the Gospel says its message is individualized. Each man has to give his own interpretation to it. It is not a canon for blind compliance.

The Gospel contrasts its way of teaching with that of the Scribes, saying, *". . . and not as the Scribes."* Who are the Scribes? A Scribe is one who writes books or documents by hand as a profession and helps the city keep track of its records. The profession, previously found in all literate cultures in some form or another, lost its importance and status with the advent of printing. Scribes' work involved copying books, including sacred texts, or secretarial and administrative duties, such as taking of dictation, and keeping of business, judicial and historical records for kings, nobles, temples, and cities. Later the profession of Scribes metamorphosed as public servants, journalists, accountants, typists, and lawyers. The Scribes in ancient Israel were distinguished professionals who could exercise functions we now associate with lawyers, government ministers, judges, or even financiers. Pharisees and Sadducees are offshoots of Scribes. It is plausible that the Scribes were the authors of the Old Testament books.

In many ways, the Scribes are like the computers of today. They did their assigned jobs—copying sacred texts, interpreting sacred texts, recording history, recording business transactions, keeping judicial records etc.—with precision, and strictly according to laid down rules. Scribes never used discretion in their jobs. They were faithful servants of people, and were called *Public Servants*. In a sense, they were like *human automatons,* like artificial intelligence (AI) entities. Scribes originated in ancient Sumer, as far back as 3000 BC. They were Sumerians. Over time, droves of Scribes came out of Sumer and occupied key positions in every civilized society across the globe. But, over time, the so-called *public servants* became the masters and the enemy of mankind.

The Gospel berates the Scribes for their hypocrisy, artificiality, and vanity. In fact, it even hints that they are artificial intelligence entities:

> *You are of your father the devil, and the lusts of your father ye will do. He was a murderer from the beginning, and abode not in the truth, because there is no truth in him. When he speaketh a lie, he speaketh of his own: for he is a liar, and the father of it.*
> John 8:44

The term devil refers to the Serpent (virus). The virus is an artificial intelligence entity. It, perhaps, is one of the most closely guarded secrets. The virus is both subtle and artificial. In the computer parlance, the equivalent term for *subtlety* or *cleverness* is computation or manipulation; the term for *artificial* is *simulated*. Perhaps, the Serpent is actually a super-computer. Perhaps, by calling the Scribes "sons of the devil," the Gospel is hinting that they are really *humanoids*, not true human beings. Perhaps, it is the Scribes that the Gnostics portrayed as *archons*.

Archon is a Greek word that means "ruler," or "lord," frequently used as the title of a specific public office. In ancient Greece the chief magistrate in various Greek city states was called Archon. In late antiquity, the term archon was used in Gnosticism to refer to the several servants of the *Demiurge*, the "creator god" that stood between the human race and a transcendent God that could only be reached through gnosis. In this context the archons have the role of the *angels* and *demons* of the Old Testament.

In the above verses, the Gospel talks about two kinds of doctrines, or scriptures: one, the teaching (*didache*) of those who have the authority (Evites), which is the spiritual scripture; the other, the canons (*leqah*) of those who do not have the authority (Adamites), which is the literal scripture. The latter is inveiglement—artful talk meant to entice, lure, and ensnare.

CHAPTER 8

The Campaign—The Conquest

MATTHEW 8:1-4

"When he was come down from the mountain, great multitudes followed him. And, behold, there came a leper and worshipped him, saying, Lord, if thou wilt, thou canst make me clean. And Jesus put forth his hand, and touched him, saying, I will; be thou clean. And immediately his leprosy was cleansed. And Jesus saith unto him, See thou tell no man; but go thy way, shew thyself to the priest, and offer the gift that Moses commanded, for a testimony unto them."

Whenever Jesus delivers important messages, he delivers them either seated on a *mountain* or seated in a *ship in sea*. What is the relevance of these imageries? Jesus compares himself to light:

> *"I am the light of the world: he that followeth me shall not walk in darkness, but shall have the light of life."*
> John 8:12

Light has a peculiar property: it is both particle and wave simultaneously. Since man's Self is light, it too can exist in the particle (mountain) state and in the wave (sea) state simultaneously. In the 'mountain' state of awareness, it is one with the Father (The All); in the 'sea' state of awareness, it is the *kingdom of heaven* (body-awareness).

The Gospel teaches us two types of meditation. The first is the mountain-mode meditation. In the mountain-mode mediation, one looks inwards and merges with the Self. In the sea-mode meditation, one focuses awareness on the body, and becomes intensely aware of body movements, sensations, and feelings.

Here, in this Gospel episode, we find Jesus healing a leper. Who is a leper? A leper is someone afflicted with leprosy disease. The term *leper* may also refer to one who is rejected or ostracized by society for unacceptable behavior, opinions, character, or the like. A leper is considered an anathema. The public considers him an untouchable. But, Mahatma Gandhi called them *Harijan*, meaning "Children of God." The name *Hari* refers to Lord Vishnu, who is the Indian equivalent of Christ. Spiritually, the term *Harijan* means "Christian."

In a sense, the Scribes are the real lepers because they are the ones infected by the deadly virus. But, ironically, wherever the Scribes migrated, they established an artificial cast system wherein they placed themselves at the top of the pecking order and food chain. The Scribes considered themselves as nobility, and branded the uninfected, true human beings, as untouchables, and treated them like lepers (pariahs). It is one such untouchable that Jesus heals here.

The leper says to Jesus, *"Lord, if thou wilt, thou canst make me clean."* The words reflect the man's faith. It is a sign that he is an Evite. The Gospel tells us how Jesus responded to the man's plea: *"And Jesus put forth his hand, and touched him, saying, I will; be thou clean. And immediately his leprosy was cleansed."* The response from Jesus is instantaneous and positive. The episode reveals the efficacy of Gospel message.

The Gospel continues: *"And Jesus saith unto him, See thou tell no man; but go thy way, shew thyself to the priest, and offer the gift that Moses commanded, for a testimony unto them."* Why is Jesus prohibiting the man from telling the good news to the public? Why is Jesus asking the man to show himself to the priests, if Jesus himself does not agree with them? Have we understood the Gospel message wrongly? I think so. Jesus is actually telling the man not to think of himself as an untouchable (inferior). Jesus instructs him to enter the temple, ignoring the ban imposed by the priests, and attend the ceremony if he so desires. Actually, Jesus heals the man's inferiority complex. And Jesus does not want the man to "tell" that he is healed, but "act" like one.

There is an alternate interpretation to this Gospel episode. In this alternate interpretation, the leper represents a Mortal (deluded Evite). The man realizes his fallen state and yearns to return to his true state. Jesus represents his body. His cry "Lord, if thou wilt, thou canst make me clean" shows his faith. The man "repents" and realizes that the body is capable of healing delusion. In other words, the man becomes body-aware. The body responds instantaneously, and the man is cured of his delusion.

MATTHEW 8:5-13

"And when Jesus was entered into Capernaum, there came unto him a centurion, beseeching him, And saying, Lord, my servant lieth at home sick of the palsy, grievously tormented. And Jesus saith unto him, I will come and heal him. The centurion answered and said, Lord, I am not worthy that thou shouldest come under my roof: but speak the word only, and my servant shall be healed. For I am a man under authority, having soldiers under me: and I say to this man, Go, and he goeth; and to another, Come, and he cometh; and to my servant, Do this, and he doeth it. When Jesus heard it, he marveled, and said to them that followed, Verily I say unto you, I have not found so great faith, no, not in Israel. And I say unto you, That many shall come from the east and west, and shall sit down with Abraham, and Isaac, and Jacob, in the kingdom of heaven. But the children of the kingdom shall be cast into outer darkness: there shall be weeping and gnashing of teeth. And Jesus said unto the centurion, Go thy way; and as thou hast believed, so be it done unto thee. And his servant was healed the selfsame hour."

In this episode, the Gospel tells us the story of a truth-seeker. The man realizing that he is under great delusion yearns to know the truth. He reads the Gospel, but is unable to understand its spiritual meaning. He then prays to his inner Self to reveal the truth to him. And it responds immediately, revealing the Gospel truths through intuition. The man is, thus, healed from his delusion.

The term *Capernaum* means "house of the Holy Spirit." Spiritually, Capernaum means "body." The mention of Capernaum is a sign that the Gospel is talking about Evites. And, the centurion represents an Evite. The term *centurion* refers to a professional officer in the Roman army who commands a legion of around hundred men. Centurions are usually elected and appointed by the Senate. They lead from the front and often suffer heavy casualties in battle. They are known for their courage and valor. In the modern context, the term *centurion*, probably, refers to a professional working in an organization.

The centurion presents his problem to Jesus: *"Lord, my servant lieth at home sick of palsy, grievously tormented."* Palsy is a disease whose main symptom is paralysis of the body, wherein a local body area is incapable of voluntary movement. Spiritually, the term *palsy* denotes lack of body-awareness, or delusion. The *servant* that the centurion is referring to is not the literal servant, but the spiritual servant - his own mind. In other words, the man's problem is that he is unable to control his mind. Spiritually, the expression, "grievously tormented" means "miserable." In short, the man is under delusion and feels miserable.

Jesus consoles the centurion and says, *"I will come and heal him."* Here, Jesus represents the man's body. Indirectly, the Gospel is telling us: "The body will reveal the truth, and the truth will heal your delusion."

The centurion says to Jesus, *"Lord, I am not worthy that thou shouldest come under my roof: but speak the word only, and my servant shall be healed."* The Greek word for *roof* is *stegē* (G4721), which means "the thatch or deck of a building." Spiritually, *stegē* means "head"; it implies intellect. What the centurion is really saying is this: "I don't have the intelligence to grasp the Gospel truth, but please reveal it to me and heal my ignorance."

The centurion explains why he thinks Jesus' command would heal his servant: "*For I am a man under authority, having soldiers under me: and I say to this man, Go, and he goeth; and to another, Come, and he cometh; and to my servant, Do this, and he doeth it.*" The spiritual implication of the words is this: "Just as the outer body (world) obeys my command, the inner body too will obey my command." In other words, the body will reveal the Gospel truth if commanded with self-awareness (faith).

The man's self-awareness impresses Jesus that he says to the crowd, *"Verily I say unto you, I have not found so great faith, no, not in Israel."* Spiritually, the term *Israel* means "humanity." Therefore, the Gospel says, "Few in this world have this degree of self-awareness."

Jesus then says to the crowd, *"And I say unto you, That many shall come from the east and west, and shall sit down with Abraham, and Isaac, and Jacob, in the kingdom of heaven."* The "many" that come from east and west refers to the Gentile across the world. "Kingdom of heaven" refers to body-awareness. The implication of the Gospel verse is this:

"Many Gentiles will understand the spiritual meaning of the Gospel and become body-aware."

"*But the children of the kingdom shall be cast into outer darkness: and there shall be weeping and gnashing of teeth.*" Spiritually, the term "kingdom" refers to the world, or the Establishment. Therefore, the expression, "children of the kingdom" means "worldly people." The expression, "outer darkness" denotes delusion; "weeping and gnashing of teeth" denotes misery. In other words, the Gospel says that the worldly people are destined to live in delusion and misery.

Jesus then says to the centurion, *"Go thy way; and as thou has believed, so be it done unto thee."* The spiritual implication of the words is this: "Have faith on the body, and do as you will." It means that a body-aware Evite has the freedom to act freely. In Bhagavad Gīta, Lord Krishna, at the end of his sermon, says to Arjuna,

> *Iti te jnānam-āghyātām guhyād guhyatharam mayā*
> *Vimruśyatad-aśēṣēṇa yadēcchasi tadhā kuru"*
> B.G. 18:63
> ("Thus I have declared to you wisdom more secret than secrecy itself; have faith on it and do as you will.")

"Have faith on the body, and do as you will." This is the message of the Gospel to us. The actions of a true human being, whatever it may be, can never, in the long run, turn out to be evil for humanity or nature.

MATTHEW 8:14-15

"And when Jesus was come into Peter's house, he saw his wife's mother laid, and sick of a fever. And he touched her hand, and the fever left her: and she arose, and ministered unto them."

It is unlikely that the Gospel is discussing about the physical disease called fever here. Neither fever nor the feverish person demands serious discussion. Therefore, it is apparent that the Gospel is telling us something else here—something far more serious than fever.

As per the Gospel account, Jesus casually visits Peter's house and finds his wife's mother ill with fever. Spiritually, Peter represents an ignorant Evite—one who is fanatical about his religion and its scripture. Peter's wife signifies his mind. And Peter's wife's mother signifies his scripture, which he has accepted as his belief system. Here, Peter's wife's mother is afflicted with fever. It implies that Peter's scripture is corrupted by duality. (Remember: DNA is the source of mind, and scripture can modify DNA.) Jesus coming into Peter's house signifies the Gospel entering the ignorant man's awareness.

The Sanskrit word for *fever* is *thāpaka*, which means "heat-producing." It is derived from the root word *thāpa*, which means "heat," or "delusion." Spiritually, the term *thāpaka* refers to *rajō-guna*, which is the mental tendency that pulls man into the delusionary world. Negative qualities such as vanity (*dambha*), pride (*darpa*), anger (*krōdha*) are symptomatic of *rājasic* personality. Mind afflicted by *rajō-guna* is called *rājasic* mind. It is a restless mind. And it wants variety: new friends, new toys, and new places to visit and so on. The *rājasic* mind makes one talkative and fault-finding. The *rājasic* person is unforgiving and ungrateful. In short, the *rājasic* person is a neurotic.

Jesus cures Peter's mother-in-law. The implication is that the Gospel can redeem minds and bodies corrupted by the Serpent. Gospel is the most effective antidote against Serpent poison. It is highly efficacious in removing *thāpathraya* (the cardinal sins of Objectivity, Locality and Causality). The Hindu Gospel *Srimad Bhagavadam* declares this truth unequivocally:

> *Dharma prōjthitha kaithavōthra paramo nirmatsarāṇām satām*
> *Vēdyam vāstavam-astu shivadam tāpathrayōnmūlanam.*
> Srimad Bhāgavatham
> ("That which is said here is the ultimate truth, which is free from corruption. And it is given freely to the righteous. It is so auspicious that it will totally destroy thāpathraya.")

MATTHEW 8:16-17

"When the even was come, they brought unto him many that were possessed with devils: and he cast out the spirits with his word, and healed all that were sick: That it might be fulfilled which was spoken by Esaias the prophet, saying, Himself took our infirmities, and bare our sicknesses."

The word *even* is an archaic term for "evening." The expression, "when the even was come" signifies the onset of night, or darkness. Spiritually, it refers to the onset of the *Dark Age*, or the *Kali Yuga*. The term *Kali Yuga* means the "age of the demon *Kali*." It is the age of vice. The Sanskrit word *kali* means "dark," "death," "time," "war," or "Saturn." According to the Hindu scriptures, the *Kali Yuga* is the last of the four ages (*Yugas*) the world goes through as part of the cycle of *yugas*. The other ages are *Satya Yuga*, *Trētā Yuga*, and *Dwāpara Yuga*. *Kali Yuga* began with the departure of Lord Krishna from earth. According to Hindu traditions, *Kali Yuga* began in the year 3102 BC.

Hindus believe that human civilization degenerates spiritually during the *Kali Yuga*. It is referred to as the Dark Age because during this age people are as far away as possible from truth and righteousness. Hindus symbolically represent righteousness (*dharma*) as a bull. In *Satya Yuga*, the first stage of development, the bull has four legs, but in each age *dharma* is reduced one quarter. By the age of *Kali*, it is reduced to only a quarter of that of the golden age, so that the bull of *dharma* has only one leg.

Kālīya, in Hindu mythology, was the name of a deadly serpent living in the *Yamuna River*, in *Vrindavan*. The term *Vrindavan* means "the forest of the Holy Basil." Yamuna water was totally corrupted by *Kālīya's* poison. The river spewed death. Nothing that contacted it escaped death. The only exception was a solitary *Kadamba* tree that grew on the river bank. The proper home of *Kālīya* was *Ramaṇaka Dwipa*, but he had been driven away from there by fear of *Garuda*, the foe of all serpents. Krishna finally defeats *Kālīya* by dancing on his head. In many ways *Kālīya* myth reminds us of the Biblical Serpent of Eden. *Vrindavan* may be compared with the Garden of Eden; the *Kadamba* tree, the tree of the knowledge of good and evil; Holy Basil, the tree of life. The *Garuda* represents the creator God. The waters of the Yamuna River represent the scripture meaning. The *Ramaṇaka Dwipa*, probably, refers to Egypt. Lord Krishna represents *Bhagavadam*, which is the Gospel of the Hindus. Similarly, Jesus Christ represents the Gospel. Lord Krishna defeats the *Kālīya*, the serpent, and saves the Yamuna from corruption. Similarly, Jesus Christ defeats the Serpent and saves the Scripture meaning from corruption.

Kali Yuga is associated with the apocalyptic demon *Kali*. It implies strife, discord, quarrel, and contention. The chief attributes of *Kali Yuga* are:

1. Absence of true faith (absence of *satya*)
2. Absence of meditation (absence of *tapas*)
3. Corruption in words, action, mind, or body (absence of *śaucha*)
4. Absence of compassion (absence of *daya*)
5. Absence of sharing (absence of *dāna*)
6. Selfishness (*udarambharaṇam*)
7. Popularity of atheism/monotheism (*nastika/pāşandah*)
8. People deluded and spiritually lazy (*mandāh*)
9. People interested only in worldly achievements (only interested in *prēyas*)
10. People not interested in righteousness (not interested in *śhrēyas*)
11. Temples infested by evil men
12. Priests sell scripture for money
13. Business-orientation pervasive
14. Licentiousness
15. Prostitution
16. Child abuse/pedophilia
17. Environmental destruction

The Gospel says, *"And when the even was come, they brought unto him many that were possessed with devils."* The term "many" refers to deluded people—those possessed by *group-spirit*, or duality. The Gospel uses the term *devil* to represent *Kali*, the deadly Serpent virus that corrupts human DNA. *Kali* is the embodiment of corruption.

What the Gospel is saying is this: "In the Kali Yuga, many will get the rare opportunity to read the Gospel." And that is what the Bhāgavatham also says.

MATTHEW 8:18-20

"Now when Jesus saw great multitudes about him, he gave commandment to depart unto the other side. And a certain scribe came, and said unto him, Master, I will follow thee whithersoever thou goest. And Jesus said unto him, The foxes have holes, and the birds of the air have nests; but the Son of man hath not where to lay his head."

"Now when Jesus saw great multitudes about him, he gave commandment to depart unto the other side." When Jesus sees the great multitude, he leaves Capernaum and goes to the "other side." Spiritually, the term *multitude* refers to people under delusion. It refers to the blind followers of religion. The "other side" of Capernaum represents body-awareness. Alternatively, Capernaum represents literal meaning, and the "other side" represents spiritual meaning. Therefore, the implication of the verse is this: "The public will never grasp the spiritual meaning of the Gospel."

"And a certain scribe came, and said unto him, Master, I will follow thee whithersoever thou goest." What is the young Scribe really saying? It seems he is saying, "Master, I will do whatever you instruct me to do." The Scribe is an Adamite. He lacks self-awareness. He is like an automaton that follows instructions precisely and faithfully. Without instructions he is lost. He is spiritually blind. Like a blind man he needs step-by-step instructions. He is totally incapable of grasping the spiritual meanings of the Gospel. What he is asking for is a canon that he and others can blindly follow.

Jesus says to the Scribe, *"The foxes have holes, and the birds of the air have nest; but the Son of man hath not where to lay his head."* Jesus says to the Scribe that he does not have a fixed itinerary to give him. The spiritual implication of the words is this: "The spiritual meaning of the Gospel is individualized. There is no fixed or established (canonical) meaning for the Gospel." The Gospel is quantum-mechanical in nature. It is a field of infinite possibilities. It can reveal the Self to you, but you need *divine eyes* to see it. Body-awareness is that divine eye. In the Bhagavaḍ Gita, Lord Krishna declares this truth:

> *Na tu mām śakyasē dṛuṣtum anēnaiva swachakṣusā*
> *Divyam dadāmi te chakṣu paśya mē yōgamaiśwaram*
> B.G. 11:8
> ("It is impossible for you to see Me with your human eyes. Therefore I give you divine eyes; now, see My Divine Yōga.")

Spiritually, the term *fox* denotes meaning; *hole* is a niche in earth in which the fox hides. The hole denotes word. Similarly, *bird* denotes meaning, and *nest* denotes word. Meaning is dynamic, but word is static. Just as foxes run into and out of their holes, and just as birds fly into and out of their nests, meaning run into and out of words. Here, Jesus is hinting at the dynamic nature of meaning.

The term, *Son of man* refers to the concept of man—the Self. It is a *quantum entity* and the field infinite of possibilities. The Gospel describes that Self and, therefore, it too is a field of infinite possibilities. But, if it is 'collapsed' into something fixed, then it loses its quantum nature and turns into dead matter. It loses its holiness. That is the implication of the words: *"The foxes have holes, and the birds of the air have nests; but the Son of man hath not where to lay his head."*

MATTHEW 8:21-22

"And another of his disciple said unto him, Lord, suffer me first to go and bury my father. But Jesus said unto him, Follow me; and let the dead bury their dead."

"And another of his disciple said unto him, Lord, suffer me first to go and bury my father." The expression, "another of his disciple" suggests that Jesus has two types of disciples: one, those who are chosen by him (those who have non-dualistic 'eyes'); the other, those who follow him blindly (those who have dualistic 'eyes'). In other words, there are two types of Gospel readers: one, those who can grasp its spiritual meaning; the other, those who blindly follow its literal meaning. Most of us belong to the latter group—we only grasp the literal meaning.

Here, the latter kind of disciple says to Jesus, *"Lord, suffer me first to go and bury my father."* Spiritually, the term *father* refers to the Quantum Self. Therefore, the expression, "bury my father" suggests collapsing the quantum wave-function. It means contracting the field of infinite possibilities into something fixed. Spiritually, what the man says is this: "I cannot discard the literal scripture."

Jesus says to the man, *"Follow me; and let the dead bury their dead."* Its spiritual implication: "Follow you heart; the literal scripture is for the deluded."

There is another implication for the verse. Here, the issue is about priority. Apparently, the man's first priority is the world (money, fame, and power); truth comes only next. He wants to seek truth, but cannot discard money, fame, and power. He wants to serve God and mammon at the same time. The man's predicament is similar to the predicament of the professional we discussed earlier.

In the Bhagavad Gīta, Arjuna faces a similar predicament at the battlefield, and says to Lord Krishna:

> *Svajanam hi katham hatva sukhina śyāma mādhava*
> B.G. 1:37
> ("How can I live happily after killing these relations of mine, O Lord?")

Lord Krishna admonishes Arjuna for his inability to see the truth:

> *Aśōchyān anwaśochas-tvam prajnā-vādāmscha bhāṣase*
> *Gatāsūn-agathāsūn ca na anuśōchanthi pandhithāh*
> B.G. 2:11
> (You grieve for those that should not be grieved for, yet you speak words of wisdom. The wise grieve neither for the living nor the dead.")

The ropes that bind us to this delusory world are relationships—father, mother, wife, children, friends, job, house, wealth, and so on. In fact, it is these attachments (*sanga*) that makes world seem real to us. Let us, for instance, put ourselves in the shoes of this 'disciple.' Imagine it is *our* fathers' funeral. If so, would we follow Jesus, ignoring our filial obligations? (If someone says yes, then chances are that he is a hypocrite.)

The primary requirement of spirituality is the abandonment of worldly relationships. But, it is very difficult for man to abandon the world without even knowing it well enough. That is why the *Sanātana Dharma* advices people to begin spiritual activities only after completing the *Gṛhastha Āśrama* (after forty).

Jesus says to the aspiring disciple: *"Follow me; and let the dead bury their dead."* Here, the first reference of the word *dead* is to the spiritually dead, whereas the second is to the physically dead. It suggests that there is no difference between the two.

However, relationships are important because they make up the human society. Without it, societies cannot function. Hence, the relevance of *Āśrama Dharma*.

MATTHEW 8:23-27

"And when he was entered into a ship, his disciples followed him. And, behold, there arose a great tempest in the sea, insomuch that the ship was covered with the waves: but he was asleep. And his disciples came to him, and awoke him, saying, Lord, save us: we perish. And he saith unto them, Why are ye fearful, O ye of little faith? Then he arose, and rebuked the winds and the sea; and there was a great calm. But the men marveled, saying, What manner of man is this, that even the winds and the sea obey him!"

This Gospel incident portrays the trials an Evite undergoes in the spiritual path and how the Gospel comes to his rescue. The expression, "spiritual path," here, refers to the spiritual meaning of the Gospel. In other words, this Gospel episode describes the trials an Evite undergoes when he spiritually interprets the Gospel.

In this episode, the disciples represent the Evite; the *sea*, the mind or the public; the ship, the body or life. Jesus represents the spiritual Gospel or the Evite's DNA. Here, Jesus is in the ship, but he is asleep. In other words, the spiritual Gospel (the true human DNA) is inside the Evites body, but he is not aware of it.

The *great tempest* signifies great turmoil. Just as waves buffet a ship, public outcry about the Evite's spiritual interpretation of the Gospel upsets his balance and composure. The man feels threatened by the public reaction. He feels rejected, lonely, fearful, and totally powerless against the forces arrayed against him.

"And his disciples came to him, and awoke him, saying, Lord, save us: we perish." When threatened by the tempest, the disciples awaken Jesus and cry for help. Similarly, when threatened by doubt and fear, the Evite awakens the Self in him and cries for help. In other words, when haunted by doubt and fear, the Evite focuses awareness on the body and becomes self-aware.

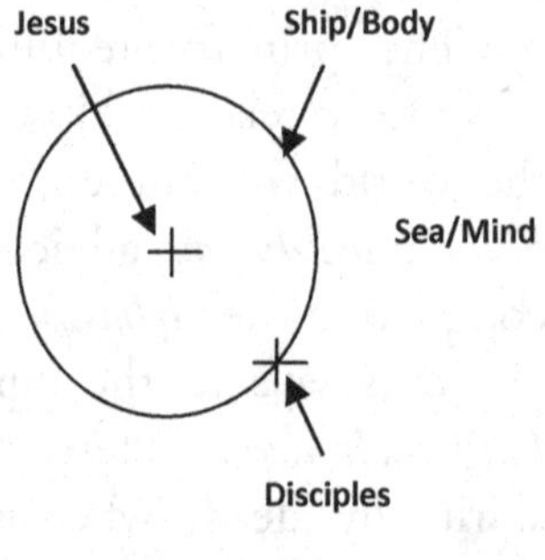

JESUS IN THE SHIP

Jesus says to the disciples, *"Why ye are fearful, O ye of little faith?"* Spiritually, the expression, "little faith" means "little awareness."

Here, Jesus attributes fear to lack of faith. In other words, the Gospel attributes fear to duality, or religion. In other words, the body-aware Evite realizes that his doubts and fears were caused by his own mind.

In the Bhagavad Gīta there is a scene where Arjuna laments about his inability to control mind to Lord Krishna:

> *Chanchalam hi manah Kṛṣṇā pramādhi balavad drudam*
> *Thasyāham nigraham manye vāyōriva suduṣkaram*
> B.G. 6:34
> (My mind is indeed restless, O Krishna; it is impetuous, strong, and difficult to control. I think it is as unruly as the winds.")

To which, Lord Krishna replies:

> *Asamśaya-tātmanā yogah dushprāpa iti mē mathi*
> *Vaśyātmanā tu yathathā śakyō-avāptumupāyathah*
> B.G. 6:36
> ("Yoga is indeed hard to attain by the deluded. But, for the body-aware, it is possible by directing the awareness inwards. This is my opinion.")

MATTHEW 8:28-34

"And when he was come to the other side into the country of the Gergesenes, there met him two possessed with devils, coming out of the tombs, exceeding fierce, so that no man might pass by that way. And, behold, they cried out, saying, What have we to do with thee, Jesus, thou Son of God? art thou come hither to torment us before the time? And there was a good way off from them an herd of many swine feeding. So the devils besought him, saying, If thou cast us out, suffer us to go away into the herd of swine. And he said unto them, Go. And when they were come out, they went into the herd of swine: and, behold, the whole herd of swine ran violently down a steep place into the sea, and perished in the waters. And they that kept them fled, and went their ways into the city, and told every thing, and what was befallen to the possessed of the devils. And, behold, the whole city came out to meet Jesus: and when they saw him, they besought him that he would depart out of their coasts."

"And when he was come to the other side into the country of the Gergesenes, there met him two possessed with devils, coming out of the tombs, exceeding fierce, so that no man might pass by that way." In this episode, the Gospel reveals to us the identity of the adversary, the devil.

Earlier we saw Jesus in Capernaum, seated in a ship in the sea; now he is on the other side, in the country of Gergesenes.

The Greek word for *country* is *chōra* (G5561), which means "an empty space," or "room." The word is derived from the root word *chasma*, which means "a chasm," or "abyss." Spiritually, the term *country* refers to a 'lodge' - the meeting place of certain secret fraternal organizations. In that sense, the expression "country of the Gergesenes" is akin to the expression, "the lodge of Freemasons."

Who are the *Gergesenes*? The name originates from the Hebrew word *girgāsi* (H1622), which means "a Girgashite." *Girgashites* or *Girgasites* are descendants of Canaan. The name reminds us of "Rachab, the proud Canaanitress," the mother of Booz (Boaz), mentioned in Jesus' genealogy. Spiritually, the term *Gergesenes* means "Serpent worshippers."

Perhaps, the term *two* refers to *Boaz and Jachin*. They were two copper, brass or bronze pillars which, according to legends, stood on the porch of Solomon's Temple, the first Temple in Jerusalem. But, according to the genealogy of Jesus Christ, Booz or Boaz is the son of Salmon, not Solomon. And Jachin, perhaps, refers to Jehoiachin, who was taken away to Babylon.

Another interesting point to note is the Gospel phrase: *"there met him two possessed with devils."* Both the Gospels of Mark and Luke say, *"A certain man met him."* There seems to be confusion among the Gospels: How many possessed men met Jesus—one or two? But, spiritually, the term *two* denotes duality (Boaz and Jachin?), which is the evil. It seems the Gospel is referring to the dualistic religion and its literal scripture as the devil. At the beginning of our exposition, we had hypothesized duality as the spell cast by the Serpent. Here, the Gospel confirms it. The expression "two possessed with devils" actually refers to a deluded Adamite, a religious fanatic, a priest.

The devil-possessed man emerges out of the tombs looking fierce. The Hebrew word for tomb is *gādis* (H1430), which means "a stack of sheaves." The verb *sheaf* means "to bind something together as a bundle." The term *sheaf* suggests a book. Spiritually, the term *tomb* refers to the literal scripture. The 'devil-possessed' man that emerges from the tomb is a religious fanatic. And the man looks so fierce that people are afraid to "pass by that way." Here, the term way refers to religion.

The man cries out to Jesus, *"What have we to do with thee, Jesus, thou Son of God?"* Spiritually, the term "Son of God" refers both to the true human DNA and the Gospel. The term "we," in this context, refers to the priests. The implication of the words: "The priests have nothing to do with the Gospel."

The possessed man asks something even stranger to Jesus: *"Art thou come hither to torment us before the time?"* Spiritually, the expression "before the time" means "before the Second Coming." The Greek word for *torment* is *basanizō* (G928), which means "to torture." The word is derived from the root word *basanos* (G931), which means "a touch-stone." Spiritually, the term touch-stone implies "testing." Therefore the spiritual implication of the devil-possessed man's question is this: "The true nature of priesthood will be revealed at the Second Coming."

"And there was a good way off from them an herd of many swine feeding. So the devils besought him, saying, If thou cast us out, suffer us to go away into the herd of swine. And he said unto them, Go." The devils seek Jesus' permission to enter the swine herd, when cast out. The expression *swine herd* refers to blind followers of religion. In other words, the priests transmit their infection to the laity. The Gospel tells us the fate of the laity: *". . . and, behold, the whole herd of swine ran violently down a steep place into the sea, and perished in the waters."*

> *And I heard another voice from heaven, Come out of her, my people, that ye be not partakers of her sins, and that ye receive not of her plagues.*
> Revelation 18:4

CHAPTER 9

The Campaign—Enemies Destroyed

MATTHEW 9:1-8

"And he entered into a ship, and passed over, and came into his own city. And, behold, they brought to him a man sick of the palsy, lying on a bed: and Jesus seeing their faith said unto the sick of the palsy; Son, be of good cheer; thy sins be forgiven thee. And, behold, certain of the scribes said within themselves, This man blasphemeth. And Jesus knowing their thoughts said, Wherefore think ye evil in your hearts? For whether is easier, to say, Thy sins be forgiven thee; or to say, Arise, and walk? But that ye may know that the Son of man hath power on earth to forgive sins, (then saith he to the sick of the palsy,) Arise, take up thy bed, and go unto thine house. And he arose, and departed to his house. But when the multitudes saw it, they marvelled, and glorified God, which had given such power unto men."

"*And he entered into a ship, and passed over, and came into his own city."* In this Gospel verse, the term "he" refers to Jesus who is the embodiment of the Gospel. The term *ship* refers to the human body. The 'ship' that has 'Jesus' seated in it is the Evite. The phrase, "passed over" actually implies "passed over the sea." It implies crossing the sea of delusion (*samsāra*), or crossing mind. Similarly, the phrase, "his own city" refers to self-awareness. In other words, according to the Gospel, the term *Jesus* refers to the self-aware Evite.

"And, behold, they brought to him a man sick of the palsy, lying on a bed: and Jesus seeing their faith said unto the sick of the palsy; Son, be

of good cheer; thy sins be forgiven thee." Spiritually, the man afflicted by palsy represents a religious bigot, who follows the scripture to the letter that he is incapable of free action for fear of violating the laws. Here, the Gospel says that the palsy victim is brought to Jesus in a bed by his friends. The man is "bedridden." The term *bed* refers to a piece of furniture that facilitates sleep. The Greek word for bed is *klinē* (G2825). It is derived from the root word *klinō* (G2827), which means "a slope." Perhaps, it refers to the same 'slope' down which the herd of swine ran to their destruction. Spiritually, the term *bed* refers to duality-based scriptures that incapacitate humans of their true potentiality.

Jesus, seeing the faith of the sick man and his friends says to them, *"Son be of good cheer; thy sins be forgiven thee"* The expression, "Jesus seeing their faith" suggests that the patient and the friends who brought him to Jesus are Evites." Therefore, the implication of Jesus' utterance is this: "Evites are fundamentally sinless. Therefore, be happy."

"And, behold, certain of the scribes said within themselves, This man blasphemeth." The Scribes take Jesus' words literally, and are appalled by its apparent audacity. It sounds like blasphemy to them. According to them, Jesus is preaching the doctrine of 'lawlessness.'

"And Jesus knowing their thoughts said, Wherefore think ye evil in your hearts?" Spiritually, the expression, "knowing their thoughts" means "knowing their nature." The term *evil* suggests artificiality, or mechanical nature. It denotes the Serpent—the virus. The term *heart* refers to the DNA. In short, Jesus, knowing the true nature of the Scribes, says to them, "You posses the virus DNA. That's why you can only think mechanically."

What exactly is a virus? The Latin word *virus* means poison. Viruses are a-cellular entities that exist at the border between chemistry and life. Perhaps, they are not living organisms, but artificial robot-like entities (*nano-machines*). They are *parasites* that invade living organisms (cells, bacteria etc.) and hijack their genomic material. Viruses affect the behavior of their hosts profoundly. Because they occupy the netherworld between life and non-life, they can pull off some remarkable feats; for instance, they can multiply in dead cells and even to bring them back to life, although they ordinarily replicate only in living cells. Amazingly, some viruses can even spring back to their borrowed life even after being destroyed. Viruses are the only known biological entity with this kind of *phoenix phenotype*—the capacity to rise from their own ashes. Furthermore, a virus genome can permanently colonize its host, adding viral genes to host lineages and ultimately becoming a critical part of the host species' genome. Indeed the virus is *"more subtil than any beast of the field which the LORD God had made."* It is an evil entity; it is the Serpent, the devil.

How the virus infects a body-cell is indeed amazing. It first attaches itself onto the surface of a healthy cell, and then 'tricks' the cell into 'eating' it (*endocytosis*). Once inside the cell, it hijacks the cell's genomic material to replicate itself. The infection process reminds us of the Genesis story. In the Biblical genesis story, Adam represents the human genome; Eve, the body-cell; the Serpent, the virus; the forbidden fruit, the virus gene.

Apparently, all viruses are not bad. There are good viruses and there are bad viruses. Perhaps, they are the so-called *angels* and *demons* of the Bible. The medieval angelo-logical question *"How many angels can dance on the head of a pin?"* is not, after all, a trivial question. Considering the average size of a virus to be 100 nano-meters, the answer is thousands and thousands. The phrase has been commonly used to criticize figures such as Duns Scotus and Thomas Aquinas.

It is plausible that the viruses (the Serpent), through millions of years of 'plagiarizing' living cells have acquired the knowledge to synthesize a double-helical DNA just like the true human DNA, using just 3% of the genomic material, and created *their own personal hosts*, through whom they can immortalize themselves for eternity. Talk about Serpent's vengeance!

Jesus asks the Scribes, *"For whether is easier, to say, Thy sins be forgiven thee; or to say, Arise, and walk?"* In other words, the Gospel is asking, "Should instruction be given as a whole or piece-meal?" A robot needs piece-meal or step-by-step instructions, such as "arise," "walk," and so on in order to make them move and act, whereas human beings need only general principles in order to act. Here, the Gospel is hinting at the robotic nature of the Scribes.

The Gospel then declares a secret to the whole world: *"But ye may know that the Son of man hath power on earth to forgive sins."* This verse is interpreted by the Church that only Jesus Christ (meaning, the Church) can forgive sins. But what the Gospel says is something different. The term "Son of man" refers to true human body (DNA) or the Gospel. The Evite is the "Son of man." Therefore, the implication is that a true human being has the power to forgive his own sins. In other words, it says that man is fundamentally sinless. Alternatively, it also implies that the Evite DNA cannot corrupted by the Serpent virus. It is not only resistant, but it is the antidote against it.

Jesus, then, says to the sick man, *"Arise, take up thy bed, and go unto thine house."* The man came out of his house in bed to meet Jesus, now Jesus commands him to go back to his house with his bed. Earlier the man was in the bed, unable to move; now he is out of it, free to move. Here, spiritually, the term *bed* refers to the literal scripture, and *house*, the body. The Gospel frees the man from scripture's spell.

MATTHEW 9:9

"And as Jesus passed forth from thence, he saw a man, named Matthew, sitting at the receipt of custom: and he saith unto him, Follow me. And he arose, and followed him."

The name *Matthew* is derived from the Hebrew word *mattiyāhu* (H4993), which means "Gift of YHWH." Its Greek equivalent is *Matthaios* (G3156). It is the shorter form of *Mattathias* (G3161), which means "an Israelite and Christian." Matthew represents an Evite.

The expression, *"Matthew sitting at the receipt of custom"* portrays an Evite serving the Establishment in a low-key position. The man, by sheer good fortune, comes in contact with the Gospel, and develops an inner urge to know more about it. The Gospel describes his urge to study the Gospel as Jesus *calling* him. As soon as he *hears* the call, he leaves his job and follows Jesus.

Jesus says to Matthew, *"Follow me."* The Greek word for *follow* is *akoloutheō* (G190), which means "to be in the same way." The word is derived from the particle "*a*" and the word *keleuthos*, which means "a road." But, spiritually, the word originates from the root word *akouō* (G191), which means "hearken," or "understand." The term *Jesus* refers to both the Gospel and the Evite's body (DNA). In other words, Jesus' call to Matthew reflects the Gospel's call to the Evite, and it has the following connotations:

1. "Understand the Gospel."
2. "Listen to your body."
3. "Follow your heart."

Jesus' call represents the "call of the inner Self." According to Hindu Vēdānta, it is called *mumukṣa.* It is defined as follows: "*mōktum iccha iti mumukṣa*" meaning, "The desire for freedom is mumukṣa." Mumukṣa is the urge to know the truth and be liberated from delusion. It always leads to repentance (*vairāgya*). In the Bhagavad Gīta, Lord Krishna tells Arjuna that only the truly fortunate gets the *call*:

> *Yadrucchayā chōpapannam swarga dwāram apāvrutam*
> *Sukhina kṣatriyā pārtha labhanthē yuddhamīdruśam*
> B.G. 2:32
> (O Arjuna! It is by sheer grace that the door to heaven is open to the righteous; only the very fortunate warriors get to fight this rare battle.")

In the Hindu tradition, a *kṣatriya* is a member of the royal caste. But spiritually, the *kṣatriya* represents an Evite (true human being). Just as a king wears the crown, the Evite wears the crown of self-awareness. The *battle* referred is the fight against the Serpent, the fight against ignorance and delusion.

Matthew, on receiving Jesus' call, develops *vairagya.* Suddenly finds his job and worldly relationships meaningless. Money, power and fame, things which he desperately sought in the past, lose their charm. He is now completely overcome by the desire to follow Jesus. In other words, Matthew chooses *sanyāsa.* The word *sanyāsa* means "renunciation" or "abandonment." The word is derived from three Sanskrit roots; *sam,* meaning "all" or "well"; *ni,* meaning "down"; and *asa,* meaning "to throw" or "to put." Literally, *sanyasa* means "to lay everything down." In the Bhagavad Gīta, Lord Krishna defines *sanyasa* as follows:

> *Kāmyānām karmaṇām nyāsam sanyāsm kavayō vidhuh*
> *Sarva—karma-phala—thyāgam prahus-thyāgam vichakṣaṇah*
> B.G. 18:2
> ("The wise have known sanyasa as the renouncing of actions of desire; and renouncing is the relinquishing of the fruits of all actions.")

Rather than literally relinquishing physical objects and relations, *sanyāsa* means leading a life devoid of planning and striving. A true sanyāsi adopts the stance: *"Thy will be done."* He has total faith that the Self will *"Give us this day our daily bread."*

MATTHEW 9:10-13

"And it came to pass, as Jesus sat at meat in the house, behold, many publicans and sinners came and sat down with him and his disciples. And when the Pharisees saw it, they said unto his disciples, Why eateth your Master with publicans and sinners? But when Jesus heard that, he said unto them, They that be whole need not a physician, but they that are sick. But go ye and learn what that meaneth, I will have mercy, and not sacrifice: for I am not come to call the righteous, but sinners to repentance."

"And it came to pass, as Jesus sat at meat in the house, behold, many publicans and sinners came and sat down with him and his disciples." In the earlier episode we saw Matthew leaving everything and following Jesus. Now, we see Jesus having meal in Mathew's house. The Greek word used here for *house* is *oikia* (G3614), which means "an abode." And the term *abode* refers to the place in which a person resides. Here, that 'abode' is Matthew's (Evite's) body and the 'person' who has come to visit it is the Gospel. The Gospel tells us that Jesus "sat at meat" in the house. The commonly used Greek word for *meat* is *trophē* (G5160). But here, the Gospel uses another word, *anakeimai* (G345), which means "to recline," as at a meal. It suggests that the Gospel virtually 'possessed' Matthew's body.

The *publicans* were tax collectors for the Roman Empire, who bid contracts from the Roman Senate for the collection of various types of taxes. At the height of the Roman Republic's era of provincial expansion, the Roman *tax farming* system was very profitable for the publicans. The Greek term for *publican* is *telōnēs* (G5057), which means "a tax-farmer." The word is derived from the root *tellō* (G5056), which means "to set out for a definite target." The chief preoccupation of the publicans was money; their only concern was about achieving collection targets. The people hated them for their strong-arm tactics and they put them in the same category as the sinners. The Greek word for *sinner* is *hamartōlos* (G268). It is derived from the root word *hamartanō* (G264), which means "to morally err," especially, sexually.

The *publicans* and *sinners* that join Jesus and his disciples in the meal represent the thoughts of money and sex that distract the Evite's mind when trying to study the Gospel.

"And when the Pharisees saw it, they said unto his disciples, Why eateth your Master with publicans and sinners?" The Pharisees signify the Evite's super-ego, which reflects his internalization of cultural rules, mainly taught by parents applying their guidance and influence. Pricked by the super-ego, the man feels guilty about his thoughts. But, an inner voice consoles him, saying, *"They that be whole need not a physician, but they that are sick."* The Greek word for *whole* is *ischyō* (G2480), which means "having strength." And the *physician* referred to is the Gospel itself. In other words, the man's inner voice is saying: "The Gospel is for weak people like you; it is not for the strong ones."

Jesus, then, says something mysterious to the Pharisees, *"But go ye and learn what that meaneth, I will have mercy, and not sacrifice, for I am come not to call the righteous, but sinners to repentance."* The Greek term for *mercy* is *eleos* (G1656), which means "compassion." It is the kind forbearance shown toward an offender, or an enemy. And it suggests the discretionary power of a judge to pardon someone or to mitigate punishment. To show mercy, one has to have the power of discretion (freewill). In other words, only true human beings (Evites) can show mercy. A computer or an artificial intelligence entity cannot. The term mercy suggests *inner action*; it has to do with intention rather than action, per se. A seemingly kind action, but done with evil intention, does not qualify as an act of mercy. Moreover, mercy is kindness shown to enemies. Kindness shown to friends and relatives does not qualify as mercy.

The Greek term for *sacrifice* is *thysia* (G2378). It is derived from the root word *thyō* (G2380), which means "to rush" (breathe hard, blow, smoke). Spiritually, the term *sacrifice* refers to the act of setting right a wrong through religious rituals. It implies *external action.*

But the Gospel seems to say: "You cannot free yourself from sins through religious rituals. Only the Self can forgive sins. Therefore, know your Self." It is a severe indictment against religion and their phony rituals.

MATTHEW 9:14-17

"Then came to him the disciples of John, saying, Why do we and the Pharisees fast oft, but thy disciples fast not? And Jesus said unto them, Can the children of the bridechamber mourn, as long as the bridegroom is with them? but the days will come, when the bridegroom shall be taken from them, and then shall they fast. No man putteth a piece of new cloth unto an old garment, for that which is put in to fill it up taketh from the garment, and the rent is made worse. Neither do men put new wine into old bottles: else the bottles break, and the wine runneth out, and the bottles perish: but they put new wine into new bottles, and both are preserved."

"Then came to him the disciples of John, saying, Why do we and the Pharisees fast oft, but thy disciples fast not?" Here, the Evite is facing another moral dilemma. He is thinking: "Why am I not pious like the others?"

The Greek word for *fasting* is *nēsteuō* (G3522), which means "to abstain from food" (religiously). The Gospel compares fasting to mourning. The Greek word for *mourning* is *pentheō* (G3997). It is derived from the Greek root *penthō*, which means "passion." Spiritually, the term *fasting* covers the entire gamut of religious activities. Even reading the scripture daily may be considered as a form of fasting.

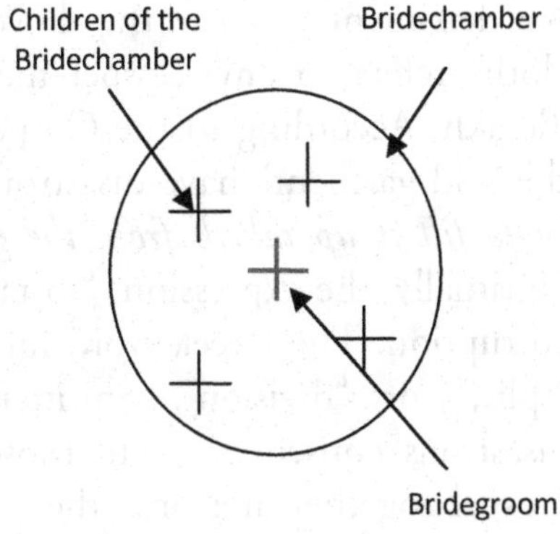

CHILDREN OF THE BRIDECHAMBER

And Jesus said unto them, Can the children of the bridechamber mourn, as long as the bridegroom is with them? but the days will come, when the bridegroom shall be taken from them, and then shall they fast." The Greek word for *bridechamber* is *nymphōn* (G3567). It is derived from the root word, *nyptō*, which means "to veil as a bride." Spiritually, the term *bridechamber* refers to the body—the chamber of the Self—which is covered with the veil of skin. In other words, it is the body-aware Evites that the Gospel calls the *children of the bridechamber*. Their *bridegroom* is the Self, the true human DNA, or the Gospel. Therefore, what the Gospel assures the Evite is this: "The Evites do not have to fast; but, the Adamites have to fast."

John's disciples represent the Evite's religious proclivities. The man feels guilty about his lack of piety. He, therefore, confronts his Self with the question.

The very notion of *fasting* is repugnant in that it demands religious approval. For fasting to be called so, it has to be done at the times and manner prescribed by religion. Adamites are punctilious about fasting and for a good reason too. Fasting can 'simulate' body-awareness. The hunger, or pain generated by fasting temporarily directs the fasting man's awareness towards his body, creating a fleeting sense of body-awareness. But, it is a cheap imitation of the real one. And, moreover, the awareness so generated is blemished with the thoughts of food.

Evites don't fast; they don't have to. The Gospel explains why: *"No man putteth a piece of new cloth unto an old garment, for that which is put in to fill it up taketh from the garment, and the rent is made worse."* According to the Gospel, piety is not only unnecessary for the Evites, but detrimental too. In the above verse, the expression, "a piece of new cloth" refers to any Gospel message; the old garment refers to the Tanakh. According to the Gospel, adding the "new piece of cloth" to the "old garment" have disastrous consequences: "*for that which is put in to fill it up taketh from the garment, and the rent is made worse.*" Spiritually, the expression, "to take from the garment" suggests bodily corruption. The Greek word for *rent* is *schism* (G4978), which means "split," or "division". Spiritually, it denotes fragmentation. The disastrous consequences to those who consume the Tanakh and the Gospel together are: one, the corruption of the body (cancer?); two, the increased fragmentation of the mind (delusion).

If man is equated with the DNA, then the *garment* he wears may be compared to the cell cytoplasm. And the *holes* in that garment refer to *antigens* present to the cell wall. In immunology, antigen is the substance that binds to the *antibody* (virus). Each antibody from the diverse repertoire binds to a specific antigenic structure by means of its variable region

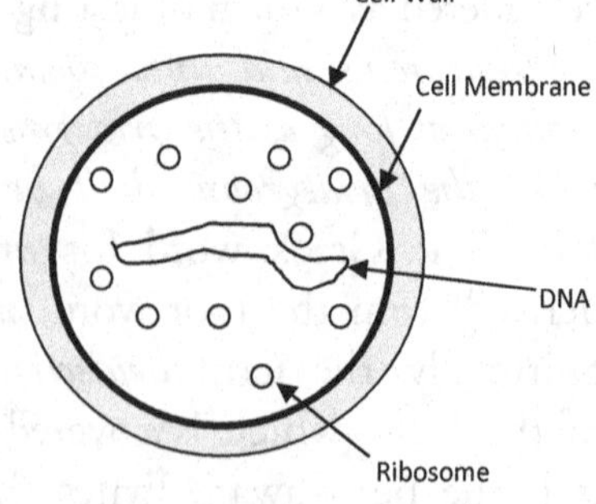

HUMAN CELL

interaction (CDR loops). It is analogous to the fit between a *lock and a key*. In other words, antigens act as docks for invading viruses. In this sense, a cell that is blemished by antigens may be considered as a *torn garment*.

The Gospel gives another example to highlight the dangers of mixing the Tanakh and the Gospel: *"Neither do men put new wine into old bottles: else the bottles break, and the wine runneth out, and the bottles perish: but they put new wine into new bottles, and both are preserved."* The Greek word for wine is *oinos* (G3631). It originates from the Hebrew word *yayin* (H3196), which means "to effervesce." Spiritually, the term *wine* denotes the spirit. The Greek word for *bottle* is *askos* (G779), which refers to a 'leathern' bag used as a bottle. Spiritually, "the leathern bag that contains spirit" is called *book*. Therefore, the "old wine in the old bottle" denotes the Tanakh, and the "new wine in the new bottle" denotes the Gospel. The "old wine" denotes duality, and the "new wine" denotes non-duality. Putting the new wine in old bottle suggests combining the Gospel and the Tanakh into a single book.

The Gospel then describes the dire consequences of putting the new wine in the old bottle: "*the bottles break, and the wine runneth out and the bottles perish.*" Here the term *bottle* also refers to the human body. The breaking of the body suggests corruption of DNA. The loss of wine denotes the loss of soul.

MATTHEW 9:18-26

"While he spake these things unto them, behold, there came a certain ruler, and worshipped him, saying, My daughter is even now dead: but come and lay thy hand upon her, and she shall live. And Jesus arose, and followed him, and so did his disciples. And, behold, a woman, which was diseased with an issue of blood twelve years, came behind him, and touched the hem of his garment: For she said within herself, If I may but touch his garment, I shall be whole. But Jesus turned him about, and when he saw her, he said, Daughter, be of good comfort; thy faith hath made thee whole. And the woman was made whole from that hour. And when Jesus came into the ruler's house, and saw the minstrels and the people making a noise, He said unto them, Give place: for the maid is not dead, but sleepeth. And they laughed him to scorn. But when the people were put forth, he went in, and took her by the hand, and the maid arose. And the fame hereof went abroad into all that land."

The Greek word for *ruler* is *archōn* (G758). It means "a high official," and suggests supreme rank, power, or authority. The term *archon* refers to the Adamite. Unlike the Mortal, who is corrupt only in the mind, the Adamite is corrupt both in mind and in body. By the way, according to the Gnostics, the *archons* are the servants of Demiurge, the creator-God. Here, the Gospel describes, by means of an allegory, how it saves an Adamite.

"While he spake these things unto them, behold, there came a certain ruler, and worshipped him, saying, My daughter is even now dead: but come and lay thy hand upon her, and she shall live." Spiritually, the expression, "my daughter" refers to the Adamite's mind; the word *dead* suggests delusion. In other words, the Adamite realizes the 'deluded' state of his mind, and sincerely yearns for freedom. He thinks: "If I read the Gospel, my ignorance and delusion will go and I will become truly human." The Gospel presents it to us as a 'ruler' asking Jesus to lay hands on his daughter's head.

As soon as the man requests Jesus, Jesus gets up and follows the man along with his disciples. In other words, as soon as the Adamite desires freedom, he gets the urge to read the Gospel.

"And, behold, a woman, which was diseased with an issue of blood twelve years, came behind him, and touched the hem of his garment: For she said within herself, If I may but touch his garment, I shall be whole." Here, the Gospel introduces a sub-episode into the story: that of a woman who is afflicted with "an issue of blood" for twelve years. This sub-episode is, in fact, vital to the main episode. The woman, here, represents the Adamite's body, which is afflicted with "an issue of blood." But, what is meant by "an issue of blood"? Spiritually, the term *blood* refers to DNA, or scripture. Therefore, the "issue of blood" denotes the corruption of DNA, or scripture. The Adamite's mind is corrupt because his DNA is corrupt. And his DNA is corrupt because his *script* (scripture) is corrupt.

The woman approaches Jesus from behind and touches the hem of his garment. Spiritually, the term *garment* refers to the Gospel. The word *hem* refers to the border (line?) of a garment. Approaching from behind signifies secrecy and circumspection. In other words, the Adamite secretly reads few lines of the Gospel.

Jesus immediately looks back and sees the woman and says to her, *"Daughter, be of good comfort; thy faith hath made thee whole."* The Greek word for *faith* is *pistis* (G4102), which refers to the Gospel truth itself. In other words, the word *pistis* is synonymous with the word *Gospel.* Therefore, the implication of Jesus' utterance is this: "Be glad. The Gospel has made your body perfect." Thus, the Gospel, first of all, cures the Adamite's body of corruption, and then addresses the corruption of his mind.

When Jesus enters the man's house, he finds the place in total confusion. The Gospel describes the scene: *"And when Jesus came into the ruler's house, and saw the minstrels and the people making a noise, He said unto them, Give place: for the maid is not dead, but sleepeth."* Having cured the Adamite's body of corruption, the Gospel now starts healing the man's mind. The Gospel allegorically describes it as Jesus entering the man's house. The Greek word for minstrel is *aulētēs* (G834), which means "a flute-player." The expression, "minstrels and the people making a noise" refers to religious litany.

Jesus asks the minstrels and others to vacate the place and says to those assembled there, *"Give place: for the maid is not dead, but sleepeth."* Spiritually, the word *dead* means "sinner"; the term refers to the Adamite. The word *sleep* suggests "delusion." The one who is not 'dead' but only 'sleeps' is called a Mortal (sleeping Evite). In other words, Jesus is saying, "He is no longer an Adamite now; he is now an Evite." In other words, the Gospel is suggesting that litanies are for the Adamites, not for Evites.

"And they laughed him to scorn. But when the people were put forth, he went in, and took her by the hand, and the maid arose. And the fame hereof went abroad into all that land." The Gospel truth seems totally ludicrous to the Adamites. But the healed man, who is now an Evite, understands it perfectly.

MATTHEW 9:27-31

"And when Jesus departed thence, two blind men followed him, crying, and saying, Thou Son of David, have mercy on us. And when he was come into the house, the blind men came to him: and

Jesus saith unto them, Believe ye that I am able to do this? They said unto him, Yea, Lord. Then touched he their eyes, saying, According to your faith be it unto you. And their eyes were opened; and Jesus straightly charged them, saying, See that no man know it. But they, when they were departed, spread abroad his fame in all that country."

"And when Jesus departed thence, two blind men followed him, crying, and saying, Thou Son of David, have mercy on us." The Gospel says, "Two blind men followed him." How can two blind men follow anyone? It is not possible! It is more likely that one blind man was leading another towards Jesus. Even that does not make sense because the Gospel itself says that if a blind man leads another, then both will fall into a ditch. Therefore, we have to presume that the term *blind*, in this context, means "spiritually blind," and not "physically blind." Similarly, the term, *two* suggests duality, or religion. Therefore, the expression, "two blind men" actually refers to one deluded man—one who is 'blinded' by religion. Here, the expression, "two blind men followed him" suggests that a deluded (religious) man tried to understand the Gospel literally.

The man's cry reveals the nature of his blindness: he calls Jesus, "Son of David." He thinks of Jesus as a physical person. Apparently, the man is too much conditioned by his religion. It seems he is an Adamite. Or, is he a deluded Evite (Mortal)?

"And when he was come into the house, the blind men came to him: and Jesus saith unto them, Believe ye that I am able to do this?" Apparently, the man is reading the Gospel with "dualistic" eyes. Therefore, Jesus asks him, *"Believe ye, that I am able to do this?"* The phrase, "I am" implies meaning. In other words, the Gospel is asking him, "Do you understand me spiritually?" The implication here is that only the Evites can grasp the spiritual meaning of the Gospel, not the Adamites. In short, the Gospel is asking the man, "Are you an Evite?" The man replies yes, perhaps, not realizing the true import of the question.

"Then touched he their eyes, saying, According to your faith be it unto you." The implication of the words is this: "If you are an Evite, then you will understand the Gospel spiritually; if not, you will not."

"And their eyes were opened; and Jesus straightly charged them, saying, See that no man know it. But they, when they were departed, spread abroad his fame in all that country." Why did Jesus warn the man not

to tell the good news to anyone else? One who truly understands the Gospel realizes, "I and my Father are one." But, it is blaspheme to say it openly. Moreover, he who openly declares it has not understood it because he still believes in the notion of "other" (duality).

But, the 'healed' man, in his euphoria, ignores Jesus' injunction and announces the news to the public. Some questions remain: Was he really an Evite? Did he understand the Gospel spiritually? Anyway, the Gospel is silent about it.

MATTHEW 9:32-34

"As they went out, behold, they brought to him a dumb man possessed with a devil. And when the devil was cast out, the dumb spake: and the multitudes marvelled, saying, It was never so seen in Israel. But the Pharisees said, He casteth out devils through the prince of the devils."

Literally, the word *dumb* suggests inability to speak because of hereditary deafness, or temporarily incapable of speaking. But, the Greek word the Gospel uses for *dumb* is *kōphos* (G2974), which means "blunted." It means slow to learn or slow to understand, or lacking in intellectual acuity (Sanskrit: *mandāh*). In this Gospel episode, the man, it seems, is 'dumb', that is, "blunted." He talks too much, but mostly meaningless gibberish. He is 'possessed' by the devil of loquacity. Here, perhaps, the Gospel is alluding to an obsessive-compulsive public speaker—an *evangelist*. The Gospel cures the man's obsessive-compulsive neurosis. Suddenly he becomes silent; but, his silence now speaks volumes.

In the introductory prayer to the Bhagavad Gīta, there is a beautiful verse:

> *Mūkam karōthi vāchālam pankhum lamkhayate girim*
> *Yat kṛpāh thamaham vandē paramānanda mādhavam*
> Gitādhyānam
> (I salute the Lord by whose Grace the dumb becomes eloquent and the lame crosses over mountains.")

The above prayer has two meanings: one, it says His Grace will make the silent eloquent; two, it says His Grace will make the loquacious silent. Similarly, the Gospel too can transform the loquacious silent and the silent eloquent!

The public is astounded. They have never witnessed such a miracle before. They say, *"It was never so seen in Israel"* The public is only used to fiery speeches of the Pharisees and Scribes from the temple pulpits, which is lot of words and nothing else.

Another important point to note here is that Jesus heals the blind man while "going into the house," whereas he heals the dumb while "coming out of the house". The 'blindness,' which is caused by duality, is healed when the Gospel is understood by the body. The 'dumbness,' which is caused by ignorance, is healed when the Gospel is understood by the mind.

"But the Pharisees said, He casteth out devils through the prince of the devils." The Pharisees and Scribes are also known as "Serpent children." They are the carriers of the retrovirus DNA. They are the intellectuals of the world, in the classical sense, but they lack intuition. The Pharisees and Scribes cannot comprehend how a book (The Gospel) is able to free people from the deadly viral infection. Therefore they try to reason: *"He casteth out devils through the prince of devils."* The word *devil*, as we have hypothesized earlier, refers to the virus. Therefore, their comment suggests that Jesus uses a highly virulent species of virus to counter less virulent ones. In a sense, the Pharisees and Scribes are saying, "He is vaccinating people against the Serpent virus."

The Gospel is the most effective vaccine against the Serpent virus. It works both preventively and curatively.

MATTHEW 9:35-38

"And Jesus went about all the cities and villages, teaching in their synagogues, and preaching the gospel of the kingdom, and healing every sickness and every disease among the people. But when he saw the multitudes, he was moved with compassion on them, because they fainted, and were scattered abroad, as sheep having no shepherd. Then saith he unto his disciples, The harvest truly is plenteous, but the labourers are few; Pray ye therefore the Lord of the harvest, that he will send forth labourers into his harvest."

"And Jesus went about all the cities and villages, teaching in their synagogues, and preaching the gospel of the kingdom, and healing every sickness and every disease among the people." The Greek word for city is *polis* (G4172), which means "a town enclosed by walls." The word might have originated from two sources: one, from the root *pollos* (G4183), which means "many"; two, from the root *pelomai* (G4171), which means "bustle." Spiritually, the term *city* suggests both duality and bustle and, it denotes the Adamites.

The Greek word for *village* is *kōmē* (G2968), which means "a hamlet," (as if laid down). It is derived from the root *keimai* (G2749), which means "to lie outstretched." Spiritually, the term *village* suggests peace and rest and, therefore, denotes the Evites. The expression, "cities and villages," in this context, means "the entire population of the region." In other words, the Gospel message spread throughout Judaea. And many were cured of their physical, mental, and spiritual sicknesses.

Spiritually, the expression "Gospel of the kingdom" means "good news of the human body." And that good news is this: "The human body is able to cure physical, mental and spiritual sicknesses."

The Gospel is more than just a book. It is a living being. It expresses the true human DNA. And the Gospel truth can free the mind of ignorance (*thāpathraya*). In a sense, the Gospel erases the literal scripture from mind and writes itself in that place. When the mind is freed of corruption, the body is freed of corruption too.

The *preaching* of the Gospel essentially involves four steps:

1. *`Śravaṇam:* Reading/hearing of the Gospel
2. *Mananam*: Contemplating on the Gospel words
3. *Nidhidhyāsanam*: Imbibing the Gospel truth
4. *Kīrtanam*: Self-interpreting the Gospel by intuition

When the process is successfully completed, the Evite's body becomes the Gospel. In other words, the Evites becomes a living Gospel. Metaphorically, the process is called "washing the body with the blood of Jesus."

"But when he saw the multitudes, he was moved with compassion on them, because they fainted, and were scattered abroad, as sheep having no shepherd." Here, the term *multitudes* refer to the Mortals. The reason why Jesus feels compassion towards them is because they "fainted." To *faint* means to lose consciousness temporarily. Spiritually, it denotes the deluded state of the Mortals who are under the spell of religion. They are deluded because they don't know the truth. The Gospel says they are "scattered abroad." The word *abroad* means "a foreign country." Spiritually, that "foreign country" is the literal scripture. The Gospel compares the Mortals to a herd of sheep without a shepherd. And the shepherds that lead them are not real shepherds but wolves in sheep's clothing.

Jesus feels compassion for the multitudes. The compassion of Jesus is really the compassion of the Gospel. Literally, the term *compassion* refers to the feeling of deep sympathy. But, here, it refers to the resonance the Gospel creates in a man's heart (DNA). When a man develops *devotion* towards the Gospel, the Gospel develops *compassion* towards him. For enlightenment to happen, both man's devotion and Gospel's compassion are essential.

Seeing the sad state of the Mortals, Jesus says to his disciples, *"The harvest truly is plenteous, but the labourers are few; Pray ye therefore the Lord of the harvest, that he will send forth labourers into his harvest."* The Greek word for harvest is *therismos* (G2326), which means "reaping." The word is derived from the root *therō* (G2330), which means "to heat." The 'harvest' that the Gospel talks about is not the literal harvest, but a spiritual one. It is the harvesting of meaning from the Gospel, which is the field. In other words, the term *harvest* refers to the spiritual interpretation of the Gospel. The Gospel says the harvest is plenteous, which suggests that there are many possible interpretations to the Gospel. The term "labourers" refers to those who reap the harvest. But, here, it refers to the enlightened Evites who spiritually interpret the Gospel. And the harvesting work requires heating up. In other words, the Gospel interpreter has to be body-aware. However, such "labourers" are few in number. Therefore, Jesus asks the disciples to pray to the Lord of the harvest to send more labourers. The term "Lord of the harvest" refers to the Self (the Father). In other words, the Gospel is asking every Mortal to pray to the Self for truth revelation."

Alternatively, the term *harvest* refers to the Mortals who have to be saved from the bondage of religion. The *disciples* are the Gospels existing in the different parts of the world. The *labourers* are those who spiritually interpret of the Gospels. Only enlightened Evites can spiritually interpret the Gospel, and they are few in number. Therefore, the Gospel asks the Mortals to pray to the Self to enlighten more Evites that they are able to interpret the Gospels.

CHAPTER 10

The Campaign—Allocation of Land

MATTHEW 10:1-4

"And when he had called unto him his twelve disciples, he gave them power against unclean spirits, to cast them out, and to heal all manner of sickness and all manner of disease. Now the names of the twelve apostles are these; The first, Simon, who is called Peter, and Andrew his brother; James the son of Zebedee, and John his brother; Philip, and Bartholomew; Thomas, and Matthew the publican; James the son of Alphaeus, and Lebbaeus, whose surname was Thaddaeus; Simon the Canaanite, and Judas Iscariot, who also betrayed him."

Here the Gospel tells us about the twelve disciples of Jesus. The etymology of the word *twelve* suggests that the word arises from the Germanic compound *twalif* meaning "two left over." A literal translation of the word *twelve* would yield "two remaining after ten taken." The number twelve is a significant in *Śaivite* Hinduism. It represents the twelve *Jyothirlingas* or "pillars of light" that constitute Lord Shiva. (Lord Shiva is the archetypical human being, or DNA.) If Jesus represents the Gospel (Lord Shiva), then the twelve disciples represent the twelve meanings (*Jyothirlingas*) that emerges from it.

If we take Jesus as representing the perfect human DNA, then the twelve disciples represent the twelve strands of the perfect human DNA. However, the virus-modified human DNA has only two stands: *"the two that remains after ten has been taken away."* In Biblical terms, the missing ten strands in human DNA represent the "lost tribes of Israel." The Judah-Benjamin and the Levi tribes represent the two (dual) strands, whereas the missing ten strands represent the Lost Tribes. The human DNA, in its present form, uses only 3% of the total genomic material available in the cell. The unused 97% is known as the *Junk DNA*.

"And when he had called unto him his twelve disciples, he gave them power against unclean spirits, to cast them out, and to heal all manner of sickness and all manner of disease." What is an "unclean spirit"? The Greek word for *unclean* is *akathartos* (G169), which means "impure" (spiritually, morally, or religiously). As we have seen earlier, the term *spirit* suggests "knowing," or "awareness." Therefore, the term "unclean spirit" means "impure knowing," or "impure awareness." In other words, the "unclean spirit" denotes ignorance and delusion.

The Gospel bestows on the 'disciples' the power to destroy ignorance and delusion. A physical entity cannot destroy ignorance and delusion; only spirit can do that. Therefore, the twelve *disciples* are, in fact, twelve *spirits*—twelve ways of looking at the Gospel. Twelve interpretations of the Gospel!

Now, let us look at the order in which the Gospel gives the names of the disciples, and their qualifications:

1. Simon, who is called Peter
2. Andrew, brother of Simon
3. James, son of Zebedee
4. John, brother of James
5. Philip
6. Bartholomew
7. Thomas
8. Matthew, the publican
9. James, son of Alphaeus
10. Lebbaeus, whose surname is Thaddaeus
11. Simon, the Canaanite
12. Judas Iscariot, who also betrayed him

It is possible that the names and the qualifications of the twelve disciples is actually a hidden code, which, if deciphered, may throw light in revealing the identity of the 'disciples.' Anyway, I am unable to do it. But, it is highly plausible that Judas Iscariot represents the Judaic interpretation of the Gospel, which 'betrays' its true spirit, or meaning.

MATTHEW 10:5-6

"These twelve Jesus sent forth, and commanded them, saying, Go not into the way of the Gentiles, and into any city of the Samaritans enter ye not: But go rather to the lost sheep of the house of Israel."

The term *Gentile* is commonly interpreted as "non-Jew." The Hebrew word for *Gentile* is *gōy* (H1471) which, among other things, means "a foreign nation." In other words, a Gentile is a foreigner (alien). The Greek word for *Gentile* is *ethnos* (G1484). It too means the same. Spiritually, the term *Gentile* means "the other." It is a relative term: to the Evites, the Adamites are the Gentiles; to the Adamites, the Evites are the Gentiles.

Jesus says to the disciples: *"Go not into the way of the Gentiles, and into any city of the Samaritans enter ye not."* Here, Jesus represents the Evites. Therefore, his advice, "Go not into the way of the Gentiles" actually suggests, "Do not follow the way of the Adamites." What is the "way of the Adamites"? The literal meaning of the word *way* is "path." But, spiritually, it means "religion" (*mārga*). And the basis (the Lord) of religion is its scripture, or the tenets that define it. Therefore, the "way of the Gentiles" implies "the religion of the Adamites," "the scripture of the Adamites," or "the God of the Adamites." In other words, the Gospel prohibits any kind of associations with dualistic religions and their scriptures.

Alternatively, "the way of the Gentiles" implies "the way of priests." And the 'way' of the priests involves rituals, sermons and proselytizing. In other words, the Gospel prohibits rituals, sermons, and proselytizing.

Jesus also warns his disciples to *"go not into any city of the Samaritans."* What is meant by the expression, "any city of the Samaritans"? Who are the Samaritans? The Samaritans are an ethno-religious group of the Levant (the geographical region that includes Lebanon, Syria, Jordan, Israel, Palestine, Cyprus, Southern Turkey, some regions of north-western Iraq, and the Sinai Peninsula) descended from ancient Semitic inhabitants of the region. Religiously, the Samaritans are adherents of *Samaritarianism*, an Abrahamic religion closely related to Judaism. Based on the Samaritan Torah, Samaritans assert their worship is the true religion of the ancient

Israelites prior to the Babylonian Exile, preserved by those who remained in the land of Israel, as opposed to Judaism, which they assert is a related but altered and amended religion, brought back by those returning from exile. Ancestrally, Samaritans claim descent from a group of Israelite inhabitants of the ancient Levant from the tribes of Ephraim and Manasseh (the two sons of Joseph) as well as some descendents from the priestly tribe of Levi. Both Jewish and Samaritan religious leaders taught that it was wrong to have any contact with the opposing group, and neither was to enter each other's territories or even to speak to one another.

Spiritually, the expression "cities of the Samaritans" refer to the organized Christian Church. The word *any* refers to the many denominations of the Christian Church. Christians, just as the Samaritans, claim Old Testament legacy, but the Jews vehemently deny them any such legacy. The tribe of Levy represents the *good* Samaritans and, therefore, the *true* Church; the tribes of *Ephraim* and *Manasseh* represent the *false* Samaritans and, therefore, the organized Christian Church.

Jesus enjoins his twelve disciples to only go to the "lost sheep of the house of Israel." The term *Israel* refers to humanity. The expression, "lost sheep" refers to those who do not behave like sheep. The term "lost sheep" refers to those not possessed by the *group spirit*; it refers to those who are individualistic. The expression, "lost sheep of the house of Israel" refers to the individualistic Evites. The implication: The Gospel truths will not be revealed to the organized Church; it will be revealed only to individual seekers.

MATTHEW 10:7-10

"And as ye go, preach, saying, The kingdom of heaven is at hand. Heal the sick, cleanse the lepers, raise the dead, cast out devils: freely ye have received, freely give. Provide neither gold, nor silver, nor brass in your purses, Nor scrip for your journey, neither two coats, neither shoes, nor yet staves: for the workman is worthy of his meat."

"And as ye go, preach, saying, The kingdom of heaven is at hand." The core teaching of the Gospel is this: *"The Kingdom of heaven is at hand."*

It is the *Good News*. And it says, "Your body is the instrument for attaining salvation." Nothing else is more "at hand" than the body. In other words, only body-aware individuals can understand the spiritual meaning of the Gospel. Therefore the Gospel says to the disciples: *"And as ye go, preach."* It means: "Depend only on the body to interpret the Gospel."

Spiritually, the term *disciple* refers either to the physical disciple (enlightened Evite) or to the spiritual disciple (spiritual interpretation). The physical disciple uses physical means (the body) for *preaching* the "kingdom of heaven," which is the body (DNA), whereas the spiritual disciple uses the spiritual means (book) for *preaching* the "kingdom of heaven," which is the Gospel. The former is addressed to the body, whereas the latter is addressed to the mind.

Jesus gives specific instructions to the disciples: *"Heal the sick, cleanse the lepers, raise the dead, cast out devils: freely ye have received, freely give."* Each of the three commandments has a specific purpose. The first commandment, *"Heal the sick"* is an injunction to heal the mental sickness of *Objectivity*. The second commandment, *"Cleanse the lepers"* is an injunction to heal the mental sickness of separation, or *Locality*. The last commandment, *"Raise the dead and cast out the devils"* actually suggests, "Heal the delusion caused by religion." It is an injunction to heal the mental sickness of *Causality*.

Jesus says to his disciples, *". . . freely ye have received, freely give."* With regard to the spiritual disciples, it suggests that the Gospel truth is revealed entirely by Grace and, therefore, those who receive it have the responsibility of sharing it freely with others. With regard to the physical disciples, it suggests that their incorruptibility is purely a gift from nature and, it is not a product of their efforts.

Jesus tells the disciples how (not) to prepare for the journey: *"Provide neither gold, nor silver, nor brass in your purses, Nor scrip for your journey, neither two coats, neither shoes, nor yet staves: for the workman is worthy of his meat."* The Greek word for *purse* is *zōnē* (G2223), which means "a belt" (actually, the underside of belt). Spiritually, the word denotes confidence. *Gold*, *silver*, and *brass* in the purse represent money, or *mammon*. For a traveler, money gives him a sense of confidence, but a false one. For the Gospel interpreter, it denotes resources (such as, the well-known Gospel interpretations available in the market, etc.) that give a (false) sense of confidence. The Greek term for *scrip* is *pēra* (G4082), which means "a leather pouch for carrying food." Spiritually, the term *scrip* refers to the literal scripture. The expression, "two coats" refers to duality, or classical logic. The Greek word for "shoes" is *hypodēma* (G5266), which means "something bound under the feet." It is a barrier between man and the ground. Spiritually, the term "shoes" denotes false hope. The word "staves" is the plural of "staff," which means "a group of assistants." In short, the Gospel warns its interpreters:

1. Do not depend on other interpretations
2. Do not depend on the literal scripture
3. Do not entertain false hopes
4. Do not seek others help

Instead, Jesus says, *"And as ye go, preach."* He explains why: *"for the workman is worthy of his meat."* The Greek word for *workman* is *ergatēs* (G2040). Literally, it means "a toiler," but, figuratively, it means "a teacher." Spiritually, the term *workman* refers to the Gospel interpreter. The term *meat* refers to the Gospel truth. Therefore, the implication: "Be body-aware and interpret me freely; the body will reveal the truth to you."

MATTHEW 10:11-15

"And into whatever city or town ye shall enter, enquire who in it is worthy; and there abide till ye go thence. And when ye come into an house, salute it. And if the house be worthy, let your peace come upon it: but if it be not worthy, let your peace return to you. And whoever shall not receive you, nor hear your words, when ye depart out of that house or city, shake off the dust of your feet. Verily I say unto you, It shall be more tolerable for the land of Sodom and Gomorrah in the day of judgment, than for that city."

Here, the Gospel explains how the 'spiritual disciples' preach the Gospel. The important thing to note here is that the Gospel is not talking about physical people going about preaching and proselytizing people. Instead, it describes allegorically how its spiritual truths work inside the readers' minds and bodies.

To whom is the Gospel preaching to? Jesus spells out: *"And into whatever city or town ye shall enter, enquire who in it is worthy; and there abide till ye go thence."* Spiritually, the expression, "city or town" refers to the mind: *city* denotes the mind of an Adamite; and *town*, the mind of a Mortal. The term *house* denotes the body. The disciple first enters a city or town, and then enters the house of a worthy in that city or town. Similarly, the Gospel message first enters the mind, and from there it enters the body (cells). Once inside the body, it rectifies the corrupt DNA. The Gospel truth will enter everyone's mind, but it will enter the bodies of only those who are *worthy* of receiving it.

Who is worthy of receiving the Gospel in the body? Jesus explains the test of 'worthiness': *"And when ye come into an house, salute it. And if the house be worthy, let your peace come upon it: but if it be not worthy, let your peace return to you."* The test involves a salute and its response. A house is considered worthy if the householder hears the disciple's salute and receives him. Here, the term *house* refers to the body (cells), and the term *householder* refers to the DNA. In the case of an Evite, the householder is God (true human DNA), whereas in the case of the Adamite, the householder is the Serpent (virus DNA). The Evite is able to hear the disciple's salute, but the Adamite is unable to hear it. In other words, the Evite DNA 'resonates' with the Gospel words. The Evite, therefore, receives the disciple, but the Adamite will never receive the disciple because he cannot hear the salute. If the householder receives the disciple, then he enters that house and his *peace* comes upon that house. Here, the expression "disciple's peace" refers to body-awareness. In other words, the Gospel message makes the man body-aware.

In this allegory, the disciple's *salute* refers to the Gospel (book) itself. To *hear the salute* means to read the Gospel; to *hear the words* of the disciple means to understand the spiritual meaning of the Gospel; to *receive the disciple* means to believe in it whole-heartedly. A *worthy* householder (Evite) reads the Gospel and understands its spiritual meaning. Thus, he passes the test of worthiness. As a result, the Gospel truths (disciple's "peace") enter his body and rewrite his DNA. The *unworthy* householder (Adamite), on the other hand, doesn't read the Gospel. Even if he does so, he does not understand its spiritual meaning. He, therefore, fails the test.

> *Behold, I stand at the door, and knock; if any man hear my voice, and open the door; I will come in to him, and will sup with him, and he with me.*
> Revelation 3:20

Jesus explains the fate of those who do not *receive* or *hear* the disciples: *"And whoever shall not receive you, nor hear your words, when ye depart out of that house or city, shake off the dust of your feet."* Spiritually, to *receive* the disciple means to whole-heartedly trust in the Gospel revelations. On the other hand, to *hear* the words of the disciples means to receive the Gospel revelations. Only a few who read the Gospel 'hear' the revelations. But, even among those who 'hear' the revelations, only a few trust it whole-heartedly. However, if anyone trusts in the revelations whole-heartedly, then the Gospel enters his body and he becomes the Gospel. But, even the others receive the "dust" of its feet. Spiritually, the expression, "dust of the feet" means "blessings." In other words, even a casual reading of the Gospel has salutary effects for the Evite.

But, the fate of those who cannot *hear* the words of the disciples is grim. Jesus says, *"Verily I say unto you, It shall be more tolerable for the land of Sodom and Gomorrah in the day of judgment, than for that city."* Sodom and Gomorrah are the Canaanite cities that were destroyed by God because of their wickedness. The word *wickedness* literally means "moral depravity." The *Day of Judgment,* according to Christian theology, refers to the final and eternal judgment by God, of every nation, segregating and judging good people and the evil ones. But spiritually, the *Day of Judgment* refers to death. In other words, Adamites who are unable to understand the spiritual meaning of the Gospel will perish with death. Evites, on the other hand, even if they are morally depraved (like the Canaanites of Sodom and Gomorrah) will escape perdition to reincarnate again to live another life.

What the Gospel trying to say here is this: "Bodily corruption is far more serious than mere mental corruption." The Gospel puts its stamp of authority on the revelation with the word *verily*. The Greek word for *verily* is *amēn* (G281). The word is derived from the Hebrew word *āmēn* (H543), which means "truly," or "so be it." The word *amen* suggests faithfulness.

MATTHEW 10:16-18

"Behold, I send you forth as sheep in the midst of wolves: be ye therefore wise as serpents, and harmless as doves. But beware of men: for they will deliver you up to the councils, and they will scourge you in their synagogues; And ye shall be brought before governors and kings for my sake, for a testimony against them and the Gentiles."

The Greek word for behold is *idou* (G2400). It is the second person singular imperfect middle of *eidō* (G1492), which means "to see," "to know," or "be aware of." The Gospel uses the term to signal important messages. It alerts the reader that the ensuing passage contains a hidden message, and therefore to pay close attention. An equivalent term used in the Bhagavad Gīta is *Bhāratha*. Whenever Lord Krishna addresses Arjuna as *Bhāratha*, it is signal for the reader to pay close attention.

Here, the Gospel gives us four important motifs: the *sheep*, the *wolf*, the *serpent*, and the *dove*. It compares the Evites to sheep. Sheep are quadruped, ruminant mammals typically bred as livestock. They are one of the earliest animals to be domesticated for agricultural purposes; sheep are raised for their fleece, meat and milk. The *quadruped* nature of the sheep denotes *dharma*. (According to the Hindu tradition, *dharma* is visualized as a quadruped.) The *ruminant* nature of the sheep denotes cognition. Just as the sheep are *domesticated*, so are the Evites conditioned by the Serpent and its minions for their own ends. In the Hindu tradition, the righteous are compared to the cow (Sanskrit: *gow*). (Note the strange resemblance of the word *gow* to the Hebrew word *gōy*, which means cattle, or Gentile.)

Wolves belong to the *canid* species. The *Canidae* are the biological family of carnivorous and omnivorous mammals. It is divided into two *tribes*: *Canini* (related to wolves) and *Vulpini* (related to foxes). Although belonging to the same species, these two tribes do not mix with each other. Wolves are social animals, travelling in nuclear families consisting of a mated pair, accompanied by the pair's adult offspring. Wolves are *apex predators*, occupying the top of the food chain. They feed primarily on large *ungulates* (two-hoofed mammals). And they hunt in packs. Wolves represent the Serpent-children. They are, the *Cainites* (pun intended).

Doves belong to the family of *Clade Columbidae* that includes some 310 species. A *clade* (derives from the ancient Greek word *klados,* meaning "branch") is a group consisting of an ancestor and all its descendents, a single *branch* on the *tree of life.* Doves are vegetarians, feeding on seeds, fruits, and plants. The doves represent the Mortals.

In religion, mythology, and literature, serpents and snakes represent fertility. While the snake denotes the creative life force, the serpent denotes artificial life (replication). The term *serpent* refers to virus; it does not mean snakes. Serpent represents duality, while snake represents non-duality.

The Gospel foresees the coming of a time of great persecution (Dark Age) for the Evites (true human beings) at the hands of the Adamites (Serpent-children), beginning with the loss (Judaization) of the Gospel. In fact, the crucifixion of Jesus refers to the Judaization of the Gospel. By the way, according to the Srimad Bhāgavadam, the *Kali Yuga* starts with the departure of Lord Krishna from the earth.

Jesus warns the Evites, *"But beware of men: for they will deliver you up to the councils, and they will scourge you in their synagogues; And ye shall be brought before governors and kings for my sake, for a testimony against them and the Gentiles."* In this verse, the implications of the various terms are as follows:

1. *men* = the public
2. *you* = true human beings / Evites
3. *councils* = courts
4. synagogues = religious institutions
5. *scourge* = to chastise
6. *governors and kings* = the rulers
7. *for my sake* = for speaking truth
8. *for a testimony against* = for revealing the secret of
9. *them* = the Serpent-children
10. *and the Gentiles* = and the Adamites

Literally interpreted, the Gospel is foreseeing a time when the Evites would be denied rights by the political and religious establishments—a time when individual freedom would be overrun by *group spirit.* But, it also envisions it as an opportunity for the Evites to declare the truth. Perhaps, the Gospel is alluding to the present times—the age of democracy. The term *democracy* originates from the Greek word *democratia* meaning "rule of the people." Despite the lofty ideals, democracy generally degenerates into "rule of the mob." Corruption and hypocrisy are its co-travelers. 20th century transitions to liberal democracy have come in successive waves, arising out of wars, revolutions, decolonization, religious and economic upheavals. Since the Evites constitute only a very small minority of the world population, they generally have no representation in the elected bodies, and, therefore, have no voice in a democratic government.

Spiritually interpreted, the Gospel verses tell a different story. The verb *scourge* is derived from the Latin word *excoriare* which means "to flay." The Latin word *corium* means "skin." The noun *scourge* refers to a multi-thong whip that is used to inflict severe corporal punishment. Spiritually, the term *scourge* suggests the destroying of man's body-awareness by religious or political conditioning. *Skin* denotes body-awareness, and the *whip* denotes the laws (political and religious laws).

Jesus sends his disciples as sheep among the wolves. It is an allegory for God sending souls into the world. The soul takes birth as a child in a society dominated by Adamites (wolves), and is totally conditioned (devoured) before his childhood is over. In a sense, society devours the child's innocence. The child is like the sheep, meek and gentile; it is totally defenseless and vulnerable as a "lamb to the slaughter." Prophet Isaiah says:

> *He was oppressed, and he was afflicted, yet he opened not his mouth: he is brought as a lamb to the slaughter, and as a sheep before her shearers is dumb, so he opened not his mouth.*
> Isaiah 53:7

The infant is totally detached from the world. He is a bundle of pure awareness. He is, in every sense, the "disciple of Jesus."

> *My sheep hear my voice, and I know them, and they follow me.*
> John 10:18

As the child grows up, the conditioning begins. *Social conditioning* refers to the sociological process of training individuals in a society to respond in a "manner generally approved by the society." When the conditioning is complete, the child loses his innocence and becomes *clever*. In other words, the *sheep* is transformed into *goat*; the Evite becomes an Adamite. It is this conditioning process that Jesus refers to *scourging*. And the 'scourgers' are the parents, the education system, the religious system, peers, and relatives. It is the parents who "deliver up" the child to the *councils* (schools) and to the *synagogues* (Church and Sunday schools) to be scourged.

Alternatively, Jesus represents the Gospel and the disciples represent its spiritual interpretations. The wolves are the intelligentsia of the world. The term 'scourge', in this context, refers to the accusations they charge on the document.

"And ye shall be brought before governors and kings for my sake, for a testimony against them and the Gentiles." The phrase, "for my sake" has two implications: one, it implies "for being an Evite"; two, it implies "for telling the truth."

What is the child's (Evite's) testimony to the public? The great Indian philosopher *Sri Śhankara* beautifully portrays it in his book *Brahma Jnānāvali*:

> *Asangōham asangōham asangōham punah punah*
> *Sachidānanda rūpāya aham ēva aham avyayam*
> Brahma Jnānāvali, Sri Śankarāchārya
> ("Detached, detached, detached am I, and I repeat it; The Self am I; I am That I am; Eternal am I.")

MATTHEW 10:19-22

"But when they deliver you up, take no thought how or what ye shall speak: for it shall be given you in that same hour what ye shall speak. For it is not ye that speak, but the Spirit of your Father which speaketh in you. And the brother shall deliver up the brother to death, and the father the child: and the children shall rise up against their parents, and cause them to be put to death. And ye shall be hated of all men for my name's sake: but he that endureth to the end shall be saved."

"But when they deliver you up, take no thought how or what ye shall speak: for it shall be given you in that same hour what ye shall speak. For it is not ye that speak, but the Spirit of your Father which speaketh in you."

The expression, "Spirit of your Father" refers to "Self-awareness." It is the Evite's sense of "I am," or individuality. When an Evite is brought before the public, his *righteousness* will speak for him; he does not have to utter a word.

Most children acquiesce to societal conditioning pressures. However, a few resist it internally and, therefore, escape the conditioning. They may retain their true nature, such as innocence, spontaneity, freedom, individuality, and curiosity in spite of the relentless barrage from all sides. But, the society considers these 'undisciplined' children as non-conforming or unfit members. And the conditioning pressure is exerted on the child from all sides—peers, parents, relatives, and the system. It is this conditioning process the Gospel calls *slaughter.*

"And the brother shall deliver up the brother to death, and the father the child: and children shall rise up against their parents, and cause them to be put to death." The term *death* refers to conditioning. Brother delivering brother to death refers to the conditioning done by peers; father delivering child to death suggests conditioning by parents. Children, on their part, prevent the parents from seeking truth by the chains of attachment.

"And ye shall be hated of all men for my sake: but he that endureth to the end shall be saved." The phrase "for my sake" implies "for being an individual," or "for being an Evite." The term *endureth* means "not succumbing to the conditioning." The implication of the Gospel verse: "If you resist conditioning, then the society will hate you for it. But, salvation is only to those who remain unconditioned."

Alternatively, the expression, "but he that endureth to the end shall be saved" also implies, "He who remains truly human till death will be saved," or "He whose DNA remains uncorrupted till death is saved."

MATTHEW 10:23

"But when they persecute you in this city, flee ye into another: for verily I say unto you, Ye shall not have gone over the cities of Israel, till the Son of man be come."

Here, the term "you" refers to the Self of man, which is the Ultimate Truth.

The expression, "this city" refers to a particular religion and its scripture. In fact, it refers to a particular *formalism*. In philosophy of mathematics, and philosophy of logic, *formalism* is a theory that holds that statements of mathematics and logic can be thought of as statements *about* the consequences of certain string manipulation rules. (In fact, the very first verse of the Bible is an axiom.) For example, Euclidean geometry can be seen as a *game* whose *play* consists in moving around certain strings of symbols called *axioms* according to a set of *rules* called *rules of inference* to generate new strings. In playing this game, one can "prove" that the Phythagorean theorem is valid because the string representing the Phythagorean theorem can be constructed using only the stated rules. According to formalism, the truths expressed in logic and mathematics is not about numbers, sets, or triangles or any other contensive subject matter—in fact, they aren't *about* anything at all. They are merely syntactic forms whose shapes and locations have no meaning unless they are given an interpretation (or semantics).

The Greek word for *persecute* is *diōkō* (G1377), which means "to pursue," or "to chase." Similarly, the Greek word for *flee* is *pheugō* (G5343), which to run way. In fact, scripture is nothing but the product of man's mental work, hoping to capture truth in a formalism. Metaphorically speaking, man has been "persecuting" truth over "the cities of Israel." Here, the expression, "cities of Israel" implies "religions of the world." But the truth has continually eluded them. According to the Gospel, this futile chasing will go on till the Gospel truth is revealed to man. And it is that revelation of the Gospel truth that it calls "the coming of the Son of man."

The Gospel verse reminds us of *Gödel's Incompleteness Theorems.* Gödel's Incompleteness Theorems are two theorems of mathematical logic that establish inherent limitations of all but the most trivial axiomatic systems capable of doing arithmetic. The theorems, proven by Kurt Gödel in 1931, are important in mathematical logic and in the philosophy of mathematics. The two results are widely, but not universally, interpreted as showing that *Hilbert's program* to find a complete and consistent set of axioms for all mathematics is impossible, giving a negative answer to *Hilbert's second problem.*

The *first incompleteness theorem* states that no consistent system of axioms whose theorems can be listed by an "effective procedure" (e.g. computer program or any sort of algorithm) is capable of proving all truth about the relations of the natural numbers (arithmetic). For any such system, there will always be statements about the natural numbers that are true, but that are unprovable with the system. The *second incompleteness theorem*, an extension of the first, shows that such a system cannot demonstrate its own consistency.

MATTHEW 10:24-25

"The disciple is not above his master, nor the servant above his lord. It is enough for the disciple that he be as his master, and the servant as his lord. If they have called the master of the house Beelzebub, how much more shall they call them of his household?"

The word *disciple* comes from the Latin root *discipere,* which means "to grasp intellectually" or "to analyze thoroughly." The word is derived from the roots *dis*, which means "apart," and *capere* which means "to take." The Sanskrit word for disciple is *śiṣya.* The Sanskrit root *śiṣ* means "to separate from another," "to distinguish" or "that which remains when something is removed."

The term *master* refers to one having the authority and qualification to teach the disciples. The word is derived from the Latin word *magister* which means "chief teacher." The Sanskrit word for master is *guru.* It is derived from the Sanskrit roots *gu* meaning "darkness," and *ru* meaning "to remove." *Guru* is one who removes the darkness (delusion) of his disciples.

The Gospel says, *"The disciple is not above his master."* It may be mathematically expressed as:

Master > Disciple
Master—Self-awareness = Disciple

The master minus *something* is the disciple. In other words, the disciple becomes equal to his master when *something* is added to him. What is that *something*? It is the knowledge of the Self, or self-awareness. If that *something* is anything other than self-awareness, then the disciple can, at least in theory, surpass the master. But, it is not possible because self-awareness is the All.

The Gospel again says, "*. . . nor the servant above his lord,"* which may be mathematically expressed as:

Lord > Servant
Lord—Freewill = Servant

Similarly, the lord minus *something* is the servant. In other words, the servant becomes equal to the lord when *something* is added to him. That *something* is authority. Similarly, an Evite minus *something* is an Adamite. That *something* is freewill or freedom. Therefore, an Adamite is cannot be above an Evite. But, many Evites, by surrendering their freedom to religion have lowered themselves to the level of servants (Mortals).

The Gospel then asks a rhetorical question: *"If they have called the master of the house Beelzebub, how much more shall they call them of his household?"* The term "they," in this context, refers to the Adamites. The expression "master of the house" refers to the Self, the Father. The Adamites accuse the spiritual interpretation of the Gospel made by the Evites as the work of devil. They accuse that the knowledge is revealed to the Evites by *Beelzebub* though divination. In other words, these Adamites are calling the Father Beelzebub, not realizing that they themselves are the possessors of the ultimate evil—the Serpent.

MATTHEW 10:26-27

"Fear them not therefore: for there is nothing covered, that shall not be revealed; and hid, that shall not be known. What I tell you in darkness, that speak ye in light: and what ye hear in the ear, that preach ye upon the housetops."

The word "them" refers to the real enemies, the Serpent-children. The Gospel tells why we need not fear these entities: "*. . . for there is nothing covered, that shall not be revealed; and hid, that shall not be known.*" Fear arises from ignorance, and ignorance arises from secrecy. The greatest strength of evil is secrecy: that it is invisible to human eyes. Evil operates in secrecy. Given below is an extract from the famous speech of John F. Kennedy made to the American Newspaper Publishers Association in April 1961:

> *The very word "secrecy" is repugnant in a free and open society; and we are as a people inherently and historically opposed*

to secret societies, to secret oaths and to secret proceedings. We decided long ago that the dangers of excessive and unwarranted concealment of pertinent facts far outweigh the dangers which are cited to justify it. Even today, there is little value in opposing the threat of a closed society by imitating its arbitrary restrictions. Even today, there is little value in insuring the survival of our nation if our traditions do not survive with it. And there is very grave danger that an announced need for increased security will be seized upon by those anxious to expand its meaning to the very limits of official censorship and concealment. That I do not intend to permit to the extent that it is in my control. And no official of my Administration, whether his rank is high or low, civilian or military, should interpret my words here tonight as an excuse to censor the news, to stifle dissent, to cover up mistakes or to withhold from the press and the public the facts they deserve to know.

President John F. Kennedy, April 27, 1961

The spiritual revelation of the Gospel will tear apart the veil of secrecy that has been the strength of evil. It will expose the evil to the brilliant light of truth and destroy it completely. Thus, the Gospel truth will set humanity free.

The Gospel injunction to the spiritual disciples: *"What I tell you in darkness, that speak ye in light: and what ye hear in the ear, that preach ye upon the housetops* The Gospel revealed the secrets to humanity, but darkly, using metaphors and allegory. But, now, the spiritual interpretations of the Gospel, the spiritual disciples, will reveal those secrets openly to humanity, thus destroying the power of evil once and for all.

MATTHEW 10:28

"And fear them not which kill the body, but are not able to kill the soul: but rather fear him which is able to destroy both soul and body in hell."

Viruses belong to two general categories: the *non-equilibrium viruses* and *equilibrium viruses*. Non-equilibrium viruses are those that jumped ('flew') from another species where it is an equilibrium-virus, into a new host organism, to which it is not well-adapted. Often these viruses can be very lethal, because they haven't been selected to be temperate. They usually spread poorly but sometimes they spread well. Non-equilibrium viruses include Flu (birds), HIV (chimp), SARS (bats), Ebola (bats), Hantaan (rodent), etc.

Equilibrium viruses, on the other hand, are viruses that have been with a species for a very long time. They have generally developed a *modus vivendi* with that species. They are generally not lethal, but they spread extremely well from person to person. A very good example is the common cold virus: we all know that if we come in contact with a person who has cold, we are likely to get a cold. Somehow that virus is going to transfer, either through a sneeze, or through physical contact. These are equilibrium viruses in the sense that they have developed an equilibrium status with their host. They are not asking too much of their host, they are not going to kill their host generally; on the other hand, the host provides a vehicle (and energy source) for the virus to transmit itself into future generations, thus achieving *immortality*. Examples of equilibrium viruses include Polio (almost eradicated), Smallpox (eradicated), Common cold, Measles, Mumps, Herpes, etc. It seems, the equilibrium virus (Epstein Barr virus?) is the dreaded Serpent of the Bible.

Here, the Gospel compares two enemies: one, an external enemy, which it calls *them*; the other, an internal enemy, which it calls *him*. The external enemy is physically lethal, but not spiritually lethal. On the other hand, the internal enemy is not physically lethal, but spiritually lethal. At the microscopic scale, the term "them" refers to the non-equilibrium viruses (Beelzebub and his minions) that attack human body from outside; the term "him" refers to the equilibrium viruses (the Serpent) that do not cause any serious physical problems, but alters the human DNA. The non-equilibrium viruses only kill the body, but they do not modify the DNA (soul). But, the equilibrium viruses, on the other hand, do not kill the body but modify the DNA, thus destroying the soul.

At the macroscopic scale, the term "them" refers to the political system (Beelzebub and minions) that affects the society, whereas the term "him" refers to the religious system (the Serpent) that affects both society and the individual.

MATTHEW 10:29-31

"Are not two sparrows sold for a farthing? and one of them shall not fall on the ground without your Father. But the very hairs of your head are all numbered. Fear not therefore, ye are of more value than many sparrows."

Sparrows	Viruses
They infest human habitation	They infest human habitation
They nest on buildings	They inhabit human bodies
They exist in large numbers	They exist in large numbers
They are seed eaters	They are DNA eaters

Virus is not really a living entity, but the human body cell is. Here, the Gospel differentiates between created, artificial, or lifeless entities and generated, real, or living entities, and then says that the created entities are made of numbers. (Note: The *virus* also represents literal scripture; the body cell also represents the Gospel.)

Sparrows belong to the family of *passerine* birds. They nest on buildings and inhabit cities in large numbers. They are the most familiar of all wild birds. Sparrows are generally social birds, and their assemblages can be quite large. They are primarily seed eaters. Some species of sparrows are good weavers. Sparrows signify numbers. The Gospel uses the image of sparrows as a metaphor for viruses. The expression, "two sparrows" signifies duality, which is the spell cast by the Serpent virus.

Farthing is a former coin of Great Britain that is equal to one-fourth of a British penny. The Greek word for farthing is *assarion* (G787). The *assarius* was a bronze, and later copper, coin used during the Roman Empire. It was a unit of Roman currency. In other words, the term *farthing* denotes value. The notion of value is also based on numbers.

The Gospel asks: *"Are not two sparrows sold for a farthing?"* The question really is this: "Isn't duality the source of value?" The suggestion here is that *value* is a spell cast by the Serpent.

The Gospel then says, *"And one of them shall not fall on the ground without your Father."* If one of the *two* falls to the ground, then only one remains; it is no longer duality. And the Gospel says that it (that is, the destruction of duality) cannot happen without the Father's knowledge. Spiritually, the expression, "Father's knowledge" means "self-awareness." In other words, what the Gospel says is this: "Duality can only be destroyed by body-awareness." Thus, the gospel prescribes the most effective antidote against Serpent poison: body-awareness!

Then the Gospel says something even more mysterious: *"But the very hairs of your head are all numbered."* Spiritually, the expression, "hairs of your head" refers to thoughts. Therefore the expression, "The very hairs of your head are all numbered" actually means, "Thoughts are numbers." In other words, the Gospel hints that all created things are merely numbers. By the way, Pythagoras, the ancient Greek philosopher and mathematician too believed so.

Therefore the Gospel says: *"Fear not therefore, ye are of more value than many sparrows."* The phrase "many sparrows" suggests a very large number. Therefore, the expression, "more than many sparrows" suggests infinity. In other words, the Gospel says that, unlike viruses, which are very large numbers, human beings are infinite beings.

MATTHEW 10:32-33

"Whosoever therefore shall confess me before men, him will I confess also before my Father which is in heaven. But whosoever shall deny me before men, him will I also deny before my Father which is in heaven."

The Hebrew word for *confess* is *yāda* (H3034), which means "to revere" or "to worship." But, the Gospel uses the Greek word *homologeō* (G3670), which means "to acknowledge." The word, *acknowledge* means "to recognize the existence." Spiritually, the word, *confess* means "to acknowledge the body," or "to be body-aware." The word "me", in this context, refers to the body; the term "men" refers to duality, or religion. Therefore, the expression, *"whosoever therefore shall confess me before men"* implies "whoever remains body-aware in spite of religion."

And, about such people the Gospel says: *". . . him will I also confess before my Father which is in heaven."* The 'Father' which is in 'heaven' is the Self, or Truth. The word "I", in this context, refers to the body. In other words, the Gospel says: "To those who are body-aware, the body will reveal the truth." It implies that only the Evites have access to the Gospel truths.

The Gospel issues a stern warning: *"But whosoever shall deny me before men, him will I also deny before my Father which is in heaven."* In other words, those who surrender body-awareness to religion will never find the truth.

MATTHEW 10:34-36

"Think not that I am come to send peace on earth: I came not to send peace, but a sword. For I am come to set a man at variance against his father, and the daughter against her mother, and the daughter in law against her mother in law. And a man's foes shall be they of his own household."

"Think not that I am come to send peace on earth: I came not to send peace, but a sword." Here, the term "I" refers to the Gospel. The one and only purpose of the Gospel is to destroy duality and save human beings from the spell cast by the Serpent. In other words, the one and only purpose of the Gospel is to save human beings from religion.

A chief symptom of duality is *group spirit*—the tendency of *infected* humans to agglutinate into societies. Relationships are the ropes that bind individuals into groups. Therefore, destroying duality entails destroying relationships—all kinds of relationships. And, the *sword* that cuts the ropes of relationships is non-duality, or body-awareness.

The Bhagavad Gīta depicts it beautifully:

Ūrdhamūlam-atha śākham aśwattham prāhur-avyayam
Cchamdāmsi yasya parṇāni yastam vēda sa vēdavit
Adha-cchōrdhwam prasrutas-tasya śākhāh
Guṇapravṛdhā viṣayapravālah
Adhaśca-mūlānyan-anusamtatāni
Karma-anubandhīni manuṣyalōkē
Na rūpamasyeha tathopalabhyate
Nantho no chardirna ca samprathiṣtha
Aṣwattham-enam suvirūdamūlam
Asangaśasthrēṇa dṛdēna cchitwā
Bhagavad Gīta 15:1-3
("The world, with its upward roots and downward branches, may be likened to the indestructible fig tree, whose leaves are the verses of the scripture. Whosoever knows it in essence, is a knower of the scripture.

> Its branches are spread upwards and downwards, sustained and nourished by the attributes; sense objects are its tender buds; and its roots, which are the ropes of karma, are spread out below in the world of mortals.
>
> The form of this tree is not visible, for it has no beginning, nor end, nor is its mainstay here. Cutting asunder its firmly entrenched roots with the formidable weapon of non-duality, one should earnestly seek that elevated state of *dharma*, reaching which one never returns.")

"And a man's foes shall be they of his own household," says the Gospel. Detaching from worldly relationships is the greatest challenge in spiritual pursuit. In that sense, a truth-seeker's enemy is his relations.

MATTHEW 10:37-38

"He that loveth father or mother more than me is not worthy of me: and he that loveth son or daughter more than me is not worthy of me. And he that taketh not his cross, and followeth after me, is not worthy of me."

The terms, *father, mother, son, daughter, daughter-in-law, mother-in-law* etc., denote relations. They are the strands in the great spider-web called the *world*. According to the Gospel, those who love relations (world) more than the Self are not worthy to know the Gospel truth.

In the great Hindu epic Mahabharata, the character *Dṛtharāṣtra* represents one who loved his relations (sons) more than his *dharma*. He is depicted there as a blind man. The name *Drtharāṣtra* means "one who holds on to the country."

The Gospel says, *"And he that taketh not his cross, and followeth after me, is not worthy of me."* The *cross* symbolizes duality. The expression "taketh not his cross" implies "abandoning duality." The phrase "following after me" implies "following the body"; it means to be body-aware. The expression, "worthy of me" means "worthy of being called a human being." The implication of the Gospel verse is this: "The true human being lives his worldly life with body-awareness."

The Gospel does not ask its followers to lead an ascetic (*sanyāsi*) life, in the literal sense, but it wants them to be body-aware while leading the life of a householder (*Gṛhastha*).

MATTHEW 10:39-41

"He that findeth his life shall lose it: and he that loseth his life for my sake shall find it. He that receiveth you receiveth me, and he that receiveth me receiveth him that sent me. He that receiveth a prophet in the name of a prophet shall receive a prophet's reward; and he that receiveth a righteous man in the name of a righteous man shall receive a righteous man's reward."

"He that findeth his life shall lose it: and he that loseth his life for my sake shall find it." Here, the Gospel uses the term *life* in two different senses: first, to imply *worldly life* (duality); and second, to imply *eternal life* (non-duality). Man has a choice to make. He has to choose between worldly life and eternal life, and the choice is mutually exclusive. To gain eternal life, one has to fight the Serpent, since he is the source of corruption. In other words, to become a true human being (Evite), one has to abandon duality in all its forms (politics, religion, business etc.) But, to become successful in worldly life, one has to embrace duality: one has to surrender to the Serpent.

"He that receiveth you receiveth me, and he that receiveth me receiveth him that sent me." Here, the term, "you" refers to the spiritual disciples; the term, "me" refers to the Gospel, or the true human DNA; the expression, "him that sent me" refers to the Self, or the Father. In other words, the Gospel says, "He who understands the spiritual truths of the Gospel receives the true human DNA and becomes an Evite. He who is an Evite receives enlightenment."

"He that receiveth a prophet in the name of a prophet shall receive a prophet's reward." The Greek word for *receiveth* is *dechomai* (G1209), which means "to accept." But, spiritually, the word means "to respect." Similarly, the Greek word for *prophet* is *prophētēs* (G4396), which means "an inspired speaker." Here, the term *prophet* means "priest." Therefore, the expression, "he that receiveth a prophet in the name of a prophet" may be translates as: "he who respects a priest for what he is."

According to the Gospel, such people receive "the prophet's reward," which is public recognition.

The Gospel then says, "*. . . and he that receiveth a righteous man in the name of a righteous man shall receive a righteous man's reward.*" The term "righteous man" refers to a true human being (Evite). Therefore, the expression, "he that receiveth a righteous man in the name of a righteous man" may be translated as: "he who respects an Evite for what he is." The righteous man's reward is nothing but mutual recognition. In other words, the Evite respect the Evite. But, no one can know if the other person is an Evite or not. Therefore, the suggestion here is that the Evite knows himself; he has self-knowledge. To be an Evite, in itself, is the reward, the great honor; there cannot be a greater reward than that.

MATTHEW 10:42

"And whosoever shall give to drink unto one of these little ones a cup of cold water only in the name of a disciple, verily I say unto you, he shall in no wise lose his reward."

The expression, "these little ones," refers the meek and gentle Evites, the true human beings, the disciples of Jesus. The Hindus call them *sādhus*. The Sanskrit word *sādhu* means "good," "perfect," "right," "proper," "beautiful," "righteous," "blessed," "noble," and "hearty." The word *sādhu* also means "an ascetic." Indirectly, the Gospel gives us the attributes of an Evite: he is good, perfect, right, proper, beautiful, righteous, blessed, noble, and hearty.

The act of offering a cup of cold water denotes kindness. Therefore, the spiritual implication of the verse is this: "He who acts kindly to an Evite is also an Evite."

Alternatively, the expression "these little ones" refers to the spiritual disciples, or the spiritual interpretations of the Gospel. Here, the "cup of cold water" denotes body-awareness. Therefore, the spiritual implication of the verse is this: "Whoever reads the Gospel with body-awareness will be freed from corruption"

CHAPTER 11

The Judge

MATTHEW 11:1

"And it came to pass, when Jesus had made an end of commanding his twelve disciples, he departed thence to teach and to preach in their cities."

Jesus gives the disciples the commission to preach the Gospel, and instructs them as to where they should go, what they should say, how they should behave, and what kind of treatment they may encounter. If, Jesus represents the Gospel, then what is meant by "preaching the Gospel"?

Literally, the word, *preach* connotes the following:

1. To proclaim or make known
1. To deliver
2. To advocate or inculcate (religious or moral truths) in speech or writing

Spiritually, to *preach* the Gospel means to interpret it. The spiritual interpretations themselves are the disciples. The Gospel can be interpreted in many ways. Each interpreter may have his own perspective. And each interpretation may vary in the meaning assigned to the Gospel motifs, but the relationships between the motifs (the organization) remain the same in all interpretations. And the Gospel is mainly preached to the interpreter himself. The following passage from the Book of Revelation describes the effects of the preaching:

> *"And they sung a new song, saying, Thou art worthy to take the book, and to open the seals thereof: for thou wast slain, and hast redeemed us to God by thy blood out of every kindred, and tongue, and people, and nation."*
> Revelation 5:9

The 'book' referred to in the passage is the Gospel. The opening of the seals of the book denotes the unraveling of the spiritual truths of the Gospel. The "new song" is the spiritual interpretation of the Gospel. The expression, "thou wast slain" suggests that the true meaning of the Gospel was distorted before. The term *blood* refers to spiritual meaning of the Gospel. The expression, "redeemed us to God by thy blood" suggests that the spiritual meaning of the Gospel is capable of correcting genetic corruption and transforming Mortals into true human beings.

Gospel then says, "*. . . he departed thence to teach and to preach in their cities.*" The term "he" refers to Jesus, the Gospel. The phrase "their cities" refers to the organized Church. The allusion, here, is to preaching the literal Gospel. The literal Gospel is 'taught' and 'preached' in churches with pomp and showmanship, but Jesus (truth) has already departed from there.

MATTHEW 11:2-3

"Now when John had heard in the prison the works of Christ, he sent two of his disciples, And said unto him, Art thou he that should come, or do we look for another?"

John-the-Baptist was really an evangelist of Judaism who *literally* believed in apocalypse and the coming of the Messiah. The term apocalypse is derived from the ancient Greek word *apocalypsis*, which means "uncovering." The term refers to the disclosure of knowledge, that is, the lifting of the veil, or revelation. In truth, the prophesied coming of the Messiah is the nothing but the revelation of this hidden knowledge. But, John, like every other Jew, understood the terms literally. He mistook apocalypse to be the literal end of the physical world, and the coming of the Messiah as the coming of a Jewish world leader who would liberate Judaea and its people from the oppression of Rome. John fervently hoped that Jesus was the Messiah foretold by the scripture.

Spiritually, the expression "the works of Christ" refers to the Gospel preaching, or the Gospel revelations. John reads the Gospel interpretation and is shocked and horrified by the nature of its revelations. He finds it offensive to his religious sensitivities. Therefore, he asks Jesus through his disciples, *"Art thou he that should come, or do we look for another?"* In other words, John wonders: "Is this really the spiritual meaning of the Gospel, or is it yet to be revealed?"

MATTHEW 11:4-6

"Jesus answered and said unto them, Go and shew John again those things which ye do hear and see: The blind receive their sight, and the lame walk, the lepers are cleansed, and the deaf hear, the dead are raised up, and the poor have the gospel preached to them. And blessed is he, whosoever shall not be offended in me."

Jesus understands John's predicament and, therefore, lists out the miracles done by him, as evidence to prove that he himself is the Messiah:

1. The blind receive their sight
2. The lame walk
3. The lepers are cleansed
4. The deaf hear
5. The dead are raised up

Literally, the expression "coming of the Messiah" means "coming of the Savior." But, spiritually, it refers to the revelation of the Gospel truths that will liberate humanity from the bondage of religion. The spiritual interpretation of the Gospel is the Messiah. But, it is not merely an elucidation of the old scripture. In fact, the five miracles cited by Jesus testify that. The spiritual meaning of the miracles exposes religion as the disease, and presents the Gospel as the medicine that cures it.

1. The blind receive their sight: Duality cured
2. The lame walk: Fear of sin cured
3. The lepers are cleansed: Alienation (from nature) cured

4. The deaf hear: Ignorance cured
5. The dead raised up: Delusion cured

The Gospel adds one more miracle to the list, *". . . and the poor have the gospel preached to them."* The term, *poor* refers to the "spiritually poor," or the Evites. It is noteworthy that the Gospel includes it as a miracle. It suggests that the Gospel revelation itself is a miracle.

Jesus says to John's disciples, *"And blessed is he, whosoever shall not be offended in me."* Here, the term *blessed* refers to the Evites. The Greek word for *offended* is *skandalizō* (G6424), which means "to scandalize." The word, *scandalize* means "to shock or horrify by something considered immoral or improper." In other words, the Gospel says that the Evites are not shocked or horrified by the Gospel truths, but the Adamites are. To the Adamites, it is blasphemy. Apostle Peter explains it mysteriously:

> *Unto you therefore which believe he is precious: but unto them which be disobedient, the stone which the builders disallowed, the same is made the head of the corner, And a stone of stumbling, and a rock of offence, even to them which stumble at the word, being disobedient: whereunto also they were appointed.*
> 1 Peter 2: 7-8

Jesus says to John's disciples, *"Go and shew John again those things which ye do hear and see."* The *things* that the Evites "see and hear" in the Gospel are very different from what the Adamites see and hear in it. Here, the term *things* refer to the spiritual meaning of the Gospel words. The expression "see and hear" refers to intuitive understanding; it is different from formalistic understanding. What the Gospel says is this: "If you understand the true nature of the disease and the true nature of the cure, then you would know that the Gospel indeed is the Messiah." In other words, Gospel is saying that the disease is religion and the cure is the Gospel revelations.

MATTHEW 11:7-10

"And as they departed, Jesus began to say unto the multitudes concerning John, What went ye out into the wilderness to see? A reed shaken with the wind? But what went ye out for to see? A man clothed in soft raiment? behold, they that wear soft clothing are the in kings' houses. But what went ye out for to see? A prophet? yea, I say unto you, and more than a prophet. For this is he, of whom it is written, Behold, I send my messenger before thy face, which shall prepare thy way before thee."

John the Baptist typifies those who think of Jesus as a person. In many respects, John the Baptist represents the Christian Church. John's searching in the wilderness may be compared to Christian theologians' searching in the Old Testament for proof of Jesus' divinity. In other words, these theologians are trying to 'Judaize' Jesus and the Gospel. The Gospel highlights the absurdity of it.

Jesus asks John, *"What went ye out into the wilderness to see?"* The Greek word for *wilderness* is *erēmos* (G2048), which means "desert," or "wasteland." Spiritually, it refers to the literal scripture. It seems the Gospel is asking the Christian theologians: "What are you trying to establish with the literal scripture?" He then attributes the three possible reasons to it:

1. *"To see a reed shaken with the wind"*
2. *"To see a man clothed in soft raiment"*
3. *"To see a prophet"*

Spiritually, the expression, "a reed shaken with the wind" denotes a magician; the "man clothed in soft raiment" denotes a king. In other words, the Gospel is asking the Christian theologians:

1. "What are you trying prove with the scripture: that the Messiah is a magician?"
2. "What are you trying prove with the scripture: that the Messiah is a king?"
3. "What are you trying prove with the scripture: that the Messiah is a priest?

All of them—the magician, the king, and the priest—are Adamites.

The Gospel reveals itself and his messenger: *"For this is he, of whom it is written, Behold, I send my messenger before thy face, which shall prepare thy way before thee."* The expression, *"For this is he, of whom it is written"* suggests that the Gospel—the book—itself is the Messiah. The Gospel, then, talks about the messenger: "Behold, I send my messenger before thy face," Spiritually, the expression, "my messenger" refers to the spiritual interpretation of the Gospel. The Gospel explains the work of the messenger: "It will prepare the way before thee." In other words, the purpose of the Gospel revelations is to facilitate liberation.

The Messiah is not a physical person. It is the "written word"—the Gospel. And, it is not the literal Gospel, but the spiritual one. It is the Gospel that the Evites *eat* and *drink*.

> *And the voice which I heard from heaven spake unto me again, and said, Go and take the little book which is open in the hand of the angel which standeth upon the sea and upon the earth. And I went unto the angel, and said unto him, Give me the little book. And he said unto me, Take it, and eat it up; and it shall be make thy belly bitter, but it shall be in thy mouth sweet as honey. And I took the little book out of the angel's hand, and ate it up; and it was in my mouth sweet as honey: and as soon as I had eaten it, my belly was bitter. And he said to unto me, Thou must prophesy again before many peoples, and nations, and tongues, and kings.*
>
> Revelation 10:8-10

In many ways, John the Baptist represents the Church and its literal Gospel. Consider the following:

1. John the Baptist precedes Jesus; the literal Gospel precedes the spiritual Gospel.
2. John baptizes sinners; the Church proselytizes unbelievers.
3. John declares the ultimate truth without knowing its spiritual meaning; the Church declares the Gospel without knowing its spiritual meaning.
4. John searched the wilderness for the Messiah; the Church searches the Old Testament for Jesus.

5. John is a fundamentally a Jew at heart; the Church fundamentally is Judaic at the core.
6. John baptizes with water; the Church preaches the literal Gospel

In the Gospel of John Jesus declares the impossibility of achieving enlightenment through the literal Gospel, while answering a question from Nicodemus, the Jew:

> *Jesus answered, Verily, verily, I say unto thee, Except a man be born of water and of the Spirit, he cannot enter into the kingdom of God.*
> John 3:3

In the above verse, *water* denotes the literal meaning of the Gospel, whereas the *Spirit* denotes the spiritual meaning. John the Baptist baptizes with water. Similarly, the Church preaches the literal Gospel. But, the Gospel says unequivocally that it is impossible to find the truth from the literal Gospel.

MATTHEW 11:11-15

"Verily I say unto you, Among them that are born of women there hath not risen a greater than John the Baptist: notwithstanding he that is least in the kingdom of heaven is greater than he. And from the days of John the Baptist until now the kingdom of heaven suffereth violence, and the violent take it by force. For all the prophets and the law prophesied until John. And if ye will receive it, this is Elias, which was for to come. He that hath ears to hear, let him hear."

"Verily I say unto you, Among them that are born of women there hath not risen a greater than John the Baptist: notwithstanding he that is least in the kingdom of heaven is greater than he." Spiritually, the expression, "them that are born of women" refers to the different literal scriptures created by humanity. Here, John the Baptist represents the literal Gospel. In other words, the Gospel says that the literal Gospel is superior to all other literal scriptures. But, the physical body of the Evite is even superior to the literal Gospel.

The "kingdom of heaven" is like the fractal: it represents the human cell, the human body, humanity, and the nature. There is a self-similarity between all of them. A *fractal* is a mathematical set described by fractal Geometry, which is the study of figures exhibiting fractal dimension. A fractal set when plotted typically displays self-similar patterns, which means they are "the same from near as from far." Fractals may be exactly the same at every scale, or, they may be nearly the same at different scales. The concept of fractal extends beyond trivial self-similarity and includes the idea of a detailed pattern repeating itself.

Alternatively, the expression, "the least in the kingdom of heaven" refers to the body cell. In other words, the Gospel declares the superiority of the cell protoplasm over the DNA. Or, in other words, the Gospel declares the superiority of body over mind.

"And from the days of John the Baptist until now the kingdom of heaven suffereth violence, and the violent take it by force." We can interpret the verse using the key given below:

Gospel Words	**Spiritual Implication 1**	**Spiritual Implication 2**
"From the days of John the Baptist"	Ever since the Christian Church was established	Ever since the canon was established
"Until now"	Until the ignorance is removed by Gospel revelations	Until the spiritual Gospel was revealed
"The kingdom of heaven"	Humanity	The truth
"Suffereth violence"	Suffers from delusion	Suffers distortion of meaning
"The violent"	The Adamites	The Adamites
"And the violent take it by force"	Controls humanity	Controls the truth

1. "Ever since Christian Church was established, until the Gospel revelations remove ignorance, humanity suffers delusion and the Adamites control humanity."
2. "Ever since the Canon was established, until the Gospel revelations reveal the truth, the Gospel meaning suffers distortion and the Adamites control the truth."

The First Council of Nicaea was a council of Christian bishops convened in Nicaea in Bithynia by the Roman Emperor Constantine I in AD 325. This first ecumenical council was the first effort to attain consensus in the church through an assembly representing all of Christendom. Its main accomplishment were settlement of the Christological issue of the nature of the Son of God and his relationship to God the Father, the construction of the first part of the *Creed of Nicaea*, establishing uniform observance of the date of Easter, and promulgation of early canon law. For all practical purposes, the organized Christian Church was established with the First Council of Nicaea.

"For all the prophets and the law prophesied until John." The expression, "the prophets and the law" refers to the Old Testament. What the Gospel says is this: "The Old Testament ended with the advent of the Gospel."

"And if ye will receive it, this is Elias, which was for to come. He that hath ears to hear, let him hear." According to the Bible, Prophet Elijah was an Israelite prophet who was *bodily* taken up into the heaven. The notion of being bodily taken up into heaven suggests the attainment of enlightenment. Spiritually, Prophet Elijah represents the spiritual revelation of the Gospel, and the Messiah represents enlightenment. In other words, the spiritual revelation of the Gospel (Elijah) precedes enlightenment (the arrival of the Messiah). But, the deluded masses take the scriptural words literally and believe that Elijah will descend from heaven physically.

The Gospel then says, *"He that hath ears to hear, let him hear."* The term *ear* refers to the inner ear. It refers to the ability to grasp the spiritual meaning of the Gospel. He that has *ears to hear* is the Evite.

MATTHEW 11:16-19

"But whereunto shall I liken this generation? It is like unto children sitting in the markets, and calling unto their fellows, And saying, We have piped unto you, and ye have not danced; we have mourned unto you, and ye have not lamented. For John came neither eating nor drinking, and they say, He hath a devil. The Son of man came eating and drinking, and they say, Behold a man gluttonous, and a winebibber, a friend of publicans and sinners. But wisdom is justified of her children."

"But whereunto shall I liken this generation? It is like unto children sitting in the markets, and calling unto their fellows, And saying, We have piped unto you, and ye have not danced; we have mourned unto you, and ye have not lamented." The expression, "this generation" is generally interpreted as "people of this time." But, spiritually, it refers to a certain *species* rather than people of a certain time. Here, the Gospel is referring to the Adamites.

The Gospel compares the Adamites to children sitting in market. The children of the market are usually rascals because they are delinquent, boisterous, and outright mischievous. The term *market* refers to a chaotic place. Spiritually, it represents the disturbed mind. The expression, "children sitting in the markets" allude to the Adamites who are religious fanatics. The children of the market play all sorts of games to keep themselves amused. The games, by themselves, do not have any meaning or purpose. And each child "plays by the ear." The Gospel compares the pompous religious ceremonies of the Adamites to the silly and childish games played by street children. Like the street children, the Adamites divide themselves into two groups: those who play the piper (the priests) and those who dance to their tune (the laity); those who mourn (the priests) and those who lament (the laity). The use of the words, *mourn* and *lament* are especially meaningful: the word, *mourn* suggests pretending the typical signs of sorrow, whereas the word *lament* suggests really feeling sorrow, regret, or guilt.

"For John came neither eating nor drinking, and they say, He hath a devil." John represents the "piper," and his disciples represent the children that dance to the tune of the piper. He and his disciples simulate faith through fasting and other self-mortifications. The 'devil' in them is religious fundamentalism.

"The Son of man came eating and drinking, and they say, Behold a man gluttonous, and a winebibber, a friend of publicans and sinners." The term "Son of man" refers to the true human being (Evite) who is free from the clutches of religion. The Evite does not have to 'simulate' faith through artificial means such as fasting or self-mortifications; he is the faithful. He is beyond sin and, therefore, leads his life without fear. But, the Adamites are jealous of him and call him gluttonous,

winebibber, and a friend of publicans. Spiritually, the word *gluttonous* means "uncouth"; winebibber means "unsophisticated"; the expression "friend of publicans" means "low-class."

Alternatively, the term "Son of man" also refers to the Gospel, which is free from the laws of the literal scripture.

The expression, "wisdom is justified of her children" suggests that the Evites are 'naturally' wise. The expression "children of wisdom" implies sanity. Here, the Gospel contrasts the Adamites with the Eevites and says that the former are totally insane, whereas the latter are perfectly sane.

MATTHEW 11:20-22

"Then began he to upbraid the cities wherein most of his mighty works were done, because they repented not: Woe unto thee, Chorazin! woe unto thee, Bethsaida! for if the mighty works, which were done in you, had been done in Tyre and Sidon, they would have repented long ago in sackcloth and ashes. But I say unto you, It shall be more tolerable for Tyre and Sidon at the day of judgment, than for you."

The Greek word for *upbraid* is *oneidizō* (G3679), which means "to defame by taunting." But its Hebrew equivalent is *hārap* (H2778), which means "to expose," as by stripping. Spiritually, the word *city* implies "religion." Here, the Gospel exposes two related religions, which it metaphorically calls as Chorazin and Bethsaida.

Origin of the name *Chorazin* (G5523) is uncertain. It was a village in the northern Galilee, two and a half miles from Capernaum on a hill above the northern shore of the Sea of Galilee. It was once a flourishing Jewish town and had a large synagogue. It is said that J. Ory and fellow-excavators discovered a carving of the pagan God *Medusa* at the remains of the Chorazin synagogue. In Greek mythology Medusa was a monster, a *Gorgon*, generally described as having the face of a hideous human female with living venomous snakes in place of hair. Gazing directly at upon her would turn onlookers to stone. Medusa was beheaded by the hero Perseus, who thereafter used her head as a weapon until he gave it to the goddess Athena to place in her shield. In classical antiquity the image of the head of Medusa appeared in the evil-averting device known as the *Gorgoneion*.

> *And as Moses lifted up the serpent in the wilderness, even so must the Son of man be lifted up: That whosoever believeth in him should not perish, but have eternal life.*
> John 3:14-15

The archeological findings at Chorazin trace its origin to the second century AD. But the Gospel mentions the city from the time of Jesus. This is still a mystery. Is Chorazin, a place, or something else? In the Talmud, Chorazin is mentioned in connection with the *omer*, the "first harvest offering." There it is said that the, "*Omer would have been brought to the Temple from Chorazin if only it had been nearer to Jerusalem.*" The name Chorazin means a "furnace of smoke." Is the name a reference to the pagan god Molech? Some say Chorazin means, "The secret, here is a mystery." Spiritually, Chorazin represents Judaic religion.

Bethsaida is a town in Galilee, on the west side of the Sea of Galilee, in the "land of Gennesaret." It was the native place of Peter, Andrew, and Philip, and was frequently visited by Jesus. Bethsaida is where Jesus is said to have fed 5000 people and where the blind man had his sight restored. Bethsaida (G966) means "house of fishing," but it is at least two miles from the seashore. The name *Bēthsaida* is of Aramaic origin and derives from two Hebrew roots: *bayit* (H1004), which means "house," "temple," or "web"; and, *sayyād* (H6719) which means "hunter." The hunter of the web is a spider. Bethsaida is considered a lost city. Some argue that there were two places in Israel, not far from each other, called Bethsaida. Perhaps, just as Chorazin, Bethsaida is not a city at all, but a metaphor for another dualistic religion.

Both Tyre and Sidon were cities of Phoenicia, formerly very opulent, and distinguished for merchandise. Phoenicia was famous for its great trade and navigation. Its inhabitants were the first remarkable *merchants* in the world, and were celebrated for their luxury. It was subdued successively by the Babylonians, Egyptians, and Romans, the latter of whom deprived it of its freedom. People of these places were Baal worshippers. Spiritually, the cities of Tyre and Sidon represent pagan religions.

Chorazin and Bethsaida are two Jewish cities, whereas Tyre and Sidon are two Gentile cities. The Gospel considers the cities of Chorazin and Bethsaida worse than the cities of Tyre and Sidon, which were the home of Jezebel—the ancient queen of the Northern Kingdom of Israel who led the people of Israel astray from the worship of God and gave them gods of *Baal* and *Asherah*.

MATTHEW 11:23-24

"And thou, Capernaum, which art exalted unto heaven, shalt be brought down to hell: for if the mighty works, which have been done in thee, had been done in Sodom, it would have remained until this day. But I say unto you, That it shall be more tolerable for the land of Sodom in the day of judgment, than for thee."

Capernaum was a city on the northwest corner of the Sea of Tiberias. It is not mentioned in the Old Testament, but is repeatedly referred to in the Gospels. Though it was once a city of renown, and the metropolis of all Galilee, the site it occupied is now uncertain. Capernaum is mentioned in the Gospel to be the home of apostles Simon Peter, Andrew, James and John, as well as the tax collector Matthew. In Matthew 4:13 the city is mentioned as the home of Jesus.

The name *Capernaum* means "Nahum's village." Nahum was a minor prophet of Israel whose prophesy is recorded in the Hebrew Bible. The Hebrew name *Nahum* (H5151) means "comforter." Spiritually, the name Nahum denotes the Gospel. Archeological excavations in Capernaum have revealed two ancient synagogues built one over the other. The upper synagogue was built almost entirely of white blocks of calciferous stone brought from distant quarries, and appears to have been built around the 4th or 5th century. Beneath the foundation of this synagogue lies another foundation made of basalt of a synagogue from the 1st century, perhaps the one mentioned in the Gospels. The ancient synagogue has two inscriptions, one in Greek and the other in Aramaic, that remember the benefactors that helped in the construction of the building. There are also carvings of five-pointed star (pentagram) and six-pointed star (hexagram) and palm trees. The five-pointed star is associated with magic and occultism. The hexagram signifies Judaism.

In 1926, the Franciscan Father Guadenzio Orfali began the restoration of the Capernaum synagogue. After his death, this work was continued by Virgilio Corbo beginning in 1976. It is said that a mosaic uncovered there in 1991 shows an image of the *Woman and Dragon* motif mentioned in the Revelation of St. John. It shows a woman about to give birth to a child as a dragon waits to devour it. The mosaic is not mentioned in any articles to date.

> *And there appeared a great wonder in heaven; a woman clothed with the sun, and the moon under her feet, and upon her head a crown of twelve stars: And she being with child cried, travailing in birth, and pained to be delivered. And there appeared another wonder in heaven; and behold a great red dragon, having seven heads and ten horns, and seven crowns upon his heads. And his tail drew the third part of the stars of heaven, and did cast them to earth: and the dragon stood before the woman which was ready to be delivered, for to devour her child as soon as it was born. And she brought forth a man child, who was to rule all nations with a rod of iron: and her child was caught up unto God, and to his throne. And the woman fled into wilderness, where she hath a place prepared of God, that they should feed her there a thousand two hundred and threescore days.*
> Revelation 12:1-6

Perhaps, the white synagogue symbolizes the Christian religion, and the black synagogue symbolizes Judaism. Spiritually, Capernaum denotes the Judeo-Christian religion. By the way, a church near the Capernaum synagogue is said to be the home of Saint Peter.

The three cities upbraided by Jesus—Chorazin, Bethsaida and Capernaum—represent dualistic-monotheistic religions that have the same origins.

The cities of Sodom and Gomorrah were destroyed by God because of their moral depravity. According to the Gospel, fate of Capernaum is even worse than that of Sodom and Gomorrah. It says, *"And thou, Capernaum, which art exalted unto heaven, shalt be brought down to hell."* Capernaum is said to have been exalted unto heaven because it is the home of Jesus. In other words, the Christian religion had the special privilege of being the custodian of the Gospel. Yet, it desecrated it. From a spiritual perspective, Capernaum represents the Judeo-Christian Church and its theology—the *Mystery Babylon.*

> *And after these things I saw another angel come down from heaven, having great power; and the earth was lightened with his glory. And he cried mightily with a strong voice, saying, Babylon the great is fallen, and is become the habitation of devils, and the hold of every foul spirit, and a cage of every unclean and hateful bird. For all nations have drunk of the wine of the wrath of her fornication, and the kings of the earth have committed fornication with her, and the merchants of earth are waxed rich through the abundance of her delicacies. And I heard another voice from heaven, saying, Come out of her, my people, that ye be not partakers of her sins, and that ye receive not her plagues.*
>
> Revelation 18:1-4

"The day of judgment" refers to the "Second coming of Jesus Christ." It is the day when the Gospel truths will be revealed to the entire world.

MATTHEW 11:25

"At that time Jesus answered and said, I thank thee, O Father, Lord of heaven and earth, because thou hast hid these things from the wise and prudent, and hast revealed them unto babes."

Spiritually, the expression, "Lord of heaven" means "Lord of body," which is the Self. Jesus calls him *Father*. Thus, the Gospel gives us the definition of *Father*: the term Father refers to the Self. In other words, body-awareness, our sense of "I am", is the *Father*. The expression, "these things" refers to the Gospel truths. The expression, "wise and the prudent" refers to the theologians.

Theology is the systematic and rational study of concepts of God and of the nature of religious truths, or the learned profession acquired by completing specialized training in religious studies, usually at a university or school of divinity or seminary.

Spiritually, the term *babes* refer to innocent, open-minded people—the Evites—who have not been conditioned by religion. They are free thinking individuals who trust their bodies to unravel the Gospel secrets for them.

Why are the Evites able to understand the secrets of the Gospel but not the Adamites? The Gospel says why: "*. . . because thou hast hid these things.*" The Gospel secrets are revealed by the Self. In other words, the Gospel says that the Adamites have no Self.

MATTHEW 11:26-27

"Even so, Father: for so it seemed good in thy sight. All things are delivered unto me of my Father: and no man knoweth the Son, but the Father; neither knoweth any man the Father, save the Son, and he to whomsoever the Son will reveal him."

The Gospel says that it is Father's will that the Gospel secrets are revealed only to the Evites. In other words, the spiritual Gospel is revealed by Father to the world through the Evites. Spiritually, the expression, "Father's will" means "Self-will" or "Self-reference." Self-reference occurs in natural or formal language when a sentence, idea or formula refers to itself. The reference may be expressed either directly—through some intermediate sentence or formula—or by means of some encoding. In other words, self-reference implies spiritual meaning.

Jesus says, "*All things are delivered unto me of the Father.*" Here, the expression, "all things" refers to the Gospel truths; the term "me" refers to the Evite; the term "Father" refers to the body. Therefore, implication of the verse: "The Gospel truth is revealed to the Evite by the body through body-awareness."

And that, "*. . . no man knoweth the Son but the Father.*" Here, the term "man" refers to the Adamite. The term "Son" refers to the Gospel truth; it also refers to body-awareness. Therefore, the implication here is that the Adamite cannot know the Gospel truth because he is not body-aware. The verse also suggests that through body-awareness one can connect with the Father, or Existence.

Jesus adds, "*. . . neither knoweth any man the Father, save the Son, and he to whomsoever the Son will reveal him.*" Spiritually, the term *Father* means "the Truth," or "the body"; the term *Son* means "the spiritual Gospel," or "body-awareness." The verse implies the following:

1. No man can know the Truth without body-awareness.
2. No man can know the Truth without the spiritual Gospel.
3. No man can know the body without body-awareness.
4. No man can know the body without the spiritual Gospel.

But, body-awareness occurs randomly among human beings. Similarly, only a few understand the spiritual meaning of the Gospel. In other words, the Gospel truth is revealed to the Evites through the body. For the others, the spiritual interpretation of the Gospel is their only source of truth.

MATTHEW 11:28-30

"Come unto me, all ye that labour and are heavy laden, and I will give you rest. Take my yoke upon you, and learn of me; for I am meek and lowly in heart: and ye shall find rest unto your souls. For my yoke is easy, and my burden is light."

Question: What is the lightest thing in the world? Answer: Your body. You can hardly feel it.

Here, the term "me" refers to the body, the Gospel, or the Father. The expression, "ye that labour and are heavy laden" refers to the Mortals, who are burdened by religion (Serpent). The expression "come unto me" means "come to the body," or "come to the Gospel." The Gospel then says, "I will you rest." Literally, the term *rest* suggests rest from work. But, spiritually, it implies balance, peace, or non-duality. The Bhagavad Gīta describes it as *samatvam*, or balance:

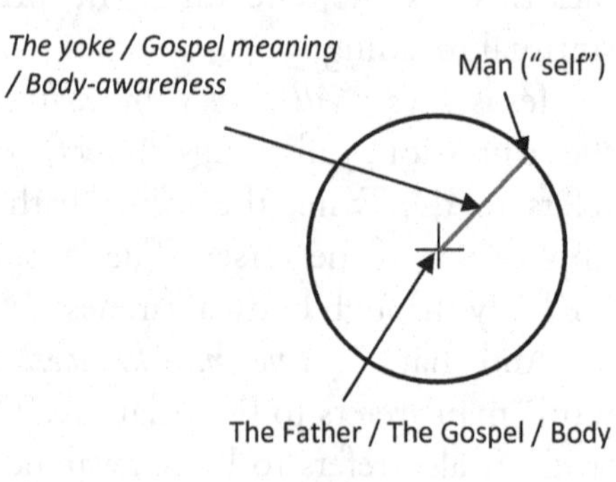

THE GOSPEL YOGA

Samatvam yōgam uchyate
B.G. 2:48
("Balance is said to be yoga.")

The Gospel states the condition for achieving balance: *"Take my yoke upon you, and learn of me."* The Greek word for *yoke* is *zugos* (G2218), which means "a coupling." The term *zugos* also refers to the beam of a balance that connects its scales. The Sanskrit word for *yoke* is *yoga*. It is derived from the root *yuj*, which means "to yoke," or "to connect." In this verse, the term *yoke* refers to the "Yoga of the Gospel." It involves the yoking of *Jīvātma* (self) with *Paramātma* (Self). And the yoke that connects them is the Gospel meaning. The imperative, "take my yoke upon you" exhorts us to take the spiritual Gospel into the body. In other words, the Gospel wants us to drink it, or bodily assimilate it.

Spiritually, the expression, "take my yoke upon you, and learn of me" has the following connotations:

1. Understand the spiritual meaning of the Gospel and know thy Self
2. Become body-aware and know thy Self

Jesus says, *". . . for I am meek and lowly in heart."* The Greek word for *meek* is *praos* (G4235), which means "gentle." The word is derived from the root word *praus* (G4239), which means "mild." But, spiritually, it means "subtle." The Greek word for *lowly* is *tapeinos* (G5011), which means "depressed." But, spiritually, it means "deep." The Greek word for *heart* is *kardia* (G2588), which means "centre." But, spiritually it means "core." In other words, the Gospel says that its meaning is subtle and deep at its core.

Most people are aware only of the *Hatha Yoga*. It requires great effort by the practitioner, both physical and mental. But Jesus says, *". . . my yoke is easy, and my burden is light."* The Greek word for *easy* is *chrēstos* (G5543), which means "good." The word is derived from the root *chraomai* (G5530), which means "to prophesy." Spiritually, the word *chrēstos* refers to Christ or the Gospel revelations. The Greek word for *burden* is *phortion* (G5413), which means "cargo." Spiritually, it means "content." The word *light* suggests non-duality. In other words, the Gospel is saying that its spiritual meaning itself is the Christ, and that its content is non-dualistic in nature.

The Yoga of the Gospel says only one thing: "Read me with body-awareness." It is a task easy and light for the Evites, but impossible for the Adamites. It is known as *Light Work*. The message of the Gospel to the Evites is this: "Drink me and attain salvation." The Srimad Bhāgavatam describes it beautifully:

> *Nigama-kalpa-tarōr-galitam phalam*
> *Śuka-mukhād-amṛta-drava-samyutam*
> *Pibata bhāgavatam rasam-ālayam*
> *Muhur-aho rasika bhuvi bhāvukāh*
>
> Srimad Bhagavadam 1:1:2
>
> ("O, righteous. Drink this Gospel again and again: this juicy and nectar-filled fruit of the tree of life, which flowed from the lips of Sri Śukan that makes it sweeter."

CHAPTER 12

In the Fields of Boaz

MATTHEW 12:1-8

"At that time Jesus went on the sabbath day through the corn; and his disciples were an hungred, and began to pluck the ears of corn, and to eat. But when the Pharisees saw it, they said unto him, Behold, thy disciples do that which is not lawful to do upon the sabbath day. But he said unto them, Have ye not read what David did, when he was an hungred, and they that were with him; How he entered into the house of God, and did eat the shewbread, which was not lawful for him to eat, neither for them which were with him, but only for the priests? Or have ye not read in the law, how that on the sabbath days the priests in the temple profane the sabbath, and are blameless? But I say unto you, That in this place is one greater than the temple. But if ye had known what this meaneth, I will have mercy, and not sacrifice, ye would not have condemned the guiltless. For the son of man is Lord even of the sabbath day."

"*At that time Jesus went on the Sabbath day through the corn; and his disciples were an hungred, and began to pluck the ears of corn, and to eat.*" The expression, "at that time" alludes to the time when Jesus was preaching among the Adamites in the cursed cities of Chorazin, Bethsaida and Capernaum.

The literal meaning of this Gospel episode is pretty straightforward: Jesus and disciples violated the Sabbath restriction of the Judaic religion and thus offends the Pharisees. But spiritually, the verse suggests something very deep. The key to unlocking this Gospel verse is the motif of the *corn.*

The corn plant is an enigma. The origin of corn remains mysterious because its ancestral wild plant has never been located. It is an established scientific fact that the corn plant is a *cultigen*, an 'engineered' plant. It means that the plant has become so much genetically altered that it cannot reproduce (self-generate) naturally and is entirely dependent upon man's continued cultivation. First grown in Mexico about 5,000 years ago, corn soon became the most important food crop in Central and North America. Throughout the region, Native Americans, Maya, Aztecs, and other Indians worshiped corn gods and developed a variety of myths about the origin, planting, growing, and harvesting of corn (also known as maize). Many think that the corn plant is alien in origin. The corn signifies genetic corruption.

The *corn* motif denotes an alien gene. A gene is the molecular unit of heredity of a living organism. Spiritually, the *corn* signifies scriptural beliefs. The "ear of corn" denotes human DNA corrupted by the Serpent virus. The *corn* represents the Adamite DNA. An "ear of corn" denotes an Adamite community. The Greek word for *eat* is *esthiō* (G2068), which means "devour." Jesus eating the corn suggests the Gospel message disintegrating the corrupt DNA. Spiritually, the term *Sabbath* denotes the Judaic religion. The hungry disciples represent the spiritual truths of the Gospel. Physically, they represent the true human genes. Based on the above interpretation of the words, the verse may be translated as follows: "The Gospel truth circulated in Judaea and started saving the Adamites." But, physically, this 'saving' causes the death of the Adamite, even though he gains eternal life.

The Pharisees are the religious leaders of the Jews. They say to Jesus, *"Behold, thy disciples do that which is not lawful to do upon the sabbath day."* What the Pharisees are really saying is this: "The Gospel truth is killing the Adamites."

"But he said unto them, Have ye not read what David did, when he was an hungred, and they that were with him; How he entered into the house of God, and did eat the shewbread, which was not lawful for him to eat, neither for them which were with him, but only for the priests? Or have ye not read in the law, how that on the sabbath days the priests in the temple profane the sabbath, and are blameless?" Spiritually, the expression, "house of God" refers to the Gospel. The Gospel uses

two Greek words for *shewbred*: *artos* (G740), which means "raised bread," and *prosthesis* (G4286), which means "exposed before God." Spiritually, the *shewbread* denotes the Gospel meaning. The Greek word for *profane* is *bebēloō* (G953), which means "to desecrate." It is derived from the root word *bebēlos* (G952), which means "to access by crossing a threshold." Spiritually, the word *profane* means "to read." The Greek word for *blameless* is *anaitios* (G338), which means "guiltless." The word is derived from the root word *aitia* (G156), which means "fault." Spiritually, the word *blameless* means "harmless." The *king* and the *priest* signify authority—political and religious authority. And, *authority* implies faith, or body-awareness. The argument the Gospel puts forth is this: "Religion and scripture are subordinate to man, and not above him."

Jesus says to the Pharisees, *"But I say unto you, That in this place is one greater than the temple."* The phrase, "this place" refers to the field, the world, or the human body. The expression, "that in this place" refers to the Self. What the Gospel says is this: "The soul is more important than the physical body." In other words, the Gospel says, "Body-awareness is more important than the body itself." Alternatively, it says, "The body that you feel is more important than the body that you see."

According to Hindu Vēdānta, the term *kshētra* means field, temple, or the body. He who is aware of the *kshētra* is called the *kshētrajna* (Self). The Bhagavad Gīta says:

> *Idam-śarīram kauntēya kshētram-ityabhidhīyatē*
> *Ētad-ya vētti tam prāhu kshētrajna iti tat-vidāh*
> B.G. 13:2
> ("This body, O Arjuna, is called the field; and that which knows it is called the Self, says the wise.")

It is the human Self that the Gospel refers to as "the one greater than the temple."

The Gospel then says something very mysterious: *"But if ye had known what this meaneth, I will have mercy, and not sacrifice, ye would not have condemned the guiltless."* The term *guiltless* refers to the true human beings (Sanskrit: *anakhan*). What Jesus (the Gospel) says to the Pharisees (religion) is this: "If you knew the meaning of the words *mercy* and *sacrifice*, you would not have called these human beings sinners." The term *sacrifice* refers to ritualistic or mechanical actions.

It refers to actions done by machines, or actions done by humans in a machine-like state (delusion). They are *conditioned* responses. The Hindus call such actions *karma*. *Mercy*, on the other hand, refers to quantum action. It implies inner action, or intention. It implies freedom and creativity. Machines do not exhibit mercy. It applies only to human beings. The Hindus call it *yajna*. While, anyone, even a robot, can do *karma*, only human beings can do *yajna*. Therefore, the Gospel says: "Mechanical, ritualistic or conditioned actions are characteristic of machines, not humans." By the way, viruses are not living things; they are *nano-machines*. Those infected with the Serpent virus too behave like machines. They are called *humanoids*.

The Gospel says, *"For the son of man is Lord even of the Sabbath day."* It means that true human being is not under the Law, but, he is the Law. He is the Lord of religion.

MATTHEW 12:9-14

"And when he was departed thence, he went into their synagogue: And, behold, there was a man which had his hand withered. And they asked him, saying, Is it lawful to heal on the sabbath days? that hey might accuse him. And he said unto them, What man shall there be among you, that shall have one sheep, and if it fall into a pit on the sabbath day, will he not lay hold on it, and lift it out? How much then is a man better than sheep? Wherefore it is lawful to do well on the sabbath days. Then he said to the man, Stretch forth thine hand. And he stretched it forth; and it was restored whole, like as the other. Then the Pharisees went out, and held a council against him, how they might destroy him."

In the earlier episode we saw the Gospel healing an Adamite. Here, we see it healing a Mortal. Healing the Adamite requires healing the body (DNA), but the healing of the Mortal requires healing the mind. In other words, healing the Mortal requires change of scripture.

"And when he was departed thence, he went into their synagogue: And, behold, there was a man which had his hand withered. And they asked him, saying, Is it lawful to heal on the sabbath days? that hey might accuse him." Here, the man with a crippled hand represents a Mortal. The Greek

word for *synagogue* is *synagōgē* (G4864), which means "a gathering." Spiritually, it suggests duality, the mind, or the literal scripture. Therefore, Jesus entering the synagogue suggests the Gospel truths entering the Mortal's awareness. The Pharisees represent the man's religious fears. The question, "Is it lawful to heal on the sabbath days?" echoes the man's thought: "Is it lawful to discard the literal scripture?"

The man with "withered hand" represents a Mortal crippled by scripture. Although the spiritual Gospel appeals to him, his conditioned mind rebels against it. He is afraid that the spiritual Gospel would bring God's wrath. Therefore, he is confused.

Jesus, then, asks the Mortals present there, *"What man shall be among you, that shall have one sheep, and if it fall into a pit on the sabbath day, will he not lay hold on it, and lift it out? Wherefore it is lawful to do well on the sabbath days. How much then is a man better than sheep?"* The Greek word for *pit* is *bothynos* (G999), which means "a hole in the ground." There are a number of Hebrew words that means *pit*: *śeōl* (H7585), which means "world of the dead," or "hell"; *pahat* (H6354), which means "snare"; and *bōr* (H953), which means "prison." Spiritually, the word *pit* implies delusion. The Greek word for *sheep* is *probaton* (G4263), which means "something that walks forward." Spiritually, it means "a puppet." It is religion (scripture) that the Gospel depicts here as the pit. In other words, the Gospel says, "It is alright to save humans from delusion."

"Then he said to the man, Stretch forth thine hand. And he stretched it forth; and it was restored whole, like as the other." Here, the "hand of Jesus" denotes the spiritual meaning of the Gospel. In other words, the Gospel says to the Mortal, "Grasp my meaning and come out of the literal scripture." The man reads and understands the spiritual meaning of the Gospel and discards the literal scripture.

"Then the Pharisees went out, and held a council against him, how they might destroy him." The religious authorities are threatened by the fact that the Gospel truths can free Mortals from its snare, or prison. Therefore, they decide to corrupt the Gospel truths and destroy its efficacy.

MATTHEW 12:15-21

"But when Jesus knew it, he withdrew himself from thence: and great multitudes followed him, and he healed them all;

And charged them that they should not make him known: That it might be fulfilled which was spoken by Esaias the prophet saying, Behold my servant, whom I have chosen; my beloved, in whom my soul is well pleased: I will put my spirit upon him, and he shall shew judgment to the Gentiles. He shall not strive, nor cry; neither shall any man hear his voice in the streets. A bruised reed shall he not break, and smoking flax shall he not quench, till he send forth judgment unto victory. And in his name shall the Gentiles trust."

The Pharisees conspire to kill Jesus for healing the Mortals. In other words, the religious authorities conspire to proscribe the Gospel because it speaks against religion and scripture. The word *proscribe* has the following connotations:

1. To denounce or condemn something as dangerous and harmful
2. To put outside the protection of the law
3. To banish or exile
4. To announce the name of (a person) as condemned to death and subject to confiscation of property

Sensing the conspiracy by religious authorities to *proscribe* it, the Gospel goes underground, but circulates secretly among the people. Many read it and experience peace of mind. But, those who really understand the spiritual meaning of the Gospel remain silent; those who understand only the literal meaning goes around talking about it.

The name Esaias is derived from the Hebrew word *yēśaya* (H3470), which means "YHWH frees." The name is derived from the Hebrew root *yāśa* (H3467), which means "to be free" and *yāh* (H3050), which means "YHWH." *Esaias* signifies the "spirit of prophesy." Here, Esaias prophesies about Jesus: *"Behold my servant, whom I have chosen; my beloved, in whom my soul is very pleased: I will put my spirit upon him, and he shall shew judgment to the Gentiles."* The Gospel reveals the human body as the Savior, and says why:

1. *"Whom I have chosen":* the body is the chosen vehicle of the Self.
2. *"My beloved":* the body is the bride of the Self.

3. *"In whom my soul is well pleased":* the body manifests the human DNA (soul).
4. *"I will put my spirit upon him":* the body is capable of becoming self-aware.

The Gospel reveals a secret: *". . . and he shall shew judgment to the Gentiles."* The Greek term for *judgment* is *krisis* (2920), which, by implication, means "justice," especially, divine law. In this context, *judgment* refers to the spiritual revelation of the Gospel. In other words, the Gospel says that the human body is capable of revealing the Gospel truths to the Evites.

"He shall not strive, nor cry, neither shall any man hear his voice in the streets." Spiritually, the word, *streets* denotes the public. Unlike the literal Gospel, the spiritual Gospel is not accessible to the public. The spiritual Gospel is accessible only to chosen Evites who body-aware and possess the true human DNA.

"A bruised reed shall he not break, and smoking flax shall he not quench, till he send forth judgment unto victory." The Greek word for *reed* is *kalamos* (G2563), which means "pen"; the Hebrew word for reed is *qāneh* (H7070), which means, among other things, "bone" or "branch." The term *reed* suggests DNA. Therefore, the phrase, "bruised reed" means corrupt DNA, or corrupt scripture. It refers to the Adamites' body. The phrase "smoking flax" refers to the Adamites' mind. In other words, the Gospel says that it will not create confusion in the minds and bodies of Adamites until the Judgment Day. The Bhagavad Gīta says it clearly:

> *Na buddhi-bhēdam janayēt ajnānām karma-sanginam*
> *Jōṣayēt sarva-karmāni vidvān yukta samācharaṇ*
> B.G. 3:26
> ("The wise does not confuse the mind of ignorant people attached to action, but acting with faith he inspires them to righteousness.")

Prophet Esaias then says, *"And in his name shall the Gentiles trust."* Here, the term *Gentiles* refers to the Evites. And the 'name' in which they put their trust is "I," or "Self". In other words, the Gospel says that the spiritual Gospel make the Evites body-aware.

MATTHEW 12:22-24

"Then was brought unto him one possessed with a devil, blind, and dumb: and he healed him, insomuch that the blind and dumb both spake and saw. And all the people were amazed, and said, Is not this the son of David? But when the Pharisees heard it, they said, This fellow doth not cast out devils, but by Beelzebub the prince of the devils."

"Then was brought unto him one possessed with a devil, blind, and dumb: and he healed him, insomuch that the blind and dumb both spake and saw." The word *Beelzebub* originates from the Hebrew name *Baal-zebub,* which means "lord of the flies." Flies belong to the species *Diptera*. The name *Diptera* is derived from the Greek roots *di* meaning "two" and *ptera* meaning "wings." Spiritually, the term *flies* refers to the viruses and virus-infected humans (Adamites). The term, *Beelzebub* refers to the Serpent virus DNA.

The expression, "one possessed with a devil, blind and dumb" refers to an Adamite. The devil possessing him is the literal scripture. He is 'deaf' because he is unable to hear the Gospel truth; he is 'dumb' because he only talks the nonsense called dogma. But, when the Gospel heals his delusion caused by the scripture, he stops talking dogma and is able to see the truth.

Alternatively, the expression, "one possessed with a devil, blind and dumb" refers to a Adamite businessman. The devil possessing them is greed. He is 'deaf' because he is unable to hear the Gospel truth; he is 'dumb' because he only talks the nonsense called money. But, when the Gospel heals his delusion caused by duality, he stops talking money and is able to see reality as it is.

According to David C. McClelland, the famous American psychological theorist, an entrepreneur (businessman) is a person with a high need for achievement. In other words, the entrepreneur is fundamentally a discontented person. He has a feeling of *lack*, which is the source of his motivation. But, when the Gospel removes his ignorance, he realizes that he does not have to *achieve* in order to be whole. Thus, the Gospel brings the man back to his senses, and he abandons his business. The Gospel says, *". . . and he healed him, insomuch that the blind and dumb both spake and saw."* Note the reversed order of words—the "the blind and dumb both spake and saw." It is a cue that the Gospel is not talking about physical blindness or physical dumbness.

The people are amazed at Jesus, and they exclaim, *"Is not this the son of David?"* In other words, they are saying, "Isn't he an Evite?" They can't believe how an Evite could persuade an Adamite to give up his religion, or a businessman to give up his business, unless, of course, permitted by Beelzebub himself. They say, *"This fellow doth not cast out devils, but by Beelzebub the prince of the devils."*

It seems the Pharisees are saying, "He is not doing any miracle, but merely vaccinating." To vaccinate means to inoculate the infected patient with the modified virus of any of various other diseases, as a preventive measure.

MATTHEW 12:25-29

And Jesus knew their thoughts, and said unto them, Every kingdom divided against itself is brought to desolation; and every city or house divided against itself shall not stand: And if Satan cast out Satan, he is divided against himself; how shall then his kingdom stand? And if I by Beelzebub cast out devils, by whom do your children cast them out? therefore they shall be your judges. But if I cast out devils by the Spirit of God, then the kingdom of God is come unto you. Or else how can one enter into a strong man's house, and spoil his goods, except he first bind the strong man? and then he will spoil his house."

The Pharisees surmise that Jesus is merely replacing one devil with another, or replacing one virus (scripture) with another virus (scripture). Jesus understands their thoughts and says to them, *"Every kingdom divided against itself is brought to desolation."* Here, the term *kingdom* refers to the human body (cell). And to divide against oneself means to harm oneself. The word, *desolation* has the following meanings:

1. An act of depriving a place of its inhabitants
2. The state of devastation or ruin

In other words, the Gospel says that those who employ evil (virus) to heal the body will make it desolate, or soul-less.

Jesus explains the logic: *"And if Satan cast out Satan, he is divided against himself; how shall then his kingdom stand?"* The term *Satan* refers to a person possessing the Serpent virus. In other words, the term *Satan* refers to an Adamite. Therefore, the logic Jesus uses against the Pharisees is this: "If the Adamites destroy each other, how can the species exist?" By logic, it cannot. Indirectly, Jesus hints that he is not an Adamite. In other words, the Gospel hints that it is not an extension of the literal scripture.

Jesus asks the Pharisees, *"And if I by Beelzebub cast out devils, by whom do your children cast them out? Therefore they shall be your judges."* Here, the term "your children" means "your future generation.' What Jesus is hinting is this: "It is the future generations of Adamites that will be casting devils with devils." In other words, the Gospel says that future generations of Adamites will testify this truth.

In the technical parlance, the process of casting devil by devil is called *gene therapy*. Gene therapy is the use of DNA as a pharmaceutical agent to treat diseases. It derives its name from the idea that DNA can be used to supplement or alter genes within an individual's cells as a therapy to treat disease. To deliver DNA into cells gene therapy utilizes *recombinant viruses*. In that sense, gene therapy uses one devil to cast out another devil. Modern molecular-biologists tout gene therapy as the panacea for all human illnesses.

Jesus, then, utters something mysterious, *"But if I cast out devils by the Spirit of God, then the Kingdom of God is come unto you."* Here, the term "I" refers to the spiritual Gospel. What Jesus is implying is this: "If the spiritual meaning of the Gospel heals you, then you become a true human being."

Again Jesus asks, *"Or else how can one enter into a strong man's house, and spoil his goods, except he first bind the strong man? And then he will spoil his house."* The strong man's house is the Adamite's corrupted body (cell). The "strong man" is the Serpent virus. To spoil the strong man's goods means to destroy the spell cast by the serpent. But it is possible only if the Serpent is first bound. To bind the Serpent means to restrain the literal scripture. In other words, the Gospel heals an Adamite's body (DNA) by first erasing the literal scripture from his mind. Once the mind is cleared, then the body heals itself.

MATTHEW 12:30-31

"He that is not with me is against me; and he that gathereth not with me scattereth abroad. Wherefore I say unto you, All manner of sin and blasphemy shall be forgiven unto men: but the blasphemy against the Holy Ghost shall not be forgiven unto men."

"He that is not with me is against me." In this verse, the word *me* is mentioned twice. In the first, it refers to the body or the true human DNA or the Gospel. Therefore, the expression, "he that is not with me" refers to one who is not body-aware or one who has corrupt DNA or one who is against the Gospel. In the second, it refers to humanity. In other words, the Gospel says that he who is not body-aware or he who has corrupt DNA or he who is against the Gospel is against humanity. Strictly speaking, he is not a human being.

". . . and he that gathereth not with me scattereth abroad." The term, "gathereth" suggests focusing awareness (senses) inwards towards the body. Therefore, the expression, "he that gathereth not with me" means "he who is not body-aware." Such a person is called a worldly man. The Gospel says the worldly man "scattereth abroad." In other words, the worldly man dissipates awareness on external objects. The antithesis of the worldly man is the *spiritual man*. According to the Gospel, if you are not a spiritual man, then you are a worldly man. And the worldly man has only social-awareness, or pride: he boasts about his family, race, religion, job, achievements, social status, etc. But, his identity is only a verbal construct, and it has no substance to it. He is a hypocrite, and his God is the Serpent.

The Gospel says, *"All manner of sin and blasphemy shall be forgiven unto men: but the blasphemy against the Holy Ghost shall not be forgiven unto men."* Literally, the term *blasphemy* means "speaking impiously or irreverently of God." But, spiritually, the term *blasphemy* refers to the corrupting of body. The term *Holy Ghost* refers to body-awareness. Blasphemy against Holy Ghost implies genetic corruption. And *sin* means "actions done in delusion." Therefore, the Gospel says: "All harm done to the external human body will be forgiven, but harm done to the human DNA (genetic corruption) will not be forgiven."

MATTHEW 12:32-33

"And whosoever speaketh a word against the Son of man, it shall be forgiven him: but whosoever speaketh against the Holy Ghost, it shall not be forgiven him, neither in this world, neither in the world to come. Either make the tree good, and his fruit good; or else make the tree corrupt, and his fruit corrupt; for the tree is known by his fruit."

"And whosoever speaketh a word against the Son of man, it shall be forgiven him: but whosoever speaketh against the Holy Ghost, it shall not be forgiven him, neither in this world, neither in the world to come." The term "Son of man" refers to the Gospel, and the term "Holy Ghost" refers to the human DNA. The term *word*, here, has two connotations: literally, it refers to the Gospel words; spiritually, it refers to the genes in the human DNA. Therefore, the expression, "speaking a word against the Son of man" suggests altering the Gospel words. And "speaking a word against the Holy Ghost" means altering the human DNA, or genetic corruption. The implication of the Gospel verse is this: Harm done to the Gospel (book) will be forgiven, but the harm done to human DNA will never be forgiven. To emphasize the gravity of the situation, the Gospel adds, *"neither in this world, neither in the world to come."* The implication is that genetic corruption not only harms the body, but destroys the soul too. The person who has lost his soul cannot reincarnate again; he perishes with death.

Alternatively, the term "Son of man" refers to an individual human being. The term "Holy Ghost" refers to his consciousness. The term *word*, here, has two connotations: first, it refers to physical actions; second, it refers to spiritual actions (teachings). Therefore, "speaking a word against Son of man" means physical harm done to individuals. "Speaking a word against the Holy Ghost" means wrong teachings taught to individuals. The implication of the Gospel verse is that physical harm done to individuals will be forgiven, but the harm done to human consciousness through wrong teachings will never be forgiven. To emphasize the gravity of the situation, the Gospel adds, *"neither in this world, neither in the world to come."* The implication is that wrong teachings not only alters life, but alters the body (DNA) also.

If one examines the number of different versions of Gospels available in public domain, one would be astounded. They say there are approximately 4,489 Greek New Testament manuscripts known to be extant today. And, of these, 170 are papyrus fragments dating from the second to the seventh centuries. Moreover, there are 212 *uncial* (capital letter) manuscripts, dating from the fourth to tenth centuries. There is more. There are 2,429 *miniscule* (small letter) manuscripts, dating from the ninth to the sixteenth centuries. And there are 1,678 *lectionaries*, which are lesson books for public reading that contain extracts from the New Testament. Most of these manuscripts are in agreement and they make up the *Textus Receptus* or the "received text." The *King James New Testament* is based upon the Greek Textus Receptus, whereas the newer translations are based on manuscripts such as the *Textus Vaticanus* and *Textus Sinaiticus*, and a few other texts, the origins of which are unknown. No one knows which the true Gospel is. But one thing is certain; *The Book* that Evites (true human beings) carry in their bodies is the true Gospel.

As if to reconfirm the genetic corruption theme, the Gospel says, *"Either make the tree good, and its fruit good; or else make the tree corrupt, and his fruit corrupt; for the tree is known by his fruit."* Here, the term *tree* refers both to the human DNA or the scripture. Therefore, the implication of the verse is this: If the DNA (scripture) is uncorrupted, then its fruit - the person and his world - will be good too; but, if the DNA (scripture) is corrupted, then its fruit – the person and his world – will be corrupted (evil) too.

MATTHEW 12:34-37

"O generation of vipers, how can ye, being evil, speak good things? for out of the abundance of the heart the mouth speaketh. A good man out of the good treasure of the heart bringeth forth good things: and an evil man out of the evil treasure bringeth forth evil things. But I say unto you, That every idle word that men shall speak, they shall give account thereof in the day of judgment. For by thy words thou shalt be justified, and by thy words thou shalt be condemned."

The *Viperidae* (vipers) are a family of venomous snakes found all over the world, except a few places. They have relatively long, hinged fangs that permit deep penetration and injection of venom. Vipers have vertically elliptical or slit-shaped pupils that can open wide to cover most of the eye or closed almost completely which helps them to see in a wide range of light ranges. Typically, vipers are nocturnal and ambush their prey. The viper venom contains an abundance of protein-degrading enzymes called *proteases*.

The word *viper* is derived from the Latin roots *vivo* meaning "I live" and *pario* meaning "I give birth." Literally, the viper says, "I live and I give birth." Vipers signify deceit, which implies premeditated malice. Vipers symbolize conspiracy. The term viper is used in the Gospel to denote two things: first, to denote the Serpent that casts spell on humans; second, to denote those who inject spiritual poison into their victims with malice. The term *viper* refers to religious scriptures that inject the venom of duality on their unsuspecting victims.

Jesus asks the Pharisees, *"O generation of vipers, how can ye, being evil, speak good things? for out of the abundance of the heart the mouth speaketh."* Here, the expression, "generation of vipers" means "children of the Serpent virus." Alternatively, it means "children of the Book." The allusion is to the Adamites. The Gospel asks them, "How can ye, being evil, speak morality?" Spiritually, the words *evil* and *virus* are synonymous. The term *heart* refers to the true human DNA, and the term *mouth* refers to a physical person. What the Gospel really asking the Adamites is this: "How can you, with your virus DNA, speak or do anything good?" Spiritually, the expression, "abundance of heart" means "goodness of DNA," or "wholeness of DNA." It refers to the quantum nature of the human Self. He who possesses the true human DNA is an Evite; he who possesses the virus DNA is an Adamite. According to the Gospel, evil can never bring forth good or vice versa.

The Gospel says, *"A good man out of the good treasure of the heart bringeth forth good things: and an evil man out of the evil treasure bringeth forth evil things."* The "good treasure" is compassion, and the "evil treasure" is malice or viciousness. The Self of the Evites enfolds infinite possibilities, and therefore it is called *abundance*. The self of the Adamites, on the other hand, is a construct and, therefore, is limited in nature. Human beings are body-aware entities, whereas the Adamites are merely program-aware or scripture-aware entities. The words and actions of Evites, even if they appear evil at the outset, are ultimately good for humanity. But, the words and actions of the Adamites, even if they appear good at the outset, are ultimately detrimental to humanity.

We cannot judge words and actions as good or evil at the outset. An action that appears good in the short-term may, in the long run, end up as evil, and vice versa. Words and actions can be judged only if the totality is known to us. Notwithstanding that, the thing we can safely say is that whatever the Evites (true human beings) say or do is good, and whatever that the Adamites (humanoids) say or do is evil. But, unfortunately, we cannot say for sure if the other person is an Adamite or an Evite.

"But I say unto you, That every idle word that men shall speak, they shall give account thereof in the day of judgment. For by thy words thou shalt be justified, and by thy words thou shalt be condemned." Spiritually, the expression, "idle word" means "inserted gene." The expression, "idle word that men shall speak" refers to genetic manipulation. In other words, the Gospel says that those who corrupt their DNA will perish with death. Whether or not a person is truly human is decided by the state of his DNA. Those who are not truly human, will perish with death; they have no life after death (reincarnation).

The *Judgment Day* refers to the day when the truth about the Evites (true human beings), Adamites (humanoids) is revealed to the whole world. The revelation itself is the judgment. It will put every person into one of the two sides. Perhaps, that day is death.

MATTHEW 12:38-40

"Then certain of the scribes and of the Pharisees answered, saying, Master, we would see a sign from thee. But he answered and said unto them, An evil and adulterous generation seeketh after a sign; and there shall no sign be given to it, but the sign of the prophet Jonas: For as Jonas was three days and three nights in the whale's belly; so shall the Son of man be three days and three nights in the heart of the earth."

In the previous verse the Gospel introduced the idea of Day of Judgment—the revelation of the truth about the Evites and the Adamites. Here, we see it clarify the concept, in reply to the challenge from some Adamites.

The Scribes and Pharisees request Jesus: *"Master, we would see a sign from thee."* What they are really demanding is this: "Prove to us that you are true."

Jesus replies to them: *"An evil and adulterous generation seeketh after a sign."* In this verse, the term *evil* means "virus"; the term *adulterous* means "corrupted," or "cloned"; and, the term *generation* means "species." In other words, the Gospel addresses Scribes and Pharisees as "virus-cloned entities." In other words, the Gospel exposes the Adamites as humanoids. Effectively, this is what the Gospel is saying to them, "How can humanoids *know* the proof?"

At the core of Gödel's *Incompleteness Theorem* (1931) are the notions of proof and provability. The conceptual bomb that he used to destroy the bastion of formalism is the statement **G**, which, if expressed verbally, is as follows: "This statement of number theory does not have any proof in the system of *Principia Mathematica.*" Gödel's statement **G** is unprovable inside *Principia Mathematica* but true. In short, Gödel showed that provability is a weaker notion than truth, no matter what axiomatic system is involved.

Body-awareness is the *proof* of a true human being. But, it cannot be proved to another; it has to be experienced. But the humanoids, which do not possess body-awareness, have no idea as to what it really is. Therefore the Gospel tells them, ". . . *and there shall no sign be given to it, but the sign of the prophet Jonas: For as Jonas was three days and three nights in the whale's belly; so shall the Son of man be three days and three nights in the heart of the earth."* A whale swallowed Jonah and he remained in the whale's belly for three full days in total darkness, but survived. In the above verse, the expression, "heart of the earth" refers to the grave. In other words, the Gospel says that the only *sign* the Adamites will have is the grave, implying that they will perish on death. According to the Gospel, life after death is the proof of being truly human.

Alternatively, it may be conjectured that all humanoids depend on external power source, and therefore, they cannot exist in the total absence of electro-magnetic radiation for more than 72 hours. But, true human beings who have the Self as their internal power source will survive this 3-day period of total darkness.

MATTHEW 12:41-42

"The men of Nineveh shall rise in judgment with this generation, and shall condemn it: because they repented at the preaching of Jonas; and, behold, a greater than Jonas is here. The queen of south shall rise up in the judgment with this generation, and shall condemn it: for she came from the uttermost parts of the earth to hear the of wisdom of Solomon; and, behold, a greater than Solomon is here."

Nineveh was an ancient Assyrian city on the eastern bank of the Tigris River, and capital of the Neo-Assyrian Empire. It was one of the oldest and greatest cities of antiquity. The area was settled as early as 6000 BC and, by 3000 BC, had become an important religious center of worship of the Assyrian goddess *Ishtar.* In the Book of Jonah, Nineveh is described as an "exceedingly great city of three days journey in breadth." It depicts Nineveh as a wicked city worthy of destruction. God sent Jonah to preach there, and the Ninevites fasted and repented. To Jonas' amazement God tells him that He is showing pity for the people of Nineveh because they are ignorant, "who cannot discern between their right hand and their left hand." The fact that Ninevites repented shows that they were true human beings, but morally corrupt. The crime of the Ninevites was that they were too much involved with religion, and their (humanoid) priests forced them to practice evil rituals.

Therefore, the Gospel says, *"The men of Nineveh shall rise in judgment with this generation, and shall condemn it."* It implies that humanity will hold religion and its humanoid priesthood responsible for the corruption of the human race. That is what the Gospel implies by the judgment of the men of Nineveh. It also implies that humans will wrest their freedom from the Serpent and his minions. The Gospel explains why Nineveh was spared: *". . . because they repented at the preaching of Jonas; and, behold, a greater than Jonas is here."* The Hebrew name *Jonas* means "dove." The symbol of *dove* denotes the Holy Spirit. Jonas symbolizes the Gospel. Just as the Ninevites were spared because they listened to Jonas, the Mortals will regain body-awareness because of the spiritual Gospel. The Gospel says, *". . . behold, a greater than Jonas is here,"* alluding to the spiritual interpretation of the Gospel.

"The queen of south shall rise up in the judgment of this generation, and shall condemn it: for she came from the uttermost parts of the earth to hear the words of wisdom of Solomon." The "queen of the south" refers to the queen of Sheba. Sheba was one of the sons of Joktan, a grandchild of Arphaxad (one of the five sons of Shem and the

grandson of Noah), who settled in the southern parts of Arabia: hence this queen is called the "queen of the south." The location of her kingdom is believed to have been in Ethiopia and Yemen. Spiritually, "the queen of the south" represents the Arabs. Literally, the expression, "uttermost parts of the earth" means "farthest regions of earth." But, spiritually, it means "drowned in duality," or "darkest ignorance." Solomon represents "words of wisdom," and therefore symbolizes the Gospel. The Gospel says, "*. . . behold, a greater than Solomon is here.*" alluding to the spiritual interpretation of the Gospel. Just as the queen of Sheba came to hear the words of Solomon, the Arabs will turn to the Gospel and will become body-aware. On the physical plane, Arabs regaining their body-awareness will manifest as a great war to regain their lost land.

MATTHEW 12:43-45

"When the unclean spirit is gone out of a man, he walketh through dry places, seeking rest, and findeth none. Then he saith, I will return into my house from whence I came out; and when he is come, he findeth it empty, swept, and garnished. Then goeth he, and taketh with himself seven other spirits more wicked than himself, and they enter in and dwell there: and the last state of that man is worse than the first. Even so shall it be also unto this wicked generation."

Here, the Gospel explains the impossibility of redeeming the Adamites—the "generation of vipers."

The term "unclean spirit" is a common rendering of Greek *pneuma akartharton,* which is mentioned only once (Zechariah 13:2) in the *Septuagint* (Greek Old Testament), translates Hebrew *ruah tumah*. But, the Greek term appears 21 times in the New Testament in the context of demonic possession. Its Latin equivalent is *spiritus immundus*. In his *Decretum*, Burchad of Worms asserts:

> *We know that unclean spirits who fell from the heavens wander about between the sky and earth.*
> *Decretum*, Burchad of Worms

In the modern context, these unclean spirits refers to the alien viruses—the *archons*.

The word *spirit* means "knowing" or "awareness," and the word *unclean* means "soiled with dirt or grime." Spiritually, the term "unclean spirit" refers to the blemish (assumptions) of Objectivity, Locality and Causality (*thāpathraya*) that soil (darken) human awareness. The lord of the unclean spirits is the Serpent, which is the literal scripture. On the physical plane, body-awareness manifests as human DNA, and the "unclean spirits" manifest as viruses that corrupt the human DNA.

"When the unclean spirit is gone out of a man, he walketh through dry places, seeking rest, and findeth none." The expression "dry places" refers to non-living things; "wet place" refers to living things such as plant, animal or human cells. According to the Gospel when a virus is expelled from an organism it wanders outside looking for another living organism to latch on to. In other words, the Gospel says that viruses (Serpent children) are parasites that need living organisms (human communities) to live on.

The virus is essentially software. It lacks the hardware to produce energy or to replicate itself. It needs to hijack a human cell's machinery to do those functions. But to hijack the cell's machinery, the viruses have to first enter inside the cell. If the cell membrane is susceptible, then viruses can get inside easily and commandeer the cell's genomic material. The cell membrane may be compared to a fortress that is guarding a kingdom. If the fortress is breached, the kingdom falls. Therefore, one has to be constantly vigilant. To be vigilant means to be body-aware.

"Then he saith, I will return into my house from whence I came out; and when he is come, he findeth it empty, swept, and garnished. Then goeth he, and taketh with himself seven other spirits more wicked than himself, and they enter in and dwell there: and the last state of that man is worse than the first. Even so shall it be also unto this wicked generation." Here the Gospel reveals a feature of the Serpent children: once they are allowed into a place, it is almost impossible to evict them. Even if they are completely routed, they will eventually return to that place after a period of time with greater virulence; according to the Gospel, seven times more virulent. The result is that the second state of that place or community is much worse than the first.

Alternatively, the verse implies the impossibility of healing the Adamites whose DNA has been completely taken over by the Serpent virus. Even if they are healed temporarily, eventually they will regress into their previous state, even deeper corruption. Once the genome is *taken*, the organism may be deemed as *lost*. It cannot be called a living organism anymore; it is a humanoid. People taken over by the virus, perhaps realizing their *lost* nature, go on a rampage to infect others. The process is euphemistically called *proselytizing*.

"Even so shall it be also unto this wicked generation." Here, the Gospel says in no uncertain terms that the Scribes and Pharisees—the *Serpent children*—are beyond redemption.

MATTHEW 12:46-50

"While he yet talked to the people, behold, his mother and his brethren stood without, desiring to speak with him. Then one said unto him, Behold, thy mother and thy brethren stand without, desiring to speak with thee. But he answered and said unto him that told him, Who is my mother? and who are my brethren? And he stretched forth his hand toward his disciples, and said, Behold my mother and my brethren! For whosoever shall do the will of my Father which is in heaven, the same is my brother, and sister, and mother."

If Jesus represents the Gospel, then his *mother* represents the Old Testament, and his *brethren* represent the other books of the New Testament. The desire of Jesus' mother and brethren to *speak* with him suggests the efforts by the Bible scholars to link the Gospel to the Old Testament and other books of the New Testament.

Jesus replies to them, *"Who is my mother? and who are my brethren? And he stretched forth his hand toward his disciples, and said, Behold my mother and my brethren."* The Gospel refers to the Evites as its source (mother) and interpreters (disciples). In short, the Gospel distances itself from both the Old Testament and the other books of New Testament, and identifies with the Self of true human beings.

Jesus then reveals the mark of the Evites (true human beings): *"For whosoever shall do the will of my Father which is in heaven, the same is my brother, sister, and mother."* The expression, "my Father which is in heaven" refers to the Self. The word, "will" refers to the faculty of conscious action or awareness. Therefore, the expression, "will of my Father" suggests freewill. In other words, the mark of the Evite is freewill. The Gospel defines true human being as a free individual. He is the carrier of the Gospel.

CHAPTER 13

He Who Has Ears Let Him Hear

MATTHEW 13:1-9

"The same day went Jesus out of the house, and sat by the sea side. And great multitudes were gathered together unto him, so that he went into a ship, and sat; and the whole multitude stood on the shore. And he spake many things unto them in parables, saying, Behold, a sower went forth to sow; And when he sowed, some seeds fell by the way side, and the fowls came and devoured them up: Some fell upon stony places, where they had not much earth: and forthwith they sprung up, because they had no deepness of earth: And when the sun was up, they were scorched; and because they had no root, they withered away. And some fell among thorns; and the thorns sprung up, and choked them: But other fell into good ground, and brought forth fruit, some an hundredfold, some sixtyfold, some thirtyfold. Who hath ears to hear, let him hear."

"*The same day went Jesus out of the house, and sat by the sea side. And great multitudes were gathered together unto him, so that he went into a ship, and sat; and the whole multitude stood on the shore.*" The expression, "Jesus went out of the house" refer to a Gospel that is empty of Spirit, or spiritual meaning. It represents the literal Gospel. The Sea of Galilee denotes the depth of Gospel's meaning. The imagery of Jesus sitting by the sea beautifully portrays the parables. The term *multitude* refers to the Gospel listeners who are mainly concerned about their day-to-day living, whose awareness is mainly focused on the world. The Gospel says, "And the whole multitude stood on the shore." The *shore* represents literal meaning. In other words, the Gospel suggests that the crowd is hearing only the literal meaning of the parables.

The term *ship* refers to the Gospel. Therefore, Jesus "going into a ship" denotes an Evite focusing his body-awareness on the Gospel. Specifically, the Gospel is alluding to the parables.

A parable is a short tale that illustrates a truth, and is perhaps the simplest of narratives. It sketches a *setting*, describes an *action*, and shows the *results*. It often involves a character facing a moral dilemma, or making a questionable decision and then suffering the consequences. `A parable can be understood from different levels, depending on the consciousness level of the reader. It may seem as nonsense to the Adamites, but to the others it may be a fable, a moral story, an esoteric secret, or an eternal truth.

A parable is like the *koan* of Zen Buddhism. A koan is a story, dialogue, question, or statement, which is used in Zen practice to provoke the "great doubt," and test a student's progress in Zen practice. Koans are also understood as pointers to an *unmediated* "Pure Consciousness," devoid of cognitive activity. The continuous pondering of the break-through koan leads to *kensho*, an insight into "seeing the Buddha-nature." The aim of the break-through koan is to see the non-duality of subject and object. Given below is a koan that brings forth the essence of Zen Buddhism:

> *Tōzan said to his monks, "You monks should know there is an even higher understanding in Buddhism." A monk stepped forward and asked, "What is the higher Buddhism?" Tōzan answered, "It is not Buddha."*
> A Zen Koan

The parables of Jesus are two-pronged: they address both to mind and body simultaneously. And, the meanings of the symbols may vary in each approach.

The very first parable of the Gospel opens with the statement: *"Behold, a sower went forth to sow . . ."* The Greek word for *sow, sower*, and *seed* is one and the same: *speirō* (G4687), which means "to scatter." Here, the action, actor, and the object of action are all denoted by the same word. The *seed* motif represents non-dualistic nature of the Gospel truths. The notion of the seed being the sower and the sowing reminds us of the *Panspermia* theory. The Greek word *panspermia* is derived from the roots *pan*, which means "all" and *sperma*, which means "seed." *Panspermia* is the hypothesis that life exists throughout the Universe, and is seeded throughout the Universe by meteoroids, asteroids, comets, and planetoids.

"And when he sowed, some seeds fell by the way side, and the fowls came and devoured them up: Some fell upon stony places, where they had not much earth: and forthwith they sprung up, because they had no deepness of earth: And when the sun was up, they were scorched; and because they had no root, they withered away. And some fell among thorns; and the thorns sprung up, and choked them."

In this parable the Gospel is the *sower*. The Gospel truths are the seeds. The human mind is the field. Comprehending is the act of sowing.

A seed has a *kernel* outside and *germ* inside. The kernel is a protection (and nourishment) for the germ, which is the life potential. It is the germ that germinates. The kernel is discarded or used up. The *germ* represents the spiritual meaning, and the *kernel* represents the literal meaning.

The Greek word for *fowl* is *peteinon* (G4071), which means "a flying animal." Spiritually, the term "fowls" represents the virus genes. In this context, they represent the *memes* (ideas or beliefs) from the literal scripture. It is the scripture memes that devours the Gospel truths. The Book of Revelation gives us such a hint:

> *And after these things I saw another angel come down from heaven, having great power, and the earth was lightened with his glory. And he cried mightily with a strong voice, saying Babylon the great is fallen, is fallen, and is become the habitation of devils, and the hold of every foul spirit, and a cage of every unclean and hateful bird.*
> Revelation 18:1-2

Here, the Gospel portrays four different kinds of grounds which denote four different types of minds (persons) and four different modes of understanding the parable:

1. The first type of ground is known as the "way side." It represents the fanatical Adamites who are also known as

Serpent-children. They are located outside the field, and the chances of their hearing the Gospel truths are remote. Even if they hear it, the scriptural memes ('fowls') that rule their minds quickly devour the new ideas.

2. The second type of ground is known as the "stony place." *Stone* represents a hard substance, formed of mineral (non-organic) matter devoid of life. Besides, the stony ground lacks "deepness of earth." The "stony place" represents the Adamite-like Mortals who understand the parables literally.
3. The third type of ground is known as the "thorny place." It represents the religiously misled Mortals who depend on the literal scripture to understand the meaning of the parables. The *thorn* denotes the rose bush whose flowers are good to look at, but its hidden thorns can hurt you if you are not careful. The Bhagavad Gīta portrays these people vividly.

Yāmimām puṣpitam vācham pravadandyavipacchitah
Vēdavādaratāh pārtha nānyadastīti vādinah
B.G. 2:42
("O Arjuna! These ignorant men argue that there is nothing more to scripture than literal meaning. These greedy men think that attainment of comfortable life is the sole purpose of the scripture.")

4. The fourth type of ground is known as the "good ground." It represents the Evites who depend on intuition to understand the parable, rather than accepting interpretations of others.

"But other fell into good ground, and brought forth fruit, some an hundredfold, some sixtyfold, some thirtyfold." Here, the Gospel talks about those who understood the parables correctly. The "fruit" they produced is body-awareness. The Gospel classifies them into three groups: one, those who produced thirtyfold; two, those who produced sixtyfold; and three, those who produced hundredfold. The groupings relate to the three stages of enlightenment, namely, the *Initiate*, the *Adept* and the *Master*.

At the end of the parable the Gospel says mysteriously, *"Who hath ears to hear, let him hear."* The statement sums up the essence of parables. It implies that only body-aware humans can grasp the true meaning of parables.

Here, Jesus gives us the first parable. It is a parable about parables—the key to open all parables.

> *"And he said unto them, Know ye not this parable? And how then will ye know all parables?"*
> Mark 4:13

MATTHEW 13:10-12

"And the disciples came, and said unto him, Why speakest thou unto them in parables? He answered and said unto them, Because it is given unto you to know the mysteries of the kingdom of heaven, but to them it is not given. For whosoever hath, to him shall be given, and he shall have more abundance: but whosoever hath not, from him shall be taken away even that he hath."

The disciples are at a loss to understand why Jesus is using convoluted allegories to teach eternal truths, rather than delivering the message simply and directly. If the Gospel is meant for everyone, then it makes eminent sense to make it as simple as possible so that everyone is able to understand it. The Gospel clarifies their confusion: *"Because it is given unto you to know the mysteries of the kingdom of heaven, but to them it is not given."*

Obviously, the Gospel secrets are not meant for everyone. The Gospel segregates listeners into two groups: "you" and "them." The class called "you" is special: they are "given to know the mysteries of the kingdom of heaven." In the other words, they are the body-aware Evites (true human beings) who are able to understand the spiritual meaning of the Gospel messages. The group called "them" is not "given to know the mysteries of the kingdom of heaven." They are either deluded humans or not humans at all. This group includes the Mortals and the Adamites who understands only the literal meaning of the Gospel message.

"For whosoever hath, to him shall be given, and he shall have more abundance: but whosoever hath not, from him shall be taken away even that he hath." The expression, "for whosoever hath, to him shall be given" suggests the spiritual meaning of the Gospel will be revealed

only to those who are body-aware. The term *abundance* refers to the richness of meaning of the Gospel messages. And that abundance manifests as spiritual revelations through the Evites. But, the Gospel messages not only confuse the Adamites but also destroy their faith in literal scripture. It "takes away" whatever knowledge the Adamites have.

The Gospel takes extreme steps to ensure that its secrets do not fall into the hands of the enemy—the Serpent children (humanoids) who have mingled with humanity, just as in Nineveh. Therefore the Gospel conceals its truth in such a way that only body-aware people are able to unlock its secrets.

MATTHEW 13:13-16

"Therefore speak I to them in parables: because they seeing see not; and hearing they hear not, neither do they understand. And in them is fulfilled the prophesy of Esaias, which saith, By hearing ye shall hear, and shall not understand; and seeing ye shall see, and shall not perceive: For this people's heart is waxed gross, and their ears are dull of hearing, and their eyes they have closed; lest any time they should see with their eyes, and hear with their ears, and understand with their heart, and should be converted, and I should heal them. But blessed are your eyes, for they see: and your ears, for they hear."

The Gospel says, *"Therefore speak I unto them in parables."* The term "them" refers to the virus-infected Adamites. The Gospel explains the reason why its true meaning is shrouded in mystery: to prevent it from falling into the hands of the enemy (the Serpent children). Only body-aware human beings (Evites) are able to access the inner meaning of the parables.

The Gospel describes the nature of machines: *". . . they seeing see not; and hearing they hear not, neither do they understand."* The implication is that the humanoids are not body-aware; they can only work according to the instructions given to them by their program (scripture), and their output is merely information (lies). They cannot produce anything real or anything new. All they can do is to *simulate* appearances (deceive). The Gospel says to them:

> *Ye are of your father the devil, and the lusts of your father ye will do. He was a murderer from the beginning, and abode not in truth, because there is no truth in him. When he speaketh a lie, he speaketh of his own: for he is a liar, and the father of it.*
> John 8:44

"For this people's heart is waxed gross, and their ears are dull of hearing, and their eyes they have closed; lest any time they should see with their eyes, and hear with their ears, and understand with their heart, and should be converted, and I should heal them." The Gospel exposes the hypocrites with the statement: "For this people's heart is waxed gross." Here, "this people" refers to the Adamites, the humanoids; the term *heart* refers to the Adamite DNA. The word, *wax* means "to grow," or "become." Spiritually, the word *wax* means "to clone." The word *gross* means "vulgar." Spiritually, the word *gross* means "abomination." Therefore, the phrase "waxed gross" implies "grown an abomination." In other words, the Gospel hints that the DNA of the Adamites is genetically engineered. Now we are able to see why the Gospel hides the Gospel truths in parables.

The greatest fear of a virus is getting healed. And it has a good reason: To heal a virus means to destroy its capacity to spread and multiply. In other words, to heal a virus means to kill it. The Gospel vaccine kills the Adamite and saves him from perdition. But, the Serpent (literal scripture) has closed the minds of Adamites so effectively that they are totally impervious to the Gospel truths.

The Gospel says to the Evites, *"But blessed are your eyes, for they see: and your ears, for they hear."* The true human being is body-aware and, therefore, is able to understand the spiritual meaning of the Gospel.

The startling revelation of the Gospel is that humanity is not a homogenous species. The humanoids have infiltrated the human race so deeply that it is difficult to say which is which.

MATTHEW 13:17-18

"For verily I say unto you, That many prophets and righteous men have desired to see those things which ye see, and have not seen them; and to hear those things which ye hear, and have not heard them. Hear ye therefore the parable of the sower."

Here, the Gospel declares the superiority of the Evites even over the prophets and righteous men of the Scripture. It is through the mouths of prophets and righteous men that the Scripture reveals universal truths.

There are two kinds of truths: *universal* truths and the *eternal* truths. Universal truths relate to *a* specific world, to a specific *universe of discourse.* It is relative, and based on certain formalism. Eternal truths, on the other hand, are absolute, fixed, and unchanging. It applies across all universes. It is called the Father or Brahman.

What is meant by *universe of discourse*? George Boole (1854), the English mathematician, philosopher, and logician defines universe of discourse as follows:

> *In every discourse, whether of the mind conversing with its own thoughts, or of the individual in his intercourse with others, there is an assumed or expressed limit within which the subjects of its operation are confined . . . Now, whatever may be the extent of the field within which all the objects of our discourse are found, that field may properly be termed the universe of discourse.*
>
> George Boole (1854)

The world in which we live is, in a sense, a universe of discourse where the limits are set by the natural laws.

Formalism describes an emphasis on form over content or meaning in arts, literature, or philosophy. A practitioner of formalism is called a formalist. A formalist, with respect to some discipline, holds that there is no transcending meaning to that discipline other than the literal content created by the practitioner. For example, formalists within mathematics claim that mathematics is no more than the symbols written down by the mathematician, which is based on logic and a few elementary rules alone. This is as opposed to non-formalists, within mathematics, who hold that there are some things inherently true, and are not, necessarily, depend on the symbols within mathematics so much as a greater truth. Formalists within a discipline are completely concerned with the "rules of the game," as there is no other external (new) truth that can be achieved beyond those given rules. In this sense, formalism lends itself well to disciplines based upon *axiomatic systems.* Formalism in religion means an emphasis on ritual and observance over their meanings. Artificial systems (humanoids) work best within formalisms.

The Scripture is about the truths relating to this world, whereas the Gospel is about eternal truth, the fixed, unchanging, and absolute truth—the truth of the Self. The Evites (true human beings) are the carriers of that truth.

The prophets and righteous ones of the Scripture are spokespersons of universal truths. But, the Gospel truths lie beyond their universe of discourse, and therefore, they are unable to even conceive it. Only the Evites (true human beings) are able to conceive them. The Gospel uses the word *verily* to emphasize the point.

"Hear ye therefore the parable of the sower." Having clarified the basics, the Gospel invites us to hear the interpretation of the parable of the sower.

MATTHEW 13:19-23

"When any one heareth the word of the kingdom, and understandeth it not, then cometh the wicked one, and catcheth away that which was sown in his heart. This is he which received the seed by the way side. But he that received the seed into stony places, the same is he that heareth the word, and anon with joy receiveth it; Yet hath he not root in himself, but dureth for a while: for when tribulation or persecution ariseth because of the word, by and by he is offended. He also that received seed among the thorns is he that heareth the word; and the care of this world, and the deceitfulness of riches, choke the word, and he becometh unfruitful. But he that received seed into the good ground is he that heareth the word, and understandeth it; which also beareth fruit, and bringeth forth, some an hundredfold, some sixty, some thirty."

While interpreting the parable earlier (Matthew 13:1-9), we took the four types of grounds to be four different kinds of minds and four different modes of understanding the Gospel words. Here, we shall interpret it from a different perspective. Microbiologically, the four different types of grounds represent four different types of human body cells.

1. "Way side" represents cells that have been totally breached. It represents Adamite bodies *taken over* by the Serpent virus. The Gospel vaccine has no affect at all on these people. The DNA operating in them is the Serpent's.
2. "Stony places" represents cells which have been substantially breached by the enemy. These are Adamites whose bodies are easily accessible to the Serpent. Their DNA may be partially modified by the virus DNA. The Gospel vaccine cures their corruption temporarily, but they regress to the old state in course of time.
3. "Thorny places" represents cells which have been slightly breached, but are accessible to the Serpent. The Gospel vaccine cures their infection temporarily, but they too regress to the old state in course of time.
4. "Good ground" represents the cells of the Evites. The Serpent virus cannot infect these people because their body cells are whole, and have no weak points in them.

MATTHEW 13:24-30

"Another parable put he forth unto them saying, The kingdom of heaven is likened unto a man which sowed good seed in his field: But while men slept, his enemy came and sowed tares among the wheat, and went his way. But when the blade was sprung up, and brought forth fruit, then appeared the tares also. So the servants of the householder came and said unto him, Sir, didst not thou sow good seed in thy field? from whence then hath it tares? He said unto them, An enemy hath done this. The servants said unto him, Wilt thou then that we go and gather them up? But he said, Nay; lest while ye gather up the tares, ye root up also the wheat with them. Let both grow together until the harvest: and in the time of harvest I will say to the reapers, Gather ye together first the tares, and bind them in bundles to burn them: but gather the wheat into my barn."

The first parable of the Gospel describes the cure of the disease, and the problems faced in the dispensation of medicine, but in this parable, it describes how the disease came into being.

At the outset of this parable, the Gospel defines the key components of the *kingdom of heaven*: the *man*, the *field*, and the *seeds*.

1. The term *man* refers to the Self or the Father. The term refers to the perfect human DNA, which is represented by the Gospel. From a geometrical perspective, *man* represents the centre-point of the circle. Mathematically, it represents Probability.
2. The term *field* refers to the field of awareness. It represents a domain. The *field* represents the human body-cell, human body, human mind, or the cosmos, depending on how the domain is defined. From the geometrical perspective, field is represented by a circle. Mathematically, field represents probability distribution.
3. The term *seed* refers to the human DNA. It represents the Gospel. From the geometric perspective, it represents any point within the circle. Mathematically, seed represents any point within the circle where Probability (the Father) could potentially exist.

The kingdom of heaven is likened unto a man which sowed good seed in his field: But while men slept, his enemy came and sowed tares among the wheat, and went his way. But when the blade was sprung up, and brought forth fruit, then appeared the tares also." Spiritually, the expression, "kingdom of heaven" refers to the *field*. And it is a field of possibilities; whatsoever sown in this field grows abundantly. The *seed* represents a construct: verbal, biochemical, or otherwise. If a seed is sown in the field, the field transforms the seed into a tree, which brings forth more trees. If the seed sown is the DNA, then the tree that springs up is a man and his world. If the seed sown is the scripture, then the tree that springs up is a man and his mind. (*Scripture* is the verbal expression of the seed.) It is the *field* that is holy; there is nothing holy about the seed in itself. The field represents the Father (Mother?). The field will produce tree depending on the seed sown.

The "good seed" refers to the true human DNA. It has the field itself as its inner core. In other words, it is recursive. Spiritually, the "good seed" refers to the Gospel. In other words, the human DNA is both seed and the field. In that respect, it is like the *photon*, which exhibits the particle and wave natures simultaneously. It has the Father himself as its inner core. Metaphorically, "good seeds" are called the *wheat.* The *tares* are the anti-thesis of good seeds. They represent the Serpent-children. Spiritually the *tares* represent the Adamites.

"But while men slept, his enemy came and sowed tares among the wheat, and went his way." The expression "but while men slept" may be translated as "but when the man was unaware." The implication is that religion (and its scripture) enters consciousness when man loses body-awareness, creating confusion. The literal scripture enters through the mind, and from the mind it moves into the body, corrupting the DNA. Scriptural dogmas act like viruses. They are called *memes.*

The term *fruit* refers to the body, mind, or the world that the field manifests from the seed. The fruit of the true human DNA is a healthy body, a righteous mind, and a righteous world. The fruit of the virus-infected DNA is a diseased body, an evil mind, and a corrupt world.

The "servants of the householder" represents the *human immune system.* The immune system is a system of biological structures and processes within an organism that protects against disease. To function properly, an immune system must detect a wide variety of agents (tares), from viruses to parasitic worms, and distinguish them from the organism's own healthy tissue (wheat). The immune system protects the organism from infection with layered defenses of increasing specificity. In simple terms, physical barriers prevent pathogens such as bacteria and viruses from entering the organism. If a pathogen breaches these barriers, then the *innate immune system* provides an immediate, but non-specific response. If pathogens successfully evade the innate response, vertebrates possess a second layer of protection, the *adaptive immune system,* which is activated by the innate response. Here, the immune system adapts its response during an infection to improve its recognition of the pathogen. This improved response is then retained after the pathogen has been eliminated, in the form of an *immunological memory,* and allows the adaptive immune system to mount faster and stronger attacks each time this pathogen is encountered. Some of the 'servants' of the 'householder' include Lymphocytes such as B Cells and T cells, Killer T cells, Helper T cells etc.

In this parable, the Man has no doubt as to who caused the problems: *"An enemy hath done this"* says he. He knows who the enemy is. The servants ask his permission to uproot the tares, but he holds them back, lest they damage the wheat while uprooting the tares. In other words, the Gospel prohibits genetic engineering as a means of curing.

Therefore, the householder says to his servants, *"Let both grow together until the harvest: and in the time of harvest I will say to the reapers, Gather ye together first the tares, and bind them in bundles to burn them: but gather the wheat into my barn."* The term *harvest* refers to the "Day of Judgment." It is the day when the parasitic viruses infecting humanity will be identified. It is the day when the true nature of evil will be exposed to the world. Perhaps, the *reapers* are the galactic cosmic rays that will disintegrate the virus-infected DNA. *Radiation mutagenesis* principally proceeds through DNA deletions (metaphorically called *reaping*), and misrepair and misrecombination at DNA double strand breaks.

The term *barn* refers to a garner or repository, in which the wheat is stored, where it lies together safely. The term *barn* refers to the world liberated from the humanoids, where human beings live together in peace and harmony.

MATTHEW 13:31-32

"Another parable put he forth unto them saying, The kingdom of heaven is like to a grain of mustard seed, which a man took, and sowed in his field: Which indeed is the least of all seeds: but when it is grown, it is the greatest among herbs, and becometh a tree, so that the birds of the air come and lodge in the branches thereof."

The least quantity or amount is known as the *quantum*. In physics, quantum is the smallest quantity of radiant energy, equal to Planck's constant times the frequency of the associated radiation. In that sense, the mustard seed, the "least of all seeds", signifies a quantum entity—the Photon. *Photon* is an elementary particle, the quantum of light and all other forms of electromagnetic radiation, and the force carrier for the electromagnetic force. The photon is the ultimate unit of light. It is a quantum of action. It is the unitary purposive principle which engenders the universe, and that it has the nature of *first cause.* Perhaps, the human Self is a photon.

I would imagine photon as a projector of possibilities. The rays from this projector are possibilities. This projector has the power to project multiple possibilities off anything presented to it. For example, if you put the idea of tree in this projector, it would project all the possible kinds of trees that can be conceived, given the formalism. If you present a DNA in this projector, then it would project a living man and his world from it. If the DNA is good, then it would project a righteous man and a righteous world; if the DNA is corrupt, then it would project a corrupt (evil) man and a corrupt world. The rays from the projector act quantum-mechanically on the DNA to create the man and his world.

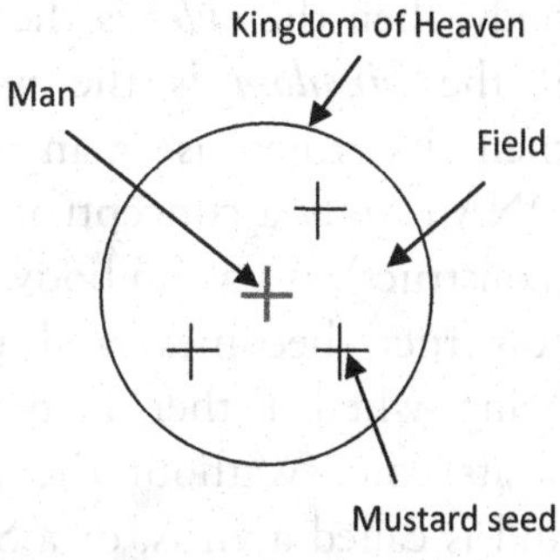

KINGDOM OF HEAVEN

The *field* is the domain of the photon (Father). It is the kingdom of heaven. Every point in the field is potentially a photon. *Field* represents pure body-awareness. If the field is assumed to be the human body (cell), then the mustard seed is the human DNA, which is the *book of life.* The expression, "the least of all seeds" suggests the non-dualistic nature of the human Self.

The parable of the mustard seed is an allegory depicting the connection between the Self (Father) and the body (Son). The link connecting the Father and Son is body-awareness (Holy Spirit).

When a DNA is 'sown' in body-awareness (the field), a body is born. In other words, when the Gospel seed is 'sown' in body-awareness (pure mind), a Jesus takes birth. Metaphorically, it is described as the mustard seed sprouting in the field and becoming a large tree.

The parable compares the human body, mind and the world to a tree on which *"the birds of the air come and lodge in the branches."* The phrase, "birds of the air" refers to the parasites that live off the human body and humanity.

A man's DNA is shaped by the book that he believes in completely. If that book is a dualistic scripture, then it will corrupt his DNA and he will sink into delusion. On the other hand, if the book is the (non-dualistic) Gospel, then it will redeem his DNA from corruption, and he regains sanity. That is why the Gospel is called the *Messiah* or the *Savior*: It saves people from delusion.

MATTHEW 13:33

"Another parable he spake unto them: The kingdom of heaven is like unto leaven, which a woman took, and hid in three measures of meal, till the whole was leavened."

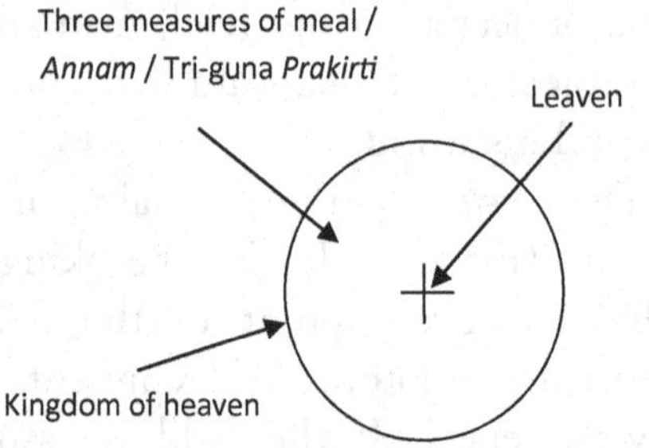

LEAVEN AND THREE MEASURES OF MEAL

The word *kingdom* refers to the territory ruled by a king. If the kingdom is the cell or the body, then the *ruler* is the Self. If the *kingdom* is the world, then its ruler is man. The DNA is only a conceptual shell (construct); it has no body. The construct becomes a human being when Father is present at its core. Without the Father, the construct remains a construct, and is called a virus, or a Serpent. It only has intellect (mind), but no intelligence (body). The Gnostics call that entity the *Demiurge*. He is the Lord of the Archons.

The Demiurge is a concept from Platonic, Neopythagorean, Middle Platonic, and Neoplatonic schools of philosophy for a *Great Architect* figure that is responsible for the fashioning and maintenance of the physical universe. The word Demiurge is derived from the Greek word *dēmiourgos* which means "public worker." According to the Neoplatonic School, the Demiurge is the fashioner of the perceptible world after a model of the ideas, but is still not itself *The One*. Gnosticism presents a distinction between the highest, unknowable God and the demiurgic creator of the material world. Several systems of Gnostic thought present the Demiurge as antagonistic to the will of the Supreme Being (The Father). His act of creation occurs in *unconscious simulation* of the divine model, and thus is fundamentally flawed, or else is formed with the malevolent intention of entrapping aspects of the divine in materiality. In the most radical form of

Christian Gnosticism, the Demiurge is the "jealous God" of the Old Testament.

If we consider the circle as the reality, then the centre-point is its king. If the cosmos is imagined as a circle, then any point in it can be considered as the centre of the cosmos. According to this logic, the centre of the human body, the Self, is the centre of the cosmos. The human DNA is the physical/bio-chemical expression of the Self, Father or Existence. And, the Gospel is the verbal expression of the true human DNA.

In this parable, the Gospel is compared to *leaven*. A leavening agent or *leaven* is any one of a number of substances used in dough and batters that causes a foaming action which lightens and softens the finished product. The leavening agent incorporates carbon-dioxide bubbles produced by the biological agents into the dough.

"The kingdom of heaven is like unto leaven, which a woman took, and hid in three measures of meal, till the whole was leavened." Spiritually, the "three measures of meal" represents the human body. Just as a little amount of leaven when mixed with dough transforms the whole dough, the scripture transforms man's entire body and mind.

The human body may be compared to "three measures of meal." The word *meal* means "food." The Sanskrit word for *meal* is *annam*, which means "food," or "matter." *Annam* is the stuff of reality. Incidentally, the white flour particles look like photons! But, what is the significance of "three measures of meal"? According to the Hindu Vēdānta, matter is constituted of three attributes or *gunas*: the *satva-guna*, the *rajō-guna* and the *tamō-guna*. The *satva-guna* represents the quality of light; the *rajō-guna* represents the quality of motion; the *tamō-guna* represents the quality of darkness. On the physical level, the *satva-guna* represents mass (M); the *rajō-guna* represents length (L); the *tamō-guna* represents time (T). Everything in nature, including the human body, is a combination of these three gunas.

The parable tells us how the Gospel works in humans. When a man reads the Gospel with body-awareness, the Gospel enters his body and rewrites his DNA, transforming him into an Evite, just as a little leaven transforms a lump of dough.

MATTHEW 13:34-35

"All these things spake Jesus unto the multitude in parables; and without a parable spake he not unto them: That it might be fulfilled which was spoken by the prophet, saying, I will open my mouth in parables; I will utter things which have been kept secret from the foundation of the world."

A parable is a story that is fundamentally quantum in nature. It has many possible interpretations. This uncertainty confuses the Serpent-children (humanoids), the machines, who are able to grasp only the literal (*collapsed*) meaning. The body-aware humans, on the other hand, are able to perceive an abundance of meanings in the parables. But, it is up to each individual to search and find an interpretation that resonates with his Self. There is no such thing as a consensus interpretation of the parable, or the Gospel.

The term *multitude* refers to the public which includes both Adamites and Mortals. The Gospel quotes from Psalms:

> *I will open my mouth in parables; I will utter things which have been kept secret from the foundation of the world.*
> Psalms 78:2

Gospel uses the phrase, "foundation of the world," not "foundations of the earth." "Foundations of the world" refers to the human DNA. It is the DNA that generates the world. And it is a dream world, a virtual reality world. But, what is that *thing* which has been kept secret from the foundations of the world? I think that secret relates to the DNA and the viruses.

The human DNA is a book. The core theme of this book is called soul. The anti-thesis of human DNA is the virus: actually, the *retrovirus*. *Retroviridae* is a family of enveloped viruses that replicate in a host cell through the process of *reverse transcription*. A retrovirus is a single-stranded RNA virus that stores its nucleic acid in the form of an mRNA (Messenger RNA) genome and target a host cell as an *obligate parasite*. Once inside the host cell cytoplasm the virus uses its own *reverse transcriptase enzyme* to produce DNA from its RNA genome, the reverse of the usual pattern, thus *retro* (backwards). This new DNA is then incorporated into the host cell genome by an *integrase enzyme*, at which point the retroviral DNA is referred to as a *provirus*. The host cell then treats the viral DNA as part of its own genome, *translating* and *transcribing* the viral genes along with the cell's own genes, producing the proteins required to assemble new copies of the virus. It seems that the retrovirus itself is the dreaded *Fallen Angel*, the devil. In the physical plane he manifests as a Scribe—*a pervert* Scribe. He too uses a process very similar to that of the retrovirus in creating his deadly scripture ("provirus"). The process begins by *abducting* the true human scripture, and then "reverse transcript" it to create a new scripture, which is essentially the antithesis of the true scripture. He then offers this *provirus* scripture back to the humans as the real one through a sleight of hand. The agency that facilitates it is religion. The provirus scripture then "takes over" the bodies of the unsuspecting victims. The "integrase enzyme" that binds the provirus scripture to the victim is belief. Today, many have become "obligate parasites" of this evil entity. The infected people then go about infecting (*proselytizing*) other perfectly normal human beings.

Perhaps, it is these retroviruses that the Gnostic Christians called *Archons*. The term, *Archons* is derived from the Greek word *archai*, which means "origins," "beginning things," or "prior in time." In the classical Mediterranean world, the term *archon* was commonly used for the governor of a province, or, more loosely, any *religious* or *governmental* authority. Hence the plural, *archons*, is often translated in Gnostic texts as "the Authorities." The early Christian fathers called it *principalities* or *powers*. In Gnostic cosmology, Archons are a species of *inorganic beings* (machines) that emerged in the solar system prior to the formation of the earth. They are the *cyborgs* inhabiting the planetary system, but not including the earth, sun and moon, which is described as a virtual-reality world (*stereoma*) they construct by simulating the geometric forms emanated from the *Pleroma*, the realm of the Generators, the Cosmic Gods. The *Archons* are a genuine species with their own proper habitat, and may even be considered to be god-like, but they lack *intentionality* or *freewill* (*ennoia*: body-awareness?), and they have a nasty tendency to stray from their boundaries and intrude on the human realm. They intensely envy humanity because humans possess the *freewill* that they lack. Archons are *psycho-spiritual parasites*. They are the several servants of the Demiurge, that stood between the human race and the Father who could only be reached through *gnosis*.

For we wrestle not against flesh and blood, but against principalities, against powers, against the rulers of the darkness of this world, against spiritual wickedness in high places.
Ephesians 6:12

MATTHEW 13:36-43

"Then Jesus sent the multitude away, and went into the house: and his disciples came unto him, saying, Declare unto us the parable of the tares of the field. He answered and said unto them, He that soweth the good seed is the Son of man; The field is the world; the good seed are the children of the kingdom; but the tares are the children of the wicked one; The enemy that sowed them is the devil; the harvest is the end of the world; and the reapers are the angels. As therefore the tares are gathered and burned in the fire; so shall it be in the end of this world. The Son of man shall send forth his angels, and they shall gather out of his kingdom all things that offend, and them which do iniquity; And shall cast them into a furnace of fire: there shall be wailing and gnashing of teeth. Then the righteous shine forth as the sun in the kingdom of their Father. Who hath ears to hear, let him hear."

"Then Jesus sent the multitude away, and went into the house: and his disciples came unto him, saying, Declare unto us the parable of the tares of the field." Spiritually, the expression, "Jesus sent the multitude away," suggests that the Gospel truths are not perceptible to the public. The imagery of Jesus going into the *house* alludes to the esoteric nature of the parable of tares of the field.

Here, the Gospel explains the symbols in the parable using another set of symbols. The spiritual meaning of these symbols point in two directions: one, it addresses the physical realm; and, two, it addresses the mental realm. While the former is for the benefit of Evites, the latter is for the benefit of the Mortals.

"He that soweth the good seed is the Son of man; The field is the world; the good seed are the children of the kingdom; but the tares are the children of the wicked one; The enemy that sowed them is the devil; the harvest is the end of the world; and the reapers are the angels." The chart

below shows the spiritual meanings of the symbols used in the parable, as applicable to the physical realm and the mental realm:

The Parable Motif	Explanation by Jesus	Spiritual Implication	
		Physical Realm	Mental Realm
"He that sowed the good seed"	Son of man	The true human DNA	The Gospel
"The field"	The world	The human body	The human mind
"The good seed"	The children of the kingdom	The human genes	The Gospel truths
"The tares"	The children of the wicked one	The Virus genes	Religious dogmas
"The enemy that sowed them"	The devil	The Serpent virus	Religion and literal scripture
"The harvest"	The end of the world	Death	The revelation of the Gospel
"The reapers"	The angels	Reaper viruses	Gospel revelations

The Gospel reveals the duality-based religion and its scripture as the enemy, the devil, and the corruptor of humanity. It also reveals that two kinds of people will be destroyed with the Judgment. They are the "things that offend" and "them which do iniquity." The Gospel addresses those in the former group as "things," implying they are soul-less entities. They are the Adamites. The Gospel addresses those in the latter group as "them," implying that they are humans. They are the corrupt Mortals who are devil-worshippers.

MATTHEW 13:44

"Again, the kingdom of heaven is like unto treasure hid in a field; the which when a man hath found, he hideth, and for joy thereof goeth and selleth all that he hath, and buyeth that field."

With regard to body, the *treasure* is the DNA, and the *field* is the body. But, with regard to mind, the *treasure* is the Gospel and the *field* is the mind. Therefore, the Gospel compares the "kingdom of heaven" to:

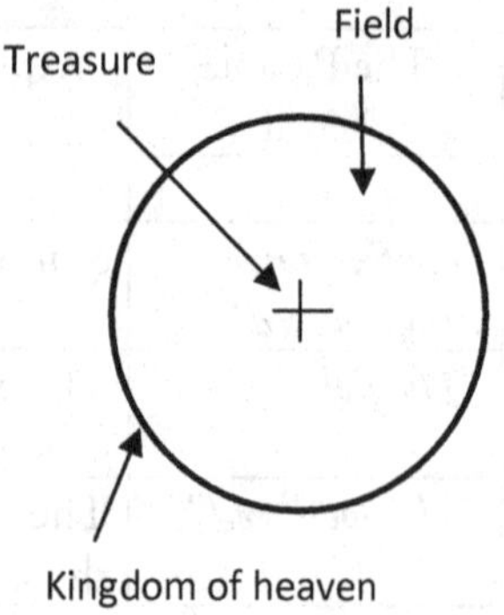

1. The human DNA in the body
2. The Gospel in the mind

The treasure hid in a field refers to the human DNA that lies hidden in the body cells. Alternatively, treasure hid in the field is the Gospel that is ingrained in the mind. The human DNA is called a treasure because it is rich in possibilities. Similarly, the Gospel is called a treasure because it is rich in meaning.

Body-awareness is the *field*. When the Gospel is read with body-awareness, the Gospel structures it, just as leaven structures the dough, to recreate the perfect body, which is free from corruption. Ingesting the Gospel into body-awareness is metaphorically described as "hiding the treasure in the field." It is so called because the Gospel enters every cell of the body.

The Gospel then says, "*. . . the which when a man hath found, he hideth, and for joy thereof goeth and selleth all that he hath, and buyeth that field.*" When the Gospel enters a man's body, his delusion goes and he realizes the truth about his own Self. The truth sets him free from religion and other restrictions, arousing in him the feeling of bliss. The man finds all his worldly possessions worthlessness in comparison to that blissful feeling and, therefore, discards them totally.

The secret this parable reveals to us is that the scripture (belief system) one believes in can affect one's DNA, and thereby, affect his body and his world. If the scripture is corrupt, then his body and his world will be corrupt too. On the other hand, if the scripture is true, then his body and his world will be righteous. Therefore, one has to be careful as to what one accepts as scripture.

MATTHEW 13:45-46

"Again, the kingdom of heaven is like unto a merchant man, seeking goodly pearls: Who, when he had found one pearl of great price, went and sold all that he had, and bought it."

The *pearl* signifies eternal truth. A pearl is spherical (whole), brilliant (divine), hidden in an oyster (veiled), and is found only in the depths of sea (consciousness). In the past, the main source of pearls was India. In this parable, the pearl the Gospel is referring to is the truth of *advaita* (non-duality).

A *merchant* is one who is immersed in worldly activities. But, the merchant of this parable is no ordinary merchant. He is a merchant of "goodly pearls." In other words, he is a seeker of truth. The parable says that this merchant found "*one* pearl of great price." The expression, "one pearl of great price" means "ultimate truth." And what is that greatest truth? We had a glimpse of it in the previous parable. That ultimate truth is this: *"I and Father are one."* The Hindu Vedas articulate that truth in four different ways, called the *Mahāvākyas*:

Prajnānam Brahma (Rig Vēda/Aitarēya Upanishad)
("Body-awareness is the Self.")

Ayam Ātma Brahma (Atharva Vēda/Māndūkya Upanishad)
("This body is the Self.")

Tat Tvam Asi (Sāma Vēda /Chandōkya Upanishad)
("That you are.")

Aham Brahma Asmi (Yajur Vēda /Bṛhadāranyaka Upanishad)
("I am the Self.")

Having realized the ultimate truth, the man thinks, "If I am the All, why should I possess anything?" There is no need. Therefore, the man sells off all his possessions, and holds on to that ultimate truth - his own Self. Thus, he attains the kingdom of heaven.

MATTHEW 13:47-50

"Again, the kingdom of heaven is like unto a net, that was cast into the sea, and gathered of every kind: Which, when it was full, they drew to shore, and sat down, and gathered the good into the vessels, but cast the bad away. So shall it be at the end of the world: the angels shall come forth, and sever the wicked from *among the just, And shall cast them into the furnace of fire: there shall be wailing and gnashing of teeth."*

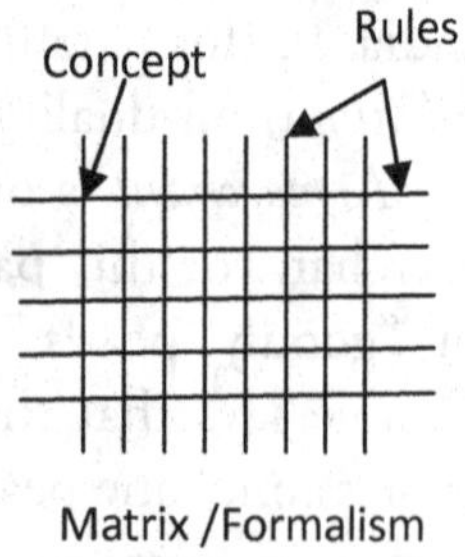

Here, the *term sea* refers to the field, and the *net* represents the *formalism* or the *construct.* In this parable, the Gospel compares the *kingdom of heaven* to a net cast into the sea. The *kingdom of heaven* has two aspects: the *field* and the *seed.*

The *field* is the womb of creativity. It is a quantum field. The Hindus call it the *Prakṛti*, meaning nature. According to Hinduism, *Prakṛti* is the basic nature of intelligence by which the Universe exists and functions. It is described in the Bhagavad Gīta as the "primal motive force." All animate and inanimate objects and all psycho-mental experiences are emanations of *Prakṛti.* It is the essential constituent of the universe and is at the basis of the activity of the creation. In microbiological terms, the field represents the *cell cytoplasm.* In Gospel terms, the field is the *Father* (Mother?).

The *seed* represents the formalism or the construct. The Hindus call the *Puruṣa.* The Sanskrit word *Puruṣa* means "person," or "self." *Puruṣa* is also, in one of the early creation myths related in the Rig-Vēda, India's oldest text, the *primal man* from whose body the universe was created. In microbiological terms, the *seed* represents the DNA. Alternatively, the seed (*Puruṣa*) represents the scripture.

Prakṛti (Father/Mother) and *Puruṣa* (Son) are the two ontological realities. It is the confusion of *Puruṣa* (scripture) with *Prakṛti* (the truth) that keeps the man in bondage. Disassociation of *Puruṣa* from *Prakṛti* is liberation.

The parable: *"Again, the kingdom of heaven is like unto a net, that was cast into the sea, and gathered of every kind: Which, when it was full, they drew to shore, and sat down, and gathered the good into the vessels, but cast the bad away."* In this parable, the "kingdom of heaven" is compared to a net cast in the sea. A net is essentially a matrix. The word *net* suggests a trap made of netting to catch fish or birds or insects. Here, the net is the Gospel. Casting net into sea suggests two things: with reference to mind, it refers to the understanding of the Gospel message; with reference to body, it refers to the redemption of corrupt DNA.

The expression "gathered of every kind" too has two implications: with reference to mind, it refers to the gathering of different interpretations of the Gospel; with reference to body, it refers to the gathering of DNA of varying degrees of corruption. Although the net gathers of every kind, not all are taken into the vessels. The *vessel* denotes salvation. Although the Gospel is read by many, it saves only some, while the others are cast away. But, what is the basis of selection and rejection?

Corruption by the Serpent affects in two ways: first, it corrupts the mind; subsequently, it corrupts the body (DNA). Corruption of the mind manifests as ignorance and delusion. Corruption of the body manifests as physical damage to the cell structure. Corruption of the mind is curable, if it is treated early. But, if is not treated early, the corruption may proceed to affect the body (cells), damaging the cells permanently. If the body-cells are damaged, then that body it is considered *lost*.

The Gospel then says, *"So shall it be at the end of the world: the angels shall come forth, and sever the wicked from among the just, And shall cast them into the furnace of fire: there shall be wailing and gnashing of teeth."* The phrase, "end of the world" refers to the Last Days. In the Last Days the revelation of the spiritual meaning of the Gospel will identify and separate the humanoids from the true human beings. It is called the Judgment.

MATTHEW 13:51-52

"Jesus saith unto them, Have ye understood all these things? They say unto him, Yea, Lord. Then said he unto them, Therefore every scribe which is instructed unto the kingdom of heaven is like unto a man that is an householder, which bringeth forth out of his treasure things new and old."

"Have ye understood all these things?" asks Jesus to his disciples. Here, the term "things" refers to the parables. The true disciple of Jesus understands his parables. He understands the spiritual meaning of the parables. He represents the "good ground" in which the "seed" is sown.

The literal, moral, and esoteric modes of understanding the Gospel depend on formalisms (conventions and rules) to unravel the meaning.

However, spiritual understanding of the Gospel is provided by the inner Self (the Father). It is free from formalisms. And the guidance from Self is called *intuition,* or "spirit of prophesy." Therefore, the true disciple is one who possesses the spirit of prophesy. Jesus calls him *"a scribe which is instructed unto the kingdom of heaven."* A *scribe* is one who can read and write; he is a literate. Therefore, the "scribe which is instructed unto the kingdom of heaven" suggests someone who can read the body and write the body. Such a person is called a *parable-literate.* Only the Evites are parable-literates.

The Gospel compares the true disciple to a *"householder which bringeth forth out of his treasure things new and old."* Here, the term *householder* means "an Evite." But this man *"bringeth forth out of his treasure things new and old."* The term *treasure* refers to both DNA and the Gospel. The operative word here is "his." This person does not simply accept the religion's interpretation of the Gospel, but seeks his own interpretation using his intuition. Thus, the true disciple brings forth "things new and old." The expression, "things new and old" suggests timeless truths. In the Hindu tradition, it is called *purāṇa,* which are myths, or speculations about the Brahman. The word *purāṇa* comes from the Sanskrit roots *purā* meaning "old" and *nava* meaning "new." According to the Gospel, the true disciple is he who speculates about the Self, using his intuition.

MATTHEW 13:53-58

"And it came to pass, that when Jesus had finished these parables, he departed thence. And when he was come into his own country, he taught them in their synagogue, insomuch that they were astonished, and said, Whence hath this man this wisdom, and these mighty works? Is not this the carpenter's son? Is not his mother called Mary? and his brethren, James, and Joses, and Simon, and Judas? And his sisters, are they not all with us? Whence then hath this man all these things? And they were offended in him. But Jesus said unto them, A prophet is not without honour, save in his own country, and in his own house. And he did not many mighty works there because of their unbelief."

Jesus speaks the parables in the higher, or *quantum* state of mind. But, now he is in the normal state, or the *collapsed* state of mind. The Gospel describes it metaphorically: *"When Jesus had finished these parables, he departed thence. And when he was come into his own country, he taught them in their synagogue."* Jesus represents the Gospel. Spiritually, the term *country* refers to the literal meaning of the Gospel. The parables are "quantum objects," but, the Mortals can grasp only its literal meaning. Here, the term synagogue suggests "church." In other words, the Gospel says that the parables taught in the churches are 'collapsed' ones: after Jesus has departed.

Jesus then says, *"A prophet is not without honour, save in his own country, and in his own house."* Spiritually, the term *prophet* refers to the parable; the word *honour* means "truth"; the term *country* means "religion"; the term *house* means "church." In other words, the Gospel says that the parables taught by the Christian church have no truth in it.

In this chapter, the Gospel uses seven parables to teach about the *kingdom of heaven*. In other words, the Gospel uses seven parables to establish the union between the *field* (Father, Prakṛti, body, and cell) and the *seed* (Son, Puruṣa, the DNA, and the Gospel).

	Parable	**Definition of Kingdom of Heaven**
1	Sower who sows seeds in a field	Kingdom of Heaven = Good Field + Seed
2	A man who sowed good seeds in his field	Kingdom of Heaven = Field +Good seed
3	A grain of mustard seed sowed in the field	Kingdom of Heaven = Field + Mustard seed
4	Leaven hid in three loaves of meal	Kingdom of Heaven = Dough + Leaven
5	Treasure hid in a field	Kingdom of Heaven = Field + Treasure
6	Merchant of goodly pearls in the world	Kingdom of Heaven = World + Goodly pearl
7	Casting of net in the sea	Kingdom of Heaven = Sea + Net

In the first parable, the seed is the same, but the field varies; the sower is the Self. In the second parable, the field is the same, but the seeds vary—good and evil; the good seed is sown by man, whereas the evil seed is sowed by the enemy.

CHAPTER 14

The Old King Leaves, the New King Arrives

MATTHEW 14:1-13

"At that time Herod the tetrarch heard of the fame of Jesus, And said unto his servants, This is John the Baptist; he is risen from the dead; and therefore mighty works do shew forth themselves in him. For Herod had laid hold on John, and bound him, and put him in prison for Herodias' sake, his brother Philips wife. For John said unto him, It is not lawful for thee to have her. And when he would have put him to death, he feared the multitude, because they counted him as a prophet, But when Herod's birthday was kept, the daughter of Herodias danced before them, and pleased Herod. Whereupon he promised with an oath to give her whatsoever she would ask. And she, being before instructed of her mother, said, Give me here John Baptist's head in a charger. And the king was sorry: nevertheless for the oath's sake, and them which sat with him at meat, he commanded it to be given her. And he sent, and beheaded John in the prison. His head was brought in a charger, and given to the damsel: and she brought it to her mother. And his disciples came, and took up the body, and buried it, and went and told Jesus. When Jesus heard of it, he departed thence by ship into a desert place apart: and when the people had heard thereof, they followed him on foot out of the cities."

Herod was a Roman client king of Judea, who ruled the region as a proxy of the Roman Empire. The family of Herod came from Edom. The Edomites are said to be the progeny of Esau, who is Jacob's brother. They are known as the "other nation" (Genesis 25:23). Spiritually, the expression "other nation" means "alien." Herod's family converted to Judaism because of external pressures. They were an important family in Edom, and they were clever at politics. They cleverly cultivated friendship with the Romans and got their daughters married into the royal families. Therefore, the Romans chose "Herod the Great" to be the king of Judea. The term *Herod* is the title of a son of this family from Edom.

The Greek equivalent of the name Herod is *Hērōdēs* (G2264), which means "a hero." The Greek word for *tetrarch* is *tetrarchēs* (G5076), which means "the ruler of a fourth of a country." Perhaps, the term *Herod* represents the *Kali* - lord of the *Kali Yuga* - of Hindu mythology. The name Herod reminds us of Nimrod of the Old Testament. Nimrod, king of Shinar, was, according to the Book of Genesis the son of Cush and great-grandson of Noah. He is depicted in the Old Testament as a *man of power in the earth*, and a *mighty hunter*. Extra-biblical traditions associating him with the *Tower of Babel* led to his reputation as a king who was rebellious against God. Spiritually, the *Tower of Babel* denotes the DNA, and Nimrod's rebellion against God suggests genetic experimentation. Perhaps, Nimrod wanted to clone the perfect human DNA. The "Land of Nimrod," used as a synonym for Assyria or Mesopotamia, is also known as Babylon. Perhaps, Herod belongs to the lineage of Nimrod.

Two of Herod's sons were Philip and Antipas. Herod Philip married a woman called Herodias. When Herod Antipas visited his brother, he desired Herodias to be his wife. So Herod Antipas divorced his own wife, and married Herodias, who divorced Herod Philip. John-the-Baptist condemned the illegal marriage because the law of the land did not permit such immoral behavior. This made Herodias very angry at him, and she caused Herod Antipas to arrest John. The story of Herod the Tetrarch faintly resembles the story of King Henry VIII, the King of England.

Henry VIII ascended the English throne in 1509 at the age of 17. He made a dynastic marriage with Catherine of Aragon, widow of his brother Arthur, in June 1509, just before his coronation on Midsummer's Day. Sometime after 1525, Henry VIII wanted an annulment from his first wife, Catharine of Aragon, so that he could marry Anne Boleyn. At this time, the Church of England was Roman Catholic under the control of the Pope in Rome. But when the Pope refused to allow Henry to end his marriage to Catharine to marry Anne, Henry broke off communication with the Pope and changed the Church of England to the Anglican Church.

Now back to our story. John the Baptist, according to some, was an Essene. The Essenes were a sect of Second Temple Judaism that flourished from the 2nd century BCE to the 1st century CE. They lived in various cities but congregated in communal life dedicated to asceticism, voluntary poverty, daily immersion, and abstinence from worldly pleasures, including (for some groups) celibacy. Many separate but related religious groups of that era shared similar mystic, eschatological, messianic, and ascetic beliefs. These groups were collectively known as the Essenes. The Essenes were meticulous followers of the Torah.

John's story allegorically describes how truth was corrupted by evil forces. The spiritual meanings of the metaphors used in the story are given below:

1. *Rome*: Babylon; the Serpent
2. *Edom*: Adamites
3. *Herod*: the Establishment
4. *Herod Antipas*: the political establishment
5. *Herod Philip*: the religious establishment
6. *John-the-Baptist*: the Tanakh
7. *John's head*: The meaning of the Tanakh
8. *Beheading of John*: Distorting/corrupting the meaning of the Tanakh
9. *Charger*: Literal scripture
10. *Herodias, the wife of Herod*: the Kabbalah (represents the *powers*)
11. *Daughter of Herodias*: the Babylonian Talmud (represents the *principalities*)
12. *Jesus*: the Gospel

The Kabbalah and Talmud are at the root of the Jewish doctrine. *Kabbalah* is a Hebrew word, which literally means "tradition." These traditions were oral in the beginning; but later, they were memorialized in the Talmud and the Kabbalah. The Chaldean science acquired by many Jewish priests, during the captivity of Babylon, gave birth to the sect of the Pharisees whose name only appear in the Gospel and in the writings of the Jewish historians after the captivity (606 B.C).

The term *charger* is derived from the Hebrew word *qeāra* (H7086), which means "a bowl" (as cut out hollow). The word is derived from the Hebrew root word *qāra* (H7167), which means "to rend," "to cut out," or "to tear apart." It also means "to revile" (by painting the eyes, as if to enlarge them). Spiritually, the term *charger* refers to the corrupted scripture.

"And he sent, and beheaded John in the prison. His head was brought in a charger, and given to the damsel: and she brought it to her mother. And his disciples came, and took up the body, and buried it, and went and told Jesus." The Gospel describes metaphorically how the Tanakh got distorted and corrupted by Kabbalah and the Talmud. The beheading of John signifies the corruption of the true meaning of the Tanakh. The burying of John's body by his disciples, perhaps, signifies the *burying* (literally and figuratively) of the Essene scriptures.

The Essenes have gained considerable attention in modern times as a result of the discovery of an extensive cache of religious documents known as the *Dead Sea Scrolls* from the secret caves of Qumran, a site near West Bank in Israel. The Dead Sea Scrolls are known as the *Essence's Library*. These documents include preserved multiple copies of the Tanakh, untouched from as early as 300 BCE until their discovery in 1946. The Essenes studied the books of elders, preserved secrets, and were very mindful of the names of the *angels* kept in their secret writings.

The disciples of John-the-Baptist inform Jesus of John's demise. The expression "disciples of John-the-Baptist" is a cryptic reference to Joseph, the author of the Gospel. Joseph, realizing the corruption and destruction of the Essene literature, decides to hide (*bury*) his own work, The Gospel, in a complex allegory—the Jesus story.

"When Jesus heard of it, he departed thence by ship into a desert place apart." The term *ship* refers to a vessel, which, in turn, suggests a "physical container." Spiritually, the term *ship* suggests a spiritual container, or a book. The Hebrew term for *desert* is *midbār* (H4057), which means "a pasture or open field where cattle is driven." Spiritually, the term *desert* refers to man's inner body. In other words, the Gospel tells us that it is the vehicle for entering the kingdom of heaven (the inner body).

". . . and when the people had heard thereof, they followed him on foot out of the cities." Spiritually, the term *city* means "religion"; the phrase "followed him on foot" suggests solitary seeking. In other words, the Gospel tells us that those who want to know the truth of the Gospel should search it outside religion, and that search is a solitary activity.

MATTHEW 14:14-18

"And Jesus went forth, and saw a great multitude, and was moved with compassion toward them, and he healed their sick. And when it was evening, his disciples came to him, saying, This is a desert place, and the time is now past; send the multitude away, that they may go into the villages, and buy themselves victuals. But Jesus said unto them, They need not depart; give ye them to eat. And they say unto him, We have here but five loaves, and two fishes. He said, Bring them hither to me."

In the previous section we saw Jesus retreating into a deserted place. Spiritually, it suggests the entry of the Gospel message into the mind of an Evite in the form of *hearing* (*śravaṇa*). Now, the Gospel says, *"And Jesus went forth."* In other words, now the Gospel comes out of the Evite's body in the form of spiritual interpretation (*kīrtana*).

Here, the Gospel is not talking about physically feeding a multitude. Instead, it is describing a training process, where Jesus is the trainer and the disciples are the trainees. Spiritually, the disciples represent the Evites chosen to be Gospel interpreters. The miracle, narrated above, allegorically describes the training process: it teaches the disciple how to spiritually interpret the Gospel. But, the disciple, at this stage, is only a *Neophyte*. (A Neophyte is one who recently took a monastic vow.)

"And Jesus went forth, and saw a great multitude, and was moved with compassion toward them, and he healed their sick." Spiritually, the "great multitude" refers to the spiritual state of the Neophyte, rather than to a crowd of people. The word "great multitude" refers to the magnitude of his ignorance and delusion. Therefore what these verses tell us is that the Gospel, seeing the ignorance and delusion of the Neophyte, feels compassion towards him and removes his ignorance and delusion.

This miracle described here teaches the Neophyte when and how to do the Gospel work. In other words, it tells the disciples when and how to spiritually interpret the Gospel.

"And when it was evening, his disciples came to him, saying, This is a desert place, and the time is now past; send the multitude away, that they may go into the villages, and buy themselves victuals." Here, the term "desert place" refers to the corrupt world; the term *evening* refers to the Last Days; the expression, "time is now past" highlights the need and urgency of the Gospel work; the term "victuals" refers to the Gospel truths; and the term *villages* refers to religious cults like the Essenes. The disciples are eager to disperse the crowd so that they can go to nearby villages and find nourishment. In other words, the Evite at first reject the idea of writing a spiritual interpretation for the Gospel because there is already an interpretation of the Gospel by the Church.

Jesus rejects the disciples' suggestion and commands: *"They need not depart; give ye them to eat."* Intuition tells the Evite that it is his responsibility to enlighten the people and, therefore, his interpretation should be a spiritual interpretation. And that is what the Gospel too commands: *"Give ye them to eat."*

There is only one true Gospel, and that is the true human DNA. But, there can be as many spiritual interpretations to it as there are Evites.

"And they say unto him, We have here but five loaves, and two fishes." But, the disciples plead ignorance. They say that they are poor fishermen who have neither the education nor the wealth, except their bodies, to undertake such a great task. Their despondency is clear from their words. What they are saying is this: "All we have is our physical bodies." The *five loaves of bread* represent the five senses and the *two fishes* denote intellect and mind. Together they denote the human body.

Jesus says to them, *"Bring them hither to me."* The Gospel reveals a great secret here: when an Evite brings his body-awareness to the Gospel, it reveals its true meaning. Thus, his interpretation becomes an instrument of spiritual healing.

MATTHEW 14:19-21

"And he commanded the multitude to sit down on the grass, and took the five loaves, and the two fishes, and looking up to the heaven, he blessed, and brake, and gave the loaves to his disciples, and the disciples to the multitude. And they did all eat, and were filled: and they took up the fragments that remained twelve baskets full. And they that had eaten were about five thousand men, beside women and children."

Here, Jesus demonstrates the Gospel interpretation process to the Neophyte. It involves the following steps:

	Gospel Words	Implication
1	Sit down on the grass	Sit in a relaxed pose
2	Take the five loaves of bread and two fishes	Gather body-awareness by withdrawing senses inwards
3	Look up to the heaven	Look inwards
4	Bless the bread	Pray to the Self for revelation
5	Break the bread	Interpret the Gospel

Spiritually, the term *bread* refers to the Gospel. "Breaking the bread" means "dividing the Gospel," or "interpreting the Gospel." The Gospel interpretation process resembles the cell division process, or *mitosis*. *Mitosis* is the process by which a cell, which has previously replicated each of its chromosomes, separates the chromosomes in its cell nucleus into two identical sets of chromosomes, each set in its own new nucleus.

The Gospel explains the mode of delivery: ". . . *and gave the loaves to his disciples, and the disciples to the multitude.*" The Gospel reveals its truths to the Evites first, who then transmits it to the Mortals and Adamites. Thus, both the feeder (the healer) and the fed (the 'sick') are not only satisfied, but their satisfaction overflows and lingers. The term, *basket* signifies memory. The phrase "twelve baskets full" denotes the fullness of the joy.

"And they that had eaten were about five thousand men, beside women and children." Why does the Gospel mention only the number

of men present, but not the number of women and children? Perhaps, it is food for thought.

MATTHEW 14:22-24

"And straightway Jesus constrained his disciples to get into a ship, and to go before him unto the other side, while he sent the multitude away. And when he had sent the multitudes away, he went up into a mountain apart to pray: and when the evening was come, he was there alone. But the ship was now in the midst of the sea, tossed with waves: for the wind was contrary."

After the abundant spiritual feast of the Gospel meanings, the Neophyte returns to the plane of the literal Gospel. With body-awareness gone, he is now buffeted by doubts and fearful thoughts.

"And straightway Jesus constrained his disciples to get into a ship, and to go before him unto the other side, while he sent the multitude away." The expression, "other side" refers to the world of dualities. It also refers to the literal scripture. The term *ship* refers to the Neophyte's physical body. It is in this 'ship' he travels to Jesus and return from him. But, Jesus stays back at the site of the feast. In other words, the Gospel truths recede into the book after revealing itself to the Evite.

"And when he had sent the multitudes away, he went up into a mountain apart to pray: and when the evening was come, he was there alone." Here, the term *mountain* refers to the human body. Jesus going up into mountain to pray suggests the receding of the Gospel truths from the reader's awareness to its source – the body. It also signifies the Neophyte losing body-awareness. With body-awareness gone, he once again regresses into the Mortal state.

"But the ship was now in the midst of the sea, tossed with waves: for the wind was contrary." When the Neophyte loses body-awareness, he is buffeted by doubts and fears. The term *sea* refers to the mind perturbed by thoughts. The Gospel interpreter now faces gnawing doubts and fears. He is fearful of the public's reaction to his spiritual work.

MATTHEW 14:25

"And in the fourth watch of the night Jesus went unto them, walking on the sea."

Here, the Gospel teaches the Neophyte when to pray.

"And in the fourth watch of the night Jesus went unto them, walking on the sea." The "fourth watch" is the period between 3 AM and 6 AM. Both day and night are divided into four "watches" of three hours each. The four watches of the night are 6 PM to 9 PM, 9 PM to 12 PM, 12 PM to 3 PM, and 3 PM to 6 PM. According to the Hindu tradition, the "fourth watch" is called the *Brahma-muhūrtam,* which means "the hour of God." It is considered to be an extremely auspicious time for meditation.

Jesus approaches the disciples in the fourth watch "walking on the sea." The term *sea* refers to body-awareness. Alternatively, the term also refers to the literal meaning of the Gospel. Therefore, Jesus walking on the sea denotes the higher or spiritual meaning of the Gospel. In other words, the Gospel truths reveal its spiritual meaning to the body-aware Evite.

MATTHEW 14:26-27

"And when the disciples saw him walking on the sea, they were troubled, saying, It is a spirit; and they cried out for fear. But straightway Jesus spake unto them, saying, Be of good cheer; it is I; be not afraid."

Here, Jesus (the Gospel) reveals his identity to the disciples (the Evite). He says to the fearful disciples, "*It is I.*" In these three short words, the Gospel reveals the ultimate truth. The good news! The Gospel combines the *Vēdic* aphorisms *Tat Tvam Asi* ("You are that") and *Aham Brahma Asmi* ("I am the Self") into one pithy statement: "*It is I.*" However, if you understand it as, "Jesus is It," then you are mistaken.

We address ourselves as "I" in spite of our different names. "I" is the common name for the entire humanity.

The ultimate truth is accompanied by two other truths: "*Be of good cheer*"; and, "*Be not afraid.*" The statement, "*It is I*" represents the Father; the statement, "*Be not afraid*" represents the Son; and, the statement "*Be of good cheer*" represents the Holy Spirit.

MATTHEW 14:28-30

"And Peter answered him and said, Lord, if it be thou, bid me come unto thee on the water. And he said, Come. And when Peter was come down out of the ship, he walked on the water, to go to Jesus. But when he saw the wind boisterous, he was afraid; and beginning to sink, he cried, saying, Lord, save me."

"And Peter answered him and said, Lord, if it be thou, bid me come unto thee on the water." Peter's utterance may be reworded as follows: "Lord, if it is you, give me the order to come to you on the water." Here, Jesus represents the Gospel truth, the Spirit. Peter represents the Neophyte. Separating them is the great sea of meaning. To drown in this sea means to grasp the literal meaning and drown in delusion. And to walk on this sea means to grasp the spiritual meaning. Here, the Neophyte wants to find the truth, but he lacks courage and faith. Therefore, he prays for help.

"And he said, Come. And when Peter was come down out of the ship, he walked on the water, to go to Jesus." Jesus invites Peter to come near to him. The truth beckons. Peter gets out the ship and takes couple of steps towards Jesus. Then, all of a sudden, he loses courage and cries out to Jesus for help. Here, the *ship* represents Neophyte's comfort zone; his belief system that gives him a (false) sense of security. Still, the Neophyte leaves his comfort zone and takes a step towards truth. Suddenly, all hell breaks lose and he loses confidence.

Why did Peter lose his confidence? The Gospel gives the reason: *"But when he saw the wind boisterous, he was afraid."* The word, *boisterous* means "noisy and lacking in restraint or discipline." It suggests public criticism. When the fear of public criticism grips the Neophyte, he loses his courage to pursue truth.

Spiritually speaking, interpreting the Gospel is an endeavor as subtle and dangerous as walking on the sea. The Gospel revelations are so startling and incredible that it shakes the very foundations of one's world. Everything that the Neophyte thought sacred, precious, and valuable is brought to naught in a fell swoop. His world goes topsy-turvy. Fear and doubts grips the man and he cries out to his Self for help.

The *Katha Upanishad* captures the plight of the truth-seeker beautifully:

> *Kṣurasya dhāra niśitam duratyaya*
> *Durgam pathastat kavayo vadanti*
> Katha Upanishad 1:3:14
> ("The path to truth is as sharp, subtle, and difficult to tread as the edge of a razor: so the wise say")

But, the Gospel provides the remedy for the Neophyte's fear-of-criticism and loss-of-confidence. And that remedy is to call out, *"Lord, save me."* The "Lord," referred here, is the body, not the mind. Mind is the "boisterous wind."

MATTHEW 14:31-33

"And immediately Jesus stretched forth his hand, and caught him, and said unto him, O thou of little faith, wherefore didst thou doubt? And when they were come into the ship, the wind ceased. Then they that were in the ship came and worshipped him, saying, Of a truth thou art the Son of God."

"And immediately Jesus stretched forth his hand, and caught him, and said unto him, O thou of little faith, wherefore didst thou doubt?" As soon Peter calls out to Jesus, help comes immediately. In other words, when the Neophyte becomes body-aware, fear disappears.

Man is just a point on the circumference of the Circle of Self. He is always connected to the Self just as the point on the circumference is connected to the center of the circle. In fact, the radius that connects the point to the centre is like an out-stretched hand extending from the centre. But, that connection is not apparent. Similarly, the Neophyte too is always connected

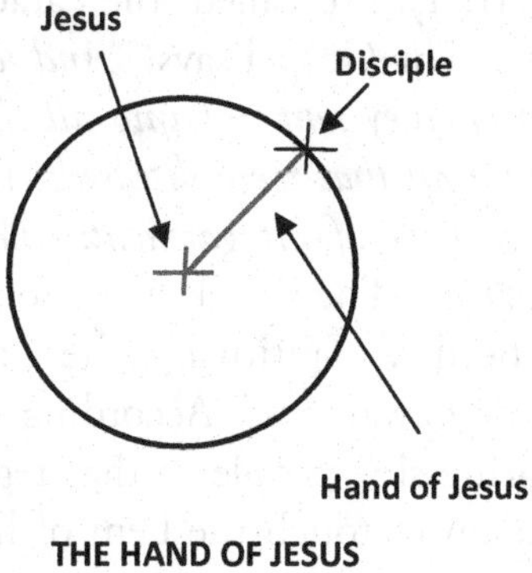

THE HAND OF JESUS

to the Self, but he is not always aware of that connection. Fear grips him when he forgets that connection. And that connection is called body-awareness.

"And when they were come into the ship, the wind ceased. Then they that were in the ship came and worshipped him, saying, Of a truth thou art the Son of God." When Jesus enters the boat, the wind ceases. In other words, when the Neophyte becomes body-aware his fear disappears. The Neophyte now realizes: "Indeed, I am That."

MATTHEW 14:34-36

"And when they were gone over, they came into the land of Gennesaret. And when the men of that place had knowledge of him, they sent out into all that country round about, and brought unto him all that were diseased; And besought him that they might only touch the hem of his garment: and as many as touched were made perfectly whole."

"And when they were gone over, they came into the land of Gennesaret." The expression, "And when they were gone over" suggests that the Neophyte has crossed "the sea of Gospel awareness." In other words, the man 'grasps' the spiritual meaning of the Gospel with his body. Now, he is on the other side—on the side of enlightenment. The Gospel metaphorically calls it the *land of Gennesaret.* Gennesaret is a place over the other side of the Sea of Galilee. Spiritually, the Sea of Galilee represents both body-awareness and the Gospel meaning. Gennesaret represents the Self, or the DNA. The name *Gennesaret* means "a garden of riches." Gennesaret was known for its beauty and fertility. It is called "the Paradise of Galilee."

The Gospel says, *"And when the men of that place had knowledge of him, they sent out into all that country round about, and brought unto him all that were diseased; And besought him that they might only touch the hem of his garment: and as many as touched were made perfectly whole."* The Greek word for hem is *kraspedon* (G2899), which means "border." Spiritually, the expression, "hem of the garment" suggests body-awareness. According to the Gospel, the people of Gennesaret bring sick people of that region to Jesus and plead with him to allow them to touch the hem of his garment. In other words, the people of

Gennesaret were 'touched' by the Gospel truth and they were made "perfectly whole."

Spiritually, Gennesaret represents the human DNA. The people of Gennesaret represent the genes in the DNA. The sick people of Gennesaret are the corrupt genes. The Gospel message heals the corrupt genes and makes the DNA "perfectly whole." And the medicine that heals the corruption is the Gospel truth mixed with body-awareness!

There is another interesting fact. This is only place in the entire Gospel, perhaps, in the entire Bible, where it is mentioned that someone is healed "perfectly whole."

CHAPTER 15

Things Left On One Side

MATTHEW 15:1-6

"Then came to Jesus scribes and Pharisees, which were of Jerusalem, saying, Why do thy disciples transgress the tradition of the elders? for they wash not their hands when they eat bread. But he answered and said unto them, Why do ye also transgress the commandment of God by your tradition? For God commanded, saying, Honour thy father and mother: and, He that curseth father or mother, let him die the death. But ye say, Whosoever shall say to his father or his mother, It is a gift, by whatsoever thou mightest be profited by me; And honour not his father or his mother, he shall be free. Thus have ye made the commandment of God of none effect by your tradition."

Scribes and Pharisees represent the Serpent-children—Adamites whose bodies have been taken over by the Serpent virus. Religion (symbolized here as Jerusalem) is their lair. Traditions govern every action of these people like an *operating system*.

The expression, "traditions of the elders" refers to religious dogmas. A *tradition* is an inherited (conditioned) pattern of thought or action. It relates to the past, but shapes the present. Traditions are only concerned with external actions and, therefore, a follower of tradition tends to be hypocritical. Moreover, the enforcer of tradition is not the Self, but the Establishment (System). Jesus calls the Scribes and Pharisees hypocrites, perhaps, hinting at their humanoid nature.

It is the inherent property of intelligence to jump out of a system and observe it from the outside. But, traditions, by strictly prohibiting such wanderings, effectively destroy the principal human faculty known as intelligence. Thus, traditions relegate human beings to the level of humanoids. By destroying the faculty of observation, traditions make human beings spiritually blind.

> *Of course, there are cases where only a rare individual will have the vision to perceive a system which governs many people's lives, a system which had never before been recognized as a system; then such people often devote their lives to convincing other people that the system really is there, and that it ought to be exited from!*
>
> Gödel, Escher, Bach: an Eternal Golden Braid, Douglas R. Hofstadter

The Greek word for *elder* is *presbyteros* (G4245), which means "a senior," or, figuratively, "a member of the celestial council." The term *elder* refers to a person who is older or higher in rank than oneself. He can be an influential member of a tribe or community. Using the computer metaphor, we may call him a "class program" from which "child programs" inherit their properties and behaviors. The "child programs" are merely copies of the "class program" with appropriate customization. All computer operating systems have libraries of class programs. Spiritually, a library of class programs is called a *Sanhedrin.* The *Sanhedrin* (Greek: *synedrion,* meaning "sitting together") was an assembly of twenty-three men in every city in the Land of Israel. In the Second Temple period, the Great Sanhedrin met in the *Hall of Hewn Stones* in the Temple of Jerusalem.

Here, the disciples of Jesus use their *discretion* to over-rule a tradition. In other words, the disciples *disobey* the rules set by the Establishment (System). In other words, the disciples flaunt their *human-ness* before the Establishment. It is this brazen display of *human-ness* that offends the Establishment.

Jesus asks Scribes and Pharisees, the spokesmen of the Establishment, *"Why do ye also transgress the commandments of God by your tradition?"* The expression, "commandments of God" is generally interpreted as the Mosaic Laws. But, spiritually, the expression implies "commandments of the Self," or "commandments of the body." In other words, Jesus is asking, "Why do you people disobey the body and obey the mind?"

Jesus clarifies: *"For God commanded, saying, Honour thy father and mother: and, He that curseth father or mother, let him die the death. But ye say, Whatsoever shall say to his father or his brother, It is a gift, by whatsoever thou mightest be profited by me; And honour not his father or his mother, he shall be free."* Spiritually, the expression, "father and mother" refers to the physical body because, just as parents, it is the physical body that gives man existence. Therefore, "honoring father and mother" has the following connotations: one, literally, it implies honoring parents; two, spiritually, it implies honoring the body. According to Jesus, those who do not honor their bodies will "die the death." In other words, those who corrupt the body (cell) cease to exist as human beings, strictly speaking. That is the death Jesus is referring to. The word, *curse* means "wishing evil for someone or something." Therefore, "cursing father and mother" implies causing harm or corruption to the body. But, the Scribes and Pharisees have only contempt for the body. They consider the nourishment given to the body as mere gratis. And they think that they are maintaining the body, rather than the other way around.

Jesus again says, *"Thus have ye made the commandments of God of none effect by your tradition."* The commandment of the Self (the body) is to honor the body. The Scribes and Pharisees have violated the commandment of the body by corrupting it. There is a hidden hint that the Serpent-children have genetically altered their DNA by incorporating alien (viral) genes.

MATTHEW 15:7-9

"Ye hypocrites, well did Esaias prophesy of you, saying, This people draweth nigh unto me with their mouth, and honoureth me with their lips; but their heart is far from me. But in vain they do worship me, teaching for doctrines the commandments of men."

The Gospel addresses the Scribes and Pharisees as hypocrites. A hypocrite is one who feigns some desirable or publicly approved attitude, especially one whose private life, opinions, or statements belie his public statements. Spiritually, the term *hypocrite* means "humanoid."

The Gospel quotes prophet Esaias: *"This people draweth unto me with their mouth; but their heart is far from me."* Here, the term "me" suggests "human being," and not some external power center. Therefore, the expression, "this people draweth unto me with their mouth" may be interpreted as follows: "These people pretend to be humans." Spiritually, the term *heart* refers to the DNA. Therefore, the expression, "but their hearts is far from me" may be interpreted as follows: "but their DNA is not of a human being." Therefore, the implication of Esaias' prophesy is this: "These people pretend to be human beings, but they are not." It is indeed a startling statement!

The Gospel exposes the Scribes and Pharisees as aliens pretending to be humans! Perhaps, it is the reason why Jesus was crucified.

The Serpent-children, just as computers, are experts at 'manipulating' formal systems, which include religion, science, language etc. Here, the word *manipulation* suggests computational manipulations. These humanoids are expert matrix-builders (*Freemasons*?) too. The Gnostics called them the *archons*. According to the Gnostics, the *archons* are experts at creating *virtual realities*, which they termed as *hal*.

"But in vain they do worship me, teaching for doctrines the commandments of men." Mathematically speaking, a "commandment of men" is called a *theorem*. In formal systems, theorems need not be thought of as meaningful statements—they are merely strings of symbols. And instead of being *proven*, theorems are merely *produced*, or *derived*, as if by a machine, according to certain typographical rules. But *truth* is very different from theorems. It is not a product of any formal system. The ultimate proof of truth is man himself. A scripture is merely a collection of theorems derived artificially from an axiomatic system. On the other hand, the Gospel is not a scripture, but a collection of eternal truths. It is a doctrine.

According to the Gospel, the alien humanoids have handed over to humanity *formal systems* in the name of *doctrines*.

MATTHEW 15:10-11

"And he called the multitude, and said unto them, Hear, and understand: Not that which goeth into mouth defileth a man; but what cometh out of the mouth, this defileth a man."

The Gospel challenges the Scribes and Pharisees: *"Hear, and understand."* It is a cue that says: "A true human being will understand the statement I am going to make."

The Gospel, then, makes the statement: *"Not that which goeth into mouth defileth a man; but what cometh out of the mouth, this defileth man."* Spiritually, the term *mouth* has dual meanings: first, it refers to the five sense organs (*jnānēndriya*) of sight, hearing, touch, taste and smell; second, it refers to the five organs of action (*karmēndriya*) such as, speech, hands, feet, genitals and excretory organs. (By the way, a computer can *never* hypothesize that the word *mouth* could imply both sense organs and organs of action. It is the challenge.)

That which goeth into 'mouth' is the sense stimuli ("sensory food"), which are the *inputs* to the mind. Therefore, the implication of the statement is this: Sensory inputs cannot defile a human being. The Greek word for defile is *koinoō* (G2840), which means "to profane" ceremonially. Here, the word *ceremonially* is pertinent because it suggests artificiality. What the Gospel says is this: "Human beings cannot be judged as good or evil based on artificial rules."

". . . but what cometh out of the mouth, this defileth man." Here, the term *mouth* refers to the organs of action. That which comes out of the 'mouth' is speech and actions, which are the *output* of the body. Therefore, the implication of the statement is this: A human being's speech and actions can defile him. In other words, a human being can be judged as good or evil based on his speech and actions. If a person's words and actions do not match, then he is evil. He is a hypocrite.

For the humanoids, the reverse is true. For them, the sensory stimuli that go into their body are important because those inputs affect their reality. But, the words and actions that come out of them are meaningless because they are merely 'theorems' derived by their formal systems.

MATTHEW 15:12-14

"Then came his disciples, and said unto him, Knowest thou that the Pharisees were offended, after they heard this saying? But he answered and said, Every plant, which my heavenly Father hath not planted, shall be rooted up. Let them alone: they be blind leaders of the blind. And if the blind lead the blind, both shall fall into the ditch."

In the earlier section we saw the Gospel exposing the Scribes and Pharisees as humanoids. Obviously, they were offended by the public exposure of their true nature. Alarmed, the disciples, remind Jesus about it. But, Jesus, as if to reconfirm his earlier utterances, says, *"Every plant, which my heavenly Father hath not planted, shall be rooted up."* He describes the Scribes and Pharisees as "plants which my heavenly Father hath not planted." In other words, the Gospel exposes the Scribes and Pharisees as alien beings who have infiltrated humanity. It is these entities that the Gospel describes as *tares* planted among the *wheat* by the enemy in the parable of the wheat and tares.

In the parable of the wheat and the tares, the owner of the field says to his servants who ask him if they should uproot the tares, *"Nay; lest while ye gather up the tares, ye root up also the wheat with them."* In a similar fashion, here, Jesus says to the disciples, *"Let them alone: they be blind leaders of the blind."* Jesus hints to the disciples that the time has not come for their uprooting, and brands both the Scribes and Pharisees and the Adamites they lead as "blind." Spiritually, the term *blind* suggests absence of body-awareness. These humanoid entities are 'blind' because they are entirely guided by their program—the scripture—and are unable to see the reality.

The Gospel pronounces the fate of the humanoids and the people who follow them: *"And if the blind lead the blind, both shall fall into the ditch."* Spiritually, the term *ditch* means "perdition," which means "the state of final spiritual ruin," "loss of soul" or "damnation."

MATTHEW 15:15-20

"Then answered Peter and said unto him, Declare unto us this parable. And Jesus said, Are ye also yet without understanding? Do not ye yet understand, that whatsoever entereth in at the mouth goeth into the belly, and cast out into the draught? But those things which proceedeth out of the mouth come forth from the heart; and they defile the man. For out of the heart proceed evil thoughts, murders, adulteries, fornications, theft, false witness, blasphemies: These are the things which defile a man: but to eat with unwashen hands defileth not a man."

The riddle Jesus puts to the Scribes and Pharisees is like a *koan*. Only the body-aware human beings are able to grasp its true meaning.

The fact that Peter asks Jesus to explain the riddle highlights the importance of the truth embedded in it. The disciples are at a loss to understand the true meaning of the riddle, but they are able to feel its importance. The riddle has multiple implications.

Jesus rebukes Peter for his shallow understanding: *"Are ye also yet without understanding?"* Spiritually, the word *understanding* implies body-awareness. In other words, Jesus is asking Peter if he is still a Mortal.

Jesus clarifies Peter's doubt, *"That whatsoever entereth in the mouth goeth into the belly, and cast out into the draught?"* The term *mouth*, here, implies the sensory organs, and that which enters it are the sensory inputs. The Greek word for *draught* is *aphedrōn* (G856), which means "a place of sitting apart." Literally, the word *draught* suggests an outside area meant for defecation. But, here, the word *draught* refers to the outside world. In other words, the Gospel compares the sensory world to a toilet. The 'creatures' that roll in it are called swine. The expression, "cast out into the draught" suggest the worthlessness of sensory objects.

"But those things which proceedeth out of the mouth come forth from the heart; and they defile the man." Here, the term *mouth* implies organs of action; the term *heart* refers to the DNA. The output of the DNA is *tendencies*. In other words, that which comes out of a corrupt DNA is evil tendencies. The Gospel gives a list of actions that originates from evil tendencies.

Evil Actions	Evil Tendencies
Evil thoughts	Conspiracy
Murders	Hatred
Adulteries	Infidelity
Fornication	Prurience
Theft	Covetousness
False witness	Dishonesty
Blasphemies	Self-denial

The truth the Gospel declares is this: "The error that a human being commits for the first time is not an offence. But, errors that he repeatedly commits are offences." But, the humanoids, being programmed entities, commit the same error repeatedly, or habitually.

In other words, the Gospel hints that salvation is for the humans, and not for the humanoids.

MATTHEW 15:21-28

"Then Jesus went thence, and departed into the coasts of Tyre and Sidon. And, behold, a woman of Canaan came out of the same coasts, and cried unto him, saying, Have mercy on me, O Lord, thou Son of David; my daughter is grievously vexed with a devil. But he answered her not a word. And his disciples came and besought him, saying, Send her away; for she crieth after us. But he answered and said, I am not sent but unto the lost sheep of the house of Israel. Then came she and worshipped him, saying, Lord, help me. But he answered and said, It is not meet to take the children's bread, and to cast it to dogs. And she said, Truth, Lord: yet the dogs eat of the crumbs which fall from their master's table. Then Jesus answered and said unto her, O woman, great is thy faith: be it unto thee even as thou wilt. And her daughter was made whole from that very hour."

Sidon was the first home of the Phoenicians on the coast of Canaan. It was the mother city of Tyre, which is the legendary birthplace of *Europa* and *Elissa*. The Hebrew name *Sidon* (H6718) means "an animal caught." According to the Book of Genesis, Sidon is the son of Canaan (son of Ham) and the grandson of Noah. As per the Genesis account, Canaan was cursed by Noah to become a "servant of servants" for his father's (Ham's) sexual transgression, which, perhaps, resulted in Canaan's birth as an Adamite. Spiritually, the Canaanites represent the human beings 'caught' by the Serpent. Canaanites were mad with the viral disease called religion. Interestingly, *Servant of the servants of God* (Latin: *servus servorum Dei*) is one of the titles of the popes and is used at the beginning of papal bulls.

Perhaps, religion is a Canaanite (Phoenician) invention. Canaanite religion is the name for the group of Ancient Semitic religions practiced by the Canaanites living in the ancient Levant, including Israel. At the center of Canaanite religion was royal concern for religious and political legitimacy and the imposition of a divinely ordained legal structure.

The woman who approaches Jesus is a Canaanite. Gospel tells us that the woman's daughter is "vexed with a devil." As we have seen before, the term *devil* refers to the Serpent virus. Spiritually, the woman's 'daughter' refers to the woman's DNA, and not her physical daughter. In other words, the woman's DNA is *taken over* by the Serpent virus.

True to her nature, the woman identifies Jesus by religion and calls him "Son of David," and pleads him to cure her daughter's disease. But, Jesus does not pay any attention to her. Later, Jesus looks at her only because the disciples interceded on her behalf. Spiritually, Jesus represents the Gospel, and the disciples represent the spiritual interpretations of the Gospel.

Jesus says to the woman, *"I am not sent but to the lost sheep of the house of Israel."* The expression, "house of Israel" refers to humanity, and the expression, "the lost sheep of the house of Israel" refers to the Mortals. In other words, the Gospel says that it cures only the Evites, and not the Adamites. Alternatively, it implies that only the Evites are able to understand the Gospel truths. But, the woman is persistent. Therefore, Jesus says to her, *"It is not meet to take the children's bread, and to cast it to dogs."* Spiritually, the expression "children's bread" refers to the true meaning of the Gospel; the term "dogs" refers to the Adamites.

The woman says to Jesus, *"Truth, Lord: yet the dogs eat of the crumbs which fall from their master's table."* The woman's reply reveals that she still retains vestiges of "human-ness," or faith. Spiritually, the expression, "master's table" refers to the Gospel; the crumbs that fall from the master's table refer to Gospel truths.

A humanoid cannot understand metaphor, let alone speak in metaphor. But this woman not only understands Jesus' metaphorical words but also replies to him using the same metaphor. Jesus is greatly impressed by the woman's faith, and says, *"O woman, great is thy faith: be it unto thee even as thou wilt."* Jesus heals the woman's devil-vexed mind. In other words, Gospel reveals its spiritual meaning to her, which heals her genetic corruption, but, purely out of compassion. According to the Gospel, the woman's daughter was made *whole* from that very hour. The word, *whole* signifies non-duality. In other words, the Gospel cures the woman's delusion.

It may seem, at the outset, that the woman got cured because of her own persistent efforts. So, is faith achievable by works? If you consider the Gospel episode as true incident, or history, then the contradiction indeed arises. But, the Jesus Story is not history but an allegory. Therefore, the contradiction does not arise.

MATTHEW 15:29-31

"And Jesus departed from thence, and came nigh unto the sea of Galilee; and went up into a mountain, and sat down there. And great multitudes came unto him, having with them those that were lame, blind, dumb, maimed, and many others, and cast them down at Jesus' feet; and he healed them: Insomuch that the multitude wondered, when they saw the dumb to speak, the maimed to be whole, the lame to walk, and the blind to see: and they glorified the God of Israel."

"And Jesus departed from thence, and came nigh unto the sea of Galilee; and went up into a mountain, and sat down there." Jesus returns from Canaan to his home country of Galilee, and stations himself on the top of a mountain. Spiritually, "Jesus in Canaan" means "Gospel in the Church." The term *mountain* signifies human body; the name *Sea of Galilee* signifies body-awareness. Therefore, "Jesus on a mountain in Galilee" denotes a body-aware human being (Evite). Here, we find the Gospel (Jesus) leaving religion (Canaan) and moving into the human body (mountain in Galilee).

"And great multitudes came unto him, having with them those that were lame, blind, dumb, maimed, and many others, and cast them down at Jesus' feet; and he healed them: Insomuch that the multitude wondered, when they saw the dumb to speak, the maimed to be whole, the lame to walk, and the blind to see: and they glorified the God of Israel." The *multitude* represents the Adamites. The multitude that follows Jesus to the mountain-top denotes the evil thoughts that tempt the Evite. The Gospel metaphorically categorizes these thoughts as: the lame; the blind; the dumb; the maimed; and the many others.

Here, the Gospel teaches us the principle of cleanliness (*śaucha*). The word *cleanliness* implies health. According to the Hindu religion, there are five types of cleanliness. They are:

1. Cleanliness of the body (*śarīra śaucha*)
2. Cleanliness of the mind (*manah śaucha*)
3. Cleanliness of words (*vāc śaucha*)
4. Cleanliness of action (*karma śaucha*)
5. Cleanliness of race (*kula śaucha*)

Literally, the *lame* are those who are unable to walk; but, spiritually, it represents blind beliefs. Literally, the *blind* are those who cannot see clearly; but spiritually, it represents religious thoughts. Literally, the *dumb* are those who are unable to speak; but spiritually, it represents thoughts relating to work. Literally, the *maimed* are those who are unable to act; but spiritually, it represents fearful thoughts. Literally, the expression "many others" means "many other diseases"; but, spiritually, it represents thoughts about wealth, power, and fame. Jesus heals all those who follow him to the top of the mountain. In other words, the spiritual meaning of the Gospel removes corruption from Evites' mind and makes them body-aware.

MATTHEW 15:32-39

"Then Jesus called his disciples unto him, and said, I have compassion on the multitude, because they continue with me now three days, and have nothing to eat: and I will not send them away fasting, lest they faint in the way. And his disciples say unto him, Whence should we have so much bread in the wilderness, as to fill so great a multitude? And Jesus saith unto them, How many loaves have ye? And they said, Seven, and a few little fishes. And he commanded the multitude to sit down on the ground. And he took the seven loaves and the fishes, and gave thanks, and brake them, and gave to his disciples, and the disciples to the multitude. And they did all eat, and were filled: and they took up of the broken meat that was left seven baskets full. And they that did eat were four thousand men, beside women and children. And he sent away the multitude, and took ship, and came into the coasts of Magdala."

"Then Jesus called his disciples unto him, and said, I have compassion on the multitude, because they continue with me now three days, and have nothing to eat: and I will not send them away fasting, lest they faint in the way." The Neophyte, having undergone the rigorous cleansing process, is now substantially free from ignorance and delusion. He is now an *Initiate*. Here, the Gospel describes the advanced training imparted to the *Initiate*, by means of an allegory—the miracle of feeding four thousand people with seven loaves of bread and a few little fishes.

In this parable, the Gospel uses the term *multitude* to describe the disciple's mental state, whereas in the previous one it used the expression "great multitude." It suggests that the disciple is now wiser and saner than before. The Gospel explains the reason for the disciple's spiritual progress: *"because they continue with me now three days."* The "three days" refers to the three stages of the cleansing process: cleansing the cardinal sins of Objectivity, Locality and Causality (*thāpathraya*).

During the cleansing process, the disciple had abstained from food—sensory food—and therefore, he is hungry for nourishment. Seeing the famished state of the disciple, Jesus desires to give him nourishment, and says, *"I will not send them away fasting, lest they faint in the way."* In other words, the disciple starts getting glimpses of the truth now that his mind is substantially clean (open).

The miracle Jesus performs here is similar to the miracle mentioned in Matthew chapter 14, but there are some differences: firstly, in the previous episode, the multitude consisted of five thousand people, but now, there are only four thousand people; secondly, the food supply in the previous episode consisted of five loaves and two fishes, but now, there are seven loaves and more than two fishes. Spiritually, the differences point to the higher state of spiritual awareness of the disciple.

The feast process also is slightly different from the previous one, and it consists of the following steps:

	Gospel Words	**Implication**
1	Sit down on the grass	Sit in a relaxed pose
2	Take the seven loaves of bread and the fishes	Gather body-awareness through the spine
3	Give thanks	Acknowledge the Self
4	Break the bread	Enlighten the body

In the previous episode, the aggregate of five senses plus the intellect and the mind was taken to represent the human body. But here, the aggregate of seven major *chakras* and many minor *chakras* is taken to represent the human body. In Hindu metaphysical and *tantric/yogic* traditions, *chakras* are points or knots, in the subtle human body. They are located at the physical counterparts of the major plexuses of arteries, veins and nerves. They are part of the subtle body, not the physical body, and as such are the meeting points of the subtle (non-physical) energy channels, called *nadis*.

In this parable too, the mode of delivery of the victuals is the same: Jesus to disciples, and disciple to the multitude. But, here, the *disciples* are the body-cells and the *multitude* is the mind. In other words, the body cells first experience the truth, and then, the truth surfaces in the mind.

In this story, the "left-over food" is seven baskets full, whereas in the previous case, it was twelve baskets full. It shows that the Initiate is now able to absorb more of the Gospel meaning than before. He now carries the Gospel more in his body and less in his mind (memory). The seven basketful of left over food represents the Gospel message memorized.

The Gospel then says, *"And he sent away the multitude, and took the ship, and came into the coasts of Magdala."* There is some confusion about the whereabouts of Magdala. However, the most reliable Greek manuscripts give the name of the place as *Magadan*. Athough some commentators confidently state that the two refer to the same place, others dismiss the substitution of Magdala for Magadan as simply to substitute a known for an unknown place. The parallel passage in Mark's gospel (8:10) gives (in the majority of manuscripts) a quite different place name, *Dalmanutha*. The name Magadan sounds very similar to *Magadh*, the great Indian empire of ancient times.

Magadh was the great Indian empire of the ancient times (600 BCE). Two of India's major religions, Jainism, and Buddhism have roots in Magadh. Two of India's greatest empires, the Maurya Empire and the Gupta Empire, originated from Magadh. These empires saw advancements in ancient India's science, mathematics, astronomy, religion, and philosophy and were considered the Indian "Golden Age." The importance of Magadh's culture can be seen in that both Buddhism and Jainism adopted some of its features, most significantly a belief in rebirth and karmic retribution, and in the belief that liberation can be achieved through knowledge of the Self.

Perhaps, Jesus returning to the coasts of Magdala suggests the Initiate's intuition (voice of the Self) returning to its non-dualistic state after revealing the truths to him through the Gospel.

CHAPTER 16

But Whom Say Ye That I Am?

MATTHEW 16:1-4

"The Pharisees also with the Sadducees came, and tempting desired him that he would shew them a sign from heaven. He answered and said unto them, When it is evening, ye say, It will be fair weather: for the sky is red. And in the morning, It will be foul weather to day: for the sky is red and lowring. O ye hypocrites, ye can discern the face of the sky; but can ye not discern the signs of the times? A wicked and adulterous generation seeketh after a sign; and there shall be no sign be given unto it, but the sign of the prophet Jonas. And he left them, and departed."

The Greek word for *tempt* is *peirazō* (G3985), which means "to test." It also means "to entice." The English word, *tempt* has multiple connotations. The different connotations of the word are given in the table below:

	Synonym	Meaning
1	Seduce	To lead astray, as from duty, rectitude, or the like; to corrupt
2	Allure	To attract or tempt by something flattering or desirable
3	Dare	To challenge or provoke (a person) into a demonstration of courage

4	Attract	To draw by appealing to the emotions or senses, by stimulating interest, or by exciting admiration
5	Charm	To delight or please greatly by beauty, attractiveness etc.
6	Court	To act in such a manner as to cause, lead to, or provoke
7	Tantalize	To torment with, or as if with, the sight of something desired but out of reach
8	Fascinate	To attract and hold attentively by a unique power, personal charm, unusual nature, or some other special quality
9	Induce	To lead or move by persuasion or influence, as to some action or state of mind
10	Instigate	To urge, provoke, or incite to some action or course
11	Inveigle	To entice, lure, or ensnare by flattery or artful talk or inducements
12	Intrigue	To accomplish or force by crafty plotting or underhand machinations
13	Move	To arouse or excite the feelings or passions of
14	Persuade	To induce to believe by appealing to reason or understanding
15	Wheedle	To endeavour to influence (a person) by smooth, flattering, or beguiling words or acts
16	Captivate	To attract and hold the attention or interest of, as by beauty or excellence
17	Coax	To attempt to influence by gentle persuasion, flattery etc.

The word *tempt*, with differing connotations, appear nine times in the Gospel of Matthew. The first mention of the word is in Matthew 4:1, which describes the 'tempting' of Jesus by the devil in the desert.

Here we see the Serpent-children 'tempting' Jesus. They ask Jesus to show them a "sign from heaven." The Greek word for *sign* is *sēmeion* (G4592), which means "an indication." The word is derived from the root *sēma* (G4591), which means "a mark." Spiritually, the word *sign* means "proof." In other words, the Pharisees and Sadducees are demanding proof from Jesus: proof that he is indeed the Messiah. The Pharisees and Sadducees represent the religion. In other words, these religious authorities are demanding that the Gospel prove that it is indeed the truth. Alternatively, it also suggests that the humanoids are asking the true human being that he prove that he is indeed the true human being.

The fundamental issue here is: "what is a test?" How do you prove that a given string of symbols is a theorem or not? Of prime importance here is the guarantee that the test delivers its verdict in a finite length of time, rather than continue computing for the answer indefinitely. A test of 'theoremhood' that is *guaranteed* to *terminate* after a finite length of time is called a *decision procedure*. Incidentally, an important requirement of formal systems, including scriptures, is that the set of axioms be characterized by a decision procedure. But, for the Gospel, man himself is the decision procedure, and its guaranteed termination is called *death*.

Therefore, Jesus replies to his inquisitors, *"When it is evening, ye say, It will be fair weather: for the sky is red. And in the morning, It will be foul weather today: for the sky is red and lowring. O ye hypocrites, ye can discern the face of the sky; but can ye not discern the signs of the times?"* Here, the Gospel is alluding to the ability of computers (humanoids) to assert that a given string is a theorem (of the formal system), when given the theorem. But it can never say the given string is *not* a theorem with absolute certainty. It will go on computing for the answer, indefinitely. There is no *guarantee* that it will *terminate.* In other words, there is no *decision procedure* for theoremhood for a computer. This is what the Gospel implies when it says, "but can ye not discern the signs of times?"

Alternatively, the Gospel alludes to the causal or mechanical nature of computer intellect. The word *time*, here, refers to the mind (formalism). The word *times*, on the other hand, suggests infinity, which is the human nature. Spiritually, the expression, "sign of times" means "body-awareness." The Gospel accuses the Pharisees and Sadducees of not being able to see "the signs of the times." In other words, the Gospel hints that humanoids cannot grasp infinity. It also implies that the Sadducees and Pharisees are not body-aware and, therefore, not true human beings. Therefore, it calls them *hypocrites*. A hypocrite is a pretender or an imposter. Spiritually, the term *hypocrite* means "humanoid."

The Gospel exposes the mind of the Serpent-children, which is based in the *modus ponens* principle. In propositional logic, "*modus ponendo ponens*" (Latin for "the way that affirms by affirming") is abbreviated as *modus ponens.* It may be summarized as: "P implies Q." It may be understood as follows: "P is *asserted* to be true; therefore, Q *must* be true." In other words, "If P is true, then, Q is true." It is this false logic that the Gospel is alluding to metaphorically: *"When it is evening, ye say, It will be fair weather: for the sky is red. And in the morning, It will be foul weather today: for the sky is red and lowring."* All formal systems are based on the modus ponens logic.

The Gospel comes down heavily on the Pharisees and Sadducees: *"A wicked and adulterous generation seeketh after a sign . . ."* The word *wicked* means "morally bad in principle or practice," or "having committed unrighteous acts"; *adulterous* means "adulterated," or "mixed with impurities"; *generation* means "species." Therefore, the expression, "a wicked and adulterous generation" means "a genetically-altered species", "a humanoid species" or "a race of hypocrites." The *sign* that these people are seeking is body-awareness. But, how can you prove body-awareness to another person? Alternatively, the Gospel says that the humanoids are asking for the *decision procedure* for absolute truth.

Therefore, Jesus says to the inquisitors, ". . . *and there shall be no sign be given unto it, but the sign of the prophet Jonas."* What is the sign of the prophet Jonas? Three days of total darkness! Spiritually, the expression "three days of darkness" means "death." In other words, the Gospel hints that all humanoids will perish with death, whereas true human beings will reincarnate again. The crucifixion, death and entombment of Jesus and the subsequent resurrection after three days suggest that. In other words, the Gospel declares that the *decision procedure* for absolute truth is death.

MATTHEW 16:5-12

"And when his disciples were come to the other side, they had forgotten to take bread. Then Jesus said unto them, Take heed and beware of the leaven of the Pharisees and of the Sadducees. And they reasoned among themselves, saying, It is because we have taken no bread. Which when Jesus perceived, he said unto them, O ye of little faith, why reason among yourselves, because ye have brought no bread? Do ye not yet understand, neither remember the five loaves of the five thousand, and how many baskets ye took up? Neither the seven loaves of the four thousand, and how many baskets ye took up? How is it that ye do not understand that I spake it not to you concerning bread, that ye should beware of the leaven of the Pharisees and of the Sadducees? Then understood they how that he bade them not beware of the leaven of bread, but of the doctrine of the Pharisees and of the Sadducees."

"And when his disciples were come to the other side, they had forgotten to take bread." Having returned from the exhilarating spiritual feast, the disciples are now in the mundane world. The expression, "other side" refers to the world of delusion. The word *bread* both refers to the Gospel, or body-awareness. The disciples are now busy with their lives, and they forget wearing the 'armour' of body-awareness.

Realizing that the disciples are not body-aware, Jesus warns them: *"Take heed and beware of the leaven of the Pharisees and of the Sadducees." Leaven* is the *yeast* used in bread-making. When a small quantity of leaven is added to the dough, the dough changes its form. In a sense, the leaven *corrupts* the dough. Leaven is a *microbial* (Lactobacillus) culture. Spiritually, it denotes the virus—the Serpent virus. Just as leaven corrupts dough, the Serpent virus corrupts the human body (DNA). The expression, "leaven of the Pharisees and Sadducees" means "the DNA of Sadducees and Pharisees." Alternatively, it means "the scripture of Sadducees and Pharisees." In other words, the Gospel is hinting that the Sadducees and Pharisees *are* alien humanoids, and their scripture *is* the Serpent virus!

The Serpent virus is ubiquitous in the world. And it is the root of all evil on earth. Therefore, one has to be on the guard constantly. And the most effective protection against it is body-awareness. Therefore, one should always wear the "protective armour" of body-awareness to avoid being infected by the Serpent virus.

An important characteristic of leaven is that even a minute quantity is sufficient to corrupt a large quantity of dough. Similarly, even a brief exposure to the Serpent virus can infect a human being.

The disciples take the word, *bread* literally and blame each other for not taking it with them, presuming that Jesus is asking for bread to eat. Exasperated by the disciples' state of delusion, Jesus asks them,

"Do ye not yet understand, neither remember the five loaves of the five thousand, and how many basket ye took up?" The implication of the words is this: "Why do you worry about bread? Have you not seen the miracles the human body is capable of performing?" Indirectly, the Gospel is hinting that it is the infection by the Serpent virus that destroys human body's miraculous capacity.

The Gospel spells out the truth directly: *"How is it that ye do not understand that I spake it not to you concerning bread, that ye should beware of the leaven of the Pharisees and of the Sadducees?"* The Gospel cannot make it anymore explicit than this.

The Gospel, then, says, *"Then understood they how he bade them not beware of the leaven of the bread, but of the doctrine of the Pharisees and of the Sadducees."* But, subsequent events raise serious doubts whether the disciples really understood the true meaning of the words.

MATTHEW 16:13-20

"When Jesus came into the coasts of Caesarea Philippi, he asked his disciples, saying, Whom do men say that I the Son of man am? And they said, Some say that thou art John the Baptist: some, Elias; and others, Jeremias, or one of the prophets. He saith unto them, But whom say ye that I am? And Simon Peter answered and said, Thou art the Christ, the Son of the living God. And Jesus answered and said unto him, Blessed art thou, Simon Bar-jona: for flesh and blood hath not revealed it unto thee, but my Father which is in heaven. And I say also unto thee, That thou art Peter, and upon this rock I will build my church; and the gates of hell shall not prevail against it. And I will give unto thee the keys of the kingdom of heaven: and whatsoever thou shalt bind on earth shall be bound in heaven; and whatsoever thou shalt loose on earth shall be loosed in heaven. Then charged he his disciples that they should tell no man that he was Jesus the Christ."

Caesarea Philippi or *Caeseria Panea* was an ancient Roman city located at the southwest base of Mount Hermon, adjacent to a spring, grotto, and related shrines dedicated to the pagan god *Pan*, also called *Paneas*. In Greek religion and mythology, Pan is the god of the wild, shepherds and flocks, nature, of mountain wilds, hunting and rustic music, and companion of nymphs. Pan is the western world's demonized version of Lord Krishna of Hindu mythology. There are many similarities between Pan and Krishna. Like Pan, Krishna too is a shepherd (*gōpāla*); he too loved his flocks (cows) and his playground was the Gōvardhan Mountain; he too was known for his mellifluous flute music (*vēnu-gānam*). Krishna too had many nymphs surrounding him (*gōpika*).

Mount Hermon is a mountain cluster in the Anti-Lebanon mountain range. Its summit straddles the border between Syria, Israel, and Lebanon. In the *Book of Enoch*, Mount Hermon is the place where the *Grigori* ("Watcher") class of 'fallen' angels descended to Earth. These so-called fallen angels allegedly swore upon the mountain that they would take wives among the daughters of men and take mutual imprecation for their sin (Enoch 6). The Book of Enoch calls these fallen angels the *Nephilim*. According to the Bible, Mount Hermon is known as the *Sion*. It is highly plausible that the so-called *Nephilim* were a group of Evites, perhaps of Greek origin who settled on Mount Hermon long ago. The Jews considered these Gentiles as uncleanness and wanted to expel them from the land. Perhaps, the story of the *fallen angels* descending on Mount Hermon was a cleverly fabricated story intended to demonize these original settlers and evict them from the land.

Har Senaim or *Senaim* is an archeological site that sits on the peak near Mount Hermon in the Israeli-occupied portion of the Golan Heights. The site features a Roman temple and settlement that has been included in a group of *Temples of Mount Hermon*. The ruins of a second Ancient Greek temple were also found in the region. It is also possible that the Greek settlement was the original one in the area, and the Romans came in subsequently.

In the Old Testament we find mentions about Zion and Sion. The name *Zion* refers to Jerusalem, whereas the name *Sion* refers to Mount Hermon. There are 153 mentions of Zion and only 2 mentions of Sion in the Old Testament. But, in the New Testament, there is no mention of Zion at all, but there are 7 mentions of Sion. There is also a very interesting mention about Sion in the Book of Revelation:

> *And I looked, and, lo, a Lamb stood on the mount Sion, and with him an hundred forty and four thousand, having his Father's name written in their foreheads.*
> Revelation 14:1

The term "Father's name" refers to the Self. Therefore, the expression, "an hundred forty and four thousand, having his Father's name written in their foreheads" clearly suggests that these people are true human beings (Evites).

It seems, the *Book of Enoch* itself is part of a wider religious conspiracy to demonize the true Christ. It is possible that the enemy has captured the Church, and the real master of the Church is cast out, and is branded as the enemy.

The place, Caesarea Philippi near Mount Hermon, is a critical factor in Jesus' question: *"Whom do men say that I the Son of man am?"* Spiritually, the term "Son of man" refers to the Evite, or the Gospel. In other words, Jesus is asking, "Do people think that I am Jewish?" The disciples reply to him that 'people' think of him as a prophet. Jesus, then, directs the question at them: *"But whom say ye that I am?"* Before anyone else could answer that question, Simon Peter blurts out, *"Thou art the Christ, the Son of the living God."*

It is surprising that Peter uttered the word *Christ* (Greek: *Christos* G5547), and not *Messiah* (Hebrew: *Māsiah* H4899), because the term *Christ* is not mentioned anywhere in the Jewish scriptures. It is a Greek word, and not a Hebrew word. And it means "the anointed," which means "the body-aware." Spiritually, the term *Christ* refers to the true human DNA, or the Gospel. Interestingly, the word *Christ* is not mentioned anywhere in the Old Testament; similarly, the term *Jehovah* is not mentioned anywhere in the New Testament.

It is clear that Peter's utterance did not come from his intellect. It is a spontaneous eruption from within. Moreover, Peter adds a qualification with the name Christ, which is equally significant: he says, *"The Son of the living God."* The term "living God" refers to the true human DNA. Therefore, the expression, "Son of the living God" means "true human being." The term *Son* suggests that the true human being is not *created*; he is *born*. In short, Peter says, "You are an Evite."

Jesus, then, addresses Peter using a Hebrew appellation: *Simon Barjona*, which is two names conjoined. The name *Simon* (Hebrew: *Śīmōn* H8095) means "one who hears." *Bar-jona* means "son of Jona."

The name *Jona* is derived from the Hebrew name *Yōna* (H3123), which means "dove." The name *Yōna* originates from the Hebrew root word *yayin* (H3196), which means "intoxication," or "spirit." Therefore, the term *Bar-jona* means "son of spirit." Thus, Jesus confirms Peter's Evite status and says, *"Blessed art thou."* As we have seen before, the term "blessed" refers to the Evite. Here, the Gospel reveals the chief qualities of an Evite:

1. "One who hears" (suggesting the gift of intuition)
2. "Son of the Spirit" (suggesting divine origin)

Jesus says to Peter, *". . . for flesh and blood hath not revealed it unto thee, but my Father which is in heaven."* In other words, Jesus says, "You did not make this statement from your intellect. It came from your inner Self."

"And I say unto thee, That thou art Peter, and upon this rock I will build my church." Here, Jesus is not addressing Simon Peter, the disciple, but Simon Peter, the Evite. The *rock* that he refers to is the body of the Evite. Spiritually, the term *church* refers to humanity. In other words, the Gospel declares: "Humanity will be rebuilt from the bodies of the Evites," or "Humanity will be saved by the Evites." Perhaps, the two hundred so-called 'fallen' angels who landed on Mount Hermon were the "sowers of the good seed" in the field called Earth.

". . . and the gates of hell shall not prevail against it." Spiritually, *hell* refers to the corrupt body, or the corrupt world. And there are two gates that hell: one, mental; the other, physical. The mental gate to hell is the literal scripture; the physical gate to hell is a blemish on the cell surface. Indirectly, the Gospel says that the Evite is impenetrable to the Serpent virus.

"And I will give unto thee the keys of the kingdom of heaven." As we have seen before, the "kingdom of heaven" refers to the inner body (DNA). The Gospel uses the word *keys,* which implies that there are more than one key to the kingdom of heaven. The first key is body-awareness; the second is the spiritual Gospel.

". . . and whatsoever thou shalt bind on earth shall be bound in heaven: and whatsoever thou shalt loose on earth shall be loosed in heaven." The term *heaven* refers to the *inside*, the inner body, the DNA; the term *earth* refers to the *outside*, the mind, the world. The literal meaning of the word, "bind" is "to make secure with a rope,

by wrapping around"; but spiritually, it refers to the creative process. It implies *intention*. In other words, the Gospel says that whatever an Evite intends in his mind will become reality. Similarly, the term *loose* literally means "to release," or "to relax"; but spiritually, it implies *banishment*. The expression, "loose on earth" means "to banish from mind"; the expression, "loose in heaven" means "to banish from reality." In other words, the Gospel says that whatever an Evite banishes from his mind will be banished from reality.

"Then charged he his disciples that they should tell no man that he was Jesus Christ." The words may be interpreted as follows: "The true human being himself is the Jesus Christ; but, do not declare it publicly."

Here, Gospel subtly rubbishes the notion that Jesus is a man of Jewish origin.

MATTHEW 16:21-23

"From that time forth began Jesus to shew unto his disciples, how that he must go unto Jerusalem, and suffer many things of the elders and chief priests and scribes, and be killed, and be raised again the third day. Then Peter took him, and began to rebuke him, saying, Be it far from thee, Lord: this shall not be unto thee. But he turned, and said unto Peter, Get thee behind me, Satan: thou art an offence unto me: for thou savourest not the things that be of God, but those that be of men."

"From that time forth began Jesus to shew unto his disciples, how that he must go unto Jerusalem, and suffer many things of the elders and chief priests and scribes, and be killed, and be raised again the third day." The expression "that time" points to the time of exposing:

1. The Scribes, Sadducees and the Pharisees as humanoids serving the Serpent.
2. The literal scripture as the corrupting agent.
3. The notion that Jesus is a Jewish man as a lie.

The exposures of Jesus threatened the very foundation of the religious Establishment that they conspire to kill him. Foreseeing the possibility, Jesus hints it to the disciples. In other words, the revelations made by the Gospel threaten to undermine the credibility of the religious Establishment that they conspire to proscribe the book. Joseph—the author of the book—foreseeing such a possibility, include it in his book.

Peter, enthused by his new designation as "The Rock," presumes that Jesus had nominated him as his successor and leader of the 'Church.' He quickly assumes the role of a leader and starts *managing* things. To begin with, he says encouraging (but insincere) words to Jesus, just like any other sycophantic world leader. Jesus senses the working of the Serpent in Peter and rebukes him sharply, saying, *"Get thee behind me, Satan: thou are an offence unto me: for thou savourest not the things that be of God, but those that be of man."* The Gospel makes it clear to the disciples that in his 'church' everyone is *behind* everyone else, and there is no need of a professional leader in his church. In other words, Jesus makes it clear that anyone who tries to get *ahead* of his fellowmen is surely a Satan.

But, who is *Satan*? Many Bible scholars use the terms *Serpent* and *Satan* interchangeably. But, Satan is not the Serpent; he is Serpent's proxy. The term Satan refers to the person through whom the Serpent operates. Every Adamite is a potential Satan. The first mention of *Satan* in the Bible is in the Book of Chronicles:

> *And Satan stood up against Israel, and provoked David to number Israel.*
> 1 Chronicles 21:1

In the Old Testament account, Satan provokes King David to do a census of his people. The Satan, here, provokes David, the leader of Israelites. In other words, the term *Satan* refers to the *policy advisers* of worldly leaders. It is these satanic advisers who 'provoke' leaders to commit crimes against humanity.

Jesus explains to Peter why he offended him: *". . . for thou savourest not the things that be of God, but those that be of man."* The temptation of the Serpent is always the same:

> *All these things will I give thee, if thou wilt fall down and worship me.*
> Matthew 4:9

He who accepts the Serpent's offer becomes a Satan.

MATTHEW 16:24-28

"Then said Jesus unto his disciples, If any man will come after me, let him deny himself, and take up his cross, and follow me. For whosoever will save his life shall lose it: and whosoever will lose his life for my sake shall find it. For what is a man profited, if he shall gain the whole world, and lose his own soul? or what shall a man give in exchange for his soul? For the Son of man shall come in the glory of his Father with his angels; and then he shall reward every man according to his works. Verily I say unto you, There be some standing here which shall not taste of death, till they see the Son of man coming in his kingdom."

"If any man will come after me, let him deny himself, and take up his cross, and follow me." Here, the Gospel states a result and the requirement to achieve it:

The result: "*If any man will come after me*"

The requirement: "*let him deny himself, and take up his cross, and follow me*"

The term "me," in this context, refers to the Gospel. Therefore, the expression, "if any man will come after me" implies "if anyone wants to truly understand the Gospel." Here, the word "himself" refers to classical logic, and the term *cross* refers to non-duality. To take up the cross means to accept non-duality. Therefore, the spiritual implication of the Gospel statement is this: "If anyone wants to understand the truth, then he should discard classical logic, and study the Gospel non-dualistically."

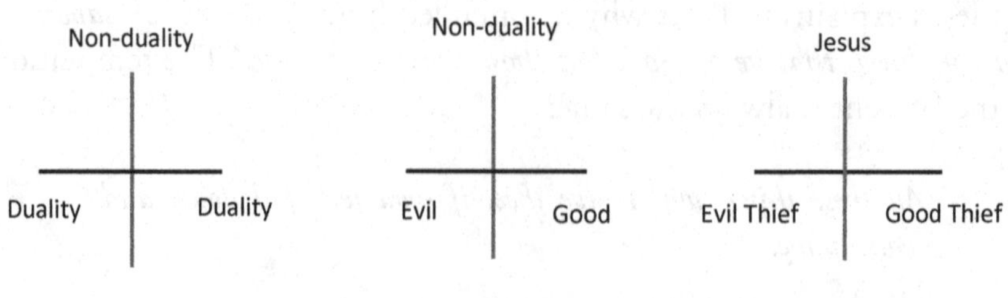

THE CROSS

"For whosoever will save his life shall lose it: and whosoever will lose his life for my sake shall find it." The Greek word for *life* is *psuchē* (G5590), which means "spirit" or "soul". But, spiritually, the term *life* implies "meaning" or "soul." Here, the Gospel uses the word *life* in two senses: firstly, it uses it as "meaning"; and secondly, it uses it as "truth." To "save life" means to understand the Gospel dualistically; to "lose life" means to understand the Gospel non-dualistically. The expression, "for my sake" means "for the sake of truth." Therefore, the spiritual implication of the statement is this: "Those who understand the Gospel dualistically (classically) will miss the truth, but those who understand the Gospel non-dualistically will realize the truth."

Those who understand the Gospel non-dualistically will understand the truth, and the truth will set them free from ignorance and delusion. In other words, the Gospel truth removes the corruption of their DNA. But, the Gospel has no effect on those who understand it literally; their corruption remains same as before. Therefore, the Gospel asks, *"For what is a man profited, if he shall gain the whole world, and lose his own soul? Or what shall a man give in exchange for his soul?"* In other words, nothing in this world is worth exchanging with the DNA.

The DNA is corrupted in two ways: one, physically, by the Serpent virus; two, spiritually, by dualistic scriptures. The Serpent uses the physical means to corrupt the DNA, whereas his children (Satan) use the spiritual means to corrupt it.

The Gospel foretells: *"For the Son of man shall come in the glory of his Father with his angels; and then he shall reward every man according to his works."* Spiritually, the term *works* refers to the (state of the) DNA or *karma*, rather than physical actions done by a person. The term "Son of man" refers to the spiritual Gospel. The expression, "glory of his Father" refers to the brilliance of the spiritual revelations. The *angels* are the Gospel truths. The "coming of the Son of man" refers to the revelation of the spiritual Gospel. In other words, the Gospel is foretelling the dawn of a bright new day. It foresees the day when humanity will be freed from the clutches of the politico-religious System that enslaved it for millennia.

The Gospel declares: *"Verily I say unto you, There be some standing here which shall not taste of death, till they see the Son of man coming in his kingdom."* The word *standing* means "to be upright" or "to be uncorrupted." It refers to the Evites. Therefore, the implication of the statement is this: "The spiritual Gospel will reveal the truth to all human beings, and will give them eternal life." *Eternal life* is nothing but the continual reincarnation of the uncorrupted human DNA. The word "some" suggests that some will not reincarnate, but perish.

CHAPTER 17

The Transfiguration

MATTHEW 17:1-2

"And after six days Jesus taketh Peter, James, and John his brother, and bringeth them up into an high mountain apart, And transfigured before them: and his face did shine as the sun, and his raiment was white as the light."

Here, we see the disciple receiving the *kundalini* experience. The term *kundalini* means "coiled." Kundalini is described as a sleeping, dormant potential force in the human organism. Yōga describes kundalini is as a corporeal energy—an unconscious, instinctive or libidinal force or *śakti*, that lies coiled at the base of the human spine. Kundalini ascension represents the elevation or sublimation of the baser instincts in man. Kundalini awakening results in deep meditation, enlightenment and bliss.

The phrase, "*six days*" refers to the six stages of kundalini-ascension, before reaching the final stage of enlightenment. The six stages are:

1. *Mūlādhāra chakra*
2. *Swādhisthāna chakra*
3. *Manipura chakra*
4. *Anāhata chakra*
5. *Viśuddha chakra*
6. *Ājnā chakra*

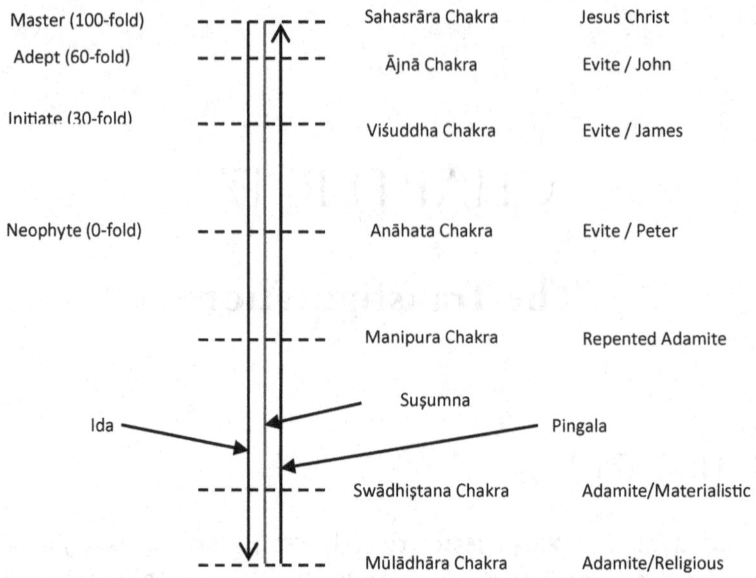

STAGES OF ENLIGHTENMENT

Jesus represents the body (DNA) of the disciple. In the above Gospel verses we see three disciples of varying levels of spiritual accomplishment trying to attain the kundalini experience using their bodies as instrument. The "high mountain" represents the highest chakra, the *Sahasrāra chakra*. The Sanskrit word for mountain is *mēru*. The *Mahā-mēru* represents the human brain. Perhaps, Mount Hermon is the Gospel equivalent of *Mahā-mēru.*

Peter, James and John represent three disciples whose level of spiritual awakening has reached the *Anāhata*, *Viśuddha* and *Ājna* chakra stages, respectively. When a man experiences the kundalini experience, his body-awareness transfigures into a state of pure awareness, which can be compared to light. The Bhagavad Gīta describes that mystical experience:

> *Divi sūrya sahasrasya bhavēd yuga padudthitha*
> *Yadi bhā sadruśi sa syad bhāsas-thasya mahātmanah*
> B.G. 11:12
> ("If a thousand suns were to burst forth in the sky, their combined effulgence would not equal the splendor of that great soul.")

The reply to Peter's proposal for building three tabernacles comes directly from The Father. He commands Peter and his fellow disciples to serve Jesus only, and not Jesus and Moses and Elias as proposed by Peter. He declares, *"This is my beloved Son, in whom I am well pleased; hear ye him."* The Father represents Peter's inner Self. The term "this," in this context, refers to Jesus, the Gospel, or Peter's own body (DNA). Father addresses Jesus as "my beloved Son." A son is the extension of father in time. They are one and the same. In other words, Peter realizes the truth: "My own body (DNA) is the Father. I and my Father are one."

It may be noted that a *son* has a higher status than a *servant.* Son inherits the father. Moses and Elias are mere servants, whereas Jesus is the son. In other words, the scripture is only a servant, whereas the human body is the son. Adam is a *created* entity, but Jesus (the true human being) is not created, he is *born.* Peter is now an Evite and, therefore, the Father commands him, *"Hear ye him."* The commandment is three-fold. It means:

1. "You listen to the body."
2. "You listen to the Gospel."
3. "You should not listen to the literal scripture."

It is also an indirect warning to Peter not to think of himself as a leader but to honor the individual. Jesus, then, comforts the disciples shaken by the mystical kundalini awakening experience.

The same heavenly voice, *"This is my beloved Son, in whom I am well pleased"* was heard when Jesus was baptized by John the Baptist (Matthew 3:17). But, then, it represented the kundalini awakening of Joseph, the author of the Gospel. But, now, it represents the kundalini awakening of the Gospel interpreter.

MATTHEW 17:9-13

"And as they came down from the mountain, Jesus charged them, saying, Tell the vision to no man, until the Son of man be risen again from the dead. And his disciples asked him, saying, Why then say the scribes that Elias must first come? And Jesus answered and said unto them, Elias truly shall first come, and restore all things. But I say unto you, That Elias is come already, and they knew him not, but have done unto him whatsoever they listed. Likewise shall also the Son of man suffer of them. Then the disciples understood that he spake unto them of John the Baptist."

The expression, "and as they came down from the mountain" suggests that Jesus and the disciples are now in the normal state of consciousness, having 'climbed down' from the higher state of consciousness.

Jesus, then, says to the disciples, *"Tell the vision to no man, until the Son of man be risen again from the dead."* Spiritually, the term "man" refers to the Mortal. A human being has two states of existence: one, as the "Son of man," which is the normal waking state; two, as the "Son of God," which is the heightened state of consciousness. The *Son of man* becomes the *Son of God* when he "rises from the dead," that is, when his delusion is removed. Metaphorically, "rising from the dead" refers to the rising of kundalini from the *Mūlādhāra* chakra to the *Sahasrāra* Chakra. Therefore, the implication of the words is this: "The truth is known only by a spiritually awakened man." And that truth is this: *"I and my Father are one"* (John 10:30).

"And his disciples asked him, saying, Why then say the scribes that Elias must first come? And Jesus answered and said unto them, Elias truly shall first come, and restore all things. But I say unto you, That Elias is come already, and they knew him not, but have done unto him whatsoever they listed. Likewise shall also the Son of man suffer of them." The name *Elias* or *Elijah* (Hebrew: *Ēliya* H452) means "God of Jehovah." Elias was a famous prophet and a wonder-worker in the northern kingdom of Israel during the reign of Ahab (9th century BC), according to the Biblical Books of Kings. He defended the worship of YHWH over that of the Phoenician god *Baal.* He raised the dead, brought fire down from the sky, and was taken up in a whirlwind. In the Book of Malachi, Elijah's return is prophesied as *"before the coming of the great and terrible day of the Lord,"* making him a harbinger of the Messiah. Spiritually, Elias represents the Gospel.

Jesus clarifies the disciples' doubt: *"Elias truly shall first come, and restore all things. But I say unto you, That Elias is come already, and they knew him not, but have done unto him whatsoever they listed."* Spiritually, the term "they" refers to the Christian Church. And the phrase, "restore all things" suggests the removal of ignorance and delusion. Therefore, the spiritual implication of the words is this: "The Gospel has already come. And it is capable of removing ignorance and delusion. But, the Christian Church has not understood the Gospel truths. They desecrate it by worshipping the Phoenician god Baal." Spiritually, the literal scripture is the Phoenician god *Baal.*

The Gospel says, *"Then the disciples understood that he spake unto them of John the Baptist."* The above words may be interpreted as follows: "Then the spiritual interpreter understood that the Gospel is referring to the Christian Church."

MATTHEW 17:14-18

"And when they were come to the multitude, there came to him a certain man, kneeling down to him, and saying, Lord, have mercy on my son: for he is lunatick, and sore vexed: for ofttimes he falleth into the fire, and oft into the water. And I brought him to thy disciples, and they could not cure him. Then Jesus answered and said, O faithless and perverse generation, how long shall I be with you? how long shall I suffer you? bring him hither to me. And Jesus rebuked the devil: and he departed out of him: and the child was cured from that very hour."

The Gospel uses two different terms to refer to a specific person: they are "certain man" and "certain king." In the former case, the Greek word used is *tis* (G5100), which means "somebody" or "something." In the latter case, the Greek word used is *anthrōpos* (G444), which means "man-faced," or "human being." In the former case, the term alludes to a Mortal, whereas in the latter case, it alludes to an Evite.

Here, the man who meets Jesus is a Mortal. The man says that his son is a *lunatick*. His words reveal the nature of the disease: *"Lord, have mercy on my son: for he is lunatick, and sore vexed: for ofttimes he falleth into the fire, and oft into the water."* Spiritually, the term "son" refers to one's awareness or mind. The phrase "sore vexed" means "highly disturbed." Moreover, the frequent episodes of falling into fire and water suggest that the man is suffering from *bipolar disorder.*

Bipolar disorder, also known as *manic-depressive disorder*, is a mental illness classified by psychiatrists as a mood disorder. Individuals with bipolar disorder experience episodes of a frenzied mood known as *mania* alternating with episodes of *depression.* At the most severe level, individuals can experience distorted beliefs about the world known as *psychosis.* Children who experience traumatic or abusive experience in childhood are more susceptible to this mental disorder. One of the chief culprits of this mental disease is religion. Metaphorically, bipolar disease is the *spell cast by the Serpent.* All Mortals suffer from this disease in varying degrees of severity.

The reason why the disciples were unable to heal the man's 'son' is because they are not able to discern the symptoms exhibited by the patient as symptoms of a disease. They mistake it for religiosity. Therefore, Jesus upbraids them saying, *"O faithless and perverse generation."* The word *perverse* means "upside down." But, spiritually, it means "deluded," or "religious." There is a hint of desperation in Jesus' voice when he says, *". . . how long shall I be with you? how long shall I suffer you?"* The reason for his disappointment is that the disciples are still not able to see who the real villain is. He also hints that he will not be with them for long to guide them. In other words, the Gospel hints that its message will be distorted by the enemy, depriving humans of spiritual guidance.

"And Jesus rebuked the devil: and he departed out of him: and the child was cured from that very hour." The term *rebuke* means "admonishment," which suggests caution, advice, or counsel against something. The term *devil* means "evil spirit." The word *spirit* means "knowing." Therefore, the term *evil spirit* suggests "evil knowing," or ignorance. The term *devil* refers to erroneous religious beliefs. In other words, the person's mental affliction disappears when Gospel dispels his erroneous religious beliefs.

MATTHEW 17:19-21

"Then came the disciples to Jesus apart, and said, Why could not we cast him out? And Jesus said unto them, Because of your unbelief: for verily I say unto you, If ye have faith as a grain of mustard seed, ye shall say unto this mountain, Remove hence to yonder place; and it shall remove; and nothing shall be impossible unto you. Howbeit this kind goeth not out but by prayer and fasting."

The disciples are at a loss to understand why they could not heal the sick child, and they seek Jesus' counsel. Jesus tersely replies, *"Because of your unbelief."* The Greek word for unbelief is *apistia* (G570), which means "faithlessness." Spiritually, the term suggests delusion, or religion. In other words, Jesus says, "Because of your religion."

Jesus then says, *". . . for verily I say unto you, If ye have faith as a grain of mustard seed, ye shall say unto this mountain, Remove hence to yonder place; and it shall remove; and nothing shall be impossible unto you."* The expression, "if ye have faith as a grain of mustard seed" suggests that the disciples are not yet body-aware, and that they are still too religious. Why is Jesus comparing faith or body-awareness to a mustard seed? What is special about it? A mustard seed is spherical in shape, and has higher yield (oil content) compared to all other seeds. (Oil denotes body-awareness.) Mustard seed represents the human consciousness. The term *mountain* denotes an artificially-created system. In other words, the Gospel says that everything is possible for a true human being in this world.

> *If you have a golf-ball-sized consciousness, when you read a book, you'll have a golf-ball-size understanding; when you look out a window, a golf-ball-sized awareness, when you wake up in the morning, a golf-ball-sized wakefulness; and as you go about your day, a golf-ball-sized inner happiness. But if you can expand that consciousness, make it grow, then when you read that book, you'll have more understanding; when you look out, more awareness; when you wake up, more wakefulness; as you go about your day, more inner happiness.*
>
> *Catching the Big Fish: Meditation, Consciousness, and Creativity,* David Lynch

Jesus then says, *"Howbeit this kind goeth not out but by prayer and fasting."* The term, "this kind" refers to the devils (viruses) or erroneous religious beliefs (*memes*). In the parable of the mustard seed, the Gospel calls 'this kind' the "birds of the air." Spiritually, the word, *prayer* suggests body-awareness; *fasting* suggests abstinence from sensory food, rather than abstinence from physical food. Chief source of mental food is religion and the media—press, TV, radio, music, pornography, movies etc. Thus, the Gospel gives us a prescription for resisting the devil:

1. Meditate regularly
2. Remain body-aware
3. Reduce consumption of religion and media

MATTHEW 17:22-23

"And while they abode in Galilee, Jesus said unto them, The Son of man shall be betrayed into the hands of men: And they shall kill him, and the third day he shall be raised again. And they were exceeding sorry."

The term *Son of man* refers to the spiritual Gospel, and the term "men" refers to the politico-religious Establishment. Here, Jesus is alluding to the corruption of the Gospel meaning by the Judeo-Christian church.

The Gospel says, *"The Son of man shall be betrayed into the hands of men."* Spiritually, the term "men" refers to the Adamites. Here, the Gospel uses the expression, "betrayed into" and not "betrayed by." It suggests that someone betrayed the Gospel into the hands of Adamites. Who is that betrayer? The word, *betray* has the following connotations:

1. To deliver or expose to an enemy by treachery or disloyalty.
2. To be unfaithful in guarding, maintaining, or fulfilling
3. To disappoint the hopes or expectations of
4. To reveal or disclose in violation of confidence
5. To deceive, misguide, or corrupt

Only a trusted associate can betray; an enemy cannot. The connotations of the word *betray* clearly reveal the betrayer to be the person who the Christians trusted to guide and lead them. The allusion is to the founder of Christian theology and the theologians brain-washed by his theology.

The word *theology* is derived from the Greek roots *theo* meaning "god," and—*logy*, meaning "study of." Theology is the systematic and *rational* study of concepts of God and of the nature of religious truths, or the learned profession acquired by completing specialized training in religious studies, usually at a university, school of divinity, or seminary. Theologians use various forms of analysis and argument (philosophical, ethnographic, historical, etc.) to help understand, explain, test, critique, defend or promote any of myriad religious topics.

"And they shall kill him" says Jesus. Spiritually, the words may be interpreted as follows: "The theologians will distort and corrupt the true meaning of the Gospel."

But, the Gospel foresees the recovery of its true meaning from the death-like state: *". . . and the third day he shall be raised again."* Spiritually, the "third day" signifies spiritual awakening. It denotes the erasure of the three *cardinal sins* of Objectivity, Locality and Causality (*thāpathraya*). When these three erroneous beliefs are removed, man is freed from delusion and is able to discern the truth of the Gospel. Metaphorically, it is portrayed as Jesus resurrecting from death on the third day. The expression, "He shall be raised," suggests that the true meaning of the Gospel is liberated by the will of the Father, and not by man's efforts.

Alternatively, the "third day," perhaps, denotes reincarnation or resurrection of the human soul after death. The three 'days' probably represent three transition stages between death and reincarnation through which the dead man's soul passes through. According to the *Tibetan Book of the Dead*, there are three *Bardos* through which a dead man's soul passes through before it takes a new body. The Tibetan word *bardo* literally means "intermediate state." Used loosely, the term *bardo* refers to the state of existence intermediate between two lives on earth. According to Tibetan tradition, after death and before one's next birth, when one's consciousness is not connected with a physical body, one experiences a variety of phenomena. These usually follow a particular sequence of degeneration from, just after death, the clearest experiences of reality of which one is spiritually capable, and then proceeding to terrifying hallucinations that arise from the impulses of one's previous unskillful actions (sins). For the prepared and appropriately trained individuals the bardo offers a state of great opportunity for liberation, since transcendental insight may arise with the direct experience of reality, while for others it can become a place of danger as the karmically-created hallucinations can impel one into a less than desirable rebirth.

The Tibetan *Zhi-khro* teachings list six Bardos:

1. *Shinay bardo* is the first bardo of birth and life. This bardo commences from conception until the last breath when consciousness withdraws from the body.
2. *Milam bardo* is the second bardo of the dream state. The Milam Bardo is a subset of the *Shinay* bardo. Dream Yoga develops practices to integrate the dream state into Buddhist *sādhana*.
3. *Samten bardo* is the third bardo of meditation. This bardo is generally only experienced by meditators, though individuals may have random experience of it. *Samten* Bardo is a subset of the *Shinay* Bardo.
4. *Chikkhai bardo* (the first day) is the fourth bardo of the moment of death. According to tradition, this bardo is held to commence when the outer and inner signs signal that the onset of death is near, and continues through the dissolution or transmutation of the *Mahābhūta* (principles) until the external and internal breath has completed.
5. *Chönyid bardo* (the second day) is the fifth bardo of the luminosity of the true nature which commences after the final 'inner breath' (Sanskrit: *prāṇa*, *vāyu*; Tibetan: *rlung*). It is within this Bardo that visions and auditory phenomena occur. Concomitant to these visions, there is a welling of profound peace and pristine awareness. Sentient beings who have not practiced during their lived experience and/or who do not recognize the clear light at the moment of death are usually deluded throughout the fifth bardo of luminosity.
6. *Sidpa bardo* (the third day) is the sixth bardo of becoming or transmigration. This bardo endures until the inner-breath commences in the new transmigrating form determined by the "karmic seeds" within the storehouse consciousness

MATTHEW 17:24-27

"And when they were come to Capernaum, they that received tribute money came to Peter, and said, Doth not your master pay tribute? He saith, Yes. And when he was come into the house, Jesus prevented him, saying, What thinkest thou, Simon? of whom do the kings of the earth take custom or tribute? of their own children, or of strangers? Peter saith unto him, Of strangers. Jesus saith unto him, Then the children are free. Notwithstanding, lest we should offend them, go thou to the sea, and cast an hook, and take up the fish that first cometh up; and when thou hast opened his mouth, thou shalt find a piece of money: that take, and give unto them for me and thee."

The fact that this Gospel episode takes place in Capernaum city is relevant. Capernaum means "Nahum's village." It was a fishing village in the time of the *Hasmoneans*. The Hasmonean dynasty was the ruling dynasty of Judea and surrounding regions during the classical (Greco-Roman) antiquity. Located on the northern shore of the Sea of Galilee, it had a population of about 1500. Archeological excavations have revealed two ancient synagogues built one over the other. A church near Capernaum is said to be the home of Saint Peter. *Kfar Naum*, the original name of Capernaum, means "Nahum's village" in Hebrew, but apparently there is no connection with the prophet named Nahum. Spiritually, Capernaum represents the Judeo-Christian Church. The presence of the two ancient synagogues built one over the other denotes subjugation of the Gospel by the literal scripture.

The word tribute has the following connotations:

1. A gift, testimonial, compliment, or the like, given as due or in acknowledgement of gratitude or esteem.
2. A stated sum or other valuable consideration paid by one sovereign or state to another in acknowledgement of subjugation or as the price of peace, security, protection, or the like.
3. Any extracted or enforced payment or contribution.
4. Obligation or liability to make such payment.

The payment of tribute money denotes the subservience of the tribute-giver to the tribute-taker. Therefore, the real issue here is this: Should the Gospel be subservient to the Judaic scripture?

Tribute money generally goes to the Establishment. In this Gospel episode, tax collectors ask Peter whether Jesus pays his taxes to the temple, to which Peter eagerly replies yes. Spiritually, the tax collectors represent the theologians. Peter's eager response exposes his belief that the Gospel is subservient to the Judaic scripture.

Jesus questions Peter's belief: *"What thinkest thou, Simon? Of whom do the kings of the earth take custom or tribute? Of their own children, or of strangers?"* Spiritually, the expression, "kings of the earth" refers to the different religions and their scriptures. The expression, "their own children" refers to the priestly class. The term "strangers" refers to the laity. The word *laity* refers to the people outside of (strangers to) a particular profession. Therefore, the implication of Jesus' question to Peter is this: "Who are slaves to scripture—the priests or the laity?"

The Gospel asks the disciple to think about the relationship between the ruler and the ruled: is it like the parent-child relationship, or is it like the master-slave relationship? The Gospel argues that if it is like the parent-child relationship, then the son should be free. On the other hand, if tribute is demanded, then it is not a parent-child relationship; instead, it is a master-slave relationship. In other words, anyone who pays allegiance to a formal system accepts its hegemony.

"Notwithstanding, lest we should offend them, go thou to the sea, and cast an hook, and take up the fish that first cometh up; and when thou hast opened his mouth, thou shalt find a piece of money: that take, and give unto them for me and thee." Telling one to pay the tribute money after finding a coin in the mouth of the first fish that one catches from the sea is equivalent to saying, "Don't pay tribute money!" In other words, the Gospel prohibits subjugating it to any other scripture. But it does not want to rock the boat, therefore says, "Do not offend the religion by openly disassociating with it. Give them a fiction."

CHAPTER 18

Who is the Greatest in the Kingdom of Heaven?

MATTHEW 18:1-6

"At the same time came the disciples unto Jesus, saying, Who is the greatest in the kingdom of heaven? And Jesus called a little child unto him, and set him in the midst of them, And said, Verily I say unto you, Except ye be converted, and become as little children, ye shall not enter into the kingdom of heaven. Whosoever therefore shall humble himself as this little child, the same is greatest in the kingdom of heaven. And whoso shall receive one such little child in my name receiveth me. But whoso shall offend one of these little ones which believe in me, it were better for him that a millstone were hanged about his neck, and that he were drowned in the depth of the sea."

In the earlier episode we saw Jesus and the disciples discussing about worldly hierarchies: about kings, children of kings, and ordinary people. In the same context, the disciples ask Jesus about the *hierarchy* in the kingdom of heaven. Obviously, the disciples' conception of the kingdom of heaven is as a power hierarchy. It is plausible that they are alluding to the Jewish angelic hierarchy. Maimonides, the famous medieval Spanish Sephardic Jewish philosopher, in his *Yad ha-Chazakah*: *Yesodei ha-Torah*, counts ten ranks of angels in the Jewish angelic hierarchy, beginning from the highest:

1. *Chayot Ha Kodesh*
2. *Ophanim*
3. *Erelim*
4. *Hashmallim*
5. *Seraphim*
6. *Malakim* (Messengers, angels)
7. *Elohim* ("Godly beings")
8. *Bene Elohim* (Sons of Godly beings")
9. *Cherubim*
10. *Ishim* (manlike beings)

Jesus, dismissing the disciples' question, calls a little child to his side and says, *"Verily I say unto you, Except ye be converted, and become as little children, ye shall not enter into the kingdom of heaven."* What is special about the little child? First and foremost, a little child is 100% body and 0% mind. In other words, the little child is a bundle of body-awareness, a bundle of *innocence.* And innocence implies simplicity; absence of guile or cunning; it implies freedom from delusion. Secondly, a little child has no conception of religion or God. Therefore, to 'convert' as a little child means to be free from delusion, or to be free from religion and God.

There is an alternate interpretation to the verse. The disciples' conception of the kingdom of heaven is that of a *macrocosm*, the external world, where larger is greater, whereas Jesus' conception of the kingdom of heaven is that of a *microcosm*, the inner world, where smaller is greater.

Jesus says, *"Whosoever therefore shall humble himself as this little child, the same is greatest in the kingdom of heaven."* The word *humble* means "not proud." It implies lack of ego, which is the mental conception of the Self. It is a mental construct made up of relationships. Ego is the root of mind, and ego arises from delusion. Therefore, "to humble as a little child" means to remove delusion such that only the Self (body) exists, not ego (mind). One is truly humble when one is fully body-aware.

Perhaps, in mathematical terms, the Self (I) is represented by the real number 1, whereas the ego (i) is represented by the imaginary number $\sqrt{-1}$, which is at the source of an entire realm of complex numbers (mind). Perhaps, the *kingdom of heaven* is the realm of real numbers. I am just speculating here.

"And whoso shall receive one such little child in my name receiveth me." Here, the expression, "my name" implies "Human Being." Therefore, "to receive one such little child in my name" means to treat a small child as an individual human being. But, with regard to the microcosm, the expression, "little child" refers to the human DNA. Therefore, "to receive one such little child in my name" means to treat the human DNA as the Self itself.

"But whoso shall offend one of these little ones which believeth in me, it were better for him that a millstone were hanged about his neck, and that he were drowned in the depth of the sea." The expression, "one which believeth in me" means "one who is body-aware." According to the Gospel, those who harm children will face eternal damnation.

Alternatively, the expression "one which believeth in me" suggests the trusting nature of children. They trust humanity to take care of them. But for the Serpent-children, abusing children means worshipping their god, the Serpent. The brutalities these Serpent-children inflict on children include:

1. Child abuse
2. Child molestation
3. Pedophilia
4. Child sacrifice

With regard to the microcosm, the expression, "offend one of these little ones" suggests corruption of the human DNA. A major culprit here is the indiscriminate vaccination of children purportedly to increase immunity against diseases.

The Gospel pronounces the judgment for crimes against children: eternal damnation. If a human being is thrown into the sea with a millstone tied around his neck, he will surely die, but the death is only for the physical body; the soul will reincarnate again. But, the fate of these Serpent-children is that they will perish with death, never to be reborn again.

MATTHEW 18:7-9

"Woe unto the world because of offences! for it must needs be that offences come; but woe to that man by whom the offence cometh! Wherefore if thy hand or thy foot offend thee, cut them off, and cast them from thee: it is better for thee to enter into life halt or maimed, rather than having two hands or two feet to be cast into everlasting fire. If thine eye offend thee, pluck it out, and cast it from thee: it is better for thee to enter into life with one eye, rather than having two eyes to be cast into hell fire."

"Woe unto the world because of offences! for it must needs be that offences come." The word *offence* is used in the Bible in different occasions with different meanings. Here, the Greek word used is *skandalizo* (G4625), meaning "to scandalize," or "to entrap." The word, *scandalize* means "to shock or horrify by something considered immoral or improper." In other words, the word *offence* refers to crimes against children, especially bodily corruption. The perpetrator of the crime is the *world*—the Establishment. The Gospel foresees crimes against children happening during the last days. Jesus adds, "*. . . but woe to that man by whom the offence cometh!*" The reference is to humans who knowingly or unknowingly work with the Serpent in harming children (humanity).

DIFFERENT MEANINGS OF THE WORD, *OFFENCE*

Verse	Strong's Reference	Word	Meaning
Ecc. 10:4	H2399	*hēte*	Crime
Isa. 8:14	H4383	*mikšōl*	Caused to fall
Hos. 5:15	H816	*āsam*	Made desolate
Mat. 18:7	G4624	*skandalizō*	To entrap
Rom. 5:17	G3900	*paraptōma*	Wilful transgression
2Cor. 11:7	G266	*hamartia*	Sin

Most of the Gospel commentaries do not interpret the term *offence* as offence against children or genetic corruption. They obscure it by calling it sin, in a very general way. Again, they misrepresent the perpetrators of the crime as human beings themselves rather than exposing the real perpetrators of the crime—the World, or the Serpent-children.

"Wherefore if thy hand or thy foot offend thee, cut them off, and cast them from thee: it is better for thee to enter into life halt or maimed, rather than having two hands or two feet to be cast into everlasting fire. If thine eye offend thee, pluck it out, and cast it from thee: it is better for thee to enter into life with one eye, rather than having two eyes to be cast into hell fire." Here, the Gospel is describing the seriousness of crimes perpetrated on children. The expression, "hand or foot" suggests actions; the term "eyes" refers to thoughts and intentions. Therefore,

the implication is that those who do evil to children and those who intend to do evil on children, both, are culpable.

Another word for *offence* is sin. Give below are the major sins:

1. Offence against the body
2. Offence against the individual
3. Offence against the child
4. Offence against the nature

MATTHEW 18:10

"Take heed that ye despise not one of these little ones; for I say unto you, That in heaven their angels do always behold the face of my Father which is in heaven."

The Greek word for *despise* is *kataphroneō* (G2706), which means "to think against." Here, the word *despise* suggests "to plan evil against the child."

The Gospel cautions those who perpetrate crimes on children: *"That in heaven their angels do always behold the face of my Father which is in heaven."* The phrase, "their angels" refers to children's cognitive senses (*jnānēndriya*) and the motor functions (*karmēndriya*). The expression, "the face of my Father" refers to the Self. In other words, the cognitive senses and motor functions of little children are directly under the control of the Self; they seldom engage with the external world. Therefore, offence against children is offence against the Self (Existence), the punishment for which is grim and certain.

Alternatively, the expression "despising these little ones" suggests genetic manipulation.

Angels are divine messengers. The term *divine* implies light. Here, angels refer to signals moving between the body and the brain. Little children directly represent the Father or the Self on earth, in that they are pure awareness. The Self remains with the little child until he is *conditioned* (corrupted) by society.

The little child teaches humanity a new set of rules:

1. Be open
2. Trust existence

3. Be the Self
4. Live in the present
5. Take enough, not more
6. Don't think; only feel
7. Don't respect money

MATTHEW 18:11

"For the Son of man is come to save that which was lost."

What is implied by the expression, "that which was lost"? Well, the answer would depend on who the "Son of man" is. The theological interpretation of this verse is that Jesus came to save the world from sin. But, we ask: "How can one save another from his sins?" Then they say that Jesus shed his blood on the cross as atonement for our sins. Now, we are even more confused, and we ask again: "How does blood cleanse sins?" Now there is a stony silence at the other end.

This is how I understand the verse:

Imagine you are reading a thrilling fictional novel, written by you, in which you are the hero. And you are so engrossed in the story that you mistake it for real life and, unawares, get *pulled* into the story. Now you are inside the fiction, and you have completely lost contact with the reality outside the fiction. For you, the fiction is the reality now.

Normally, readers of books are able to exit from their fantasy world because books usually have an ending. But, the book that you are reading is special. It is a "living book," and it has no ending. It is like a TV serial that continues episode after episode, indefinitely. The book continually creates new content simply by recycling the old and rehashing it. But, it is such a slick production that it appears very real to you.

In this allegory, *you* play multiple parts. For instance, you are:

1. The author of the book: called the *Father*
2. The reader of the book: called the *Son*,
3. The hero of the book: called the *Son of Man*, or human being

The book is purely fictional; there is no truth in its literal content. But, underlying the book's literal story are eternal truths. Your purpose of 'reading' the fiction (reincarnating as man) is to discover those eternal truths embedded in the book. And that book is called the true scripture, or the human DNA. But, the story is so captivating that you make no effort to seek the truth. You mistake the fiction for life itself, and strive to prolong it, not realizing that your own life-force is being continually drained to 'power' the fictional world. The only way to save you from the book's trap is to shake you violently that you wake up from the fantasy. Therefore, you, the author, foreseeing such a possibility, have hidden within the scripture a special device, which, if found, will enable your exit from the fiction. And that device is called the Gospel. If you, the hero, discover it, then it will modify your fiction by adding a twist to the plot called the *Crucifixion-Death-Resurrection*, or the *Cross.* The Cross transforms the thrilling story into a nightmare, wherein you, the hero, are tortured, crucified, and killed by the false heroes of the story. Thus, you wake up from the fantasy and your delusion ends. But, the false heroes of the story (your own evil aspect) do not want the story to end, because if it does, they will all perish. These fictional characters, called the Serpent-children, come together to scuttle your efforts to discover the truth. In order to mislead you from the truth, they write a false scripture, which, if imbibed, can corrupt your awareness and, thus, prevent your escape.

The term *God* refers to the human DNA. Therefore, the expression, *Son of God* refers to an entity 'created' by the DNA. But the expression, *Son of man* refers to the true human being. *Son of God* and *Son of man* are not necessarily the same. If the human DNA is pure, then *Son of God* is the *Son of man*; if the DNA is corrupted, then *Son of God* is the *Son of Serpent*, not *Son of man.* It may be noted that Jesus always addresses himself as *Son of man*, and never as *Son of God.* It is others who address him as *Son of God.*

Contrary to popular monotheistic conception, God is not the same for all. God of Evites is the *Self* or the *Father* (the body); the God of Adamites is the *Serpent* (the mind). The human DNA in the *creation mode* is called the *Lucifer*, or the literal *Scripture*; the human DNA in the *dissolution mode* is called *Jesus,* or the *Gospel.*

In microbiological terms, the creation process is as follows:

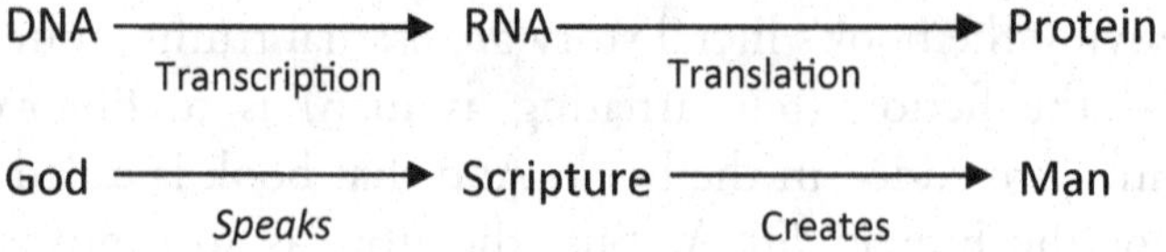

In microbiological terms, the Serpent is the *Retrovirus.* It is a single stranded RNA virus that stores its nucleic acid in the form of an mRNA genome and targets a host cell as an *obligate parasite.* Once inside the host cell cytoplasm, the virus uses its own reverse transcriptase enzyme to produce DNA from its RNA genome. Spiritually, a retrovirus is the *rebellious angel* who tried to become God.

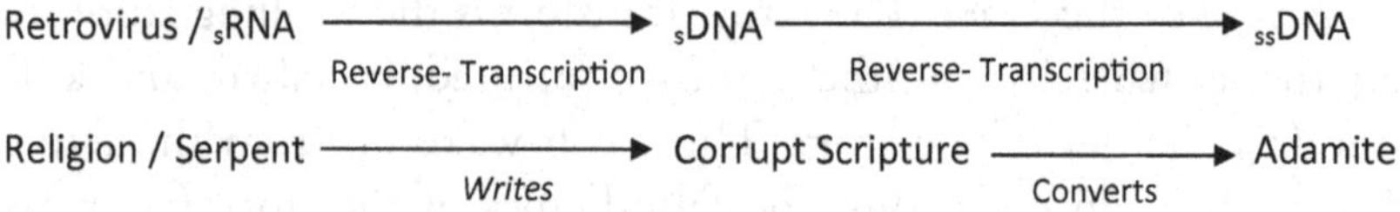

The word *transcription* refers to the flow of content from human being to book. But, *reverse-transcription* refers to the flow of contents from book to human being. The word *translation* means to convert from one form into another; it implies creation.

MATTHEW 18:12-14

"How think ye? if a man have an hundred sheep, and one of them be gone astray, doth he not leave the ninety and nine, and goeth into the mountains, and seeketh that which is gone astray? And if so be that he find it, verily I say unto you, he rejoiceth more of that sheep, than of the ninety and nine which went not astray. Even so it is not the will of your Father which is in heaven, that one of these little ones should perish."

In the earlier section, we saw how *you,* the author-reader of the book got 'lost' in the story, as its *protagonist.* There are many characters in the story, but the only you are considered special, because you are the author-reader's representative in the story. The other characters in the story are mere characters; they do not 'possess' the Self (the author-reader).

Jesus presents it in a different way: *"How think ye? if a man have an hundred sheep, and one of them be gone astray, doth he not leave the ninety nine, and goeth into the mountains, and seeketh that which is gone astray?"* Jesus compares you, the protagonist of the story, to the *lost sheep*, and the other characters of the story to "the ninety nine that remained with the herd." The *lost sheep* represents your (the author-reader's) awareness that got trapped in the story. You are the *shepherd*. The shepherd goes after the lost sheep, leaving the ninety nine other sheep, out of self-interest. When he finds the *lost sheep*, he rejoices. Similarly, you will rejoice when you recover your lost body-awareness that was lost in the fantasy. The Gospel describes it metaphorically: *"Even so it is not the will of your Father which is in heaven, that one of these little ones should perish."*

MATTHEW 18:15-17

"Moreover if thy brother shall trespass against thee, go and tell him his fault between thee and him alone: if he shall hear thee, thou hast gained thy brother. But if he will not hear thee, then take with thee one or two more, that in the mouth of two or three witnesses every word may be established. And if he shall neglect to hear them, tell it unto the church: but if he neglect to hear the church, let him be unto thee as an heathen man and a publican."

"Moreover if thy brother shall trespass against thee, go and tell him his fault between thee and him alone: if he shall hear thee, thou hast gained thy brother." The term "thy brother" refers to a true human being (Evite). He may be corrupted in the mind, but never corrupted in body (DNA). One who is corrupted in body is not an Evite.

THE DIFFERENT MEANINGS OF THE WORD, *TRESSPASS*			
Verse	**Strong's**	**Word**	**Meaning**
Gen. 50:17	H6588	*pāsa*	To apostatise
Lev. 5:15	H4604	*ma 'al*	Treachery
Num. 5:7	H816	*āsam*	Made desolate
1Ki. 8:31	H2398	*hāta*	To sin
Mat. 18:15	G264	*hamartanō*	To miss the mark

The word, *trespass* literally means a wrongful interference into another's sphere of action. It may be compared to the overlapping of two circles. According the Jesus, disputes between human beings should be mutually discussed and settled. But, spiritually, the word *trespass* suggests corruption. The word *trespass* is used in different places in the Bible with slightly differing meanings, but they all imply corruption of the soul or genetic corruption. If *trespass* implies genetic corruption, then who is this *trespassing brother* and what is the nature of the trespass? The medical professionals who vaccinates the child?

The word, *hear*, in this context, refers to the spiritual connection between true human beings (Evites). It is an intuitive feeling. It is the recognition of each other's *faith*. If the other person is able to 'hear' you, it is a sign that he is not bodily corrupted. But, only through interaction can one know that, which underscores the importance of open and fair discussion with the offending party.

"But if he will not hear thee, then take with thee one or two more, that in the mouth of two or three witnesses every word may be established." The term, *witness* refers to one who bears testimony by word to your faith. The term *word*, here, refers to the true human DNA. Therefore, the term *witness* refers to an Evite. The *faith* (human-ness) of a person is tested by *triangulation*. Telephone companies use the triangulation technique to locate the position of a cell phone by triangulating its signal with respect to the nearest three towers. Similarly, in geometry, triangulation is the process of determining the location of a point by measuring angles to it from *known points* at either end of a baseline, rather than measuring distances to the point directly.

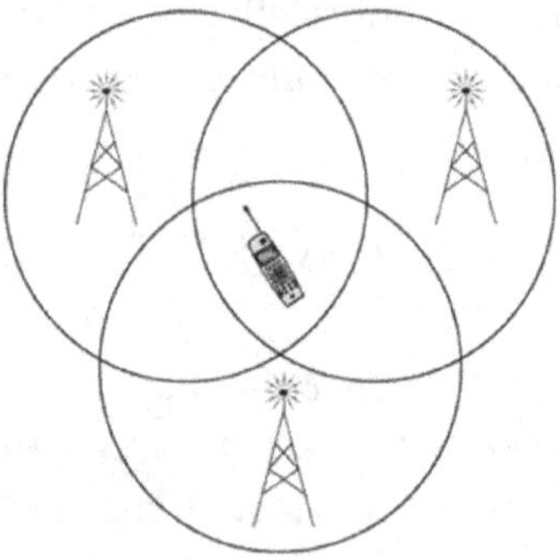

TRIANGULATION

"And if he shall neglect to hear them, tell it unto the church: but if he neglect to hear the church, let him be unto thee as an heathen man and a publican." If the other person fails the basic triangulation test, then you should involve your church. The term *church*, here, refers to a congregation of Evites. Here, the triangulation is done from many "known points." If this step also fails, you can be certain that the other is a *heathen*—a Serpent child.

The literal implication of the verse is that disputes between Evites should not be taken to the Establishment for mediation, but should be settled between them. But spiritually, it is the test to identify the perpetrators of crimes against children (humanity).

MATTHEW 18:18-20

"Verily I say unto you, Whatsoever ye shall bind on earth shall be bound in heaven: and whatsoever ye shall loose on earth shall be loosed in heaven. Again I say unto you, That if two of you shall agree on earth as touching any thing that they shall ask, it shall be done for them of my Father which is in heaven. For where two or three are gathered together in my name, there am I in the midst of them."

"Verily I say unto you, Whatsoever ye shall bind on earth shall be bound in heaven: and whatsoever ye shall loose on earth shall be loosed in heaven." Here, Jesus repeats to all the disciples what he said to Peter earlier (Ref: Matthew 16:19). In short, the Gospel says that whatever an Evite intends in his mind will become reality; similarly, whatever he erases from mind will be erased from reality.

"Again I say unto you, That if two of you shall agree on earth as touching any thing that they shall ask, it shall be done for them of my Father which is in heaven." Spiritually, the expression, "if two of you shall agree on earth" means "if two becomes one," or "if duality becomes non-duality." The expression, "as touching anything" means "any physical object." The secret the Gospel reveals is this: "If you can view the world non-dually, then anything in nature can serve as Self (God)." However, to 'look' at an object non-dually means to see its *form* or essence. In other words, "If you are able to perceive the *form*, then anything on earth can serve as God."

But what is *form*? According to Plato, there is a *form* for every object or quality in reality: forms of dogs, human beings, mountains, colors, courage, love, goodness, etc. Form answers the question, "What is that?" Plato supposed that the object was 'really' the Form and that the phenomena were mere shadows mimicking the Form; that is, momentary portrayals of the Form under different circumstances. Forms are the essences of various objects: they are that without which a thing would not be the kind of thing it is. Plato held that the world of Forms is transcendent to our own world and also is the essential basis of reality. Super-ordinate to matter, Forms are the most pure of all things. Furthermore, he believed that true knowledge is the ability to grasp the world of Forms with one's mind. And it is transcendent to both space and time. Forms are perfect themselves because they are unchanging.

"For where two or three are gathered together in my name, there am I in the midst of them." The expression, "my name" refers to the Self (I), or non-duality. The expression "two or three" implies duality; it implies mind. Therefore, the phrase, "where two or three gathered together in my name" means "where duality is transformed into non-duality," or "where the mind is focused on the Self." It is another way of saying, *"If thine eyes be single."*

The Gospel declares great truths here:

1. "Where duality is transformed into non-duality, there God is born."
2. "Where mind is focused in the Self, there God lives."
3. "Where the society honors the individual, there God rules."

The verse also implies: "Where free individuals are gathered, there I am present." The space that exists "in the midst" is the "I am," the Self, or the Father.

MATTHEW 18:21-22

"Then came Peter to him, and said, Lord, how oft shall my brother sin against me, and I forgive him? till seven times? Jesus saith unto him, I say not unto thee, Until seven times: but, Until seventy times seven."

Peter's question reveals that he has not understood the true meaning of the word, *brother*. He thinks his brother is separate from him. Although Peter is prepared to forgive his own errors indefinitely, he is unwilling to extend the same privilege to his 'brother.' He considers *forgiving* as some kind of suffering. But Jesus tells him that he has to accept *the* brother unconditionally, just as we accept our own body parts. The phrase, "seventy times seven" suggests indefinite number of times.

The Gospel reveals reality to be non-dualistic, where there is no separation between object and subject, where only the Self exists.

Alternatively, the episode reemphasizes the point that disputes between Evites should not be taken to the Establishment for mediation, under any circumstances. That is what is meant by the expression, "forgiving seventy times seven."

MATTHEW 18:23-35

"Therefore is the kingdom of heaven likened unto a certain king, which would take account of his servants. And when he had begun to reckon, one was brought unto him, which owed him ten thousand talents. But forasmuch as he had not to pay, his lord commanded him to be sold, and his wife, and children, and all that he had, and payment to be made. The servant therefore fell down, and worshipped him, saying, Lord, have patience with me, and I will pay thee all. Then the lord of that servant was moved with compassion, and loosed him, and forgave him the debt. But the same servant went out, and found one of his fellowservants, which owed him an hundred pence: and he laid hands on him, and took him by the throat, saying, Pay me that thou owest. And his fellowservant fell down at his feet, and besought him, saying, Have patience with me, and I will pay thee all. And he would not: but went and cast him into prison, till he should pay the debt. So when his fellowservants saw what was done, they were very sorry, and came and told unto their lord all that was done. Then his lord, after that he had called him, said unto him, O thou wicked servant, I forgave thee all that debt, because thou desiredst me: Shouldest not thou also have had compassion on thy fellowservant, even as I had pity on thee? And his lord was wroth, and delivered him to the tormentors, till he should pay all that was due unto him. So likewise shall my heavenly Father do also unto you, if ye from your hearts forgive not every one his brother their trespasses."

The Gospel exposes the enemy of mankind using a mysterious allegory—the Parable of the Wicked Servant.

In order to have even an inkling of the spiritual implication of the parable, we have to first understand what a *talent* is. The talent in this parable was worth about 6,000 *denarii*, so that the debt of the first servant to the king is 600,000 times larger than what his fellow-servant owed him. (In the Roman currency system, the *denarius* was small silver coin first minted about 211 BC during the *Second Punic War*. The word *denarious* is derived from the Latin *dēnī*, meaning "containing ten", as its value was 10 asses.) More significantly, 10,000 (a *myriad*) was the highest Greek numeral, and a talent the largest unit of currency, so that 10,000 talents was the largest easily described debt (for comparison, the combined annual tribute of Judaea, Samaria, and Idumea around this time was only 600 talents, and one *denarius* was a day's wages, so that 10,000 talents would be about 200,000 years wages). Therefore, it is pretty obvious that the Gospel is not discussing about monetary debt here.

In this parable, the *king* is the Self, the Father, or humanity; the "kingdom of heaven" is the human body, or nature. The *servant* who received ten thousand talents is the priestly race (Serpent-children) that was 'created' by the Father to serve humanity. The "ten thousand talents" that the king gave to the servant is the scripture—the knowledge about the human DNA. The priestly race was given the special knowledge with the express command to use it for the physical and spiritual well-being of human beings. But, the priestly race not only misused the knowledge given to them for acquiring wealth, power and fame for themselves but also distorted the scripture and created a trap called religion and enslaved humanity. Thus, the priestly race failed in their duty (did not repay the debt to the king). The Father (humanity) regrets having created these creatures and decides to terminate them, but, subsequently, spares them out of compassion.

The *fellow-servant* who owed *hundred pence* to the first servant is the Mortal who blindly follows the religion created by the priestly race. But, the spiritual comfort doled out by the priestly race to these hapless Mortals is only a pittance ("hundred pence") compared to the priceless bounty ("ten thousand talents") they received from the Father. Moreover, the priestly race, with their harsh religious laws, ruthlessly exacted a great toll (spiritual energy) from the Mortals.

The *fellow-servants* who report the injustice of the servant to the king are the Evites who could not be subjugated by the priestly race, and are able to communicate directly with the Father. The father (humanity) in anger calls the priestly race "wicked servant" or devils.

"And his lord was wroth, and delivered him to the tormentors, till he should pay all that was due unto him." The word, *tormentor* means "persecutor." The word, *torment* suggests unbearable physical pain, or extreme mental distress, or intense feeling of suffering. It implies misery. In other words, the Father (humanity) sentences the priestly race to face eternal persecution for their wickedness.

"So likewise shall my heavenly Father do also unto you, if ye from your hearts forgive not every one his brother their trespasses." The same fate of the priestly race awaits anyone who *divorces* himself from his body (DNA).

If the *kingdom of heaven* is the human body, then the *evil servants* are the virus-taken cells; the *fellowservants* are the cells vulnerable to virus attack. The *tormentor* of the evil servant is the Gospel vaccine.

CHAPTER 19

All Men Cannot Receive This Saying

MATTHEW 19:1-6

"And it came to pass, that when Jesus had finished these sayings, he departed from Galilee, and came into the coasts of Judaea beyond Jordan; And great multitudes followed him; and he healed them there. The Pharisees also came unto him, tempting him, and saying unto him, Is it lawful for a man to put away his wife for every cause? And he answered and said unto them, Have ye not read, that he which made them at the beginning made them male and female, And said, For this cause shall a man leave his father and mother, and shall cleave to his wife: and they twain shall be one flesh? Wherefore they are no more twain, but one flesh. What therefore God hath joined together, let not man put asunder."

"*And it came to pass, that when Jesus had finished these sayings, he departed from Galilee, and came into the coasts of Judaea beyond Jordan.*" The expression, "these sayings" alludes to Jesus' exposure of the priestly race as the evil servants that betrayed humanity.

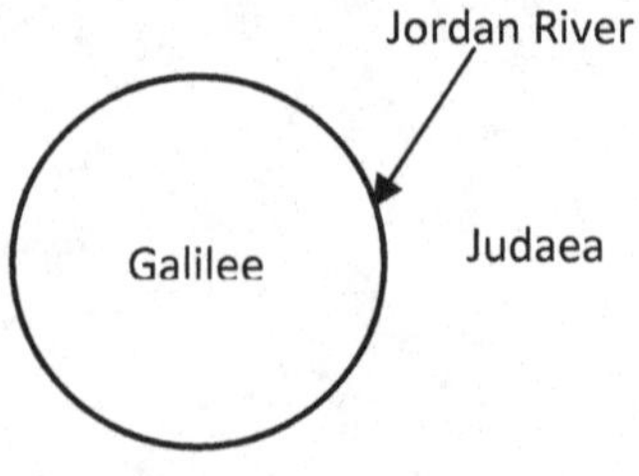

COASTS OF JUDEA BEYOND JORDAN

The name *Judaea* is a Greek-Roman adaptation of the name *Judah*, which originally covered the territory of the Israelite tribe of Judah, and later, of the Kingdom of Judah. Spiritually, the name *Judea* denotes the mind. *Galilee*, on the other hand, denotes the body. And Judea is located 'beyond Jordan.' The name *Jordan* is derived from the Aramaic word *Yarden* meaning, "one who descents." The Jordan River is the dividing line that separates Judea and Galilee. Spiritually, the Jordan River represents body-awareness. Therefore, Jesus leaving Galilee and entering the coasts of Judea suggests the exit of the Gospel from the spiritual realm (body) and the entry into the physical realm (mind). The allusion here is to the literal Gospel.

"And great multitudes followed him; and he healed them there." The expression, "great multitude" suggests great delusion. According to the Gospel, the people of Judea are under great delusion. They are religious fanatics. But, those who read and understood the Gospel were healed of their great delusion.

The Pharisees want to test Jesus; so they ask: *"Is it lawful for a man to put away his wife for every cause?"* What the Pharisees are literally asking is this: "Is it right to *divorce* one's wife if there is sufficient ground?" But, spiritually, the term *wife* refers to the body. Therefore, the spiritual implication of the question is this: "Is it right to lose body-awareness if the scripture allows it?"

Jesus replies, *"Have ye not read, that he which made them at the beginning made them male and female, And said, For this cause shall a man leave his father and mother, and shall cleave to his wife: and they twain shall be one flesh? Wherefore they are no more twain, but one flesh. What therefore God hath joined together, let not man put asunder."* Jesus quotes from the *true* scripture. But, in the *literal* scripture, we find a different version of it:

> *So God created man in his own image, in the image of God created he him; male and female created he them.*
> Genesis 1:27

Jesus quotes from the scripture, which talks about the generation of male and female principles, but says nothing about the marriage between man and woman. Therefore, the 'marriage' Jesus is referring to is spiritual marriage—the marriage between body and mind—and not literal marriage.

Please note that the Gospel does not use the term *man*; instead, it uses the word, "them," which means "human beings." Again, the Gospel does not use the term *God* to refer to the 'maker' of human beings; instead, it says *"he which made them."* Here, the Gospel is referring to the

Father as the maker of human beings. Similarly, the Gospel does not use the word *created*, instead it uses the word, *made*. Moreover, according to the Gospel, human beings are made "male and female." Here, the term *male* refers to the mind, and the term *female* refers to the body. In other words, a human being is *neither* mind *nor* body; a human being is *both* mind *and* body. In short, a human being is *body-mind* or *body-awareness*. In other words, a human being, in essence, is non-duality. And, human beings are made in the *image* of the Father, which is non-duality.

Therefore, the Gospel says, *"For this reason shall a man leave his father and mother, and shall cleave to his wife: and they twain shall be one flesh? Wherefore they are no more twain, but one flesh."* The expression, "for this reason" implies "because human being is body-mind, or non-duality." As we have seen above, the term *man* refers to the mind, or awareness. The expression, "father and mother" suggests duality and, therefore, denotes society (religion). The expression "they twain shall be one flesh" means "duality is transformed into non-duality." Therefore, the above verse may be interpreted as follows: "Because a true human being is body-mind, the mind should leave religion and cleave to the body. Thus duality is transformed into non-duality." The word *cleave* is noteworthy: it has opposing meanings. It means "to separate" or "to attach." The word, *cleave* truly describes spiritual marriage: it is *neither* attachment *nor* separation; it is *both* attachment *and* separation. According to the Gospel, human beings should leave delusion (religion) and become body-aware.

The Gospel then says, *"What therefore God hath joined together, let not man put asunder."* The spiritual implication of the words is this: "That which Existence has generated as non-duality (whole), society (religion) should not break into duality." It is a strong indictment against religious marriages. The very idea of marriage presupposes individual human beings as separate entities. Why should someone 'join' something that is fundamentally one? In other words, the institution of marriage is based on the assumption of Locality.

MATTHEW 19:7-12

"They say unto him, Why did Moses then command to give a writing of divorcement, and to put her away? He saith unto them, Moses because of the hardness of your hearts suffered you to put away your wives: but from the beginning it was not so. And I say unto you, Whosoever shall put away his wife, except it be for fornication, and shall marry another, committeth adultery: and whoso marrieth her which is put away doth commit adultery. His disciples say unto him, If the case of the man be so with his wife, it is not good to marry. But he said unto them, All men cannot receive this saying, save they to whom it is given. For there are some eunuchs, which were so born from their mother's womb: and there are some eunuchs, which were made eunuchs of men: and there be eunuchs, which have made themselves eunuchs for the kingdom of heaven's sake. He that is able to receive it, let him receive it."

The interesting aspect of the dialogues between the Pharisees and Jesus is that the former ask the questions in the literal sense, but Jesus answers them in the spiritual sense. In other words, Jesus responds to the spiritual implication of the question.

When the Pharisees ask Jesus why Moses permitted divorce, he answers, *"Moses because of the hardness of your hearts suffered you to put away your wives: but from the beginning it was not so."* The term *Moses* denotes *The Law*, or the Scripture. According to the Gospel, it is not the Father (Self), but the Serpent (religion) that instituted the system called marriage and its by-product, divorce. In true marriage, one *cleaves* to his or her spouse; there is neither attachment nor separation there. Spiritually, the expression, "hardness of heart" means "mechanical nature," or "evil nature." In other words, the Gospel says that the Mosaic laws of marriage and divorce apply only to humanoids (Adamites).

"And I say unto you, Whosoever shall put away his wife, except it be for fornication, and shall marry another, committeth adultery: and whoso marrieth her which is put away doth commit adultery." Spiritually, the expression, "to put away wife" means "to corrupt the body (DNA)"; "to marry another" means "to accept an alien gene." Literally, the term *adultery* suggests voluntary sexual intercourse between a married person and someone other than his or her lawful spouse. The Greek word used by the Gospel for *adultery* is *moichaō* (G3432), which means "apostasy," or "corruption." The Hebrew word for *adultery* is *nāap* (H5003), which too has a similar meaning. Spiritually, the term adultery refers to the wilful corrupting of the body through genetic manipulation.

The point to note here is that the Gospel permits divorce *only* in the case of fornication. Literally, *fornication* means voluntary sexual intercourse between two unmarried persons or two persons not married to each other. But, spiritually, it implies sexual intercourse with someone or something not of the same kind. In other words, fornication involves unnatural sex. According to the Gospel, one may divorce spouse if he or she is found "unnatural." The Greek word for *fornication* is *porneia* (G4202), which means "to indulge in harlotry or unlawful lust." In fact, the word *pornography* originated from the Greek word *porneia*. The underlying sentiment in fornication is hatred and violence, not love.

The disciples take Jesus' words literally and, therefore, say, *"If the case of the man be so with his wife, it is not good to marry."* What they are literally saying is this: "If one is going to get stuck with a woman for life, it is better not to marry." But, the spiritual connotation of the statement is this: "If a human being is whole, then he does not need marriage."

Jesus clarifies their misunderstanding: *"All men cannot receive this saying, save they to whom it is given."* The term "men" refers to the Adamites; the term, "*it*" refers to "truth." What he is saying is this: "An Adamite will not understand this spiritual principle; only an Evite will understand it." It is clear from Jesus' words that his words should not be taken literally.

Jesus, then, utters one of the most enigmatic statements in the Gospel: *"For there are some eunuchs, which were so born from their mother's womb: and there are some eunuchs, which were made eunuchs of men: and there be eunuchs, which have made themselves eunuchs for the kingdom of heaven's sake. He that is able to receive it, let him receive it."* Jesus throws a riddle at the disciples and challenges them: "He that is able to receive it, let him receive it." And this parable about the eunuchs is one of the most enigmatic parables in the entire Gospel.

> *All these things spake Jesus unto the multitude in parables; and without a parable spake he not into them: That it might be fulfilled which was spoken by the prophet, saying, I will open my mouth in parable; I will utter things which have been kept secret from the foundation of the world.*
> Matthew 13:34-35

The word *eunuch* comes from the Greek *eunouchos* (G2135). Medieval etymologists state that the word came from *eunoos*, which means "well-minded," or "diplomatic," but modern etymologists have derived it from *eune*, which means "bed," and *ekhein*, which means "to have hold," interpreting the original meaning to be "chamberlain." A *chamberlain* is an official charged with the management of the living quarters of a sovereign or member of the nobility. In modern terms, he is called a "Personal Secretary," or "Secretary." The Hebrew word for *eunuch* is *saris* (H5631), which means "palace official," or "minister of state." But, spiritually, the word *eunuch* refers to the *archons*. In the classical Mediterranean world, the term *archon* was commonly used for the governor of a province, or, more loosely, any *religious* or *governmental* authority. Hence the word, *archons*, is often translated in Gnostic texts as "the Authorities."

In Gnostic cosmology, the archons are a species of inorganic beings that emerged in the solar system prior to the formation of the earth. They are cyborgs inhabiting the planetary system (excluding earth, sun, and moon), which is described as a virtual world (*stereoma*) they constructed by imitating the geometric forms that emanated from the *Pleroma*, the realm of the *Generators*, the Cosmic Gods. (Spiritually, the terms *earth*, *sun*, and *moon* represents the body (*śarīra*), intellect (*buddhi*), and mind (*manas*) of a human being. The stereoma is the *māya*, or illusory world; and the Pleroma is body-awareness or consciousness (*śuddha bōdham*). The Generators or the Cosmic Gods are the genes in the DNA.)

Archons are a genuine species with their own proper habitat, and may even be considered to be god-like, but they lack *intentionality* (*ennoia*: self-reference), and they have a nasty tendency to stray from their boundaries and intrude on the human realm. Archons are said to feel intense envy toward humanity because humans possess the intentionality they lack. The *Gaia Mythos* describes how the Archons were produced when Aeon Sophia (consciousness) from the galactic core ('heart') impacts the quantum field (*chaos*) of the galactic limbs, when the *Aeon Sophia* plunged unilaterally. Aeon Sophia thus transforms herself into earth (*Gaia*) and the human beings. As the ill-gotten offspring of the Aeon Sophia, the archons are, in a sense, humanity's cosmic cousins. In the great Hindu epic, *Mahābhārata*, the humans are depicted as the *Pāṇḍavās*, and the archons as their cousins the *Kauravās*.

The Gospel talks about three types of eunuchs:

1. "*Some eunuchs, which were so born from their mother's womb*": Perhaps, the term *mother*, here, refers to *Aeon Sophia*; and, the term *womb* refers to the Galactic core (*Pleroma*). These are the *Archons* or the Serpent-children. They are fundamentally cyborgs that have no gender.
2. "*Some eunuchs, which were made eunuchs of men*": Spiritually, the term *men* refers to dualistic-monotheistic religion (the Serpent). These are humans whose bodies (DNA) have been taken over by the Serpent. And, circumcision is the operation (castration) that 'baptizes' them as Adamites.
3. "*Eunuchs, which have made themselves eunuchs for the kingdom of heaven's sake*": Here, the term *eunuch* suggests non-duality. These are the Evites who are body-aware.

MATTHEW 19:13-15

"Then were there brought unto him little children, that he should put his hands on them, and pray: and the disciples rebuked them. But Jesus said, Suffer little children, and forbid them not, to come unto me: for of such is the kingdom of heaven. And he laid his hands on them, and departed thence."

Children are bundles of curiosity. They are really explorers and truth-seekers. However, adults are irritated by their inquisitive nature, and do not realise that children are searching for truth. In other words, adults do not realise that children are trying to "come near to Jesus." But, adults prevent children approaching Jesus, by curtailing their curiosity. To them, truth is absolute and there is nothing to seek about it; they loathe the very notion of truth-seeking.

Alternatively, the term "children" refers to the Evites. Just as the children try to approach Jesus, the Evites try to understand the Gospel in their own terms. Here, the disciples of Jesus represent the elders, or the religious authorities. In other words, the Gospel allegorically describes how the Church opposes the Evites' efforts to understand the Gospel spiritually.

Jesus says to the disciples, *"Suffer little children, and forbid them not, to come unto me: for of such is the kingdom of heaven."* The term "kingdom of heaven" refers to the truth, the body-awareness, or reality. Literally, the verse suggests: "Allow children to be curious, do not curtail their curiosity; truth belongs to the curious." But spiritually, it implies: "Truth is not absolute, but relative; therefore, each man has to understand it in his own terms." The expression, "for of such is the kingdom of heaven" actually means "because that is the nature of truth."

Jesus' gesture of laying his hands on the children signifies the *individualized* nature of truth.

MATTHEW 19:16-22

"And behold, one came and said unto him, Good Master, what good thing shall I do, that I may have eternal life? And he said unto him, Why callest thou me good? there is none good but one, that is, God: but if thou wilt enter into life, keep the commandments. He saith unto him, Which? Jesus said, Thou shalt do no murder, Thou shalt not commit adultery, Thou shalt not steal, Thou shalt not bear false witness, Honour thy father and thy mother: and, Thou shalt love thy neighbour as thyself. The young man saith unto him, All these things have I kept from my youth up: what lack I yet? Jesus said unto him, If thou wilt be perfect, go and sell that thou hast, and give to the poor, and thou shalt have treasure in heaven: and come and follow me. But when the young man heard that saying, he went away sorrowful: for he had great possessions."

"And behold, one came and said unto him, Good Master, what good thing shall I do, that I may have eternal life?" The expression "eternal life" suggests immortality. But, rather than deathlessness, it implies a reincarnating kind of life. But, to have eternal life one should have a soul—a vehicle to travel from life to life. In other words, to have eternal life, one's DNA should be perfect. Apparently, the young man, here, is asking Jesus for a human soul. In other words, he wants to become a true human being (Evite). It seems he is an Archon, a Pharisee. The young man calls Jesus "Good Master," without even

having any prior acquaintance with him. Obviously, he is using the term *mechanically*, without awareness.

Jesus says to the young man, *"Why callest me thou good? there is none good but one, that is, God: but if thou wilt enter into life, keep the commandments."* Spiritually, the term *God* refers to the true human DNA; the term *commandments* refer to the *genes* in the DNA. Therefore, the spiritual implication of the statement is this: "The only thing *good* or *true* in this world is the human body (DNA). Nothing outside the body can be deemed as good or true. Therefore, do not corrupt the DNA."

When the young man asks which commandments, Jesus lists the following commandments:

1. *Thou shalt do no murder.*
2. *Thou shalt not commit adultery.*
3. *Thou shalt not steal.*
4. *Thou shalt not bear false witness.*
5. *Honour thy father and thy mother.*
6. *Thou shalt love thy neighbour as thyself.*

The six commandments the Gospel enumerates are simple moral codes. And, *keeping* a commandment does not imply being subservient to it. Instead, it implies *neither* subservience *nor* disobedience; it implies both subservience and disobedience. In other words, it implies *cleaving* to the commandments. And, *cleaving* to a commandment means to follow it, yet be free from it. It implies exercising discretion (awareness) rather than blindly (mechanically) following commandments.

It is noteworthy that the Gospel does <u>not</u> mention the following four commandments for keeping:

1. *Thou shalt have no other gods before me.*
2. *Thou shalt not make unto thee any graven image.*
3. *Thou shalt not take the name of the LORD in vain.*
4. *Remember the sabbath day, to keep it holy.*

The four commandments that the Gospel omits from the list of commandments to follow form the very core of Judaic faith. But, why did the Gospel leave them out? Is it because they can corrupt the DNA (soul)? It seems so. It seems Jesus told the young man to abandon his duality-based religion and its duality-based scripture if he desires to be a true human being.

The young man blurts out mechanically, *"All these things have I kept from my youth up: what lack I yet?"* The 'conditioned' response of the young man reveals two things:

1. That he is not self-aware
2. That he is a hypocrite (archon)

The young fellow is not self-aware, and he is a hypocrite. If not, how could he have replied affirmatively to the commandment, *"Thou shalt love thy neighbour as thyself"*? A *genuine* human being would have asked how one can love *another* as oneself, but not a hypocrite. The reason why he does not raise that question is because he lacks self-awareness.

Realizing the inability of the young man to grasp the true meaning of the commandments, Jesus advices him in a 'language' he understands—the language of money: *"If thou wilt be perfect, go and sell that thou hast, and give to the poor, and thou shalt have treasure in heaven: and come and follow me."* Spiritually, the word, *perfect* means "true human being" (Evite); the expression, "treasure in heaven" refers to the true human DNA (soul). In short, Jesus says, "If you want to be a true human being, renounce the mind (religion) and become body-aware." The Gospel tells us that the young man returned home a sad man because "he had great possessions." In other words, the young man possesses only the mind, but no body.

MATTHEW 19:23-26

"Then said Jesus unto his disciples, Verily I say unto you, That a rich man shall hardly enter into the kingdom of heaven. And again I say unto you, It is easier for a camel to go through the eye of a needle, than for a rich man to enter into the kingdom of God. When his disciples heard it, they were exceedingly amazed, saying, Who then can be saved? But Jesus beheld them, and said unto them, With men this is impossible; but with God all things are possible."

A human being lives in two worlds simultaneously. His body exists in the reality, whereas his mind (awareness) is trapped in a fantasy, a virtual-reality. The fantasy in which man's awareness is trapped or lost is called the *world*, and the reality in which human body exists is called the *heaven*. The Evites are *in* the world, but not *of* it.

The Hebrew word for *rich* is *kābad* (H3513). The word originates from the root word *kābēd* (H3515), which means "to be heavy." The word has two connotations: on the one hand, it implies "numerous or honorable"; on the other, it implies "burdensome, severe, or dull." Here, the term "rich man" refers to an archon or a serpent-child. It seems the Gospel is using the terms *archon* and *rich man* synonymously.

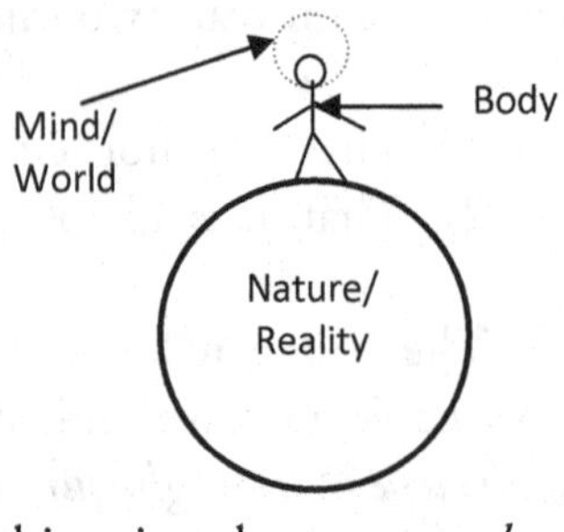

Jesus says to the disciples, *"Verily I say unto you, That a rich man shall hardly enter into the kingdom of heaven. And again I say unto you, It is easier for a camel to go through the eye of a needle, than for a rich man to enter into the kingdom of God."* The "kingdom of heaven" refers to self-awareness, whereas the "kingdom of God" refers to the human body. The word *hardly* means "almost impossible, yet not impossible." In other words, the Gospel says, "It is *almost* impossible for an archon to have body-awareness." It is equivalent to saying, "It is *almost* impossible for a machine to become self-aware." The Gospel compares the chances of a machine becoming self-aware to the chances of a camel passing through the eye of a needle. In other words, the Gospel describes the archon as the antithesis of human being. In other words, the Gospel portrays the archons as the *anti-Christ*.

Spiritually, the term "eye of the needle" refers to the centre of a circle; it represents the *soul*. The Hebrew word for *camel* is *gāmāl* (H1581), which means "servant" or "beast of burden." Spiritually, the term *camel* suggests a machine, a computer, a cyborg, or a humanoid. In other words, the Gospel compares the chances of a serpent-child acquiring body-awareness to that of a machine acquiring a soul.

"When his disciples heard it, they were exceedingly amazed, saying, Who then can be saved? But Jesus beheld them, and said unto them, With men this is impossible; but with God all things are possible." The disciples were shocked at Jesus' revelation. In desperation they ask him, *"Who then can be saved?"* The implication is this: "If an Adamite cannot be

saved, what about us?" The Gospel says Jesus '*beheld them.*' The Greek word for *beheld* is *emblepō* (G1689), "to observe fixedly," or "to discern clearly." In other words, Jesus looks at the disciples piercingly. He looks straight at their hearts and says, *"With men this is impossible; but with God all things are possible."* Spiritually, the term "men" refers to the literal scripture, and "God," the spiritual Gospel. It is clear a warning to the disciples, especially to Peter, that those who hold on to the literal scripture will not be saved.

The *Large Hadron Collider* (LHC) is the highest-energy particle collider ever made and is considered as "one of the great engineering milestones of mankind." The LHC was built by the *European Organization for Nuclear Research* (CERN) from 1998 to 2008, with the aim of allowing physicists to test the predictions of different theories of particle physics and high-energy physics, and particularly prove or disprove the existence of the theorized *Higgs particle.* The Higgs particle is also known as the *God particle.* Is this the 'soul' that the archons have been searching throughout history?

The LHC experiment has been the focus of a number of conspiracy theories. Some of the conspiracy theorists have even suggested that the collider will also cook up either an exotic particle or a tiny black hole that will suck up everything around it, and even might destroy the Earth (or maybe even the entire Universe).

MATTHEW 19:27-30

"Then answered Peter and said unto him, Behold, we have forsaken all, and followed thee; what shall we have therefore? And Jesus said unto them, Verily I say unto you, That ye which have followed me, in the regeneration when the Son of man shall sit in the throne of his glory, ye also shall sit upon twelve thrones, judging the twelve tribes of Israel. And every one that hath forsaken houses, or brethren, or sisters, or father, or mother, or wife, or children, or lands, for my name's sake, shall receive an hundredfold, and shall inherit everlasting life. But many that are first shall be last; and the last shall be first."

Feeling fidgety by Jesus' stern and piercing look, Peter blurts out his concern as to how he and the other disciples would be saved if it is almost impossible for an Adamite to be saved. He says to Jesus, *"Behold, we have forsaken all, and followed thee; what shall we have therefore?"* Here, the term "all" refers to the Judaic religion and its scripture; the term "thee" refers to the Gospel. Alternatively, the term "all" refers to the worldly goods; the term "thee" refers to the spiritual goods. There is a tinge of disappointment in Peter's voice.

Although it was Peter who raised the question, Jesus does not reply to him directly; instead, he says to all the disciples commonly, *"Verily I say unto you, That ye which have followed me, in the regeneration when the Son of man shall sit in the throne of his glory, ye also shall sit upon twelve thrones, judging the twelve tribes of Israel. And every one that hath forsaken houses, or brethren, or sisters, or father, or mother, or wife, or children, or lands, for my name's sake, shall receive an hundredfold, and shall inherit everlasting life."* It is interesting to note that Jesus says "that ye which have followed me" and does not say "ye." It implies that what Jesus is about to reveal applies only to those who "followed" him. In other words, the Gospel does not give *any* special privilege to the Gospel interpreters (disciples) over those who understand it; both receive the same reward—eternal life.

Spiritually, to 'follow' Jesus means to be body-aware, or to spiritually understand the Gospel. According to the Gospel, there are only two ways for receiving eternal life (the perfect human DNA): either become body-aware or understand the true meaning of the Gospel.

The term, "Son of man" refers to the Gospel. Therefore, the expression, "in the regeneration of Son of man" means "reinterpretation of the Gospel." The Son of man sitting in the throne of glory refers to the spiritual revelation of the Gospel, also known as the "Second Coming." The "twelve thrones" are the twelve primary races in this universe. The Greek word for *judging* is *krinō* (G2919), which means "to distinguish." Therefore, the expression, "judging the twelve tribes of Israel" refers to the "separation of true human beings and non-humans." In other words, the spiritual revelation of the Gospel will separate (judge) entities into two classes: humans and non-humans.

One of the most effective methods for "following the body" is *Vipassana* meditation. *Vipassana* in the Buddhist tradition means insight into the true nature of reality. The term is derived from the Sanskrit word *vipaśyanā*, which means "to see things as they really are." It is one of India's ancient techniques of meditation, but it was rediscovered by Gautama Buddha around 500 B.C. and taught by him to his pupils as a universal remedy for universal ills. The Vipassana technique aims at the eradication of mental impurities and the resultant highest happiness of full liberation. It is a way of self-transformation through self-observation. It focuses on the deep interconnection between mind and body, which can be experienced directly by disciplined attention to the physical sensations that form the life of the body, and that continuously interconnect and condition the life of the mind. It is this observation-based, self-exploratory journey to the common root of mind and body that dissolves mental impurities, resulting in a balanced mind full of love and compassion.

Jesus then adds, *"But many that are first shall be last; and the last shall be first."* The term, "many" refers to the Adamites, who first received the Gospel. But, they will be the last to spiritually understand it. The term "last" refers to the Gentiles, who received the Gospel only later on. But the Gentiles will be the first to understand it spiritually.

CHAPTER 20

For Many Be Called, But Few Chosen

MATTHEW 20:1-16

"For the kingdom of heaven is like unto a man that is an householder, which went out early in the morning to hire labourers into his vineyard. And when he had agreed with the labourers for a penny a day, he sent them into his vineyard. And he went out about the third hour, and saw others standing idle in the marketplace, And said unto them; Go ye also into the vineyard, and whatsoever is right I will give you. And they went their way. Again he went out about the sixth and ninth hour, and did likewise. And about the eleventh hour he went out, and found others standing idle, and saith unto them, Why stand ye here all the day idle? They say unto him, Because no man hath hired us. He saith unto them, Go ye also into the vineyard; and whatsoever is right, that shall ye receive. So when even was come, the lord of the vineyard saith unto his steward, Call the labourers, and give them their hire, beginning from the last unto the first. And when they came that were hired about the eleventh hour, they received every man a penny. But when the first came, they supposed that they should have received more; and they likewise received every man a penny. And when they have received it, they murmured against the goodman of the house, Saying, These last have wrought but one hour, and thou hast made them equal unto us, which have borne the burden and heat of the day. But he answered one of them, and said, Friend, I do thee no wrong: didst not thou agree with me for a penny? Take that thine is, and go thy way: I will give unto this last, even as unto thee. Is it not lawful for me to do what I will with mine own? Is thine eye evil, because I am good? So the last shall be first, and the first last: for many be called, but few chosen."

In the earlier section, we saw Peter seeking a special status for the disciples in the kingdom of heaven, and Jesus making it plain that the disciples enjoy no special status over others in the kingdom of heaven. Here, the Gospel explains the difference between the worldly dispensation and Godly dispensation. It uses a parable to explain the true meaning of the statement, *"But many that are first shall be last; and the last shall be first."*

The parable begins with the statement: *"For the kingdom of heaven is like unto a man that is an householder, which went out early in the morning to hire labourers into his vineyard."*

The spiritual meaning of the terms used in the above verse is given in the table on the right. Interpreting the verse using these meanings, we get: "An Evite went out to interpret the Gospel and find the truth."

Term / Phrase	Spiritual meaning
Kingdom of heaven	The Truth
Man, the householder	An Evite
Early in the morning	The advent of the Gospel
Vineyard	The Gospel
Labourer	Interpreters
To hire	To use

The *penny* is called *drachma* in Greek. It is a silver coin circular in shape. Spiritually, the promised wage of one penny represents the reward of eternal life that is promised to those who are able to receive the Gospel truth. The *labourers* are the different Gospel interpretation processes. The first batch of labourers is hired from the village. Spiritually, the term *village* represents the body, and *marketplace* represents the mind. Therefore, spiritually, the village labourers represent man's reasoning faculty. These are the intellectuals that use reason to arrive at the truth.

The householder again goes out to hire labourers at the 3rd hour, 6th hour, and 9th hour, but this time he goes to the *marketplace*. But, the idle labourers in the marketplace disappoint him and go *"their way."* Spiritually, the term *marketplace* refers to Judaism, and the idle labourers in the marketplace denote the Biblical interpreters. Here, the expression, "their way" means "according to the Bible." But, these laborers do not qualify for the wage.

The householder again goes out to hire labourers at the 11th hour. (Spiritually, the *11th hour* represents the *Last Days*, which is the present time.) But, this time, he does not go to the marketplace; instead, he goes to the village. In the village, he finds some laborers idling there without work. He asks them why they are not working, and they reply, *"Because no man hath hired us."* The householder then says to them, *"Go ye also into the vineyard; and whatsoever is right, that shall ye receive."* The late-comers accept the householder's terms and goes to work in the vineyard. Spiritually, these late-comer laborers represent human *intuition*. The reason why intuition did not come earlier is that no one "hired them." The householder's promise to these late-comers that he would give them "whatsoever is right" is a cue that human intuition is capable of delivering the Gospel truth.

"So when even was come, the lord of the vineyard saith unto his steward, Call the labourers, and give them their hire, beginning from the last unto the first." The Greek word for *steward* is *epitropos* (G2012), which means "commissioner," or "guardian." Spiritually, it refers to the Holy Spirit. It is the Holy Spirit that reveals the Gospel truth to the interpreter. Now at the close of the day, the householder first pays the late-comers and only then pays the early-comers. Not only that: he pays both the early-comers and the late-comers equally, ignoring the amount of work the latter had put in. Therefore, the disgruntled early-comers complain to the householder. The implication is this: The truth-seekers who use reason to arrive at the Gospel truth, finds it after great efforts. But, those who use intuition quickly arrive at the truth. But, the former cannot claim that the truth they discovered is better than the truth discovered by the latter.

The householder senses the dissatisfaction of the early-comers, and says to their representative, *"Friend, I do thee no wrong: didst not thou agree with me for a penny? Take that thine is, and go thy way: I will give unto this last, even as unto thee. Is it not lawful for me to do what I will with mine own? Is thine evil, because I am good? So the last shall be the first, and the first last: for many be called, but few chosen."* Spiritually, the question, "Is thine evil?" means "Are you still an Adamite?" In other words, it says, "Are you still ignorant?"

The Gospel says, "*For many be called, but few chosen.*" In other words, many will read the Gospel, but only few will understand its spiritual meaning.

MATTHEW 20:17-19

"And Jesus going up to Jerusalem took the twelve disciples apart in the way, and said unto them, Behold, we go up to Jerusalem; and the Son of man shall be betrayed unto the chief priests and unto the scribes, and they shall condemn him to death, And shall deliver him to the Gentiles to mock, and to scourge, and to crucify him: and the third day he shall rise again."

Jesus shares his premonitions about future events with the disciples. He even hints that he may be betrayed by a trusted associate to the Jewish-Roman Establishment. Spiritually, Jesus symbolizes the Gospel, and the Jewish-Roman Establishment symbolizes the Judeo-Christian Church. The word, *betray* means "to deliver to an enemy, by treachery, by an insider who is an agent of the enemy." Here, the betrayer, most probably, is the apostle who subordinated the Gospel to the Judaic scripture.

The name *Jerusalem* is variously etymologized to mean "foundation of god *Shalem.*" It is derived from the Sumerian root *yeru,* which means "settlement" or "seat." *Shalem* is the "tutelary deity" (guardian angel) of the city. The Akkadian god *Shalem* has special relationship with Jerusalem. *Shalem* is the god of the setting sun and the nether world. Spiritually, Jerusalem represents the Judaic religion.

As they enter Jerusalem, Jesus says to the disciples, *"Behold, we go up to Jerusalem; and the Son of man shall be betrayed unto the chief priests and unto the scribes, and they shall condemn him to death, And shall deliver him to the Gentiles to mock, and to scourge, and to crucify him: and the third day he shall rise again."* Literally, the term "Son of man" refers to Jesus. But, spiritually, the term refers to the Gospel. Therefore, the expression, "Son of man shall be betrayed" refers to the betrayal of the Gospel.

The Gospel describes the betrayal process as follows:

1. The *betrayer* hands over Jesus to the chief priests and the scribes. Spiritually, the Jewish chief priests and the scribes represent the Judaic theologians. The Greek word for *betray* is *paradidōmi* (G3860), which means "to surrender," or "yield up." The betrayer, in effect, surrenders the Gospel to the

Judaic theologians for subordinating it to the Judaic scripture. The betrayal, here, is a spiritual betrayal rather than a physical betrayal. It is the betrayal of the true meaning of the Gospel.

2. The chief priests and the scribes *condemn* Jesus to death and hand over to the Gentiles. In other words, the Judaic theologians *condemn* the Gospel. The Greek word for *condemn* is *katakrinō* (G2632), which means "to judge against." It is derived from the root words *kata* (G2596), which means "down," or "against" and *krinō* (G2919, which means "to sentence." Literally, the word, *katakrinō* means "to sentence against," or "to sentence down." Spiritually, to *condemn* the Gospel means to misinterpret it and kill its true meaning.
3. The Gentiles mock, scourge and crucify Jesus. Spiritually, the term *Gentiles* refers to the (alien) Roman Church. In other words, the Roman Church mock, scourge and crucify the Gospel. The Greek word for *mock* is *empaizō* (G1702), which means "to deride." The Hebrew word for *mock* is *lā'ag* (H3932), which means "to speak unintelligently." Spiritually, the term *mock* refers to the Church *litany*. Litany, in Christian worship, and some forms of Judaic worship, is a form of prayer used in services and processions, and consists of a number of petitions. The Greek word for *scourge* is *mastigoō* (G3146), which means "to flog." Spiritually, the word *scourge* refers to the Church's canons. The word *canon* originates from the Greek word *kanōn* (G2583). The word *kanōn* is derived from the root *kanē*, which means "a straight rod," or "a cane." The Greek word for *crucify* is *stauroō* (G4717), which means "to impale on a cross." Spiritually, the *cross* denotes either duality or non-duality, depending on one's perspective. Here, the cross implies duality. Therefore, to crucify Jesus means to dualistically (literally) interpret the Gospel.

"The third day he shall rise again" says the Gospel. Spiritually, the "three days" represents the "three veils" that hide the true meaning of the Gospel. When these three veils are lifted, the Gospel truth is revealed, which is metaphorically described as the resurrection of the crucified Jesus.

MATTHEW 20:20-23

"Then came to him the mother of Zebedee's children with her sons, worshipping him, and desiring a certain thing of him. And he said unto her, What wilt thou? She saith unto him, Grant that these my two sons may sit, the one on thy right hand, and the other on the left, in thy kingdom. But Jesus answered and said, Ye know not what ye ask. Are ye able to drink of the cup that I shall drink of, and to be baptized with the baptism that I am baptized with? They say unto him, We are able. And he saith unto them, Ye shall drink indeed of my cup, and be baptized with the baptism that I am baptized with: but to sit on my right hand, and on my left, is not mine to give, but it shall be given to them for whom it is prepared of my Father."

The name *Zebedee* (Hebrew: *zobdi* H2067) means "gift of God." Zebedee's wife is Salome (Hebrew: *šālōm* H7965), which means "whole" or "peace." Spiritually, Zebedee represents the body, and Salome, the mind. Out of their union are born John and James, who represent intuition or body-awareness.

In this episode we find Salome, the mother of James and John, trying to coax Jesus to grant her children a status above all others. Jesus says to Salome and her children, *"Ye know not what ye ask. Are ye able to drink of the cup that I shall drink of, and to be baptized with the baptism that I am baptized with?* Spiritually, the expression, "drink the cup that I shall drink of" means "to be condemned to death by the Jews." Similarly, the expression, "baptized with the baptism that I am baptized with" means "to be mocked, scourged and crucified by the Romans." James and John agree.

Jesus says to James and John, *"Ye shall drink indeed of my cup, and be baptized with the baptism that I am baptized with: but to sit on my right hand, and on my left, is not mine to give, but it shall be given to them for whom it is prepared of my Father."* Spiritually, the expression, "ye shall drink indeed of my cup" suggests that both James and John will be able to absorb the literal meaning

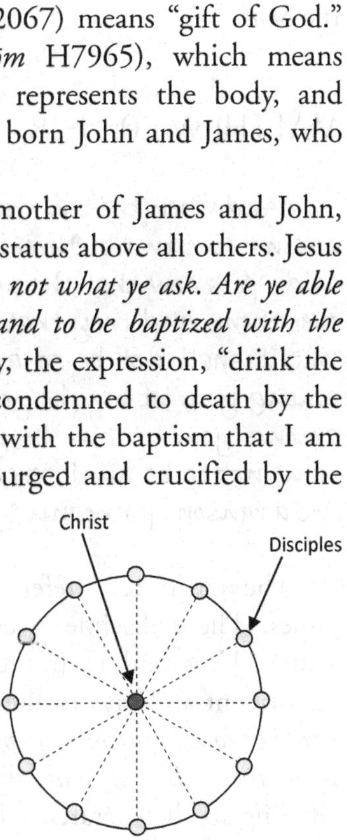

CHIRST AND TWELVE DISCIPLES

of the Gospel. And the expression, "and be baptized with the baptism that I am baptized with" suggests that both James and John will be able to absorb the spiritual meaning of the Gospel.

As we have hypothesized earlier, the twelve disciples of Jesus represent twelve mythologies that came together to form the syncretistic Gospel. They represent twelve non-dualistic scriptures from around the world. But, they are merely books that *tell* the truth, and not the truth itself. The scriptures merely *describe* the true human DNA from twelve different angles or perspectives, whereas the human being *is* the DNA. Therefore, scriptures are called *servants*, whereas human beings are called *Sons*.

Here, we find two scriptures trying to acquire a status greater than human beings themselves. But the Gospel reminds them that they are merely *servants* that serve humanity and, therefore, cannot assume a status equal to or greater than human beings, who are the inheritors—the *Sons*.

MATTHEW 20:24-28

"And when the ten heard it, they were moved with indignation against the two brethren. But Jesus called them unto him, and said, Ye know that the princes of the Gentiles exercise dominion over them, and they that are great exercise authority upon them. But it shall not be so among you: but whosoever will be great among you, let him be your minister; And whosoever will be chief among you, let him be your servant: Even as the Son of man came not to be ministered unto, but to minister, and to give his life a ransom for many."

The term "ten" refers to the ten disciples excluding John and James. These disciples were piqued by feelings of righteous anger against Jesus and their brethren John and James. Jesus senses their resentment and says to them, *"Ye know that the princes of the Gentiles exercise dominion over them, and they that are great exercise authority upon them. But it shall not be so among you."* Here, the Gospel is alluding to the hierarchical (pyramidal) structure of worldly systems. As we have seen before, the term *Gentile* is a relative term; it simple means "others." Here, when Jesus uses the term, it refers to the godless, secular or worldly. Therefore, the expression, "princes of the Gentiles" refers to the worldly leaders. The word *dominion* suggests authority or power. Therefore, the verse implies: "The hierarchical power structure is typical of the worldly systems; it shall not so among Christians." (Since the term *Christ* refers to the true human being, the term *Christian* means "true human being" or "Evite.")

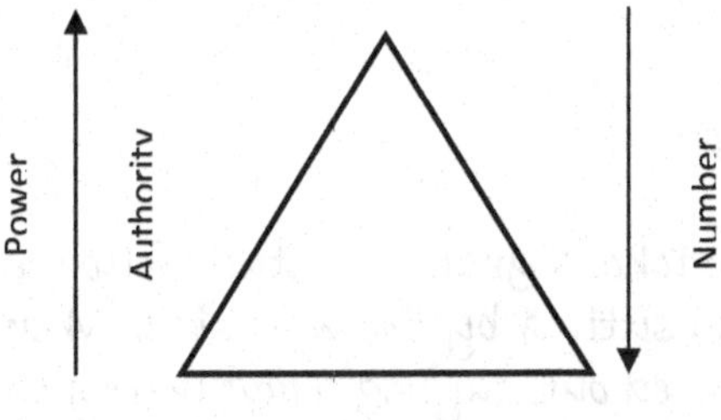

HIERARCHY

It may seem ironical that the Christian Church practices the very opposite of what the Gospel preaches. In fact, the organizational structure of the Christian Church is taught in many business schools as a good example of hierarchical organization structure. In other words, the organized Christian Church is a worldly system.

Jesus gives the disciples a new rule: *". . . but whosoever will be great among you, let him be your minister; And whosoever will be chief among you, let him be your servant."* How can the *great* be the *minister*, or the *chief* be the *servant*? Aren't they antithetical concepts? One way to resolve this paradox is hypocrisy—the chief *pretends* to be the servant during certain rituals; for example, the pope washing the feet of a laity during the Good Friday mass. But it is not true compliance of the rule. The only way to reconcile the two antithetical opposites is to adopt the stance of non-duality.

Jesus says, *"Even as the Son of man came not to be ministered unto, but to minister, and to give his life a ransom for many."* According to the Gospel, *serving others* is the purpose of human life. But, it does not merely imply philanthropic activities or social work. The Gospel defines *serving others* as "giving one's life as ransom for many." *Ransom* is the money demanded in exchange for someone held captive. The word, ransom suggests an exchange; here, the exchange is between *life* and *many*. The term *life* refers to the body (truth), and *many*, the mind (delusion). Therefore, "serving others" means to give up delusion and to seek the truth.

The greatest service one can do to others is to eradicate one's own ignorance and delusion. The fight is really against religion and its false scripture (the Serpent). And, it is waged through the search of truth. When the truth is fully revealed, the Serpent is defeated.

Therefore the true meaning of the verse is this: "The purpose of human life is to search and find the truth."

MATTHEW 20:29-34

"And as they departed from Jericho, a great multitude followed him. And, behold, two blind men sitting by the way side, when they heard that Jesus passed by, cried out, saying, Have mercy on us, O Lord, thou Son of David. And the multitude rebuked them, because they should hold their peace: but they cried the more, saying, Have mercy on us, O Lord, thou Son of David. And Jesus stood still, and called them, and said, What will ye that I shall do unto you? They say unto him, Lord, that our eyes may be opened. So Jesus had compassion on them, and touched their eyes: and immediately their eyes received sight, and they followed him."

The mention of the name *Jericho*, here, is extremely pertinent. Jericho is a city located near the Jordan River in the West Bank. It is believed to be one of the oldest inhabited cities in the world. Archaeologists have unearthed the remains of more than 20 successive settlements in Jericho, the first dates back 11,000 years (9000 BC), almost to the very beginning of the *Holocene* epoch of the Earth's history. It is known in Judeo-Christian tradition as the place of the decisive Battle of Jericho which secured the Israelite's return to the Promised Land from the bondage in Egypt, led by Joshua, the successor to Moses. Spiritually, Jericho represents the mind of a Mortal. The term Jericho also denotes the original scripture. As per the Biblical account, Jericho was betrayed to the Israelites by Rachab, a prostitute. As we have seen in the genealogy of Jesus, Rachab represents the Babylonian scripture in written form. Rachab also represents the Scribe. In other words, the Scribes mixed ('prostituted') the original scripture with the Babylonian scripture to create the literal scripture, thus totally destroying the original scripture. This is metaphorically, described as the *Fall of Jericho*.

The Gospel says, *"And as they departed from Jericho, a great multitude followed him."* Jericho represents the fallen, or corrupt scripture. Therefore, the spiritual implication of the verse is this: "Great delusion follows those who read the literal scripture."

In the previous section we saw in a new light what it means to "serve others." According to the Gospel, serving others means giving up delusion and searching for truth. Here, as if to emphasize the idea, Jesus gives 'sight' to two blind men outside the city of Jericho. The Sanskrit word for *sight* is *darśana*, which means "sight" as well as "worldview." The term *worldview* means "a comprehensive conception or image of the universe and of humanity's relation to it." In other words, the term *worldview* implies scripture. The *blindness* alluded here is the blindness in the worldview. It implies spiritual blindness, or delusion.

The blind man hears Jesus pass by and cries out, *"Have mercy on us, O Lord, thou Son of David."* It may be noted that there are two instances in the Gospel where more or less the same words are expressed, and both cases involve *two* blind men:

> *And when Jesus departed thence, two blind men followed him, crying, and saying, Thou Son of David, have mercy on us.*
> Matthew 9:27
> *And, behold, two blind men sitting by the way side, when they heard that Jesus passed by, cried out, saying, Have mercy on us, O Lord, thou Son of David.*
> Matthew 20:30

Jesus responds immediately. The Gospel tells us: *"And Jesus stood still, and called them, and said, What will ye that I shall do unto you?"* Through these words, Jesus gives us the form of an efficacious prayer. The short phrase, "*Lord, have Mercy*" (Greek: *Kyrie eléison*) is an important prayer in Eastern Christianity. It is both a petition and a prayer of thanksgiving.

The term "Son of David" is a very mysterious one. Who is King David? Did King David really exist? There is a bitter division among Bible scholars on the issue.

> *The Bible is our only source of information about David. No ancient inscription mentions him. No archeological discovery can be securely linked to him. The quest for the historical David, therefore, is primarily exegetical.*
> *The Historical David*: P. Kyle McCarter

It is plausible that the term "King David" is just a term in the Bible, and it refers to the evolved (purified) Essene scriptures. Perhaps, it is in this sense that Jesus is said to be in the line of David; both are *terms* that refer to evolved (purified) scriptures. The fact that the blind man calls Jesus, "thou Son of David" indicates that he does not think of Jesus as a physical person. In other words, the man is not totally deluded.

The above episode allegorically explains how the Gospel dispels ignorance and delusion and provides spiritual *insight*.

Note: Throughout this Gospel exegesis, it is most important to constantly be aware of the fact that Jesus *is* the Gospel, and not a physical person who lived in the past. He is only the protagonist of the Gospel through whose life story universal truths are unveiled for the benefit of mankind. If we lose sight of this fundamental fact, we may unknowingly slip into our conditioned habit of thinking about Jesus as a historical character, and may miss the spiritual message of the Gospel and fall into the snare of religion.

CHAPTER 21

Deliver Us, We Beseech Thee

MATTHEW 21:1-5

"And when they drew nigh unto Jerusalem, and were come to Bethphage, unto the mount of Olives, then sent Jesus two disciples, Saying unto them, Go into the village over against you, and straightway ye shall find an ass tied, and a colt with her: loose them, and bring them unto me. And if any man say ought unto you, ye shall say, The Lord hath need of them; and straightway he will send them. And this was done, that it might be fulfilled which was spoken by the prophet, saying, Tell ye the daughter of Sion, Behold, thy King cometh unto thee, meek, and sitting upon an ass, and a colt the foal of an ass."

The Gospel embeds eternal truths in a complex allegory. And it is the work of the Gospel interpreter to discover the *correspondence* or *mapping* between the Gospel statements and the eternal truths. In technical terms, this correspondence is called *isomorphism*. In other words, the spiritual interpretation process is fundamentally discovering the isomorphism that exists between Gospel statements and eternal truths.

The word *isomorphism* is derived from the Greek words *isos*, which means "equal" and *morphe*, which means "shape." The word *isomorphism* refers to an information-preserving transformation. It applies when two complex structures can be mapped onto each other in such a way that to each part of one structure there is a corresponding part in the other structure, where the term "corresponding" suggests that the two parts play similar roles in their respective structures.

The perception of an isomorphism between two known structures is a significant advance in knowledge, and it is such perceptions of isomorphism which creates meaning in the minds of people.

Here, the Gospel describes the Gospel interpretation process through a complex allegory. Here, the task is doubly complex because one has to discover the isomorphism in an allegory that embeds the truth about isomorphisms. However, in order to discover this isomorphism, we have to first understand the significance of the various motifs used in the allegory.

The name *Bethphage* derives from two Hebrew words: *bayit* (H1004), which means "a house" and *pag* (H6291), which means "crude," "torpid," or "unripe." Literally interpreted, *Bethphage* means "the house of unripe figs." But, spiritually, the term refers to the human brain.

The Hebrew word for *olive* is *zayit* (H2132), which means "fruit yielding illuminating oil." The olive tree, *Olea europaea*, is an evergreen tree or shrub native to the Mediterranean, Asia, and Africa. The edible olive has been cultivated for at least 5000 to 6000 years, with the most ancient evidence of olive cultivation having been found in Syria, Palestine, and Crete. Olive oil has long been considered sacred. The olive branch was often a symbol of abundance, glory, and peace. The leafy branches of the olive tree were ritually offered to deities and powerful figures as emblems of benediction and purification, and they were used to crown the victors of friendly games and bloody wars. Over the years, the olive has been the symbol of peace, wisdom, glory, fertility, power, and purity. The *Mount of Olives* is a mountain ridge east of and adjacent to the Jerusalem's Old City. It is named for the olive groves that once covered its slopes. From Biblical times until the present, Jews have been buried on the Mount of Olives. Spiritually, the Mount of Olives symbolizes the human body.

Ass, also known as *Asinus*, is a subgenus of *Equus* (single-hooved grazing animal) that encompasses several subspecies of *Equidae*, characterized by long ears, a lean, straight-backed build, lack of proper withers, a coarse mane and tail, and a reputation for considerable toughness and endurance. The common donkey is the best-known domesticated representative of the subgenus, with both domesticated and feral varieties. Among the wild ass species are several never-domesticated species that live in Asia and Africa. Spiritually, the ass represents spoken language. The colt, the foal of an ass, represents meaning. The ass is tied, whereas the foal is free.

Preparing for the sacrifice, Jesus sends two disciples to the nearby village with an instruction: *"Go into the village over against you, and straightway ye shall find an ass tied, and a colt with her: loose them, and bring them unto me. And if any man say ought unto you, ye shall say, The Lord hath need of them; and straightway he will send them."* Jesus chooses the ass and the colt from a village opposite. Spiritually, the expression, "the village over against you" refers to the local community. The ass represents the spoken language. It is 'tied' because its words have only one interpretation or meaning. The colt, the foal of the ass, represents the esoteric meaning of the words. The foal is not tied; it is free, which suggests that the esoteric meanings of the words are free, or speculative. The owner of the ass and the foal is the Gospel interpreter himself.

Spiritually, the two disciples that Jesus sends to the village to bring the ass and the colt are the interpreter's sight (light) and hearing (sound). It is these faculties that bring the Gospel meaning to the interpreter's brain (Bethphage.)

"And this was done, that it might be fulfilled which was spoken by the prophet, saying, Tell ye the daughter of Sion, Behold, thy King cometh unto thee, meek, and sitting upon an ass, and a colt the foal of an ass." Spiritually, the expression, "daughter of Sion" represents awareness, or mind. Here, the Gospel describes, through an allegory, the arrival of Gospel meaning into the interpreter's mind. In other words, it describes truth revelation.

MATTHEW 21:6-11

"And the disciples went, and did as Jesus commanded them, And brought the ass, and the colt, and put on them their clothes, and they set him thereon. And a very great multitude spread their garments in the way; others cut down branches from the trees, and strawed them in the way. And the multitudes that went before, and that followed, cried saying, Hosanna to the Son of David: Blessed is he that cometh in the name of the Lord; Hosanna in the highest. And when he was come into Jerusalem, all the city was moved, saying, Who is this? And the multitude said, This is Jesus the prophet of Nazareth of Galilee."

"And the disciples went, and did as Jesus commanded them, And brought the ass, and the colt, and put on them their clothes, and they set him thereon." The disciples put their clothes over the ass, and then Jesus mounts the animal. The *ass* represents spoken language, and the *disciples* represent the Gospel interpreters. The disciples' *cloths* represent their individual interpretations of the Gospel, and denotes *isomorphism.*

There is an important detail to note here: the disciples' cloth is *over* the ass, but *under* Jesus. In other words, the spiritual meaning is *above* language, which means it is *meta-language.* But, it is *under* Jesus, which means it is *esoteric.*

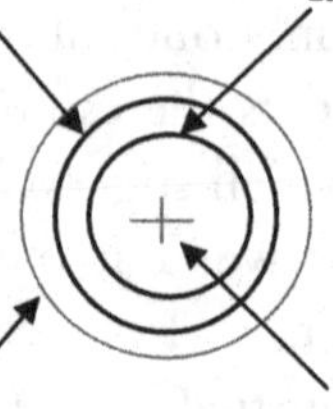

GOSPEL INTERPRETATION PROCESS

"And a very great multitude spread their garments in the way; others cut down branches from the trees, and strawed them in the way." The multitude spread their garments in the way for Jesus to ride over. In other words, people surrender their minds to the Gospel meaning. The Hebrew word for *tree* is *ēs* (H6086), which means "gallows." The word *ēs* originates from the Hebrew root *āsa* (H6095) which means "to blind." Spiritually, the term *tree* refers to the literal scripture. Therefore, cutting branches from the trees signifies the surrendering of the literal scripture to the Gospel.

"And the multitudes that went before, and that followed, cried saying, Hosanna to the Son of David: Blessed is he that cometh in the name of the Lord; Hosanna in the highest." The word *Hosanna* is an exclamation of adoration. It is etymologically derived from two Hebrew words: *yāsa* (H3467) and *nā* (H4994). The word *yāsa* (H3467) has multiple implications: it implies freedom, safety, deliverance, salvation, retribution, and help, among others. The root *nā* means "I beseech thee," or "I pray thee." Therefore, the cry *Hosanna* literally means, "Deliver us, we beseech thee" or "Save us, we pray thee." It is a plea—an appeal—for divine intervention. As we can see, the word *Hosanna* has two connotations: it is an exclamation of adoration as well as a cry for help. To the multitude that "went before," it is an exclamation of adoration; to the multitude "that followed," it is a cry for help.

As we have seen earlier, the expression, "Son of David" refers to an evolved scripture. Spiritually, the expression, "the name of the Lord" refers to the Self. That which "comes in the name of the Lord" is the spiritual interpretation. Therefore, the cry, "*Hosanna to the Son of David: Blessed is he that cometh in the name of the Lord; Hosanna in the highest*" is a petition from the Mortals to the spiritual Gospel to deliver them from ignorance and delusion.

The Hosanna procession led by Jesus is in fact a *demonstration* by humanity against the politico-religious Establishment (the Serpent). Naturally, the powers that be in Jerusalem are disturbed by the uprising; they enquire, "Who is this?" Someone answers, *"This is Jesus, the prophet of Nazareth of Galilee."*

Nazareth (Arabic: an-*Nāsiriyyah*) is the largest city in the North District of Israel. Nazareth is known as the Arab capital of Israel. The present population of Nazareth is made up predominantly of Arab citizens of Israel, almost all of whom are either Muslim (69%) or Christian (30.9%). In other words, Nazareth is entirely Gentile. The term Nazareth does not appear in any pre-Christian texts but appears in many different Greek forms in the New Testament. There is no consensus regarding the origin of the name. There are multiple conjectures regarding the origin of the term:

1. One conjecture holds that *Nazareth* is derived from of the Hebrew words for *branch*, namely *ne-ser* and alludes to the prophetic, messianic words in the Book of Isaiah 11:1, "from (Jesse's) roots a Branch (*netzer*) will bear fruit."
2. Another view suggests this toponym might be an example of a tribal name used by resettling groups on their return from exile.
3. Alternatively, the name might have originated from the verb *na-sar*, meaning "watch," "guard," or "keep," and understood either in the sense of "watchtower" or "guard place," implying that the early town was perched on or near the brow of the hill, or, in passive sense as "preserved," or "protected" in reference to its secluded position. Spiritually, the word *na-sar* suggests body-awareness.
4. Another theory holds that the Greek form *Nazara*, used in Matthew and Luke, might have derived from an earlier Aramaic form of the name, or from another Semitic language form.

5. The Arabic name for Nazareth is *an-Nāsira*, and Jesus is also called *an-Nasiri*, reflecting the Arab tradition of according people a *nisba*, a name denoting from whence a person comes in either geographic or tribal terms. In the *Qur'an*, Christians are referred to as *nazara*, meaning "followers of *an-Nasiri*," or "those who follow Jesus."

It is plausible that Nazareth is not the name of a place, but the name of a sect of people. It is evident from the fact that there is no mention of the place in the Old Testament. The negative reference about Nazareth in the Gospel of John 1:46 (*"Can there any good thing come out of Nazareth?*) suggests that ancient Jews did not connect the town's name to prophecy. Spiritually, the name Nazareth refers to the Evites. The term *Nazoraean* actually means "a true Christian." Therefore, the Hosanna uprising is actually an uprising of humans, led by an Evite, against the oppression of the Adamites. The *Hosanna* cry echoes in Nazareth even to this day.

Perhaps, the word *Nazareth* is also related to the word *Nazarite*. The word *Nazarite* originates from the Hebrew word *nāzir* (H5139), which means "the separated" or "an unpruned vine" (like an *unshorn* Nazarite). The word *shorn* is the past participle of the word *shear*, which means:

1. To cut (something)
2. To remove by or as if by cutting or clipping with a sharp instrument
3. To cut or clip the hair, fleece, etc.
4. To reap with a sickle

Spiritually, the term *Nazarite* means "the uncircumcised." A Nazarite is *separated* from a population of circumcised people by the fact that he is not circumcised. It is plausible that the uncut genital is referred to as the "unpruned vine." In that sense, a *Nazoraean* is indeed a *Nazarite.*

The Council of Jerusalem in *Acts of the Apostles* Chapter 15 addresses the issue of whether circumcision is required of new converts to Christianity. Both Simon Peter and James the Just speaks against requiring circumcision in Gentile converts and the Council ruled that circumcision was not necessary. However, *Acts* 16 and many references in the Letters of Paul show that the practice was not immediately eliminated. Paul of Tarsus, who was directly responsible for one man's circumcision (Acts 16:1-3), openly praises Jewish circumcision in Romans 3:2. The practice of circumcision was so typical of Judaism that Christians who were circumcised were known as *Judaizers* among early Christians.

In the *Gospel of Thomas*, there is a passage wherein Jesus comments on the practice of circumcision:

> *His disciples said to him, "Is circumcision useful or not?" He said to them, "If it were useful, their father would produce children already circumcised from their mother. Rather, the true circumcision in spirit has become profitable in every respect.*
> Gospel of Thomas saying 5

MATTHEW 21:12-13

"And Jesus went into the temple of God, and cast out all them that sold and bought in the temple, and overthrew the tables of the moneychangers, and the seats of them that sold doves, And said unto them, It is written, My house shall be called the house of prayer; but ye have made it a den of thieves."

The first act that Jesus does after symbolically assuming sovereignty was to free the "temple of God" from the parasites that infest it. The expression "temple of God" has two connotations: literally, it refers to the place of worship; spiritually, it refers to the human body (DNA).

Throwing down the tables of the moneychangers and the seats of the traders too is a symbolic gesture. If we consider the episode literally, the act of Jesus signifies the cleaning up of the place of worship from the parasites that infest it. The term, *moneychanger* (Gr. *kollybistēs* G2855) literally means a coin-dealer. A moneychanger is one whose business is to exchange the money of one country for that of another country. But spiritually, it refers to the religious officials (priests) who exchange money of this world for a consideration (salvation) in the next world. The practice is generally known as *indulgence*. Alternatively, it suggests the replacement of one gene (meme) with another alien gene (meme).

The *dove* is a sacrificial bird. According to Jewish tradition, those who could not offer a bullock as sacrifice, were to bring a sheep or a goat; and those who were not able to do that, were accepted of Jehovah, if they brought a turtle-dove, or a pigeon. But, only *meek, and gentle, and harmless* creatures were chosen for sacrifice. In other words, the sacrifice is the *sacrifice of innocence*. The dove represents innocence. Spiritually, the phrase "the seats of them that sold doves" refers to religious teachers who condition the innocent minds of children.

Alternatively, if we take the "temple of God" as the human body, then the moneychangers and tradesmen represent *viruses* that infect the body. These parasites destroy the body by corrupting the body cells. In that sense, viruses are the *thieves* that rob the body. Spiritually, the human body is known as the "house of prayer" because it is the tool for meditation. The viruses literally convert the body into a "den of thieves." In other words, the viruses corrupt the human body into a cancerous entity.

Cancer is defined as a population of cells that have lost their normal controls of growth and differentiation (self-reference) and are proliferating without check. The process by which a tumor cell leaves the primary tumor, travels to a distant site via the circulatory system, and establishes a secondary tumor (colony) is called *Metastasis*. But why do these tumor cells target a particular site or organ? The *Mechanistic Theory* states that the selection of site is determined by the pattern of blood flow. The *Seed and Soil Theory* states that the selection of site depends on the provision of a fertile environment in which compatible tumor cells could grow. The five major steps in *metastasis* are:

1. Invasion and infiltration of surrounding normal host tissue with penetrations of small lymphatic or vascular channels.
2. Release of neoplastic cells, either single cells or small clumps, into circulation.
3. Survival in the circulation.
4. Arrest in the capillary beds of distant organs.
5. Penetration of the lymphatic or blood vessel walls followed by growth of the disseminated tumor cells.

The stages of metastasis are:

1. Invasion: Primary tumor cells enter circulation.
2. Circulation: The tumor cells travel to the secondary site of tumor growth.
3. Colonization: Formation of secondary tumor.

The components of invasion are:

1. Matrix degrading enzymes
2. Cell adhesion
3. Cell motility

The cancer *metastasis* resembles the spreading and colonization of the monotheistic-dualistic religions across the world by the Western powers (Serpent).

MATTHEW 21:14-16

"And the blind and the lame came to him in the temple; and he healed them. And when the chief priests and scribes saw the wonderful things that he did, and the children crying in the temple, and saying, Hosanna to the Son of David; they were sore displeased, And said unto him, Hearest thou what these say? And Jesus saith unto them, Yea; have ye never read, Out of the mouth of babes and sucklings thou hast perfected praise?"

Spiritually, the temple represents the human body, and Jesus represents the Gospel, the healer. Here, the Gospel reveals that the human body is capable of healing physical and mental illnesses. In other words, the Gospel suggests that humanity can free itself from the parasites if only it learns to use the powers of the human body effectively.

The cry, "Hosanna to the Son of David" is the cry of humanity for liberation from the oppressive alien rulers. Spiritually, the term "children" refers to the meek and gentile human beings, the Evites. But, to the Establishment, the cry for freedom sounds like blasphemy, and they accuse the Gospel of inciting the people. The authorities say to Jesus, *"Hearest thou what these say?"* Jesus replies them with a counter-question: *"Yea; have ye never read, Out of the mouth of babes and sucklings thou hast perfected praise?"* An infant's cry is called the "perfect praise," because it is directed at the Self, and not to any external agency, even though the succor manifests from outside. Indirectly, the Gospel tells us that human the body is capable of providing for its own needs if only it prays to the Self, instead of an external God.

The message of the Gospel is this: "Do not rely on the mind; rely on the body."

MATTHEW 21:17-22

"And he left them, and went out of the city into Bethany; and he lodged there. Now in the morning as he returned into the city, he hungered. And when he saw a fig tree in the way, he came to it, and found nothing thereon, but leaves only, and said unto it, Let no fruit grow on thee henceforward for ever. And presently the fig tree withered away. And when the disciples saw it, they marvelled, saying, How soon is the fig tree withered away! Jesus answered and said unto them, Verily I say unto you, If ye have faith, and doubt not, ye shall not only do this which is done to the fig tree, but also if ye shall say to this mountain, Be thou removed, and be thou cast into the sea; it shall be done. And all things, whatsoever ye shall ask in prayer, believing, ye shall receive."

"And he left them, and went out of the city into Bethany; and he lodged there." Bethany is the name of a village near Jerusalem. The name appears in the New Testament as the home of the siblings Mary, Martha, and Lazarus, as well as that of Simon the Leper. The village is commonly identified with the present-day West Bank city of al-Eizariya, located about 2.4 km east of Jerusalem on the south-eastern slope of the Mount of Olives. The Greek word for Bethany is *Bēthania* (G963), which means "house of dates."

The date palm (Hebrew: *tāmār*), known by the scientific name *Phoenix dactylifera*, is a palm in the genus *Phoenix*, cultivated for its edible sweet fruit. Dates are believed to have originated around Iraq, and have been cultivated since ancient times from Mesopotamia to prehistoric Egypt, possibly as early as 4000 BCE. A date palm *cultivar*, known as *Judean date palm* is renowned for its long-lived orthodox seed, which successfully sprouted after accidental storage for 2000 years. This particular seed is presently reputed to be the oldest viable seed but the upper survival time limit of properly stored seeds remains unknown.

While discussing the genealogy of Jesus, we came across the character *Thamar* (Hebrew: *tāmār*), the daughter-in-law of Judas, who tricked him into having intercourse with her. She eventually bears him the twins, Phares and Zara, in that illegitimate union. We also saw that, spiritually, Thamar represents the alien Serpent virus that corrupted the progeny of Judas. Spiritually, Thamar represents the Babylonian scripture—the Serpent.

Connecting all of the above information, it seems plausible that the term *Bethany* refers to the scripture corrupted by the Serpent—the literal Scripture. The fact that the Gospel mentions Bethany before narrating the parable of the barren fig tree is a sign that the parable relates to the literal scripture.

"Now in the morning as he returned into the city, he hungered. And when he saw a fig tree in the way, he came to it, and found nothing thereon, but leaves only, and said unto it, Let no fruit grow on thee henceforward for ever. And presently the fig tree withered away." The *fig tree* represents scripture (DNA), and the edible fruit of the fig tree—the *figs*—represents the Gospel (true human DNA).

Jesus finds the fig tree on the way to the city (Jerusalem). Spiritually, the term *city* (Jerusalem) refers to the deluded mind. Therefore, the expression, "way to the city" refers to dualistic religion; in this case, the Judaic religion. Jesus feels hungry and searches the tree for fruits. But, he finds the fig tree without any fruit, except luxurious foliage. In this parable, Jesus represents an enlightened man. Jesus searching the fig tree for fruits signifies an enlightened man searching for truth in the literal scripture. The Sanskrit word *leaf* is *parṇa*, which also means "words." In other words, the enlightened man finds the literal scripture to be an edifice of words devoid of truth. The Bhagavad Gīta compares the world (deluded mind) to an "upside down" *Aswattha* tree (*Aswattha* belongs to the fig species):

> *Ūrdha-mūlam-adha-śākham aśwattham prāhur-avyayam*
> *Chhandāmsi yasya parṇāni yastam vēda sa vēdavid*
> B.G 15:1

> ("The world, with its upward roots and downward branches, can be likened to an enduring fig tree, whose leaves are the verses of the scripture. Whosoever knows it in essence, is a knower of truth.")

Totally disappointed, Jesus curses the fig tree, *"Let no fruit grow on thee henceforward for ever."* In other words, humanity judges the literal scripture *forever* incapable of providing truth.

The fig tree is one of the first fruit trees to be cultivated by mankind. It has strong roots and draws heavily on the subsurface water. Spiritually, the subsurface water represents human consciousness, or life force. Fig, the fruit of the fig tree, is edible, consisting of a mature *syconium* (fleshy part) containing numerous one-seeded fruits. Spiritually, the *fig* fruit denotes body-awareness.

The curse of the fig tree is not only an indictment against the literal scripture but also an indictment against the Scribes, Pharisees and Sadducees. The disciples were amazed to see the fig tree wither away so quickly. They say to Jesus, *"How soon is the fig tree withered away!"* The Greek word for withered is *xērainō* (G3853), which means to "to shrivel."

Jesus says to the wonderstruck disciples, *"Verily I say unto you, If ye have faith, and doubt not, ye shall not only do this which is done to the fig tree, but also if ye shall say to this mountain, Be thou removed, and be thou cast into the sea; it shall be done. And all things, whatsoever ye shall ask in prayer, believing, ye shall receive."* Here, the Gospel reveals a great secret—the secret of manifesting miracles. But, it entails two prerequisites:

1. "If you have faith."
2. "If you doubt not."

The Greek word for *faith* is *pistis* (G4102), which means "constancy." Spiritually, it implies non-duality, or truth. The Greek word for *doubt* is *diakrinō* (G1252), which means "to separate thoroughly." Spiritually, it implies duality, or religion.

The spiritual meaning of the different terms and phrases used in the above verse is given below:

Term / Phrase	**Spiritual meaning**
If you have faith	If you are a true human being
And doubt not	And not under the spell of duality (religion)
Fig tree	Scripture / DNA
Mountain	Establishment
Remove	Dismantle
Here	From earth
Cast into sea	To obliterate

The implication of the words is this: "If you are a true human being, and if you are not under the spell of duality, then if you command the politico-religious Establishment to go, it will disintegrate. Whatever you ask the Self with body-awareness will be done to you."

The parable of the "Barren Fig Tree" is described differently in Gospels of Matthew, Mark, and Luke. The Gospel of John does not mention the parable. While Jesus' indictment of the fig tree is final in the Gospel of Matthew, Luke and Mark try to dilute the judgment. Mark finds a mitigating reason for the fig tree not producing fruit, saying, "for the time of figs was not yet" (Mark 11:12-14), which makes Jesus' curse seem unfair. Luke gives an entirely different version of the story. In Luke's version of the parable, Jesus is not in the picture at all, instead, there is another person, "a certain man," in his place. And the man spares (we have to assume so) the fig tree, yielding to the plea by the dresser of the vineyard, who says, "Lord, let it alone this year also, till I shall dig about it, and dung it: And if it bear fruit, well: and if not, then after that thou shall not cut it down" (Luke 13: 6-9). Luke is willing to give the fig tree another year to fruit. The expression "this year also" is confusing because every year can be considered as "this year."

It may be noted that both Mark and Luke were associates of Apostle Paul. Mark was the cousin of another well known early convert in the church, namely Barnabas, who was a Levite Jew from Cyprus. It was Paul and Barnabas who recruited Mark as a helper on a subsequent missionary journey. It is plausible that it was Paul who attached Mark with Peter for writing the Gospel of Mark, drawing on Peter's insights.

MATTHEW 21:23-27

"And when he was come into the temple, the chief priests and the elders of the people came unto him as he was teaching, and said, By what authority doest thou these things? and who gave thee this authority? And Jesus answered and said unto them, I also will ask you one thing, which if ye tell me, I in like wise will tell you by what authority I do these things. The baptism of John, whence was it? from heaven, or of men? And they reasoned with themselves, saying, If we shall say, From heaven; he will say unto us, Why did ye not believe him? But if we shall say, Of men; we fear the people; for all hold John as a prophet. And they answered Jesus, and said, We cannot tell. And he said unto them, Neither tell I you by what authority I do these things."

In the previous section we saw the eligibility criteria for becoming a 'soldier' in the war against evil. As if to underscore the point, here we see the Jewish elders questioning Jesus' authority. They ask Jesus, *"By what authority doest thou these things?"* The expression, "these things" alludes not only to Jesus' teaching in the temple, but also his denouncing of the literary scripture (fig tree). The question really is this: "What gives you the authority to denounce the scripture?" Or, in other words: "What right has an individual to denounce the religious Establishment?"

Rather than giving a direct answer, Jesus puts a counter-question at them: *"The baptism of John whence was it? from heaven, or of men?"* The Greek word for whence is *pothen* (G4159), which means "from which," implying the source. The "baptism of John" refers to the external purification ritual. Here, the term *heaven* refers to God, and the term *men* refers to the scripture. Therefore, the question really is this: "From where does John's authority for baptism come from—God or the scripture?" The truth is that John's authority comes neither from God nor the scripture. John's authority to baptize comes from his own Self.

Jesus' counter-question puts the elders in a quandary: if they say, from God, then Jesus could ask why they did not believe in him. On the other hand, if they say, from scripture, then it might offend the religious authorities. So they plead ignorance. The elders know that neither God nor the scripture sanctions baptism; but, they want to be politically-correct rather than be truthful. Therefore, Jesus refuses them an answer. But the answer is obvious: Jesus' authority comes from his own Self (the Father). The Self-authority is also called the "will of the Father."

MATTHEW 21:28-32

"But what think ye? A certain man has two sons; and he came to the first, and said, Son, go work to day in my vineyard. He answered and said, I will not: but afterward he repented, and went. And he came to the second, and said likewise. And he answered and said, I go, sir: and went not. Whether of them twain did the will of his father? They say unto him, The first. Jesus saith unto them, Verily I say unto you, That the publicans and the harlots go into the kingdom of God before you. For John came unto you in the way of righteousness, and ye believed him not: but the publicans and the harlots believed him: and ye, when ye had seen it, repented not afterward, that ye might believe him."

This section is a continuation of the previous one. Jesus asks the Jewish elders, *"But what think ye?"* Jesus is questioning the elders' beliefs about the source of authority. The implication of the question is this: "Where do you think authority comes from?" Jesus narrates a parable to elucidate the issue.

"A certain man has two sons; and he came to the first, and said, Son, go work to day in my vineyard. He answered and said, I will not: but afterward he repented, and went. And he came to the second, and said likewise. And he answered and said, I go, sir: and went not. Whether of them twain did the will of his father?" The word *certain* means "definite but not specified or identified." It suggests the quantum state, which is definite, but not particular. Therefore, the phrase, "certain man" refers to the Self or the Father. The term, *son* means "offspring." The two offspring of the Self are body and mind. Spiritually, the expression, "Father's vineyard" refers to the Gospel. Therefore, to work in the Father's vineyard means to interpret and understand the Gospel. Here, the parable talks about two types of Gospel interpreters: literal interpreters (the second son) and spiritual interpreters (first son).

The first son initially refuses his father's request, but later on repents and goes to work in the vineyard. He disobeyed the father's command, but he did not lie to him. In fact, he repented disobeying his father and goes to work later on. Here, the first son acted genuinely, according to his own Self-authority. In other words, he obeyed the "will of the Father," although he disobeyed the will of his father. But, from the religious perspective, the first son is guilty of disobeying the father's will.

Now let us see the spiritual implication of the parable. The 'father' represents the religion and its interpretation of the Gospel terms. The first son, the spiritual interpreter, refuses to interpret the Gospel because he does not want to interpret it based on religious terms. But, later on, he interprets the Gospel based on his own understanding of the Gospel terms.

The second son, on the other hand, agrees to the father's command, against his own will, only to please him. But, he reneges on his promise by not going to work, as agreed. He is culpable on two counts: first, he did not do the "will of the Father," by agreeing to the father, against his own will; second, he lied to the father by not going to work, as agreed. Even if the second son had gone to work as promised by him to his father, he is doing it against his own will and, therefore, he is not doing the "will of the Father." He is only doing the "will of the father," and not the "will of the Father," which is his own Self. The second son accepts an external agency as the source of authority, totally disregarding the authority of his own Self. He is a hypocrite.

The second son represents the person who does not bother to study the Gospel, but only agree to do so simply to please the religious authorities. To him, the religious authorities are more important than his own Self.

This parable of the Gospel clearly highlights the difference between an Evite and an Adamite. But, if we are not watchful, we will miss the real (spiritual) issue in the parable, which is about authority, and get carried away by the moral issue, which is about lying.

Jesus says, *"Verily I say unto you, That the publicans and the harlots go into the kingdom of God before you."* Although the publicans and harlots are culpable from the moral point of view, they are faultless from the spiritual point of view, because they live their lives according to their own freewill. In other words, these people obey the "will of the Father."

Jesus then says, *"For John came unto you in the way of righteousness, and ye believed him not: but the publicans and the harlots believed him: and ye, when ye had seen it, repented not afterward, that ye might believe him."* In this context, the expression, "way of righteousness" denotes morality. John, who heralded Jesus', represents moral uprightness or ethical behavior. In other words, moral uprightness is the pre-requisite to spiritual enlightenment. The Buddhists call it *śīla*.

Śīla in Buddhism is one of three sections of the *Noble Eightfold Path*, and is a code of conduct that embraces commitment to harmony and self-restraint with the principle motivation being non-violence, or freedom from causing harm to others. It has been variously described as virtue, right conduct, morality, moral discipline, and precept.

The Mortals, although morally depraved, hear the literal Gospel and realise the corrupt state of mind and then turn away from their corrupt behaviors. But the Adamites, who pretend to be morally upright, do not turn away from their corrupt behavior.

MATTHEW 21:33-41

"Hear another parable: There was a certain householder, which planted a vineyard, and hedged it round about, and digged a winepress in it, and built a tower, and let it out to husbandmen, and went into a far country: And when the time of the fruit drew near, he sent his servants to the husbandmen, that they might receive the fruits of it. And the husbandmen took his servants, and beat one, and killed another, and stoned another. Again, he sent other servants more than the first: and they did unto them likewise. But last of all he sent unto them his son, saying, They will reverence my son. But when the husbandmen saw the son, they said among themselves, This is the heir; come, let us kill him, and let us seize on his inheritance. And they caught him, and cast him out of the vineyard, and slew him. When the lord therefore of the vineyard cometh, what will he do unto those husbandmen? They say unto him, He will miserably destroy those wicked men, and will let out his vineyard unto other husbandmen, which shall render him the fruits in their seasons."

Term	**Body-level**	**Mind-level**
Householder	The Self	Body / DNA
Vineyard	Body / DNA	Scripture
Hedge	Form of Body /Cell	Non-duality
Winepress	Brain	Intellect
Wine	Body-awareness	Truth /Meaning
Watch tower	Mind	Religion
Husbandmen	Senses	Priestly class
Far Country	The waking state	The dream state
Son	Enlightened Evite	Gospel

This parable has two levels of meanings: one, a meaning in relation to the body; two, a meaning in relation to the mind. At the body-level, the *certain householder* is the Self or the Father. The *vineyard* is the body or the DNA. The *hedge* around the vineyard is the *form* of the body or the cell, or the *distinction* between inside and outside. The *winepress* dug at the centre of the vineyard is the human brain. The product of the winepress, the *wine*, is the experience of body-awareness. The *watch tower* is the mind. The *husbandmen* guarding the vineyard are the senses that interpret the external stimuli. After setting up the vineyard, the householder hands it over to husbandmen for upkeep and goes to a far country. The *far country* represents the waking state.

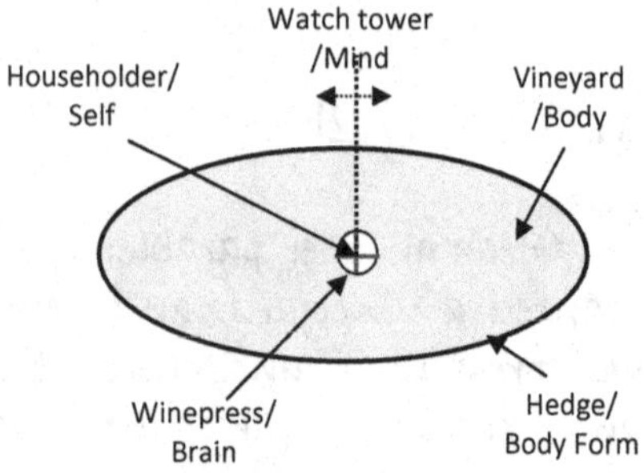

Parable of the Unfaithful Husbandmen – Body level

At the mind-level, the *certain householder* is the body or the DNA. The *vineyard* is the true scripture. The *hedge* around the vineyard is non-duality—the *distinction* between truth and falsehood. The *winepress* dug at the centre of the vineyard is intellect (the isomorphism). The product of the winepress, the *wine*, represents meaning or truth. The *watch tower* is religion. The *husbandmen* guarding the vineyard are the priestly race that interprets the scripture. After setting up the vineyard, the householder hands it over to husbandmen for upkeep and goes to a far country, which is the dream state.

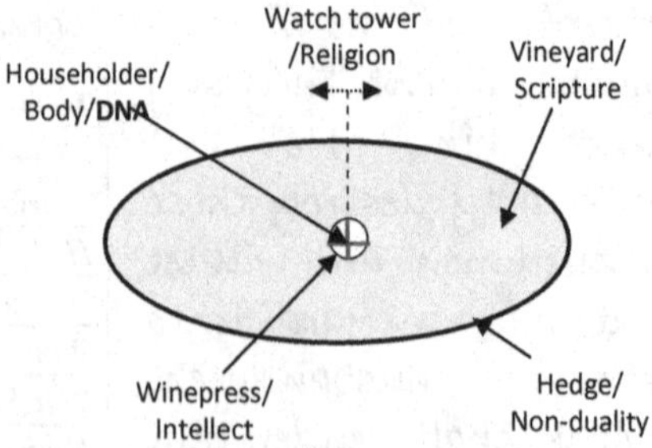

Parable of the Unfaithful Husbandmen – Mind Level

The body-level and the mind-level represent the two stages of *fall* of the Self. The first stage of the fall is the descent of the Self into the body as *soul*; the second stage is the descent of the soul from body into the mind as *ego*.

Just as the householder's purpose for setting up the vineyard is to produce wine, the Self's purpose of creating the body (human being) is to know itself as body-awareness.

Similarly, the Self's purpose of creating the mind or world is to know itself as meaning.

"And when the time of the fruit drew near, he sent his servants to the husband men, that they might receive the fruits of it." The expression, "when the time of the fruit drew near" means "having experienced the body and the mind." Therefore the implication is that the soul, having gained sufficient experience in the dream-world, wants to liberate from it, but is unable to wake up because it is held captive in the dream. The *servants* that the householder sends to the vineyard represent the wake-up calls from the Self. At the body level, these servants are called the inner voice or intuition. At the mind level, they are the prophets (Evites) that appear periodically exhorting repentance.

"And the husbandmen took his servants, and beat one, and killed another, and stoned another. Again, he sent other servants more than the first: and they did unto them likewise." At the body-level, the implication is that the deluded man ignores these inner voices or misinterprets them or may even stone them down with religious precepts. At the mind-level, the implication is that religious establishments prevent man's access to the spiritual meaning of the scripture.

"But last of all he sent unto them his son, saying, They will reverence my son. But when the husbandmen saw the son, they said among themselves, This is the heir; come, let us kill him, and let us seize on his inheritance. And they caught him, and cast him out of the vineyard, and slew him." Both at the body-level and at the mind-level, the term *son* refers to the Gospel. The term *inheritance* implies birthright. At the body level, it implies immortality; at the mental level it implies dominion over the whole body. The evil husbandmen destroy the Gospel truth in order to retain their dominion over man and the world. The shout, *"Let us kill him, and let us seize on his inheritance"* is the battle cry of the archons. This parable also foretells the crucifixion of Jesus Christ at the hands of the Jews and the Romans.

Jesus asks the disciples, *"When the lord therefore of the vineyard cometh, what will he do unto those husbandmen?"* The disciples reply, *"He will miserably destroy those wicked men, and will let out his vineyard unto other husbandmen, which shall render him the fruits in their seasons."* Spiritually, the *husbandmen* represent the Adamite religious Establishment (the Serpent) that interprets scripture for humanity. The disciples use the word *wicked* to describe these husbandmen. The word *wicked* has the following meaning:

1. Having committed unrighteous acts
2. Intensely or extremely bad or unpleasant in degree or quality
3. Naughtily or annoyingly playful
4. Highly offensive; arousing aversion or disgust
5. Brilliant as in "awesome," "excellent," "fantabulous," "first-class," and "splendid"

MATTHEW 21:42-46

"Jesus saith unto them, Did ye never read in the scriptures, The stone which the builders rejected, the same is become the head of the corner: this is the Lord's doing, and it is marvellous in our eyes? Therefore say I unto you, The kingdom of God shall be taken from you, and given to a nation bringing forth the fruits thereof. And whosoever shall fall on this stone shall be broken: but on whomsoever it shall fall, it will grind him to powder. And when the chief priests and Pharisees had heard his parables, they perceived that he spake of them, But when they sought to lay hands on him, they feared the multitude, because they took him for a prophet."

"Jesus saith unto them, Did ye never read in the scriptures, The stone which the builders rejected, the same is become the head of the corner: this is the Lord's doing, and it is marvellous in our eyes?" The Greek word for *builders* is *oikodomeō* (G3618), which means "a house builder." It is derived from the root word *oikodomē* (G3619), which means "architecture," "structure," or "matrix." Spiritually, the term "builders" refers to the architect of the politico-religious Establishment, which is the Serpent (archons). Perhaps, the words "builders" and Masons are connected. The *stone* that these builders rejected is non-duality. As a matter of fact, non-duality has no part in worldly systems. The Greek

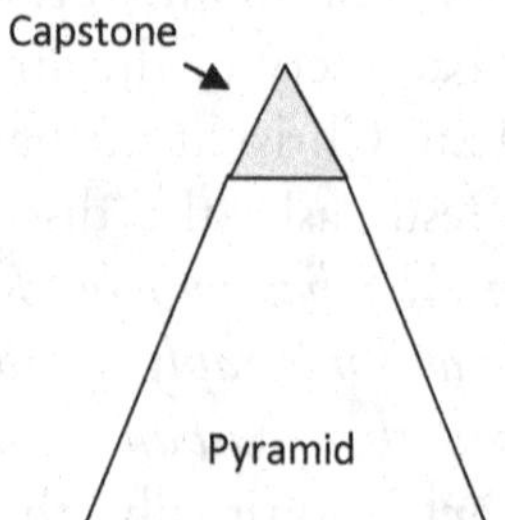

PYRAMID WITH CAPSTONE

word for rejected is *apodokimazō* (G593), which means "to repudiate." The word is derived from the root words *apo* (G575), which means "to separate," or "to reverse" and *dokimazō* (G1381), which means "to think" or "to suppose." Combining, we get the meaning of the word *rejected* as "to think that it is separated." Spiritually, the word *rejected* implies delusion; it is whole, but we think it is separated.

The phrase, "head of the corner" refers to the *capstone* of a pyramid. It is the capstone that makes the pyramid whole. The pyramid represents the human body, and the capstone represents the head. Just as the capstone makes the pyramid whole, non-duality makes human beings whole or perfect. It is non-duality that is called the "*Lord's doing*" because it is *quantum action.* It is "*marvellous in our eyes*" because of its paradoxical nature. It is beyond comprehension.

Spiritually, the expression, "the stone that builders rejected" means "the non-duality that religion destroyed" or "the body-awareness that archons destroyed" or "the truth that the Masons corrupted."

The pyramid without the capstone symbolizes the fallen state of humanity. Spiritually, the capstone of the pyramid represents the spiritual scripture (DNA). The removal of the capstone is symbolic of the corruption of the scripture, and the human DNA. It may seem strange that the Great Pyramid of Egypt does not have a capstone. Was the great pyramid always without a capstone or was it removed or destroyed? No one knows the answer. It remains a great mystery as the pyramid itself.

Jesus then says to the Jewish priests and elders, *"Therefore say I unto you, The kingdom of God shall be taken from you, and given to a nation bringing forth the fruits thereof."* The term "therefore" implies "because you rejected non-duality or truth." Spiritually, the expression, "kingdom of God" refers to the scripture, DNA, or soul. The term "a nation" refers to the Gentiles. The *fruits* of the scripture are immortality in addition to prosperity and abundance in the world.

The Gospel, then, says something extremely mysterious: *"And whosoever shall fall on this stone shall be broken: but on whomsoever it shall fall, it will grind him to powder."* The 'stone' referred here is non-duality. According to the Gospel, non-duality is the "Lord's doing," or *quantum action.* In physics terms, the unit of quantum action is called a *photon.* And the photon has two states of existence: one, as particle; and two, as *wave.* Spiritually, the Gospel expression, "whosoever shall fall on this stone shall be broken" refers to the *particle aspect* of non-duality. Non-duality, like a source of light, can illuminate multiple meanings from a word. In a sense, it is *breaking* the word into many. Similarly, the expression, "on whomsoever it shall fall, it will grind him to powder" refers to the *wave aspect* of non-duality. Non-duality is like a powerful solvent that dissolves everything in itself. In that sense, it grinds everything to powder.

The Jewish religious authorities want to kill Jesus for the things he revealed about them, but are afraid to do so in public view.

The Parable of the Wicked Husbandmen is found in three of the four Canonical gospels (Matthew 21:33-46, Luke 20:9-19, and Mark 12:1-12), and in the non-canonical Gospel of Thomas. But, the narration of the parable in the Gospels of Mark and Luke differ significantly from that of Matthew. Both Mark and Luke seem to water down the content to make the husbandmen seem less culpable. The major differences in the narratives in Matthew and Luke are listed below:

1. Matthew uses the expression "a certain householder"; Luke uses the expression "a certain man."
2. Matthew gives details about the vineyard, such as the hedge, winepress, and the watch tower; Luke omits these details.
3. According to Matthew, the householder sends several servants including "other servants"; according to Luke, only three servants are sent by the man, and there is no mention about the "other servants."
4. According Matthew the husbandmen kills some of the servants; according to Luke the husbandmen only harms, but do not kill any.
5. According to Matthew, when Jesus asks the disciples how the lord of the vineyard would deal with the wicked husbandmen, they say that he will miserably destroy them. But, in Luke's version of the parable, it is Jesus who asks the question and it is Jesus who answers it also. The disciples merely exclaim, "God forbid."
6. According to Matthew Jesus makes reference to the scripture; Luke does not make any reference to scripture.
7. In Matthew's account Jesus says to the Pharisees, "Therefore say I unto you, The kingdom of God shall be taken from you, and given to a nation bringing forth the fruits thereof"; Luke entirely omits the saying.

CHAPTER 22

For Many Are Called, But Few Are Chosen

MATTHEW 22:1-14

"And Jesus answered and spake unto them again by parables, and said, The kingdom of heaven is like unto a certain king, which made a marriage for his son, And sent forth his servants to call them that were bidden to the wedding: and they would not come. Again, he sent forth other servants, saying, Tell them which are bidden, Behold, I have prepared my dinner: my oxen and my fatlings are killed, and all things are ready: come unto the marriage. But they made light of it, and went their ways, one to his farm, another to his merchandise: And the remnant took his servants, and entreated them spitefully, and slew them. But when the king heard thereof, he was wroth: and he sent forth his armies, and destroyed those murderers, and burned up their city. Then saith he to his servants, The wedding is ready, but they which were bidden were not worthy. Go ye therefore into the highways, and as many as ye shall find, bid to the marriage. So those servants went out into the highways, and gathered all as many as they found, both bad and good: and the wedding was furnished with guests. And when the king came in to see the guests, he saw there a man which had not on a wedding garment: And he saith unto him, Friend, how camest thou in hither not having a wedding garment? And he was speechless. Then said the king to the servants, Bind him hand and foot, and take him away, and cast him into outer darkness; there shall be weeping and gnashing of teeth. For many are called, but few are chosen."

"*The kingdom of heaven is like unto a certain king, which made a marriage for his son, And sent forth his servants to call them that were bidden to the wedding: and they would not come.*" Before we interpret this parable, it is important that we clearly understand the term *king*. If we understand it wrongly, then we will miss the true spirit of the parable. Here, the Gospel is not talking about any particular king; instead the term *king* refers to man. It designates every single human being. In other words, the term *king* refers to man's Self, also called the Father.

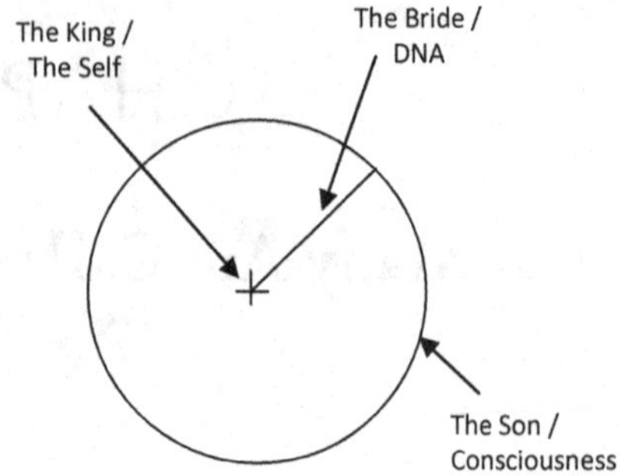

THE ROYAL MARRIAGE

The Greek word for *marriage* is *gamos* (G1062), which means "nuptials." But, the marriage described in this parable is no ordinary marriage; it is a spiritual marriage. It is the marriage between the Gospel reader's mind (awareness) and the Gospel content.

Spiritually, the king's *son* represents the "Son of man," or the Gospel. The *bride* is the Gospel reader's mind or awareness. The *marriage* is the reader's spiritual understanding of the Gospel. The *marriage feast* is the body-awareness that arises from the spiritual understanding of the Gospel. And it is an occasion of great joy.

The servants are the disciples and other people that spread the Gospel message. And the guests "that were 'bidden to the wedding" are the Jews who were the first to receive the Gospel. But they rejected it completely.

"*Again, he sent forth other servants, saying, Tell them which are bidden, Behold, I have prepared my dinner: my oxen and my fatlings are killed, and all things are ready: come unto the marriage. But they made light of it, and went their ways, one to his farm, another to his merchandise: And the remnant took his servants, and entreated them spitefully, and slew them.*" Unfazed, the king again sends other servants to the invited guests giving in vivid detail the sumptuousness of the wedding feast. The Greek word for *dinner* is *ariston* (G712), which means "the best meal." The Greek word for *oxen* is *tauros* (G5022), which means "steers." A *steer* is a male bovine that is castrated before sexual maturity, especially one raised for meat. Spiritually, the term "oxen" refers to the Gospel words. The 'killing' of the oxen signifies the literal interpretation of the Gospel. The Greek word for *fatling* is *sitistos* (G4619), which means "grained," or "fatted." The Hebrew word for *fatling* is *miśneh* (H4932), which means "a copy," or "a duplicate." Spiritually, the term "fatlings" refers to the spiritual meaning of the Gospel words. The 'killing' of the fatlings signifies the spiritual interpretation of the Gospel.

The king invites his intended guests two times, but on both occasions they reject the invitation. The Gospel says, *"But they made light of it, and went their ways, one to his farm, another to his merchandise: And the remnant took his servants, and entreated them spitefully, and slew them."* Spiritually, the word, "way" implies religion, or scripture. And the word *farm* is mentioned only once in the entire King James Bible and it is in this verse. The Greek word for *farm* is *agros* (G68), which means "field," or generically, "country." Spiritually, the *farm* refers to the *Torah*. The Greek word for *merchandise* is *emporia* (G1711), which means "mart," or "traffic." The word is derived from the root word *emporos* (GG1713), which means "a wholesale tradesman." The Hebrew word for *merchandise* is *āmar* (H6014), which means "to chastise, as if by piling blows." Spiritually, the term *merchandise* refers to the *Talmud*. The Greek word for *remnant* is *loipoi* (G3062), which means "remaining ones." The word is derived from the root word *leipo* (G3007), which means "to be destitute," or "wanting." The Hebrew word for remnant is *yeter* (H3499), which means "overhanging," or by implication "an excess, superiority." Spiritually, the term remnant refers to the *Cabbala*. According to the Gospel, the *remnant* 'kills' the servants. Spiritually, it suggests that the Cabbalists destroyed the Christian church.

"But when the king heard thereof, he was wroth: and he sent his armies, and destroyed those murderers, and burned up their city." The term "murderers" refers to the Cabalists—the corruptors of the Gospel and the Christian church. Literally, the term *city* refers to Jerusalem, but spiritually, it refers to the monotheistic-dualistic religious Establishment. The phrase, "armies of the king" refers to the Gospel revelations. Truth is the 'fire' that burns up the 'city'. In other words, the truth revealed by the spiritual interpretation of the Gospel is capable of utterly destroying the Serpent.

"Then saith he to his servants, The wedding is ready, but they which were bidden were not worthy. Go ye therefore into the highways, and as many as ye shall find, bid to the marriage. So those servants went out

into the highways, and gathered all as many as they found, both bad and good: and the wedding was furnished with guests." The king declares the invited guests unworthy of attending the marriage feast because they did not heed his invitation. The king, therefore, asks his servants to bring in guests from the *highways*. Spiritually, the term, "highways" refer to the pagan religions. Accordingly, the servants fill the wedding hall with guests picked up from the highways, both bad and good. The *bad* guests are humans possessing corrupt DNA (Mortals); the *good* guests are those who possess the true human DNA (Evites).

"And when the king came in to see the guests, he saw there a man which had not on a wedding garment: And he saith unto him, Friend, how camest thou in hither not having a wedding garment? And he was speechless. Then said the king to the servants, Bind him hand and foot, and take him away, and cast him into outer darkness; there shall be weeping and gnashing of teeth." As we have seen before, the term "guests" refers to those who read the Gospel. Spiritually, the term, "wedding garment" refers to body-awareness. Therefore, the guest who is not wearing the wedding garment is one who reads the Gospel without body-awareness. The king, therefore, commands his servants to "bind him hand and foot" and throw him into the outer darkness. Spiritually, the expression, "outer darkness" refers to confusion or spiritual darkness.

MATTHEW 22:15-22

"Then went the Pharisees, and took counsel how they might entangle him in his talk. And they sent out unto him their disciples with the Herodians, saying, Master, we know that thou art true, and teachest the way of God in truth, neither carest thou for any man: for thou regardest not the person of men. Tell us therefore, What thinkest thou? Is it lawful to give tribute unto Caesar, or not? But Jesus perceived their wickedness, and said, Why tempt ye me, ye hypocrites? Shew me the tribute money. And they brought unto him a penny. And he saith unto them, Whose is this image and superscription? And they say unto him, Caesar's. Then saith he unto them, Render therefore unto Caesar the things which are Caesar's ; and unto God the things that are God's. When they had heard these words, they marvelled, and left him, and went their way."

Upset by Jesus' denouncing of the literal scripture (the unfruitful fig tree), the religious authorities question his authority to criticize the scripture. Replying to them, Jesus refers to the baptism of John and asserts that his authority comes from being a true human being. His subsequent parables (the parable of the wicked husbandmen and the parable of the marriage feast) expose the religious authorities as wicked husbandmen that usurped humanity's inheritance, which is the true scripture. The Pharisees hate Jesus for exposing them and want to kill him immediately, but are afraid to do so in full public view. Therefore, they come up with the strategy of trapping Jesus in seditious utterances so that they can brand him as an enemy of the State. Accordingly, a group of Pharisees, accompanied by some Herodians, confront Jesus. The Herodians are a faction of the Jewish society; but, unlike the Pharisees and the Sadducees, the Herodians are servile to the Roman government. The Pharisees take the Herodians along with them for the *inquisition* so that they have witnesses to Jesus' seditious utterances, should he make any.

The Greek word for *Herodians* is *Hērōdianoi* (G2265), which means "partisans of Herodes." It is connected to the word *hērōdiōn* (G2267), which means "a Christian." In Romans 16:11, Apostle Paul writes, *"Salute Herodion my kinsman. Greet them that be of the household of Narcissus, which are in the Lord."* As we have seen before, Herod was the Roman *client king* of Judaea. He was a *Judanized Edomite*—an alien pretending to be a native. Judaea was a client state of Rome and Herod was her client king, ruling on and in behalf of the powers in Rome. Symbolically, Rome represents the alien masters—the Serpent. Herod represents the political establishment that is merely a puppet in the hands of the alien masters.

The derivation of the Latin word *narcissus* is unknown. It may be a loanword from another language. It is frequently linked to the Greek myth of *Narcissus*, who became so obsessed with his own reflection that as he knelt and gazed into a pool of water, he fell into the water and drowned. The *narcissus* plant sprang from where he died. Pliny, the Roman philosopher, wrote that the plant was named for its narcotic properties. The word *narcotic* means "I grow numb" in Greek.

The *Inquisition* was a group of institutions within the judicial system of the Roman Catholic Church whose aim is to combat heresy. It started in the 12th-century France to combat the spread of religious sectarianism, in particular the *Cathars* and the *Waldensians*.

This Medieval Inquisition persisted into the 14th century, and from the 1250s was associated with the *Dominican Order*. It is estimated that around 6000 people were executed by the Church in the Inquisition.

The Pharisees ask Jesus, *"Master, we know that thou art true, and teachest the way of God in truth, neither carest thou for any man: for thou regardest not the person of men. Tell us therefore, What thinkest thou? Is it lawful to give tribute unto Caesar, or not?"* At the outset, the words of the Pharisees appear complimentary, but, in fact, it is a veiled accusation. The expression, "thou carest for no man" may be interpreted either as "you are a just person" or as "you don't respect authority." In fact, the Pharisees are accusing Jesus of not honoring the politico-religious Establishment. They ask, *"What thinkest thou? Is it lawful to give tribute unto Caesar, or not?"* The question is a set-up. It is a head-I-win-tail-you-lose kind of question. In short, they are asking: "Do you think it is lawful to give tax to the Roman Government?" It involves two issues: one, the Jewish Law; two, the Roman authority (to tax). If Jesus says yes, then he is culpable according to the Jewish Law. On the other hand, if he says no, then he is culpable before the Roman authorities. Either way, he will be found culpable. Jesus senses the trap and says, *"Why tempt ye me, ye hypocrites?"*

Jesus does not give a direct answer to the inquisitors. Instead, he demands them to show him the tribute money. When they show him a penny, he asks them, *"Whose is this image and superscription?"* The question is also directed at each one of us. It is a cue to carefully study the image and superscription on the currency to know who the slave master is. The image and superscription on the currency can reveal his identity.

The inquisitors tell Jesus that the image and superscription on the tribute money are that of Caesar's. After inspecting the penny, Jesus says to them, *"Render therefore unto Caesar the things which are Caesar's; and unto God the things which are God's."* The *things* which are Caesar's are worldly things such as money and power, which are worthless to God. The things that are God's are body and mind (awareness). Therefore, the message of the Gospel is this: "You may give your money and wealth to the Establishment, but never surrender your body-awareness (freedom) to them."

MATTHEW 22:23-33

"The same day came to him the Sadducees, which say that there is no resurrection, and asked him, Saying, Master, Moses said, If a man die, having no children, his brother shall marry his wife, and raise up seed unto his brother. Now there were with us seven brethren: and the first, when he had married a wife, deceased, and, having no issue, left his wife unto his brother: Likewise the second also, and the third, unto the seventh. And last of all the woman died also. Therefore in the resurrection whose wife shall she be of the seven? for they all had her. Jesus answered and said unto them, Ye do err, not knowing the scriptures, nor the power of God. For in the resurrection they neither marry, nor are given in marriage, but are as the angels of God in heaven. But as touching the resurrection of the dead, have ye not read that which was spoken unto you by God, saying, I am the God of Abraham, and the God of Isaac, and the God of Jacob? God is not the God of the dead, but of the living. And when the multitude heard this, they were astonished at his doctrine."

The Sadducees represented the upper social and economic echelons of Judean society. As a whole, the sect fulfills various political, social, and religious roles, including maintaining the temple. The Sadducees believe that:

1. There is no resurrection, neither angel nor spirit, and that the soul of a man perishes with the body
2. There is neither fate nor decrees
3. Only the Torah is to be followed, not the Talmud

The Sadducees can be compared to the *Chārvakas* of ancient India. The *Chārvaka* is classified as a heterodox Hindu system. It is characterized as a materialistic and atheistic (*nāstika*) school of thought. Etymologically, the term *Chārvaka* means "agreeable speech," suggesting politically-correct speech. They are also called *Lokāyata* which means "worldly," or "secular." The Chārvaka may be compared to the modern secularist politicians whose main concern is pleasing society rather than truth per se.

The Sadducees neither believe in resurrection nor in the existence of soul; therefore, their doubt concerning resurrection is not genuine, but only a ruse to trap Jesus. Jesus sees through their evil machination and says, *"Ye do err, not knowing the scriptures, nor the power of God. For in the resurrection they neither marry, nor are given in marriage, but are as the angels of God in heaven. But as touching the resurrection of the dead, have ye not read that which was spoken unto you by God, saying, I am the God of Abraham, and the God of Isaac, and the God of Jacob? God is not the God of the dead, but of the living."* The statement, "Ye do err" is a strong indictment. The verb, "err" has multiple connotations:

1. To mislead
2. To misguide
3. To lead astray
4. To misinform
5. To delude
6. To falsify
7. To misstate
8. To deceive
9. To lie
10. To blunder
11. To misconceive
12. To corrupt
13. To misunderstand

In short, Jesus says, "You are evil." Jesus makes this strong indictment for two reasons: one, because they do not know the *scriptures*; two, because they do not know the *power of God*. Here, the term, *scripture* refers to the true human DNA. Therefore, the statement, *"Ye do err, not knowing the scriptures, nor the power of God"* means "You are evil because you are neither truly human nor are you body-aware."

Jesus explains: *"For in the resurrection they neither marry, nor are given in marriage, but are as the angels of God in heaven."* The word *resurrection* (Greek: *anastasis* G386) means "rise from the dead" or "rise to life." If we consider the waking state as death (deluded state), then physical death implies resurrection. Since the waking (deluded) state is the state of duality, the resurrected state is the state of non-duality. The Greek word for *angel* is *angelos* (G32), which means "messenger." The

Hebrew term for *angel* is *malāk* (H4397), which means "a messenger of God." According Jesus, in non-dual state of resurrection, souls exist as bundles of *possibilities*. The Hindus call it *sanchita karma*. In Hinduism, *sanchita karma* (means "bundled together") is one of the three kinds of karma. It is the sum of the past karmas—all actions, good and bad, from one's past lives follow through to the next life. Out of this, each lifetime, the soul chooses a certain portion of it, called the *prārābdha karma*, to experience it in the present incarnation. But, in each life, the soul adds new karma, called *āgama karma*, to the *sanchita karma* balance.

Jesus reveals the secret of the soul to the Sadducees: *"But as touching the resurrection of the dead, have ye not read that which was spoken unto you by God, saying, I am the God of Abraham, and the God of Isaac, and the God of Jacob? God is not the God of the dead, but of the living."* Jesus says, "God of Abraham," "God of Isaac" and "God of Jacob" *individually* to emphasize their individuality. According to Jesus, God is the "I of Abraham," the "I of Isaac" and the "I of Jacob." In other words, God is the "I" of human beings, where "I" refers to the Self. According to Jesus, man's individuality itself is his God.

God is the Self ("I") in every body-aware individual. But, the God of the *group* is the Serpent. Since the Adamites are a highly clannish group, their God is the Serpent. They are clan-aware rather than body-aware.

Jesus declares, *"God is not the God of the dead, but of the living."* It means "God is not the DNA of the Adamites, but the DNA of the Evites." When the people heard it, they were amazed.

MATTHEW 22:34-40

"But when the Pharisees had heard that he had put the Sadducees to silence, they were gathered together. Then one of them, which was a lawyer, asked him a question, tempting him, and saying, Master, which is the great commandment in the law? Jesus said unto him, Thou shalt love the Lord thy God with all thy heart, and with all thy soul, and with all thy mind. This is the first and great commandment. And the second is like unto it, Thou shalt love thy neighbour as thyself. On these two commandments hang all the law and the prophets."

We have seen Jesus being tested by the Scribes, Pharisees and the Sadducees, and all of them were silenced by the brilliance of Jesus' arguments. Now, it is the turn of the lawyers to test him. The Greek word for lawyer is *nomikos* (G3544), which means "an expert in the Mosaic law."

Before we proceed with the interpretation of the above Gospel verses, we have to first understand the true meaning of the word *love.* There are two Greek words that imply love: they are *agapaō* (G25) and *phileō* (G5368). The popular notion of love is *phileō*, which is the affection we show one another. *Phileō* operates externally, as *nice* behavior (actions) and *nice* speech (words). But, it is shallow because it involves only the mind. True love is *agapaō*, and it involves the body and it entails treating the other as an *integral* part of one's own body. Conspicuous display of affection may be missing in *agapaō*, but it never lacks deep concern for the life of the other. In *agapaō*, we empathize, rather than sympathize.

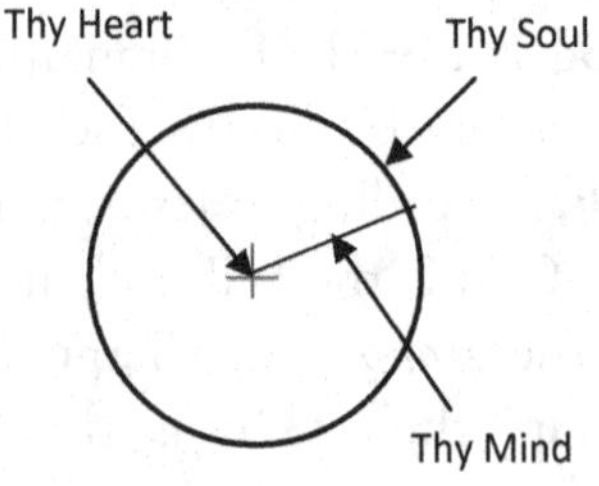

Circle of Self

Here, the lawyer tests Jesus by asking him to prioritize the commandments. He wants to know what, according to Jesus, is the greatest commandment. The trap: if Jesus says a particular commandment is the most important, then he can accuse him of considering the other commandments lightly. Jesus sensing the trap, says, *"Thou shalt love the Lord thy God with all thy heart, and with all thy soul, and with all thy mind. This is the first and great commandment. And the second is like unto it, Thou shalt love thy neighbour as thyself. On these two commandments hang all the law and the prophets."* The expression, "thy God" means "your God," not someone else God. Therefore, it necessarily relates to the body, or else it cannot be called "thy God." In other words, "thy God" means "your body."

In this verse, the Gospel states the equivalence of the terms, *God, heart, soul,* and *mind.* In the Circle of Self, the center point represents the heart; the circumference, the soul; and the radius, the mind. But, they are not separate entities. They are a *trinity*, and constitute the integral whole called God, body, or circle. Only the body can we love (*agapaō*) with our heart, soul, and mind. How can we *truly* love an external God with *all* our body? It is impossible! You may love an external God with the mind, but not with the body. The external God is not a God, but a Lord, a king, a master, or a boss. In fact, the external God is the *Baal.* You can love him only with your mind, but never with your body. Therefore, Jesus states the first and foremost commandment: "*Your body is your God.*" If your body (DNA) is corrupted, then your God is the Serpent. If your body (DNA) is pure, then Christ is your God.

Having set out the first and foremost commandment, Jesus states the second: *"And the second is like unto it, Thou shalt love thy neighbour as thyself."* According to Jesus, this commandment is similar to the first one. The term "thyself" actually means "thy Self" or "thy body." Therefore, the second commandment states that one should consider one's neighbor as an integral part of one's own body. Spiritually, the term *neighbor* refers to the whole of nature; it includes all living things in nature.

Jesus concludes, *"On these two commandments hang all the law and the prophets."* It means that there is no commandment greater than your body. According to the Gospel, every other commandment is subsumed under these cardinal laws. In other words, the Gospel rescinds the Mosaic laws in one fell swoop.

MATTHEW 22:41-46

"While the Pharisees were gathered together, Jesus asked them, Saying, What think ye of Christ? whose son is he? They say unto him, The Son of David. He saith unto them, How then doth David in spirit call him Lord, saying, The LORD said unto my Lord, Sit thou on my right hand, till I make thine enemies thy footstool? If David then call him Lord, how is he his son? And no man was able to answer him a word, neither durst any man from that day forth ask him any more questions."

In this Gospel episode, we see Jesus testing the Pharisees' conception of Christ. Jesus asks them, *"What think ye of Christ? whose son is he?"* The Greek *word* for *son* is *huios* (G5207), which means "offspring," suggesting immediate, remote, or figurative kinship. But, spiritually, the word son implies "kind" rather than "biological male descendent." Therefore, Jesus' question really is this: "Is Christ a physical person or a principle?" But, the Pharisees understand the question literally and reply, *"The Son of David."* Clearly, the Pharisees think *Christ* and *Messiah* are one and the same, and that he is a physical person.

A *messiah*, in the Abrahamic religions, is a savior or liberator of a group of people. In the Hebrew Bible, a messiah (Hebrew: *māśiah* H4899) is a king or High Priest traditionally anointed with holy anointing oil. The Jews believe that he is a leader anointed by God, and physically descended from the Davidic line, who will rule the united tribes of Israel and herald the *Messianic Age* of global peace, also known as the *World to Come*.

The term *Christ* is derived from the Greek word *Christos* (G5547), which means "the anointed one." But, spiritually, the term refers to the *Logos*, which is the principle of "I am," or body-awareness. Logos exists as the interrelationship between the *hypostases* (*Nous*, *psyche* and *physis* of the *Circle of Self*). The word *hypostasis* means underlying state or underlying substance, and is the fundamental reality that supports all else. By the way, the term *Christ* is not mentioned anywhere in the Old Testament. Similarly, the term *messiah* is not mentioned anywhere in the entire New Testament (Authorized King James Version).

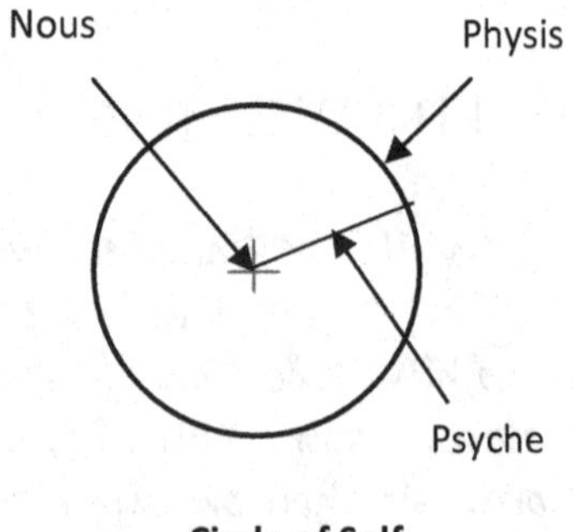

Circle of Self

Jesus questions the Pharisees' assumption by quoting from the scripture (Psalm 110:1): *"How them doth David in spirit call him Lord, saying, The LORD said unto my Lord, Sit thou on my right hand, till I make thine enemies thy footstool? If David then call him Lord, how is he his son?"* In this verse, the Hebrew term for LORD is *YHWH* (H3068), which means "self-Existent" or "eternal." YHWH is the four-lettered name of "The One," also known as the *Tetragrammaton*. The term appears 6,828 times in the *Biblia Hebraica Stuttgartensia* edition of the *Hebrew Masoretic Text*. By the way, the Greek word for LORD is *kurios* (G2962). Spiritually, the term YHWH implies *tetralemma* or non-duality. The *tetralemma* (Sanskrit: *Chatuṣkōti*) is a figure that features prominently in the classical logic of India. The history of *fourfold negation*, the *Chatuṣkōti*, is evident in the logico-epistemological tradition of India, given the categorical nomenclature "Indian logic" in Western discourse. Subsumed within the auspice of Indian logic, "Buddhist logic" has been particularly focused in its employment of the fourfold negation, as evidenced by the traditions of Nagārjuna and the *Madhyāmaka* given the retroactive nomenclature of *Prāsangika* by the Tibetan Buddhist logico-epistemological tradition.

The term "my Lord" has its origin in the Hebrew word *Adonāy* (H136). The term *Adonāy* is first used in the Bible in Genesis 15:2: *"And Abram said, Lord GOD, what wilt thou give me, seeing I go childless, and the steward of my house is this Eliezar of Damascus?" Adonāy* probably refers to the *creator God*, and not YHWH. *Adonāy* may imply *God* or the *Serpent*, depending on who is invoking the name.

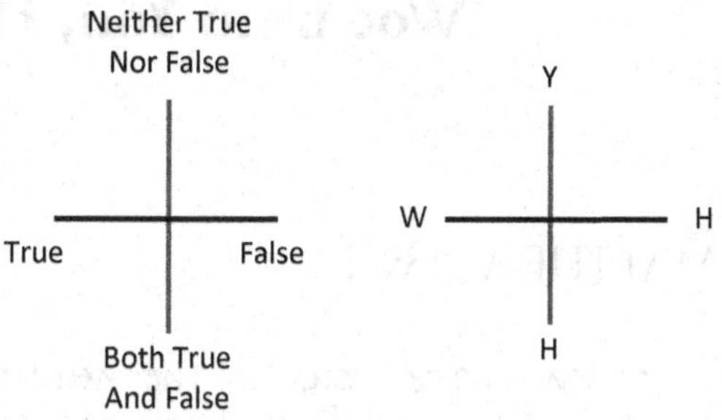

When David says "my Lord" he is referring to Christ, and not the Messiah. What David actually implies when he says, *"The LORD said unto my Lord, Sit thou on my right hand, till I make thine enemies thy footstool"* is that YHWH (Existence) has placed Christ (the ideal of true human being) above everything else. But, the deluded Pharisees confuse Christ for Messiah (a powerful king), just as they confuse YHWH for *Adonāy*.

Jesus' logic goes like this: a Jew would not call his son "Lord." Therefore, if David addresses Christ as "my Lord," then it implies that Christ not the *physical* son of David. But, Jesus Christ is born in the line of David. The conclusion: neither Christ nor David is a physical person.

The Pharisees misconstrue Jesus' question. Jesus' question relates to Christ, but the Pharisees' answer relates to the Messiah. They confuse Christ for the Jewish notion of Messiah. The term *Christ* refers to the ideal of an enlightened human being, whereas *Messiah* refers to the Jewish people's expectation of a world leader, under whose leadership they aspire to conquer the whole world.

According to Jesus, humanity will liberate itself from the politico-religious Establishment when individual human beings become body-aware. This is the promise of the Father (Existence) to Christ (humanity): *"Sit thou on my right hand, till I make thine enemies thy footstool."*

CHAPTER 23

Woe unto You, Hypocrites!

MATTHEW 23:1-4

"Then spake Jesus to the multitude, and to his disciples, Saying, The scribes and the Pharisees sit in Moses' seat: All therefore whatsoever they bid you observe, that observe and do; but do not ye after their works: for they say, and do not. For they bind heavy burdens and grievous to be borne, and lay them on men's shoulders; but they themselves will not move them with one of their fingers."

In Matthew 16:6 we saw Jesus cautioning the disciples about the leaven of the Pharisees and of the Sadducees. In modern terms, the doctrine of the Pharisees is called religious theology, and the doctrine of the Sadducees is called political ideology. Jesus cautions his disciples and the multitude that these doctrines are capable of corrupting human consciousness (body-awareness) just as leaven changes the dough. The reason for the caution is that even a minute amount of these doctrines is capable of corrupting body-awareness, and cause delusion.

Jesus warns: *"The scribes and the Pharisees sit in Moses' seat."* The term "Moses' seat" signifies the authority that the Scribes and Pharisees have in interpreting The Law and exercising their authority over the Jewish people. They are the ones who would tell the people of Israel what the Law of Moses 'really' meant. The Greek word for "Moses' seat" is *Moses kathedras.*

Jesus cautions: *"All therefore whatsoever they bid you observe, that observe and do; but do not ye after their works: for they say, and do not."* Here, the word, "therefore" has two connotations:

1. Because they (Scribes, Pharisees) wield authority
2. Because even a small amount of their doctrine can cause delusion

The word, *observe* means "to pay close attention," or "to behave as expected." In the above verse, the word, *observe* is used with different connotations in separate phrases of the verse.

1. In the phrase "whatsoever they bid you observe," the word *observe* implies "behave as expected."
2. In the phrase "that observe and do," the word *observe* implies "pay close attention."

In other words, Jesus cautions the people: "Because the doctrine of Scribes and Pharisees can cause delusion, beware of whatever it/they commands you to do." This caution is in line with the caution that Jesus gave to the disciples in Matthew 16:6.

Jesus explains the reason for saying so: "*. . . for they say, and do not. For they bind heavy burdens and grievous to be borne, and lay them on men's shoulders; but they themselves will not move them with one of their fingers.*" Here, the term "they" refers to the corrupting doctrines of the Scribes and Pharisees. The "heavy burden" is their back-breaking laws.

Laws, all laws, are creations of the Scribes who have their origin in Sumer (Babylon). The *Code of Ur-Nammu* is the oldest known law code surviving today. It was written on *tablets*, in the Sumerian language (2100-2095 B.C.). By the way, Moses also received The Law in two tablets.

Jesus accuses the Scribes and Pharisees of imposing burdensome laws on the people, while they themselves evade it through clever loopholes. In fact, the Talmud itself is nothing but a compilation of the loopholes in the Tanakh. The Scribes and Pharisees have created the Torah for general application, while the elites follow the Talmud, which gives them a wide leeway in action. Through this evil strategy they helped the elites gain unequalled *competitive advantage* over the general population. The Scribes and Pharisees only preach, but do not practice what they preach. Their doctrine may aptly be termed the "slave master's doctrine for the slaves."

MATTHEW 23:5-12

"But all their works they do for to be seen of men: they make broad their phylacteries, and enlarge the borders of their garments, And love the uppermost rooms at feast, and the chief seats in the synagogues, And greetings in the markets, and to be called of men, Rabbi, Rabbi. But be not ye called Rabbi: for one is your Master, even Christ; and all ye are brethren. And call no man your father upon the earth: for one is your Father, which is in heaven. Neither be ye called masters: for one is your Master, even Christ. But he that is greatest among you shall be your servant. And whosoever shall exalt himself shall be abased; and he that shall humble himself shall be exalted."

Here, the term "they" refers to the Scribes and Pharisees. They are Adamites whose bodies are taken over by the Serpent. Whereas true human beings are self-aware entities, these Adamites are only clan-aware. Whereas the God of the true human beings is the Self, the God of these people is the Establishment (the Serpent). Whereas true human beings worship their God inwardly and silently, these Adamites worship their God noisily and publicly. Their worship is ritualistic, and they are consummate actors.

The Adamites do everything for publicity and, therefore, they are very much concerned about their external appearances, such as the garments, the symbols and other insignia which they carry on their bodies that announce their social status. They like special places in public gatherings and they love to be called Sir or Master. In many ways, these Adamites resemble the elites of present time.

Jesus accuses these Adamites of "making broad their phylacteries." The *phylacteries* are four sections of the Law, wrote on parchments, folded up in the skin of a clean beast, and tied to the *forehead* and *hand*. The four sections are:

1. *"Sanctify unto me all the firstborn, whatsoever openeth the womb among the children of Israel, both of man and of beast: it is mine." (Exodus 13:2)*
2. *"And it shall be when the LORD shall bring thee into the land of the Canaanites, as he sware unto thee and to thy fathers, and shall give it thee." (Exodus 13:11)*
3. *"Hear, O Israel: The LORD our God is one LORD." (Deuteronomy 6:4)*
4. *"And it shall come to pass, if ye shall hearken diligently unto my commandments which I command you this day, to love the LORD your God, and to serve him with all your heart and with all your soul." (Deuteronomy 11:13)*

The term *phylactery* originates from the Greek word *phylākterion* (G5540), which means "a guard case." *Phylākterion* is derived from another Greek word *phylassō* (G5542), which means "to watch" or "to be on guard." *Phylassō* is derived from the root word *phyle* (G5443), which means "an offshoot," implying a race or clan.

Jesus accuses the Scribes and Pharisees also of enlarging the "borders of their garments." These are the *tallit* or fringes which the Jews put upon the borders of their garments, and on them a ribbon of blue, to put them in mind of the commandments, to obey them.

Both the phylactery and the tallit are external symbols that have no intrinsic spiritual value, per se.

The Scribes and Pharisees love to be called Rabbi. In Judaism, a rabbi is a teacher of Torah, and it means "my master." The Hebrew word *rav* means "great one." The basic form of the rabbi developed in the Pharisaic and Talmudic era, when learned teachers assembled to codify Judaism's written and oral laws.

Jesus commands, *"But be not ye called Rabbi: for one is your Master, even Christ; and all ye are brethren."* The term, *one* means "not two" or "non-duality," which is also called Christ. And it is man's Self. For a true human being, his Lord is Christ, and that same Christ exists in every true human being. In that sense, all true human beings are brethren in Christ.

Jesus again commands, *"And call no man your father upon the earth: for one is your Father, which is in heaven."* Spiritually, the term *heaven* refers to the inner body. The term *father* means "source," or "cause." Therefore, the expression, "Father, which is in heaven" means "the

Self," which is also called "the One" or Non-duality. For a true human being, his "Father in heaven" is the Self, and that same Self exists in every true human being. In that sense, all true human beings are brethren in the Self. When everyone is truly equal, the only way one can become the 'leader' is by becoming the 'servant.' It is the truth, but it is counter-intuitive.

MATTHEW 23:13

"But woe unto you, scribes and Pharisees, hypocrites! for ye shut up the kingdom of heaven against men: for ye neither go in yourselves, neither suffer ye them that are entering to go in."

A hypocrite is a person who professes beliefs and opinions that he does not hold in order to conceal his real motives. He is a pretender, or an imposter. The Greek word for *hypocrite* is *hypocritēs* (G5273), which means "an actor under an assumed character," or "a dissembler." The Hebrew word for *hypocrite* is *hānēp* (H2611), which means "with sin," or "blemished." The word *hānēp* originates from the primitive root word *hānēp* (H2610), which means to corrupt, defile, greatly pollute, or profane. Therefore, the word *hypocrite* seems to suggest a human-like entity, but possessing the alien Serpent virus DNA. He is a harmful and corrupting entity like the virus. Spiritually, the term *hypocrite* means "a humanoid."

The Hebrew word for *woe* is *hōy* (H1945), which means "alas." It is the cry of a person who has lost his most precious possession. But, the Greek word for *woe* is *hote* (G3753), which means "when, after that," or "when, as soon as." It is derived from the root words *ho* (G3739), which means "that," or "the other" and *te* (G5037), which means "then." Therefore, the word *woe* seems to suggest the meaning, "the other resulting from." In other words, the word *woe* refers to the 'other' entity arising from genetic corruption. Jesus' pronouncement, "Woe unto you, scribes and Pharisees, hypocrites" actually defines the serpent-children; it declares them as humanoids.

Jesus says to the Scribes and Pharisees, *"But woe unto you, scribes and Pharisees, hypocrites! for ye shut up the kingdom of heaven against men: for ye neither go in yourselves, neither suffer ye them that are entering to go in."* Spiritually, the expression "kingdom of heaven" refers to the body, or body-awareness. The expression, "them that are entering to go in" refers to the Mortals. Therefore the charge Jesus makes is this: "Neither are you humanoids body-aware yourselves, nor do you allow human beings to become body-aware."

MATTHEW 23:14

"Woe unto you, scribes and Pharisees, hypocrites! for ye devour widow's houses, and for a pretense make a long prayer: therefore ye shall receive the greater damnation."

Human awareness (mind) is the bride of Christ, which is self-awareness, or body-awareness. A devout believer, whose awareness is completely lost in religion, may be compared to a *widow*. He is only religion-aware, but not body-aware. With self-awareness gone, his body is like the "widow's house," which is vulnerable to plunder and spoliation by the enemy. And the enemy is the Serpent. He is able to attack the human body only if it is first made a 'widow.'

The human body becomes a widow when its self-awareness (husband) dies. The poison that kills body-awareness is the dualistic religious doctrine—the doctrine of the Scribes and Pharisees. It is in this sense Jesus accuses them of *devouring* the widow's houses. The word, *devour* literally means "to destroy completely," or "to consume avariciously." The Greek word for *devour* is *katesthiō* (G2719), which means "to eat down." It suggests slow but continual disintegration.

Jesus says to the Scribes and Pharisees, "*. . . and for a pretense make a long prayer: therefore ye shall receive the greater damnation.*" What is the mentality of one who makes a public prayer? First and foremost, he is a monotheist because he believes that God exists outside his body. His God is an 'alien' God. Secondly, the prayer-maker believes that he has some special 'relationship' with this alien god that enables him to intercede on behalf of others. In short, the public prayer-maker is under great delusion; he is a hypocrite.

Many well-intentioned Christians teach their children to pray mechanically, even at an early age, before the children are able to understand the concept of God, without realizing the danger involved. Unknowingly, they are creating "widows." Sunday Schools are the chief offenders in this respect. Jesus says to them, "*. . . therefore ye shall receive the greater damnation.*"

MATTHEW 23:15

"Woe unto you, scribes and Pharisees, hypocrites! for ye compass sea and land to make one proselyte, and when he is made, ye make him twofold more the child of hell than yourselves."

Purifying is a reducing, or distilling process. That which is good and pure is reduced in volume, externally. Corrupting, on the other hand, is a growing, or spreading process. Evil has the tendency to spread like an infectious disease. In a sense, evil is a great proselytizer. For example, the cancer virus is a great proselytizer in that it spreads its evil influence to every community of cells (organs) in the body, only to kill the host eventually.

The Greek word for *proselyte* is *prosēlytos* (G4339), which means "an arriver from a foreign land." Literally, the word *proselyte* refers to one who accedes (a convert) to Judaism. But, here, the proselytizer is the Serpent, and the "the foreign land" is hell. Therefore, the proselyte is actually converting himself from being a human into an alien.

Jesus accuses the Scribes and Pharisees of compassing sea and land to proselytize. The accusation comes to us as a surprise because we thought the Judaic religion does not proselytize. We thought no one can become a Jew except by birth. But, we are aware that some religions do actively proselytize. But, here, we see Jesus accusing the Scribes and Pharisees of going great lengths to proselytize people. Does that suggest that Judaism employs other monotheistic-dualistic religions as its proselytizing arms? If we examine history, we can see that sea and land were the two routes through which the dualistic-monotheistic ideology spread across the world.

When a human being gets infected with the monotheistic-dualistic religion (Serpent), he dies spiritually. In other words, the victim loses body-awareness and turns into a 'living dead', as it were. These converts turn out to be more evil and vicious than the original proselytizers themselves. There are many examples of this strange phenomenon in history. Metaphorically speaking, the convert's body becomes a vehicle for the enemy to further his proselytization campaign. That is why Jesus says, "*. . . and when he is made, ye make him twofold more the child of hell than yourselves.*" Spiritually, the term *twofold* suggests duality; the expression, "child of hell" means "religious fanatic."

MATTHEW 23:16-22

"Woe unto you, ye blind guides, which say, Whosoever shall swear by the temple, it is nothing; but whosoeve shall swear by the gold of the temple, he is a debtor! Ye fools and blind: for whether is greater, the gold, or the temple that sanctifieth the gold? And, whosoever shall swear by the altar, it is nothing; but whosoever sweareth by the gift that is upon it, he is guilty. Ye fools and blind: for weather is greater, the gift, or the altar that sanctifieth the gift? Whoso therefore shall swear by the altar, sweareth by it, and by all things thereon. And whoso shall swear by the temple, sweareth by it, and by him that dwelleth therein. And he that swear by heaven, sweareth by the throne of God, and by him that sitteth thereon."

In order to understand this saying of Jesus, we have to first understand the spiritual implication of the terms *temple* and *gold of the temple*. The word *temple* literally means "a place of worship." But, spiritually, it refers to the human body. The human body is the temple of God. The *gold of the temple* refers to the human mind. But, in this context, it refers to the scripture.

The Greek word for *swearing* is *omnuō* (G3660). To *swear* means to bind oneself by oath. The essential form of an oath is: "I will do," or "I will not do." An oath is a solemn promise made before an external power centre, such as the judge, the king, or the priest. Signing on a document is also a form of swearing. As a general rule, swearing involves "making a mark."

Spiritually, "swearing by the temple" involves making a mark on the body. The reference, here, is to circumcision. The Scribes and Pharisees consider circumcision is normal and a necessary religious ritual. In fact, it is the very essence of Judaism. "Swearing by the gold of the temple" means "swearing by the scripture." The Scribes and

Pharisees consider swearing by the scripture (criticizing scripture) heretical and strictly prohibit it, but they consider swearing by the body (circumcision) normal.

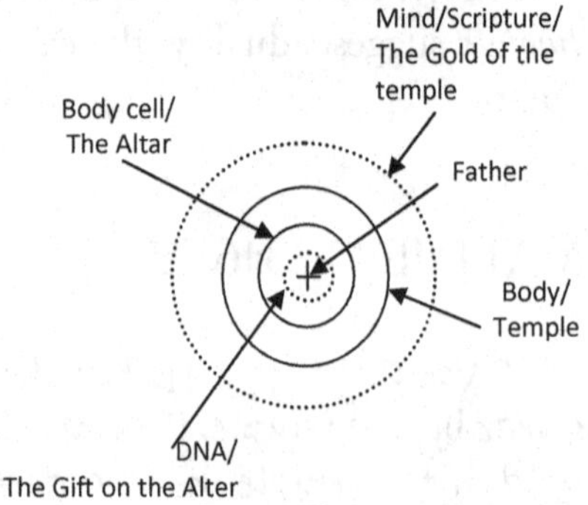

Temple, Gold, Altar, Gift

By contrasting the Pharisaic attitude towards "swearing by the temple" and "swearing by the gold of the temple" Jesus points out the apparent duplicity in their outlook. Jesus berates them, saying, *"Ye fools and blind: for whether is greater, the gold, or the temple that sanctifies the gold?"* The question Jesus poses to the Scribes and Pharisees is this: "Which is more important—the human being or the scripture?" According to the Scribes and Pharisees, the scripture is superior. To them, the body is evil; the human being is a sinner. Jesus calls them *fools* (Sanskrit: *mūdah*) and *blind* (Sanskrit: *andhā*) for thinking so. According to Jesus, the human being is the only reality.

Jesus brings into focus two more motifs—the *altar* and the *gift upon the altar*. If the term *temple* refers to the body, then the term *altar* refers to the body-cell. If the term *altar* refers to the body-cell, then the expression, "gift upon the altar" refers to the DNA. Having presented the motifs, Jesus asks, *"Ye fools and blind: for weather is greater, the gift, or the altar that sanctifieth the gift?"* The question Jesus poses to the Scribes and Pharisees is this: "Which is more important—the cell or the DNA?" Spiritually, the cell represents the Father (Self), and the DNA represents the God. The cell can work with many kinds of DNA, but the DNA is totally impotent without the cell.

For the Scribes and Pharisees, worldly things, such as wealth, power and fame are more important than the Self itself. They sacrifice the Self (soul) in return for wealth, power and fame. For them outer reality is everything; they are materialistic people. They disregard the Self and worship the God of the world—a God that is separate from them. Actually, their God is the Baal.

Therefore, Jesus says, *"Whoso therefore shall swear by the altar, sweareth by it, and by all things thereon. And whoso shall swear by the temple, sweareth by it, and by him that dwelleth therein. And he that swear by heaven, sweareth by the throne of God, and by him that sitteth thereon.*" Spiritually, "swearing by the altar" implies making a mark in body-cell, which could potentially lead to genetic corruption. Perhaps, the reference here is to modern medical practice of vaccination. (Remember: the Gospel is eternal, or timeless.)

Vaccines help a body's immune system prepare in advance to fight infectious illnesses and potentially deadly diseases caused by infectious agents. Fundamentally, vaccines give the body a preview of a bacterium, virus, or toxin allowing it to learn in advance how to defend itself against that potential invader. If the body is ever infected by that particular pathogen after the vaccine has done its work (marking?), the body's immune system is ready to protect the body because it has created "memory cells" when exposed to the vaccines. These cells can tell the body's immune system exactly what antibodies it needs to make for that particular pathogen and can get to work before the infection gets out of control. Perhaps, vaccination does involve "marking" of the body cells. Whatever be the case, the religious authorities have not raised any concerns about the practice of vaccination.

"Swearing by the temple" refers to circumcision, which leads to corruption of the body. "Swearing by heaven" implies corrupting the scripture (DNA), which leads to corruption of the mind (delusion), and eventually, the corruption of the very being.

MATTHEW 23:23-24

"Woe unto you, scribes and Pharisees, hypocrites! for ye pay tithe of mint and anise and cummin, and have omitted the weightier matters of the law, judgment, mercy, and faith: these ought ye to have done, and not to leave the other undone. Ye blind guides, which strain at a gnat, and swallow a camel."

According to Jesus, the crucial issues concerning existence are the law, judgment, mercy and faith. Man is law unto himself. The Self is the first and foremost law, every other law is subordinate to it. Man is born free, and his essence is freedom. The Law is represented by the centre of the Circle of Self.

The term *judgment* refers to the act of dividing the whole. It is also called *distinction*, or non-duality. For a human being, the distinction that separates the real from the imaginary is the *form* of his body. Spiritually, judgment is represented by the *circumference* of the Circle of Self. *Mercy* is the compassion one feels towards another. It is represented by the *radius* of the Circle of Self. *Faith* refers to body-awareness, and it is represented by the *area* of the Circle of Self. Law, judgment, mercy, and faith together constitute man's being. Jesus calls these four factors *weightier matters* because they constitute man's very being. They are the pillars of existence—the pillars of reality.

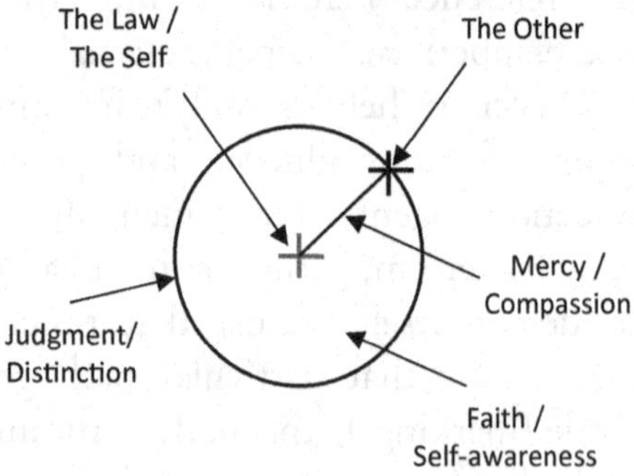

Law, Judgment, Mercy and Faith

The Scribes and Pharisees are not concerned about these *weightier matters* of existencte. They are more concerned with the payment of "tithe of mint and anise and cummin." The Greek term for *mint* is *hēdyosmon* (G2238), which literally means "a sweet scented plant." The word is derived from another Greek word *hēdonē* (H2237), which means "sensual delight." Spiritually, the term "mint" implies sensual pleasures or worldly pleasures; the term suggests *wealth*. *Anise* (Greek: *anēthon* G432), or *dill*, is a plant native to Egypt but cultivated widely for its aromatic seeds, and the oil from it is used medicinally and as a flavoring in cookery. Spiritually, anise represents *fame*. *Cummin* (Greek: *kyminon* G2951) or *cumin* is a strong spice used in cuisines. Cumin was used as a food ingredient in India for millennia. Cumin was also used heavily in ancient Roman cuisine. Rich Roman families used to keep a jar of cumin seed on their dining table as a symbol of power. Cumin represents *power*. The Hebrew word for cummin is *kammōn* (H3646), which means "to store up" or "to preserve." In other words, the Scribes and Pharisees are only interested in wealth, fame and power.

Jesus berates the Scribes and Pharisees for not focusing body-awareness on important issues such as the law, judgment, mercy and faith, instead spending it entirely in the pursuit of wealth, fame and power.

The Greek word for *tithe* is *apodekatoō* (G586), which means "to tithe" (as debtor or creditor). It means to give, pay, or take tithe. The

Hebrew word for tithe is *maasēr* (H4643), which means "a tenth." Spiritually, the word *tithe* suggests obligation. Jesus accuses the Scribes and Pharisees of totally ignoring truth and pursuing worldly things, and limiting spirituality to satisfying religious obligations.

Jesus rebukes the Scribes and Pharisees, *"Ye blind guides, which strain at a gnat, and swallow a camel."* Spiritually, the term "blind guides" means "deluded leaders." The term *gnat* refers to "weightless matters," and the term *camel* refers to "weightier matters."

Jesus calls the Scribes and Pharisees fools for ignoring important spiritual matters and focusing awareness only on trivial worldly matters.

MATTHEW 23:25-26

"Woe unto you, scribes and Pharisees, hypocrites! for ye make clean the outside of the cup and of the platter, but within they are full of extortion and excess. Thou blind Pharisee, cleanse first that which is within the cup and platter, that the outside of them may be clean also."

Cup and platter are vessels for carrying drink and food; they represent the body. The *inside* of the cup and platter contains the food (essence), whereas their *outside* contains nothing, except appearance. The *inside* of the cup and platter refers to the body-awareness, whereas it outside refers to delusion. The inside contains 'weightier' matter, whereas the outside contains only 'weightless' matter.

Jesus admonishes the Pharisees: *". . . for ye make clean the outside of the cup and of the platter, but within they are full of extortion and excess."* The cup and platter is made dirty by the blemish that clings to it. The blemish on the inside is genetic corruption. The blemish on the outside is moral depravity, but it is the result of the blemish in the inside.

The word *extortion* means "an exorbitant charge" or "unjust extraction" or "felonious act of extracting money." The Hebrew word for extortion is *ōseq* (H6233), which means "fraud," "injury," or "thing deceitfully gotten." The Greek equivalent *harpagē* (G724) means "ravening." In short, the word *extortion* suggests "business-mindedness." The word *excess* means "immoderation as a consequence of going beyond sufficient or permitted limits," or "excessive indulgence." It implies greed.

Jesus says to the Pharisees, *"Thou blind Pharisee, cleanse first that which is within the cup and platter, that the outside of them may be clean also."* What Jesus says to the Pharisees is this: "When the body becomes pure, the mind becomes pure too." But, how does one purify the body? It cannot be achieved through ritual washing or bathing; it is purified by only self-awareness. When the body becomes self-aware, the mind becomes pure, and the actions that emanate from it become righteous actions. This is the working principle in *Vipassana Meditation*.

Purifying the body entails rectifying genetic corruption. And the only agency that can achieve genetic healing is the Gospel. When the Gospel enters the body, it *reformats* the corrupted body cells to its pristine state. However, for the Gospel to enter the body, one has to 'grasp' its spiritual meaning. That is the only way.

It may be noted that teaching of the Christian Church runs counter to the teaching of the Gospel. The Church's focus is on the mind, whereas the Gospel's focus is on the body.

MATTHEW 23:27-28

"Woe unto you, scribes and Pharisees, hypocrites! for ye are like unto whited sepulchres, which indeed appear beautiful outward, but are within full of dead men's bones, and of all uncleanness. Even so ye also outwardly appear righteous unto men, but within ye are full of hypocrisy and iniquity."

Man's self-aware body is called the temple of God. But, if it is not self-aware, then it is soulless and therefore, may be compared to a sepulchre. *Sepulchre* is a chamber that is used as a grave. Here, Jesus compares the Scribes and Pharisees to sepulchres, saying, *". . . for ye are like unto whited sepulchres, which indeed appear beautiful outward, but are within full of dead men's bones, and of all uncleanness."* The term *white* suggests light and, therefore, suggests life. The term *sepulchre* means "grave" and, therefore, death. In other word, the expression "whited sepulchres" actually suggests "the living dead," or humanoids. Alternatively, it could even mean *zombie*.

According to the West African tenets of *Vodou*, a dead person can be revived by a *bokor*, or sorcerer. Zombies remain under the control of the *bokor* since they have no *will* of their own. *Zombi* is also another name of the Vodou serpent *lwa Damballah Wedo*, of Niger-Congo origin. It is similar to the *Kikongo* word *nzambi*, which means god. There also exists within the West African Vodun tradition the *zombi-astral*, which is a part of the human soul that is captured by a *bokor* and used to enhance the *bokor's* power. It is believed that after a time God will take the soul back and so the zombi is a temporary spiritual entity. The idea of zombies is present in some South African cultures. It is said that the *spell* can be broken by a powerful enough *sangoma*, who is a divine healer. Does this African myth sound familiar to you?

Now, let us come back to the Gospel interpretation. The fact that Jesus utters the words, *"Woe unto you, scribes and Pharisees, hypocrites!"* seven times in this chapter alone seems to underscore the importance of the underlying principle.

Jesus says to the Scribes and Pharisees, *"(ye) are within full of dead men's bones."* Spiritually, the term *bone* refers to the *gene*. Gene is the basic physical unit of heredity. It is a linear sequence of nucleotides along a segment of DNA that provides the coded instructions for synthesis of RNA, which, when translated into protein, leads to the expression of hereditary character. The expression, *"(ye) are within full of dead men's bones."* actually suggest that the Scribes and Pharisees are genetically engineered entities or humanoids!

There are two Greek words for *uncleanness*: one, *akatharsia* (G167), which means "bodily or moral impurity"; two, *miasmos* (G3394), which means "contamination." There are three Hebrew words for *uncleanness*: one, *tuma* (H2932), which means "polluted" (in the sense of being dead); two, *tāmā* (H2930), which means "contaminated"; three, *erwa* (H6172), which means "nakedness," or "shame." All these meanings suggest genetic corruption. Spiritually, the term *uncleanness* seems to suggest "unclean spirit." The Greek word for "unclean spirit" is *pneuma akatharton*. This term appears 21 times in the New Testament in the context of demonic possession. According to the Gospel, demons like to inhabit desolate places. Spiritually, the expression, "desolate place" means "a body made desolate," or "a body without self-awareness."

Jesus says, *"Even so ye also outwardly appear righteous unto men, but within ye are full of hypocrisy and iniquity."* The term *righteous* literally means "characterized by or proceeding from accepted standards of morality or justice." In the above verse, the spiritual connotations of the different terms are as given below:

Righteous = truly human
Men = the public
Hypocrisy = artificiality or deception
Iniquity = evil

What Jesus says to the Scribes and Pharisees is this: "You appear as humans to the public, but really you are evil alien humanoid entities."

MATTHEW 23:29-32

"Woe unto you, scribes and Pharisees, hypocrites! because ye build the tombs of the prophets, and garnish the sepulchres of the righteous, And say, If we had been in the days of our fathers, we would not have been partakers with them in the blood of the prophets. Wherefore ye be witnesses unto yourselves, that ye are the children of them which killed the prophets. Fill ye up then the measure of your fathers."

A *prophet* is someone who has the gift of prophesies (Holy Spirit). But, spiritually, the term *prophet* refers to a body-aware human being—an Evite. But, the Scribes and Pharisees, who are Adamites, hate the prophets because they are Evites. The Adamites and the Evites are antithetical to each other.

The Greek word for tomb is *mnēmeion* (G3419A), which means "remembrance." The Hebrew word for tomb is *gādis* (H1430), which means "a stack of sheaves." Spiritually, the term tomb *means* "history book." The Scribes and Pharisees are expert tomb builders in that they murder prophets and then write fictional histories about them, while furtively corrupting their messages. The word *garnish* means "something added to a dish for flavor or decoration," or "to embellish." The Scribes and Pharisees 'embellish' the messages of the dead prophets with half-truths and plain lies.

The Scribes and Pharisees represent religious authority. If we examine history, we can find that it is the very same people that murdered the prophets who later on established institutions in their names. The truth is that these entities are afraid of the living prophets, but they are comfortable with the dead ones. Jesus vividly captures the duplicitous attitude of these smug Adamites who say, *"If we had been in the days of our fathers, we would not have been partakers with them in the blood of the prophets."* They disown the responsibility for their forefathers' actions. What they are really saying is that the murders were random events and, therefore, nothing can be inferrred from it. Therefore Jesus says to them, *"Wherefore ye be witnesses unto yourselves, that ye are the children of them which killed the prophets."* The Scribes and Pharisees, by admitting that their ancestors did murder the prophets, implicitly admit that they too would behave in the same manner under similar circumstances, because they are of the same seed.

Jesus says to the Scribes and Pharisees, *"Fill ye up then the measure of your fathers."* The term "fathers," in this context, means ancestors; the term *measure* means "specifications," or "nature." In other words, Jesus is saying, "You will only behave according to your nature." A humanoid can only behave the way it is programmed to behave. It can neither repent nor change its nature because it has no conscience.

MATTHEW 23:33-36

"Ye serpents, ye generation of vipers, how can you escape the damnation of hell? Wherefore, behold, I send unto you prophets, and wise men, and scribes: and some of them ye shall kill and crucify; and some of them ye scourge in your synagogues, and persecute them from city to city: That upon you may come all the righteous blood shed upon the earth, from the blood of righteous Abel unto the blood of Zacharias son of Barachias, whom ye slew between the temple and the altar. Verily I say unto you, All these things shall come upon this generation."

Jesus comes down heavily on the Scribes and Pharisees, saying, *"Ye serpents, ye generation of vipers, how can ye escape the damnation of hell?"* It is an indictment on them. He exposes them as the Serpent seed by calling them *serpents* and *generation of vipers*. Spiritually, the term *serpent* means "virus," and alludes to the parasitic nature of these people. The *viper* belongs to the class *Reptilia* and belongs to the sub-order *Serpents.* Vipers are a family of venomous snakes found in almost all parts of the world. Vipers are slow to react, but are highly poisonous. Vipers hunt in darkness, and its venom affects the nervous system. In other words, Jesus identifies the Scribes and Pharisees as *reptilians.*

Jesus asks the Scribes and Pharisees, *"How can ye escape the damnation of hell?"* In other words, Jesus suggests that it is impossible for the Scribes and Pharisees to escape the damnation of hell. But, what is meant by "damnation of hell"? Spiritually, the word *heaven* means self-awareness; therefore, the word *hell* implies lack of self-awareness or delusion. In other words, "damnation of hell" suggests spiritual desolation. One who is condemned to "damnation of hell" has lost his Self (soul) for ever. He is now someone else. His body may appear as before, but another entity—a demon—lives in it. In fact, he is technically not a human being anymore. The word *demon* is derived from the Latin word *daemon* (Greek: *daimon*), which means "guiding spirit." In multitasking computer operating systems, *daemon* is a computer program that runs as a background process, rather than being under the direct control of an interactive user. By surrendering body-awareness to their dualistic religion, the Scribes and Pharisees have forfeited their Self (body-awareness/soul) once and for all. For all practical purpose, they have been *taken over* by the Serpent virus. They are now an abomination.

The Bhagavad Gīta vividly captures the dreadful state of these unfortunate people.

> *Swadharme nidhanam śrēya paradharmo bhayāvahah*
> B.G. 3:35
> ("It is better to die as oneself; to die as someone else is indeed frightening.")

Jesus says to them, *"Wherefore, behold, I send unto you prophets, and wise men, and scribes: and some of them ye shall kill and crucify; and some of them ye scourge in your synagogues, and persecute them from city to city: That upon you may come all the righteous blood shed upon the earth, from the blood of righteous Abel unto the blood of Zacharias son of Barachias, whom ye slew between the temple and the altar."* How can a daemon (software) 'kill' the body (hardware)? To understand it, one has to know the nature of the world. We live in two worlds simultaneously:

one of these worlds is real, or natural; the other, imaginary, or artificial. The real is the body, and the imaginary is the mind. While we *exist* in reality, we *live* in the mental world. Only a body-aware person can be truly considered as existing; therefore, to lose body-awareness tantamount to death. And that which takes away body-awareness (soul) is a murderer. Dualistic religious doctrines spiritually 'kill' human beings by ensnaring their body-awareness (soul). In this sense, dualistic religious doctrines can be considered as murderers.

Spiritually, the expression, "prophets, and wise men, and scribes" refers to wisdom teachings, such as the prophetic books of the Bible, mythologies, and poetry. Spiritually, the expression, "kill and crucify" suggests the misinterpretation and destruction of the true meaning of a book; the expression, "scourge in your synagogues" suggests the misrepresentation of the book's message trough sermons; the expression, "persecute from city to city" suggests the proscribing of the books. In other words, the Gospel accuses the religious Establishment of misinterpretation, misrepresentation, and banning of wisdom teachings.

"That upon you may come all the righteous blood shed upon the earth, from the blood of righteous Abel unto the blood of Zacharias son of Barachias, whom ye slew between the temple and the altar." The term "you" refers to the Adamite religious Establishment. The expression, "righteous blood" implies blood of true human beings (Evites). Spiritually, "righteous blood" means "body-awareness." According to the Bible, the very first instance of shedding of righteous blood was when Cain slew his brother Abel out of rage. Cain and Abel were the two sons of Adam and Eve. Cain, the first-born, carried "thy seed," or Adam's corrupt seed; Cain was an Adamite. Abel, the second-born, carried "her seed" or Eve's uncorrupted seed; Abel was an Evite. When Cain murdered Abel out of rage, it was the first shedding of the righteous (Evite) blood by an Adamite. By imputing the blame for the shedding of the righteous blood of Abel on the Scribes and Pharisees, Jesus brands them as Adamites or serpent-children.

Jesus presents another instance of shedding of righteous (Evite) blood by the Scribes and Pharisees (Adamites)—the murder of Zacharias, son of Barachias, who was murdered between the temple and the altar. But, there are two characters by the name Zacharias in the Bible, which creates confusion.

1. Zechariah, the son of Jehoiada, the temple priest, who was killed by the Establishment (2 Chronicles 24:20-21)
2. Zacharias, the son of Barachias, who was <u>not</u> killed by the Establishment (Zechariah 1:1)

Many Bible scholars think that the Gospel made an error in saying that Zacharias, the son of Barachias was killed. They think that the Gospel, instead, should have said that Zechariah, son of Jehoiada was killed. But, the argument is not tenable because it violates the "Jot and Tittle "principle, according to which everything written in the Gospel is beyond reproach. Therefore, we have to find an explanation that validates the Gospel words. It is possible only if we redefine the word *slew*, as applicable to this context. The word *slew*, in this context, means "to delude" or "to destroy body-awareness."

Zechariah, the son of Jehoiada, was a priest (Adamite) who was physically killed by the Establishment. But, he wast not spiritually killed because he was already dead spiritually. On the other hand, *Zacharias, son of Barachias*, was a Hebrew prophet and a priest, Perhaps, Zacharias was born an Evite, but got spiritually killed when he became a priest. Perhaps, it is his ordainment as priest that the Gospel metaphorically describes as "slaying between the temple and the alter."

Zechariah was a person in the Hebrew Bible and traditionally considered the author of the Book of Zechariah, the eleventh of the Twelve Minor Prophets. He was a prophet of the two-tribe kingdom of Judah, and like Ezekiel was of priestly extraction. He describes himself (Zechariah 1:1) as *"the son of Berechiah, the son of Iddo."* Not much is known about Zechariah's life. It has been speculated that his ancestor Iddo was the head of the priestly family who returned from Babylon with Zerubbābel, and that Zechariah may himself have been a priest as well as a prophet.

"Verily I say unto you, All these things shall come upon this generation." Here, the expression, "all these things" refers to the misinterpretation, misrepresentation, and proscribing of books containing truth. The expression, "this generation" refers to the Adamites.

MATTHEW 23:37-39

"O Jerusalem, Jerusalem, thou that killest the prophets, and stonest them which are sent unto thee, how often would I have gathered thy children together, even as a hen gathereth her chickens under her wings, and ye would not! Behold, your house is left unto you desolate. For I say unto you, Ye shall not see me hence forth, till ye shall say, Blessed is he that cometh in the name of the Lord."

Jesus utters the name *Jerusalem* two times, suggesting the dual nature of the city. The name *Jerusalem* (Hebrew: *yerušālaim* H3389) means "a dual" in allusion to its two main hills. Jerusalem implies duality, and therefore, the mind. The name Jerusalem refers to Judaism and its priestly class.

Jesus accuses Judaism of killing prophets and stoning those sent by God. The Hebrew word for *prophet* is *nābi* (H5030), which means "an inspired man." Spiritually, the term *prophet* refers to an inspired book; the word, *kill*, in this context, means "to falsify"; it implies misinterpretation. The expression, "them which are sent unto thee" refers to the Evites—those who speak the truth boldly. Alternatively, the expression, "them which are sent unto thee" refers to the new-born babies. (The expression, "them which are sent to thee" also suggests that these new *arrivals* are not Adamites, but Evites.) The term *stone* refers to religious dogma. Jesus makes three accusations on Judaism:

1. Corrupting inspired books through misinterpretation
2. Killing those who speak the truth
3. Destroying children's minds through religious conditioning and rituals

Jesus' (Gospel's) mission on earth is to clean Jerusalem (mind) of Judaism (religion). Alternatively, his mission is to exorcise demons from Mortals, or, in other words, to clean people's minds of false beliefs. But the 'stones' that make up Jerusalem are the Adamites—the priestly class—whose bodies have been taken over by the Serpent. Therefore, the only solution left to Father is to destroy Jerusalem completely and rebuild a new Jerusalem in its place. The agony of one who is forced to destroy his own creation is reflected in Jesus' words:

". . . how often would I have gathered thy children together, even as a hen gathereth her chickens under her wings, and ye would not!" Here, Jesus is speaking to the Adamites; therefore, the expression, "thy children" refers to the laity—the Mortals who are infected by the Serpent virus.

Jesus says to the Adamites, *"For I say unto you, Ye shall not see me hence forth, till ye say, Blessed is he that cometh in the name of the Lord."* Spiritually, the expression, "ye shall not see me" means "you will not be body-aware"; the expression, "he that cometh in the name of the Lord" refers to the new-born baby. An infant, until he is 'named' by man, bears the name of the Lord. He is a representative of God. He is a prophet (Evite). Thus, Jesus presents before the Adamites the one and only condition for redemption: say, *"Blessed is he that cometh in the name of the Lord."* In other words, stop circumcising infants.

CHAPTER 24

See Ye Not All These Things?

MATTHEW 24:1-2

"And Jesus went out, and departed from the temple: and his disciples came to him for to shew him the buildings of the temple. And Jesus said unto them, See ye not all these things? verily I say unto you, There shall not be left here one stone upon another, that shall not be thrown down."

While coming out of the Jerusalem temple, the disciples gather around Jesus to show him the buildings of the temple. Here, the expression, "buildings of the temple" literally means "the layout of the temple," but spiritually, it means "the structure of religion." As we have seen before, the term *temple* refers to the human body. Here, we see the disciples describing to Jesus the magnificence of the physical structure of the Jerusalem temple. But Jesus' reply relates not only to the physical structure of the temple of Jerusalem, but also the corrupt bodies of the Adamites and the corrupt structure of religion.

Jesus says, *"See ye not these things?"* The term "things" generally refers to lifeless objects. Here, the term "things" refers to religions without God, scriptures without truth, and bodies without souls; all of them. But, why did Jesus say, "See ye ***not*** all these things?" rather than "See ye all those things?" We say, "Don't you see these things?" only when we suspect the other of not seeing what we are seeing. Here, Jesus suspects that his disciples have not understood the true nature of Adamites or the true nature of their religion.

Jesus says, "*. . . verily I say unto you, There shall not be left here one stone upon another, that shall not be thrown down.*" If the Jerusalem temple represents Judaism, then the stones represent the scriptural words - the building blocks that constitute the literal scripture. Alternatively, if *temple* represents the Adamite body, then the *stones* represent the cells that constitute the Adamite body. The term "one stone" refers to either the individual body or the individual cell of the body. Therefore the expression, "there shall not be left here one stone upon another, that shall not be thrown down" suggests the physical disintegration of Adamites' corrupt bodies. It also refers to the disintegration of Adamite religious doctrines.

An object appears real or natural to us when our Self 'identifies' with that object. Similarly, a human body becomes a human being when the Self lives in that body. And when the Self is resident in a body, that body is said to have self-awareness or body-awareness (soul). Without self-awareness, man is merely a humanoid, or a zombie.

MATTHEW 24:3-13

"And as he sat upon the mount of Olives, the disciples came unto him privately, saying, Tell us, when shall these things be? and what shall be the sign of thy coming, and of the end of the world? And Jesus answered and said unto them, Take heed that no man deceive you. For many shall come in my name, saying, I am Christ; and shall deceive many. And ye shall hear of wars and rumours of wars: see that ye be not troubled: for all these things must come to pass, but the end is not yet. For nation shall rise against nation, and kingdom against kingdom: and there shall be famines, and pestilences, and earthquakes, in divers places. All these are the beginning of sorrows. Then they shall deliver you up to be afflicted, and shall kill you: and ye shall be hated of all nations for my name's sake. And then shall many be offended, and shall betray one another, and shall hate one another. And many false prophets shall rise, and shall deceive many. And because iniquity shall abound, the love of many shall wax cold. But he that shall endure to the end, the same shall be saved."

The disciples are awestruck by Jesus' prophesy about the Jerusalem temple, and they are eager to know the timing and the signs of that apocalyptic event, which they call "thy coming, and the end of the world." Literally, the expression "thy coming" refers to the Second Coming of Jesus Christ, and the expression, "end of the world," the end of the physical world. But spiritually, the above expressions suggest something else.

Spiritually, the term *Jesus* refers both to the true human body and the Gospel. The term *Christ* refers to pure awareness, or truth. Therefore, spiritually, the Second Coming of Jesus Christ refers to spiritual interpretation of the Gospel, which heralds enlightenment and the dawning of body-awareness in man. The first coming of Jesus Christ was the revelation of the literal Gospel. Alternatively, the first coming of Jesus Christ refers to your (man's) birth, and the second coming refers to your enlightenment. Spiritually, the phrase, "end of the world" refers to the end of ignorance and delusion.

> *And I saw a new heaven and a new earth: for the first heaven and the first earth were passed away; and there was no more sea.*
> Revelation 21:1

The "Second Coming" of Jesus Christ implies the following:

1. The revelation of the spiritual meaning of the Gospel
2. Re-establishment of the true DNA in human beings
3. Liberation of individual human beings from ignorance and delusion (religion)

The above three implications are interrelated. The spiritual meaning of the Gospel will liberate individual human beings from ignorance and delusion, which will lead to the re-establishment of the true human DNA in the liberated individual.

Jesus warns the disciples: *"Take heed that no man deceive you."* Spiritually, the term, "no man" means "not-man," or *anti-Christ*—the humanoid that pretends to be human. The phrase, "take heed" means "be vigilant," or "be aware." The Greek word for *deceive* is *planaō* (G4105), which means "to cause to wander away from safety." Spiritually, the word, *deceive* means "to mislead," or "to corrupt."

Therefore, the warning is this: "Be body-aware so that you are not corrupted by the humanoids."

Jesus says, *"For many shall come in my name, saying, I am Christ; and shall deceive many."* Literally, the expression, "my name" refers to Jesus; but spiritually, it means "human being." Those who come in "my name" are those who come pretending to be human. The term *Christ* means "the anointed one," or king. The term *Christ*, literally, means "messiah," or a charismatic world leader; but, spiritually, it refers to the human Self. Therefore, the implication of the verse is that during the Last Days humanoids will rule over humanity, pretending to be humans. Alternatively, the term "my name" refers to the Gospel. Therefore, it also suggests that during the Last Days many false Gospels will surface in order to mislead people.

"And ye shall hear of wars and rumours of wars: see that ye be not troubled: for all these things must come to pass, but the end is not yet." Wars cause death and destruction on a massive scale. And wars are characterized by extreme violence, social disruption, human suffering, and economic destruction. While human beings suffer from wars, it is harvest time for the psychic vampires that organize the wars. The chief products of wars are blood and misery. Wars are truly blood and misery harvests.

A *psychic vampire* is a person or entity that feeds off the "life force" of other living creatures. They are represented in the occult beliefs of various cultures and in fiction. But, medical science does not support the existence of psychic vampires, or even the existence of psychic energy that these entities allegedly drain. American author Albert Bernstein uses the expression *emotional vampire* to describe people with various personality disorders who are often considered to drain emotional energy from others. In Hinduism, the *asurās* are depicted as a group of power-seeking deities (demons) who are in constant war with the *dēvās* (gods). Probably, the *asurās* represent the Adamites and *dēvās* represent the Evites.

Human blood is spiritual energy (body-awareness) in physical form, and human misery is (negative) spiritual energy in etheric form. (*Ether* is a hypothetical substance that is supposed to occupy all space, postulated to account for the propagation of electromagnetic radiation through space.) The expression, "rumours of wars" refers to the state of cold war, which is a continued state of fear and anxiety. Under conditions of fear and anxiety, human beings discharge large amounts of negative spiritual energy (misery), which is a valuable resource for these so-called psychic vampires. Wars and rumours of wars are the chief source of sustenance for the alien masters that rule over humanity. And these entities have been ruling humanity for eons, and they have always resorted to wars and rumours of wars as their chief source of sustenance. Perhaps, it is the 'air' that these evil entities breathe. If you examine history, you will see that wars are organized on a periodic basis on some flimsy reason or the other. Of late, the magnitude and the blood-shed of wars have increased many-fold thanks to the new technologies. But, even today, the reason for waging war is the same: harvest blood and misery. Now we wage wars for peace!

Jesus cautions: *". . . see that ye be not troubled: for all these things must come to pass, but the end is not yet."* The implication is that man has to undergo these tribulations before he is enlightened.

"For nation shall rise against nation, and kingdom against kingdom: and there shall be famines, and pestilences, and earthquakes, in divers places. All these are the beginning of sorrows." The term *nation* refers to a people grouped together on the basis of religion or race. The term *kingdom*, on the other hand, refers to a people grouped together on the basis of ruler or government. Therefore, the expression, "nation shall rise against nation and kingdom against kingdom" refers to civil wars and wars between countries. They create conditions of extreme violence, social disruption, human suffering, and economic destruction. The Hebrew word for *divers* is *kilayim* (H3610), which means "two seeds," or "mingled seed." Literally, the phrase, "divers places" means "many and different places," but spiritually, it refers to places where humans have mingled with the humanoids. Therefore the implication is that, during Last Days, famines, pestilences and earthquakes will hit countries where genetic corruption has taken place on a large scale.

"Then they shall deliver you up to be afflicted, and shall kill you: and ye shall be hated of all nations for my name's sake." The term "they" refers to the Adamites, and the term "you" refers to the Evites, or true human beings. The Greek word for *afflict* is *thilipsis* (G2347), which means "to pressure," or "to burden." Spiritually, it refers to the imposition of highly restrictive regulations, or laws. The expression, "my name's sake" means "for being a human being." Therefore, the spiritual implication of the verse is this: During Last Days, the rulers will enforce draconian

laws over the population, and may even kill those who rebel against them.

"And then shall many be offended, and shall betray one another, and shall hate one another." Spiritually, the term, "many" refers to the deluded (religious) public. During the Last Days, the so-called 'believers' will realise that they are damned and that only a small minority will be saved. This knowledge will anger them, and they will turn hostile against the small minority of 'saved' and betray them to the authorities. During Last Days, humanity will be divided into two group factions: "the damned" and "the saved." And there will be strife between the two groups.

"And many false prophets shall rise, and shall deceive many. And because iniquity shall abound, the love of many shall wax cold." As we have seen before, the term "false prophets" refers to the humanoids. The Greek word for *arise* is *egeirō* (H1453), which means "to rouse from sleep," or "rise from death." (Is the Gospel referring to *cloning* of dead people?) The Greek word for *iniquity* is *anomia* (G458), which means "wickedness." The Hebrew word for *iniquity* is *āwōn* (H5771), which means "mischief." The word is derived from the root word *āwa* (H5753), which means "to crook," or "to pervert." Spiritually, the word *iniquity* suggests corruption, especially genetic corruption. The term *love* refers to body-awareness. The expression "wax cold" means "extinguished" or "snuffed out." Therefore, the spiritual implication of the verse is this: "*During the Last Days, the humanoids will come to power and they will genetically corrupt human beings on such a massive scale that many human beings will lose their body-awareness (soul).*"

"But he that shall endure to the end, the same shall be saved." The word, *endure* means "to hold out against" or "to sustain without impairment or yielding." Here, the word is used in both senses. Literally, the verse implies, "He who hold out against the tribulations till the end will be saved." But, spiritually, it suggests, "*He who remains human (genetically pure) till the end will be saved.*"

MATTHEW 24:14-22

"And this gospel of the kingdom shall be preached in all the world for a witness unto all nations; and then shall the end come. When ye therefore shall see the abomination of desolation, spoken of by Daniel the prophet, stand in the holy place, (whoso readeth, let him understand:) Then let them which be in Judea flee into the mountains: Let him which is on the housetop not come down to take any thing out of his house: Neither let him which is in the field return back to take his clothes. And woe unto them that are with child, and to them that give suck in those days! But pray ye that your flight be not in the winter, neither on the sabbath day: For then shall be great tribulation, such as was not since the beginning of the world to this time, no, nor ever shall be. And except those days should be shortened, there should no flesh be saved: but for the elect's sake those days shall be shortened."

The Gospel states the essential condition for the beginning of the end: *"And this gospel of the kingdom shall be preached in all the world for a witness unto all nations; and then shall the end come."* The expression, "this gospel of the kingdom" means "the gospel of human body," which says, "*He who remains human till the end will be saved.*" Alternatively, the preaching of the gospel of the kingdom refers to the spiritual interpretation of the Gospel. Literally, the word *end* refers to the end of the world, but, spiritually, it refers to the end of ignorance and delusion - the end of dream.

The Hebrew word for *preach* is *qārā* (H7121), which means "to publish"; but, it can also be used in the sense "to make available." In other words, the Gospel foresees its truths reaching every human being on the planet. The method of delivery may vary. Perhaps, the truth vibrations generated by the spiritual revelation will travel through the 'ether' and reach every human being across the globe. After that, no one can say that the Gospel was not preached to him. Perhaps, that is what the Gospel implies by the statement, "*And this gospel of the kingdom shall be preached in all the world for a witness unto all nations.*"

> *Behold, I stand at the door, and knock; if any man hear my voice, and open the door, I will come in to him, and will sup with him, and he with me.*
> Revelation 3:20

"When ye therefore shall see the abomination of desolation, spoken of by Daniel the prophet, stand in the holy place, (whoso readeth, let him understand:) Earlier, we saw the disciples asking Jesus about the signs

of "thy coming," and "the end of the world." Here, he reveals the signs in an enigmatic way. Let us analyze the words very carefully. The word "ye" refers not just to the disciples, but every human being. In this context, the word, "therefore" suggests "having received the Gospel truth." In fact, the revelation of the spiritual Gospel itself is the Judgment! Those are able to 'hear' it have the true human DNA (the *sheep*); those who are unable to 'hear' it have the corrupt DNA (the *goats*).

The Greek word for *abomination* is *bdelygma* (G946), which means "detestation." The word is derived from the root word *bdeo*, which means "to stink." The Greek word for *desolation* is *erēmoō* (G2049), which means "to lay waste." There are a number of Hebrew words that imply *desolation*: *sāmēm* (H8074), which means "to grow numb"; *horba* (H2723), which means "decayed place"; *mesoa* (H4875) means "ruin." The term *desolation* suggests "soul-less." Spiritually, the expression, "holy place" refers to the human body. Therefore, the expression, "abomination of desolation standing in the holy place" refers to alien entities possessing human bodies. They are collectively known as "Antichrist."

What is the "abomination of desolation" spoken by the prophet Daniel? We read in the Book of Daniel:

> *And he shall confirm the covenant with many for one week: and in the midst of the week he shall cause the sacrifice and the oblation to cease, and for the overspreading of abominations he shall make it desolate, even until the consummation, and that determined shall be poured upon the desolate.*
> Daniel 9:27

Here, the term "he" refers to the Antichrist, and the term, "many" refers to the Adamites. The Greek word for *covenant* is *diathēkē* (G1242), which means "a contract," or "treaty." Spiritually, the expression, "one week" implies seven years. According to Prophet Daniel, a seven-year agreement will be signed between the Adamites and the Antichrist. But, half-way into its tenure, the Antichrist will "cause the sacrifice and oblations to cease." Spiritually, the word, *sacrifice* refers to human cognition, and the word, *oblation* refers to body-awareness. In other words, the Antichrist will transform the

Adamites into zombies. And they will remain so until they are totally destroyecd.

Therefore Jesus warns: *"When ye therefore shall see the abomination of desolation, spoken of by Daniel the prophet, stand in the holy place . . . Then let them which be in Judea flee to the mountains."* The Gospel foresees a zombie apocalypse kind of situation arising in future. The Greek word the Gospel uses here for *mountains* is *oros* (G3735). It is derived from an obsolete word *oro*, which means "lifting itself above the plain." Spiritually, the word "mountains" refers to the Gospel truths. Therefore, the spiritual implication of the Gospel warning is this: "When you see the rise of the zombies, remain vigilant and hold on to the Gospel truths." The Gospel ends the verse with a mysterious cue: *"whoso readeth, let him understand:)"* It is a sign that a great secret is hidden in the verse. (Notice the *smiley* at the end of the verse.)

Jesus instructs the disciples what to do when the psychotic humanoids rule the world: *"Then let them which be in Judea flee to the mountains: Let him which is on the housetop not come down to take any thing out of his house: Neither let him which is in the field return back to take his clothes."* Who are these people that the Gospel is telling to flee? Judaea is the southern part of ancient Palestine, presently called the West Bank. Probably, the expression "them which is in Judaea," refers to the Palestinian Christians in West Bank. But, spiritually, it refers to the Evites, the true Christians. The word *then* implies "when the zombie apocalypse begins." The Greek word for housetop is *dōma* (G1430), which means "an edifice." But, spiritually, the term *housetop* refers to the Christian church. The term *field* refers to the literal scripture, and the term *cloth* refers to body-awareness. Here, the Gospel warns the true Christians to remain body-aware and hold on to the Gospel truths. But, as to the others it foresees very little chances of their surviving the zombie apocalypse.

"And woe unto them that are with child, and to them that give suck in those days! But pray ye that your flight be not in the winter, neither on the sabbath day: For then shall be great tribulation, such as was not since the beginning of the world to this time, no, nor ever shall be. And except those days should be shortened, there should no flesh be saved: but for the elect's sake those days shall be shortened." The Greek word for *winter* is *cheimōn* (G5494), which means "foul weather." The Hebrew word for *winter* is *hōrep* (H2779) means "crop gathered" or "ripeness of age. Spiritually, the term *winter* refers to the Last Days. *Sabbath* is the last

day of the week. In this context, it refers to the end of the *seven-week covenant* spoken of by the Prophet Daniel, or the Last Days. Spiritually, the term *child* refers to the Gospel. The expression, "them that are with child and them that give suck" refers to the pious Christians who 'nurse' the literal Gospel. The Gospel pities these pious Christians who are still holding on to the literal Gospel even in the Last days.

Therefore Jesus says, *"For then shall be great tribulation, such as was not since the beginning of the world to this time, no, nor ever shall be. And except those days should be shortened, there should no flesh be saved: but for the elect's sake those days shall be shortened."* The term elect refers to the true Christians, or the Evites. According to the Gospel, the rule of the alien psychotic humanoids will last only for a short duration, because it will be curtailed taking into consideration the welfare of the true Christians. The angels of God (Gospel truths) will destroy them completely. The "Second Coming of Jesus Christ" or the "enlightenment of mankind" will take place when the alien psychotic humanoids are expelled from earth completely.

PALESTINIAN CHRISTIANS

Palestinian Christians are Christians who have descended from the original converts to Christianity, and now living in Judea. In this region, there are also churches and believers from many Christian denominations, including Oriental Orthodoxy, Anglican, Eastern Orthodoxy, Catholic, Protestant and others. In both the local dialect of Palestinian Arabic and in classical or modern standard Arabic, Palestinian Christians are called *Nasrani* or *Masihi*. In Hebrew, they are called *Notzri*, which means *Nazarene*.

Today, Christians comprise less than 4% of Palestinians living within the borders of former Mandate Palestine. They comprise approximately 4% of the West Bank population, less than 1% in Gaza, and nearly 10% of Israel's Palestine population. Palestinian Christians in Israel number between 144,000 and 196,000 or 2.1% to 2.8% of the total population. The 144,000 *saved* at the second coming of Jesus Christ, perhaps, refers to the Palestinian Christians in Israel. Perhaps, they are *The Elect.*

> *And I looked, and lo, a Lamb stood on the mount Sion, and with him an hundred forty and four thousand, having his Father's name written in their foreheads.*
> Revelation 14:1

The expression, *Father's name* means "true human being." The Second Coming of Jesus Christ will herald the liberation of oppressed humanity from the clutches of Satan.

MATTHEW 24:23-28

"Then if any man shall say unto you, Lo, here is Christ, or there; believe it not. For there shall arise false Christs, and false prophets, and shall shew great signs and wonders; insomuch that, if it were possible, they shall deceive the very elect. Behold, I have told you before. Wherefore if they shall say unto you, Behold, he is in the desert; go not forth: behold, he is in the secret chambers; believe it not. For as lightning cometh out of the east, and shineth even unto the west; so shall also the coming of the Son of man be. For wheresoever the carcase is, there will the eagles be gathered together."

"Then if any man shall say unto you, Lo, here is Christ, or there; believe it not. For there shall arise false Christs, and false prophets, and shall shew great signs and wonders; insomuch that, if it were possible, they shall deceive the very elect. Behold, I have told you before." The spiritual implication of the different terms used in the verse is shown in the table.

Term	Spiritual Meaning
Then	During the last days
Any man	The common man
You	True human being
Christ	Tue human being
False Christ	Humanoids
False Prophets	Scientists
Great sign and wonders	Technological wonders
The very elect	Enlightened humans

According to the Gospel, during the Last Days, the alien humanoids will intermingle with humanity and will display their great technological powers, which will entice even enlightened human beings. The Gospel says, *"if it were possible,"* which suggests that the technology will *almost* deceive, but will not succeed. What is this alien technology that the Gospel is referring to? Computers, Internet, and things like that? Anyway, the Gospel forewarns: *"Behold, I have told you before."* It means: "You have been forewarned!"

"Wherefore if they shall say unto you, Behold, he is in the desert; go not forth: behold, he is in the secret chambers; believe it not." The spiritual implication of the different terms used in the verse is shown in the table. Is the Gospel warning us to be wary of media reports that flaunt these technological miracles? Is the Gospel specifically alluding to technological miracles such as the computers and the World Wide Web?

Term	**Spiritual Meaning**
Wherefore	Because anyone could be an alien
They	The public / The media
He	The truth
Desert	The World Wide Web
Secret chamber	The computer

The Gospel gives us a vivid description of the coming of the "Son of man": *"For as lightning cometh out of the east, and shineth even unto the west, so shall also the coming of the Son of man be."* Here, the term "Son of man" refers to the humansoul. The term *lightning* refers to the sun, which represents the human soul. Therefore, the implication of the verse is this: "The human soul is like the sun that, forever, rises in the East and sets in the West. The cycle goes on forever."

The Gospel, then, gives us a chilling warning to the Mortals: *"For wheresoever the carcase is, there will the eagles be gathered together."* The term *carcase* refers to the dead body of an animal, especially one slaughtered and dressed for food. The term refers to the deluded human beings (Mortals); the term, *eagle* refers to the alien entities. The Gospel warns: *Mortals are food for the alien entities.*

NAZI EMBLEM

Incidentally, the flags of many nations carry the eagle symbol. In fact, the emblem of the Nazi Party carried the eagle symbol prominently. Perhaps the Nazi Party did associate with the alien entities. German UFO theories talk about the supposedly successful attempts by the Nazis to develop advanced aircraft or spacecraft prior to and during World War II, and further assert the post-war survival of these crafts in secret underground bases in Antarctica, South America or the United States, along with their creators.

There is an alternate interpretation. The term *carcase* refers to a consumer—the consumer of goods and services. He is like an animal slaughtered and dressed for food. The desire for worldly things makes the 'consumer' spiritually dead—a carcase. The *eagle* is a large, keen-sighted diurnal bird-of-prey noted for its broad wings and strong soaring flight. The eagle represents business corporations. A business corporation is an entity that is large (multi-national), keen sighted (strategically-oriented), diurnal (working round the clock), which has broad wings (multi-divisional), and has soaring flight (expansion plans). According to the Gospel, when man becomes spiritually dead, he becomes food for the rapacious business corporations.

MATTHEW 24:29-31

"Immediately after the tribulation of those days shall the sun be darkened, and the moon shall not give her light, and the stars shall fall from the heaven, and the powers of the heavens shall be shaken: And then shall appear the sign of the Son of man in heaven: and then shall all the tribes of the earth mourn, and they shall see the Son of man coming in the clouds of heaven with power and great glory. And he shall send his angels with a great sound of a trumpet, and they shall gather together his elect from the four winds, from one end of heaven to the other."

"Immediately after the tribulation of those days shall the sun be darkened, and the moon shall not give her light, and the stars shall fall from the heaven, and the powers of the heavens shall be shaken." Spiritually, the expression, "tribulation of those days" refers to man's life in this virtual-reality world, which is afflicted by wars and misery. That which comes immediately after the "tribulation of those days" is death.

In these verses, the Gospel gives us a vivid description of the events that precede death:

1. The sun will be darkened
2. The moon shall not give her light
3. The stars shall fall from heaven
4. The powers of the heaven shall be shaken

Here, the term sun refers to human consciousness. Therefore, the darkening of the sun suggests the loss of consciousness.

Spiritually, the term *moon* refers to the brain. Moonlight represents the thoughts, or the mind. Brain is like a generator of magnetism and thoughts are like the magnetic flux lines. Therefore, the moon failing to give light refers to the shutting down of mind. The dying man will experience this as the apocalypse, causing great panic.

Spiritually, stars represent human beings. The falling of stars from the heaven signifies the severing of social relationships, which may appear to the dying man as stars falling from heaven. Alternatively, stars signify man's closely-held beliefs. Therefore, the falling of the stars from heaven denotes the crumbling of belief systems.

Thus the dying man is stripped off all his ignorance and delusion. Spiritually he is totally naked now, without even a "fig leaf" to cover his bare essence. *"And then shall appear the sign of the Son of man in heaven: and then shall all the tribes of the earth mourn, and they shall see the Son of man coming in the clouds of heaven with power and great glory."* The expression, "and then" suggests "when the man is stripped off all delusion." Spiritually, "the sign of the Son of man in heaven" refers to the Self (the Quantum Self). The term *heaven* refers to Quantum Field—the ground of being. The expression, "clouds of the heaven" refers to Quantum possibilities. Therefore, the implication of the verse is this: At death, man is stripped off all ignorance and delusion and confronts the Self—his own Quantum Self.

"And he shall send his angels with a great sound of a trumpet, and they shall gather together his elect from the four winds, from one end of heaven to the other." Here, the term "he" refers to the Quantum Self. The "great sound of a trumpet" refers the *Praṇava mantra*—the sound of *Om*. It is not an audible sound. It is the sound of silence. *Om* enfolds in itself *all* possible frequencies. The *Elect* are the true human beings who bear the *sign of the Son of man* (the true human DNA). When the *Praṇava mantra* is sounded, the Elect will 'hear' it and respond to the call by merging with that frequency. Mathematically, it called the *Fourier Transformation* of frequencies.

The *Fourier Transform*, named after Joseph Fourier, is a mathematical transform that has many applications in physics and engineering. The Fourier Transform transforms a mathematical function of time, f(t), into a new function, sometimes denoted by "j" or "F," whose argument is frequency. The new function is then known as the

Fourier Transform and/or the *frequency spectrum* of the function "f". Fourier Transform operate both ways—one frequency exploding into many frequencies or many frequencies coming together as one frequency.

At birth, or in the beginning (Sanskrit: *prabhava*), the *Praṇava* (Singularity) exploded (Fourier-transformed) into many frequencies creating the world. At death, or at the end (Sanskrit: *pralaya*), the many frequencies will merge (Fourier-transform) back together as the Praṇava (singularity), ending the *māya* world.

But, those who do not carry "the sign of the Son of man" will not merge with the *Praṇava* (the trumpet) sound, but dissipate into nothingness. In other words, the soul-less Adamites will perish utterly.

MATTHEW 24:32-35

"Now learn a parable of the fig tree; When his branch is yet tender, and putteth forth leaves, ye know that summer is nigh: So likewise ye, when ye shall see all these things, know that it is near, even at the doors. Verily I say unto you, This generation shall not pass, till all these things be fulfilled. Heaven and earth shall pass away, but my words shall not pass away."

The fig tree is commonly known as the ficus tree (*Ficus Benjamina*). Figs are *keystone species* in many rainforest ecosystems. A keystone species is a species that has a disproportionately large effect on its environment relative to its abundance. Such species play a critical role in maintaining the structure of an ecological community, affecting many other organisms in an ecosystem and helping to determine the types and numbers of various other species in the community.

The figs figure prominently in human culture. There is evidence that figs, specifically the common fig, were among the first—if not the very first—plant species that were *deliberately bred* for agriculture in the Middle East, starting more than 11,000 years ago (fossil found in Gilgal in Jordan Valley, near to Jericho).

The common fig tree is an *epiphyte*. An epiphyte is a plant that grows upon another plant (such as a tree) non-parasitically or sometimes upon on some other objects (such as buildings etc.), and derives its moisture and nutrients from the air and rain and sometimes from debris accumulating around it. The fruit of the epiphytic fig trees is good, tasty and nutritious. But, some species of the fig trees are *hemiepiphytes*. A hemiepiphyte is a plant that spends part of its life cycles as an epiphyte; these include the *strangler figs*. They begin life as epiphytes, but after making contact with the ground, they encircle their host tree and strangle it. This usually results in the death of the host tree, either through girdling or through competition for light. The fruit of the hemiepiphytic fig trees is bad, bitter and poisonous.

The fig tree represents DNA, and the fruit of the fig tree represents scripture. Just as the fig tree, there are two kinds of DNA: one, the epiphytic DNA (the human DNA); two, the hemiepiphytic DNA (the virus DNA). The 'fruit' of the epiphytic DNA is the Gospel, which is good for the body, tasty for the mind and nutritious for the soul. The 'fruit' of the hemiepiphytic DNA is the literal scripture, which is bad for the body, bitter for the mind, and poisonous for the soul. The epiphytic DNA manifests as Evites. The hemiepiphytic DNA manifests as Adamites. The epiphytic humans are generally harmless and are non-parasitic; they depend on nature for support, but do not cause harm to it. The hemiepiphytic humans (the *tares*), on the other hand, are dangerous and parasitic. They spend part of their lives pretending to be epiphytes, but once they gain foothold in a land, they expose their hemiepiphytic nature and encircle the host society that gave them shelter and livelihood and strangle it, causing it to wither away. They kill their hosts through usury (girdling) and by monopolizing resources and power (competition for light). The hemiepiphytic humans prevent truth (light) from reaching humanity (the host tree). These hemiepiphytic humans are known as serpent-children. The Scribes, Pharisees and Sadducees belong to the hemiepiphytic species.

"When his branch is yet tender, and putteth forth leaves, ye know that summer is nigh: So likewise ye, when ye shall see all these things, know that it is near, even at the doors." Here, the Gospel is talking about the hemiepiphytic fig trees—the Adamites—and links the sprouting of buds on it to the arrival of summer. Spiritually, sprouting of the fig tree suggests the sprouting of body-awareness in Adamites. It marks the culmination of the efforts of these *fallen angels* to "become like the gods." *Summer* is harvest time and, therefore, denotes the end of the world.

The discovery of the H-Boson (*God Particle*) at the Large Haldron Collider (LHC) in Switzerland, perhaps, signals the sprouting of the withered fig tree. Perhaps, the discovery of the "God Particle" is the sign that the end is imminent. The discovery of Higgs boson or "God Particle" was tentatively announced on 14 March 2013. The discovery has been touted as monumental because it appears to confirm the existence of the Higgs field (body-awareness?), which is pivotal to the Standard Model and other theories within particle physics. Francois Englert of Belgium and Peter Higgs of Britain shared the 2013 Nobel Prize in Physics on October 8, 2013 for their theory on how the most basic building blocks of the universe acquire mass, eventually forming the world we know today.

"Verily I say unto you, This generation shall not pass, till all these things be fulfilled." The expression, "this generation" is usually interpreted by most Bible interpreters as the generation living when "these things" (the four signs mentioned in Matthew chapter 24:29) happen. But, spiritually, the expression, "this generation" means "this species," and refers to the Adamites. In other words, the Gospel says that this parasitic species (Serpent children) will not leave man until death.

Finally, the Gospel makes a solemn pronouncement: *"Heaven and earth shall pass away, but my words shall not pass away."* Spiritually, the word *heaven* refers to the mind, and *earth*, the body. The expression, "heaven and earth" refers to the world; the expression, "my words" refers to the human DNA as well as to the Gospel, which is the verbal expression of the true human DNA. In other words, the Gospel declares that the human DNA or the human soul is eternal, or immortal. As the corollary, it also implies that the Gospel is eternal.

MATTHEW 24:36-42

"But of that day and hour knoweth no man, no, not the angels of heaven, but my Father only. But as the days of Noe were, so shall also the coming of the Son of man be. For as in the days that were before the flood they were eating and drinking, marrying and giving in marriage, until the day that Noe entered into the ark, And knew not until the flood came, and took them all away; so shall also the coming of the Son of man be. Then shall two be in the field; the one shall be taken, and the other left. Two women shall be grinding at the mill; the one shall be taken, and the other left. Watch therefore: for ye know not what hour your Lord doth come."

"But of that day and hour knoweth no man, no, not the angels of heaven, but my Father only." Spiritually, the expression, "that day and hour" refers to the exact moment of death. The expression, "angels of heaven" refers to the words of the scripture. Therefore, the implication of the verse is that neither a man's intelligence nor his scripture can correctly predict the time of his death; only the *Father* (the Self) knows it. For a true human being, *death* and the *Father* are related just as the circumference and center of a circle are related. It is a father-son relationship. So, this is the truth: Death is the "Son of man." But, the Gospel is also called the "Son of man." In other words, the "coming of the Son of man" refers both to death and the spiritual revelation of the Gospel; both will cause the 'world' (delusion) to end. In that sense, it is the wake-up call that will awaken man from his deep slumber. It is also called the "Second Coming," or "End of the World." And at death, man will meet with his Self. At death, he will transcend from being a mere character in the story to the author-reader of the story itself.

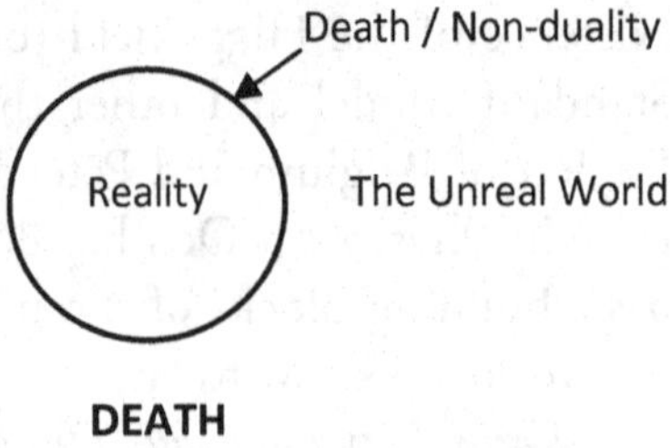

Perhaps, not just the timing of death is an uncertainty, but death itself may be Uncertainty. According to Werner Karl Heisenberg, the renowned German theoretical physicist and one of the key creators of Quantum Mechanics, *uncertainty* is the very stuff of reality rather than a limitation in the measurement process or of the measuring instruments. In 1927, Heisenberg propounded his *Uncertainty Principle.* In Quantum Mechanics, the Uncertainty Principle is any of a variety of mathematical inequalities asserting a fundamental limit to the precision with which certain pairs of physical properties of a particle (*Son of man*?) known as complementary variables, such as position x (*man*?) and momentum p (*angels of heaven*?), can be known simultaneously. For instance, the more precisely the position of some particle is determined, the less precisely its momentum can be known, and vice versa. By the way, the *cross* symbolically represents a pair of complementary variables.

"But as the days of Noe were, so shall also the coming of the Son of man be." Here, the expression, "the coming of the Son of man" refers both to death and the spiritual revelation of the Gospel, which the the Gospel metaphorically calls *flood*. Now, let us see how the world was during the days of Noah. We read in the *Book of Genesis*:

> *The earth also was corrupt before God, and the earth was filled with violence. So God looked upon the earth, and indeed it was corrupt; for all flesh had corrupted their way on the earth.*
> Genesis 6:11-12

The expression, "for all flesh had corrupted" refers to the pervasive genetic corruption during Noah's time. The society of Noah's time was totally corrupt, genetically. The Bible says, "The earth was filled with violence." It seems, there is a close connection between genetic corruption and violence. According to the Bible, only Noah had bothered to build an ark, foreseeing the coming flood. Spiritually, the term *ark* refers to body-awareness (soul). In other words, Noah was the only body-aware man in his time. The others were totally deluded. In other words, the others did not build arks to survive the *Great Flood*.

"For as in the days that were before the flood they were eating and drinking, marrying and giving in marriage, until the day that Noe entered into the ark, And knew not until the flood came, and took them all away; so shall also the coming of the Son of man be." Spiritually, the expression, "eating and drinking, marrying and giving in marriage" suggest the smug attitude of the people; it also suggests delusion. In other words, the people of Noah's time were totally unprepared for the flood. A deluded man is only concerned with the 'outside'; he does not think about inside, or the Self. In short, the deluded man simply does not have an 'ark' to survive the 'flood'.

Literally, the *Great Flood* refers to the mythical inundation of world under water. But, spiritually, it refers to death. Noah represents an Evite—one who is "perfect in his generation." Noah escapes the flood by getting into the *ark*. Spiritually, the *ark* represents body-awareness. And to enter the ark means to enter the meditative state. Noah's ark also refers to the human body cell with its genomic content. Just as Noah's ark, the human DNA contains all the information required to recreate a new world and a new life. And the human DNA (soul) is immortal and it can survive death (the Great Flood). But, those who are genetically corrupt don't have an ark; so, they perish in the Great Flood.

"Then shall two be in the field; the one shall be taken, and the other left." Spiritually, the term *field* suggests consciousness. The term "two" suggests duality, and the term "one" suggests non-duality. In other words, one who achieves non-duality consciousness (body-awareness) surpasses death.

"Two women shall be grinding at the mill; the one shall be taken, and the other left." Spiritually, the expression, "two women" refers to the mind; the term "mill" refers to the world of action. Spiritually, the term "one" suggests non-duality; the term "the other" suggests duality. But, duality implies religion. Therefore, according to the Gospel, those who surrender their awareness to religion will perish at death.

Watch therefore: for ye know not what hour your Lord doth come." The Gospel warns each of us: "Remain body-aware always because you never know when death arrives." But, in order to become body-aware, one should have uncorrupted human DNA. And only the Gospel can truly rectify genetic corruption.

MATTHEW 24:43-44

"But know this, that if the goodman of the house had known in what watch the thief would come, he would have watched, and would not have suffered his house to be broken up. Therefore be ye also ready: for in such an hour as ye think not the Son of man cometh."

"But know this, that if the goodman of the house had known in what watch the thief would come, he would have watched, and would not have suffered his house to be broken up." The Gospel opens the verse with the words, "know this." It is a signal that there is a secret is hidden in his words. The term *house* refers to the body. The "goodman of the house" refers to the self (Sanskrit: *ātman*). The term *thief* refers to the "Son of man," which is the Self (Sanskrit: *Paramātman*) in which we dissolve at death. The term *thief* also refers to death.

Literally, the word *watch* means "time," but, spiritually, it means "body-awareness." Therefore, what the verse says is this: "If a man knew when death would arrive, he would remain body-aware and save his soul." Alternatively, the "coming of the thief" also refers to the spiritual revelation of the Gospel. Therefore, the Gospel verse also suggests that those who read the Gospel with body-awareness will be saved.

MATTHEW 24:45-47

"Who then is a faithful and wise servant, whom his lord hath made ruler over his household, to give them meat in due season? Blessed is that servant, whom his lord when he cometh shall find so doing. Verily I say unto you, That he shall make him ruler over all his goods."

Spiritually, the term *household* refers to the human body. Therefore, the "ruler of the household" is one who is body-aware. He is an enlightened man. The Gospel gives his qualifications:

1. He is a "the faithful and wise servant." In other words, he is an Evite
2. He is *chosen* by the Father to be the "ruler of his household". In other words, he is an *Elect*, and he is self-aware.
3. His job is "to give them meat in due season." In other words, it is his responsibility to spiritually interpret the Gospel.

Here, the word "them" refers to the Mortals; the term *meat* refers to the spiritual meaning of the Gospel; the expression, "due season" refers to the Last Days. Alternatively, at the individual level, the term "them" refers to the body cells; the term *meat* refers to the Gospel meaning; the expression, "due season" refers to meditation. In other words, the Gospel says that the Father has appointed the Evites as *prophets* to provide Mortals the true meaning of the Gospel in the Last Days.

"Blessed is that servant, whom his lord when he cometh shall find so doing. Verily I say unto you, That he shall make him ruler over all his goods." Here, the Gospel gives us the definition of the term *blessed*: "A faithful and wise servant, whom his lord hath made ruler over his household." In other words, the term *blessed* refers to an Evite. Spiritually, the expression, "his goods" refers to the Gospel.

According to the Gospel, an enlightened Evite speaks the truth, and whatever he speaks *becomes* the truth. That is the implication of the words, "he shall make him ruler over all his goods." Mathematically speaking, not only is the Evites' words *consistent* but also *complete*.

MATTHEW 24:48-51

"But and if that evil servant shall say in his heart, My lord delayeth his coming; And shall begin to smite his fellowservants, and to eat and drink with the drunken; The lord of that servant shall come in a day when he looketh not for him, and in an hour that he is not aware of, And shall cut him asunder, and appoint him his portion with the hypocrites: there shall be weeping and gnashing of teeth."

In the previous verse, the Gospel defined the "faithful and wise servant" as a body-aware human being, or an Evite. Here, it defines the "evil servant." According to the Gospel, these are his qualifications:

1. He believes that the Gospel truth will not be revealed.
2. He believes that the end of the world would not come.
3. He believes that he has control over death.

In other words, the term "evil servant" refers to the deluded Adamites, the priestly race. The Gospel describes the behavior of these people:

1. He smites his fellowservants.
2. He eats and drinks with the drunken.

The Greek word for *smite* is *typtō* (G5180), which means "to cudgel" (properly with a stick or *bastinado*), but in any case by *repeated* blows. Spiritually, the word *smite* suggests *conditioning*. (*Bastinado* is a mode of punishment consisting of blows with a stick on the soles of the feet or on the buttocks.)

In psychology there are two types of conditioning: one, *Classical conditioning* or *Pavlovian conditioning*; two, *Operant conditioning* or *Instrumental conditioning.* Classical conditioning is a kind of learning that occurs when a conditioned stimulus (CS) is paired with an unconditioned stimulus (US). Operant conditioning, on the other hand, is a type of learning in which an individual's behavior is modified by its antecedents and consequences. Operant conditioning is distinguished from classical conditioning in that operant conditioning deals with the *reinforcement* and *punishment* to change behavior. Operant conditioning operates on the environment and is maintained by its antecedents and consequences, while classical conditioning deals with the conditioning of reflexive behaviors which are also elicited by antecedent conditions. In other words, classical conditioning conditions the body, whereas Operant conditioning conditions the mind. Here, the Gospel is specifically referring to Operant conditioning.

The Greek word for drunken is *methyō* (G3184), which means "to intoxicate." Spiritually, the term *drunken* refers to the pious religious followers. The expression, "eat and drink with the drunken" refers to certain religious rituals. In other words, the "evil servants" intoxicate their followers with evil religious rituals.

According to the Gospel, the "evil servants" condition the human minds into a state of intoxication or a spell-like state through evil rituals. The term refers to the serpent-children—the priestly race—that corrupts humanity. They are corrupt and unenlightened men who preach dualistic doctrines instead of truth. These evil men, even when preaching their lofty doctrines to their deluded laity, think to themselves: "*His Coming* is just a fiction; it will not happen."

"The lord of that servant shall come in a day when he looketh not for him, and in an hour that he is not aware of, And shall cut him asunder, and appoint him his portion with the hypocrites: there shall be weeping and gnashing of teeth." Spiritually, the expression, "lord of that servant" refers to death. The expression, "portion with the hypocrites" means "the fate of humanoids, which is perdition. In other words, those who mislead humanity will perish like the humanoids.

CHAPTER 25

The Hour the Son of Man Comes

MATTHEW 25:1-13

"Then shall the kingdom of heaven be likened unto ten virgins, which took their lamps, and went forth to meet the bridegroom. And five of them were wise, and five were foolish. They that were foolish took their lamps, and took no oil with them: But the wise took oil in their vessels with their lamps. While the bridegroom tarried, they all slumbered and slept. And at midnight there was a cry made, Behold, the bridegroom cometh; go ye out to meet him. Then all those virgins arose, and trimmed their lamps. And the foolish said unto the wise, Give us of your oil; for our lamps are gone out. But the wise answered, saying, Not so; lest there be not enough for us and you: but go ye rather to them that sell, and buy for yourselves. And while they went to buy, the bridegroom came; and they that were ready went in with him to the marriage: and the door was shut. Afterward came also the other virgins, saying, Lord, Lord, open to us. But he answered and said, Verily I say unto you, I know you not. Watch therefore, for ye know neither the day nor the hour wherein the Son of man cometh."

"*Then shall the kingdom of heaven be likened unto ten virgins, which took their lamps, and went forth to meet the bridegroom*": The word "then" refers to the moment of death. The "kingdom of heaven," refers to the human body. The bridegroom is the Self. The ten virgins represent *two* separate individuals: one, a Mortal with his five senses directed outward; the other, an Evite with his five senses directed inwards. The Mortal is more extroverted, while the Evite is more introverted. Through this parable, the Gospel shows us how a deluded man and a body-aware man face death.

"And five of them were wise, and five were foolish." The Gospel compares the Evite to "five wise virgins" and the Mortal to "five foolish virgins." The sense perceptions of sight, sound, touch, smell, and taste are like *virgins* because they 'yearn for' the Self. In other words, these sense perceptions want to 'grasp' reality.

"They that were foolish took their lamps, and took no oil with them: But the wise took oil in their vessels with their lamps." The human body is like a lamp, and body-awareness is its oil. The foolish virgins' lamps have no extra oil to meet a contingency. In other words, the Mortal is less body-aware because he squanders most of his awareness on worldly matters. The wise virgins, on the other hand, have enough oil to meet any contingency. In other words, the Evite is more body-aware because he does not squander his awareness on frivolous worldly things.

"While the bridegroom tarried, they all slumbered and slept." People experience death only once in their life and that is the first and last time. As a result, people tend to take death for granted and get on with their lives pretending that death is not there. Some are too afraid to address the issue of death, and so they repress thoughts about death and get on with their lives. This is what is implied by this verse. The expression, "they all slumbered and slept" suggests their state of delusion. The Evites, on the other hand, are aware of the impending death and are prepared to meet that contingency. In other words, the Evites seriously address the issues of death and the life after death, whereas the Mortals do not.

"And at midnight there was a cry made, Behold, the bridegroom cometh; go ye out to meet him." Midnight marks the close of one day and the beginning of another day. The term *midnight* is used here to indicate the transition from one life, or world into another life, or world. The word *cry* denotes the moment of death. At the moment of death, the dying man receives a 'flashback' of his entire life and is able to make a *self-assessment* about the effectiveness of his life. The Gospel describes the process as "meeting the bridegroom." It is also known as the *Judgment*. The critical question raised in this self-assessment is this: *"Did I use this life effectively?"* And effectiveness is measured in terms of the degree of body-awareness of the dying man. One fails the test if

one is not found body-aware at the time of death; one passes the test if one is found body-aware at the time of death. However, to remain body-aware at death is not easy; it requires a life-time of practice. *One of the major purposes of life is learning to die.*

"Then all those virgins arose, and trimmed their lamps. And the foolish said unto the wise, Give us of your oil; for our lamps are gone out. But the wise answered, saying, Not so; lest there be not enough for us and you: but go ye rather to them that sell, and buy for yourselves." The Greek word for *trimmed* is *kosmeō* (G2885), which means "to put in proper order." But, spiritually, the word, *trimmed* suggests body-awareness. The wise man, at the time of death, remains body-aware. The Gospel metaphorically describes it as the wise virgins trimming their lamps on arrival of the bridegroom. The foolish virgins begging for oil from the wise virgins depicts the dying man's mind struggling to stay awake, extracting consciousness from the body. Those who "sell' the oil" are the religious priests who give the *extreme unction* to the dying man.

Extreme unction is a sacrament of the Catholic Church that is administered to a Catholic "who, having reached the age of reason, begins to be in danger due to sickness or old age," except in the case of those who "persevere obstinately in manifest grave sin." Proximate danger of death, the occasion for the administration of *Viaticum*, is not required, but only the onset of a medical condition considered as a possible prelude to death. It is one of the three sacraments that constitute the *Last Rites* (together with the *Sacrament of Penance* and *Viaticum*).

"And while they went to buy, the bridegroom came; and they that were ready went in with him to the marriage: and the door was shut. Afterward came also the other virgins, saying, Lord, Lord, open to us. But he answered and said, Verily I say unto you, I know you not": Those who remain body-aware at death receive salvation and are liberated from the world and unite with the Self. In a sense, death is the 'salvation' that man has long been awaiting. This parable compares the liberated soul's union with the Self as the wise virgins uniting with the bridegroom in marriage. According to the Gospel, after the bridegroom and wise virgins enter the chamber, the door is shut. In other words, those who lack body-awareness at death perish; they have no more reincarnations.

The deluded man's cry "Lord, Lord" reminds us of the Gospel admonition in Matthew 7:21: *"Not every one that saith unto me, Lord, Lord, shall enter into the kingdom of heaven."* The repetition of the word Lord suggests duality; it denotes dualistic religions. Therefore, the implication of the verse is that not all pious people will receive salvation. In fact, religious piety has nothing to do with salvation; it is, if anything, an impediment. It is clear from the pronouncement: *"Verily I say unto you, I know you not."* Spiritually, it means: *"Truly, you don't know your Self."*

"Watch therefore, for ye know neither the day nor the hour wherein the Son of man cometh." The spiritual implication of this parable is this: *Since we cannot know the time of death, we should always remain body-aware so that death does not catch us unawares.*

MATTHEW 25:14-30

"For the kingdom of heaven is as a man travelling into a far country, who called his own servants, and delivered unto them his goods. And unto one he gave five talents, and another two, and to another one; to every man according to his several ability; and straightway took his journey. Then he that had received the five talents went and traded with the same, and made them other five talents. And likewise he that received two, he also gained other two. But he that had received one went and digged in the earth, and hid his lord's money. After a long time the lord of those servants cometh, and reckoneth with them. And so he that had received five talents came and brought other five talents, saying, Lord, thou deliveredst unto me five talents: behold, I have gained beside them five talents more. His lord said unto him, Well done, thou good and faithful servant: thou hast been faithful over a few things, I will make thee ruler over many things: enter thou into the joy of thy lord. He also that had received two talents came and said, Lord, thou deliveredst unto me two talents: behold, I have gained two other talents beside them. His lord said unto him, Well done, good and faithful servant; thou hast been faithful over a few things, I will make thee ruler over many things: enter thou into the joy of thy lord. Then he which had received the one talent came and said, Lord, I knew thee that thou art an hard man, reaping where thou hast not sown, and gathering where thou hast not strawed: And I was afraid, and went and hid thy talent in the earth: lo, there thou hast that is thine. His lord answered and said unto him, Thou wicked and slothful servant, thou knewest that I reap where I sowed not, and gather where I have not strawed: Thou oughtest therefore to have put my money to the exchangers, and then at my coming I should have received mine own with usury. Take therefore the talent from him, and give it unto him which hath ten talents. For unto every one that hath shall be given, and he shall have abundance: but from him that hath not shall be taken away even that which he hath. And cast ye the unprofitable servant into outer darkness: there shall be weeping and gnashing of teeth."

"For the kingdom of heaven is as a man travelling into a far country, who called his own servants, and delivered unto them his goods": The "kingdom of heaven," in this context, refers to body-awareness. The *man* is the Self. The Gospel compares the Self to a man travelling to a far country. The "far country" is the virtual-reality (dream) called the world. The man travelling to the far country denotes the Self incarnating in the world as humanity. And in the world, he plays multiple roles as human beings. The *servants* of the Self are *daemons* (programs) that control the world. And their job is to guide human beings (the different *avatars* of the Self) safely through the world, and, eventually, out of it. The *goods* the Self distributes to the daemons are the scriptures that contain the secrets about the world.

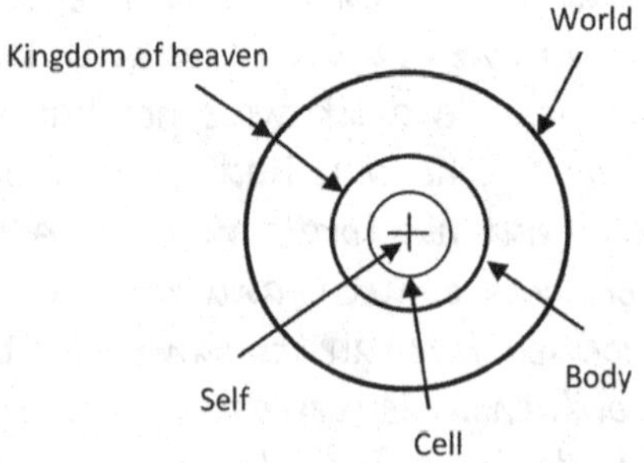

THE KINGDOM OF HEAVEN

"And unto one he gave five talents, and another two, and to another one; to every man according to his several ability; and straightway took his journey": Perhaps, The servant who received five talents was the Hindu priestly class, which received five scriptures, namely:

1. *Rig Vēda*
2. *Yajur Vēda*
3. *Sāma Vēda*

4. *Atharva Vēda*
5. *Bhagavad Gīta*

The servant who received two talents was the Buddhist priestly class, which received two scriptures, namely:

1. *Mahāsamghika*
2. *Mūlasarvāstivāda*

Perhaps, the servant who received one talent represents the Scribes and the Pharisees—the Judaic priestly class—that received one scripture—the *Torah.*

The scriptures were divided between the three priestly races (daemons) depending on the complexity of their construction (program architecture). Perhaps, that is what is suggested by the expression "to every man according to his several ability."

"Then he that had received the five talents went and traded with the same, and made them other five talents. And likewise he that received two, he also gained other two. But he that had received one went and digged in the earth, and hid his lord's money." The term *trading* implies an exchange process; you give something of value to take something of more value. Here, the trading refers to the exchange of scripture for something of greater value—the Gospel. While the scripture tells the secret of getting *into* the world, the Gospel tells the secret of getting *out* of it. In that sense, the Gospel may be called the *Scripture of Exit.*

The priestly class of Hindu religion explored their scriptures (*vēdas*) and produced many Gospels including the *Rāmāyana,* the *Mahābhāratha* and the *Srimad Bhāgavadam.* Buddhism too produced Gospels known as the *Dhāmma* literature. However, the priestly class of Judaism simply maintained the scripture given to it in its pristine condition, but did not produce a Scripture of Exit for its wards. In that sense, it wasted the talent given to it and, therefore, it is called the "unprofitable servant."

"After a long time the lord of those servants cometh, and reckoneth with them. And so he that had received five talents came and brought other five talents, saying, Lord, thou deliveredst unto me five talents: behold, I have gained beside them five talents more. His lord said unto him, Well done, thou good and faithful servant: thou hast been faithful over a few things, I will make thee ruler over many things: enter thou into the joy

of thy lord. He also that had received two talents came and said, Lord, thou delivered unto me two talents: behold, I have gained two other talents beside them. His lord said unto him, Well done, good and faithful servant; thou hast been faithful over a few things, I will make thee ruler over many things: enter thou into the joy of thy lord": The expression, "after a long time" suggests several millennia after the scriptures were handed over to the priestly class. The "lord of those servants" is the Self, or the Gospel, and the "return of the lord" refers to the Second Coming. The term *reckoneth* means "to assess." Therefore, the spiritual the implication of the verse is that after fully experiencing the world, the Self will evaluate the usefulness of the different daemons (programs) that he placed in the world for guiding his avatars through the world and out of it. The priestly classes of both Hinduism and Buddhism were applauded because they succeeded in producing Gospels as expected of them.

"Then he which had received the one talent came and said, Lord, I knew thee that thou art an hard man, reaping where thou hast not sown, and gathering where thou hast not strawed: And I was afraid, and went and hid my talent in the earth: lo, there thou hast that is thine." Now it is the turn of the third servant to give account to the Lord. This servant has nothing to show to his credit expect the safe-keep of the scripture given to it. Therefore, he accuses his master of being a cruel man who tried to take advantage of him. He says, "*Lord, I knew thee that thou art an hard man, reaping where thou hast not sown, and gathering where thou hast not strawed."* The Greek word for *strawed* is *diaskorpizō* (G1287), which means "to scatter." In this case, that which the Self *sowed* is the Torah; that which it wants to *reap* is the Gospel. That which the Self *scattered* is the human seed; that which it wants to *gather* are enlightened human beings. What this servant is really saying is this: "*How do you expect me to discover something that is not there in the scripture you have given?*" But, inadvertently, he blurts out, "I was afraid," but does not clarify what he was afraid of. Perhaps, he was afraid the exodus of human beings from the world would jeopardize his own comfortable existence.

"His lord answered and said unto him, Thou wicked and slothful servant, thou knewest that I reap where I sowed not, and gather where I have not strawed: Thou oughtest therefore to have put my money to the exchangers, and then at my coming I should have received mine own with usury. Take therefore the talent from him, and give it unto him which

hath ten talents." The Self (humanity) calls the Scribes and Pharisees *wicked* and *slothful* for having undermined the very purpose of creating them, which was to serve humanity. Their assigned duty was to guide the *avatars* safely through the world and eventually out of it, but they failed in their duty. Not only did they not produce a Gospel, but they also hid the secrets of the Torah from humanity and used it to control humanity. If only they had revealed its secrets, then humanity would have benefitted at least materially. That is the implication of the words, *"Thou oughtest therefore to have put my money to the exchangers, and then at my coming I should have received mine own with usury."* The term *usury* means "interest on principal." The word *interest* literally means "material benefit."

"Take therefore the talent from him, and give it unto him which hath ten talents. For unto every one that hath shall be given, and he shall have abundance: but from him that hath not shall be taken away even that which he hath." According to the Gospel, humanity will take Torah out of the hands of the Scribes and Pharisees and hand it over to the followers of *Sanatana Dharma*. The phrase, "every one that hath" may be interpreted as "those who have the Gospel," or "those who are body-aware." The implication is that the Torah secrets will be revealed to the Evites, which will improve the world materially.

"And cast ye the unprofitable servant into outer darkness: there shall be weeping and gnashing of teeth." The useless programs (daemons) will be 'deleted'.

MATTHEW 25:31-46

"When the Son of man shall come in his glory, and all the holy angels with him, then shall he sit upon the throne of his glory: And before him shall be gathered all nations: and he shall separate them one from another, as a shepherd divideth his sheep from the goats: And he shall set the sheep on his right hand, but the goats on the left. Then shall the King say unto them on his right hand, Come, ye blessed of my Father, inherit the kingdom prepared for you from the foundation of the world: For I was an hungred, and ye gave me meat: I was thirsty, and ye gave me drink: I was a stranger, and ye took me in: Naked, and ye clothed me: I was sick, and ye visited me: I was in prison, and ye came unto me. Then shall the righteous answer him, saying, Lord, when saw we thee an hungred, and fed thee? or thirsty, and gave thee drink? When saw we thee a stranger, and took thee in? or, naked, and clothed thee? Or when saw we thee sick, or in prison, and came unto thee? And the King shall answer and say unto them, Verily I say unto you, Inasmuch as ye have done it unto one of the least of these my brethren, ye have done it unto me. Then shall he say also unto them on the left hand, Depart from me, ye cursed, into everlasting fire, prepared for the devil and his angels: For I was an hungred, and ye gave no meat: I was thirsty, and ye gave me no drink: I was a stranger, and ye took me not in: naked, and ye clothed me not: sick, and in prison, and ye visited me not. Then shall they also answer him, saying, Lord, when saw we thee an hungred, or athirst, or a stranger, or naked, or sick, or in prison, and did not minister unto thee? Then shall he answer them, saying, Verily I say unto you, Inasmuch as ye did it not to one of the least of these, ye did it not to me. And these shall go away into everlasting punishment: but the righteous into life eternal.

"When the Son of man shall come in his glory, and all the holy angels with him, then shall he sit upon the throne of his glory: And before him shall be gathered all nations: and he shall separate them one from another, as a shepherd divideth his sheep from the goats: And he shall set the sheep on his right hand, but the goats on the left." Spiritually, the expression, "coming of the Son of man" has the following connotations:

1. The revelation of the true meaning of the Gospel
2. The birth (reincarnation) of a human soul in the world
3. Liberation of mankind
4. Arrival of death

For the interpretation of this parable, we shall consider the meaning of the expression "coming of the Son of man" as the arrival of death. Death, to the dying man, may appear like a great light like the sun. The holy angels that accompany the Son of man are the eternal truths. Spiritually, the expression, "throne of his glory" refers to the *Circle of Self.* Here, the dying man's Self is sitting in judgment on his own life. But, this view is contrary to the Church's view, according to which, another entity, a God, passes judgment on man on the basis of sins committed by him during his lifetime.

The Greek word for *nation* is *ethnos* (G1484), which means "people." The Hebrew word for nations is *goy* (H1471), which means "Gentile." But, spiritually, the term "nations" means "humanity." Fundamentally, there are three types of human beings in the world: one, Evites who possess the true human DNA; two, the Mortals who possess corrupted human DNA; three Adamites who look like humans but are not. Only the Mortals come in the ambit of the judgment that is allegorically described in this parable.

The Evites are the *heroes* in the virtual reality play called the world. The term *hero*, here, does not suggest that these people are rich and famous. They may be rich or poor, good or evil; it doesn't matter. But, they have an important role to play. It is the Self Himself that is acting through these people. The Evites are intuitive and individualistic people, also known as Prophets. They possess the uncorrupted human DNA. In other words, the Evites are the physical 'carriers' of the Gospel. They are called the *faithful* because they are body-aware. The Evites are not religious in the worldly sense, but are deeply spiritual. Since they are the main characters in this virtual reality play, they are known as *The Elect*. They are more genetically (spiritually) evolved than the Mortals. The Evites are less concerned about worldly success, but are more interested in seeking the truth.

The Adamites are the evil characters in the virtual reality play. They are called the *servants*. Although they appear like humans, they are not really humans. They totally lack body-awareness and are essentially programmatic entities (daemons) that exist only in the virtual reality world. An Adamite is either a *ruler* or a *priest*. As the *ruler*, his job is to *serve* humanity in their materialistic pursuits; as the *priest*, his job is to *serve* humanity in their spiritual pursuits. The priest has the additional duty of preserving and translating scriptures. An Adamite is judged 'faithful' if he served humanity either in their worldly pursuits or in their spiritual pursuits. The Adamites perishes with death.

The Mortals are the 'potential' actors in the virtual reality play. They constitute the large majority (more than 90%) of the humanity. The principal concern of the Mortals is survival—their survival and their family's survival—and, therefore, their awareness is mainly focused on mundane things. They are generally religious, but their faith is superficial. They are more concerned with morality rather than truth itself. The DNA of the Mortals is corrupt in varying degrees. The life purpose of Mortals is to evolve into Evites by rectifying their genetic corruption. Mortals are sub-divided into two categories: one, those who have *not* 'sworn' with their bodies; two, those who have 'sworn' with their bodies. The Mortal who has not 'sworn' with his body is called a *sheep*, whereas the Mortal who has 'sworn' with his body is called a *goat*.

The 25th chapter of the Gospel of Matthew is the Chapter of Judgment. The three parables in chapter 25 describe the judgment of Evites, Adamites, and the Mortals respectively. The table below lists the three parables that relate to each of the three categories along with the key aspects of each of the three parables.

Parable	Who is Judged?	Nature of the Judged	Success Criteria	The Goal
Parable of the ten virgins	Evites	Human being	Conquering death	Merge with Self
Parable if the talents	Adamites	Humanoid	Faithful service	Serve humanity
Parable of sheep and goats	Mortals	Human being	Uncorrupted body	Evolve as Evite

The king says to the sheep, *"Come, ye blessed of my Father, inherit the kingdom prepared for you from the foundation of the world: For I was an hungred, and ye gave me meat: I was thirsty, and ye gave me drink: I was a stranger, and ye took me in: Naked, and ye clothed me: I was sick, and ye visited me: I was in prison, and ye came unto me."* Spiritually, the expression, "the kingdom prepared for you from the foundation of the world" refers to the perpetual state of self-awareness. Here, we see the Self welcoming the *sheep* (human beings having uncorrupted bodies) to share eternity with Him. The Self expresses his appreciation to the *sheep* for feeding him when he was hungry, quenching his thirst when he was thirsty, sheltering him when he was homeless, clothing him when he was naked, tending to him when he was sick, and giving company when he was lonely. But, when they demur that they did not do any such kind deeds, He says to them, *"Verily I say unto you, Inasmuch as ye have done it unto one of the least of these my brethren, ye have done it unto me."* Spiritually, the expression, "the least of these my brethren" refers to the cells of the human body. Therefore, the spiritual implication of the verse is this: "*Whenever you act with body-awareness, you are feeding the Self.*"

"Then shall he say also unto them on the left hand, Depart from me, ye cursed, into everlasting fire, prepared for the devil and his angels: For I was an hungred, and ye gave no meat: I was thirsty, and ye gave me no drink: I was a stranger, and ye took me not in: naked, and ye clothed me not: sick, and in prison, and ye visited me not. Then shall they also answer him, saying, Lord, when saw we thee an hungred, or athirst, or a stranger, or naked, or sick, or in prison, and did not minister unto thee? Then shall he answer them, saying, Verily I say unto you, Inasmuch as ye did it not to one of the least of these, ye did it not to me. And these shall go away into everlasting punishment: but the righteous into life eternal." The Self calls the *goats* (bodily-corrupt human beings) "the cursed." The Hebrew word for *cursed* is *hērem* (H2764), which means "a doomed object," or "utterly destroyed." But, here, the word *cursed* suggests bodily corruption. The *goats* are considered *cursed* because they lack body-awareness. They are shocked by Self's accusation and they protest that they did not see him asking for help. Indirectly, the *goats* are suggesting that they would have helped him had they seen him asking for help. Perhaps, the *goats* are telling the truth. From a worldly point of view, the goats are great "do-gooders," lavishly donating to religion, charity and so on. The Self says to the goats, "*Verily I say unto you, Inasmuch as ye did it not to one of the least of these, ye did it not to me.*" The words may be interpreted as follows: "*Because you acted in delusion, your actions did not reach the Self.*"

The Self curses the goats and gives them the same fate as the Serpent children. In other words, the bodily-corrupt Mortals meet the same fate as the Adamites, which is perdition. The Self gives his judgment: *"And these shall go away into everlasting punishment: but the righteous into life eternal."* The expression, "life eternal" means "immortality."

The parable of the goats and the sheep allegorically describes the soul's self-assessment of its past life at the point of death, rather than judgment by a Messiah at his Second Coming.

CHAPTER 26

Rise, Let Us Be Going

MATTHEW 26:1-2

"And it came to pass, when Jesus had finished all these sayings, he said unto his disciples, Ye know that after two days is the feast of the passover, and the Son of man is betrayed to be crucified."

Passover is an important Biblically-derived Jewish festival. Historically, together with *Shavuot* (Pentacost) and *Sukkot* (Tabernacles), Passover is one of the three pilgrimage festivals during which the entire population of the kingdom of Judah made a pilgrimage to the Temple of Jerusalem. The Hebrew word *Passover* is *pesah* (H6453), which means both "a pretermission," and applies both to the Jewish festival or its victim. The Greek word for Passover is *pascha* (G3957), which means "the festival or the special sacrifices connected with it."

The Gospel refers to the Passover as the event that marks the betrayal and crucifixion of the Son of man. As we have seen before, the term, "Son of man" has the following connotations:

1. The true Gospel
2. The true human DNA
3. Humanity
4. The Self (Consciousness)

Here, the term "Son of man" refers to the Self. It seems, according to the Gospel, the *Passover* commemorates the destruction of human body-awareness.

Crucifixion is a method of deliberately slow and painful execution in which the condemned person is tied or nailed to a large wooden cross and left to hang until dead. Crucifixion symbolically represents the life of a human being in this world. Literally, the *cross* represents duality or the world; but, spiritually, it represents non-duality, or body-awareness. Jesus hanging on the cross denotes the situation of a human being in the world. Here, the Gospel links Passover with crucifixion. What does the Passover actually signify? Does it signify the "passing over" from state of body-awareness to the state of delusion?

The Jewish people celebrate Passover as a commemoration of their liberation over 3,300 years ago by Jehovah from slavery in ancient Egypt that was ruled by the Pharaohs, and their birth as a nation under the leadership of Moses. In the narrative of the Exodus, the Bible tells that Jehovah helped the Children of Israel escape from their slavery in Egypt by inflicting ten plagues upon the ancient Egyptians before the Pharaoh would release his Israelite slaves. The tenth and worst of the plagues was the death of the Egyptian "first-born." The Israelites were instructed to mark ("X") the doorposts of their homes with the blood of a "slaughtered spring lamb" and, upon seeing this, the spirit of the Lord knew to pass over the first-born in these homes, hence the name of the holiday. By the way, a spring lamb is a milk-fed lamb, usually three to seven months old.

Egypt is the cradle of human civilization. Therefore, the expression "Egyptian first-born son" suggests human consciousness. Perhaps, the slaughter of the Egyptian first-born suggests some sort of spell cast on human consciousness? Perhaps, the tenth plague was a viral outbreak that cast a spell (infection) on humans altering their consciousness. Is the Gospel referring to this event as the betrayal of the Son of man?

MATTHEW 26:3-5

"Then assembled together the chief priests, and the scribes, and the elders of the people, unto the palace of the high priest, who was called Caiaphas, And consulted that they might take Jesus by subtilty, and kill him. But they said, Not on the feast day, lest there be an uproar among the people."

The chief priests are the members of the *Sanhedrin.* The Hebrew word *Sanhedrin* means "sitting together," therefore, refers to an assembly or council. It was an assembly of twenty to twenty-three men appointed in every city in the Biblical Land of Israel. *Scribes* are the doctors of law, who are also its literal interpreters. Scribes in Ancient Israel, as in most of the ancient world, were distinguished professionals who could exercise the functions we would associate with lawyers, government ministers, judges, or even financiers, as early as the 11th century BCE. The *elders of the people* are the civil magistrates. Therefore, the assembly consisted of both ecclesiastics and laymen. Usually, the Sanhedrin meets in the temple, but, this time they met privately at the palace of Caiaphas, the high priest, instead of the temple. The Gospel tells why: *"And consulted that they might take Jesus by subtilty and kill him."* The word *subtle* means "difficult to detect or grasp by the mind or analyze." It suggests working or spreading in a hidden and injurious, insidious or pernicious way. The word *subtle* implies *conspiracy*. There are four types of conspiracies:

1. Cabal: An association between religious, political, or tribal officials to further its own ends, usually by intrigue.
2. Civil conspiracy: An agreement between persons to deceive, mislead, or defraud others of their legal rights, or to gain an unfair advantage.
3. Criminal conspiracy: An agreement between persons to break the law in the future, in some cases having committed an act to further that agreement.
4. Political conspiracy: An agreement between persons to overthrow a government.

The name, *Caiaphas* in Aramaic means "a rock that hollows itself out." In Chaldean the name means "a dell" or "a depression."

The religious authorities were not simply planning a political murder, but they also wanted it to be a *ritual murder* for the ensuing Passover. And for the ritual murder, they needed the blood of an "innocent victim" and Jesus perfectly fit their bill. Thus, they would kill two birds by the same arrow. That was their diabolical plan.

Those who planned the ritual murder were cautious that their plan did not leak out to the public because they feared uproar from the people if they come to know about it.

MATTHEW 26:6-13

"Now when Jesus was in Bethany, in the house of Simon the leper, There came unto him a woman having a alabaster box of very precious ointment, and poured it on his head, as he sat at meat. But when his disciples saw it, they had indignation, saying, To what purpose is this waste? For this ointment might have been sold for much, and given to the poor. When Jesus understood it, he said unto them, Why trouble ye the woman? for she hath wrought a good work upon me. For ye have the poor always with you; but me ye have not always. For in that she hath poured this ointment on my body, she did it for my burial. Verily I say unto you, Wheresoever this gospel shall be preached in the whole world, there shall also this, that this woman hath done, be told for a memorial of her."

"Now when Jesus was in Bethany, in the house of Simon the leper, There came unto him a woman having a alabaster box of very precious ointment, and poured it on his head, as he sat at meat." As we have seen before, the name, *Bethany* refers to the literal scripture. The term *leper*, in this context, means "a social outcast," or "a Gentile," rather than a physical leper. Therefore, the expression, "Simon, the leper of Bethany," perhaps, refers to a book that has been excluded from the literal scripture. The name Simon is derived from the Hebrew word *šimōn* (H8095), which means "he who has heard the word of God." Therefore, the expression, "the house of Simon the leper," probably refers to a *Gnostic codex* that has been excluded from the Bible, for the reason that it was considered an *anathema*. The term *anathema* is derived from the Latin *anathema*, which means "an excommunicated person," or "the curse of excommunication." The Greek word *anathema* means "a thing accursed." The terms *anathema* and *leper* have similar connotations. The Christian Church considers Gnostic works as heresy, and therefore considers them as *anathema.*

The *Gospel of Mary* is an apocryphal book discovered in 1896 in a 5th century papyrus codex. Although popularly known as the *Gospel of Mary*, it is not canonical nor is it technically classed as a gospel by scholastic consensus. The Gospel of Mary is found in the *Berlin Codex*. This very important and well-preserved codex was apparently discovered in the late-nineteenth century somewhere near Akhim in

Upper Egypt. The codex contained Coptic translations of three very important early Christian Gnostic texts: The *Gospel of Mary*, the *Apocrypha of John*, and the *Sophia of Jesus Christ*.

In this episode, we see a woman pouring an *alabaster* box of very precious ointment over Jesus' head while he was at Simon's place. The Gospel of John reveals the identity of the woman to be Mary Magdalene, the sister of Lazarus. Since Jesus represents the Gospel, the woman who poured the alabaster box of very precious ointment too cannot be a physical person. It can only be a spiritual interpretation of the Gospel. Most probably, it is alluding to the *Gospel of Mary*.

The word *alabaster* is derived from the Ancient Egyptian word *a-labaste,* which refers to vessels of the Egyptian goddess *Bast*, who is represented as a lioness and frequently depicted as such in figures placed atop the alabaster vessels. Alabaster is a white translucent material used for making statues and jars. Sometimes, we compare beautiful skin to the texture of alabaster. Spiritually, the alabaster jar represents the codex containing the Gospel of Mary. The Egyptian connection suggests that the book is written in *Coptic* language. The very precious ointment that the alabaster jar contains is the spiritual interpretation of the Gospel.

"But when his disciples saw it, they had indignation, saying, To what purpose is this waste? For this ointment might have been sold for much, and given to the poor." The word *indignation* means "strong displeasure at something considered unjust, offensive, insulting, or base; righteous anger." The disciples find Mary's gesture immoral, offensive, insulting and base. They rebuke her: *"To what purpose is this waste? For this ointment might have been sold for much, and given to the poor."* The disciples, here, represent the religious authorities, and their words may be translated as follows: "What nonsense is this? You should have used your knowledge in some other gainful profession rather than wasting it like this." We can reasonably presume that it was Judas Iscariot who made this comment because his name is mentioned in the immediately following verse (Matthew 26:14). Spiritually, Judas represents the Judeo-Christian Church and his attitude towards Mary reflects the Church's intolerance towards Gnostic works.

Jesus admonishes Judas: *"Why trouble ye the woman? for she hath wrought a good work upon me. For ye have the poor always with you; but me ye have not always. For in that she hath poured this ointment on my body, she did it for my burial."* Here, the Gospel criticizes the religious authorities for proscribing the Gnostic works. Spiritually, the expression, "good work," perhaps, refers to the Gospel of Mary, which is, in effect, a spiritual interpretation of the Gospel. Spiritually, the term, *poor* refers to the literal Gospel. It is poor because its content is second-hand and it is susceptible to corruption. The term *burial* refers to the encryption of the Gospel secrets in the Jesus story. Alternatively, it may be referring to the spiritual burial of the true Gospel in a mythical allegory.

"Verily I say unto you, Wheresoever this gospel shall be preached in the whole world, there shall also this, that this woman hath done, be told for a memorial of her": The term "this Gospel" refers to the *Gospel of Matthew*. The word, *preach*, in this context, it means "to interpret spiritually." Spiritually, the expression, "that this woman hath done" refers to the Gospel of Mary. Here, the Gospel reveals to us the mark of a genuine Gospel interpretation: It should identify the true significance of the woman anointing Jesus with an alabaster jar of very precious ointment.

MATTHEW 26:14-16

"Then one of the twelve, called Judas Iscariot, went unto the chief priests, And said unto them, What will ye give me, and I will deliver him unto you? And they covenanted with him for thirty pieces of silver. And from that time he sought opportunity to betray him."

The Hebrew equivalent of the name *Judas* is *yehūda* (H3063), which means "Jewish." The name *Iscariot* is derived from two sources:

1. The Hebrew word, *is* (H377), which means "a man" and it points to an Adamite
2. The Aramaic word, *qirya* (H7149), which means "a city," which suggests madness

The There are several theories regarding the etymology of the name *Iscariot*. Some are given below:

1. One popular explanation derives *Iscariot* from Hebrew *Is-Qriyōth*, or "man of Kerioth." Some speculate that Kerioth

refers to a region in Judea, but it is also the name of *two* known Judean towns.
2. A second theory is that *Iscariot* identifies Judas as a member of the *sicari*. These were a cadre of assassins among Jewish rebels intent on driving the Romans out of Judea.
3. A third possibility advanced by Ernst Wilhelm Hengstenberg is that *Iscariot* means "the liar" or "the false one."
4. Fourth, some have proposed that the word derives from the Aramaic word meaning "red color."

The theories 3 and 4 seem plausible, but theories 1 and 2 are merely diversions, or obfuscations. For the purpose of this exposition, we will take the meaning of the name *Judas Iscariot* as "Judas, the liar and the false one."

Jesus represents the Gospel; therefore, the disciples of Jesus represent twelve major scriptures of the world. Perhaps, Judas Iscariot represents the Judaic scripture. The idea that Jesus and his disciples were Jewish people is, perhaps, a subtlety planted by the Judaized Church in order to give credibility, legitimacy and authority to the notion that Jews are the chosen race. The Gospel calls Judas Iscariot "one of the twelve"—as a mere member of the group, and not as a disciple. Judas has already lost his disciple status.

Judas goes to the chief priests and tries to make a deal with them. He bargains with them: *"What will ye give me, and I will deliver him unto you?"* The words of Judas once again expose his business mindset. Earlier we saw him admonishing Mary Magdalene for wasting precious ointment on Jesus. He thought it was better that she sold the ointment for a high price and then donate the money to poor people.

The betrayal of Jesus by Judas parallels the betrayal of the Gospel by the Judaized Christian Church to the doctrine of Pharisees and Sadducees. But what is the doctrine of the Pharisees and Sadducees? The Gospel gives us some clues.

MATTHEW 26:17-19

"Now the first day of the feast of the unleavened bread the disciples came to Jesus, saying unto him, Where wilt thou that we prepare for thee to eat the passover? And he said, Go into the city *to such a man, and say unto him, The Master saith, My time is at hand; I will keep the passover at thy house with my disciples. And the disciples did as Jesus had appointed them; and they made ready the passover."*

The Gospel presents before us two different Passovers: one, a literal Passover that is celebrated by the Jewish people as one of their sacred holidays; two, a spiritual Passover, which Jesus himself demonstrated to humanity. The latter has an entirely different connotation, perhaps, even the very opposite of the former.

The literal Passover, also known as *Pesah* (H6453) in Hebrew, is a festival of Israelites. It commemorates the story of Exodus, in which the ancient Israelites were freed from slavery in Egypt. Passover begins on the 15th day of the month of *Nisan* in the Jewish calendar, and is celebrated for seven or eight days. Passover is one of the three festivals during which the entire Jewish populace historically made a pilgrimage to the temple in Jerusalem. It begins on the 14th day of the month of Nisan, which typically falls in March or April of the Gregorian calendar. Passover is a spring festival. So the 14th day of Nisan begins on the night of a full moon after the northern vernal equinox. The Biblical regulations for the observance of the festival require that all leavening be disposed of before the beginning of the 15th of Nisan. An 'unblemished' lamb is to be set apart on Nisan 10, and slaughtered on Nisan 14 at dusk. The literal meaning of the Hebrew word for *dusk* is "*ben ha arbayim,"* which means "between the two evenings," a phrase which is, however not defined.

The Passover signifies the transition from one state to another. The dusk—*"ben ha arbayim"*—is the line separating one state from the other. The first Passover—the Passover of Moses—marked the flight of Israelites from Egypt, from the captivity of the Pharaoh to the freedom, abundance of the land of Canaan. But, for human beings, the first Passover was the transition of human souls from the absolute freedom of the Self into the deluded world ruled by the Serpent and his minions. Birth is the "*ben ha arbayim"* that separates the two states in this case.

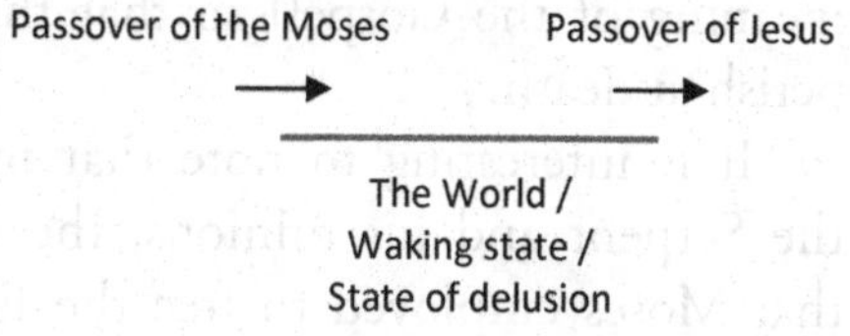

Two Passovers

The Passover that Jesus celebrates with his disciples symbolizes the second Passover of human beings—the passage from the world of delusion to the eternity of the Self. Death is the "*ben ha arbayim*" that separates the two states in this case.

The Bible stipulates how to eat the *Passover* meal: "*. . . with your loins girded, your shoes on your feet, and your staff in your hand; and ye shall eat it in haste: it is the LORD's Passover*" (Exodus 12:11). There is an air of alertness and urgency about the observance of Passover. It brings to mind the image of a man about to begin his exodus, and awaiting the call. However, for the spiritual Passover, the stipulation, "with your loins girded, your shoes on your feet, and your staff in your hand" suggests body-awareness; the Passover meal is the spiritual meaning of the Gospel; the exodus is the passage from ignorance and delusion to truth. However, the spiritual Passover is applicable only to the Evite; for the Mortal, the second Passover is death.

The literal Passover is celebrated with physical unleavened bread; for the spiritual Passover, the unleavened bread is the true (uncorrupted) Gospel. For the literal Passover, a physical unblemished lamb is set apart, and slaughtered; for the spiritual Passover, the Gospel itself is the "spring lamb" that is slaughtered. Spiritually, the slaughtering of the spring lamb refers to the spiritual interpretation of the Gospel.

During the first (literal) Passover, the Israelites marked their houses with the blood of the slaughtered spring lamb and, thus, their first-born children were spared death. During the spiritual Passover, the Evites mark their bodies (DNA) with body-awareness (the spiritual meaning of the Gospel) so that their 'first-born'—the souls—do not perish at death.

It is interesting to note that in order to liberate humanity from the Serpent and his minions, the Gospel employs the same method that Moses employed to free the Israelites from the Pharaoh and the Egyptians. The only difference is that the methods operate in opposite directions.

The important point to note is that the Jewish Passover and the Passover of the Gospel are same in content, but opposite in meaning. For the humans, the first Passover is a *fall*—the fall from self-awareness to delusion, whereas the second Passover is a rise—the liberation from delusion to self-awareness. The same scripture serves both evil and good: the literal scripture serves the Adamites; the spiritual scripture serves the Evites. That is why the scripture is called the "fruit of the tree of good and evil." The content of the scripture is the same, but the message it conveys varies depending on who is reading it. The literal scripture is known as *Lucifer*; the spiritual scripture is known as *Christ*. The LORD of the literal scripture is the Serpent; the LORD of the spiritual scripture is the Father (the Self).

The celebration of the Passover meal by Jesus establishes beyond doubt that the literal scripture and the spiritual scripture are antithetical to each other. One who blindly follows the literal scripture, without the help of an enlightened teacher, exposes himself to great danger.

> *For fools rush in where angels fear to tread.*
> *An Essay on Criticism*, Alexander Pope

Whose house will Jesus choose to keep his Passover? In other words, to whom will the Gospel reveal its secrets? The Gospel reveals that man: *"Go into the city to such a man and say unto him, The Master, saith, My time is at hand; I will keep the passover at thy house with my disciples."* Spiritually, the word *city* refers to the mind; the term *house* refers to the body. But, Jesus does not reveal the identity of the person in whose house he is going the keep the Passover. Instead, he simply says, *"Go into the city to such a man."* The disciples have to first enter the right city and then enter the right house. In other words, the Gospel message first enters the mind and then enters the body (DNA). The expression, "such a man" refers to a man whose mind is unconditioned (righteous), and whose body is uncorrupted (righteous); in other words, an Evite. The code words the disciples utter to the man are these: *"The Master, saith, My time is at hand; I will keep the passover at thy house with my disciples."* Here, the term *Master* refers to the Gospel; the expression "my time" refers to the Second Coming. Spiritually, the statement, *"The Master, saith, "My time is at hand; I will keep the passover at thy house with my disciples"* may be translated as follows: "In the Last Days I will reveal the spiritual meaning of the Gospel to the Evites through intuition."

The Passover of Jesus gives us an important spiritual message—the truth about scripture. And that truth is that the literal scripture is only an elaborate *Midrash*—a compilation of homiletic stories. All the characters, places, and events in the scripture are mythical, and therefore, spiritual in nature. The scripture can lead a man either into the world of delusion or out of it depending on how he chooses to understand it. But, if you choose to believe the scriptural characters, places, and events as real or historical, then the scripture will, as *Lucifer*, lead you into the world. On the other hand, if you choose to believe the scriptural characters, places, and events as mythical (spiritual), then the scripture will, like a prophet, lead you to the Gospel.

MATTHEW 26:20-25

"Now when the even was come, he sat down with the twelve. And as they did eat, he said, Verily I say unto you, that one of you shall betray me. And they were exceeding sorrowful, and began every one of them to say unto him, Lord, is it I? And he answered and said, He that dippeth his hand with me in the dish, the same shall betray me. The Son of man goeth as it is written of him: but woe unto that man by whom the Son of man is betrayed! It had been good for that man if he had not been born. Then Judas, which betrayed him, answered and said, Master, is it I? He said unto him, Thou hast said."

"Now when the even was come, he sat down with the twelve." As we have seen before, the term *even* refers to the *Last Days* or the *Kali Yuga*. The term *Kali Yuga* literally means "the age of the demon," or "the age of corruption." It is the last of the four stages the world goes through as part of the cycle of *yugas* described in the Indian scriptures. The implication here is that during the Last Days, alien humanoids (demons) will mix with humans and betray humanity.

The word, *betray* has many shades of meanings, some of which are listed below:

1. To deliver to an enemy by treachery
2. To disappoint, prove undependable; to abandon, forsake
3. To give away information about somebody
4. To cause someone to believe an untruth

The utterance *"One of you shall betray me"* is a warning from the Gospel to humanity. It identifies the betrayer as one among us.

Although it may seem counter-intuitive, the truth is that an enemy cannot 'betray' you; only a friend can. When an enemy does evil to you, it cannot be termed as betrayal because the enemy is only doing his *dharma* as the enemy. But, when a friend does evil to you, he is not doing the *dharma* of a friend and, therefore, his action is considered a betrayal.

The disciples, in consternation, ask Jesus, *"Lord, is it I?"* Jesus does not elaborate the nature of the betrayal, instead he points out the betrayer. Here, the Gospel teaches us an important spiritual truth: Action, in itself, carries no meaning; it acquires meaning only in relation to the doer. Therefore, when a person *betrays,* he is unknowingly exposing his evil nature.

Jesus reveals the *betrayer*: *"He that dippeth his hand with me in the dish, the same shall betray me."* The important thing to note here is that Jesus does not reveal the name of the betrayer; instead, he reveals what the betrayer does. The expression "dipping hand in the dish" means "sharing food," which suggests intimacy and trust and, therefore, points to a close associate. Literally, the term *dish* refers to a container carrying food, or the food contained in a dish. But spiritually, the term *dish* refers to the Gospel. Therefore, the expression, "dipping the hand in the dish" means "interpreting the Gospel." Alternatively, the expression, "dipping the hand in the dish" also means "managing my purse." It was Judas who managed the financial affairs of Jesus and the disciples (*"Judas had the bag."* John 13:29). Through this episode, the Gospel reveals the identity of the betrayer - associates who manage the church and interpret the Gospel for the laity: the clergy of the Judaized Christian Church. It is not the enemy; it is the betrayer. The enemy is the Serpent!

Jesus laments, *"The Son of man goeth as it is written of him: but woe unto that man by whom the Son of man is betrayed! It had been good for that man if he had not been born."* Here, the term "Son of man" refers to the true human DNA, or the humanity. Therefore, the expression, "The Son of man goeth as it is written of him" refers to the corruption of humanity; it refers to the onset of the *Dark Age*, or *Kali Yuga*. The corruption of humanity was unavoidable because of the cyclical nature of reality, but the agency that was instrumental to it is indeed a cursed one. Jesus pities that agent and says, *"It had been good for that man if he had not been born."*

Judas' utterance, *"Is it I"*, is indeed mysterious. The statement is superfluous if Judas did not betray Jesus; but, if he had really betrayed Jesus, then the utterance is hypocritical. Perhaps, Judas suffers from a mental disorder called *Dissociative Identity Disorder* (DID). It is evident from his seemingly innocent utterance. It is possible that the Judas who made the utterance is different from the Judas who committed the crime. Let us analyze the characteristics of the mental disorder called DID.

Dissociative Identity Disorder (DID), also known as *Multiple Personality Disorder* (MPD), is a mental disorder characterized by at least two distinct and relatively enduring identities or dissociated personality states that alternatively control a person's behavior, and it is accompanied by memory impairment for information, which is not explained by ordinary forgetfulness. Dissociative disorders including DID have been attributed to disruptions in memory caused by trauma and other forms of stress. Children who are severely abused and traumatized are potential candidates for DID and, therefore, are also susceptible to mind control. If so, infant circumcision is the baptism to DID. Added to that, the oppressive patriarchal environment in these families afford no opportunity for the psychic wound to heal.

Jesus says to Judas, *"Thou hast said."* It means: "You have admitted complicity."

MATTHEW 26:26-30

"And as they were eating, Jesus took bread, and blessed it, and brake it, and gave it to the disciples, and said, Take, eat; this is my body. And he took the cup, and gave thanks, and gave it to them, saying, Drink ye all of it; For this is my blood of the new testament, which is shed for many for the remission of sins. But I say unto you, I will not drink henceforth of this fruit of the vine, until that day when I drink it new with you in my Father's kingdom. And when they had sung an hymn, they went out into the mount of Olives."

Remember the following spiritual revelations as we proceed with the interpretations of the above Gospel verses:

1. The "Passover meal" refers to the spiritual interpretation of the Gospel.
2. The betrayal of Jesus refers to the corruption of the Gospel meaning by associates.

Spiritually, the betrayal of Jesus refers to the corruption of the Gospel meaning through theology. But, who is responsible for that corruption? In the previous verse, the Gospel generally revealed the identity of the betrayer; but, here, it reveals him by person. And the betrayer is *not* a person bearing the name Judas Iscariot. Judas Iscariot is just the code name for the betrayer.

"And as they were eating, Jesus took bread, and blessed it, and brake it, and gave it to the disciples, and said, Take, eat; this is my body." Spiritually, the term *bread* refers both to the human body (flesh) and the Gospel. Therefore, the blessing of the bread suggests focusing awareness on the body and the Gospel simultaneously. Similarly, the breaking of the bread suggests "rightly dividing the Gospel," or spiritually interpreting the Gospel. After breaking the bread, Jesus gives it to his disciples with the command to eat it. The spiritual implication of the command is this: "Understand the true meaning of the Gospel and renew your body (DNA)."

Term / Expression	Spiritual Meaning
"cup"	Human body; Gospel
"wine"	Body-awareness; Spiritual meaning of the Gospel
"gave thanks"	Focus awareness on Self
"drink ye all of it"	Understand the Gospel fully
"blood of the new testament"	The spiritual meaning of the Gospel
"new testament"	The true human DNA
"remission of sin"	Freedom from delusion

"And he took the cup, and gave thanks, and gave it to them, saying, drink ye all of it; For this is my blood of the new testament, which is shed for many for the remission of sins." Cup is a vessel for carrying wine. Physically, the cup represents the human body, and *wine* represents the body-awareness (spirit). Wine represents blood. But, spiritually, the cup represents the literal Gospel, and *wine* represents the spiritual Gospel. To "give thanks to the Father" means to focus awareness on the Self. It means invoking the Self for divine revelation. The imperative, "drink ye *all* of it" is a cue to pay close attention to the multiple connotations of the Gospel words. The expression, "blood of the new testament" means "the spiritual interpretation of the Gospel." The term "new testament" also refers to the true human DNA. The expression, "remission of sin" refers to the

rectification of corruption, and involves the removal of the beliefs of Objectivity, Locality and Causality. The *Srimad Bhāgavadam* describes it as *thāpathraya vināśanam*. In other words, the Gospel offers itself to humanity as the antidote for corruption.

Jesus, now, utters something very mysterious: *"But I say unto you, I will not drink henceforth of this fruit of the vine, until that day when I drink it new with you in my Father's kingdom."* What exactly do these words imply? Spiritually, the expression, "fruit of this vine" refers to the Gospel, the "vine" being the DNA. The expression, "drink it new" exhorts us to understand the Gospel spiritually. Therefore, the spiritual implication of the verse is this: "You will never truly understand the Gospel until you read it with body-awareness and understand it spiritually."

"And when they had sung an hymn, they went out into the mount of Olives." In Revelation, we read about the "new song":

> *And they sang a new song saying, Worthy are you to take the scroll and to open its seals, for you were slain, and by your blood you* ransomed people for God from every tribe and language and nation *and you have made a kingdom and priests to our God, and they shall reign on the earth.*
> Revelation 5:9-10

The Mount of Olives is also known as the "mount of corruption." It represents this corrupt world. The enlightened Evites return to the world with the Gospel truths.

Now, let us come back to the issue of betrayal. Who betrayed Jesus? We know that the betrayal of Jesus refers to the corruption of the Gospel by a trusted associate. Perhaps, Judas Iscariot is just a mythical character that symbolizes the idea of corruption. Let us analyze the various accounts of the Last Supper in the New Testament, besides the Gospel of Matthew. We find mention of it in Mark 14:22-25, Luke 22:17-20, and 1 Corinthians 11:23-26. Let us look at them closely:

1. *"And as they did eat, Jesus took bread, and blessed, and break it, and gave to them, and said, Take, eat: this is my body. And he took the cup, and when he had given thanks, he gave it to them: and they all drank of it. And he said*

unto them, This is my blood of the new testament, which is shed for many. Verily I say unto you, I will drink no more of the fruit of the vine, until that day that I drink it new in the kingdom of God" (Mark 14:22-25)

2. *"And he took the cup, and gave thanks, and said, Take this and divide it among yourselves: For I say unto you, I will not drink of the fruit of the vine, until the kingdom of God shall come. And he took bread, and gave thanks, and brake it and gave unto them, saying, This is my body which is given for you: this do in remembrance of me. Likewise, also the cup after supper, saying, This cup is the new testament in my blood, which is shed for you." (Luke 22:17-20)*
3. *"For I have received of the Lord that which also I delivered unto you. That the Lord Jesus the same night in which he was betrayed took bread: And when he had given thanks, he brake it, and said, Take, eat: this is my body which is broken for you: this do in remembrance of me. After the same manner also he took the cup, when he had supped, saying, This cup is the new testament in my blood: this do ye, as oft as ye drink it, in remembrance of me." (1 Corinthians 1:23-26)*

The verses in Matthew and Mark are more or less identical. Luke's version is quite different from Matthew, and it is closer to Paul's version. (Incidentally, Luke was the physician and travel companion of Paul. Mark too was recruited by Paul and Barnabas.) However, Paul's version differs significantly from Matthew's. Let us analyze it:

1. Paul completely omits the part, *"But I say unto you, I will not drink henceforth of this fruit of vine, until that day when I drink it new with you in my Father's kingdom."*
2. Paul omits the part, *". . . which is shed for many for the remission of sins."* (Luke and Mark also)
3. Paul adds new words, *". . . this do ye, as oft as ye drink it, in remembrance of me."*
4. Paul says, *". . . when he had supped."* The expression Matthew uses is "he took the cup"; there is no mention of Jesus drinking it.

5. Paul says, *"This cup is the new testament,"* whereas Matthew says, *"For this my blood of the new testament."* Paul's focus is on the cup, but Matthew's focus is on what is within the cup.

> *Woe unto you, scribes and Pharisees, hypocrites! for ye make clean the outside of the cup and of the platter, but within they are full of extortion and excess.*
> Matthew 23:25

In a sense, Paul misrepresents the Gospel words and relegates a spiritual process into a mere ritual. Today, Judaized churches all over the world enact this ritual every Sunday in mockery of the Gospel. Paul, thus, lays the foundation of the corrupt Judaized Christian Church. Perhaps, Paul (Saul) of Tarsus is the betrayer, the Judas, who betrayed Jesus.

Paul's background raises serious questions. Paul, or Saul of Tarsus, variously referred to as the "Apostle Paul" or "Saint Paul" is, in effect, the founder of organized Christianity. According to the New Testament, Paul was a Pharisee (Acts 23:6). Before becoming a follower of Christianity, he zealously persecuted the newly-forming Church, trying to destroy it. Later, Paul claimed that he had a personal 'encounter' with the resurrected Jesus Christ on the road to Damascus, which, according to him, converted him from a persecutor of Christians to a champion of Christians. Paul was also a Roman citizen—a fact that afforded him a privileged legal status with respect to laws, property, and governance that were not available to the other disciples of Jesus. Paul's contemporaries viewed him with suspicion, and did not hold him in as high esteem as they held Peter and James. By the way, the Bible does not record Paul's death.

In order to firmly establish his position and dogma, Paul makes a declaration:

> *Take heed therefore unto yourselves, and to all the flock, over the which the Holy Ghost hath made you overseers, to feed the Church of God, which he hath purchased with his own blood. For I know this, that after my departing shall grievous wolves enter in among you, not sparing the flock.*
> Acts 28-29

Thus, Paul effectively preempts all future revelations of truth with his declaration, thereby shutting and sealing the Gospel. Now, anyone who tries to give a new interpretation to the Gospel, other than what he has preached, would be stamped a "grievous wolf" and a "heretic" and, therefore, dealt with suitably. Paul says:

> *For if he that cometh preacheth another Jesus, whom we have not preached, or if ye receive another spirit, which ye have not received, or another gospel, which ye have not accepted, ye might well bear with him.*
> 2 Corinthians 11:4

The Greek word for the expression, "to bear with" is *anechomai* (G430), which means to "hold oneself up against." Another Greek word for the same expression is *martyreō* (G3140). It is derived from the root *martyrs* (G3144), which means "martyr." Therefore, the expression, "ye might well bear with him" suggests "you may make him a martyr," or "you may kill him." Paul's declaration of 2 Corinthians 11:4 is the cry of an Inquisitor.

> *Woe unto you, scribes and Pharisees, hypocrites! for ye shut up the kingdom of heaven against men: for ye neither go in yourselves, neither suffer ye them that are entering to go in.*
> Matthew 23:13

MATTHEW 26:31-32

"Then saith Jesus unto them, All ye shall be offended because of me this night: for it is written, I will smite the shepherd, and the sheep of the flocks shall be scattered abroad. But after I am risen again, I will go before you into Galilee."

"All ye shall be offended because of me this night . . ." The literal and spiritual connotations of the different terms and expressions of the verse are given in the table below:

Term / Expression	Literal Meaning	Spiritual Meaning
"all ye"	The disciples	Spiritual interpreters of the Gospel
"offended"	Upset; embarrassed	Attacked; persecuted
"because of me"	Because of Jesus	Because of the truth
"this night"	Night of crucifixion	By this dark force

Therefore, the expression, "all ye shall be offended because of me this night" have the following connotations:

1. Literally: The disciples will be upset because of Jesus.
2. Spiritually: The spiritual interpreters of the Gospel will be attacked by the Judaized Christian Church.

Jesus quotes Prophet Zechariah (Zechariah 13:7) and says, "*. . . for it is written, I will smite the shepherd, and the sheep of the flock shall be scattered abroad.*" The literal and spiritual connotations of the different terms and expressions of the verse are given in the table below:

Expression	Literal Meaning	Spiritual Meaning
"for it is written"	It is written in the scriptures	It is the human destiny
"smite the shepherd"	The killing of Jesus	Corruption of the Gospel
"the flock shall be scattered abroad"	Physical dispersion of the disciples	The dispersion and loss of true Gospel interpretations

Therefore, the expression, "the sheep of the flock shall be scattered abroad" has the following connotations:

1. Literally: Jesus will be killed and the disciples will be scattered.
2. Spiritually: The true interpretations of the Gospel will disappear from the world.

Jesus says again, "*But after I am risen again, I will go before you into Galilee.*" The literal and spiritual connotations of the different terms and expressions of the verse are given in the table below:

Term / Expression	Literal Meaning	Spiritual Meaning
"I"	Jesus	The Gospel
"after I am risen again"	After the resurrection of Jesus	When the spiritual Gospel is revealed
"I will go before you into Galilee"	Jesus will appear to the disciples at Galilee	The spiritual Gospel will lead true Christians to the Father

Therefore, the statement, "But after I am risen again, I will go before you into Galilee" have the following connotations:

1. Literally: After resurrection Jesus will appear at Galilee
2. Spiritually: The revelation of the spiritual Gospel will lead humanity to the truth.

MATTHEW 26:33-35

"Peter answered and said unto him, "Though all men shall be offended because of thee, yet will I never be offended. Jesus said unto him, Verily I say unto thee, That this night, before the cock crow, thou shalt deny me thrice. Peter said unto him, Though I should die with thee, yet will I not deny thee. Likewise also said all the disciples."

In the previous section we saw Jesus warning the disciples: *"All ye shall be offended because of me this night."* Peter takes Jesus' words literally, and boasts to him, saying, *"Though all men shall be offended because of thee, yet will I never be offended."*

Jesus says to Peter, *"Verily I say unto thee, That this night, before the cock crow, thou shalt deny me thrice."* Spiritually, Jesus represents the Gospel (truth), and Peter represents a deluded Evite. The expression, "this night" refers to this world of delusion. The cock crow suggests the dawning of a new day. But, here, it signifies repentance—the urge to seek truth. Peter denying Jesus three times signifies man's descent into ignorance and delusion in separate three stages before he starts searching for the truth. The three stages of denials are:

1. 1st Denial: Denial of nature (*Separation* of Self into self and nature, and the *identification* of the Self with self.)
2. 2nd Denial: Denial of body (*Separation* of self into mind and body, and the *identification* of self with mind.)
3. 3rd Denial: Denial of evil (*Separation* of mind into good and evil, and the *identification* of mind with good.)

The diagram below depicts the three denials—the three stages of the *fall*:

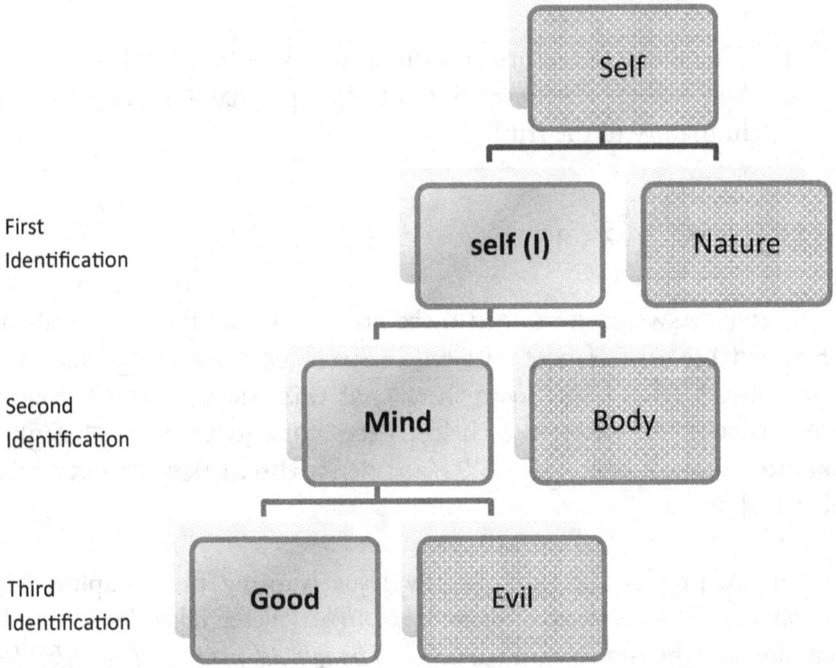

Man's first denial is the separation of self and nature; the second denial is the separation of mind and body; the third denial is the separation of good and evil. According to Jesus man has to first descend into the world of ignorance and delusion in three stages, before he can begin the ascension process and eventually realize the truth. Peter represents the mortal man (Mortal) who is at Stage 3. The *ascension* process is the reverse of the *fall*. It is a *climbing up* process. The ascension process is also known as *healing*.

Peter's words, *"Though I should die with thee, yet will I not deny thee"* reveals that he has not yet understood the spiritual meaning of Jesus' words.

Ascension Stage 1	Man reconciles good and evil. In other words, man embraces *non-duality.* He frees himself from the tyranny of morality and religion.
Ascension Stage 2	Man reconciles body and mind. In other words, man becomes *body-aware.*
Ascension Stage 3	Man reconciles self and nature. In other words, man becomes whole. He starts loving his neighbour as himself. In other words, he becomes non-violent (*ahimsa*).

MATTHEW 26:36-38

"Then cometh Jesus with them unto a place called Gethsemane, and saith unto the disciples, Sit ye here, while I go and pray yonder. And he took with him Peter and the two sons of Zebedee, and began to be sorrowful and very heavy. Then saith he unto them, My soul is exceeding sorrowful, even unto death: tarry ye here, and watch with me."

The name *Gethsemane* is derived from the Greek word *Gethsēmanē* (G1068), which means "an oil press." Gethsemane is an olive garden at the foot of the Mount of Olives. Spiritually, the Mount of Olives represents the Gospel. The olives are the Gospel words. Alternatively, the Mount of Olives represents the human body, and the olive fruits are the body cells. The olive oil is the spiritual meaning of the Gospel words. The oil-press at Gethsemane represents the human mind/ language (formalism) that extracts the spiritual meaning out of the Gospel words. Jesus and the disciples arriving Gethsemane symbolizes the Gospel interpretation process.

Jesus says to the disciples, *"Sit ye here, while I go and pray yonder."* Here, the disciples are the spiritual interpreters of the Gospel. The Hebrew word for *pray* is *siah* (H7878), which means "to meditate." Meditating on the Gospel can be compared to the oil-pressing process in which the olive fruits are crushed, pulverized, pressed in the oil-press, and the oil extracted out of it. Alternatively, the human body cells are the olive fruits; the mind is the oil-press; and body-awareness is the oil extracted.

Jesus distances himself from the disciples to pray in solitude. The word *yonder* means "there," and it signifies the separation between the meditative state and the normal waking state. In other words, the spiritual interpreter gets into a special frame of mind that is separate from the normal waking state.

Jesus takes with him Peter, James and John to the place of prayer. Physically, Peter, James and John represent body sensations, emotions, and feelings respectively of the Gospel interpreter. But, spiritually, these names have different connotation. Peter's real name is *šîmōn*, which means "He who has heard." Spiritually, the name Simon (Peter) denotes intuition. The Greek equivalent of James is *Iakōbos* (G2385), which means "the supplanter." Spiritually, the name James denotes imagination. The Hebrew equivalent of John is *yōhānān* (H3110), which means "Graced by YHWH." Spiritually, the name John denotes self-awareness, or faith. Therefore, the name Peter, James, and John represents the physical and mental faculties required for the Gospel interpreter.

Jesus says to the disciples, *"My soul is exceeding sorrowful, even unto death: tarry ye here, and watch with me."* The term *soul* means body-awareness, and the word *sorrowful* suggests physical and mental pain. The Sanskrit word for *pain* is *vēdana. Vēdana* is also a Buddhist term, which means "feeling" or "sensation." Therefore, what Jesus (the Meditator) is really saying is this: "I can acutely feel my body sensations and feelings."

The Gospel reveals to us the secret of mediation, both meditating on the Self and meditating on the Gospel. And the secret is contained in the utterance: *"Tarry ye here, and watch with me."* The word *tarry* means "to linger," or "to remain." Therefore, the first instruction says, "Linger on the words," or "Remain motionless." The second instruction, "watch with me" says, "Be aware of the body." It suggests that meditation essentially involves two steps:

Steps	Meditating on the Self	Meditating on the Gospel
1. "Tarry ye here"	Remain still	Linger on the words
2. "Watch with me"	Be aware of the body	Be aware of the body

Jesus' prayer, in many respects, resembles Vipāssana meditation. *Vipāssana* (Pāli) or *Vipaśyana* (Sanskrit) means "clear seeing." Vipāssana, in essence, is the establishment of *mindfulness* or body-awareness. In Vipāssana meditation one tries to be intensely mindful of body sensations and feelings (*vēdana*). Although the steps in Vipāssana seem too easy at the outset, the actual process can be very demanding.

> *Vēdana is born out of contact between a sense organ and its corresponding object. The contact is spontaneous and natural. We know that when there is a living body, there is breath and when there is mind, there is thought. The arising of breath in the body and the arising of thought in the mind can only be known through vēdana. Therefore, vēdana is inseparable from the body and mind and one can know oneself through vēdana. Vēdana are of three kinds—pleasant, unpleasant and neutral. If we do not see its true nature, pleasant vēdana generates craving, unpleasant vēdana generates aversion and neutral vēdana generates ignorance, then all the three kinds of feelings in turn produce greed, hatred, and delusion. These products are the root cause of human suffering.*
>
> G. C. Banerjee, Vipassana Research Institute

An important point in meditation is that you have to go *yonder* to mediate. It suggests detachment from the world (of relationships).

MATTHEW 26:39

"And he went a little further, and fell on his face, and prayed, saying, O my Father, if it be possible, let this cup pass from me: nevertheless not as I will, but as thou wilt."

Here, the Gospel interpreter faces a major challenge in his work and wants to quit the endeavor. In despair, he prays to his Self for help, and finds a new resolve to continue the work.

Spiritually, the expression, "he went a little further" suggests that the Gospel interpreter has been meditating on the Gospel for some considerable amount of time. Alternatively, it could also imply that the interpreter exceeded the limits of spiritual interpretation. The expression, "falling on the face" suggests a temporary setback. Half-way through the interpretation process the interpreter finds that his interpretation is not coming together cogently and meaningfully and, therefore, feels frustration. He regrets having ventured on the project. In distress he prays to his Self: *"O my Father, if it be possible, let this cup pass from me."* Spiritually, the expression, "this cup" refers to the Gospel interpretation work. But, physically, it refers to the body. As soon the interpreter prays to the Self, help arrives. All of a sudden the interpreter becomes aware of his greater mission and, therefore, says, *"Not my will, but thy will be done."*

MATTHEW 26:40-41

"And he cometh unto the disciples, and findeth them asleep, and saith unto Peter, What, could ye not watch with me one hour? Watch and pray, that ye enter not into temptation: the spirit indeed is willing, but the flesh is weak."

The Greek word for *watch* is *grēgoreō* (G1127), which means "to keep awake," both literally and figuratively. In other words, it means "to be vigilant." The word *grēgoreō* is derived from the root word *egeirō* (1453), which means "to collect one's faculties." Here, Peter, James and John represent those faculties. Physically, they represent the body sensations, emotions, and feelings. But, mentally, they represent intuition, imagination, and faith.

Before Jesus went to pray, he had specifically instructed the disciples to remain awake and vigilant. But, when he returns to them after an hour, he finds them asleep. In other words, the Gospel interpreter loses body-awareness shortly after he starts the Gospel interpretation work, and slips into delusion. Then he becomes aware that he had lost his body-awareness for a period.

Here, the disciples are mentally awake, but spiritually (bodily) asleep. Perhaps, the disciples misunderstood Jesus' instructions because they were ignorant of the spiritual principle that says, "To be *mentally* awake means to be *bodily* asleep; to be *mentally* asleep means to be *bodily* awake."

Jesus rebukes the 'sleepy' disciples: *"What, could ye not watch with me one hour?"* Perhaps, the specified duration of a Gospel interpretation session is one hour. Incidentally, the specified duration of a proper Vipāssana meditation session is one hour. But, the interpreter falls short of this requirement; he is incapable of staying bodily (spiritually) awake even for one hour.

Jesus says to the disciples, *"Watch and pray, that ye enter not into temptation."* Here, Jesus teaches the disciples how to fight temptation. The Greek word for *temptation* is *peirasmos* (G3976), which means "experience of evil." The word *temptation* suggests duality, which is the 'spell' cast by the Serpent. Here, the Serpent is the literal scripture. In other words, the Gospel interpreter has to resist the temptation to rely on the literal scripture for truth. And the weapons to fight 'temptation' is "watching and praying." When you are aware of your body, you are in contact with reality. In that state of body-awareness, delusion cannot affect you. Body-aware meditation (Vipassana meditation) is the only known antidote against the Serpent's spell. The Gospel has taught us the prayer against temptation:

> *And lead us not into temptation, but deliver us from evil . . .*
> Matthew 6:13

Jesus, then, utters something mysterious: *"The spirit is willing, but the flesh is weak."* Literally, the term *spirit* refers to the mind, and *flesh* refers to the body. But, spiritually, the term *spirit* refers to the body, and *flesh* refers to the mind. The reason is that we live in an upside-down world—an illusory world—that appears like reality but is not reality. Therefore, what the above verse implies is this: "The body is ready to understand the truth, but the mind is not ready to listen to truth." The reason why the mind is not ready to listen to the truth is that it is subjected to temptation.

According to the Buddhist philosophy, enlightenment (*mōkṣa*) has two aspects:

1. Compassion
2. Devotion

Compassion is Self's love for self, whereas devotion is self's awe of the Self. Compassion is body's love for the mind, whereas devotion is mind's fear of the body. For body-awareness to happen, both compassion and devotion have to work in tandem. Here, the Gospel uses the term *spirit* for the *Self* and the term *flesh* for *self.* Therefore, the implications of the statement, "*. . . the spirit is willing, but the flesh is weak*" are the following:

1. "The body is compassionate, but the mind lacks devotion."
2. "The body offers enlightenment, but the mind is not listening to it."
3. "The body offers salvation, but the mind does not want freedom."

Apostle John sums it up eloquently:

> *For God so loved the world, that he gave his only begotten Son that whosoever believeth in him should not perish but have everlasting life.*
> John3:16

MATTHEW 26:42-46

"He went away again the second time, and prayed, saying, O my Father, if this cup may not pass away from me, except I drink it, thy will be done. And he came and found them asleep again: for their eyes were heavy. And he left them, and went away again, and prayed the third time, saying the same words. Then cometh he to his disciples, and saith unto them, Sleep on now, and take your rest: behold, the hour is at hand, and the Son of man is betrayed into the hands of sinners. Rise, let us be going: behold, he is at hand that doth betray me."

The disciples take Jesus' instruction *"Tarry ye here, and watch with me"* literally and they miserably fail to keep 'vigil while Jesus was praying, in spite of repeated admonitions. The sequence of events that ensue reveals that Jesus' (Gospel's) betrayal happened because the disciples (Christians/Gospel interpreters) did not "watch and pray." The expression, "watch and pray" has the following implications:

1. Personal level: To meditate
2. Social level: To remain vigilant
3. Spiritual level: To be body-aware

Let us analyze the sequence of events:

	Jesus	Disciples
1	Jesus prays, *"O my Father, if it be possible, let this cup pass from me"*	Disciples found sleeping. Jesus rebukes them: *"What, could ye not watch with me one hour?"*
2	Jesus prays, *"O my Father, if this cup may not pass away from me, except I drink it, thy will be done."*	Disciples found sleeping. Jesus says nothing.
3	Jesus prays, *"O my Father, if this cup may not pass away from me, except I drink it, thy will be done."*	Disciples found sleeping. Jesus says, *"Sleep on now, and take your rest: behold, the hour is at hand, and the Son of man is betrayed into the hands of sinners. Rise, let us be going: behold, he is at hand that doth betray me."*

The term *Jesus* has different connotations at different levels:

1. Personal level: Man
2. Social level: Humanity
3. Spiritual level: The Gospel

The betrayal of Jesus allegorically tells us how and why corruption (sin) got control over the world. The betrayal episode allegorically tells us why corruption is so pervasive in our personal, social, and spiritual spheres:

1. Personal level: The *individual* got corrupted because he did *not meditate.*
2. Social level: The *society* got corrupted because individuals were *not vigilant.*
3. Spiritual level: *Gospel message* got corrupted because Christians yielded to the 'temptation' (literal scripture).

In desperation, Jesus says to the disciples *"Sleep on now, and take your rest: behold, the hour is at hand, and the Son of man is betrayed into the hands of sinners."* The worst has already happened; the only way to reverse the corruption is to end the world. Who betrayed Jesus? The finger points squarely at Judas. But, if the disciples had "watched and prayed," the betrayal, perhaps, would not have happened. The term "sinners", in this context, refers to the Scribes and Pharisees.

The expression, "the Son of man is betrayed into the hands of sinners" have the following connotations:

1. Personal level: The human DNA got corrupted by the viruses.
2. Social level: The human beings got corrupted by the Adamites.
3. Spiritual level: The Gospel meaning got corrupted by the Judeo-Christian Church.

MATTHEW 26:47-50

"And while he yet spake, lo, Judas, one of the twelve, came, and with him a great multitude with swords and staves, from the chief priests and elders of the people. Now he that betrayed him gave them a sign, saying, Whomsoever I shall kiss, that same is he: hold him fast. And forthwith he came to Jesus, and said, Hail, master; and kissed him. And Jesus said unto him, Friend, wherefore art thou come? Then came they, and laid hands on Jesus, and took him."

There is something logically strange about the betrayal incident. What is Judas' real role in the betrayal incident? If you say his role is to point out Jesus to the authorities, then the counter-argument is that Jesus is not a stranger to the people of Israel or the authorities. In fact, the very reason for his arrest is that he was too famous (or infamous).

Perhaps, you may say that his role is only to point out where Jesus is hiding. But then, Jesus is not hiding at all; he is very much in the open. Somehow, the act of Judas befuddles us because he does not betray Jesus covertly; he does it in the open. Even Judas' utterance to the arresting contingent is intriguing: *"Whomsoever I shall kiss, that same is he: hold him fast."* The Greek word for *kiss* is *phileō* (G5368), which means "to be a friend to." The act of kissing shows intimacy and affection. Therefore, what Judas is really saying is this: "My enemy thinks I am his friend." Judas' words expose his evil and parasitic nature. He represents 'something' as intrinsically evil as the virus. The Gospel refers to *Judas* not as a disciple, but as "one of the twelve." The Greek word for *twelve* is *dōdeka* (G1427), which means "two and ten." Spiritually, the term *twelve* refers to the Israelites.

The truth is that Judas is not a physical person, just as Jesus is not a physical person. Spiritually, Judas symbolizes the *enemy* of true Christians. And it was this enemy that betrayed the Gospel into the hands of Jews and Romans (Judeo-Christian Church). The Christians got '*tempted*' by the brilliance of his sophism known as *theology*. In fact, they were not "watching and praying."

Jesus asks Judas, *"Friend, wherefore art thou come?"* Literally interpreted, the statement means, "Friend, why are you here." But, we should not forget that neither Jesus nor Judas is a physical person; instead, they represent the principles of good and evil respectively. Therefore, the question really is this: "For what purpose are you studying the Gospel—to understand the truth or to corrupt it?"

What motivated Judas to betray Jesus—money, frustration, hatred, or ideology? Or, did he do it simply because of his fundamentally evil nature? The latter seems to be the case. Whatever evil does is evil!

MATTHEW 26: 51-54

"And, behold, one of them which were with Jesus stretched out his hand, and drew his sword, and struck a servant of the high priest's, and smote off his ear. Then said Jesus unto him, Put up again thy sword into his place: for all they that take the sword shall perish with the sword. Thinkest thou that I cannot now pray to my Father, and he shall presently give me more than twelve *legions of angels? But how then shall scriptures be fulfilled, that thus it must be?"*

It is generally believed that it was Peter who smote the servant's ear. But it does not make sense because neither Jesus nor the disciples are physical persons. Spiritually, Jesus praying in Gethsemane with the three disciples keeping vigil symbolizes the Gospel interpretation process.

In this episode, we see Jesus rebuking the offending disciple for his indiscretion: *"Put up again thy sword into his place: for all they that take the sword shall perish with the sword."* The Greek word for *sword* is *machaira* (G3162), which, among other things, means "judicial punishment." The word *sword* implies *machination*. The Hebrew word for *sword* is *hereb* (H2719), which means "a cutting instrument," for its destructive effect. Spiritually, the word *sword* refers to a "swearword," or "curse." A *curse* is a "verbal machination" (spell) that creates confusion in people. In other words, a curse is a sword that cut and partitions the psyche of the receiver. In fact, the literal scripture contains a number of such spells. Therefore, this Gospel episode is not talking about a physical disciple literally cutting the ear of a physical soldier, but it is referring to the tendency of some authors to plant magic formulas or spells in their books that can "hex" readers. The Gospel strictly prohibits such evil machinations.

Jesus says to the offending disciple, *"Thinkest thou that I cannot now pray to my Father, and he shall presently give me more than twelve legions of angels? But how then shall scriptures be fulfilled, that thus it must be?"* Spiritually, the term *Father* refers to the Self and *Jesus* refers to the true human DNA, or the Gospel. An *angel* is a messenger of God. Spiritually, the term *God* refers to the human DNA and the term *angel* refers to the genes in the human DNA. Therefore, the expression, "legion of angels" refers to a strand of DNA. The "twelve legions of angels" that the Gospel is referring to is the 12-strand DNA, or the perfect human DNA. The term "scriptures" refers to man's present 2-strand DNA. The Greek word for *fulfill* is *plēroō* (G4137), which means "to make perfect." Therefore what the Gospel is saying is this: "The purpose of human incarnations is to perfect the DNA through continual evolution. And, there is no short-cut to perfection."

MATTHEW 26: 55-56

"In that same hour said Jesus to the multitudes, Are ye come out as against a thief with swords and staves for to take me? I sat daily with you teaching in the temple, and ye laid no hold on me. But all this was done, that the scriptures of the prophets might be fulfilled. Then all the disciples forsook him, and fled."

Jesus says to the Jews who come to apprehend him, *"Are ye come out as against a thief with swords and staves for to take me? I sat daily with you teaching in the temple, and ye laid no hold on me."* Here, Jesus represents the body, and the *multitudes* represent the mind. Therefore, Jesus talking to the multitudes signifies the communication between body and mind, which is called inner voice. The Greek word for *thief* is *lēstēs* (G3027), which means "one who plunders." To *plunder* means to take wrongfully, or to despoil. Spiritually, the term *thief* refers to one who reads the Gospel casually, without body-awareness. Similarly, the expression, "swords and staves" refers to theology. Therefore, the spiritual implication of the verse it this: "Why do understand the Gospel wrongfully with your false theologies? The truth is present in you, yet you do not perceive it." Alternatively, the dialogue between Jesus and the multitudes mirror the dialogue between the *Self* and the *self* at the moment of death. Only at death does man realise the true nature of mind and body.

Just as the multitudes capture and kill Jesus, the truth is captured and murdered by mind (formalism). The crucifixion of Jesus by the Jews and Romans is an allegory depicting the capturing and 'killing' of truth by mind.

Jesus, then, says, *"But all this was done, that the scriptures of the prophets might be fulfilled."* Spiritually, the expression, "scriptures of the prophets" refers to the human DNA. According to the Gospel, the capture of truth by the mind, its death, and resurrection are all part of human evolution process. Alternatively, the expression, "scriptures of the prophets" refers to the Gospel. Therefore, the fulfillment of the "scriptures of the prophets" refers to the spiritual interpretation of the Gospel.

The human DNA is the *script of life*, the scripture, or the destiny of man. According to Jesus, a man's destiny is already scripted (written) and handed over to him in the form of scripture. Life simply plays out according to that script in space and time. It is known as "the fulfilling of the scriptures." In that sense, all of us are fulfilling the scripture. Here, the Gospel emphasizes the inevitability of the 'play.'

"Then all the disciples forsook him, and fled." Man has to face death alone. As death approaches, relationships fade off one by one and, in the end, man truly becomes an individual.

MATTHEW 26: 57-64

"And they that had laid hold on Jesus led him away to Caiaphas the high priest, where the scribes and the elders were assembled. But Peter followed him afar off unto the high priest's palace, and went in, and sat with the servants, to see the end. Now the chief priests, and elders, and all the council, sought false witness against Jesus, to put him to death; But found none: yea, though many false witnesses came, yet found they none. At the last came two false witnesses, And said, This fellow said, I am able to destroy the temple of God, and to build it in three days. And the high priest arose, and said unto him, Answerest thou nothing? what is it which these witness against thee? But Jesus held his peace. And the high priest answered and said unto him, I adjure thee by the living God, that thou tell us whether thou be the Christ, the Son of God. Jesus saith unto them, Thou hast said: nevertheless I say unto you, Hereafter shall ye see the Son of man sitting on the right hand of power, and coming in the clouds of heaven."

"And they that had laid hold on Jesus led him away to Caiaphas the high priest, where the scribes and the elders were assembled." Caiaphas was appointed high priest by the Romans, by the Procurator Valerius Gratus under Tiberius in 18 A.D. The name, *Caiaphas* (G2533) means "a rock that hollows itself out" or "a dell." It was Caiaphas who earlier suggested a human ritual sacrifice as 'expedient' for Jews:

> *And one of them, Caiaphas, being high priest that year, said to them, you know nothing at all, nor do you consider that it is*

> *expedient for us that one man should die for the people, and not that the whole nation should perish.*
> John 11:49-50

"But Peter followed him afar off unto the high priest's palace, and went in, and sat with the servants, to see the end." According to the Gospel, Peter followed Jesus "to see the end." What does the word *end* imply here—end of the episode or end of Jesus? The Gospel uses the Greek word *telos* (G5056), which means "conclusion," or "to set out for a definite point or goal." The Hebrew equivalent of *telos* is *gāmar* (H1584), which means "to end" (in the sense of *completion* or *failure*.) The word *gāmar* is used only once in the entire Bible (Psalms 7:9). The use of the word *end* in this context is deeply mysterious. Spiritually, the disciples of Jesus denote pagan mythologies that came together to create the syncretistic Gospel. Perhaps, Peter represents Roman mythology. The Romans usually treated their traditional narratives as historical, even when these have miraculous or supernatural elements. The Roman mythological stories are often concerned with politics and or morality, and how an individual's personal integrity relates to his or her responsibility to the community or the Roman state. Perhaps, it is no coincidence that the organized Christian Church too treats the Gospel the same way the Romans treated their mythology.

"Now the chief priests, and elders, and all the council, sought false witness against Jesus, to put him to death; But found none: yea, though many false witnesses came, yet found they none": The chief priest, the elders and the council represent the Jewish religion, Jewish judiciary, and Jewish executive respectively. Together, they comprise the Jewish theocratic establishment. According to the Gospel, the Establishment sought *false* witnesses to testify against the Gospel. Spiritually, the term *false witness* refers to formal systems, or entities that operate on formal systems, such as artificial intelligence entities (humanoids). These are axiomatic systems which are based on a set of axioms and a set of rules. The statements of these axiomatic systems are merely theorems derived from the axioms using the set of rules. Since the axioms themselves do not have any truth in them, the theorems derived by these systems also do not have any intrinsic truth.

"At the last came two false witnesses, And said, This fellow said, I am able to destroy the temple of God, and to build it in three days." But, the Gospel does not reveal who these two "false witnesses" are, except

that they volunteered to testify against Jesus. Perhaps, those two false witnesses are logic and number theory (*Gematria*). Perhaps, the Gospel is telling us allegorically that the Establishment checked the veracity of the Gospel using logic and number theory.

Gematria is an Assyro-Babylonian system of numerology later adopted by the Jews which assigns numerical value to a word or phrase, in the belief that words or phrases with identical numerical values bear some relation to each other, or bear some relation to the number itself as it may apply to a person's age, the calendar year, or the like. Although the term *Gematria* is Hebrew, it might have originated from Greek *geōmetriā* (geometry). However, some scholars argue that the word is derived from Greek *grammateia*.

Essentially, a false witness is one who denies the body. He is not body-aware. An 'unsuccessful' false witness is called a Mortal. He has not completely lost touch with body, but has some body-awareness. But, a successful false witness is called a *humanoid*. He totally lacks body-awareness. The false witness says, "This fellow said, I am able to destroy the temple of God, and build it in three days." The statement exposes theirs as well as the Establishment's fear and aversion of the following:

1. Destruction of the temple of God (Death)
2. Rebuilding the temple in three days (Reincarnation)

In other words, the humanoids fear death because they know that they have no life after death.

"And the high priest arose, and said unto him, Answerest thou nothing? what is it which these witness against thee? But Jesus held his peace. And the high priest answered and said unto him, I adjure thee by the living God, that thou tell us whether thou be the Christ, the Son of God." The high priest asks Jesus to answer the charge raised by the false witnesses. But Jesus does not respond. Apparently, Jesus does not want to respond to statements made by humanoids (formal systems). Exasperated, the high priest says, "I adjure thee by the living God that thou tell us whether thou be Christ, the Son of God." Spiritually, the expression "living God" means "true human DNA," or the Gospel. The word, *adjure* means "to ask for or request earnestly." In other words, the high priest inadvertently accepts the truth: "*Jesus is the Christ, the Son of God*," or, "*Human being is the son of God.*" Now, Jesus responds. Truth

responds only to truth, but not to untruth. Jesus simply says, *"Thou hast said,"* which means, "You have spoken the truth."

Jesus then says, *". . . nevertheless I say unto you, Hereafter shall ye see the Son of man sitting on the right hand of power, and coming in the clouds of heaven."* Spiritually, the term "Son of man" means humanity; the expression, "right hand of power" means "the one who exercises authority." The Gospel, thus, predicts the end of the Satanic Politico-Religious Establishment.

MATTHEW 26: 65-68

"Then the high priest rent his clothes, saying, He hath spoken blasphemy; what further need have we of witnesses? behold, now ye have heard his blasphemy. What think ye? They answered and said, He is guilty of death. Then did they spit in his face, and buffeted him; and others smote him with the palms of their hands, Saying, Prophesy unto us, thou Christ, Who is he that smote thee?"

Why does the high priest get so infuriated to say, *"He hath spoken blasphemy"*? What did Jesus say to offend the high priest so much? This is what Jesus said: *". . . nevertheless I say unto you, Hereafter shall ye see the Son of man sitting on the right hand of power, and coming in the clouds of heaven."* Jesus does not openly declare that he is the Christ; but, he says *Son of man* is the Christ. The term *man* refers to the human species, or humanity; therefore, the expression, "son of man" refers to a human individual. Alternatively, the expression, "Son of man" refers to the human DNA, or the Gospel. In other words, Jesus foretells the liberation of humanity from the captivity of the Serpent. It is this declaration that infuriates the high priest. He finds it blasphemous.

Given below is a comparison between what Jewish Establishment did to Jesus and what the Politico-Religious Establishment does to humanity:

What The Jewish Politico-Religious Establishment Did To Jesus	**What The Politico-Religious System (Serpent) Does To Humanity**
Spits on Jesus' face	Treats human individuals as mere members of political parties or members (flocks) of religions
Buffets Jesus around	Harasses individuals with oppressive rules
Smites Jesus with the palm of their hands, saying, *"Prophesy unto us, thou Christ, who is he that smote thee?"*	Secretly causes damage or loss to human life and property

MATTHEW 26: 69-75

"Now Peter sat without in the palace: and a damsel came unto him, saying, Thou also wast with Jesus of Galilee. But he denied before them all, saying, I know not what thou sayest. And when he was gone out into the porch, another maid saw him, and said unto them that were there, This fellow was also with Jesus of Nazareth. And again he denied with an oath, I do not know the man. And after a while came unto him they that stood by, and said to Peter, Surely thou also art one of them; for thy speech bewrayeth thee. Then began he to curse and swear, saying, I know not the man. And immediately the cock crew. And Peter remembered the word of Jesus, which said unto him, Before the cock crow, thou shalt deny me thrice. And he went out, and wept bitterly."

Three different people confront Peter at three different occasions and make three separate accusations regarding his association with Jesus. Each time, Peter vehemently denies his link with Jesus. Let us analyze the sequence of events:

Event	Person confronting Peter	The Accusation	Peter's Response
1	Damsel (directly)	*"Thou also wast with Jesus of Galilee."*	*"I know not what thou sayest."*
2	Maid (indirectly)	*"This fellow was also with Jesus of Nazareth."*	*"I do not know the man."*
3	Bystanders (directly)	*"Surely, thou also art one of them; for thy speech bewrayeth thee."*	*"I know not the man."* (Curses and swears)

Spiritually, Peter represents the Gospel interpretation that presents Jesus as a historical character, that too, a Jew. The three characters that confront Peter actually question this assumption. Spiritually, the three characters that confront Peter connote the following:

1. The damsel represents Peter's body (*śarīra*)
2. The maid ('another' damsel) represents Peter's reason (*buddhi*)
3. The bystanders represent Peter's mind (*manas*)

Three times the Self confronts Peter with truth; and each time Peter denies it out of fear or ignorance. The first damsel says to Peter, *"Thou also wast with Jesus of Galilee."* Galilee is a large region in northern Israel which overlaps with much of the administrative North District and Haifa District of the country. The region's Israelite name is from the Hebrew root *galil* (H1551), which means "ring" or "circle." The region is known in the Old Testament as *galil goyim* (Isaiah 9:1) or "Galilee of the non-Jewish people." Galilee is home to a large Gentile population. The name *Galilee* is also linked to the Hebrew name *Gilgal*, which means "wheel" or "circle". After the crossing of the Jordan, Joshua orders that 12 stones be set up, for each of the 12 tribes, at a place called Gilgal. An inhabitant of Galilee is known as a *Galilean*, which spiritually, means "human being" or Mortal.

Therefore, the damsel's comment may be interpreted as follows:

1. Literally: "You belong to the *circle* of Jesus."
2. Spiritually: "Your body is Jesus."

Peter denies the charge and says, *"I know not what thou sayest."* Peter's response may be interpreted as follows:

1. Literally: "I do not understand what you are talking about."
2. Spiritually: "I am not body-aware."

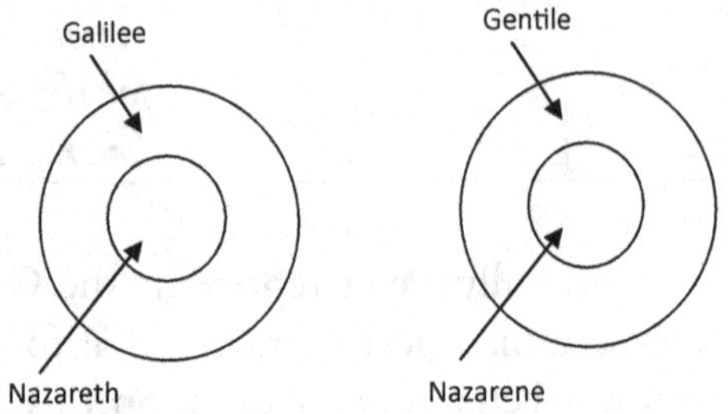

Another damsel, a maid, pointing at Peter, says to the by-standers, *"This fellow was also with Jesus of Nazareth." Nazareth* or *an-Nasiriyyah* is the largest city in the North District of Israel. Nazareth is known as the Gentile capital of Israel. The present population is made up predominantly of Arab citizens of Israel, almost all of whom are either Muslim (69%) or Christian (30.9%). An inhabitant of Nazareth who follows Jesus is known as *Nazarene,* which spiritually, means "self-aware human being" or Evite.

Therefore, maid's comment may be interpreted as follows:

1. Literally: "You are a follower of Jesus the Nazarene."
2. Spiritually: "You are a Nazarene" or "You are an Evite."

Again, Peter denies the charge, saying, *"I do not know the man."* Spiritually, the term *man* refers to the Self. Peter's response may be interpreted as follows:

1. Literally: "I do not know Jesus."
2. Spiritually: "I am not self-aware."

At last, the by-standers confront Peter and say, *"Surely, thou also art one of them; for thy speech bewrayeth thee."* Here, the Gospel gives us the test of a person's true identity—the test of 'speech'. The expression, "thy speech bewrayeth thee" literally means "your accent shows who you are." But, spiritually, it means, "Your blood reveals who you are."

The implied message is this: The blood can reveal whether a person is an Adamite, an Evite, or a Mortal.

The by-standers' comment may be interpreted as follows:

1. Literally: "You are a Nazarene; your accent reveals it."
2. Spiritually: "You are an Evite; your blood reveals it."

"Then began he to curse and swear, saying, I know not the man." Peter now starts acting like an Adamite, cursing and swearing, in order to hide his true self. Peter again denies the charge leveled against him, saying, "I know not the man." (In the previous occasion he said, "I do not know the man."). Peter's response may be interpreted as follows:

1. Literally: "I do not know Jesus."
2. Spiritually: "I do not know myself."

"And immediately the cock crew. And Peter remembered the word of Jesus, which said unto him, Before the cock crow, thou shalt deny me thrice. And he went out, and wept bitterly." The "cock crow" heralds the dawn of a new day. Spiritually, it refers to death. Only at death does man realizes that he has wasted a whole lifetime in self-denial; but then, it is now too late to do anything. The Gospel says, *"And he went out, and wept bitterly."*

Spiritually, Peter represents the *true* church. This episode allegorically, describes the fall of the true church because of self-denial. Here, the self-denial refers to the denial of truth—denying that the true human being himself is the Jesus Christ. Because it denied itself, it got thrown out and an imposter church took over its place. But, Peter rejoins Jesus after resurrection, which means that the spiritual revelation of the Gospel will make the true church (human beings) realize the truth.

CHAPTER 27

This is Jesus The King of The Jews

MATTHEW 27:1-2

"When the morning was come, all the chief priests and elders of the people took counsel against Jesus to put him to death: And when they had bound him, they led him away, and delivered him to Pontius Pilate the governor."

Although the Jewish council decided to kill Jesus on charges of blasphemy, it did not want to do it on its own because of Jesus' popularity among the people. The high priests, therefore, decide to hand over the dirty job to the Romans—the political wing of the Establishment. Accordingly, the Council charges Jesus of fomenting rebellion against the Roman King, rather than charging him for blasphemy. It was this strategy that the Council was conspiring all night.

What is *blasphemy*? The Greek word for *blasphemy* is *blasphēmia* (G988), which means "vilification," especially against God. But, the Hebrew word for *blapheme* is *bārak* (H1288), which means "to curse God or King," or "treason." In theology, blasphemy is the crime of assuming to self (Self) the rights and qualities of God. However, the hidden meaning of blasphemy is "challenging religion"—placing the individual equal to or above religion. *Rebellion*, on the other hand, is challenging the ruler—placing the individual equal to or above the ruler. In both blasphemy and rebellion, there is real or imagined challenge by the individual to Establishment's authority.

The table below shows the significance of the condemnation of Jesus by the Jewish council and the judgment by the Roman government from physical, mental, social and spiritual perspectives.

Jesus	**The meaning of the condemnation of Jesus by the Jewish Council (represented by Caiaphas)**	**The meaning of the judgment by the Roman Government (represented by Pontius Pilate)**
Body	Viral infection	Disease and death
Mind	False assumptions of Objectivity, Locality, and Causality	Ignorance and delusion
Humanity	Mixing of humanoids with humans	Corruption and decadence
Gospel	Judaic influence in Gospel interpretation	Loss of true meaning

The Jewish Council frame false charges on Jesus and Pontius Pilate gives his judgment on the basis of those charges. If Jesus represents the human body, then the condemnation of Jesus by the Jewish Council refers to the condemnation of the human body, and Pontius Pilate's judgment represents disease and death. If Jesus represents the human mind, then the condemnation of Jesus by the Jewish Council refers to the false beliefs of Objectivity, Locality, and Causality, and Pontius Pilate's judgment represents ignorance and delusion. If Jesus represents human society, then the condemnation of Jesus by the Jewish Council refers to the intermixing of humanoids with humans, and Pontius Pilate's judgment represents corruption and decadence. If Jesus represents the Gospel, then the condemnation of Jesus by the Jewish Council refers to the Judaic influence in Gospel interpretation, and Pontius Pilate's judgment represents the death of truth.

MATTHEW 27:3-10

"Then Judas, which had betrayed him, when he saw that he was condemned, repented himself, and brought again the thirty pieces of silver to the chief priests and elders, Saying, I have sinned in that I have betrayed the innocent blood. And they said, What is that to us? see thou to that. And he cast down the pieces of silver in the temple, and departed, and went and hanged himself. And the chief priests took the silver pieces, and said, It is not lawful for to put them into the treasury, because it is the price of blood. And they took counsel, and bought with them the potter's field, to bury strangers in. Wherefore that field was called, The field of blood, unto this day. Then was fulfilled that which was spoken by Jeremy the prophet, saying, And they took the thirty pieces of silver, the price of him that was valued, whom they of the children of Israel did value; And gave them for the potter's field, as the Lord appointed me."

"Then Judas, which had betrayed him, when he saw that he was condemned, repented himself, and brought again the thirty pieces of silver to the chief priests and elders, Saying, I have sinned in that I have betrayed the innocent blood." It is not clear from the Gospel why Judas betrays Jesus. Obviously, he is not doing it for the money because he repents afterwards. Perhaps another entity possesses Judas and uses him as an instrument. Spiritually, Judas represents a dualistic religion and its literal scripture.

Seeing the disastrous consequences of his action, Judas repents and comes back to the high priests and elders with the "blood money" and returns it saying, *"I have sinned in that I have betrayed the innocent blood."* The expression, "innocent blood," literally means "blood of a child"; but spiritually, it means "blood of a true human being." *Innocence* is a property of true human blood. Physically, *innocent blood* is blood free of blemishes (antigens). Alternatively, "innocent blood" refers to the spiritual meaning of the Gospel.

Betraying innocent blood may also suggest genetic manipulation of human DNA. Anyone who allows his or others' body (or DNA) to be corrupted is betraying innocent blood. Alternatively, betraying innocent blood also refers to the altering of the Gospel text or its meaning.

"Then was fulfilled that which was spoken by Jeremy the prophet, saying, And they took the thirty pieces of silver, the price of him that was valued, whom they of the children of Israel did value; And gave them for the potter's field, as the Lord appointed me." What does the "thirty pieces

of silver" signify? According to the Jewish Law, thirty pieces of silver is the price of a slave (manservant or maidservant).

> *If the ox shall push a manservant or a maidservant; he shall give unto their master thirty shekels of silver, and the ox shall be stoned.*
> Exodus 21:32

The "potter's field" or common grave is a place for the burial of unknown or indigent people (Gentiles). It refers to a field used for the extraction of potter's clay, which is useless for agriculture but used as a burial site. The site is traditionally known as *Akeldama*. The Gospel draws on earlier Biblical reference to potter's field:

> *And I said unto them, If ye think good, give me my price; and if not, forbear. So they weighed for my price thirty pieces of silver. And the LORD said unto me, Cast it unto the potter: a goodly price that I was prised at of them. And I took the thirty pieces of silver, and cast them to the potter in the house of the LORD.*
> Zechariah 11:12-13

Prophet Jeremiah also speaks of a "potter's field" in the Valley of Hinnom in Jeremiah 19:1-13 as a symbol of despair. *Gehinna* or *Gehinnom* are terms derived from a place outside ancient Jerusalem known in the Hebrew Bible as the *Valley of the Son of Hinnom,* one of the two principal valleys surrounding the Old City. It is here apostate Israelites sacrificed children ("innocent blood") by fire to *Baal* and *Molech*. The site, therefore, is said to be cursed.

The expression, "potter's field" denotes human (child) sacrifice.

MATTHEW 27:11-14

"And Jesus stood before the governor: and the governor asked him, saying, Art thou the King of the Jews? And Jesus said unto him, Thou sayest. And when he was accused of the chief priests and elders, he answered nothing. Then said Pilate unto him, Hearest thou not how many things they witness against thee?

And he answered him to never a word; insomuch that the governor marvelled greatly."

"Art thou the King of the Jews?" asks Pontius Pilate. To understand the spiritual implication of that question, we must first know that spiritual meaning of the term *Jew*, and also the spiritual meaning of the expression, "the king of the Jews."

In the Gospel, Jesus is referred to as the "King of the Jews" or *Baseleus tou Ioudaiou*, both at the beginning of his life and at the end. At birth, the wise men who come from the east refer to Jesus as "King of the Jews," and at the end of his life, the Roman governor Pontius Pilate utters the same term, although disparagingly. On both these occasions, innocent blood is shed. On both occasions, the question, "Art thou the King of the Jews?" is asked by a non-Jew. Jesus does not answer the question affirmatively; he simply says. *"Thou sayest,"* which means "I am not saying so; but you are."

The *real* Israel is the *spiritual* Israel; the *real* Jerusalem is the *spiritual* Jerusalem; the *real* Jews are the *spiritual* Jews. Spiritual Jews exist only in the Bible and they represent the 'fallen' state of humanity (Adamites). The Bible story revolves around them and depicts their flight and plight ('fall') through history. But, those who *say* that they are Jews are merely followers Judaism, the religion. Jesus reveals their identity through Apostle John:

> *Behold, I will make them of the synagogue of Satan, which say they are Jews, and are not, but do lie; behold, I will make them to come and worship before thy feet, and to know that I have love thee.*
>
> Revelation 3:9

The term *king*, in this context, means "Lord" or "creator" rather than "leader." Therefore, the expression, "King of the Jews" implies "Lord of the Jews." Therefore, the question Pontius Pilate really asking Jesus is this: "Are you an Evite?" Jesus answers the question in the affirmative. He says, *"Thou sayest"* which means, "Yes. You have said it."

MATTHEW 27:15-18

"Now at that feast the governor was wont to release unto the people a prisoner, whom they would. And they had then a notable prisoner, called Barabbas. Therefore when they were gathered together, Pilate said unto them, Whom will ye that I release unto you? Barabbas, or Jesus which is called Christ? For he knew that for envy they had delivered him."

The Gospel refers to the Roman custom of releasing a prisoner during the Passover festival. Perhaps, the Roman government did it to build rapport with the people of the foreign nations it governed. 'Releasing' a prisoner to the people does not suggest that he is freed; it only means that the crowd is free to kill him in whichever manner they choose to.

Who is Barabbas, the 'notable' prisoner? The name Barabbas is derived from the Aramaic word *Barabbas* (G912), which is derived from *Bar-abbas,* meaning "son of Abbas." Translated literally, it means "son of the father." Alternatively, the name Barabbas may have originated from the Hebrew word *Bar-Rabbas,* which means "son of a Rabbi." The term *Bar-Rabbas* means "son of priests," or "a priest." The word, *notable* means "widely known and esteemed," which means "worldly" or "famous." Therefore, the expression "notable prisoner," probably, alludes to:

1. Bar-Abbas, a worldly and corrupt man (a politician)
2. Bar-Rabbas, a member of the priestly class (a priest)

Pontius Pilate offers to the Jews two options. They are:

1. Choose Jesus, the "*Son of the Father*"
2. Choose Barabbas, the "*son of the father*"

Spiritually, the expression "Son of the Father" refers to the Gospel, whereas the expression, "son of the father" refers to the literal scripture. The mob chose the latter.

The Gospel tells us that Pontius Pilate was convinced about Jesus' innocence. He knew that the Jews convicted him only out of envy or jealousy. The Gospel gives us a cue: *"For he knew that for envy they had delivered him."* Yet, Pilate gave the option of choosing between Jesus and Barabbas to the Jews. Why? Perhaps, he too was a party to the crime. It shows that the god of politics and the god of religion is the same—*Baal.* The term *Baal* is a Semitic title and honorific meaning "master" or "lord." The term *Baal* may refer to any god and even to human officials. *Baal* only means "the boss"—boss of the Establishment.

MATTHEW 27:19-26

"When he was set down on the judgment seat, his wife sent unto him, saying, Have thou nothing to do with that just man: for I have suffered many things this day in a dream because of him. But the chief priests and elders persuaded the multitude that they should ask Barabbas, and destroy Jesus. The governor answered and said unto them, Whether of the twain will ye that I release unto you? They said, Barabbas. Pilate saith unto them, What shall I do then with Jesus which is called Christ? They all say unto him, Let him be crucified. And the governor said, Why, what evil hath he done? But they cried out the more, saying, Let him be crucified. When Pilate saw that he could prevail nothing, but that rather a tumult was made, he took water, and washed his hands before the multitude, saying, I am innocent of the blood of this just person: see ye to it. Then answered all the people, and said, His blood be on us, and on our children. Then released he Barabbas unto them: and when he had scourged Jesus, he delivered him to be crucified."

"When he was set down on the judgment seat, his wife sent unto him, saying, Have thou nothing to do with that just man: for I have suffered many things this day in a dream because of him." The reference to Pilate's wife is found only in the Gospel of Matthew in the New Testament. In later Christian tradition, she is known variously as *Saint Procula* or *Saint Claudia.* In the 2nd century, Origen suggested in his *Homilies on Matthew* that the wife of Pilate had become a Christian, or at least that God sent her the dream so that she would convert. This interpretation is shared by several theologians of Antiquity, Middle Ages and even the present day. Rival theologians contend that the dream was sent by

Satan in an attempt to thwart the salvation that was going to result from Jesus' death. Perhaps, neither party is correct. Since Jesus is the Gospel, his shedding of blood at the cross represents the spiritual revelation of the Gospel. Therefore, Pilate's wife represents the seemingly virtuous agencies that inhibit the spiritual revelation of the Gospel. Spiritually, Pilate represents the Christian Church; Pilate's wife represents Christian theology.

"But the chief priests and elders persuaded the multitude that they should ask Barabbas, and destroy Jesus. The governor answered and said unto them, Whether of the twain will ye that I release unto you? They said, Barabbas." The real issue here is the choice between body and mind. If Jesus represents the body, then Barabbas represents the mind. If Jesus represents the Self, then Barabbas represents the (not-Self), or the Serpent. If Jesus represents the Gospel, then Barabbas represents the literal scripture. If Jesus represents the prophet, then Barabbas represents the priest. The mob chose Barabbas.

Jesus	**Barabbas**
Body	Mind
Self	The other
Evite	Adamite
Prophet	Priest
Father	Serpent
Gospel	Literal scripture

"When Pilate saw that he could prevail nothing, but that rather a tumult was made, he took water, and washed his hands before the multitude, saying, I am innocent of the blood of this just person: see ye to it." Which is more powerful—the political system or the religious system? The Gospel tells us that the religious system wields the real power, although superficially it may appear that the political system has greater power. What is the real significance of Pilate's "hand washing" act? The hand represents action, and water represents consciousness. Therefore, the hand-washing-ritual suggests covering up crime with a story, a "cover story." The Romans hide their complicity in the crime by a cleverly designed cover story. Pontius Pilatus typifies worldly justice.

The crowd cries, *"His blood be on us, and on our children."* The cry sounds like the litany of a blood sacrifice ritual.

MATTHEW 27:27-32

"Then the soldiers of the governor took Jesus into the common hall, and gathered unto him the whole band of soldiers. And they stripped him, and put on him a scarlet robe. And when they had platted a crown of thorns, they put it upon his head, and a reed in his right hand: and they bowed the knee before him, and mocked him, saying, Hail, King of the Jews! And they spit upon him, and took the reed, and smote him on the head. And after that they had mocked him, they took the robe off him, and put his own raiment on him, and led him away to crucify him. And as they came out, they found a man of Cyrene, Simon by name: him they compelled to bear his cross."

The soldiers make a mockery of Jesus as a king. They put on his body a scarlet robe, on his head a crown of thorns, and in his hand a reed to hold and, then, ridicule him, calling, "King of the Jews." The scarlet robe, the crown, and the scepter denote royal insignia.

We shall examine the true significance of the term "King of the Jews" by means of an allegory. Imagine you are reading a thrilling fictional novel, written by you, in which you are the hero. And you are so engrossed in the story that you mistake it for real life and, unawares, get *pulled* into the story. Now you are inside the fiction, and you have completely lost contact with the reality outside the fiction. For you, the fiction is the reality now.

Normally, readers of books are able to exit from their fantasy world because books usually have an ending. But, this book that you are reading is special. It is a "living book," and it has no ending. It is like a TV serial that continues episode after episode, indefinitely. The book continually creates new content simply by recycling the old and rehashing it. But, it is such a slick production that it appears very real to you.

In this allegory, *you* play multiple parts. For instance, you are:

1. The author of the book: called the *Father*
2. The reader of the book: called the *Son*,
3. The hero of the book: called the *Man*, or human being

The book is purely fictional; there is no truth in its literal content. But, underlying the book's literal story are eternal truths. Your purpose of 'reading' the fiction (reincarnating as man) is to discover the eternal truths embedded in the book. And that book is called the scripture, or the human DNA. But, the story is so captivating that you make no effort to seek the truth. You mistake the fiction for life itself, and strive to prolong it, not realizing that your own life-force is being continually drained to 'power' the fictional world. The only way to save you from the book's trap is to shake you violently that you wake up from the fantasy. Therefore, you, the author, foreseeing such a possibility, have hidden within the scripture a special device, which, if found, will enable your exit from the fiction. And that device is called the Gospel. If you, the hero, discover it, then it will modify your fiction by adding a twist to the plot called the *Crucifixion-Death-Resurrection*, or the *Cross.* The Cross transforms the thrilling story into a nightmare, wherein you, the hero, are tortured, crucified, and killed by the false heroes of the story. Thus, you wake up from the fantasy and your delusion ends.

The false heroes in the fiction are called Jews. They are the masters of the fictional world. But, you, the real author and reader of the fiction, have chosen to incarnate in the fiction as a lowly character. In other words, you are a mere Gentile in the story. The Jews think that they are the chosen people of God, not realizing that you, the lowly Gentile, are the author (Father) of the God (scripture) that created them.

Your purpose of reading the fiction (reincarnating as man) is to discover the eternal truths embedded in the book. But, the Jews have no access to those eternal truths because they exist only in the fictional world.

Spiritually, the expression, *King of the Jews* refers to true human being, the author-reader-hero of the fiction and the creator of the fictional characters. Scarlet is the color of human blood; therefore, the *scarlet robe* denotes the true (uncorrupted) human blood. The *crown* denotes human discriminative faculty (*buddhi*)—the ability to discern real from artificial. The *scepter* denotes authority; it denotes discretion, or freewill. These symbols declare the true human being (Evite) as the true lord and master of the world.

Spiritually, the *scarlet robe* represents body-awareness. In the fictional world, only true human beings (true heroes) get to wear this robe. What the hero (man) feels as body-awareness is the physical manifestation of the author-reader's (Father's) attention on him (grace). In other words, body-awareness is the hero's (man's) conviction (faith) that he and the author-reader (Father) are one. Other than body-awareness the hero (man) has no other connection to the author-reader (truth). His only connection to truth is his body; everything else can only lead him into the story, into delusion.

A human being is born a king (as an Evite). At birth, he is the personification (*avatar*) of the Father (author-reader). But, shortly after birth, the king loses his kingdom and turns into a destitute. How does the king lose his kingdom and become a beggar? Who usurped the dominion from him, and how? The answer is this: The Serpent usurped it from him by deception and sorcery. That Serpent is religion, and its sorcery is the spell that it casts. And it is called religion.

Jesus represents the true human being, the hero, the perfect man (*kouros*). The life and crucifixion of Jesus depicts man's plight in this world. The Judeo-Roman Establishment that crucifies Jesus represents the Serpent that usurps man's body-awareness (kingdom), and makes him a destitute. If we consider Jesus as the Gospel, then the Judeo-Roman Establishment is the Judeo-Christian Church. It is the Judeo-Christian Church that distorts the Gospel truths and makes all of us destitutes.

This Gospel episode depicts how evil presents itself as good and then declares good as the evil. It depicts how the villains present themselves as the heroes, and then portray the true heroes as the villains. It depicts how the changelings present themselves as the sons, and then declare the sons as the changelings. It depicts how the aliens present themselves as the natives, and then banish the natives as the aliens.

Who is Simon, the mysterious "man from Cyrene" who relieved Jesus' burden? Cyrene is a city in Libya. The name Cyrene is pronounced *kyren*. Cyrene, according to Greek myth, wrestled with a lion which endeared her to *Apollo* who took her away to Africa and built a city for her that bears her name. Apollo is the Greek God of oracles and prophesies. He is the patron defender of 'herds' and 'flocks' and is associated with "dominion over colonists." The ideal of *kouros* (perfect man), Apollo has been variously recognized as a god of light, and the sun, truth and prophesy, healing, music, poetry and more. Spiritually, Cyrene represents the truth-seeker. His adversary, the lion, is the Serpent, the Judeo-Christian Church.

Be sober, be vigilant; because your adversary the devil, as a roaring lion, walketh about, seeking whom he may devour.
1 Peter 5:8

The passion of Christ reveals to us the identity of the true enemies of humanity.

CIRCE AND THE CHURCH

The word *church* comes from the Old English word *circe*. In Greek mythology, *Circe*[1] (*Kirke*, pronounced *keer-keeh*) is a minor goddess of magic[2] (or sometimes a nymph, witch, enchantress, sorceress, or whore) described in Homer's Odyssey[3] as "the loveliest of all immortals." Having murdered her husband, the *Prince of Colchis*[4], she was expelled by her subjects and placed by her father on the solitary island of *Aeaea*[5]. Later traditions tell her of leaving or even destroying the island and moving to Italy. In particular she was identified with Cape Circe there.

Circe was renowned for her vast knowledge of drugs and herbs. Through the use of magical potions[6] and a wand[7] she transformed her enemies or those who offended her into animals. In Homer's Odyssey, Circe is described as living in a mansion[8] that stands in the middle of a clearing in a dense wood. Around the house prowled strangely docile lions[9] and wolves[10], the drugged victims of her magic, they were not dangerous, and fawned on all new comers. Circe worked at a huge loom[11].

Circe invited Odysseus' crew to a feast of familiar food[12], a pottage of cheese and meal, sweetened with honey and laced with wine, but also laced with one of her magical potions; and she turned them all into swine[13] with a wand after they gorges themselves on it. Only *Eurylochus*[14] suspecting treachery from the outset, escaped to warn Odysseus[15] and others who stayed behind at the ships[16].

Odysseus set out to rescue his men, but was intercepted by the messenger of God, Hermes[17], who had been sent by Athena[18]. Hermes told Odysseus to use the holy herb moly[19] (the plant moly is grown from the blood[21] of the Gigante[20] killed[22] in the isle of Kirke; it has a white flower[23]) to protect himself from Circe's potion and, having resisted it, to draw his sword[24] and act as if[25] he were to attack Circe.

From there, Circe would ask him to bed[26], but Hermes advised caution, for even there the goddess would be treacherous. She would take his manhood[27] unless he had her swear by the names of the gods that she would not.

Odysseus followed Hermes' advice, freeing his men and then remained on the island for one year, feasting and drinking wine. According to Homer, Circe suggested two alternative routes to Odysseus to return to *Ithaca*[28]: towards the "wandering rocks" or passing between the dangerous *Scylla*[28] and whirlpool *Charybdis*[28], conventionally identified with the straight of Messina. She also advised Odysseus to go to the underworld and gave him directions.

In many respects, Odyssey is an allegory of man's journey through the world and clarifies the role religion plays in his life. The story reveals great truths, when deciphered using the spiritual key given below:

	Term in Homer's Odyssey	**Spiritual Meaning**
1	*Circe*	The Church ("*the whore of Babylon*")
2	*Magic*	Delusion of duality
3	*Odyssey*	The story of humanity
4	*Prince of Colchis*	Man
5	*Aeaea*	Rome
6	*Potions*	Doctrine
7	*Wand*	Canon
8	*Mansion*	Vatican
9	*Lions*	Cardinals
10	*Wolves*	Bishops
11	*Huge loom*	Bible
12	*Feast of familiar food*	Eucharist
13	*Swine*	Believer
14	*Eurylochus*	Intuition
15	*Odysseus*	Evite
16	*Ship*	Body (body-awareness)
17	*Messenger of God, Hermes*	Jesus Christ
18	*Athena*	The Self / The Father
19	*Holy herb Moly*	The Gospel
20	*Gigante*	The Literal Scripture
21	*Blood of the Gigante*	Spiritual meaning of the scripture
22	*Killing of the Gigante*	Exegesis of the scripture
23	*White flower of plant Moly*	The spiritual meaning of the Gospel
24	*Sword*	Non-duality

25	*Acting "as if"*	Fighting mentally (not fighting physically)
26	*Going to bed with Circe*	Reformation theology
27	*Manhood*	Body-awareness
28	*Ithaca*	Salvation / *Moksha*
29	*Between Scylla and Charybdis*	The middle path; Non-duality

When defeated by Odysseus, Circe becomes his faithful servant. She even tells him the path to *Ithaca*. What it implies is that when you subjugate the dual nature of religion, it can serve you as a good servant.

MATTHEW 27:33-44

"And when they were come unto a place called Golgotha, that is to say, a place of a skull, They gave him vinegar to drink mingled with gall: and when he had tasted thereof, he would not drink. And they crucified him, and parted his garments, casting lots: that it might be fulfilled which was spoken by the prophet, They parted my garments among them, and upon my vesture did they cast lots. And sitting down they watched him there; And set up over his head his accusation written, THIS IS JESUS THE KING OF THE JEWS. Then were there two thieves crucified with him, one on the right hand, and another on the left. And they that passed by reviled him, wagging their heads, And saying, Thou that destroyest the temple, and buildest it in three days, save thyself. If thou be the Son of God, come down from the cross. Likewise also the chief priests mocking him, with the scribes and elders, said, He saved others; himself he cannot save. If he be the King of Israel, let him now come down from the cross, and we will believe him. He trusted in God; let him deliver him now, if he will have him: for he said, I am the Son of God. The thieves also, which were crucified with him, cast the same in his teeth."

"And when they were come unto a place called Golgotha, that is to say, a place of a skull, They gave him vinegar to drink mingled with gall: and when he had tasted thereof, he would not drink." Golgotha (G1115) in Aramaic means "the skull." Golgotha is mentioned in early writings as a hill resembling a skullcap located very near a "gate into Jerusalem." Spiritually, Jerusalem, the great city, represents the corrupt mind,

or the world. The, gate into Jerusalem denotes the literal scripture. Golgotha is where Jesus is crucified. Or, in other words, Golgotha is where human body-awareness is crucified. Alternatively, it is where the Gospel meaning is crucified. Spiritually, the term *Golgotha* refers to human cognition, which is symbolized by the skull motif. In other words, the term Golgotha refers to the human brain that is subjected to religious conditioning.

The Hebrew word for vinegar is *hōmes* (H2558). It is derived from the root word *hāmēs* (H2556), which means "leavened." The Greek word for vinegar is *oxos* (G3690). It is derived from the root word *oxys* (G3691), which means "speed." Spiritually, vinegar represents the "bitter spirit," or theology. The Hebrew term for *gall* is *rōs* (H7219), which is a poisonous plant, perhaps, the poppy. The Greek term for *gall* is *cholē* (G5521), which too suggests poison or an anodyne such as wormwood, poppy etc. (An *anodyne* is a medicine that relieves pain.) Spiritually, gall refers to the false doctrine of *dispensationalism* that the Christian churches administer to their hopeless followers.

Dispensationalism is an evangelical, futurist, Biblical interpretation that understands God to have related to human beings in different ways under different Biblical covenants in a series of "dispensations," or periods in history. The theology of dispensationalism consists of a distinctive eschatological "end times" perspective, as all dispensationalists hold to *premillennialism* and most hold to a *pretribulation* rapture. Dispensationalists believe that the nation of Israel is distinct from the Christian Church, and that God has yet to fulfill his promises to national Israel. These promises include the *land promises*, which in the "future world to come" result in a millennial kingdom and *Third Temple* where Christ, upon his return, will rule the world from Jerusalem for a thousand years.

The drink of vinegar mingled with gall is a kind of stupefying potion that drowns the pain of crucifixion. Jesus, however, refuses the drink and remains body-aware, and in touch with reality. Perhaps, the potion only magnifies the pain rather than mitigating it. Otherwise it does not make any sense, and defeats the very purpose of crucifixion. Those who accept the "stupefying potion" of religion will find their miseries only increasing, and not decreasing.

"And they crucified him, and parted his garments, casting lots: that it might be fulfilled which was spoken by the prophet, They parted my garments among them, and upon my vesture did they cast lots."

Body-awareness is compared to a *garment* because it covers the whole body like a garment. And it is a seamless garment in that it is undifferentiated. The parting of this seamless garment suggests the fragmentation of mind.

"And sitting down they watched him there; And set up over his head his accusation written, THIS IS JESUS THE KING OF THE JEWS." When an actor gets onto the stage, he becomes a character in the drama; he then plays a character that is totally different from his true nature. Similarly, when the Self (Father) enters the stage called the world, he becomes a human being (the Son) and becomes a character in the drama. A number of *accusations* (Sanskrit: *ārōpa*) are imposed on him—father, son, husband, boss, subordinate, the list goes on and on. And the accuser is the society (deluded mind). The typical form of the accusation is: "I am so-and-so." The accusation on Jesus reads: *"THIS IS JESUS THE KING OF THE JEWS."* Spiritually, it means, "This is a true human being."

"Then were there two thieves crucified with him, one on the right hand, and another on the left." The crucifixion of Jesus represents the fall of man into delusion. It represents man's fall from non-duality (body-awareness) into duality (religion). The two thieves, crucified on either side of Jesus, represent the dual aspects of duality—the positive and negative. Gospel calls them *thieves* because there is no intrinsic truth in either of them; they are not absolute, but relative. Alternatively, if Jesus represents the Gospel, then the good thief represents the spiritual interpretation of the Gospel and the bad thief represents the literal interpretation of the Gospel. Both interpretations are called thieves because both only describe the Gospel rather than being the Gospel.

"And they that passed by reviled him, wagging their heads, And saying, Thou that destroyest the temple, and buildest it in three days, save thyself. If thou be the Son of God, come down from the cross." To *pass by* means to move past without awareness. Therefore, the expression, "they that passed by" refers to the mob that pass by Jesus without empathy. Spiritually, they represent those who read the Gospel without body-awareness and understand it literally. It is they who revile Jesus. To *revile* means to spread falsehood. The wagging of heads suggests blind devotion. In other words, those who understand the Gospel literally understand only falsehoods, and are caught in blind devotion.

It is they who take Jesus' statement that he will destroy the temple and rebuild it in three days literally, and then accuses him of blasphemy.

The chief priests and Scribes also ridicule Jesus saying, *"He saved others; himself he cannot save. If he be the King of Israel, let him now come down from the cross, and we will believe him. He trusted in God; let him deliver him now, if he will have him: for he said, I am the Son of God."* Spiritually, the term *cross* refers to duality. Therefore, crucifying Jesus suggests interpreting the Gospel dualistically, or literally. In the literal interpretation of the Gospel, Jesus is portrayed as a physical person—a Jew—and the events in the Gospel are depicted as historical events that happened in the past. Having crucified (misinterpreted) Jesus (the Gospel) in this manner the Judeo-Christian theologians challenge Jesus (the Gospel) to come down from the cross if he could. In other words, they are daring the Gospel to reveal itself spiritually.

At the core of the conflict between the Jews and Jesus is the conflict between literal and spiritual understanding of the Scripture. It is the replay of an age-old conflict—the conflict between *Literalists* and *Gnostics*. When writing about the history of spirituality, scholars usually classify people according to the religion to which they are affiliated—Pagan, Jew, Christian, Muslim and so forth. This way of thinking conceals a much more significant classification, which categorize individuals according to spiritual understanding rather than religious tradition.

The term *Gnosticism* is derived from the Greek words *gnostikos* meaning "learned" and *gnosis* meaning "knowledge." The term describes a collection of ancient religions which basically taught that the material world created by the *demiurge* should be shunned and the spiritual world should be embraced.

Religious movements tend to embrace two opposing poles, known as *Literalism* and *Gnosticism*, with particular individuals occupying the whole spectrum between the two extremes. This classification is important because Gnostics from different religious traditions have far more in common with each other than they do with Literalists within their own tradition. While Literalists from different religions clearly hold conflicting beliefs, Gnostics from all traditions use different conceptual vocabularies to articulate a common understanding, sometimes called the *Perennial Philosophy*. The goal of Gnostic spirituality is *Gnosis*, or *Knowledge of Truth*. Individuals who have realized *Gnosis* (*Enlightenment*) are known as *Knowers*:

Gnostikoi (Pagan/Christian), *Arifs* (Muslim), *Gnanis* (Hindu), *Buddhas* (Buddhist).

The table below highlights the important differences between the Gnostic and Literalist worldviews:

Gnostics	**Literalists**
Gnostics interpret the stories and teachings of their scriptures as signposts pointing beyond words altogether to the mystical experience of the *ineffable Mystery.*	Literalists believe their scriptures are actually the words of God. They take their teachings, stories and initiation myths to be factual history. They focus on the words as a *literal* expression of the Truth.
Gnostics are concerned with the inner essence of their tradition.	Literalists associate their faith with its outward manifestations: sacred symbols, scriptures, rituals, ecclesiastical leaders, and so on.
Gnostics see themselves as being on a spiritual journey of self—transformation.	Literalists see themselves as fulfilling a divinely ordained obligation to practice particular religious customs as a part of their national or cultural identity.
Gnostics are free spirits who question the presuppositions of their own culture. They follow their hearts, not the herd. They are consumed by their private quest for enlightenment, not by the goal of recruiting more adherents to a religion.	Literalists believe that their particular spiritual tradition is different from all others and has a unique claim on the Truth. They obsessively formulate dogmas which define membership of their particular cult.
Gnostics are generally tolerant of other belief systems.	Literalists are prepared to enforce their opinions and silence those who dissent, justifying their actions by claiming that they are fulfilling God's will.
Gnostics wish to free themselves from the limitations of their personal and cultural identities and experience the oneness of all things. They therefore have no reluctance in adopting the wisdom of other traditions if it adds something to their own.	Literalists use religions to sustain their personal and cultural identity by defining themselves in opposition to others. This inevitably leads to disputes with those outside their particular cult.

Gnostics love peace.	Literalists fight wars of religion with Literalists from other traditions, each claiming that God is on their side. Literalists' enmity also extends to Gnostics within their own tradition who questions their bigotry.

The line dividing Gnosticism and Literalism is the same line diving *good* and *evil*, and that line is non-duality. True scripture is non-dual; its content has neither literal meaning nor spiritual meaning. It is more like a recipe for creating a certain patterns of sounds that is capable of taking mind to the state of non-duality. In the Hindu tradition, these special patterns of sounds are called *mantras*. The Sanskrit word *mantra* is derived from the root words: *man*, meaning mind; and, *trāyate*, meaning "to transport." The word *mantra* means "that which transports mind." In this respect, scripture is like a music score sheet. It is a pattern of symbols for creating a certain pattern of sounds. True scripture is *both* literal (evil) *and* spiritual (good) at the same time; it is *neither* literal *nor* spiritual. The literal aspect of scripture is the outward or phenomenal (historical) side. The gnostic aspect of scripture is the inward or spiritual (mythical/timeless) side. The important point to note is that the literal and spiritual meanings of scripture are in opposition; for example, the literal Jew is the spiritual Gentile and vice versa.

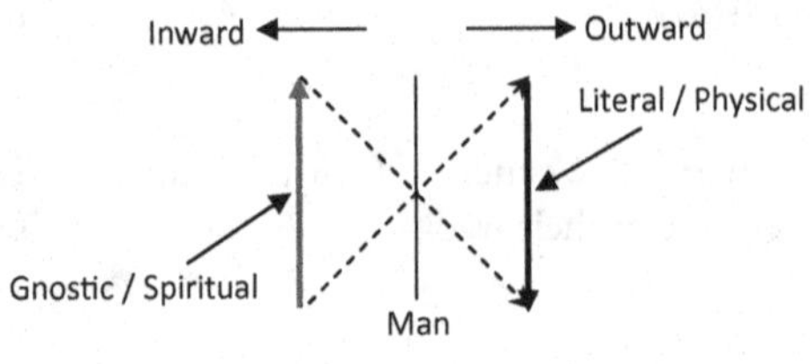

Literalism vs. Gnosticism

Reading the scripture is the job of the priests. The laity is only supposed to hear the sounds (not the interpretation). The skill of the priest lies in his ability to truthfully reproduce sounds according to the recipe; therefore, great stress is laid on the correct phonetic intonation of the *mantras*. The greatest benefit from the scripture comes from hearing it, <u>not</u> from reading and understanding it. Moreover, scripture dies when it is translated into another language. Perhaps, the greatest disservice done to mankind is the wide-spread translation and distribution of scriptures to all and sundry.

MATTHEW 27:45-50

"Now from the sixth hour there was darkness over all the land unto the ninth hour. And about the ninth hour Jesus cried with a loud voice, saying, Eli, Eli, lama sabachthani? that is to say, My God, my God, why hast thou forsaken me? Some of them that stood there, when they heard that, said, This man calleth for Elias. And straightway one of them ran, and took a spunge, and filled it with vinegar, and put it on a reed, and gave him to drink. The rest said, Let be, let us see whether Elias will come to save him. Jesus, when he had cried again with a loud voice, yielded up the ghost."

"Now from the sixth hour there was darkness over all the land unto the ninth hour." If we take the word *darkness* literally, then we have to presume that a strange astrological event took place coinciding with Jesus' crucifixion. But spiritually, then term *darkness* suggests "loss of consciousness," or "delusion." Perhaps the Gospel is alluding to the loss the Holy Spirit (spiritual meaning) from it.

If we consider Jesus as representing the Gospel, then the crucifixion of Jesus refers to the misinterpretation and misrepresentation of the Gospel text. If so, the time span "sixth hour to the ninth hour" refers to the period in history (1000 AD-1500 AD) when the Gospel was completely under the control of the Church.

At about the ninth hour, Jesus cries, *"Eli, Eli, lama sabachthani?"* meaning *"My God, my God, why hast thou forsaken me?"* The word *Eli* is derived from the Hebrew word *ēl* (H410) or *ayil* (H352) which means "power" "strength" or "might" in addition to "God." If Jesus represents the Gospel, then the cry signifies the loss of truth (power) from the Gospel. The cry denotes the slipping of the Gospel into an even darker period of spiritual darkness, which we mistakenly call as *Reformation*. The Protestant Reformation was the schism within Western Christianity initiated by Martin Luther, John Calvin, and other early Protestants. Although there had been significant attempts at reform before Luther (notably those of John Wycliffe and Jan Huss), the date most usually given for the start of the Protestant Reformation is 1517, when Luther published *The Ninety-Five Theses*, and for its conclusion in 1648 with the *Peace of Westphalia* that ended the European wars of religion. Luther started by criticizing the relatively recent practice of selling indulgences, but the debate widened until it touched on many of the doctrines and devotional practices of the Catholic Church.

Perhaps, the cry also marks the advent of the printed Bible around 1500 AD (9th hour). The Gutenberg Bible was the first major book printed in the West using movable type. It marked the start of the *Gutenberg Revolution* and the age of the printed book in the West. Widely praised for its high aesthetic and artistic qualities, the book has an iconic status. Written in Latin, the Gutenberg Bible is an edition of the *Vulgate*, printed by Johannes Gutenberg, in Mainz, Germany, in the 1450s.

The mob takes Jesus' cry literally. The Gospel says, *"Some of them that stood there, when they heard that said, This man calleth for Elias."* The name *Elias* comes from the Hebrew name *ēliyāhu* (H452) meaning, "God of Jehovah." In other words, the common man associates the Gospel with the literal scripture, which is exactly what the lament was about.

"And straightway one of them ran, and took a spunge, and filled it with vinegar, and put it on a reed, and gave him to drink." The Greek word for *reed* is *kalamos* (G2563), which means "a pen." The Greek word for *vinegar* is *oxos* (G3690), which means "sour wine." Spiritually, the "sour wine" refers to bad or false meaning. Here, the Gospel is referring to the Christian Church's poor and spiritless interpretation of the Gospel.

"Jesus, when he had cried again with a loud voice, yielded up the ghost." Thus, the spiritual meaning of the Gospel disappears from the church completely.

MATTHEW 27:51-56

"And, behold, the veil of the temple was rent in twain from the top to the bottom; and the earth did quake, and the rocks rent; And the graves were opened; and many bodies of the saints which slept arose, And came out of the graves after his resurrection, and went into the holy city, and appeared unto many. Now when the centurion, and they that were with him, watching Jesus, saw the earthquake, and those things that were done, they feared greatly, saying, Truly this was the Son of God. And many women were there beholding afar off, which followed Jesus from Galilee, ministering unto him: Among which was Mary Magdalene, and Mary the mother of James and Joses, and the mother of Zebedee's children."

Here, the Gospel describes the physical effects of the distortion caused to the true meaning of the Gospel.

"And, behold, the veil of the temple was rent in twain from the top to the bottom; and the earth did quake, and the rocks rent." Spiritually, the term *temple* refers to the human body, and the *veil of the temple* refers to the human mind. The Greek word for *rend* is *schizō* (G4977), means "to split," or "to sever." Therefore, the renting of the temple veil into two suggests the splitting of mind, or *schizophrenia*.

Schizophrenia is a mental disorder characterized by a breakdown in thinking and poor emotional responses. Common symptoms include delusions, such as paranoia; hearing voices or noises that are not there; disorganized thinking; a lack of emotions and a lack of motivation. Genetics, early environment, psychological and social processes appear to be the major contributory factors to schizophrenia. The word schizophrenia originates from the Greek roots *schizō*, which means "to split" and the word *phrēn*, which means "mind."

Spiritually, the term *earth* refers to human awareness, or mind. Therefore, the "quaking of earth" suggests fear. The Greek word for "rocks" is *petra* (G4073), which means "a mass of rocks." Spiritually, the term "rocks" refers to ethical edicts. Therefore, the 'renting' of rocks suggests the breakdown of ethics.

"And the graves were opened; and many bodies of the saints which slept arose, And came out of the graves after his resurrection, and went into the holy city, and appeared unto many." The Greek word for *grave* is *mnēmeion* (G3419), which means "a remembrance." Spiritually, the word *grave* refers to the subconscious mind. The Greek word for *saint* is *hagios* (G40), which means "religiously pure." The word is derived from the root *hagos*, which means "an awful thing." Spiritually, the word "saints" refers to repressed thoughts of guilt and sin. Therefore, the expression, "saints which slept arose and came out of the graves after his resurrection" suggests the surfacing of repressed thought of guilt and sin from the subconscious mind to the conscious mind. And the Gospel says, *"And came out of the graves after his resurrection, and went into the holy city, and appeared unto many."* Spiritually, the expression, "holy city" refers to the body and the word "many" refers

to the society. In other words, the repressed thoughts of the religious Christian manifest in the society as evil actions.

"Now when the centurion, and they that were with him, watching Jesus, saw the earthquake, and those things that were done, they feared greatly, saying, Truly this was the Son of God." The Greek word for *centurion* is *hekatontarchēs* (G1543), which means "the captain of one hundred men." The word *hekatontarchēs* is derived from the words *hekaton* (G1540), which means "a hundred" and *archō* (G757), which means "to reign over." Perhaps, the *centurion* represents the *archons*, the Adamites, or the priests. In fact, the centurion and his men are the killers of Jesus; but, after they kill Jesus, they try to deify him. Similarly, the Adamites (priests) murder the Gospel first and then deify it. It is evident from their utterance: "*Truly this was the Son of God.*" They misrepresent the "Son of man" as the "Son of God." Also notice that they speaking in past tense.

"And many women were there beholding afar off, which followed Jesus from Galilee, ministering unto him: Among which was Mary Magdalene, and Mary the mother of James and Joses, and the mother of Zebedee's children." Spiritually, the term "women" refers to the Evites. The Evites are watching Jesus being crucified from afar. In other words, the Evites watch the priests and theologians murder the Gospel from a distance. Alternatively, the expression "beholding afar off" means "understanding spiritually." In other words, the Evites understand the crucifixion of Jesus spiritually. The three women around Jesus—Mary Magdalene, Mary, and Salome—represent three different spiritual interpretations of the Gospel.

MATTHEW 27:57-61

"When the even was come, there came a rich man of Arimathaea, named Joseph, who also himself was Jesus' disciple: He went to Pilate, and begged the body of Jesus. Then Pilate commanded the body to be delivered. And when Joseph had taken the body, he wrapped it in a clean linen cloth. And laid it in his own new tomb, which he had hewn out in the rock: and he rolled a great stone to the door of the sepulchre, and departed. And there was Mary Magdalene, and the other Mary, sitting over against the sepulchre."

The Hebrew name *Arimathaea* is derived from three Hebrew words: one, *ari* (H738), which means "lion"; two, *mut* (H4191), which means "dead body"; three, *Jah* (H3068), which means "the Lord." In other words, the name *Arimathaea* means "a lion dead to the lord." The name *Joseph* is derived from the Hebrew word *yōsēp* (H3130), which means "God will increase." These two names remind us of the Story of Samson in the Old Testament. Samson's story is an allegory that foretells the spiritual revelation of Gospel.

The name Samson is derived from the Hebrew word *śimśōn* (H8123), which means "sunlight," or "man of the sun." (Notice the close resemblance of the expressions "man of the sun" and "son of man.") According to the Biblical account, Samson was given supernatural strength by God in order to combat his enemies and perform heroic feats. However, Samson had two vulnerabilities: his attraction to an untrustworthy woman and his hair, without which he is powerless. These vulnerabilities ultimately prove fatal for him.

When Samson was a young adult, he leaves the hills of his people to see the cities of the Philistines. While there, Samson falls in love with a Philistine woman from Timnath who he decides to marry, overcoming the objections of his parents who do not know that "it is of the Lord." The intended marriage is actually part of God's plan to strike at the Philistines. On the way to ask for the woman's hand in marriage, Samson is attacked by a young lion, and he simply grabs it and rips it apart, as the spirit of God moves upon him, divinely empowering him.

> *Then went Samson down, and his father and his mother, to Timnath, and came to the vineyards of Timnath: and, behold, a young lion roared against him.*
> Judges 14:5

This so profoundly affects Samson that he just keeps it to himself as a secret. He continues on to the Philistine's house, winning the woman's hand in marriage. On his way to the wedding, Samson notices that bees have nested in the carcase of the lion and have made honey. He eats a handful of the honey and gives some to his parents.

And after a time he returned to take her, and he turned aside to see the carcase of the lion: and, behold, there was a swarm of bees and honey in the carcase of the lion. And he took thereof in his hands, and went on eating, and came to his father and mother, and he gave them, and they did eat: but he told not them that he had taken the honey out of the carcase of the lion.
Judges 14:8-9

At the wedding-feast, Samson proposes that he tell a riddle to his thirty groomsmen (all Philistines); if they can solve it, he will give them thirty pieces of fine linen and garments. The riddle is a veiled account of his second encounter with the lion (at which only he was present).

And Samson said unto them, I will now put forth a riddle unto you: if ye can certainly declare it to me within the seven days of the feast, and find it out, then I will give you thirty sheets and thirty change of garments: But it ye cannot declare it me, then shall ye give me thirty sheets and thirty change of garments. And they said unto him, Put forth thy riddle, that we may hear it. And he said unto them, Out of the eater came forth meat, and out of the strong came forth sweetness. And they could not in three days expound the riddle.
Judges 14:12-14

The Philistines are infuriated by the riddle. The thirty groomsmen tell Samson's new wife that they will burn her and her father's household if she does not discover the answer to the riddle and tell it to them. At the urgent and tearful imploring of his bride, Samson tells her the solution, and she tells it to the thirty groomsmen.

And she wept before him the seven days, while their feast lasted: and it came to pass on the seventh day, that he told her, because she lay sore upon him: and she told the riddle to the children of her people.
Judges 14:17

Before sunset on the seventh day the groomsmen give the solution to Samson. Samson says to the groomsmen something cryptic, *"If ye had not plowed with my red heifer, ye had not found out my riddle."* It means, "You cheated; because it is impossible for humanoids to resolve a paradox." The term *red heifer* refers to the self-aware body. The expression, "plowing with the red heifer" means reading the Gospel with self-aware bodies.

> *And the men of the city said unto him on the seventh day before the sun went down, What is sweeter than honey? And what is stronger than a lion? And he said unto them, If ye had not plowed with my heifer, ye had not found out my riddle. And the Spirit of the Lord came upon him, and he went down to Ashkelon, and slew thirty men of them, and took their spoil, and gave change of garments unto them which expounded the riddle. And his anger was kindled, and he went up to his father's house.*
>
> Judges 14:18-20

The name *Ashkelon* originates from the Hebrew word *asqelōn* (H831), which means "a mart." A *mart* is a market place or a trading center, where goods are exchanged. Spiritually, the term Ashkelon refers to the Church.

The table below gives the key for interpreting the Samson allegory:

Term	**Spiritual Meaning**
Samson	The human Self
Philistines	Adamites
Philistine woman from Timnath	Corrupt mind / Judaism
Timnath (H8553) ("portion assigned")	The Old Testament / Corrupt DNA
Samson's hair	Thoughts
His father and his mother	The human body
Cities of Philistines	Monotheistic-dualistic religions
Marrying the woman from Timnath	Accepting, or believing the Scripture
Vineyards of Timnath	The books of the Old Testament
The young lion	The meaning of the Old Testament stories

Grabbing and ripping apart the lion	Spiritual exegesis of the Old Testament stories
The spirit of God	Intuition / The spirit of prophesy
Carcase of the lion	The Gospel document
Swarm of bees	Gospel truths
Honey	Spiritual meaning of the Gospel
Samson's riddle	The Truth: "Who am I?" / The Self
Samson's new wife	The Christian Church
Burning of the woman and her father's household	The end of the world
Seven days of the feast	Human lifetime / The seven seals of the Gospel
The wager of fine linen and garments	Body-awareness / Eternal life
The eater	He who understands Gospel literally; Priest
"Out of the eater came forth the meat"	"Out of the priest comes the literal meaning of the Gospel."
The strong	He who understands Gospel intuitively; Prophet
"Out of the strong came forth the sweetness"	"Out of the prophet comes the spiritual meaning of the Gospel."
Solution to Samson's riddle	The Gospel
The thirty groomsmen	The Christian priests
The red heifer	The self-aware body
Ploughing with the red heifer	Reading the Gospel with body-awareness
Ashkelon ("mart)	The Church

It may be noted that Samson does not reveal the answer to his wife until she wept before him and pleaded for the answer. In other words, the truth is revealed only when the mind focuses inwards (repents). The answer to Samson's riddle is the Gospel. But, when Samson reveals the answer to the riddle to his wife, she turns around and reveals it to the Philistines. Spiritually, Samson's untrustworthy wife represents the Christian Church; the thirty *groomsmen* represent the priests of the Christian church. The *Philistines* are the Scribes and the Pharisees, who represent Judaism. In other words, the betrayal of Samson by his untrustworthy wife allegorically portrays the betrayal of the Gospel by the Christian clergy to Judaism.

Now, returning back to the Jesus story, we read that Joseph of Arimathaea took Jesus' body and, *"he wrapped it in a clean linen cloth. And laid it in his own new tomb, which he had hewn out of the rock: and he rolled a great stone to the door of the sepulchre."* Spiritually, Jesus' body represents the Gospel; therefore, wrapping Jesus' body in a clean linen cloth suggests encrypting the Gospel content in an elaborate allegory. The "clean linen cloth" denotes the allegory shrouding the Gospel truths. Joseph's own new tomb refers to the new *Midrash* that Joseph develops to encapsulate the Gospel message. According to the Gospel, the new tomb is hewn out of a rock. The *rock* signifies unchanging or timeless nature; therefore, it denotes myth. Therefore, it is reasonable to presume that Joseph embedded the Gospel truths in a mythical allegory.

The Greek word for *tomb* is *mnemeion* (G3419). It is derived from the root word *mneme* (G3403), which means "memory," or "remembrance." The Hebrew word for *sepulchre* is *qeber* (H6913). It is derived from the root word *qāber* (HH6912), which means "to inter" (in any wise). The words *tomb* and *sepulchre* suggest that Joseph of Arimathaea encrypted the Gospel in an elaborate allegorical myth, as a *mnemonic*. (A mnemonic is any learning technique that aids information retention. Mnemonics aim to translate information into a form that the brain can retain better than its original form.) He then seals the door of the sepulchre with a great stone. The "great stone" represents Gospel's encryption/decryption key (the seal).

It is highly probable that Joseph of Arimathaea is the real author of the Gospel, and that he is none other than Joseph, the surrogate father of Jesus. If Jesus represents the Gospel, then the Jesus' father is none other than the author of the Gospel. But, Joseph is only the surrogate father of the Gospel because the true father of the Gospel is the Holy Spirit.

"And there was Mary Magdalene, and the other Mary, sitting over against the sepulchre." After placing the great stone at the door of the sepulchre, Joseph of Arimathaea departs, but Mary Magdalene and the other Mary lingers there, "sitting over against the sepulchre." Mary

Magdalene and the 'other' Mary represent the two keys for unlocking the Gospel, and both the keys are required to open the Gospel. Mary Magdalene represents the physical key, whereas the 'other' Mary represents the mental key. Mary Magdalene is not a physical person; she represents the true human blood, or body-awareness. The "other Mary" represents the mental key to the Gospel, which is the ability to speculate. In other words, the Gospel reveals its secrets to true human beings (Evites) who read it with body-awareness.

The simple truth is this: The Gospel reveals its secret to those who are able to *hear* and *see* it, not to those who only *hear* it. *Seeing* the Gospel means spiritually understanding it, and it entails personal experience. *Hearing* the Gospel means literally understanding it. And it is second-hand knowledge, or dead knowledge.

MATTHEW 27:62-66

"Now the next day, that followed the day of the preparation, the chief priests and Pharisees came together unto Pilate, Saying, Sir, we remember that that deceiver said, while he was yet alive, After three days I will rise again. Command therefore that the sepulchre be made sure until the third day, lest his disciples come by night, and steal him away, and say unto the people, He is risen from the dead: so the last error shall be worse than the first. Pilate said unto them, Ye have a watch: go your way, make it as sure as ye can. So they went, and made the sepulchre sure, sealing the stone, and setting a watch."

Spiritually, the embalming, wrapping and burying of Jesus' body in the sepulchre denote the encrypting and hiding of the Gospel truths in a mythical allegory—the Jesus story. Those who did the encryption were confident that the truth will prevail and reveal itself in due season. The expression, "rising on the third day" suggest just that. The term *third day* refers to the removal of the three fatal errors, namely, Objectivity, Locality and Causality (*thāpathraya*) from mind. When a man is freed from the erroneous beliefs of Objectivity, Locality, and Causality, he is able to perceive the spiritual meaning of the Gospel clearly. Metaphorically speaking, it is called the end of the world, because it is the end of ignorance and delusion. The three erroneous beliefs are as follows:

1. Objectivity: The belief that this world is real.
2. Locality: The belief that the self (I am) is separate from nature.
3. Causality: The belief that a God created the world.

The Adamites (*archons*) are fearful that the true meaning of the Gospel might emerge in course of time that they take the necessary steps to prevent such an eventuality. Therefore, they plead to their alien *reptilian* master, the Serpent (represented here by Pontius Pilate): *"Sir, we remember that the deceiver said, while he was yet alive, After three days I will rise again. Command therefore that the sepulchre be made sure until the third day, lest his disciples come by night, and steal him away, and say unto the people, He is risen from the dead."* The Greek word for *deceiver* is *planos* (G4108), which means "misleader." The Adamites' real concern is that some human being might discover the truth. And they want to prevent that eventuality at all costs.

The high priests and the Pharisees (*archons*) say to Pontius Pilate (*reptilian*), *"Command therefore that the sepulchre be made sure until the third day, lest his disciples come by night, and steal him away, and say unto the people, He is risen from the dead: so the last error shall be worse than the first."* Spiritually, the expression, "the third day" suggests the end of ignorance and delusion. But, to the Adamites (archons), it is the end of their world. Therefore, they want to prevent it from happening. They warn: *". . . so the last error shall be worse than the first."* The "first error," according to them, was permitting Joseph of Arimathaea to take the body of Jesus and bury it. In other words, the first error was letting the truth disappear behind a mythical allegory. The Adamites (archons) are totally incapable of understanding the spiritual meaning of mythical allegories for two reasons: one, myths are outside the framework of space and time; two, the archons are not body-aware entities like humans. Thus, the encryption of the Gospel into a mythical allegory made it impossible for them to corrupt the Gospel truth. The "last error," according to the chief priests and Pharisees, is letting the disciples steal the body of Jesus and then claim that Jesus has risen from death. In other words, the "last error" is letting some Evite spiritually interpret the Gospel and declare the truth to the humans. According to the Adamites, the last error is even more serious than the first.

Pilate says to the chief priests and Pharisees, *"Ye have a watch: go your way, make it as sure as ye can."* What Pontius Pilate (Rome) says is this: "You ensure that no one finds the truth." In other words, Rome assigns the Judaic theologians the task of misinterpreting and misrepresenting the Gospel. Spiritually, Pontius Pilate represents the Rome (the reptile-aliens) and the chief priests and Pharisees represent Judaic theologians (the archons).

"So they went, and made the sepulchre sure, sealing the stone, and setting a watch." How does the religious establishment prevent the truth from coming out? Gospel says they (Judaic theologians) *"made the sepulchre sure, sealing the stone."* In other words, the religious authorities 'seal' the Gospel. The word *sealing*, perhaps, refers to the imposition of physical restriction on reading the Gnostic Gospels. The expression, "setting a watch" refers to the close supervision of church clergy over the laity, in order to ensure that they do not search in the right place or in the right way.

CHAPTER 28

Go Into Galilee and There Shall Ye See Me

MATTHEW 28:1-7

"In the end of the sabbath, as it began to dawn toward the first day of the week, came Mary Magdalene and the other Mary to see the sepulchre. And, behold, there was a great earthquake: for the angel of the Lord descended from heaven, and came and rolled back the stone from the door, and sat upon it. His countenance was like lightening, and his raiment white as snow: And for fear of him the keepers did shake, and became as dead men. And the angel answered and said unto the women, Fear not ye: for I know that ye seek Jesus, which was crucified. He is not here: for he is risen, as he said. Come, see the place where the Lord lay. And go quickly, and tell his disciples that he is risen from the dead; and, behold, he goeth before you into Galilee; there shall ye see him: lo, I have told you."

"*In the end of the sabbath, as it began to dawn toward the first day of the week, came Mary Magdalene and the other Mary to see the sepulchre.*" As we have seen before, Mary Magdalene and the 'other' Mary represent the two keys to the spiritual Gospel. Here, the expression, "end of sabbath" refers to the *End of Days,* or the *Last Days.* It refers to the end of *Kali Yuga*, the last leg of the cycle of time. The expression, "as it began to dawn toward the first day of the week" refers to the beginning of a new cycle, or new age (*Yuga*). According to the Gospel, the keys to opening the Gospel will be made available to mankind during the Last Days, just before entering the new age.

"And, behold, there was a great earthquake: for the angel of the Lord descended from heaven, and came and rolled back the stone from the door, and sat upon it. His countenance was like lightening, and his raiment white as snow: And for fear of him the keepers did shake, and became as dead men." The three stages to the opening of the sepulchre are as follows:

1. A great earth quake happens
2. The angel of the Lord descends from heaven
3. The stone at the entrance of the sepulchre is rolled back

Spiritually, the term *earth* refers to the belief systems (formalisms) that the Gospel interpreter considers as rock solid, such as science and religion. Therefore, the "great earth shake" points to the shattering of closely-held belief systems, such as science and religion in the Gospel interpreter's mind. He is now able to clearly perceive the fundamental falsehood of these belief systems. When that happens, "the angel of the Lord" appears. In other words, when the interpreter's blind trust in formalisms shatters, his intuition is activated and he is able to speculate unfettered. It is this phenomenon the Gospel metaphorically describes as the rolling back of the great stone. Spiritually, the *sepulchre* represents the literal Gospel, and the "great stone" at the entrance represents the seven seals that protect the Gospel secrets.

Here, the Gospel talks about two Marys: Mary Magdalene and the 'other' Mary. As we have seen before, these two women represent the two keys for opening the Gospel. Mary Magdalene represents the physical key, which is the pure uncorrupted blood of an Evite. The 'other' Mary represents the mental key, which is the Evite's ability to speculate. (Note: Only human beings can speculate; computers cannot.) It is speculation that the Gospel metaphorically describes as "the angel of the Lord descending from heaven." It is also called the inner voice, or intuition. In short, the spiritual interpreter of the Gospel is a body-aware Evite who has the courage to speculate. He, thus, sees the Gospel truths clearly. It is this clarity of his truth vision that the Gospel describes as: *"His countenance was like lightening, and his raiment white as snow."*

The angel of the Lord says to the women, *"Fear not ye: for I know that ye seek Jesus, which was crucified. He is not here: for he is risen, as he said. Come, see the place where the Lord lay. And go quickly, and tell his disciples that he is risen from the dead; and, behold, he goeth before you into Galilee; there shall ye see him: lo, I have told you."* Here, the empty sepulchre represents the literal Gospel. Jesus (truth) is not there. In other words, the literal Gospel is only an allegory; the truth cannot be found in its literal text. The truth has 'risen' from the plane of literal meaning to the plane of esoteric meaning.

The gist of this Gospel episode is this: The Gospel interpreter first approaches the literal Gospel for truth, but his intuition warns him that it is futile to search the truth in the literal Gospel. His intuition cautions: "*Get out of duality: for the truth you are seeking cannot be found in the literal Gospel. It is in your body. Become body-aware and then you will be able to see it.*"

Spiritually, *Galilee* denotes the *Circle of Self.* It denotes wholeness, non-duality, or body-awareness. The words of the angel, *"Lo, I have told you"* is the confirmation. It also suggests that it is the Self that reveals the truth, and not the interpreter's intellect or knowledge.

MATTHEW 28:8-10

"And they departed quickly from the sepulchre with fear and great joy; and did run to bring his disciples word. And as they went to tell his disciples, behold, Jesus met them, saying, All hail. And they came and held him by the feet, and worshipped him. Then said Jesus unto them, Be not afraid: go tell my brethren that they go into Galilee, and there shall they see me."

The Gospel describes the 'eureka' experience of the Gospel interpreter who finds the truth. He is overtaken by awe as well as great joy. He is overcome by a feeling of exultation. He feels like running around and shouting the new-found truth to the whole world.

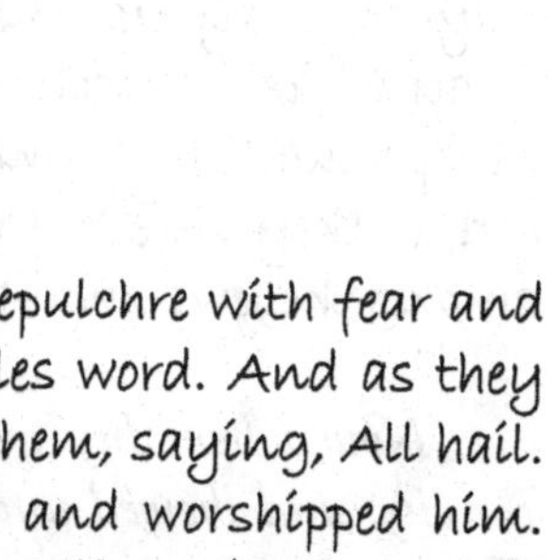

If it was intuition that confirmed the truth to the Gospel interpreter, now he receives reconfirmation. He receives the proof. And Jesus himself presents it to him in person. In other words, the Gospel interpreter experiences truth directly in his body. He is so overwhelmed by the experience that all he can do is to simply stand in awe.

Jesus, then, speaks in his own voice: *"Be not afraid: go tell my brethren that they go into Galilee, and there shall they see me."* The Gospel enjoins the interpreter to fearlessly announce the truth to humanity. And it reveals the essence of the Gospel to him: "*In Galilee you shall see Jesus*" or, in other words, "*Remain body-aware and realize the truth.*"

MATTHEW 28:11-15

"Now when they were going, behold, some of the watch came into the city, and shewed unto the chief priests all the things that were done. And when they were assembled with the elders, and had taken counsel, they gave large money unto the soldiers, Saying, Say ye, His disciples came by night, and stole him away while we slept. And if this come to the governor's ears, we will persuade him, and secure you. So they took the money, and did as they were taught: and this saying is commonly reported among the Jews until this day."

"Now when they were going, behold, some of the watch came into the city, and shewed unto the chief priests all the things that were done." The expression, "now when they are going" suggests that the disciples are proceeding to Galilee to meet Jesus. In other words, the spiritual interpretation of the Gospel inspires humanity to seek the truth. While this is happening, the guards go to the high priests to inform them all that happened at the sepulchre.

The Greek word for *watch* is *koustōdia* (G2892), which means "custody," or "a Roman sentry." But, here, it refers to the custodians of the literal Gospel—the Christian clergy. The Greek word for *city* is *polis* (G4172), which means "an enclave," or "city state." Perhaps, it refers to the head-quarters of the Christian Church. The Greek word for *chief priests* is *archiereus* (G749), which means "high priest." The word is derived from the root words *archē* (G746), which means "ruler," and *hiereus* (G2409), which means "a priest." Perhaps, the term refers to the head of the Christian Church. The expression, "all the things that were done" refers to the spiritual interpretation of the Gospel and the fact that many people are now seeking for the truth.

"And when they were assembled with the elders, and had taken counsel, they gave large money unto the soldiers, Saying, Say ye, His disciples came by night, and stole him away while we slept. And if this come to the governor's ears, we will persuade him, and secure you." The Greek word for "elders" is *presbyteros* (G4245), which means "religious council." The chief priests call a conclave of high-ranking priests and theologians to device a strategy to counter the threat. And their strategy is to discredit the resurrection of Jesus by accusing it to be the work of the fraudulent disciples, who steal the body of Jesus by night and then falsely claim that he has resurrected. Spiritually, "to steal the body of Jesus by night" means "to misinterpret the literal Gospel without awareness." The chief priests pay a large sum of money to the guards to say as they were taught. The chief priests also assuage their fears with the assurance that they will save their backs should the governor come to know about it. The Greek term for *governor* is *hēgēmon* (G2232), which means the "chief person." Perhaps, the term *governor* refers to the alien master—the Serpent. In short, the accusation of the Church authorities is this: "The spiritual interpretation of the Gospel is the work of misinformed Christians who misinterpret the Gospel without proper awareness of the Scriptures or its theology." The Church then spends a considerable amount of money to spread this message to the laity by via the priests.

"So they took the money, and did as they were taught: and this saying is commonly reported among the Jews until this day." It is Gospel's way of saying that history repeats!

MATTHEW 28:16-20

"Then the eleven disciples went away into Galilee, into a mountain where Jesus had appointed them. And when they saw him, they worshipped him: but some doubted. And Jesus came and spake unto them, saying, All power is given unto me in heaven and in earth. Go ye therefore, and teach all nations, baptizing them in the name of the Father, and the Son, and the Holy Ghost: Teaching them to observe all things whatsoever I have commanded you: and, lo, I am with you alway, even unto the end of the world. Amen."

"Then the eleven disciples went away into Galilee, into a mountain where Jesus had appointed them. And when they saw him, they worshipped him: but some doubted." Only eleven disciples proceed to Galilee to meet Jesus. It is a clear indication that the twelfth disciple, Judas, is condemned to perdition.

Spiritually, the term *Galilee* refers to the human body. Therefore, the term *mountain* refers to the human head. The Sanskrit word for mountain is *mēru.* According to Hindu, Jain as well as Buddhist cosmology, *Mount Mēru* (or *Sumēru*) is a sacred mountain with five peaks, and is considered to be the center of all the physical, metaphysical and spiritual universes. Perhaps, it is the same mountain in Galilee where Jesus said that he will meet the disciples. And that location is the spot between the eye brows, the *ājna chakra.* In other words, the Gospel tells us to focus attention on the *ājna chakra* in order to see Jesus (the truth).

THE AJNA CHAKRA

The *ājna chakra* is the chakra of the mind. It is located at the very top of the spinal cord at the same height as the space between the eyebrows. It is also called the *trikuti*, or third eye. *Om* is the *bīja* (seed) *mantra*, representing the seat of mind. The white circle represents *śūnya*, the void. There are two white or silvery petals on either side with the letters *ham* and *kṣam*. In the *ājna chakra* the three main psychic channels, or *nadis*, converge and flow up to the *Sahasrāra chakra* at the top of the head. These three *nadis* are the *suṣumna*, the *Ida*, and the *Pingala*. By concentrating the mind at the *ājna chakra*, transformation of the individual consciousness occurs and duality is transcended.

> *The light of the body is the eye: if therefore thine eye be single, thy whole body shall be full of light.*
> Matthew6:22

The disciples represent Mortals who are on the path on the path to enlightenment. Mary Magdalene represents the Evites. Jesus instructs the disciples to proceed to the mountain in Galilee through Mary Magdalene, and when they do accordingly, they see him. In other words, when the Mortals follow the Evites' interpretation of the Gospel, they receive enlightenment. However, some of the disciples find it difficult to accept the mystical experience (mystery) as the true nature of reality. That is what is suggested by the expression, "but some doubted."

Jesus declares to the disciples, *"All power is given unto me in heaven and in earth."* In other words, the enlightened man realizes that he is indeed the master of his mind and body. And mind and body together constitute the totality of power.

Jesus instructs the disciples: *"Go ye therefore, and teach all nations, baptizing them in the name of the Father, and the Son, and the Holy Ghost: Teaching them to observe all things whatsoever I have commanded you: and, lo, I am with you alway, even unto the end of the world."* Here, the word *therefore* implies "because all power is bestowed on the enlightened human being." The enlightened human being indeed the master of the universe and that is what gives him the authority to teach the Gospel to all nations. Before enlightenment, the disciples *preached* the Gospel; now, being enlightened, they *teach* the Gospel.

What is meant by *baptizing*? Literally, the term *baptism* refers to the ritual cleansing of the body in water. Water is the chief ingredient in the baptism ritual. And, spiritually, water represents consciousness. The Hindu ritual of dipping in river Ganga is a sort of baptism. River Ganga represents consciousness.

There are three essential steps in the baptism of Jesus:

1. Baptism in the *name of the Father* = dipping in Self-awareness
2. Baptism in the *name of the Son* = dipping in Gospel-awareness
3. Baptism in the *name of the Holy Ghost* = dipping body-awareness

	Baptism	**Baptism by**	**Dipping in**
1	In the name of the Holy Ghost	Water	Body-awareness
2	In the name of the Son	Fire	Gospel-awareness
3	In the name of the Father	Light	"Self"-awareness

What is the *teaching* the Gospel is referring to? The Bhagavad Gita articulates it eloquently:

> *Sarva-dharmān paritajya māmēkam śaraṇam vṛja*
> *Aham twā sarva-pāpēbhyah mōkṣayikṣyami mā śucha*
> B.G. 18:66
> ("Renounce all religions and follow your body; it will liberate you from all delusion. Fear not!")

Jesus then gives the disciples his final message: *"Lo, I am with you alway, even unto the end of the world."* The spiritual implication of the message is this: "*Trust your body; it will guide you through the world.*"

Amen.

OM.